Exam 70-548: *Designing and Developing Windows-Based Applications Using the Microsoft .NET Framework*

Note: Exam objectives are subject to change at any time without prior notice and at Microsoft's sole discretion. Please visit the Microsoft Learning Certification Web site (*www.microsoft.com/learning/mcp/*) for the most current listing of exam objectives.

Microsoft®

MCPD Self-Paced Training Kit (Exam 70-548): Designing and Developing Windows®-Based Applications Using the Microsoft® .NET Framework

Bruce Johnson and Mike Snell
of Grand Masters,
with Shawn Wildermuth

PUBLISHED BY
Microsoft Press
A Division of Microsoft Corporation
One Microsoft Way
Redmond, Washington 98052-6399

Library of Congress Control Number: 2006938196

Printed and bound in the United States of America.

1 2 3 4 5 6 7 8 9   QWT   2 1 0 9 8 7

Distributed in Canada by H.B. Fenn and Company Ltd.

A CIP catalogue record for this book is available from the British Library.

Microsoft Press books are available through booksellers and distributors worldwide. For further information about international editions, contact your local Microsoft Corporation office or contact Microsoft Press International directly at fax (425) 936-7329. Visit our Web site at www.microsoft.com/mspress. Send comments to *tkinput@microsoft.com*.

Microsoft, Microsoft Press, Active Directory, ActiveX, BizTalk, Excel, Internet Explorer, Jscript, MSDN, Outlook, SQL Server, Visio, Visual Basic, Visual Studio, Win32, Windows, Windows Mobile, Windows NT, Windows Server, and Windows Vista are either registered trademarks or trademarks of Microsoft Corporation in the United States and/or other countries. Other product and company names mentioned herein may be the trademarks of their respective owners.

The example companies, organizations, products, domain names, e-mail addresses, logos, people, places, and events depicted herein are fictitious. No association with any real company, organization, product, domain name, e-mail address, logo, person, place, or event is intended or should be inferred.

Acquisitions Editor: Ken Jones
Project Editor: Denise Bankaitis
Technical Reviewer: Tony Northrup
Editorial Production: nSight, Inc.
Indexer: Nancy Guenther

Body Part No. X13-47925

Dedication

I would like to thank my wife, Carrie; my daughter, Allie; and my son, Ben, for their patience and understanding while I took on another long, nights-and-weekends project.

—Mike Snell

I'd like to thank my wife, Alisa, and our four children—Kyle, Cameron, Gillian, and Curtis—for their love and support. They're the ones who have to put up with the pressure of deadlines, and they do so with more patience than I could.

—Bruce Johnson

About the Authors

Shawn Wildermuth

Shawn Wildermuth is a Microsoft C# MVP and is the founder of Wildermuth Consulting Services, LLC, a company that is dedicated to delivering software and training solutions in the Atlanta, Georgia, area. He goes by the moniker "The ADO Guy" and can be found on his Web site at *http://adoguy.com*. He is also a speaker on the International .NET Association (INETA) Speaker Bureau and has appeared at several national conferences to speak on a variety of subjects. Shawn is also the author of the book *Pragmatic ADO.NET* (Addison-Wesley, 2002), the co-author of *MCTS Self-Paced Training Kit (Exam 70-536)* (Microsoft Press, 2006), and the co-author of the upcoming *Prescriptive Data Architectures* for Addison-Wesley. He has been writing articles for a number of years for a variety of magazines and Web sites, including MSDN, MSDN Online, DevSource, InformIT, Windows IT Pro, The ServerSide .NET, ONDotNet.com, and Intel's Rich Client Series. Shawn has enjoyed building data-driven software for more than 20 years.

Mike Snell

Mike Snell has more than 15 years of experience as a software architect and consultant. He has led a number of enterprise-level projects building client solutions on the Microsoft platform. He has delivered training and mentoring to hundreds of developers. Presently, Mike runs the Microsoft Consulting Practice at CEI (*http://www.ceiamerica.com*) in Pittsburgh, Pennsylvania. There, with his team of consulting architects, he helps CEI's diverse client base build mission-critical software.

Mike is also recognized as a Microsoft Regional Director (*http://msdn.microsoft.com/isv/rd/*), a Microsoft Certified Solution Developer (MCSD), and a Project Management Professional (PMP).

In addition to the MCPD training guides for the Web and Windows exams, Mike is also the co-author of the titles *Visual Studio 2005 Unleashed* (Sams, 2006) and *Visual Basic Programmer's Guide to the .NET Framework Class Library* (Sams, 2002).

Bruce Johnson

Bruce Johnson is a partner with ObjectSharp Consulting and a 25-year veteran of the computer industry. The first half of his career was spent working in the trenches—otherwise known as the UNIX field. But the past 14 years have been spent on projects at the leading edge of Windows technology, a leading edge that has migrated from C++ through the myriad versions of Visual Basic and ASP, right up to the present incarnations in .NET 3.0. Bruce's experience includes the creation of commercial Web applications, the implementation of Web Services in a financial institution, and the building of a larger number of Windows Forms applications.

As well as having fun with system design and development, Bruce has also given more than 200 presentations at conferences and user groups across North America. He has written columns and articles for numerous magazines, and he attempts to write regular posts on his blog at *http://www.objectsharp.com/blogs/bruce*. With the publication of this book, he can pretty much guarantee that the activity on the blog will increase from recent levels.

Kristy Saunders

Kristy Saunders has more than 14 years of experience as a software developer and consultant. She currently works and lives in the Portland, Oregon, area, where she applies her passion for creating high-quality user experiences to architecting and building applications that serve the eLearning community.

Contents at a Glance

Table of Contents

What do you think of this book? We want to hear from you!

Microsoft is interested in hearing your feedback so we can continually improve our books and learning resources for you. To participate in a brief online survey, please visit:

www.microsoft.com/learning/booksurvey/

7   Component Development

What do you think of this book? We want to hear from you!

Microsoft is interested in hearing your feedback so we can continually improve our books and learning resources for you. To participate in a brief online survey, please visit:

www.microsoft.com/learning/booksurvey/

Introduction

This training kit is designed for developers who plan to take the Developer (PRO) Exam 70-548: Designing and Developing Windows-Based Applications by Using the Microsoft .NET Framework. In addition, developers who work on a team in a medium or large-scale development environment in a professional capacity will benefit from this training kit.

We assume that before you begin using this kit, you are familiar with creating Microsoft Windows-based applications using Microsoft Visual Studio .NET 2003 or 2005. You should have at least three to four years professional, on-the-job experience to benefit the most from this training kit. You should also have a working knowledge of Microsoft Visual Basic or C#. In addition, you should have worked on a team throughout the software development life cycle, and be familiar with technical envisioning and planning, design and development, and stabilizing and releasing software.

MORE INFO Exam Preparation Guide

You can go online to find more information on preparing for this exam. Microsoft has published a Preparation Guide that details the skills measured by the exam, the audience profile, your study options, and more. You can find this information at *http://www.microsoft.com/learning/exams/70-548.asp*.

This training kit will help you prepare for the exam. The training kit is broken down into the following sections:

- Envisioning and Designing an Application
- Designing and Developing a User Interface
- Designing and Developing a Component
- Designing and Developing an Application Framework
- Testing and Stabilizing an Application
- Deploying and Supporting an Application

Hardware Requirements

This training kit contains practice exercises that will help you with the exam contents. The following hardware is recommended for running Visual Studio 2005 to complete the practice exercises:

- Computer with a 600 MHz or faster processor
- 192 MB of RAM or more
- 2 GB of available hard disk space

- DVD-ROM drive
- 1,024 x 768 or higher resolution display with 256 colors
- Keyboard and Microsoft mouse, or compatible pointing device

Software Requirements

The following software is required to complete the practice exercises:

- One of the following operating systems:
  - Windows 2000 with Service Pack 4
  - Windows XP with Service Pack 2
  - Windows XP Professional x64 Edition (WOW)
  - Windows Server 2003 with Service Pack 1
  - Windows Server 2003, x64 Editions (WOW)
  - Windows Server 2003 R2
  - Windows Server 2003 R2, x64 Editions (WOW)
  - Microsoft Windows Vista
- Visual Studio 2005 (A 90-day evaluation edition of Visual Studio 2005 Professional Edition is included on DVD with this book.)
- Microsoft SQL Server 2005 Express Edition running on your computer. (This can be installed as part of Visual Studio.)

IMPORTANT Visual Studio Team Suite

To complete the lab exercises for Chapter 13, Lesson 1, you will need to have Microsoft Visual Studio 2005 Team Edition for Software Developers installed on your computer. This is available as part of Visual Studio 2005 Team Suite. You can download a free 180-day trial version of Visual Studio 2005 Team Suite from http://www.microsoft.com/downloads /details.aspx?FamilyId=5677DDC4-5035-401F-95C3-CC6F46F6D8F7&displaylang=en. You will need to uninstall Visual Studio 2005 Professional to install Visual Studio Team Suite on the same computer.

To complete the lab exercises for Chapter 13, Lesson 1, you will need:

- 256 MB of RAM or more
- 3.3 GB available disk space to download Visual Studio Team Suite
- 2 GB available disk space to install Visual Studio Team Suite
- One of the following operating systems:
  - Microsoft Windows 2000 with Service Pack 4
  - Windows XP with Service Pack 2
  - Windows Server 2003 with Service Pack 1
  - Windows Vista

Using the CD and DVD

A companion CD and an evaluation software DVD are included with this training kit. The companion CD contains the following:

- **Practice tests** You can reinforce your understanding of the exam content by using electronic practice tests that you customize to meet your needs from the pool of Lesson Review questions in this book. You can also practice for the 70-548 certification exam by using tests created from a pool of 300 realistic exam questions. These questions give you many practice exams to ensure that you're prepared to take the real thing.
- **Code** Many chapters in this book include sample files associated with the lab exercises at the end of every lesson. Each exercise has a project or solution you can use to start the exercise and a version of the completed exercise for your review (or if you get stuck).
- **An eBook** An electronic version (eBook) of this book is included for times when you don't want to carry the printed book with you. The eBook is in Portable Document Format (PDF), and you can view it by using Adobe Acrobat or Adobe Reader.

The evaluation software DVD contains a 90-day evaluation edition of Visual Studio 2005 Professional Edition in case you want to use it with this book.

How to Install the Practice Tests

To install the practice test software from the companion CD to your hard disk, complete the following steps:

1. Insert the companion CD into your CD drive and accept the license agreement. A CD menu appears.

   NOTE **If the CD menu doesn't appear**

   If the CD menu or the license agreement doesn't appear, AutoRun might be disabled on your computer. Refer to the Readme.txt file on the CD-ROM for alternate installation instructions.

2. Click Training Kit Exam Prep and follow the instructions on the screen.

How to Use the Practice Tests

To start the practice test software, follow these steps:

1. Click Start/All Programs/Microsoft Press Training Kit Exam Prep. A window appears that shows all the Microsoft Press training kit exam prep suites installed on your computer.
2. Double-click the lesson review or practice test you want to use.

NOTE Lesson reviews vs. practice tests

Select the (70-548) Designing and Developing Windows-Based Applications by Using the Microsoft .NET Framework *lesson review* to use the questions from the "Lesson Review" sections of this book. Select the (70-548) Designing and Developing Windows-Based Applications by Using the Microsoft .NET Framework *practice test* to use a pool of 300 questions similar to those in the 70-548 certification exam.

Lesson Review Options

When you start a lesson review, the Custom Mode dialog box appears so that you can configure your test. You can click OK to accept the defaults, or you can customize the number of questions you want, how the practice test software works, which exam objectives you want the questions to relate to, and whether you want your lesson review to be timed. If you're retaking a test, you can select whether you want to see all the questions again or only those questions you missed or didn't answer.

After you click OK, your lesson review starts.

- To take the test, answer the questions and use the Next, Previous, and Go To buttons to move from question to question.
- After you answer an individual question, if you want to see which answers are correct— along with an explanation of each correct answer—click Explanation.
- If you'd rather wait until the end of the test to see how you did, answer all the questions and then click Score Test. You'll see a summary of the exam objectives you chose and the percentage of questions you got right overall and per objective. You can print a copy of your test, review your answers, or retake the test.

Practice Test Options

When you start a practice test, you choose whether to take the test in Certification Mode, Study Mode, or Custom Mode:

- **Certification Mode**   Closely resembles the experience of taking a certification exam. The test has a set number of questions, it's timed, and you can't pause and restart the timer.
- **Study Mode**   Creates an untimed test in which you can review the correct answers and the explanations after you answer each question.
- **Custom Mode**   Gives you full control over the test options so that you can customize them as you like.

In all modes, the user interface you see when taking the test is basically the same but with different options enabled or disabled depending on the mode. The main options are discussed in the previous section, "Lesson Review Options."

When you review your answer to an individual practice test question, a "References" section is provided that lists where in the training kit you can find the information that relates to that question and provides links to other sources of information. After you click Test Results to score your entire practice test, you can click the Learning Plan tab to see a list of references for every objective.

How to Uninstall the Practice Tests

To uninstall the practice test software for a training kit, use the Add Or Remove Programs option in Windows Control Panel.

Microsoft Certified Professional Program

The Microsoft certifications provide the best method to prove your command of current Microsoft products and technologies. The exams and corresponding certifications are developed to validate your mastery of critical competencies as you design and develop, or implement and support, solutions with Microsoft products and technologies. Computer professionals who become Microsoft-certified are recognized as experts and are sought after industry-wide. Certification brings a variety of benefits to the individual and to employers and organizations.

MORE INFO   All the Microsoft certifications

For a full list of Microsoft certifications, go to *http://www.microsoft.com/learning/mcp/default.asp*.

Technical Support

Every effort has been made to ensure the accuracy of this book and the contents of the companion CD. If you have comments, questions, or ideas regarding this book or the companion CD, please send them to Microsoft Press by using either of the following methods:

E-mail: tkinput@microsoft.com

Postal Mail:

Microsoft Press
Attn: MCTS Self-Paced Training Kit (Exam 70-548): *Designing and Developing Windows-Based Applications by Using the Microsoft .NET Framework*
One Microsoft Way
Redmond, WA 98052–6399

For additional support information regarding this book and the CD-ROM (including answers to commonly asked questions about installation and use), visit the Microsoft Press Technical Support Web site at *http://www.microsoft.com/learning/support/books/*. To connect directly to the Microsoft Knowledge Base and enter a query, visit *http://support.microsoft.com/search/*. For support information regarding Microsoft software, connect to *http://support.microsoft.com*.

Evaluation Edition Software Support

The 90-day evaluation edition provided with this training kit is not the full retail product and is provided only for the purposes of training and evaluation. Microsoft and Microsoft Technical Support do not support this evaluation edition.

Information about any issues relating to the use of this evaluation edition with this training kit is posted to the Support section of the Microsoft Press Web site (*http://www.microsoft.com /learning/support/books/*). For information about ordering the full version of any Microsoft software, please call Microsoft Sales at (800) 426-9400 or visit *http://www.microsoft.com*.

Chapter 1
Application Requirements and Design

Projects are almost always envisioned and funded by stakeholders and upper management. They have the idea; you know how to write the software. You need to be able to work with business analysts to get the ideas onto paper and drive consensus for the vision before you will be trusted with the budget to execute the project. You need to show that you understand the business problem you will be trying to solve and that you can translate their vision into tangible software. This means being able to evaluate requirements and then recommend, evaluate, and refine a design for the application.

This chapter looks at how you move from the vision, goals, and requirements of an application to a proposed solution. This process involves recommending technologies, defining a design, and then vetting your recommendations through the creation of a prototype. You then need to demonstrate the feasibility of the project (and your design) to the visionaries and stakeholders. Ultimately it will be their confidence in your proposed solution that determines if a project gets funded and moves from idea to implementation.

Exam objectives in this chapter:
- Evaluate the technical feasibility of an application design concept.
  - ❏ Evaluate the proof of concept.
  - ❏ Recommend the best technologies for the features and goals of the application.
  - ❏ Weigh implementation considerations.
  - ❏ Investigate existing solutions for similar business problems.
- Create a proof-of-concept prototype.
  - ❏ Evaluate the risks associated with the proposed technology or implementation.
  - ❏ Validate that the proposed technology can be used in the application.
  - ❏ Demonstrate to stakeholders that the proposed solution will address their needs.

Lessons in this chapter:

Before You Begin

To complete the lessons in this chapter, you should be familiar with developing Microsoft Windows applications with Microsoft Visual Studio 2005 using Visual Basic or C#. In addition, you should be comfortable with all of the following tasks:

- Reviewing goals and requirements for a Windows application.
- Detailing the functional specifications for a Windows application.
- Being aware of how .NET architectures and related technologies solve specific business problems.
- Creating solutions using Windows Forms.
- Understanding object-oriented development concepts.
- Reading and working with class diagrams and other technical models.

Real World

Mike Snell

Requirements are just a starting point—or at least they should be. I've had many customers who feel that once they've documented their requirements their job is nearly over. Many seem to feel that requirements get dumped into Visual Studio and out comes an entire system. I am exaggerating, of course. However, I am routinely asked to give a fixed-price bid, for instance, to a set of requirements. This is absurd and dangerous at best. On larger projects it is negligent, in my opinion. There is just too much risk involved. I explain it to customers like this: "I can estimate how long it takes a developer, given a particular architecture, to code a screen, a business object, a database table, a stored procedure, a service, and so on. However, I can't tell you how long it takes (or how much it costs) to satisfy a requirement."

What is required, of course, is decomposition of those requirements. This means analysis, the creations of use cases, a functional specification, a solution architecture, possibly a prototype, logical models, and physical models. This is hard work. However, it serves to validate and refine the requirements as well as eliminate a lot of risk. These deliverables also lead to artifacts (forms, classes, tables, and so on) that can be estimated based on complexity factors. The result is less risk to the project team (and stakeholders) and higher confidence that what is being built is what is actually required.

Lesson 1: Evaluate Requirements and Propose a Design

Reaching a common understanding among the developers, the business, and the users is the principal goal of application requirements. Nearly all enterprise applications built by professionals define and document requirements. How those requirements get documented, agreed-to, and are managed is often different on a per-project basis.

As an example, the Microsoft Solutions Framework (MSF) for Agile Software Development defines a work item for what it calls a quality of service (QOS) requirement. This work item represents a requirement that can be classified as a performance, load, availability, stress, accessibility, serviceability, or maintainability requirement. The same methodology includes another work item called a scenario. A scenario is the MSF term for use case. A *use case* defines a path of user activity through the system to reach a specific goal. Together, these work items (QOS and scenario) represent the user view (scenario) and the nonfunctional view (QOS) of the system.

Consider another example: MSF for Capability Maturity Model Integration (CMMI) defines a work item it calls, simply, requirement. This requirement work item, however, has a number of subtypes. These subtypes include: scenario, quality of service, safety, security, functional, operational, and interface. This methodology groups all requirements together but then allows them to be subgrouped by a category. These subgroups are pretty granular. However, they can be reclassified based on some standard requirement groups such as: user requirements (scenario), nonfunctional requirements (QOS, safety, security), and functional requirements (functional, operational, and interface).

These two examples are simply the beginning. The definition of software requirements have been discussed, debated, and written about for many years. There are many good books out there dedicated solely to the subject of requirements. There are also many standards and methods that all take a slightly different perspective on software requirements. Our intent is not to change the way you write requirements. Enough is common among these methods to make them all viable. Rather, we will establish a simple baseline for talking about requirements. We will then discuss how you evaluate requirements and recommend solutions based on those requirements.

After this lesson, you will be able to:
- Recognize poor requirements and propose improvements.
- Evaluate a set of application requirements for their completeness and feasibility.
- Recommend technologies based on a set of requirements.
- Investigate and evaluate existing alternatives to your recommendations.
- Define a high-level application design based on requirements and recommendations.
- Determine whether an application's design is feasible and practical.

Estimated lesson time: 40 minutes

What Makes a Good Set of Application Requirements?

A good requirement set includes requirements that are defined from multiple perspectives. This makes a lot of sense. All projects have multiple influences. The business (or executive sponsorship) has a set of objectives and goals for the application. Users define specific tasks they need to accomplish. Developers and testers need to know what features will be required to make this application a success. There are also requirements around supporting and maintaining the application, around performance and scalability, and more. The goal is to get enough of these requirements defined so as to eliminate unknowns (risk) and to build the right project.

For our purposes we will define four types of requirements: business, user, functional, and quality of service. Together, these categories represent the necessary perspectives required to define the requirements for the vast majority of (if not all) business applications. They provide a common understanding from the business through to the developer. They also allow the quality assurance team to ensure that the application stays focused and on track. Let's take a look at each requirement category in further detail.

Business Requirement

A *business requirement* defines what the business believes to be important for the success of the project. The business typically represents management or stakeholders who are funding the project. They often define requirements in terms of vision or goals for the application. However, these goals need to be turned into real, tangible requirements.

As an example, consider a business requirement that states, "The new version should allow us to sell the application to new markets." This is a great goal for the system. It helps justify the expense of the development in that it will open up new sales channels and markets and hence increase revenues and profits. However, this goal needs to be translated into real business requirements. Real high-level business requirements derived from this goal might look as follows:

- The system must include metadata support for all named concepts. This will allow companies in different markets to rename these concepts based on their terminology.
- The system must implement an open standard for the exchange of sales data. This will allow all markets to interoperate with the application.
- The application must support the definition of feature packs for specific markets. A feature pack is a set of features that can be turned on or off as a group (think add-in). The application's core should not depend on features inside a given feature pack.

You can see that these are tangible requirements tied to what was a goal for the application: support multiple markets. It is also important to note that these are *high-level requirements*, that is, requirements without detailed specifications. That's okay. The requirements can be kept and tracked at a high level. An application architect or systems analyst will have to translate requirements into specifications and design. However, the specifications and design should not alter, add to, or take away from the requirements. If you see this happening, you need to update your requirements and get them revalidated as appropriate and necessary.

User Requirement

User requirements are the tasks the users must be able to accomplish in order to meet the objectives of their jobs. Most developers do not have the luxury of a business analyst and are therefore used to receiving or documenting user requirements. This typically involves sitting with users and discussing what exactly they do (or need to do) to help them. The following are all high-level user requirements:

- A customer service representative must be able to place an order for a customer.
- A user must be able to query the on-hand inventory to determine the number of units of a given product that are in stock.
- Users must be able to view their order histories in a list. They must be able to select an order from the list and view its details.

These are not use cases and are not specifications. The first question a business analyst might ask, for example, is "how?" How does a customer service representative place an order for a customer? The user will then typically detail a number of steps that are involved in this process. These steps represent the use case for "customer rep places order for customer." This use case helps understand the requirement. In addition, an architect or systems analyst should define the specifications for the given requirement. This will include the information developers need to know such as: what constitutes an order, what fields are required, what rules will be processed, and so on.

Functional Requirement

Functional requirements or *functional specifications* are the features the developers must build in order to satisfy the other requirements. These requirements are typically defined in great detail to help developers understand exactly what it is they need to develop. The functional requirements are typically written by a technical lead or architect. They are not the requirements of the users or the business.

A functional requirement, for example, might be to create a administrative user interface for managing the settings of an application. The functional requirement should include the name of the form, the controls used on the form, the input validation rules, the security rules, the classes that should be called to support the form's functionality, and so on.

As you can see, functional requirements can be very detailed. It is often better to do functional design rather than to write functional requirements. This allows you to take advantage of application models, tools such as Visual Studio, and some code (or pseudo code) to define the functionality of the system. Developers often understand these items better. In addition, it saves you the time of documenting these items in two places (in a document and in the physical models).

Quality of Service Requirement

Quality of service (QOS) requirements define the contractual, or nonfunctional, requirements for the system. QOS requirements do not typically represent specific user problems. Rather, they define the requirements around things like performance, scalability, and standards. These requirements should not be overlooked. They need to be defined and considered when doing application architecture and development. The following are examples of QOS requirements:

- All screens should load from the database within 5 seconds given a local area network (LAN) connection.
- The application should scale to 15 concurrent users with the current database setup (see server specification).
- The application should automatically update itself across the LAN connection.
- The system should use Windows-integrated security to identify users and partition data based on a user's group affiliation.

You can see that QOS requirements are very important. They further define what the application must support from a nonfunctional perspective. You must get this information up-front to make wise decisions on how you recommend and implement technologies for a given business problem.

Exam Tip   Pay close attention to the exact requirements for any given question on the exam. You need to satisfy all the requirements listed in the question and only those requirements listed in the question. Do not assume anything; pay close attention to only what is written. You have to eliminate the urge to use what your experience tells you and focus solely on what is written in the question.

Use Cases vs. Requirements

Use cases and requirements are not the same thing. Use cases are a Unified Modeling Language (UML) model meant to describe a set of user steps to accomplish a task. Requirements define what must be created to satisfy the user's needs. Together, they provide a good view of how the user sees the system. However, you should be wary if you encounter attempts to do away with one in favor of the other.

This happens most often with regard to use cases trying to supplant requirements. This is sometimes even successful. These situations are almost always highly agile, involve the client on a day-to-day basis, have small teams, and do not involve a geographically distributed work force. If this is your environment, you might be able to leverage use cases in lieu of requirements. What you want to avoid, however, is cluttering your use cases with a ton of specification detail to the point that you can't find the use case anymore. For more traditional environments you should consider starting with either requirements or use cases and build the missing item. You typically need both to be successful.

Requirements and uses cases have two different goals. Requirements define what needs to be created for the system to be successful. They are useful for defining scope and determining if you have met objectives. Requirements are often traced all the way through the implementation process. Project managers and testers create requirements traceability matrices that define how each requirement is realized through the system.

Use cases, on the other hand, are meant to define a set of steps to reach a common user goal. Use cases are more about the process by which a user reaches a requirement. They help architects, developers, and testers understand how people work and how the system should accommodate their activities. They are not, done correctly, requirements.

Evaluate the Requirements for the Application

When you are presented with a set of requirements, you need to be able to evaluate them and determine if they are complete, feasible, and sufficient. We have already discussed the categories of requirements that must be present to make a complete set: business, user, functional, and QOS. You next need to look at these requirements and determine whether they are sufficiently well-documented. The following represent criteria, or questions, that you can use to determine whether the requirements are sufficient:

- **Requirement perspectives**   Are all requirement perspectives considered? Do you have a definition of the business, user, and QOS requirements? Can you derive the functional requirements and design from this set of requirements?

- **Unambiguous**   Is each requirement written using specifics? Can each requirement be acted upon? You want to make sure that there are no soft requirements. You want to eliminate phrases like "the application should be easy to use" from the requirements. This is a goal. A requirement would indicate something like "the application should implement a task pane of common users' actions from a given feature."

- **Complete**   Are the requirements complete? You need to identify missing elements in the requirements. You should also indicate where further clarification of one or more requirements is warranted. Perhaps, for example, some requirements need further fleshing out through use cases. If you are having trouble understanding a requirement or designing to it, then it's not complete.

- **Necessary**   Are all the requirements actually necessary to satisfy the goals of the application? This is the opposite of complete. Sometimes business analysts, developers, and architects can add things to the system that are not really required. You need to keep a close eye out for scope creep by means of overzealous requirement definitions.

- **Feasible**   Are the requirements as documented really feasible? You need to review the requirements against known constraints such as budget, timeline, and technology. It's better to raise red flags during the requirements definition phase than to wait until the project is already over budget.

Thinking of your requirements in these terms will make everyone's job much easier. A good set of requirements will lead to good architecture, good testing, and high user acceptance.

Recommend the Best Technologies for the Application

There is a big difference between defining application architecture and recommending technologies for an application. These tasks often get intermingled and confused. One should not be a substitute for another. Architects and developers should be asked to look at the requirements for a system and make technology recommendations. These technology recommendations in conjunction with the requirements will drive a lot of the application's architecture. Therefore, technology recommendations should come prior to application architecture.

The decision to recommend one technology over another should be driven solely by the requirements. A developer should evaluate the requirements and choose the right technologies to fit. However, in all practicality these decisions sometimes have more to do with what is available than what is the best. If you are faced with this dilemma, you should factor it directly into your decision process. Make it a requirement to leverage as much existing hardware and software as you can. If this is validated and justified, you can respect the requirement.

For our purposes we will take a look at how you might recommend certain technologies over others based solely on the user, business, and QOS requirements (and not on what is available or convenient). Of course, to make recommendations you must have some familiarity with certain technologies and know how those technologies can be brought to bear on a given solution.

A Windows application can be broken down into a core set of application layers or components. These items make up the bulk of your technology recommendation opportunities. It makes sense to review the layers and components that define a Windows application. The following discussion lists each of these items, defines the options that are available, and provides a decision tree that will help guide you toward recommending one technology over another.

Client

The *client* represents how your application will be presented to the users. The client is the user's interface into the application. It is what the users see and use every time they work with the application. The following items represent some of the many Windows client technology options available to you:

- **Windows Client**   This represents the standard Windows client. This is a forms-based interface. This interface is built as either a single document interface (SDI) or a multiple document interface (MDI) application. An SDI interface has a single, main form that may load other forms into panels or tabs. Each form is typically a different type. An MDI application has a container that loads forms. These forms often represent multiple versions of the same type. Word, Excel, and Visual Studio are MDI examples.

You recommend this solution when you require a rich, interactive user interface and plan to leverage the resources of the user's desktop. This model requires the .NET Framework on each desktop. The application may connect to shared data on the LAN or even occasionally call out to a Web service or use remoting.

- **Smart Client**   Represents a client that is deployed through a Web browser but that runs as a Windows application on the client's machine. Smart Clients provide a high degree of user interactivity but still work with a Web server to leverage the pervasiveness of the Internet.

  You recommend this solution when you need to build a Web-based application with a very high degree of user interactivity and you can control the client's operating system. This solution depends on Windows and the .NET Framework being deployed on a user's desktop.

- **Microsoft Office Client**   Represents a client that is built with Microsoft Word, Microsoft Excel, or Microsoft Outlook as the principal user interface. You may still call back to a Web server through Web services to exchange data. However, users leverage the familiar paradigm of Office to get their work completed.

  You recommend an Office client when you are building applications that take advantage of the capabilities of Office (such as spreadsheet or contact management). You also need to ensure that the target version of Office is deployed on each user's desktop.

- **Windows Mobile**   Represents clients that are enabled through handheld devices running the Windows Mobile operating system.

  You would recommend this solution when users are highly mobile and need access to information over their handheld devices.

Third-Party Controls

Third-party controls represent developer controls not shipped by Microsoft or embedded in the editions of Visual Studio 2005. You will want to explore the controls that are available to you in order to weigh build versus buy decisions. For example, if your application requires that you integrate with a credit card processor, you should explore the many components available for you to do so. In most scenarios, third-party controls can eliminate risk, reduce costs, and increase delivery time. Some of the many control categories that are available include: charting, scheduling, navigation, user interface styling, licensing, reporting, integration, spreadsheets, data grids, and many more.

Application Server

Your Windows solution might or might not require an application server. An *application server* represents the server that you will recommend to run your code in your middle tier. This is code that is shared by the clients and typically processes business rules and accesses data stores. Most standard Windows clients do not require an application server. However, if you are building a client-server architecture, Smart Client, or service-oriented architecture (SOA), then you will need an application server.

Typically, architects and developers recommend the software and not many of the hardware specifications. When recommending an application server for your solution, you should consider the version of Internet Information Server (IIS) required, the version of the .NET Framework you need to target, and the security constraints of the application.

Application Libraries

An *application library* is a set of components (and, many times, source code) that you can download and use in your solution. An application library typically encapsulates a set of features that are common to a lot of applications. For example, the Microsoft Enterprise Library provides features for caching, error management, configuration, and more. You need to review your application's requirements and determine if these libraries can be used to help ensure best practices and higher quality.

Similar to application libraries are application frameworks. A *framework* is a set of base classes and components that abstract a lot of the architectural plumbing away from the developer. Frameworks try to offer a cohesive solution to many architecture problems. These typically include managing state between application layers, physically distributing the layers of an application, handling plumbing, and more.

Security

You need to be able to recommend security technologies that you can use to meet the security requirements of the application. For example, you need to determine whether you should implement a custom security model or use Windows security in your application. This typically depends on the user base. If you are writing for the corporate audience and are on a Windows network, it's best to integrate your solution with Active Directory directory service. If, on the other hand, your users are not on the same domain and connect across the Internet using a Smart Client, then you should consider creating a custom security solution that manages credentials in another data store. Other security recommendations might include how you store and encrypt data and how you connect to that data.

Data Storage

Data storage represents how your application will store and access its data. A lot of options are available. You need to let the requirements of the application lead you toward the best solution. The following represent some of the options that might be available to you:

- **File-based storage**   This represents storing your data in files in the application's file system. File-based solutions typically involve storing data as Extensible Markup Language (XML).

You would recommend this only on small applications where a database solution is not available or warranted.

- **SQL Express**   SQL Express is a free database solution available from Microsoft. It provides a starting point for creating small project databases. It also provides a file-based solution for developers looking to embed SQL in their application.

  You should consider this option when you are constrained by costs, can limit your database requirements to a single CPU, a single gig of RAM, and a 4 GB database size, and do not require many of the advanced features of a full database solution.

- **SQL Everywhere**   SQL Everywhere (also called SQL Mobile) provides a small, lightweight, highly functional database for handheld devices.

  You should recommend this option when you are building mobile solutions that store and retrieve data locally to the handheld device.

- **SQL Server editions and options**   The SQL Server family includes standard and enterprise editions. These versions include features like reporting services, analysis services, data mining, notification, and more. If you encounter these requirements, you need to be aware of how these services can help.

- **Other data storage**   A number of other options are available to you for your solutions. You may, for example, have a requirement to retrieve your data from an Oracle database or a DB2. In either case you can recommend the right .NET data provider to do so.

MORE INFO   SQL Server editions

There are a lot of editions of SQL Server—one to fit every need. For a good overview of what is available to you, search *http://www.microsoft.com/sql/* for "SQL Server 2005 Features Comparison." This provides an item-by-item comparison of features.

This should give you a good overview of what to expect when recommending technologies for your Windows solutions. Your task should be to focus on the requirements, review them, and make recommendations based solely on these requirements. You should not, for example, be recommending a SQL Express database for an enterprise application with hundreds of concurrent users. Rather, you need to respect these and other requirements and recommend the right solution for the job.

Quick Check

1. Name the common types, or categories, of requirements.
2. What is a quality-of-service (QOS) requirement?
3. What are the characteristics of a good requirement?

> **Quick Check Answers**
> 1. Requirements should be seen from multiple perspectives. These include business, user, functional, and quality of service (QOS).
> 2. A QOS requirement defines a contractual requirement that the system must meet. These requirements are often used to define scalability, performance, and other nonfunctional requirements.
> 3. A good requirement should be unambiguous, complete, necessary, and feasible.

Investigate Existing Solutions for Similar Business Problems

When you make your technology recommendations, it is wise to consider existing solutions to similar business problems. If you find an existing bit of software, a product, or a third-party component, you can sometimes buy and not build from scratch. This can save you valuable design, development, and test cycles. For example, you should consider software that might even exist already in your own organization. Often this software can be componentized to support multiple applications. If you resist the urge to reinvent, you keep the development team focused on just the features that make your application unique. The following are some common technologies to consider when looking at making alternate recommendations for your Windows solutions:

- **Corporate assets** You should always look internally first. Companies spend a lot of money every year solving the same problem many times. You might find that you can take some existing code, turn it into a component, and use it for multiple applications.
- **Third-party components and libraries** We discussed this earlier. There are some great things available to you for a low cost in terms of creating reports, charts, and other features.
- **BizTalk Server** Provides a solution for managing business process and integration. The latest version, 2006, provides integration with Visual Studio 2005. It also provides adapters for key applications in the industry. You should consider recommending this solution when you have a lot of system integration around key business processes.
- **Host Integration Server** Provides a server product for integrating with IBM mainframes. This includes connecting with data sources, messaging, and security. You should consider recommending this when you have to build an application that has a high degree of interoperability with IBM mainframes.

Create a High-Level Application Design

You have your application requirements. You have evaluated these requirements and confirmed them as good. You then put together a technology recommendation based on the requirements. Your next step is to define a model for the application's high-level design. This design should help document and explain the application you intend to create. It therefore must define the technologies that you intend to use and indicate how these technologies will be connected.

How you model your application design is not as important as just modeling it. There are many tools that will allow you to define an application design. You can create boxes and arrows in Visio or you can use Visual Studio 2005 Team Architect. The latter provides the application diagram for defining applications, their connectivity, and their configuration. You might not have this tool available to you, but it makes for a good model of what should be in your high-level application design. Let's take a look.

Visual Studio Team Architect Application Diagram

You add items to your application diagram using the Toolbox in Visual Studio 2005. Figure 1-1 shows the application diagram Toolbox. Note that you can drag application types from the Toolbox onto the designer. This allows you to indicate which technologies you are recommending for a given solution. You can define Windows applications, ASP.NET Web services, ASP.NET applications, and more. In addition, there are a number of endpoints that you can attach to an application. An architect uses these endpoints to configure which applications communicate and through what means. Let's look at an example.

Figure 1-1   The application diagram Toolbox.

Figure 1-2 provides a sample application diagram. Note that the application is defined as having two user interfaces. It defines an Office application for reporting on product quality issues (ProductQualityMetrics) and a Windows Smart Client application for the product support team (ProductSupportAdminDesk). The diagram also defines a couple of Web service applications (ReportingServices and ProductSupportServices) and two databases (ReportDb and ProductSupport).

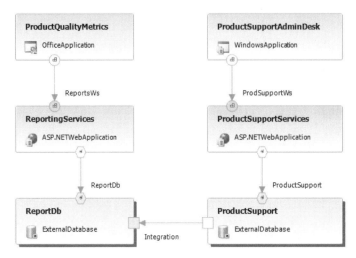

Figure 1-2   An application diagram.

Each application on the diagram can be configured in terms of the settings and constraints that are required for the application. Think of this as your application configuration plan. For example, the ProductSupportAdminDesk client application might define constraints on the client's operating system and version of the .NET Framework. Figure 1-3 shows the Setting And Constraints window in Visual Studio for this application. Note that you define these parameters through this interface. The example indicates that clients must be running Windows XP, Service Pack 2, and the .NET Framework Version 2.

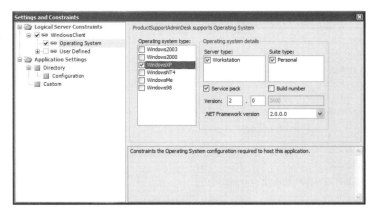

Figure 1-3   The Settings And Constraints window.

Defining the application's requirements, making your technology recommendation, and creating a high-level design are the necessary risk-aversive steps to begin your project. You will use this information to define a prototype, refine your design, and begin creating detailed specifications and an application architecture. We will cover the prototyping process in the next lesson.

MORE INFO　Creating Detailed Design

We will cover the process of creating physical models for developers (layers, class, activity, sequence) in Chapter 2, "Decompose Specifications for Developers."

Lab: Evaluate Requirements and Propose a Design

In this lab, you will evaluate a list of application requirements. You will use these requirements to make design and technology choices and propose an application design.

▶ Exercise: Review Requirements and Recommend Technologies

For this exercise, review the following set of application requirements. You will then follow the steps listed below to arrive at a set of recommendations for the application. The following are key requirements for the application:

R1　Department managers will use the data for report metrics. They need to have access to this data offline for additional analysis. Therefore, the data should be accessible to this group when connected or disconnected from the LAN.

R2　Our product support team will also use the application. They will enter customer and product support requests from their desks at the office.

R3　The system needs to support up to 100 concurrent users.

R4　Users should not have to manually log on to the application. It needs to recognize their network logons and passwords.

R5　The application should integrate with the product and order systems. When a support ticket is generated, the support ticket should be associated with the right product and customer order.

R6　The application needs to send product defect notices as daily extracts to the product quality tracking system.

1.　Review the application requirements and determine which client technology you should implement based on the specifics in the requirements.

R1 indicates you should consider a Smart Client or an Office application using Excel to support disconnected data reporting scenarios.

R2 does not dictate a user interface (UI). However, if the team is totally internal, a Smart Client solution would work well for them, too.

2. Determine a data storage mechanism for the application.

   R1 indicates you might need to consider a local storage option on the client. This could be isolated storage, SQL Everywhere, or even Excel.

   R3 indicates a large enough workforce that you will want to support a SQL Server standard back-end for data collection and storage.

3. What additional technologies should you consider for this solution? Consider cost-effective products that satisfy some of these requirements.

   R5 indicates integration around a couple of business processes. You should explore the potential of using BizTalk server to aid in this effort.

   R6 indicates sending data extracts. Again, BizTalk might be warranted. You should also consider SQL Server Integration Services (SSIS). You might consider a prototype to evaluate which will work best in this scenario.

Lesson Summary

- Application requirements should be defined from multiple perspectives. This includes the business (or executive sponsorship), the users, the developers (functional), and quality of service (nonfunctional).

- Your functional requirements or functional specifications are better off being defined through application modeling tools. You should not have to document this both in a requirements document and again through application modeling.

- A good requirement should be unambiguous. It should not read like a goal. Rather, it should be measurable and actionable. It should not be left for interpretation.

- You should verify all your requirements as necessary to the success of the system. Those that are not should be set aside.

- It is important that developers and architects right-size their recommendations based on real requirements. They should not recommend technologies because they are cool or available. Rather, they should do careful analysis and make proper recommendations.

- You should always review your recommendations against existing solutions. There might be an off-the-shelf product you can use or an internal company asset.

- You should start the process of validating your recommendations by creating a high-level application design. This should include your recommendations in terms of technologies, how these technologies integrate to form a solution, and any configuration parameters and constraints of these items.

Lesson Review

You can use the following questions to test your knowledge of the information in Lesson 1, "Evaluate Requirements and Propose a Design." The questions are also available on the companion CD if you prefer to review them in electronic form.

NOTE Answers

Answers to these questions and explanations of why each answer choice is right or wrong are located in the "Answers" section at the end of the book.

---

1. You have been given the requirement, "users in the system should be able to scroll through long lists of data without pause in the application to retrieve more data from the database." This is an example of what type of requirement?

   A. Business requirement

   B. Quality of service requirement

   C. User requirement

   D. Functional requirement

2. Requirements are essential for which of the following? (Choose all that apply.)

   A. Verifying the implemented application as acceptable.

   B. Defining the steps a user will take to accomplish a given task.

   C. Defining a common understanding of scope among the business, the users, and the project team.

   D. Determining the technologies that should be used for the application.

3. Given the following requirements, which client technology would you recommend?

   ❑ Users must be able to enter new data as well as view and update existing data. These processes will be controlled through the business rules surrounding each data element.

   ❑ The application should support up to 50 users.

   ❑ Users will access the application from their corporate desktops and laptops.

   ❑ The users expect a highly interactive experience with the application.

   ❑ The application must be easy to deploy and update.

   ❑ The application features should be accessible both online and offline.

   A. Microsoft Office application using Excel

   B. Standard Windows Client

   C. Windows Mobile Client

   D. Windows Smart Client

4. Given the following requirements, which data storage technology would you recommend?

   ❏ Users should be able to work with the application when they are not connected to the LAN.

   ❏ The application's data is retrieved and aggregated from multiple sources on a monthly basis. After the updated is posted, users should receive their updated data.

   ❏ The application should have a small footprint on the user's machine or device.

   A. SQL Enterprise

   B. SQL Express

   C. SQL Everywhere (Mobile)

   D. SQL Standard

Lesson 2: Create a Proof-of-Concept Prototype to Refine an Application's Design

You have reviewed your application requirements and received sign-off from the business. You have created your technology recommendations and they also have been given the go-ahead. This means you are ready to start physical modeling and coding, right? In some cases this might be true. However, for larger applications with higher risks it can be a great risk-reduction step to first create a prototype. A prototype will help verify some of the requirements that are still a bit fuzzy and will confirm your technology recommendations.

In this lesson we will look at how you might create a prototype to answer questions from the requirements and the technology recommendations. We will look at how you can use this prototype to help increase the confidence in the project and reduce a lot of the risks associated with it. A prototype is often the step needed to get skeptical project stakeholders to green-light your project.

After this lesson, you will be able to:

- Choose the type of prototype required for your specific situation.
- Understand the difference between a mockup and a proof-of-concept.
- Evaluate high-level design decisions through a prototype.
- Evaluate the effectiveness of your prototype.
- Demonstrate the feasibility of the project to stakeholders through the prototype.

Estimated lesson time: 20 minutes

Real World

Mike Snell

I see prototypes as a great way to evaluate risky technology recommendations. I run into a lot of projects where architects and developers want to recommend the latest thing because they have heard all the hype. However, they might have never used it, and the hype might be just that. A prototype can help them verify their assumptions before it is too late.

On a recent project I had both the client and the architect requesting a third-party set of user interface controls that neither had experience with. Both had reviewed them online and believed they would offer the features needed to do some hefty interactive, pivot-table-like reporting. In addition, both were ready to jump into SSIS for data integration; neither had ever even installed SQL 2005, let alone worked with it at length. I raised both of these risks to the project stakeholders. We agreed that a small prototype phase was in order before anyone (the developers or the client) would commit to this project.

> It turned out that the UI tools made the user interface too complex for the target user group. The third-party tools could be used, but they needed a lot of work to make them easy to use. This project time would have been missed if it were not for the prototype. SSIS, on the other hand, turned out to be great for the target solution. In fact, the prototype uncovered some additional areas where it could be used. All in all, the small prototype phase reduced risk and increased predictability—something for which all projects should strive.

What Constitutes a Good Prototype?

A good prototype answers the questions left open from the requirements and technology recommendations. The problem is that a lot of times these questions are not so much asked, but just exist. This is what we call a gap. There might be a gap between what a user defines as a requirement or scenario and what it is the user really wants to see. There might be a gap between what a developer has defined for the application architect and what the project stakeholders understand. There might be a gap between a new architecture that an architect has read about and is proposing and what is truly required. These gaps exist whether they are defined or not. A prototype is meant to reduce the overall project risk by closing some of these gaps.

Mockups and Proof-of-Concept Prototypes

There are many types of prototypes. Some projects create UI prototypes. Others might prototype an architecture consideration. Still others might look at the feasibility of using a specific technology such as BizTalk or Host Integration Server. In fact, every project might have different needs around a prototype. However, for our purposes these prototypes can be classified into two principal groups: mockups and proof-of-concept.

Mockup

A *mockup* is meant to verify the requirements and use cases through the creation of a number of key forms in the system. Mockups are also called *horizontal prototypes* because they take a single horizontal picture of the application. They do not go deep (or vertical) into the other layers of the application like the business objects and the database. Mockups are a great way to determine if the requirements are complete and understood. They also help validate the use cases, the navigational structure, and some of the logical interactions of the application.

Mockups do have shortcomings. They do not prove out any of the architecture of the system. They also do not validate the technology decisions. Mockups, however, are a great tool to move from words on paper to something much more tangible. Users often have different opinions when they see something as a picture versus a bunch of text in a document. Mockups are also useful for defining how the application will look and behave. This removes ambiguity from the implementation and builds early consensus on what will be delivered. The effect is a smoother, faster transition to real, working code once development gets started.

Proof-of-Concept

A *proof-of-concept prototype* is meant to validate the requirements and confirm the technology recommendations and high-level design. A proof-of-concept prototype is also called a *vertical prototype* because it looks at the application across the entire stack or layers of the application (UI, services, business objects, database). Proof-of-concept prototypes have also been called *reference architectures* because they provide a reference to the development team on just how the system should work from top to bottom. This removes ambiguity, creates a standard, and eliminates a lot of risk.

You create a proof-of-concept prototype by choosing a key use case (or set of use cases) of the application and then building it out through each layer of the design. It makes more sense to prove out a riskier use case than to work with a well-known use case. The latter might be easy, but it lacks the risk reduction you are looking for with a proof-of-concept.

The Prototyping Process

There are many ways to create mockup style prototypes. You can use Visual Studio to create screens that connect to dummy data and wire up the navigation. You can also use drawing tools like Visio to simply lay up images that represent the mockup. You might even decide to draw the screens on a whiteboard, index cards, or even sticky notes. The process for creating mockups should, however, involve the user. It should be highly interactive because it really is just an extension of the requirements.

A proof-of-concept prototype should, of course, be created with Visual Studio and any other tools (third-party controls, BizTalk, SSIS, and so on) you are trying to review. You can often get developer (or trial) editions of the software for this purpose. If you intend to evaluate, for instance, the feasibility of creating a Smart Client user interface, you should define one using Visual Studio and an application server. Proof-of-concept prototypes are a lot more involved than just a mockup. However, their intent is not only to validate key requirements but also to confirm key design decisions.

Create a Prototype to Evaluate Key Design Decisions

You must make a lot of key design decisions when recommending any technology. These, like all design decisions, come with a certain amount of risk. The risks are usually related to the ability of the technology to satisfy all the requirements and the developer's solid grasp of just how that technology works. The following are all risks that you should consider reducing when proposing technologies. Each of these risks can be mitigated through the creation of a proof-of-concept prototype.

Confirm the Client Technology and Application Container

The application container is the shell that houses the application and provides base services. In a Windows scenario this is understood to be a main form with the navigation, status indicator, and base functionality like undo, cut, copy, paste, autoupdate, and so on. You might decide to create an SDI or an MDI application. As an alternative, you might consider creating a Windows mobile application.

The time to define your application container is in the prototype phase. This allows the technical leaders of the application to set this very key decision on how developers will add forms to the system. This also removes the ambiguity around this key factor. Finally, defining the application container through the prototype gives users a better understanding of how the system will operate as a whole. You will not implement everything that that container defines, but they can see it there and understand how it will work as a whole.

Define User Interface Elements to Confirm Requirements

An application prototype also helps you understand your scope. You should work to understand the many forms that will be required for your application. You should try to list each of these screens and categorize them by type. A screen type helps you group similar screens. The following are some screen types you might consider:

- **Data entry form**   Represents a form where you are requesting the user to enter data for the application.
- **Data list form**   This is a form that displays a list of data. This list might require paging, sorting, filtering, and so on.
- **Wizard**   You might have a set of forms (or tabs) that work together as a wizard to capture user data.
- **Report**   You might have a number of report-like forms in the system. These reports might allow for filtering of the data through parameters or viewing the data graphically.
- **Property page**   Represents a form that is used to set and select various properties or settings. These screen types are sometimes implemented in panels or in separate dialog boxes.
- **Navigation and action panes**   These forms are employed by the user to navigate within the system or select key actions. Think of the folder pane in Outlook as an example. Depending on your application, you might have one or more of these screen types per module.

When you define the screens and group them, you should also consider their complexity. Complexity of the screen can be defined in terms of its functionality (read versus write), the number of elements on the screen, the user interactivity, and the access to and from the screen. Having this measure of complexity for each screen will help you better understand the overall scope for your project.

Next, you should create a working prototype of at least one of each screen type. This will ensure that users and developers of the system understand the screen type. You might also end up creating reusable base forms or user controls to help during implementation. Having a set of implemented screen types will also add to the overall reference architecture for the development team.

Finally, you might wish to define the actual user interface (UI) look and feel as part of the prototype phase. This step usually involves creating designs and working with the users to validate those designs. Having these designs up front will help set standards for the application and mitigate further risks and possible delays.

Evaluate Web Service and Remoting Recommendations

If you intend to recommend Web services or remoting as part of your application architecture, then you need to evaluate them for their effectiveness relative to your constraints. A prototype can help in this regard. When creating the proof-of-concept you need to consider all of the following with respect to Web services and remoting:

- How will users be connected to the application server?
- How will the application behave when there is no connection or the connection is slow? Are the results acceptable to the users or do you have to consider design alternatives?
- How will you manage transaction reliability and ensure no data loss? Will all calls to the application server be synchronous?
- How will you manage concurrency issues? Will the last user to save unknowingly overwrite some else's changes?
- How will you manage the security for the services on the application server?

Evaluate Your Proposed Security Model

Your security model should be part of the prototype. This will provide insight into what is required to support the security requirements. When you define a prototype, consider all of the following with respect to security:

- **Feasibility**   You need to be sure that what you are proposing is feasible. If, for instance, you are proposing that each user authenticate through an Active Directory account, you need to make sure all users have such accounts or that they can be created.
- **Authentication**   You need to confirm your choice for user authentication. Will you need to implement authentication by saving user credentials in a database? Or can you use Windows authentication?
- **Authorization**   You need to confirm your authorization strategy. You might need to filter data based on a user's access rights. You might even need to control this on a field-by-field basis in a business object. You also need to define how you intend to access key

resources in the application. Are there files that need to be checked against an access control list? How should the database connection string be stored securely?

- **Connectivity between resources**   You need to validate the feasibility of your proposed high-level design. This might be less of a prototype task and require some discussions with your infrastructure team. For instance, there might be firewall rules that prevent some of your communication decisions between clients and application servers.

- **Data security and encryption**   You need to understand what data in the system is sensitive and requires additional considerations. For example, some data may require that it be encrypted when passed between application layers or stored in the database.

- **Application and data access**   Some features and data in the system will require that you log their use and access. You need to determine which user activities need to be logged, how you intend to do the logging, and how you plan to manage the data in the access log.

Evaluate Third-Party Applications or Controls

Unless you are very familiar with your third-party control or application recommendations, these represent an important piece to consider in the prototype. In fact, any technology that is not familiar should be prototyped. If, for example, you intend to use Windows Workflow Services for the first time, you need to validate your assumptions through a proof-of-concept. Some third-party control categories you should consider prototyping and evaluating include:

- **General UI**   You might be using these to create unique user interface elements and navigation constructs.

- **Grid control**   You might require a specialized data grid control to manage report-like or spreadsheet-like features.

- **Licensing**   You might need to control licensing for your application or control.

- **Charts and reports**   You might have a requirement to create charts and graphs for the reporting or dashboard features.

- **Data transformation and exchange**   You might use a tool or controls to handle data import and transformation or to generate export files.

Evaluate Proposed Data Access and Storage Methods

A proof-of-concept is also a good time to evaluate your recommendations on data access and storage. If, for example, you are proposing SQL Everywhere be loaded on PDAs and other mobile devices to support offline and synchronization requirements and you have never done so, you need to prototype. Again, this will help you evaluate your decision in terms of feasibility, practicality, and level of effort.

Evaluate Your State Management Decisions

State management is not just for Web applications. Your Windows applications must also manage state effectively. *Application state* defines how data gets moved and persisted throughout the layers of an application. There are a number of things to validate around your state management decisions. Some of these include the following:

- **Shared state**   Do users have to be able to share application state like in an auction system? If so, how will this state be shared from one client to another? Through an application server?

- **State persistence**   How will state be maintained on the user's desktop? Does the user have offline access to this state?

- **Saving state**   How will state move from in memory to at rest? Will it be saved locally? How will it get to the database?

- **Caching**   If you have an application server, can some application state be cached on that server and shared? What are the ramifications of the caching strategy in terms of reading old data, updating the cache, and consuming server resources?

Confirm and Refine the Recommended Architecture

Your prototype is also the chance to refine your architecture recommendations. If, for example, you are proposing creating a framework for the application, then now is the time to validate the feasibility of that framework. You might have the functional requirement to eliminate the need for developers to manage saving and retrieving object data, for example. This type of framework needs to be reviewed and validated through a proof-of-concept.

You might also look to prove out how you will partition the layers of the application. A good reference architecture will demonstrate to a developer how the code should behave and where it should be located. For example, if you create a user interactivity layer for the application that should be used to house user interface code, then you should prototype just what code goes in this layer and how the controls of the user interface might interact with this code. Prototypes are often as much about validating proposed architectures as they are about evaluating or demonstrating recommended technologies.

Quick Check

1. What is the primary purpose of creating a prototype?
2. What is the difference between mockups and a proof-of-concept prototype?
3. What is meant by the term reference architecture?

> **Quick Check Answers**
>
> 1. A good prototype answers the questions left open from the requirements and technology recommendations.
> 2. Mockups are a horizontal view of the application at the user interface level. A proof-of-concept takes a vertical slice of the application and implements it across the layers.
> 3. A reference architecture is an implementation of the architecture across the application layers. For example, this might include a Windows Form, a set of business objects, the data access methods, and the data storage solution—all for a single feature or use case.

Demonstrate the Feasibility of the Design

You need to evaluate and prove the effectiveness of the prototype. Remember that your intent is to better understand and better establish the requirements and design recommendations. The prototype is meant to build confidence and foster a sense of mutual understanding between users, stakeholders, and the developers—before it's too late.

You should go into the prototype phase expecting to find issues with the requirements and design. Do not be afraid to make changes to your assumptions, your design, or your requirements. That is the point. You need to find conflicts between documented requirements and what is practical and feasible. For this reason, you should spend time evaluating the effectiveness of your prototype. You should consider all of the following:

- **Missing or poor requirements** Did you identify requirements that were incomplete or ambiguous? Were there areas that required additional clarification or use cases?
- **Design challenges** What portions of the application will present additional design challenges? Identify areas that will need more focus. Also, consider if you need to extend the prototype session to complete this effort.
- **Technology recommendations** Are there different recommendations that you would make based on the prototype? Did your recommendations satisfy everything you had hoped?
- **Level of effort** The prototype should help you understand how much effort will be required to build the application. Take a look at what was required for the reference architecture. Now make sure that you have enough time built into the project based on this effort (obviously adjusted for the skills of the team).
- **Usability** A good gauge of the prototype is, "Does it seem natural to the users or do they require training to work with the screens?" If they lean toward the latter, you need to keep working.

Finally, you need to take what you've learned from the prototype and put together a presentation for the stakeholders. This will help formally communicate what you've learned and accomplished during the prototype phase. These demos will help the stakeholders make the decision to release funds to get the project to the next level.

Lab: Create a Proof-of-Concept Prototype

The best way to ensure your understanding of this material is to create an actual proof-of-concept prototype. You can use this practice section as your aid for creating a prototype for your next project.

▶ **Exercise: Create a Prototype for Your Project**

Use this exercise as a guide for creating a project prototype. If you don't have a new project, consider each item in the exercise relative to your last (or your current) project. If you were not able to create a prototype for this project, ask yourself "What risks might I have eliminated if I had created a prototype?" or "How would things have gone smoother if we had started with a prototype?"

1. Read through the application requirements and use cases. Identify the forms that might be required to satisfy the application. List each form and the primary functionality of the form. Look for similarities between the forms. Use these similarities to define form types or groupings.

2. Identify areas of the requirements that seem gray or incomplete. Match these areas to the form types you identified in the previous task. Create a user interface mockup for each of these forms. Review the mockups with the users and get their feedback.

3. Review your proposed architecture with the development team. Find out what questions they have. Do they understand it the same way you understand it? Create a reference implementation of the architecture through the layers. Review this reference architecture with the team and find out if they now have a better understanding.

4. Confirm the key design decisions you made for the application through the prototype. This might include verifying your security model, understanding how you will use Web services or remoting, or validating your data management technique. You should choose to validate any items that seem risky or not fully understood.

5. Update the requirements, recommendations, and design based on the prototype. Be sure to track changes. Review how many changes resulted from the prototype.

6. Try to create an accurate estimate of the time it will take to complete the project. Can you get other developers to agree to these estimates? Do you feel the estimates are accurate and complete? If not, what would make them more accurate and complete?

7. Document the lessons the prototype taught you. Put them together in a presentation. This should include your original assumptions, the evaluation, and the revised assumptions as a result of the prototype effort. In addition, add the key screens and other items to the presentation. Take this presentation to the stakeholders and get their feedback.

Lesson Summary

- A prototype is meant to fill in the gaps that remain between the paper definition and the reality of implementation.
- You can define user interface mockups to validate the user interface and navigation of the system.
- A proof-of-concept prototype takes a vertical slice of the application and implements it across the layers. This is also called a reference architecture.
- You can define mockups using index cards, sticky notes, whiteboards, or a drawing tool such as Visio.
- Proof-of-concepts should use the target technologies for their creation. There are developer evaluation versions of nearly all the technologies you might recommend.
- A Windows prototype should confirm the recommended client type, the application container, the user interface elements (or form types), the use of an application server, your security model, the third-party controls you've recommended, the proposed data access and storage methods, your state management decisions, and your overall high-level design.
- You should review your prototype to confirm its effectiveness. You need to be comfortable making changes based on your prototype; that is the intention. You also should use the prototype to demonstrate the feasibility of the project to stakeholders.

Lesson Review

You can use the following questions to test your knowledge of the information in Lesson 2, "Create a Proof-of-Concept Prototype to Refine an Application's Design." The questions are also available on the companion CD if you prefer to review them in electronic form.

NOTE Answers

Answers to these questions and explanations of why each answer choice is right or wrong are located in the "Answers" section at the end of the book.

---

1. Review the following questions you need to answer with your prototype. Based on these questions, what type of prototype should you create?
   - ❑ How will users access data when offline?
   - ❑ How will the data be retrieved from and saved to the database?
   - ❑ How will the business rules of the application be enforced?

   A. Vertical prototype
   B. Horizontal prototype
   C. Database prototype
   D. Mockup prototype

2. You need to confirm the estimates for your project. Which of the following prototype steps should you take? (Choose all that apply.)

    A. Create a reference architecture.

    B. Define the screens, their types, and their complexities.

    C. Create a working prototype of each unique element defined by the application.

    D. Update the requirements based on the findings from your prototype.

3. Which of the following should you consider when evaluating your proposed security model? (Choose all that apply.)

    A. User authentication method

    B. User authorization methods

    C. Resources control

    D. Connectivity

4. You need to evaluate the effectiveness of your prototype. Which of the following might lead you to believe your prototype was effective? (Choose all that apply.)

    A. A number of gaps were identified in the requirements.

    B. The use cases were validated as correct and sufficient.

    C. Certain areas of the application were exposed as requiring additional focus in terms of design.

    D. The new technologies that were recommended worked just as expected.

Chapter Review

To further practice and reinforce the skills you learned in this chapter, you can perform the following tasks:

- Review the chapter summary.
- Review the list of key terms introduced in this chapter.
- Complete the case scenarios. These scenarios set up real-world situations involving the topics of this chapter and ask you to create a solution.
- Complete the suggested practices.
- Take a practice test.

Chapter Summary

- You need to look at the requirements of your application from multiple perspectives. These perspectives should include the user, the business, the developers (functional requirements), and the quality of service (or nonfunctional) requirements. Requirement should not be ambiguous. Instead, they should be clear, measurable, and actionable.
- Developers need to be able to look at a set of requirements and make some technology recommendations. These recommendations should be based solely on the requirements of the system. You should not recommend too much or too little. You should do careful analysis and make recommendations that fit these requirements. Don't always assume a build-it stance to satisfy requirements. You should consider how an off-the-shelf product or internal asset might increase time-to-market and reduce overall risk.
- Application prototypes come in many forms. However, two common forms include mockups and proof-of-concept. A mockup helps validate the user interface and navigation of the system. A proof-of-concept prototype takes a vertical slice of the application and implements it across the layers. This helps eliminate risks in the design and gives the developers a reference on which they can model their work. You should create an application prototype to confirm the recommended client technology, the application container, the user interface elements (or screen types), the use of an application server, your security model, the third-party controls you've recommended, the proposed data access and storage methods, your state management decisions, and your overall high-level design.
- You need to make sure your prototype is effective. It should not simply demonstrate that you can create simple user interface elements to satisfy basic requirements. Rather, it needs to target the risky, or unknown, elements in the system. You need to evaluate your prototype and make sure it does just that. A prototype means changes to the requirements and recommendations. That is the point.

Key Terms

Do you know what these key terms mean? You can check your answers by looking up the terms in the glossary at the end of the book.

- application library
- application server
- business requirement
- client
- data storage
- framework
- functional requirement
- functional specification
- horizontal prototype
- mockup
- proof-of-concept prototype
- quality of service (QOS) requirement
- reference architecture
- third-party control
- user requirement
- vertical prototype

Case Scenario

In the following case scenario, you will apply what you've learned about evaluating requirements, recommending technologies, and creating a prototype. You can find answers to these questions in the "Answers" section at the end of this book.

Case Scenario: Evaluate Requirements and Propose an Application Design

You are a senior developer at a large healthcare organization. The organization provides proactive healthcare services for its members. This organization has undergone a lot of growth in recent years, and an audit determined that there are a lot of departments with duplicated effort. One such pocket was with respect to member management and how calls (or touches) to members are logged and tracked. Member information was found to be on no fewer than three different systems; each of these systems had its own rules for managing this information and tracking members and organizational reach to these members. An initiative has been started to define an application that unifies member management and centralizes tracking of membership reach.

Interviews

You attend a meeting to brainstorm on the high-level requirements for the system. This meeting includes key project stakeholders, user representatives, and IT staff. The lead business analyst and yourself are co-facilitating this meeting. The following represent statements made during the meeting:

■ **Member services manager**   "We need to establish best practices around how we store and access member data. Each member should be tracked only once. All data related to this member should be available to help our member representatives assist our members. Member data includes profile information, demographics, in-house family information, and family history. In addition, a full medical record should be on file for each member. Each call by a member representative may collect some portion of this data.

"Member representatives need to be aware of the many services we offer, the steps required to allow members to access these services, the supporting documents, and so on. This will help us provide better services to keep people healthy.

"My team is really busy. They can't be expected to look for new information around process guidance. Instead, they need to be alerted (through e-mail or when they log on) about content that is pertinent to them. In fact, the system should force member representatives to confirm that they've read this information.

"The application should be fast. The member representatives are on the phone with the member. Neither should have to wait more than 5 seconds for an answer to any query.

"We have a fairly high turnover among member representatives across all departments. This application should reduce the training time for new hires.

"We need a clean user interface. The application should be easy to use and approachable. We want the member representatives to get to information quickly and efficiently with no confusion.

"Member representatives should be able to search for member data using any data point of the member's profile: last name, address, phone, and so on.

"When a member representative is contacted by a member, the representative goes through a set of questions to determine how we can best help. Each of these questions helps further evaluate the member's need and get the member to a set of steps that can help. These questions and help steps evolve over time. We need to establish a way for the various malady specialists to modify, review, and approve these questions and steps. No question or step should be changed without the approval of the appropriate specialist or manager.

"It would be nice if members could update their own information in the system. This will help keep the data from getting old. New members would be created by a member representative."

■ **Statistical Reporting and Analysis** "We need to crunch numbers on the member data every quarter. It's important that we not trace this data back to individual members or member representatives. Rather, we need to do statistical modeling to determine the overall health of our membership. This is done through a third-party application using proprietary, complex algorithms. The data we need is defined by the MemberExtract schema and should be provided as comma-separated values (CSV).

"Right now each department has its own reporting needs. It would be nice to consolidate all reports into a few common views. These views can be filtered by user and department. If individual users or groups want more reporting, they should be able to modify these base reports."

■ **IT manager** "This application should take advantage of the investment we have made in the user's desktops and the Windows operating system. A rich client should be considered.

"There will be approximately 200 internal users managing member data for over 40,000 members. All these users have corporate accounts in Active Directory. This application should expect no more than 100 concurrent users at any given time."

■ **Development manager** "Other applications will also require access to this central store of member data. Therefore we would like to create a set of services that allow this access. This data should be returned as XML because not all of these other applications are not Windows-based. We have created a server to provide this information at *http://contoso/ members/memberservice.asmx*. Two service methods are planned: *GetMembers(searchCriteria)* and *UpdateMember(memberData)*.

"We are considering using .NET 2.0 for the application. The development team has little experience with this technology. They have written some VB 6 applications previously. It would be nice if they had some examples to follow."

Questions

While thinking about the statements listed above, answer the following questions.

1. What are the user requirements of the system?
2. What are the business requirements of the system?
3. What are the QOS (or nonfunctional) requirements of the system?
4. Which requirements represent functional requirements of the system?
5. Which requirements need more detail to make them unambiguous and more actionable?
6. What security model would you recommend for the application?
7. What third-party tools should you consider for the application?
8. What data storage mechanism might you recommend for the application?
9. What areas of the application seem like they require additional research through prototyping?

Suggested Practices

To help you successfully master the exam objectives presented in this chapter, complete the following tasks.

Evaluate Requirements and Propose a Design

For this task you should consider completing both practices. If you do not have an application to work with, consider an application that you have used recently. These practices will give you a better feel for your understanding of the material.

- **Practice 1**   Spend some time with your business analysts to define application requirements. Work with users to elicit these requirements. Try documenting the requirements and then presenting them back to the users. Refine them based on their feedback. Evaluate these requirements to confirm they are not ambiguous but can be measured.

- **Practice 2**   Take a look at the requirements you created in Practice 1 and consider the technologies you would recommend based on these requirements. Alternatively, find an older set of requirements. Look at these with a fresh set of eyes. How would you solve these requirements given today's tools and technologies?

Create a Proof-of-Concept Prototype to Refine an Application's Design

This task should be common to most senior-level developers. If, however, you have not participated in this process with users, you should strongly consider executing Practice 1. Practice 2 should help you understand how a technology model answers a few questions but presents more. Only a prototype can answer many of these questions.

- **Practice 1**   Work with users to define a user interface. Use index cards or a large whiteboard. Have the users describe a scenario of what they need the application to do. You should then draw how the user interface will enable this scenario. This should help you understand expectations, navigation concerns, and interactivity.

- **Practice 2**   Define a simple, high-level application design. Document a set of assumptions for the design. Present this design to a small group of developers in a meeting. Listen to how these developers expect to implement the system. List their concerns; try not to elaborate on your design. Now review the list and consider how these questions might be answered through a prototype.

Take a Practice Test

The practice tests on this book's companion CD offer many options. For example, you can test yourself on just the content covered in this chapter, or you can test yourself on all the 70-548 certification exam content. You can set up the test so that it closely simulates the experience of taking a certification exam, or you can set it up in study mode so that you can look at the correct answers and explanations after you answer each question.

MORE INFO **Practice tests**

For details about all the practice test options available, see the section titled "How to Use the Practice Tests" in this book's Introduction.

Chapter 2

Decompose Specifications for Developers

In the previous chapter we looked at defining the requirements of an application, recommending technologies, and creating a prototype to verify those requirements and recommendations. The next step in the software development life cycle is to determine both logical and physical models for the application. The logical models help everyone understand the objects and relationships in the system. The physical models allow developers to implement features using code and other tools. This chapter examines how you start with documented requirements and technology recommendations and build to a physical design for your application.

This chapter also looks at how you review requirements and use cases and at how you define a logical model. We then discuss how you apply your technology recommendations and constraints to that logical model. The result will be a set of physical models that take into account both the logical understanding of the application and the physical abilities of the technology. This physical model will be implemented by developers.

Exam objectives in this chapter:
- Evaluate the technical specifications for an application to ensure that the business requirements are met.
  - ❏ Translate the functional specification into developer terminology, such as pseudo code and UML diagrams.
  - ❏ Suggest component type and layer.

Lessons in this chapter:

Before You Begin

To complete the lessons in this chapter, you should be familiar with developing Microsoft Windows applications with Microsoft Visual Studio 2005 using Visual Basic or C#. In addition, you should be comfortable with all of the following:

- Reviewing requirements and use cases for an application.

- Detailing the functional specifications for an application.
- Knowledge of how .NET architectures and related technologies solve specific business problems.
- Creating solutions based on Windows.
- Object-oriented development concepts.
- Reading and working with Unified Modeling Language (UML) (class diagrams and other physical models).
- Using Microsoft Visio.

Real World

Mike Snell

I find that object role modeling (ORM) diagrams are not understood or often used by developers or architects. I think this is a mistake. A recent project I was working on illustrated this for me (again).

We started the project with a set of very detailed requirements provided by the business analysts (BAs) and more than 150 use cases to help us understand how those requirements were realized. In addition, there was a complete working version of the old application we were replacing. The company wanted to rewrite its existing system using .NET. They hired us because they felt constrained by the current system in terms of what could be done. Our job was to make sure these constraints were lifted going forward.

I suggested we create ORM diagrams for the entire system as a next step. I received a lot of pushback because this looked like a lot of work. The BAs and even some of the architects thought they already understood the system. I convinced them to give it a try; we could scrap it if it proved fruitless.

We started with a small section and saw how it went. The first meeting was tough. We scheduled an hour and got stuck on many relationships that the use case had one way, the requirements had a slight variation on, and the BAs believed to have been written in stone for years. However, when we modeled the facts, we uncovered these different interpretations. We ended up spending almost four hours debating and documenting the right relationships. This pattern continued for a few days until we caught a rhythm and finished the effort in about a week.

In the end everyone on the team had a new appreciation for how the logical model really existed. It seemed this logical model had been clouded by the years of the physical implementation. As it turned out, this was also the key to unlocking their prior constraints and opening up the application for easier implementation and future extensibility. Everyone that participated in this effort came away with a new respect for ORMs.

Lesson 1: Define Objects and Their Relationships (Create a Logical Model)

It is important to discover the logical objects, relationships, and attributes that you are modeling with software. After all, the software is meant to solve real business problems for real people. The items that your software will represent are considered logical because they either exist, or are thought to exist, as real and actual concepts. For example, the concept of a pharmacist filling a prescription for a patient is a tangible, logical set of objects and relationships.

Your logical model should not change once you have agreement on it—that is, unless the real-world concepts on which it is based change. This is unlike software concepts that are affected by technology and other constraints. The logical model gives everyone on the team (users, business analysts, architects, developers, and so on) an understanding of the system from a logical viewpoint. This viewpoint is also more approachable compared to the technical, physical models.

This lesson describes how ORM diagrams work, how they are read, and how you create them. We will first cover the basics of ORM. We will then look at how you can use this tool to document your understanding of the application's requirements in the form of logical relationships.

After this lesson, you will be able to:

- Determine the principal objects (entities) in your system based on the requirements and use cases.
- Determine the logical relationships between objects.
- Determine the attributes (properties, fields) of an object.

Estimated lesson time: 20 minutes

Object Role Modeling (ORM)

ORM is the process of creating a diagram to represent real-world concepts that define or influence your software. An ORM diagram includes the primary objects (also called entities) in the system, the relationships between those objects, and the attributes (and even attribute values) that define those objects. We use the ORM notation to create this logical representation between objects. We could use entity-relationship (ER) diagrams, but they are primarily associated with databases. In addition, class diagrams are associated with physical, object-oriented development. ORMs, on the other hand, offer a purely logical modeling tool for users, business analysts, and developers.

You create ORMs by decomposing the user requirements and use cases for your application and pulling out the objects, relationships, and attributes. We will cover this process later in the lesson. First, however, we should look at how to model this information and how to understand the ORM notation.

The ORM Notation

The ORM notation offers a number of shapes and connectors to define your logical model. However, for the most part you can simplify your approach to the notation by understanding a few primary concepts. We will distill our discussion down to these primary concepts. Once you've grasped these items you can represent 95 percent or more of your models. These primary concepts include object (or entity), relationship (or fact), and cardinality.

ORM Objects

Objects are represented in ORMs by an oval with the name of the object in the oval. Remember, these are logical models. Therefore an *ORM object* is any noun in the requirements or use case. They do not have to be full-blown physical objects or primary entities. Rather, they represent the logical things that make up the system. For example, consider the following pseudo use case about an application:

1. A customer searches through the inventory to find a product (sports memorabilia, jersey, pack of cards, hat, and so on) to purchase.
2. The customer then enters payment details (credit card number, name on card, security code, and expiration date) and purchases the given product.
3. The system creates an order and receipt for the customer.

In this mini use case, the following would all be considered objects: customer, inventory, product, payment details, order, and receipt. These might seem obvious. However, sports memorabilia, jersey, pack of cards, hat, credit card number, credit card name, credit card security code, and credit card expiration date are also objects in ORM terms. Figure 2-1 shows these items as objects on an ORM diagram.

NOTE   **Visio and ORMs**

Microsoft Visio provides an ORM diagramming tool. If you have the standard Microsoft Office edition, you can create an "ORM Diagram." This is simply a drag-and-drop diagram. If you have Visio for Enterprise Architects (ships with certain versions of Visual Studio), you can create what is called an "ORM Source Model." This is an advanced ORM tool. It provides a fact editor that makes defining objects and relationships much easier. You can also validate your assumptions through examples. Both diagrams are in the database category as they seem to relate to building logical database models. However, ORMs should not be thought of as simply a database tool.

Figure 2-1   Objects on an ORM diagram.

ORM Relationship

An *ORM relationship* defines how two or more objects are related to one another. A relationship between objects in an ORM diagram is represented as a line connecting the objects. Along this line will be a rectangle divided into segments based on the number of objects in the relationship. This is typically two segments because most relationships you model are between two objects (called a binary relationship). However, if you are modeling a relationship that exists among three objects (called a ternary relationship), you need to define all three relationships.

Let's look at some examples. Consider the mini use case we wrote previously and the objects we derived from it. The use case defines relationships among each of these objects. These relationships are represented in Figure 2-2. Note that we have identified a ternary relationship between customer, product, and order. Both customer and product come together to form an order.

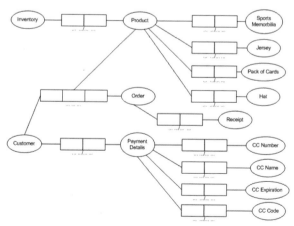

Figure 2-2   ORM relationships.

ORM Facts

One of the things still missing from our diagram is the facts that define the relationship. A fact indicates how two (or more) items are related. This is also called the *fact model* for your application. Facts don't change. They represent how objects really relate to one another.

You define facts on an ORM diagram by adding text beneath the relationship shape. Note that in Figure 2-2 there is an ellipsis (...) on either side of a slash (/) under each relationship shape. You define the relationship by replacing the ellipsis with text. The slash indicates how you read the relationship. The text on the left side of the slash reads from left to right. The text on the right side of the slash defines the inverse of the relationship. Figure 2-3 shows the model with the facts defined. As an example, you read the first fact as "Inventory has Product" and the inverse as "Product is in Inventory."

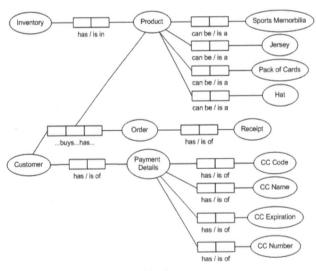

Figure 2-3   ORM relationship facts.

ORM Constraints

The final thing missing from our model is the constraints. *ORM constraints* define how the objects participate in the relationship. This includes defining which items are mandatory and the multiplicity of the relationship. Mandatory items are indicated by a closed (or filled) circle attached to either end of the connection. This closed circle indicates that the given object is mandatory in the relationship. That is, the related item does not exist without the other item.

Multiplicity indicates whether two objects relate to one another as one-to-one, one-to-many, or many-to-many. Multiplicity is indicated with a series of arrows over the relationship shape. Figure 2-4 shows the multiplicity options for ORM relationships.

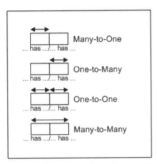

Figure 2-4   ORM relationship multiplicity.

Figure 2-5 shows these constraints applied to our sample diagram. For example, you can now read the first relationship (between Inventory and Product) as, "The inventory has one or more products and each product is in a single inventory." This gives you a very good understanding of your system in terms of objects and the facts that exist between those objects.

Figure 2-5   The ORM with cardinality.

Driving ORMs from Requirements and Use Cases

You saw in our previous example that we were able to define an ORM diagram from a simple use case. Most use cases and requirements are much more detailed than our simple example. You will want to go over these requirements and use cases line-by-line and pull out the objects and facts. The objects are easy because they are represented by nouns. The relationships (or facts) are the verb phrases that indicate a connection between objects.

When you first start your ORM diagram, the objects and facts will come fast and easy. As you get a few use cases in, however, you will identify fewer and fewer new objects and fewer new facts. Instead, you might find that you need to rethink or refactor the way you are looking at certain items. You need to look at each statement in the specifications and determine if your ORM diagram supports the statements found there. If it doesn't, either the statement or the ORM diagram must change. Once these items are aligned, you should have a solid understanding of how the items in your software relate.

Quick Check

1. What is the primary purpose of a logical model of your requirements and use cases?
2. How do you read the relationship between two objects?

Quick Check Answers

1. A logical model defines the facts in the domain for which you are building software. Creating a logical model of your requirements will both validate the requirements and provide a solid understanding of the domain.
2. The relationship is read from left to right using the text on the left side of the slash under the relationship shape. The inverse relationship is read in the opposite direction, using the text on the opposite side of the slash.

Using the ORMs to Identify Objects, Properties, Methods, Entities, and Fields

Your ORM diagram is a logical view of your objects and relationships. As you continue your design process you will use the logical model (ORMs and logical architecture) along with your technology recommendations to drive physical models. Your logical models should not change. However, when you apply these logical models to your target technology, you will make decisions that might confuse and even contradict your logical model. This is okay because you need to make trade-offs when moving to the physical model.

We will look at this process in more detail in Lesson 3, "Create Application (Physical) Models for Developers." The basic concept, however, is that you find the items in the ORM diagram that have the most relationships. These are also items that give an interesting perspective on the system (like customer or order). These will become your primary database entities and your classes. The items that relate to these primary entities will themselves sometimes become subentities (with their own definition) or they might become database fields and object properties. The relationships will form the basis for your database-stored procedures and your application methods.

Lab: Create a Logical Model

In this lab, you will review a number of high-level application requirements and a simple use case. You will use this information to define the logical objects in the domain and their relationships to one another. You will do so in the context of an ORM diagram.

▶ **Exercise: Review Requirements and Define a Logical Model**

For this exercise, review the following application requirements and simple use case. Then follow the steps listed below to determine the objects and facts in this domain. The following are the requirements and use case with which you will be working.

Requirements

R1   The application should be accessible to the entire customer service representative (CSR) team of 350.

R2   The system needs to support up to 200 CSRs taking orders.

R3   A CSR will enter customer details prior to taking the order.

R4   A CSR must be able to check a product against inventory on hand.

R5   A CSR can help a customer find a product by selecting a product category and product subcategory.

R6   A customer order should decrement on-hand inventory. Another customer should not be able to order a product if it is depleted from inventory.

Use Case: Customer Places Order with CSR

1.   CSR takes incoming customer call.

2.   CSR asks the customer for the customer's profile. Profile includes name, address, and phone number.

3.   The system presents a list of product categories to the CSR. Product categories include memorabilia, trading cards, jerseys, and hats.

4.   CSR asks the user for product characteristics in order to find a given product.

5.   Once found, the system checks the product against inventory to ensure its availability.

6.   CSR asks the active customer for the customer's payment details for the order (credit card number, name, security code, and expiration) and indicates to the system to place the order.

7.   System decrements the inventory, creates a shipping notice, and generates a receipt ticket number for the customer.

Lab Steps

The following are the steps you should follow for this lab. These steps will lead you to determine the objects in the domain as defined in the requirements and use case listed above.

1. Determine the objects in the domain. Go through the requirements and use case and pull out all the nouns. Review those nouns and determine if any represent the same thing. If so, refactor the requirements and use case to use a single representation of any nouns.

    For example, user, customer, and active customer are all the same thing. In addition, customer details and profile are the same. You should find things like this and decide on a single term for the entire system.

2. Create an ORM diagram using Visio. Add the nouns as objects on the diagram.

    Your objects should include the following: customer, application, CSR, CSR team, system, order, profile, product, product category, product subcategory, inventory, customer call, customer name, customer address, customer phone number, memorabilia, trading cards, jerseys, hats, product characteristics, payment details, credit card number, credit card name, credit card security code, credit card expiration, shipping notice, receipt ticket number.

3. Review the list of objects. Remove any objects that you know are not of interest to your logical model.

    These might include application, CSR team, system, and customer call.

4. Define the facts in the system. Go back through each requirement and each line of the use case. Read the phrases that indicate or imply a relationship. Try to model each fact, indicating both the left-to-right relationship and the inverse.

    Your fact database should include the following facts (and their inversions):

    - ❑ Order creates Receipt Ticket Number
    - ❑ Receipt Ticket Number is of Order
    - ❑ Order creates Shipping Notice
    - ❑ Shipping Notice is of Order
    - ❑ Product Category has Product Sub-Category
    - ❑ Product Sub-Category is of Product Category
    - ❑ Product is in Product Sub-Category
    - ❑ Product Sub-Category groups Product
    - ❑ Product is in Product Category
    - ❑ Product Category groups Product
    - ❑ Profile has Phone

- ❏ Phone is of Profile
- ❏ Profile has Address
- ❏ Address is of Profile
- ❏ Profile has Name
- ❏ Name is of Profile
- ❏ Customer has Profile
- ❏ Profile is of Customer
- ❏ Payment Details has CC Security Code
- ❏ CC Security Code is of Payment Details
- ❏ Payment Details has CC Name
- ❏ CC Name is of Payment Details
- ❏ Payment Details has CC Card Expiration
- ❏ CC Card Expiration is of Payment Details
- ❏ Payment Details has CC Number
- ❏ CC Number is of Payment Details
- ❏ Customer has Payment Details
- ❏ Payment Details is of Customer
- ❏ Customer places Order
- ❏ Order is of Customer
- ❏ Order has Product
- ❏ Product defines Order
- ❏ Product is in Inventory
- ❏ Inventory tracks Product
- ❏ Customer orders Product
- ❏ Product ordered by Customer

5. Define the constraints on your facts. Go through each fact and verify it with the requirements and the use case. When doing so, consider any constraints that apply to the fact. This should include determining which ends of the relationship are mandatory and the multiplicity of the relationship.

6. When you're done, lay out your facts on an ORM diagram. Your diagram should look like the one in Figure 2-6.

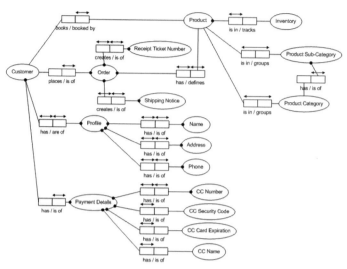

Figure 2-6   The facts in an ORM diagram.

Lesson Summary

■ A logical model is important (and is called a logical model) because your software represents real and actual concepts. These concepts do not typically change. You need to have a solid grasp of these concepts to make sure your software meets the demands of these real-world concepts.

■ An object role modeling (ORM) diagram is used to model the logical objects in your software. This includes the relationships between those objects and the constraints that should be put on those relationships.

■ ORM diagrams should be thought of as a purely logical view of your objects. It should not represent your classes or your database. You can use your ORMs to drive toward your database and class diagrams. However, this typically means trade-offs to support the technology. The ORMs do not require such trade-offs. Instead, they should stay faithful to the logical concepts that your software represents.

■ The ORM notation uses an oval to represent an object, a line with a relationship box to represent a relationship, and arrows over the box to represent multiplicity. You can write out the relationship as text under the relationship shape on the diagram.

Lesson Review

You can use the following questions to test your knowledge of the information in Lesson 1, "Define Objects and their Relationships (Create a Logical Model)." The questions are also available on the companion CD if you prefer to review them in electronic form.

1. Consider the following statement about your application: "A manager should be sent a shipping exception report in e-mail on a daily basis from the logistics system. If the shipping schedule for an order can't be verified or is in conflict, the manager must manually assign that shipment to a truck, driver, and route." Which of the following represents the logical objects defined in the previous statement?

   A. Order, Shipment, Truck, Driver, Route

   B. Manager, Report, Logistics System, Order, Shipment

   C. Manager, Shipping Exception Report, E-mail, Logistics System, Shipping Schedule, Order, Shipment, Truck, Driver, Route

   D. E-mail Shipping Report, Verify Shipping Schedule, Assign Shipment

2. Consider the following statement about an application: "A corporate user logs a support request for access to one or more applications." Suppose you have the following objects: Corporate User, Support Request, Application Access. How would you model the relationships to the Support Request object?

   A. A single unary relationship

   B. Two binary relationships

   C. A single ternary relationship

   D. A quaternary relationship

3. Consider the following statement about an application: "A supervisor approves timesheets." How would you write this fact and the inverse of this fact? (Choose all that apply.)

   A. Supervisor approves Timesheet

   B. Supervisor has Approval

   C. Timesheet approved by Supervisor

   D. Approval is of Supervisor

4. Consider the following fact, read left to right: "Shipping Slip has Ship-to Address." What constraints would you attach to this relationship?

   A. Closed circle on Shipping Slip, an arrow over the left side of the relationship shape.

   B. Closed circle on Ship-to Address, an arrow over the right side of the relationship shape.

   C. No circles, an arrow over the left side and another arrow over the right side of the relationship shape.

   D. Closed circle on Shipping Slip, a single, long arrow that covers both the left and right sides of the relationship.

Lesson 2: Define Application Layers (Create a Logical Architecture)

A logical architecture helps developers understand how a system is put together, how it works, and how they should add code to it. Logical architectures are not required to make your application work; instead, they are simply a means to explain how it works. It is very difficult for most developers to simply look at code, or even walk through code, and get a feel for exactly how the application works. Therefore it can be helpful to define a logical understanding of the layers, components, and communication paths in your system. This also helps architects design the system.

This lesson looks at how you can create and use logical architecture models. We will first look at defining the layers of your application. We will then cover creating a component model. Finally, we will examine how you can describe the communication between the layers and components.

> **After this lesson, you will be able to:**
> - Define the logical layers of your application and indicate what code should go into each layer.
> - Indicate the communication paths and protocols between the layers in your system.
> - Create a logical architecture to define your application.
>
> **Estimated lesson time: 20 minutes**

Define the Layers of Your Application

The logical layers of your system represent how you plan to divide your code into logical pieces or groups. For example, a three-tier system might define layers to include the user interface, business objects, and database layer. These are considered logical layers because the code is divided logically by what it represents. Physically, the code libraries themselves may run in the same process. In this case layers are combined for technical trade-offs (or physical reasons). As an example, think of a Windows application that defines a set of business objects and stores them inside the same executable as the user interface. These objects run in the same process. However, the code is logically separated; user interface (UI) code goes in the UI layer and business object code goes in the business object layer.

What Does It Mean to Have Application Layers?

The term "layer" can be thought of as similar to the term "tiers." "Tiers" was preferred for a time because applications were being built as two-tier and three-tier designs. Tiers in a three-tier application, for example, include the user interface, middle tier, and database tier. A two-tier application has a user interface working with a database directly. The abstraction of code into tiers allows for the innovation (or replacement) of the user interface or database code without rewriting the guts of the business logic.

This last concept—the ability to abstract portions of an application so that they can evolve independently—pushed application architectures toward *n*-tier. More tiers were added to the application. For example, a database tier can be divided into a database abstraction layer for the business objects, a database utility (or helper) layer, stored procedures, and the database technology itself. The user interface tier might be split between the strict UI code (events and layout operations) and the code that calls the middle tier. The middle tier can also be divided into subtiers. All of these splits represent what we refer to as application layers. Thinking in terms of layers is easier than considering all of these items as tiers in an *n*-tier design. You can define a name to each layer and the system is easier to understand.

Layers provide a clean, logical way to look at an application. Application layers are typically organized from top to bottom. The top is where the user activity happens. The bottom is where the data is stored when at rest. Your application *state*, the data that moves from database to the user interface, is passed through the layers (from top to bottom and back again). Each layer in the middle represents a view of the state in your application or a service that works on that state. For example, the user interface translates state for display to the user. The business layer works on state and applies business rules to it. The database layer knows how to save state to the database. To gain a logical understanding of a system you must define the layers and how state is passed among them (the communication paths). Of course, that presents your high-level, logical architecture. You still need to group features into components and define component models.

Layers of a Windows Application

A Windows application can be divided into a number of logical layers. Your decision on which layers to implement and enforce typically depends on your quality of service (QOS) requirements. For example, if your application is a stop-gap, possibly throwaway, system with low scalability and maintainability concerns, you might choose to implement only a couple of layers (UI and database). If, on the other hand, you are optimizing your architecture for varied physical deployments, high scalability, multiple user interfaces (Smart Client, Mobile, Reports, and so on), and a high degree of reuse, then you will opt to abstract your application into many more logical layers—you might even decide to create a framework that supports your layers.

Most enterprise-level applications written today employ some version of the three primary layers: user interface, middle tier, and database. Each of these layers might then be divided into additional layers. The following discussion presents each of these layers and some of their common divisions. Any combination of these layers may make up a Windows application.

User Interface   A user interface layer provides a window to the application for users. This layer is typically responsible for getting data from the middle tier and displaying it to the user. It is also responsible for controlling how a user interacts with that data. This includes data entry, validation, creating new elements, search, and so on. The UI layer is also in charge of getting the user's modifications back to the middle tier for processing. The user interface layer is often a layer by itself. However, it is also sometimes divided into one or more of the following additional layers:

- **Presentation (or user experience)**   This layer defines only the presentation portion of the user interface. This is the portion responsible for laying out the user interface. Think of this code as the code inside of the *FormName.Designer.cs, InitializeComponent* method in C#. Visual Basic hides this code from the developer. In both cases, Visual Studio is trying to abstract the code for the forms engine and promote the use of the form designer tools.

- **User interface code**   This layer is where developers place the code to interact with the user interface. The layer is typically embedded with the form. There is a partial class associated with each form in both VB and C#. You put your code in this class and it gets compiled with the form. The code that goes in this layer is to respond to events such as loading a form or clicking a button. You might decide to abstract the code to respond to these items into a separate user interface interaction layer. The code that would get compiled with the form would then simply delegate calls to this layer. This will increase your reuse if you intend to implement different forms that do the same thing or a new user interface.

- **Business logic interaction code**   You might create this layer if you do not wish to tie the code used to interact with your business layer (middle tier) to the user interface code. This can be helpful if you intend to plan for the replacement of your user interface. For example, you might create a Windows-based client today but have a plan to move to Extensible Application Markup Language (XAML), an Office Client, or something even further out.

Middle Tier   The middle tier is where you house your business logic. This is often referred to as just the business layer. However, this tier typically includes a lot more than just business logic. It might include components for handling caching, logging, error management, and so on. You might use the Microsoft Enterprise Library (or a similar library) in this tier. The middle tier typically runs on an application server such as Windows Server and Internet Information Services (IIS). However, you can create your own middle tiers (using things like Windows services and sockets). The middle tier is sometimes divided into one or more of the following additional layers:

- **Business layer (or business services)**   This layer is where you put your domain objects and their business rules. You might be writing stateless components that work with Enterprise Services, real object-oriented business objects that run in process, or simple data transfer objects (DTOs) with processing services that work across remoting channels. In any case, most applications define a business layer. This isolates the business logic so it can be reused, remain stable (as UIs get rewritten and modified), be easier to change, and so on. As an example, a business layer object might be an *Invoice* class. It might contain properties that define an invoice and methods that save and load the object. These methods and properties will define the business rules for the given object. These rules should be validated before the object is sent to another layer for processing.

■ **Application layer (or application services)**   This layer represents the plumbing to make your application work. This plumbing typically solves QOS requirements such as "the application must log errors or cache data for performance." You want to keep this code isolated from your business logic. Sometimes this code gets put into a framework. You can also consider the Microsoft Enterprise Library as part of the application layer. Examples of an application layer might include a *Log* class that contains methods to log certain events, such as errors.

■ **Database layer (or database services)**   This layer abstracts the retrieval and storage of data in your database. This code is sometimes combined with the business layer. However, this tight coupling can make the code harder to understand, more brittle to change, and less reusable. As an example, the database layer might contain static (or shared) methods that work to save and retrieve data from the database on behalf of the business layer. An example might include an *InvoiceData* class with a method like *GetInvoice* that returns a *DataSet* with invoice data. The database abstraction layer is often part of the database layer. However, it typically does not reside on the database server but on the middle-tier application server. That is why it is discussed here.

Database Layer   The database layer represents how you manage the data in your application. For most enterprise applications this means a relational database, such as Microsoft SQL Server. The database layer is responsible for saving, retrieving, and ensuring the integrity of your data. The database "tier" is sometimes divided into one or more of the following additional layers:

■ **Database layer**   See the previous "Middle Tier" section.

■ **Stored procedures**   This layer represents the SQL or managed code used to select, insert, update, and delete data with the database. It also includes any database-defined functions you might create.

■ **Integration services**   This layer represents how the database works with other data sources for integration purposes. In SQL Server this is SQL Server Integration Services (SSIS) or the older Data Transformation Services (DTS).

■ **Database tables, log, and indexes**   This layer represents the actual data in the system, the log of activity, and the indexes used by the database software.

Quick Check

1. What is the purpose of logical application layers?
2. What is the intent of creating multiple (3+) application layers?

Quick Check Answers

1. Logical application layers help developers and architects understand how a system works and where to write their code.
2. You abstract code into a layer to mitigate risk. You might be trying to increase reuse, you might be worried about layers changing independently, you might be trying to increase scalability, or you might be trying to isolate developers. The decision to create more than two layers typically revolves around support QOS requirements.

Define Communication Between Layers

The application layers define the logical abstractions you intend for the code in the system. You will need to consider how you intend to deploy these logical layers in a physical environment. The environment might constrain your deployment options, or you might have other concerns. For example, you might not be allowed to create a Smart Client designed to work with an application server across an Internet channel. You might have a restriction that the application server exposed across an Internet channel can't connect directly into your database server. In this case you might have to deploy your business logic layer on the application server and your database layer code on another server inside the firewall. The server housing the database layer could then communicate with the database. Clearly, it's important that you be aware of these issues when defining your layers. Imagine if you coupled the layers in the prior example and did not find out about this constraint until it was time to deploy the project. You would be scrambling to decouple this code and would face certain delays and increased costs.

Another deployment issue you need to consider is the communication paths and protocols between the layers. This might not be a concern if you are creating a simple, stand-alone Windows application. However, if you are building anything at the enterprise level, it most likely connects to data in some manner. As you saw in the section of Chapter 1, "Application Requirements and Design," titled "Create a High-Level Application Design," you can use tools like Visual Studio Team Architect to set these constraints, indicate the communication paths, and define the ports in terms of security and protocol. For your logical architecture, you may decide to simply indicate the layers in the system and their intent and draw arrows between the layers that communicate. On each arrow you may indicate the intended communication like Hypertext Transfer Protocol (HTTP), Transmission Control Protocol/Internet Protocol

(TCP/IP), Simple Object Access Protocol (SOAP), and so on. Figure 2-7 shows an example of a logical architecture.

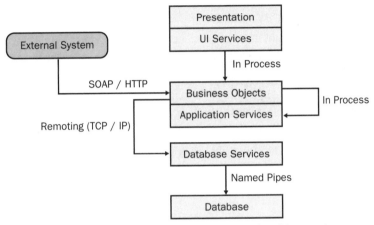

Figure 2-7 An application layer diagram (logical architecture).

This diagram shows the logical layers of the application. Note that, based on deployment constraints, the UI code (presentation and UI services), the business object layer, and the application services layer will all execute in the same process. There is also an external system that will connect to some of the business logic through a Web service. The database services code will be deployed on a different server. Therefore the communication to this server is through remoting. Finally, the database services code will be the only layer communicating directly to the database; it will do so across named pipes.

Lab: Define Logical Application Layers

In this lab, you will define the logical layers of an application. You will start by reviewing a number of design goals and some functional requirements. You will use this information to propose the logical layers of a solution architecture. You will also add physical constraints to those layers in terms of communication paths and deployment options.

▶ **Exercise: Review Requirements and Define Logical Application Layers**

For this exercise, review the following design goals and some functional requirements. Then follow the steps listed below to determine the application layers and communication paths. The following are the requirements with which you will be working.

Design Goals / Functional Requirements

G1   The application should be accessible to any employee on the corporate network through a Windows application interface.

G2   The user interface should be easy to deploy and update.

G3   The business processing rules should be extracted into their own set of classes and methods. For now, these rules belong to only this application.

G4   The database access code will be created by a database developer and not the developer of each module. All data access should be encapsulated in a common area.

G5   All common application functions should be grouped together. We are considering using Microsoft Enterprise Library or something similar to provide these services to the various layers of the application.

G6   We are targeting an existing application server for the deployment of the shared business layer. Clients will access this server through remoting.

G7   We plan to use the relational database to manage the data and data transactions in the system. This database is accessible from the application server through TCP/IP. Individual clients will not be able to access the database directly.

Lab Steps

1. Determine the user interface layers that you would define.

    G1 indicates that this is a Windows client application. This means Windows Forms and user controls. G2 indicates easy deployment and updating. For this reason you might suggest creating a Smart Client application. These facts might lead you to a single layer for the Windows user interface. This layer would combine both presentation and the code to interact with the business objects on the server.

2. Determine the layers you would define for the middle tier.

    G3 indicates that the business rules should be abstracted into their own layer. G5 indicates that there are common services for the entire application. These facts should lead you to recommend both a business logic layer and an application services layer.

3. Determine the layers you would define for the data tier.

    G4 indicates that a single, separate developer will be working on data access methods. This should warrant a separate layer for the database services.

4. Draw the recommended layers on a diagram. Figure 2-8 shows a representation.

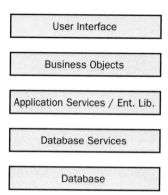

Figure 2-8   The proposed application layers.

5. Determine the communication paths between the layers.

   The design goals indicate that the user interface layer should interact only with the business objects. It should not call the other services directly. The business objects layer should work with the application services layer. It also works with the database services to store and retrieve data. The database layer should work with the application services layer and the database.

6. Determine the physical processes that will execute each layer in the system.

   The user interface will run on the client. The business objects, application services, and database services can all run on the same machine and in-process. G6 indicates an application server for this. It also indicates that the client will access this server through remoting. The database server is another machine. The application server should connect to this through TCP/IP. Figure 2-9 shows a representation of your final, logical, layered architecture.

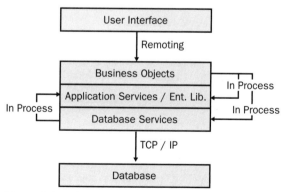

Figure 2-9   The completed logical application layers.

Lesson Summary

- You define the logical layers of your application in order to help developers and architects understand how your system works and where their code logically fits.
- A logical architecture indicates the layers in the system and the communication paths between those layers.
- You abstract code into layers to help mitigate risk and increase reusability. You might also have design goals that you are satisfying with the logical layers in your application.
- An ASP.NET application is usually split between the user interface layers (presentation and form interaction code), the middle tier (business logic and application services), and the database tier (database abstraction code and the database itself).

Lesson Review

You can use the following questions to test your knowledge of the information in Lesson 2, "Define Application Layers (Create a Logical Architecture)." The questions are also available on the companion CD if you prefer to review them in electronic form.

NOTE Answers

Answers to these questions and explanations of why each answer choice is right or wrong are located in the "Answers" section at the end of the book.

---

1. Which are the following are benefits of defining application layers? (Choose all that apply.)
   A. Increase code reuse.
   B. Make your code more understandable.
   C. Indicate the library (.dll) that code should go into.
   D. Make your code more maintainable.

2. You have decided to create a separate presentation layer for your user interface. Which of the following code items belong in this layer? (Choose all that apply.)
   A. Windows Forms
   B. Business rules processing
   C. User controls
   D. Database access code

3. You are writing an application that has the following constraints:
   - ❑ The application needs to be written in a very short time.
   - ❑ The application will not be reused. The company is already working on a replacement. However, that will take longer to develop.
   - ❑ The application should support about 10 users.
   - ❑ The application will be accessed by means of a single Windows form.
   - ❑ The application logic is not very complex.
   - ❑ The application will be deployed on each user's desktop (client). Each client will have access to a single SQL Server machine.

   Considering these constraints, what application layers would you recommend?
   - A. Presentation → User → Activity → Business Objects → Database
   - B. User Interface → Business Services → Database
   - C. User Interface → Database
   - D. User Interface → Application Services → Database

Lesson 3: Create Application (Physical) Models for Developers

The physical models for an application indicate how developers should build a system. These are technical models using a technical notation such as UML or the Visual Studio Class Designer. The models take the information from the requirements, use cases, technology recommendations (or high-level architecture), and logical models (ORMs and application layers) and define the components, classes, methods, and messaging between objects.

This lesson looks at how you can define components from the modules, submodules, and layers in your application. It then looks at building class models based on the domain you defined in the ORMs. Next, we cover the purpose of some additional UML models (sequence, collaboration, and activity) that help you understand your system better. Finally, we explore how you can use pseudo code to help developers better understand your intent.

NOTE **The Unified Modeling Language (UML)**

This lesson (and this book) is not meant to be a definitive primer on UML. There are many good books out there that tackle that subject. Rather, in this lesson we will cover the basic overview of the UML models as they relate to physical models for developers. We will not cover the intricacies of the notation, nor will we cover all of the many models. If you are totally unfamiliar with UML, you should consider some additional reading on this subject.

> **After this lesson, you will be able to:**
> - Understand the purpose of a component diagram.
> - Understand the purpose of a class diagram.
> - Understand the purpose of an activity diagram.
> - Understand the purpose of sequence and collaboration diagrams.
> - Create pseudo code to aid developers.
>
> **Estimated lesson time: 35 minutes**

> ### Real World
> *Mike Snell*
>
> Developers and UML do not always mix well. I have seen many development teams who believe they are hindered by the structured notation of UML. The developers in these environments feel UML is too complex or the effort is too burdensome for the reward. They still end up creating application models. However, their models are usually boxes and arrows or long sections of text that read like sequence diagrams or flowcharts. I have also seen the opposite (although more rare). These teams are UML-crazy. They require every model for every object, method, system interaction, activity, and so on. These teams typically produce more models than code. What is needed, I think, is a practical approach.
>
> I suggest my teams use the pieces of UML that make sense, when they make sense. If a better (structured) tool exists, use that. For example, if they are having a hard time understanding how objects communicate, they create a sequence diagram. If they have a complex method, they create an activity diagram. These models are not required; they are used when they are useful. We use UML because it is a standard. Lately, we have also been using the Visual Studio Class Designer to create our physical class diagrams. This is a great tool that also saves us time because it stays in sync with the code.

Create a Component Diagram

A *component diagram* is used to indicate the components (or code packages) that you will create for your application. A *component* is made up of logically related classes grouped together in a single, deployable unit. You can think of a component as a DLL, control, or Web service. Component diagrams are useful for indicating physical dependencies and physical deployment (in conjunction with a deployment diagram). This section looks at how you determine the components in your system and how you create a component diagram.

Defining Application Components

When you are working through your requirements, use cases, and logical model, you also work to put things into logical groupings. For example, consider the requirements and use cases for a client billing system. You will want to group the requirements into modules like engagement manager, client accounts, projects, invoicing, and so on. You then might break these modules into submodules and define the set of features within each module and submodule.

You want to follow a similar technique for the code elements of your application. You should group the code into physical components that will be used to indicate which library contains a given set of code. These components may follow the same lines as your application layers, or they may follow your modules or even features. For example, if you follow your application lay-ers, you may have a UserInterface component, a BusinessObjects component, and so on. Or you may decide to break out some of these layers into multiple components. You may create a EngagementManager component, an Invoice component, and so on. Each of these may con-tain business logic for a given module. However, this physical distribution may be based on the choice to encapsulate each module of the application.

Create a Component Diagram

You create a component diagram by adding components to the diagram and then setting their dependencies. Figure 2-10 shows an example component diagram. The components are rep-resented with the rectangles that include the two smaller rectangles on their left. Note that each component name is preceded with text indicating its logical layer and then two colons. This text represents the components package. A UML package is a logical grouping of compo-nents, classes, and other objects. Here we are using packages to group components by logical layers. For example, the *ClientBillingUI* component is inside the *User Interface* package.

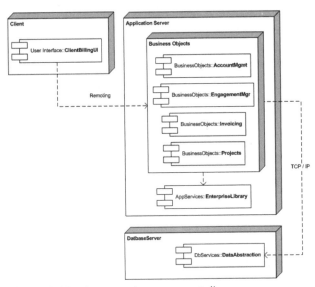

Figure 2-10   An example component diagram.

The outer boxes that surround the components are called nodes. A UML node indicates a deployment container. This is typically a physical piece of hardware. For example, the user interface is running on the *Client* node; the business objects and application services are all on the *Application Server* node. We have also used the node concept to group the business objects. This cuts down on the arrows required to indicate all the dependencies in the diagram.

Create a Class Diagram

A *class diagram* defines the structure of the classes (methods and properties) and the relationship between those classes. A class diagram defines the specification of the system. The classes in the model are static representations of your objects. The model is not meant to show how these classes interact, nor does it show the classes as objects. Rather, it shows the definition of the classes, how they are related, and how they are defined in terms of one another (and in terms of object-oriented design).

The UML defines a model for creating class diagrams. This model represents a notation for things like methods, properties, inheritance, associations, data types, and so on. The notation is meant to be technology-agnostic. It is focused on object-oriented concepts and not a particular technology such as .NET or Java. Visual Studio 2005, however, now provides a class diagramming tool. This tool is not meant to follow the UML notation. However, it too defines classes, properties, methods, enumerations, inheritance, dependencies, and so on.

The principal benefit of using Visual Studio is that it is a "live" model. It represents a two-way synchronization with your code and your diagram. If you build your class models in Visual Studio, you get the code stubbed out as well. If you change your code, the model gets updated. Therefore, as code gets modified, your model is automatically updated. For this section we will leave the UML and talk about designing classes with the Class Designer.

Define Classes for Your Application

The classes in your application should derive from your solution architecture (or framework) and your business domain. The solution architecture classes you define are dependent on that architecture. For example, if you intend to create a central class for handling the logging of errors, then you create a class called *Logger* or similar. Or if you want a base class for managing object security, you create that as part of your framework. The same is true for other framework-like classes such as a database helper class or a cache management class, and so on.

The business domain classes also need to respect your solution architecture. If, for example, your architecture dictates that each class knows how to save and create itself from the database, then you need to design your business classes accordingly. Perhaps you would create a common interface, for example. As another example, if you are creating your business model using a pattern like DTO, then you need to create simple domain classes with only fields or properties and then create a set of domain services to work with these classes. The point is, how you define your business domain classes depends on the technical constraints of your overall solution architecture.

The makeup of your business domain itself should be defined based on your logical model. The *business domain* refers to which classes you will define, which classes are made up of other objects (inheritance and encapsulation), and the properties of your classes. If you look back at your ORM diagrams, you will find your primary entities. These are the principal objects that link to a lot of other objects in the model. These objects can be thought of as the "perspective" objects. That is, they are the objects that you most typically start with and examine the relationships from their perspective. They are usually easy to pick out. For example, a *Project* or *ClientAccount* object in a client billing application will end up with a lot of links and be considered as important from a point of view. These objects also participate heavily in the feature set, modules, submodules, requirements, and use cases. The other objects in your ORM are sometimes bit players in the domain. Other times they end up as simply properties, or even values of properties, of a class.

To create your business domain (class diagram) you should look through your ORMs and pick out the domain objects and their properties. You then need to apply the physical constraints of your technology choices and the constraints of your solution architecture to the class diagram. The result should be a domain model that stays true to your logical model and supports your technology choices.

Create a Class Diagram

The Class Designer in Visual Studio provides a notation that should be easy to pick up for those used to working with UML. The notation represents classes as rectangles. These rectangles (like UML classes) are split into multiple sections (usually in two). The top grouping in the class contains the properties of the object; the bottom contains the methods. The notation also allows for the display of things like fields and nested types. Figure 2-11 shows an example class diagram for illustration purposes.

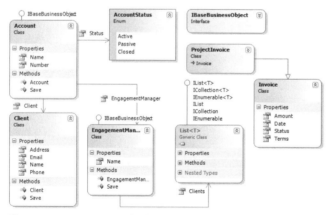

Figure 2-11   An example class diagram.

The Visual Studio 2005 Class Designer has a visual representation of a number of object-oriented elements. These elements include all of the following:

- **Class**   Represented as a rectangle with properties and methods. In Figure 2-11, Account, Client, List, EngagementManager, and Invoice are all classes.

- **Interface** An interface is represented like a class but has a different color (green). In Figure 2-11, IBaseBusinessObject is an interface.
- **Implement interface** The interfaces that a class implements are represented with the lollipop icon extending from the top of the object. For example, Account in Figure 2-11 implements IBaseBusinessObject.
- **Association / Aggregation** A property that is of a specific type in your domain is indicated by an arrow with the property name on the line of the arrow. Status is an example from Figure 2-11.
- **Inheritance** A class that inherits another class is indicated with the open-ended arrow head (similar to UML). In Figure 2-11, ProjectInvoice inherits the Invoice class.
- **Enumeration** An enumeration is indicated as a rectangle that is not rounded off (like the classes are). Figure 2-11 has the enumeration AccountStatus.
- **Other Items** The notation allows you to see a number of additional items. These include *Abstract Class*, *Struct*, *Delegate*, and a *Comment*. You can also show members of the .NET Framework (note that Figure 2-11 shows *List<T>* from the *Generic* namespace). In addition, you can modify the model to show data types and parameters.

Create a Sequence Diagram

A *sequence* diagram shows object interaction during execution (or run time). The model demonstrates the lifetime of these objects and shows the message exchange between them. Object-oriented programming results in a lot of small objects interacting with one another. The objects call one another through a sequence (or chronology) to get work done for the application. The many objects making many calls to one another can make it difficult to understand how they come together to form a complete solution. A sequence diagram is meant to illustrate and clarify just how these objects talk to one another to form a specific solution.

The UML notation dictates how you create sequence diagrams. Objects are listed as rectangles at the top of the diagram with lifelines extending from them. An object *lifeline* is an indication of how long an object will live before it is disposed of or made ready for garbage collection. The objects themselves are described in the rectangle that sits atop this lifeline. The description that goes in the rectangle is meant to describe an instance of the class. For this reason you typically write the description as "*an Object*" or "*the Object*," where object is the name of the class or variable representing the class.

Figure 2-12 shows an example sequence diagram. In this example, EditClientUI, Client, ClientService, and ClientDB are all objects. This example is meant to show how these objects work together to support the use case, edit client. The design has a user interface form (EditClientUI), a domain object (Client), an object service for managing the domain object (ClientService), and a database abstraction class for the object (ClientDB).

Notice the long rectangles that extend along the lifeline of each object. These rectangles indicate when an object is created and when it goes out of scope. For example, the ClientDB object is created twice by the ClientService during this process.

The messages that pass between objects are indicated by the arrows from one lifeline to another. These messages are meant to be read from top to the bottom, left to right (as a sequence). Each message represents a method call, property call, or return value. For example, the GetClient message represents a call to the *GetClient* method of the ClientService object. The calls to the Client.Name, Client.Email, and related properties are also depicted. Return calls are shown as a dashed arrow; *return confirmation* is an example. All the messages depicted in Figure 2-12 are synchronous. You can also indicate asynchronous messages by using an arrow that has only its lower half.

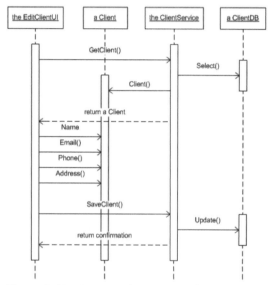

Figure 2-12   An example sequence diagram.

Collaboration Diagram

A collaboration diagram shows the same type of interaction between objects as a sequence diagram does. However, the collaboration diagram allows you to lay out the objects in any way you like. The actual sequence is dictated by numbered messages (and not by the model's constraints). Figure 2-13 shows the same sequence diagram shown in Figure 2-12 as a collaboration diagram.

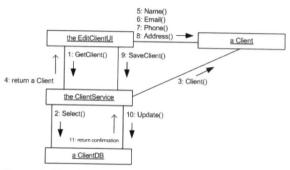

Figure 2-13 An example collaboration diagram.

Create an Activity Diagram

The UML defines the activity diagram as an answer for flowcharting and workflow definition. An *activity diagram* allows you to indicate activities that happen one after another and in parallel. For this reason, the activity diagram is sometimes used to model workflow and the business process associated with use cases. However, the principal intent of an activity diagram is to be a physical model that helps developers understand complex algorithms and application methods. This is the use of the model that we will discuss here.

Figure 2-14 shows an example activity diagram of a constructor for the fictitious Contact class. The closed black circle indicates the start of the method. The arrows indicate the processing flow. Each rounded rectangle indicates an activity in the method. You can see that the example starts with the Get Contact Details activity and moves from one activity to another. You can think of these activities as markers in your method (or even commented sections). These are the things the method must do.

The activity diagram allows you to indicate branches or decisions that must be made in the code. These are represented by the diamonds. The control that comes off of each side of the branch is guarded. That is, it must be labeled as a Boolean condition that must be met in order for the code to flow in that direction. The first branch in the example is a decision on whether or not the application is online (as opposed to not being connected to a network). If it is online, the control moves to Check Cache. If not, the control moves to Pull From Cache.

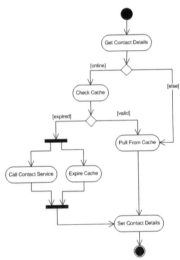

Figure 2-14   An example activity diagram.

The activity diagram also allows you to indicate parallel processing (or multithreading). You do so with a *fork*. The fork indicates that two processes are happening at once. In the example, both Call Contact Service and Expire Cache are forked and in parallel. Once any parallel processing is complete, it is *joined*. The figure shows a join for the two items executing in parallel. Finally, once the processing is complete, you use a black circle with an outer ring to indicate the completion of the activity.

Create Pseudo Code

An effective developer model that is often overlooked is pseudo code. *Pseudo code* is not a diagram or a model; it is text that is written like you write code. It does not follow a specific language or notation. It does, however, offer a codelike view of a method for developers who prefer to see code (or are more used to it than models). It can also be an easier (and faster) way to express concepts for architects and designers who are not used to writing up a lot of diagrams (and might also prefer code).

Pseudo code is what you make it. You should strive to mimic some of the structure of your chosen language just to help your developers read it. If, for example, you use C#, you might put curly braces in your pseudo code. If you use VB, you should consider using *end* statements. However, the code will not compile, will make strange assumptions that code should not make, will take shortcuts, and will generally break the rules. That is the whole point. It is not meant to be real code. The following is an example of some pseudo code for the method defined in Figure 2-14:

```
' VB
Public New
  If Application.Online
    GetCache()
 If Cache.Expired
     New Thread.execute (call ContactService)
     Cache.Expire
     Thread.wait for completion
   Else
     GetCache(me)
   End
  Else
    GetCache(me)
  End
  Me.Name = contact.name() … set all properties
End

// C# public Contact() {
  If Application.Online {
    GetCache()
 If Cache.Expired
     New Thread.execute (call ContactService)
     Cache.Exipre
     Thread.wait for completion
  } else {
    GetCache(me)
  } else {
    GetCache(me)
  }
  Me.Name = contact.name() … set all properties
}
```

Lab: Create Physical Models

In this lab, you will work to define a few physical models for an application. You will first work to create a class diagram. You will then define object interaction diagrams (both collaboration and sequence).

▶ **Exercise 1: Review Object Relationships and Define a Class Diagram**

For this exercise, you will first review a few architectural goals for a Windows application. You will then look at an ORM diagram (Figure 2-15) for a portion of the application that allows an engagement manager to set up a new project in the client tracking system. You will then work with the design goals and the ORM to define the business services layer. You will specify the business domain using a class diagram.

Architecture Goals

■ All business logic should be encapsulated into a separate business domain layer.
■ Each business object should know how to save, update, load, and delete itself.

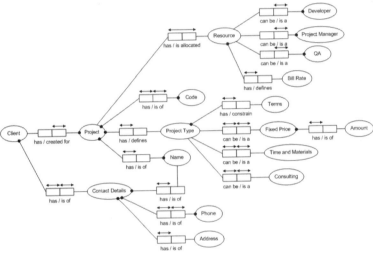

Figure 2-15   The project subsystem ORM.

Lab Steps

The following steps will lead you through this exercise.

1. Use Visual Studio 2005 to create a new Windows application (File | New | Project). You can call this application what you wish; you can either create a VB or C# Windows application.

2. Add a class diagram to the application (Project, Add New Item, select Class Diagram). You can name this diagram whatever you like.

3. Determine the primary objects in the system. Review the ORM (Figure 2-15) and determine which objects have many links from them. Review your choices. Add a class to the diagram for each primary object you chose. Figure 2-16 shows an example.

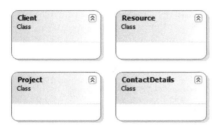

Figure 2-16   The primary objects from the ORM.

4. Determine the objects from the ORM that represent simple properties of your domain objects. These are objects from the ORM that did not end up as primary objects, are not relationships, and are not considered values of properties. Add these properties to each class in the model using the Class Details window (right-click a class and choose Class Details). Figure 2-17 shows an example.

Figure 2-17   Object properties from the ORM.

5. Determine the association relationships between the classes. These relationships represent properties that link the objects together. You define these relationships using the Association tool from the Class Designer toolbox. After selecting the Association tool, click and drag from the class that has the association to the class that is the association. Figure 2-18 shows the class diagram with the associations. The properties Projects and Resources were defined as the generic collection, *List<T>*, where *T* must be an instance of Project and Resource respectively. These properties are shown as double arrows. You can show these associations once you define the property by right-clicking it in the model and choosing Show As Collection Association.

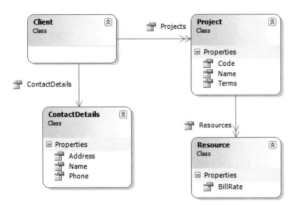

Figure 2-18 Association relationships.

6. Determine the enumerations you wish to define based on the model. These are items that define a property in terms of values. You create an enumeration using the Enum tool on the toolbox. Figure 2-19 shows an example.

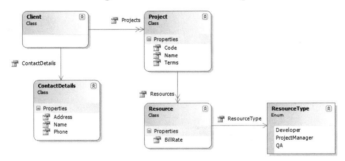

Figure 2-19 Enumerations added to the model.

7. Determine which objects represent base classes and which should implement inheritance. The ORM model indicates a *Project Type* object. This could be thought of as an enumeration. However, some of the types have their own values. Therefore, you might consider creating an inheritance structure. You do so by adding the new classes to the model, one for each *Project Type*. You then drag the Inheritance tool from the child class to the base class. Figure 2-20 shows an example.

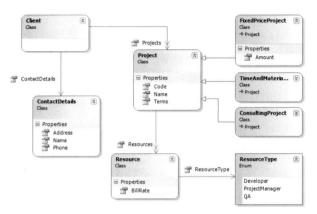

Figure 2-20   Inheritance added to the model.

8. Determine any interfaces you wish to define for the system. The architecture goals indicate that each business object needs to save, load, update, and delete itself. Therefore, you might consider implementing a common interface for your business objects. You do so by adding an *Interface* object from the toolbox. You then indicate the methods and any properties that are part of this interface. You can then use the Inheritance tool to indicate which objects implement this interface. Figure 2-21 shows the class model with the IBusinessObject interface.

Figure 2-21   An interface added to the model.

▶ **Exercise 2: Create an Interaction (Sequence) Diagram**

For this exercise, you will review a use case that describes a user submitting an issue to a support system. You will then use this use case along with a description of the classes in your system to create a sequence diagram. The sequence diagram is meant to describe how the physical model realizes the use case.

CAUTION   Visio for Enterprise Architects

This lab assumes that you are using Visio for Enterprise Architects. If you do not have this, you can still use a drawing tool to draw a sequence diagram that mimics the lab.

Submit Trouble Ticket Use Case

Precondition: User has logged onto the system.

1. A user wants to submit an incident report to the trouble ticket system.
2. The system generates a new trouble ticket for the user.
3. The system takes the user to the SubmitIssue form in the application.
4. The user enters the details of the incident.
5. The system saves the incident and generates a trouble ticket tracking number.
6. The tracking number is sent back to the user for tracking purposes.

Book Trip Architecture Model

- User: class represents a user in the system.
- SubmitIssue: a form in the application that allows a user to submit an incident report.
- IncidentReport: a class that represents an issue or incident.
- TroubleTicketService: a class that contains methods for submitting a trouble ticket.

Lab Steps

The following steps will lead you through this exercise.

1. Open Visio and create a new UML Model Diagram (File | New | Software | UML Model Diagram).
2. Add the classes to the model. In the Model Explorer, right-click Top Package and choose New | Class. Name each class and click OK. You should add the following classes from the architecture model: User, IncidentReport, SubmitIssueUI, TroubleTicketService.
3. Define methods for each class. For this exercise, we will simply define those methods we intend to use for the sequence diagram. If you had created your class diagram previously, you would use the full class description as an input into the sequence diagram.

You add a method to a class in Visio by right-clicking the class in the Model Explorer and choosing New | Operation. This opens up the UML Operation Properties dialog box. You can use this dialog box to name your operation and indicate its return type, its visibility, and any parameters that are required. You add parameters by clicking the Parameters category on the left side of the dialog box.

Create the following operations along with their parameters:

```
TroubleTicketService.GetIncidentReport(user)
TroubleTicketService.SubmitIncident(incidentReport)
User.Load(id)
IncidentReport.Load(user)
IncidentReport.SetIncidentDetails(description, date, repeatSteps)
```

4. Add a sequence diagram to the UML model. Right-click Top Package in the Model Explorer and choose New | Sequence Diagram.

5. Drag an Object Lifeline shape onto the diagram for each primary object in the interaction. Double-click each object to define its instance. Select a class from the model as the Classifier. Indicate an instance name in the Name field.

6. You should have an object lifeline (in order) for a SubmitIssueUI, a User, an IncidentReport, and the TroubleTicketService.

7. Align the tops of each object lifeline. Extend each lifeline down about half of the page.

8. Add an activation (long rectangle) to the lifeline of each of your objects. You will use this activation to indicate when the object is created and when it gets disposed of.

9. Begin connecting your objects using messages. Each message is defined by a method on the object that is being called. For example, the first message you should create will be from SubmitIssueUI to User. The message should be the *Load(id)* method. Review the use case and the architecture model and continue to connect objects. Your final sequence diagram should look similar to Figure 2-22.

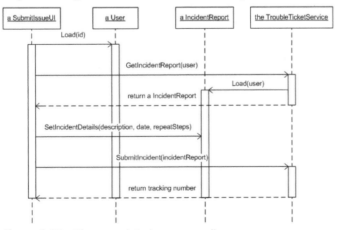

Figure 2-22 The completed sequence diagram.

Lesson Summary

- A component is a group of logically related classes and methods.

- A component diagram represents the components in your system and shows how they work with one another to form a solution. You can show the deployment of components onto nodes. A node typically represents a piece of hardware (like a server).

- A class diagram illustrates the static specification of classes. This includes methods, properties, fields, and so on. It also shows relationships like inheritance and encapsulation. The Visual Studio 2005 Class Designer allows you to model classes, structures, enumerations, interfaces, and abstract classes.

- You define the classes in your system, called the business domain, using the logical model (ORMs) and the technological constraints of your solution architecture. The ORM diagrams help define the primary objects in your business domain. These objects link to a lot of other objects in the model. The objects to which they link might end up as properties, property values, or other objects.

- A sequence diagram depicts the messages between objects over a sequence of events. The sequence diagram typically shows multiple objects across a use case.

- A collaboration diagram shows the sequence of events between objects as numbered messages. The collaboration diagram is a lot like a sequence diagram; however, it allows you to show the objects in any spatial layout.

- An activity diagram indicates the activities in an algorithm or method that happen one after another and in parallel. An activity diagram is like a flowchart.

- Pseudo code is code-like text that is written to show a code-like view of a method. Pseudo code helps developers who prefer to see code to understand a complex algorithm or method.

Lesson Review

You can use the following questions to test your knowledge of the information in Lesson 3, "Create Application (Physical) Models for Developers." The questions are also available on the companion CD if you prefer to review them in electronic form.

NOTE   Answers

Answers to these questions and explanations of why each answer choice is right or wrong are located in the "Answers" section at the end of the book.

---

1. You have been instructed to define the physical specification for developers. Which model would you use?

    A. Component diagram

    B. Collaboration diagram

    C. Pseudo code

    D. Class diagram

2. Which of the following are differences between a sequence diagram and a collaboration diagram? (Choose all that apply.)

    A. A sequence diagram shows message calls over time. A collaboration diagram shows asynchronous messaging.

    B. A sequence diagram uses the model to illustrate sequence and order. A collaboration diagram illustrates this through numbered messages.

    C. A sequence diagram has object lifelines and shows when objects are created and destroyed. A collaboration diagram does not show this information.

    D. A sequence diagram enforces the layout of objects across the top of the page. A collaboration diagram allows you to lay out objects in any spatial manner you choose.

3. Which of the following are good uses for an activity diagram? (Choose all that apply.)

    A. Defining class interactions and groupings

    B. Modeling complex algorithms

    C. Showing a sequence of business events or workflows

    D. Modeling multithreaded methods

4. Which of the following statements are true about a component diagram? (Choose all that apply.)

    A. A component diagram has a node that represents physical hardware.

    B. A component diagram allows you to indicate the communication protocols between servers.

    C. A component diagram can show the logical layers of the application.

    D. A component diagram illustrates which objects reference each other.

Chapter Review

To further practice and reinforce the skills you learned in this chapter, you can perform the following tasks:

- Review the chapter summary.
- Review the list of key terms introduced in this chapter.
- Complete the case scenarios. These scenarios set up real-world situations involving the topics of this chapter and ask you to create a solution.
- Complete the suggested practices.
- Take a practice test.

Chapter Summary

- A logical software model is designed to represent real and actual concepts from your business domain. The logical model should change only if these concepts change. You can model this domain using object role modeling (ORM) diagrams. These diagrams represent objects as ovals. They show relationships between the objects using a rectangle that is split in two. You define text under each side of this rectangle in order to describe the relationship from left to right and the inverse. You place arrows over the relationship rectangle to represent multiplicity. Finally, you can indicate which object or objects are required of the relationship by placing a closed circle on the line pointing to the required object.

- A logical architecture (think layers or tiers) indicates how your system logically works and where (in which layer) developers need to put their code. This model also shows the communication paths between the layers. For example, it can indicate if the user interface should talk directly to the database layer (or not). Layers also mitigate risk and increase reusability. Most enterprise-level Windows applications define layers for the user interface (presentation and form interaction code), the middle tier (business logic and application services), and the database tier (database abstraction code and the database itself).

- You can use UML and Visual Studio to create physical models for developers. These physical models include component diagrams, class diagrams, activity diagrams, and interaction diagrams (sequence and collaboration). You create a component diagram to show the logical grouping of classes (into components) and the relationships (references) between these components. The component diagram can also show how components are deployed onto nodes (hardware). You create a class diagram to define the static specification of the classes in your domain. A class diagram defines classes, their methods and properties, inheritance and encapsulation, interfaces, enumerations, and so on. You create interaction diagrams to show how objects interact at run time. The UML defines both the sequence and the collaboration diagram to illustrate this information. A sequence diagram depicts messages between objects over time (left to right, top-down). A collaboration diagram shows the object call sequence as numbered messages between objects. You can choose how to lay out a collaboration diagram. The sequence diagram notation dictates this for you. You create an activity diagram to illustrate workflow or the activities in a complex algorithm. An activity diagram shows both synchronous parallel activities. Think of an activity diagram like a flowchart.

Key Terms

Do you know what these key terms mean? You can check your answers by looking up the terms in the glossary at the end of the book.

- activity diagram
- business domain
- class diagram
- code
- collaboration diagram
- component
- component diagram
- layers
- multiplicity
- object role modeling (ORM)
- pseudo code
- sequence diagram
- state (or application state)

Case Scenario

In the following case scenario, you will apply what you've learned about decomposing specifications for developers. You can find answers to these questions in the "Answers" section at the end of this book.

Case Scenario: Evaluate User Inputs and Create Physical Models

You are a senior developer for a company whose principal business is creating custom-fit rollers and tubing. There is an existing Windows application that allows the sales team to create quotes and send them to customers by means of fax and e-mail. You have been approached by the sales management team to add features to this application. They would like to be able to set various product pricing and job scheduling thresholds. If a salesperson goes beyond these thresholds, the quote should be routed to a sales manager for approval. This application should cut down on overpromising to customers and underbidding by the sales team. You have been assigned the task of implementing the approval process for these quotes. You have been given a use case and design goals for review.

Use Case: Approve Quote

Precondition: User has logged onto the system (typically in response to an e-mail notification indicating a pending approval request). System has recognized the user as part of the Sales Manager group. The sales manager has selected the menu option Approve Pending Quotes.

1. System displays a list of pending quotes to the sales manager. Quotes are ordered by submittal date and time.
2. Sales manager selects a quote from the list to review and approve.
3. System displays the details of the quote, including customer name, address, and contact details. The quote also shows a promised production date, the shipping terms (express, 3-day, or ground), the payment terms (charge account, net 10, net 30, other), and the salesperson.
4. The system also displays a list of products on the quote. Each product contains the following information: product code, description, price per unit, discount per unit, and quantity ordered. In addition, a flag is set for each product, indicating if it requires a custom build or if there are products already in inventory.
5. Finally, the system highlights any items that are outside the bounds of a threshold. Thresholds can be set for each product's discount price, the production date (relative to current date), and the payment terms. Supervisor looks for any irregularities with the timesheet.
6. The sales manager reviews the quote irregularities. If the sales manager approves the quote, the sales manager indicates that approval to the system.

   Post-condition: System marks the selected quote status as approved. The quote is then "locked" and can't be edited or have its status changed unless an administrator or sales manager moves the status to reopen.

Alternate Case: Reject Quote

Precondition: Use case follows the Approve Quote case through step 5.

1. The sales manager reviews the quote irregularities and decides not to approve the quote. The sales manager indicates to the system that the quote should be rejected.
2. System asks the sales manager to provide a reason for rejection.

3. System sends a notification to the salesperson whose quote was rejected, asking the salesperson to make modifications to the quote and then resubmit.

Post-condition: System has marked the quote's status as rejected. The quote is open for editing by the salesperson and requires resubmission.

Design Goals / Functional Requirements

- The quote approval application should be built as an extension to the existing system.
- The quote threshold business rules should be encapsulated. Each business object should know how to save and retrieve itself from the database.
- Sales managers should be able to approve a quote from the Windows application or directly from a corporate e-mail account.
- The application server can access the database server directly because this application sits on the corporate local area network (LAN).

Questions

While thinking about the specifications (use case and design goals) listed above, answer the following questions.

1. How would you model the domain of the use case using an ORM diagram?
2. What would a logical architecture model (application layers) look like for this specification?
3. What would a high-level class diagram look like for this specification?
4. How would you create a sequence diagram to describe the object interaction concerning the approval portion of the use case?

Suggested Practices

To help you successfully master the exam objectives presented in this chapter, complete the following tasks.

Define Objects and Their Relationships (Create a Logical Model)

Many developers have never created ORMs. However, they make a great approach to defining a logical model based on requirements and user scenarios. Consider this task to make sure you get experience in creating ORMs. This will help you master this objective.

- **Practice 1** Review requirements and use cases of a new system that has just been designed (preferably) or an older system that you might have worked on. Use this information to define an ORM diagram using Visio. Review this logical representation with a business analyst or user who provided input into the use cases. Determine if the use case really intended the results of the ORM.

- **Practice 2**   Use the ORM you created for Practice 1. Compare it to the domain model (classes or database) that was defined for the system. Determine why trade-offs were made with respect to the ORMs. Consider if these were mistakes or if the technology dictated an alternate solution. Consider how that might affect the understanding of the system without the ORMs.

Define Application Layers (Create a Logical Architecture)

This task should be common to most senior-level developers. They often think of systems in terms of layers. If, however, this is not your experience, you can use this task to better master this objective.

- **Practice 1**   Look back at a few existing projects you worked on. Try to describe the layers of the application. If you can't describe them, try and trace the code. Is the code spread out in many places across the application or was there a disciplined effort to contain the code?
- **Practice 2**   Using the layers you created as part of Practice 1, try to find justification for these layers within the nonfunctional requirements and design goals.

Create Application (Physical) Models for Developers

Class modeling is where application design and coding meet. If you've never before created class models (or are unfamiliar with the Visual Studio 2005 Class Designer), this task will provide a good overview of how to use class modeling to help you better structure your code. In addition, if you need more work with UML, follow the practices listed below to create key UML diagrams.

- **Practice 1**   Use Visual Studio 2005 to create a class diagram (or model an existing set of classes). Use the tool to add new methods, properties, and classes to your application.
- **Practice 2**   Create a sequence diagram to describe how a feature of your application works. Pick a feature that you've implemented. Start with its use case and see how well you can describe the messages between your objects without looking at the code. Then compare the sequence diagram to the implemented code.
- **Practice 3**   Convert your sequence diagram from Practice 2 into a collaboration diagram.
- **Practice 4**   Consider the next method you intend to write. Draw an activity diagram to describe the method before you write it. Determine if this helped you in understanding the method before you wrote the code.

Take a Practice Test

The practice tests on this book's companion CD offer many options. For example, you can test yourself on just the content covered in this chapter, or you can test yourself on all the 70-548 certification exam content. You can set up the test so that it closely simulates the experience of taking a certification exam, or you can set it up in study mode so that you can look at the correct answers and explanations after you answer each question.

MORE INFO   Practice tests

For details about all the practice test options available, see the section titled "How to Use the Practice Tests" in this book's Introduction.

Chapter 3
Design Evaluation

Before you can start to build your application, it is important to take time to review your designs and ensure that you are building the right Microsoft Windows-based application features. In this chapter we will delve into the complexities of evaluating the logical and physical designs.

Exam objectives in this chapter:
- Evaluate the logical design of an application.
  - ❏ Evaluate the logical design for performance.
  - ❏ Evaluate the logical design for maintainability.
  - ❏ Evaluate the logical design for extensibility.
  - ❏ Evaluate the logical design for scalability.
  - ❏ Evaluate the logical design for security.
  - ❏ Evaluate the logical design against use cases.
  - ❏ Evaluate the logical design for recoverability.
  - ❏ Evaluate the logical design for data integrity.
- Evaluate the physical design of an application. Considerations include the design of the project structure, the number of files, the number of assemblies, and the location of these resources on the server.
  - ❏ Evaluate the physical design for performance.
  - ❏ Evaluate the physical design for maintainability.
  - ❏ Evaluate how the physical location of files affects the extensibility of the application.
  - ❏ Evaluate the physical design for scalability.
  - ❏ Evaluate the physical design for security.
  - ❏ Evaluate the physical design for recoverability.
  - ❏ Evaluate the physical design for data integrity.

Lessons in this chapter:

Before You Begin

To complete the lessons in this chapter, you should be familiar with VB or C# and be comfortable with the following tasks:

- Successfully complete all lessons in Chapters 1 and 2.
- Use SQL Server Management Studio to attach databases.
- Be familiar with SQL Server Management Studio's Database Designer.

Real World

Shawn Wildermuth

I have been unfortunate. I have survived a number of situations in my past where creating the design was thought of as the last impediment to getting to the start of coding. Just because you create a design does not mean it's a good design. No matter how bright or well-intentioned I have been in creating a design, it is rarely right the first time.

Some years ago I had a boss who insisted on your asking every technical question you had to a teddy bear that he left in the hall. As much as I felt silly doing it, I did learn that vocalizing a problem or design would solve my problem more often than not. Evaluating a design is like that.

Evaluating a design with a team of professionals has become a certain step in every successful project I have worked on in the last 15 years. The team that reviews a design does not have to be the best and brightest. Often the epiphany of a poor design choice comes from the mere presenting of a design, not just letting my coworkers tear it apart.

Lesson 1: Evaluating the Logical Design

Before you can begin the process of actually creating your Windows-based application based on the design, you will need to evaluate the design for correctness and completeness. By completing this evaluation, you can ensure that any potential problems with the design are caught as early in the process as possible to reduce the cost of fixing any design flaws.

> **After this lesson, you will be able to:**
> - Evaluate a logical design for standard design criteria.
>
> **Estimated lesson time: 10 minutes**

Evaluation of the Logical Design

In Chapter 2, "Decompose Specifications for Developers," you worked from use cases to a logical design of your system. Once you have a logical design for a proposed system, you need to evaluate the design based on a set of standard evaluation criteria. In general, this means evaluating the design for performance, maintainability, extensibility, scalability, availability, recovery, data integrity, and use case correctness. In general, you can group these evaluations into run time evaluation (performance, scalability, availability, recoverability, and security); architectural evaluation (maintainability and extensibility); and requirements evaluation (business use case).

Performance Evaluation

Although the logical design of a system is a high-level design, there are performance considerations that you can evaluate. The two types of evaluation you need to make to the logical design are to review the system tiers and to review the abstraction layers.

As you review the logical design, you should also ensure that the design is not over-designed into too many tiers. Typically, designing a Windows application into three logical tiers is sufficient. Creating additional logical tiers usually indicates a poor design unless there is a well thought-out reason for the additional tiers.

You should review the levels of abstraction for particular entities to make sure that there are very specific reasons to abstract out particular parts of the design. In particular, you should be looking for extraneous and unnecessary levels of abstraction. Additional levels of abstraction can affect performance by forcing the flow of data across too many objects. By removing extraneous levels of abstraction, you can ensure that the design has a high level of performance.

Typically, the level at which you can do a performance evaluation of the logical design is limited to finding redundancies. The level of detail required to determine other performance problems is just not available in the logical design.

Scalability Evaluation

The logical design review is also the place where you should be evaluating the design for scalability. Scalability simply refers to the ability to adapt to increasing the load on the system as the number of users increases. In a logical design, the most important part of handling scalability is to make sure that you have a separate logical middle tier. Remember, the logical design is not supposed to specify how you will actually deploy an application on a physical machine. Instead, it should allow for a robust design that can accommodate scalability concerns. You can address these concerns by making sure that the logical design keeps the entire middle tier as a separate distinct part of the design.

Isolating different parts of an application into separate logical tiers is important to scalability because it allows for scaling out of an application. For example, you could start with all the tiers of your application physically within the same machine. As the application matures, you might find it helps performance to be able to move the tiers to separate machines. It gives you the flexibility to move the database tier to a separate machine and even move the middle tier to a separate machine. This isolation of the tiers logically gives you the flexibility to learn about how your application uses machine resources and allows you to change it as needed without having to rewrite the entire application.

Availability and Recoverability Evaluation

Your logical design should also take into account the availability and recoverability of your project. High availability is the characteristic of a design that allows for failover and recovery from catastrophic failures. This includes failover ability, reliable transactions, data synchronization, and disaster preparedness. Because the logical design is a fairly high-level view of the design, you can't deal with all of these availability concerns at the logical level. Instead you should ensure that your entities can deal with availability solutions.

Your entities will be able to handle high-availability solutions in several ways:

- Use reliable transactions (for example, database transactions, Microsoft Message Queuing [MSMQ] transactional messaging, or distributed transactions like Enterprise Services or Distributed Transaction Coordinator [DTC] transactions).
- Be able to deal with failure by supporting rebuilding of corrupted files and configurations in case of a failure of saving data outside a transaction.
- Allow for failover to different databases or other data services (for example, Web services) centers in case of catastrophic hardware failure.

Security Evaluation

In evaluating the security of the logical design of a Windows-based application, you will need to ensure that the application will be able to protect its secrets. Windows-based applications typically will need to access security information in order to do the work they're required to do. If you have a Windows-based application that uses a database, you will need to ensure that the connection information that the application uses is securely placed. This is important because as nefarious persons get ahold of your application, you do not want them to have access to your data. For example, let's say that you have a Windows-based application that is used to access sales information for salespeople. A copy of this application might be installed on the laptop of a salesperson. If this laptop is subsequently stolen, how do you ensure that the data that the application uses is secure?

You can secure data in your Windows-based application in several ways: use secure authentication, encrypt sensitive data (like configuration data), limit local caching of data to only when absolutely necessary, and use authentication to help prevent unauthorized access to the software itself.

The first line of defense in securing an application is how users are authenticated. In any authentication system you will need to determine how to handle the credentials (for example, usernames and passwords). If you are using domain Windows Authentication (for example, Active Directory directory service), then your authentication mechanism will automatically meet the organization's security requirements. But if you are using a custom authentication scheme (for example, storing credentials in a database or flat file), you will need to deal with securing that information. Typically, storing passwords at all is a security risk. If you are using a custom authentication scheme, you should store a hash-value of the password to allow you to confirm that a password matches without having to actually store the password. In other words, if your stored hash of the password matches a hash of the credential's password, then it's a good password. By avoiding actually storing the password, you are less at risk of someone who has access to the database getting access to every account in the system.

MORE INFO   ADO.NET Security Best Practices

For more information on best practices for ADO.NET, see the ADO.NET Security Best Practices in the .NET Framework SDK (*http://msdn2.microsoft.com/en-us/library/hdb58b2f.aspx*).

For almost every application there is sensitive data that can be dangerous in the wrong hands—for example, logon information to a Web service or database server that allows access to sensitive data. By encrypting this data based on Windows Data Protection (more often called the Data Protection Application Programming Interface [DPAPI]), you can encrypt data where it's only decryptable by a specific user. DPAPI allows you to encrypt data without having shared secrets (as is common with *System.Security.Cryptography*).

MORE INFO   The Data Protection API

For more information on how the Data Protection API (DPAPI) can help you secure your applications, see the article "Windows Data Protection" at *http://msdn.microsoft.com/library/en-us/dnsecure/html/windataprotection-dpapi.asp*.

In addition to encrypting data, you should allow for local caches of data to be minimized on machines. Keeping local copies of data is dangerous because those caches are susceptible to being accessed by people who do not have access to the data through your application. In addition, caches can be copied to easily hidden pieces of hardware (for example, universal serial bus [USB] memory devices) for use outside your control. If you do need to keep local caches (for example, for an application that is not always connected to a company's servers), then protecting any sensitive data in the cache becomes paramount. Let's say you have a cache of data that contains medical record information. Protecting that data from prying eyes is your responsibility.

You should also ensure that your logical design protects you against certain types of security attacks that do not require intrusion into your network. The most important to guard against are SQL-injection attacks. SQL-injection attacks are possible if you are building SQL statements on the fly. You can protect against SQL-injection attacks by using either stored procedures or parameterized queries when talking to the database. By using stored procedures or parameterized queries, you can ensure that any data inserted into a SQL statement is treated as data and not evaluated as part of the statement.

MORE INFO **Preventing SQL injection**

For more information on best practices for ADO.NET, see "Data Points," by John Papa, on MSDN Magazine on the Microsoft Web site (*http://msdn.microsoft.com/msdnmag/issues/05/05/DataPoints/*).

Lastly, you should also review that auditing is used to monitor your application. Auditing is helpful in detecting what users are doing in your application to monitor unauthorized access to certain parts of a system. Auditing should not only include usage monitoring but also should log attempts to access the system improperly. For example, every time a user logs on unsuccessfully, an auditing of that activity should be logged. The reasoning behind that level of auditing is to allow you to detect attempts to break into your system. If a single user attempts to log on hundreds of times over and over, you can assume that someone is trying to hack a password in your system by brute force. Detecting that sort of behavior can allow you to stop intruders before they get started.

Quick Check

1. How should you use Windows Authentication?
2. How do you prevent compromising the database connection string in a Windows application?
3. What should you do to prevent intruders from compromising your .NET assemblies?

Quick Check Answers

1. For Windows applications, Windows Authentication should be used for authentication only if the application is being deployed within an organization that is using domain security. For shrink-wrapped applications, you should use another form of authentication.

2. To prevent users from using connection strings from the application in other nefarious ways, you should encrypt any secrets, including connection strings.

3. You should sign your assemblies with strong names to ensure that they can't be replaced by any code except for the original publisher of the Windows application.

Maintainability Evaluation

Ninety cents out of every development dollar are used to maintain a system, not build it. That makes the maintainability of a system crucial to its long-term success. Evaluation for maintainability starts here in the logical design.

The maintainability in the logical design is based on segmenting of elements of the logical design into a specific tier of the design. Specifically, each element of the logical design should belong to one (and only one) tier of logical design. The most common problem with a logical design in the realm of maintainability is in entities that cross the data/user interface boundary. For example, if you have an entity in the logical design that is meant to store data about a customer, that same component should not also know how to expose the customer as a Windows Forms control. Separating each of those pieces of functionality will ensure that changes to the user interface and the data layer are separate. Intermingling user interface and middle tiers inevitably creates code that becomes harder and harder to maintain.

Extensibility Evaluation

While reviewing the logical design, it is important that you view extensibility in your design from two distinct perspectives: "Can I extend other components?" and "Are my components extensible?".

You should evaluate the logical design and determine what entities in your design can be built on top of other components. Usually this means determining what classes to extend from the .NET Framework itself. You should also look at what classes you could use in your own code to build these new objects on. For example, if you look at a customer entity in the logical design, you might have a common base-class that does data access for your entity objects. On the other hand, you might derive those classes from a class in the .NET Framework (for example, *Component* class) in order to get built-in behaviors.

It is important that you look for ways to reuse existing code to complete your design instead of rebuilding everything from scratch. Finding components inside the .NET Framework as well as in your existing code base (if any) to use as the basis of your components will improve the quality of your project (that is, old code usually means better code) as well as decrease development costs.

In your logical design you should also look for ways to ensure that the code you write is extensible. One of the reasons we write object-oriented code is to allow code reuse. The more of your design that can be reused, the better the investment in the technology you will make.

Data Integrity Evaluation

Your logical design should also imply how the data that the Windows-based application will work with remains integral during the full life cycle of the application. This means that you will need to ensure not only that the database has a full set of schema (including primary keys, foreign keys, and data constraints) but also that the client code determines the correct type of data concurrency to use for your application.

The decision that you make about what type of concurrency to use (optimistic versus pessimistic) will affect the overall safety and performance of your middle tier. With optimistic concurrency, rows are not locked when read by a user. Therefore, if a user wants to update a row, the application has to first determine if another user has modified the row. With pessimistic concurrency, the application locks rows as it reads them. This prevents other users from modifying the row, guaranteeing that the row doesn't change while the user is viewing it, and allowing the user to change the row at any time.

Typically, optimistic will perform better but will increase the chance that data changes between updates. Optimistic concurrency implies that data will be ensured to not have changed between the time of retrieving data and saving changes. During that time, if data has changed you will need to determine the best way of handling those changes. Optimistic concurrency generally performs better because there are fewer locks (database and logical locks) on the data so more clients can access data concurrently.

On the other hand, choosing pessimistic concurrency ensures that the data that a client is changing can't change during the time that the client is working with that data. In all but the severest cases, optimistic concurrency is the right decision because it scales out better and performs well.

Business Use Case Evaluation

At the point of the logical design review you will need to review the business use cases to ensure that what you have designed continues to meet those needs. You might assume that, since the design was spawned from the use cases, this evaluation is not necessary, but that would be wrong. Much in the way that each listener changes a conversation that travels around a room, it is common and easy for a design to make assumptions about what it thinks the use cases are. This review of the use cases against the design will almost always find inconsistencies (or ambiguities) that need to be addressed in the logical design.

Lesson Summary

- Evaluating a logical design for run time attributes such as performance, scalability, availability, recoverability, security, and data integrity will ensure that the logical design will result in the one best suited to fulfill the requirements.

- Evaluating a logical design for architectural issues such as maintainability and extensibility will ensure that the Windows-based application can efficiently mature as a product.

- Evaluating a logical design for completeness against the business use cases will ensure that the logical design meets or exceeds the real reason the Windows-based application is being written.

Lesson Review

You can use the following questions to test your knowledge of the information in Lesson 1, "Evaluating the Logical Design." The questions are also available on the companion CD if you prefer to review them in electronic form.

NOTE Answers

Answers to these questions and explanations of why each answer choice is right or wrong are located in the "Answers" section at the end of the book.

---

1. What are some ways to protect sensitive data in your Windows-based application? (Choose all that apply.)
   A. Require authentication to use your application.
   B. Use Web services to get data to and from the database.
   C. Encrypt sensitive data that is required on the client (for example, configuration data).
   D. Limit the use of local caches of data on the client.

2. Which of the following methods can you use to increase availability and recoverability of an application? (Choose all that apply.)
   A. Stored procedures
   B. Reliable transaction support
   C. File and configuration recovery
   D. Database failover

3. How many different logical tiers can each component in your design belong to?

    A. One.

    B. Two.

    C. As many as required.

    D. A component should not be tied to a specific tier of the design.

Lesson 2: Evaluating the Physical Design

Once you have completed the evaluation of the logical design, the physical design is next. This evaluation will entail reviewing the concrete details of how the architecture of the Windows-based project will be constructed, both in terms of physical layout on disk as well as separation within a network.

After this lesson, you will be able to:
- Evaluate the physical design of your Windows-based application against standard design criteria.

Estimated lesson time: 10 minutes

Evaluation of the Physical Design

The physical design of a Windows-based application includes how the project is going to look when it's deployed and ready for use. The big difference in this evaluation and the evaluation of the logical design is the level of concrete details of the design. This includes the client deployment (for example, how the application will be delivered to the client machines) as well as the network topology of what code and data will exist on what type of machine.

Much like the logical design, the evaluation of the physical design is broken up into a series of evaluation categories. These include performance, maintainability, extensibility, scalability, availability, and security evaluations.

Performance Evaluation

The performance evaluation of the physical design starts with a review of the different aspects of the physical design. These aspects include content, network, and database implementations. Each of these design aspects can impair the final performance of the Windows-based application.

As you perform an evaluation of the content of your Windows-based application, you should test the application for the performance of the system both at startup time and for the long term. Improving the startup time of an application can affect the acceptability to the users of the application. This often means profiling the system to see what startup costs are happening, including just-in-time (JIT) processing and library loading. Often the evaluation of the performance at startup can be combated with the perceived speed instead of the real speed. Adding a "splash screen" to give users something to occupy their eyes while they wait can improve the perceived performance in appreciable ways. You might find that precompiling the intermediate language (IL) to machine code (using the nGen tool) will improve your startup time, but it should be used only for applications that do not change often.

In reviewing the long-term usage of an application, you will need to ensure that the design limits the number of long-used objects in your application. Although keeping data cached on the client can help in many situations, overuse of cached data will affect the performance not only of your application (as the heap gets fragmented) but also the system in general if your application consumes more resources than it actually needs.

Next, you should review the network implementation of the project. The performance of a Windows-based application can be greatly improved or destroyed depending on how the middle tier is implemented in the physical design. You should look at how the middle tier is implemented to determine whether access to the tier is helping or hurting performance. There are no hard and fast rules about the right implementation, but separating your middle tier into a separate class of machine in the physical design is not always necessary. Typically, you would choose to separate the user interface tier and the middle tier into separate machines if the middle tier will tax the application by using a lot of memory or processor cycles. Because of the added expense of remotely accessing the data (across machine boundaries), it's often more economical (performance-wise) to keep the middle tier on the same machine as the application.

Lastly, you need to review the database implementation to ensure that it's performing adequately. As part of your performance evaluation you should check the database operations to make sure they're performing as expected (both in isolation and under load testing). If this evaluation finds fault, there are a myriad of ways to tune the database, but they are too numerous to explain in this training kit.

Scalability Evaluation

The scalability evaluation of the physical design is much like the evaluation of the logical design; you need to determine if the system can handle adapting to larger loads. You do this by reviewing the physical design to make sure that all components (custom components written for the project, as well as first-party and third-party components used in the project) are compatible with moving from an in-process usage to a middle-tier scenario. This usually entails ensuring that all components can handle being efficiently moved across process boundaries.

Availability and Recoverability Evaluation

In reviewing the availability of your Windows-based application, you will need to determine what level of availability is required for the application. For example, if you are running a mission-critical customer relationship management (CRM) system it becomes very important that you can handle failover to different machines and even data centers if you have a catastrophic failure (for example, hardware failure, interruption of Internet access, and so on). On the other hand, if you're building a small internal application, availability is not crucial to your success. At this time you should ensure that your physical design takes into account the actual availability requirements. This includes more than just making sure that the deployment strategy takes this into account; it should also include support for how to have backup databases and Web servers available with the correct version of the code and data. There are different strategies, but usually you will want to use a failover clustered database server for local availability.

The flip side of availability is recoverability. Even if you don't need to support failover to new machines, data centers, and so on, you will likely need to support recovering from a failure. This means you need a strategy for backing up any data in the system. This includes database data, event data (for example, MSMQ and Event Logs), and any other transient data that are crucial to your business.

Security Evaluation

When reviewing the security of your physical design, you should be aware of the physical design of any communication between your Windows-based application and any servers. For example, if your application will access a database server, you will need to ensure that access to that server is secure. Within your organization this might not be a problem because firewalls and the like should keep people out. But as people are becoming more and more mobile, you will need to deal with an application that can be run outside of your network. In that case you should use a virtual private network (VPN) to provide safe access to your internal servers. You should never expose your servers to the bare Internet just to allow these remote applications to work. If using a VPN isn't possible, then creating proxies to the server (for example, Web services) is acceptable, but often at a performance penalty and by incurring the cost of securing the Web servers.

Real World

Shawn Wildermuth

Securing Windows-based applications in this world of mobile professionals is becoming more and more difficult. Many organizations I have dealt with have tried to avoid creating a VPN to allow mobile professionals to work by using all sorts of other solutions (for example, Web services, terminal services, and so on). In almost every case it was easier to simply support a VPN.

If your design uses click-once deployment, you will need to ensure that the Web servers that are exposing the application are secured like any other Internet-facing server. If you think that a little server with a click-once application on it is not apt to be hacked, you are just inviting trouble.

Maintainability Evaluation

In reviewing the maintainability of the physical design, you should pay attention to the common-sense approach of the code base. This means that components should use common directory structures and have directory structures of the project mirror namespace usage as much as possible. The key to maintainability is making the code base easy to navigate.

Extensibility Evaluation

The physical makeup of any Windows-based application can really affect how extensible it is. In general, your review of the extensibility should include a review of what controls and other components are written as part of the project. Where possible, the location of these controls and components should be as centrally located as possible so that they can be used in applications if possible. Writing the same control for different applications is just tedious. Alternatively, copying components from one project to the other destroys the ability for each application that uses a particular component to get the benefits of bug fixes and improvements to the control.

MORE INFO Designing for extensibility

For more information on making your designs extensible, please see the .NET Framework documentation (*http://msdn2.microsoft.com/en-us/library/ms229028.aspx*).

Data Integrity Evaluation

Finally, you should do an evaluation of the data integrity for your physical design. Unlike the evaluation you conducted against the logical design, this evaluation should include evaluation from the user interface down to the database. Data constraints that are included in the database schema will ensure that the data stays consistent, but you should also include that same constraint higher in the code to reduce the need to go to the database just to find a data inconsistency. For example, if you have a check constraint in the database to make sure that Social Security numbers are nine digits, your user interface should have validation of that fact so that, if an invalid Social Security number is entered, it is easier to report that to the user to fix than to wait for the data to be sent to the database just to receive a failure message.

Lesson Summary

- Evaluating the physical design should ensure that the deployed project meets the full requirements of a project.
- This physical design evaluation will review the performance, scalability, availability, recoverability, security, maintainability, extensibility, and data integrity of the designed system.

Lesson Review

You can use the following questions to test your knowledge of the information in Lesson 2, "Evaluating the Physical Design." The questions are also available on the companion CD if you prefer to review them in electronic form.

NOTE Answers

Answers to these questions and explanations of why each answer choice is right or wrong are located in the "Answers" section at the end of the book.

---

1. Should your middle tier always physically exist on a machine separate from your Windows-based application?

    A. Yes

    B. No

2. Should you enforce data integrity constraints outside the database (in addition to inside the database)?

    A. Yes

    B. No

3. Should you use a VPN if you need to allow external usage of internal servers?

    A. Yes

    B. No

Chapter Review

To further practice and reinforce the skills you learned in this chapter, you can perform the following tasks:

- Review the chapter summary.
- Review the list of key terms introduced in this chapter.
- Complete the case scenarios. These scenarios set up real-world situations involving the topics of this chapter and ask you to create a solution.
- Complete the suggested practices.
- Take a practice test.

Chapter Summary

- Taking the Object Role Model that was generated as part of the design work and creating a database design is a key part of any Windows-based application design.
- Taking the time to evaluate the logical design of your Windows-based application will help refine a design as well as ensure that the code that is written from the design is exactly what is required for the project.
- Performing a review of the physical design will ensure that your design is going to meet the requirements and also perform well once deployed.

Key Terms

Do you know what these key terms mean? You can check your answers by looking up the terms in the glossary at the end of the book.

- logical design
- optimistic concurrency
- pessimistic concurrency
- physical design

Case Scenarios

In the following case scenarios you will apply what you've learned about how to do data design. You can find answers to these questions in the "Answers" section at the end of this book.

Case Scenario 1: Review the Logical Design of a CRM Application

You work for a small company that needs a CRM application. You will need to create a system that can hold common CRM data, such as customers, salespeople, and orders.

Interviews

Following is a company manager's statement:

- **Engineering Manager** "We will be creating a new CRM application. Our design team has created a logical design that describes the different elements. We need to evaluate the logical design."

Questions

Answer the following questions for the design team.

1. How will you review the design for business case completeness?
2. How are you going to handle a maintainability review of the design?

Case Scenario 2: Review the Physical Design of a CRM Application

You work for a small company that needs a CRM application. You will need to create a system that can hold common CRM data, such as customers, salespeople, and orders.

Interviews

Following is a company manager's statement:

- **Engineering Manager** "We will be creating a new CRM application. Our design team has created a physical design showing the different elements as they will exist on specific machine types. We need to review this design."

Questions

Answer the following questions for the design team.

1. How will you evaluate the security of the physical design?
2. How will you evaluate the extensibility of the physical design?

Suggested Practices

To successfully master the objectives covered in this chapter, complete the following tasks.

Evaluate a Logical Design

For this task, you should complete at least Practice 1. You can do Practice 2 for a more in-depth understanding of logical design evaluation.

- **Practice 1**   Take the logical design from Chapter 2 and evaluate it based on the criteria in Lesson 1.
- **Practice 2**   Create a set of recommendations based on the review of the logical design.

Evaluate a Physical Design

For this task, you should complete at least Practice 1. You can do Practice 2 for a more in-depth understanding of physical design evaluation.

- **Practice 1**   Take the physical design from Chapter 2 and evaluate it based on the criteria in Lesson 2.
- **Practice 2**   Create a set of recommendations based on the review of the physical design.

Take a Practice Test

The practice tests on this book's companion CD offer many options. For example, you can test yourself on just one exam objective, or you can test yourself on all the 70-548 certification exam content. You can set up the test so that it closely simulates the experience of taking a certification exam, or you can set it up in study mode so that you can look at the correct answers and explanations after you answer each question.

MORE INFO   Practice tests

For details about all the practice test options available, see the "How to Use the Practice Tests" section in this book's Introduction.

Chapter 4

Define a Common User Interface Layout

A professional application should have a consistent and stable user interface that provides an intuitive way to access features. To provide such an interface, you need to consider the audience for your application, their requirements, and the way in which the business carries out its work. In addition, users have come to expect a lot from a rich Microsoft Windows user interface. This includes things like easy-to-use navigation, context menus, highly interactive forms, graphical and audio feedback, and more. From a user's perspective, the visual interface is the application. Therefore, you will want to define your interface standards and build consistent, intuitive interfaces for your users.

This chapter covers the task of defining a user interface for your application based on user requirements and business goals. We will first look at how you identify the taxonomy of the application based on goals, workflow, and user navigation needs. Next, we will look at how you implement the user interface in a consistent and appropriate manner. Finally, in Lesson 3 we will examine how you choose specific controls to handle various user interface scenarios.

Exam objectives in this chapter:

- Choose an appropriate layout for the visual interface.
  - Decide the content flow within the application.
  - Evaluate user navigation needs.
  - Identify the goal of the UI.
  - Ensure the congruency and consistency of the user experience throughout the application.
  - Choose techniques to control the layout.
- Evaluate a strategy for implementing a common layout throughout the UI.
  - Suggest an applicable UI standard based on the application specification. Considerations include MDI, SDI, control grouping, and so on.

- Choose an appropriate control based on design specifications.
  - ❏ Evaluate the type of data that must be captured or displayed.
  - ❏ Evaluate available controls. Considerations include standard .NET Framework controls and custom, internally developed, and third-party controls.
  - ❏ Evaluate the manner in which available controls are implemented in previous and ongoing projects or applications.
  - ❏ Evaluate the user demographic.
  - ❏ Evaluate the user environment.

Lessons in this chapter:

Before You Begin

To complete the lessons in this chapter, you should be familiar with developing Windows applications with Microsoft Visual Studio 2005 using Visual Basic or C#. This chapter does not focus on the technical details of creating Windows applications. This should be a prerequisite to reading the chapter. The focus here will be primarily on the definition and organization of the user interface to meet the user needs of the application. You should be comfortable with all of the following tasks:

- Creating Windows form-based applications to solve business problems.
- Using the set of Windows controls to implement common user scenarios.
- Object-oriented development concepts.
- Reading and working with application requirements and user scenarios.

Real World

Mike Snell

Users see and judge an application primarily through its user interface. Developers have to respect this fact. No matter how wonderfully a specific application workflow, business rule engine, or algorithm is implemented, it goes completely unnoticed by users. They can see and touch only the user interface. I have seen this proven out many times.

I recall a recent project where the team had spent many long days across multiple weeks to prepare an application for a big user demonstration. The application contained a lot of complex logic that required a lot of hard work. The demo was ready to go; the development team was excited because they had just implemented some of the most complex code of their lives. During the demo, however, users continued to interrupt the demonstration to point out issues with the user interface and usability. There were layout issues, spelling mistakes, poor field labeling, and inconsistent use of buttons. The developer doing the demonstration continued to dismiss these issues as "cosmetic." The code behind the demo worked wonderfully, he would point out. At the end of the demo the user stakeholders indicated their displeasure with the progress of the application; they did not like what they saw. This issue escalated and it took a lot to smooth it over. We cleaned up the user interface and did the demo again to a much better reception. The execution code did not change; the presentation did.

This example illustrates the importance of the user interface. It also shows how the technical team and users can often get out of synchronization. A best practice is to always show a real, professional user interface to the user community. In addition, use real example data. Test data is just a bunch of garbage that's distracting to users. These steps will go a long way to show application progress from the user's perspective.

Lesson 1: Evaluate Requirements and Choose an Appropriate Layout for the Visual Interface

A primary goal of a good visual interface is to organize features is such a way as to align them with the way in which users think about the work they perform with the application. This can be difficult. It requires part business analyst and part user interface developer. You need to be able to review user scenarios and requirements and consider common UI constructs to propose a solution. This skill comes with a lot of experience. This lesson helps to define the items you should consider when defining a layout for your Windows visual interface.

After this lesson, you will be able to:

- Identify the user and business goals for the application as they relate to the visual interface.
- Define the taxonomy for your application, including the grouping of features and the organization of work tasks.
- Determine the appropriate navigation structure for your application based on the goals and requirements of the application.

Estimated lesson time: 30 minutes

Identify the Goals of the User Interface

Different applications have different goals for the visual interface. These goals, in most business scenarios, typically relate to the use of the software. For example, if your application will involve many users entering data on a day-to-day basis, you might have the goal of creating a fast, rich, and powerful Windows user interface. If, on the other hand, your application will be used only by a select few individuals a couple of times per month, then users might prefer a UI that walks them through this task (like a wizard). You need to be able to recognize user interface goals and then translate them into technical decisions about the UI layout.

The Origin of UI Goals

User interface goals come from the business requirements, the user requirements, and potentially the use cases. You should be able to read through these items and pull the UI goals out of them. You should document the UI goals in a common area that defines the user interface. Each goal should have a corresponding result or decision that makes the goal attainable and tangible. For example, the goal "the application should be easy to use" is a great goal, but only by defining the actionable items around the goal can you build a consensus that the design of the application will meet the goal.

If you dig through your use cases and requirements and can't find the visual interface goals, you should consider a brainstorming session with the users. In this session you should ask the users what is important to them with respect to the application. Users will typically offer a lot of adjectives about the UI and perhaps some examples. You can take these adjectives and present possible user interface layout options with respect to each adjective. You can discuss the trade-offs and ramifications of each choice with the user. This exercise will help users determine the type of visual interface they desire. It will also help the team build consensus on this important topic.

Common UI Goals/Adjectives

When we talk about a Windows user interface, we typically use a common set of adjectives to describe the goals that define how we want the UI to look, feel, and behave. These adjectives are the starting point. They work to define to goals for the user interface. You then need to translate these goals into decisions and actions that will define your user interface. It's important to have a common understanding of what is meant by each of these adjectives and what actions typically result from prioritizing your application toward one or more of these adjectives. The following are some of the common adjectives that are used to define UI goals for Windows applications.

NOTE   Windows and Web user interfaces

This chapter (and this book) assumes you have already decided upon a Windows user interface. This is not to discount Web UIs. If you are at the early stages of an application, you might still be deciding between a Windows and a Web interface. We will not go into this topic here. However, you can search the MSDN Library for the topic "Choosing between Windows Forms and Web Forms" for more information.

Accessible   The term "accessible" typically relates to the application's ability to reach a broad audience. If you are building your application for a select few well-known individuals, your accessibility concerns might be low. If, however, you intend to reach as many computer users as possible, you should optimize for accessibility. The goal of having a highly accessible application might translate into one or more of the following tangible decisions:

- Support for a high-contrast user interface for users who do not see color depths and need high contrast (black and white, for example)
- Support for both visual and audio cues for users who can't hear (or have no sound on their computer) or those who have limited sight and would benefit from sound cues
- Support for large fonts for users who have trouble reading small text on computer screens
- Support for multiple input devices such as keyboard-only controls and shortcuts that will work with input devices such as speech control

---

MORE INFO   **Accessible regulations and the Certified for Windows logo**

For more information on building accessible Windows applications, including how to obtain the Certified for Windows logo, search "Creating an Accessible Windows-based Application" in the MSDN Library.

Easy To Use   The term "easy to use" is the most overused goal for user interfaces. Nobody is looking for a hard-to-use application. Everyone wants their application to be easy to use. Ease of use typically translates into less time and money spent in training and an increase in user productivity.

You need to define a tangible definition of easy to use for the given application. This definition should take into account the habits of the users, their requirements, and how often they will use the application. For example, consider an application that has existed for years with a non-standard UI. You might make the decision to rewrite the application but still employ a similar, nonstandard UI so that users do not require retraining. A new user might find this UI unfamiliar and very hard to use. However, the application might be considered easy to use because it's so familiar to the established user base.

Another extreme might be an application that employs wizards for every task in order to make these tasks easy for users to perform. A user needs little training to walk through a single step at a time in a wizard. However, this UI might backfire if the application is used often by many users. The more familiar users get with it, the more cumbersome it might become. Users will complain of having many repetitive clicks to complete what will seem like a simple operation.

You need balance. You need to evaluate which features users will use often and therefore will be willing to invest their time in to learn. The more use a user has for these features, the more power and advanced features the user will desire. Those features that are used less often might be implemented using simple step-by-step user paradigms. This removes the burden from the users of having to learn and remember these types of features where their investment will not have such a significant payback.

Familiar   The goal "the application should seem familiar to users and follow defined Windows standards" is often unspoken. However, it can be the deciding factor that determines if your user interface is acceptable. You do not want to invent new paradigms for working with data. Instead you want to leverage the knowledge a user has built up by working with similar applications and similar concepts. The more familiar the application can seem to the user base, the more likely it will be accepted and considered easy to use by those who have to work with it.

A familiar application means following established standards for Windows. For example, menus should appear in the same place, menu items should have familiar names for familiar features, and toolbars should have familiar icons. These are just a few of the many established Windows standards. You should also consider where you place OK and Cancel buttons on your form, how you name these items, how you align text, how much space you put between input controls, and so on. Similarly, if your users are used to working with Microsoft Office for specific tasks, you should not force them into a simple UI without the many tools and options of an Office document. Rather, you might consider extending Office and implementing your features within Microsoft Word, Microsoft Excel, or Microsoft Outlook. Making your features behave like other Windows features can go a long way toward increasing usability and the feeling of a polished, professional application.

NOTE   Windows XP and Vista standards

Microsoft publishes the Visual Guidelines for both Windows XP and Windows Vista. UI developers and designers should be familiar with these guidelines as they dictate standards like fonts, colors, icons, and so on. You can download these guidelines from *http://www.microsoft.com/whdc/ Resources/windowsxp/*.

Inductive (vs. Deductive)   An inductive user interface (IUI) is a user interface that leads a user through application tasks, sometimes step by step. These interfaces also provide simple interfaces with a lot of instructional text on the interface itself. Users do not typically require a lot of training to work with IUIs; they do not have to deduce what a screen is asking of them or how to work with it. Rather, the IUI tries to simplify each task, present instructions, and guide a user through each step. In addition, if a user makes a mistake, the user can easily correct it when working with an IUI.

Users typically do not come right out and ask for an IUI. Rather, they might ask for IUI concepts or refer to similar applications. They might say they want their Windows application to behave like a Web application with the back and forward buttons, or they might compare their needs to applications like Microsoft Money or the Task Pane features inside Office. When you hear comments like these, think IUI.

An IUI is often best for applications that users do not use that often or do not intend to invest a lot of time in learning the interface or reading the application's help files. In these cases an IUI is perfect. A user might work with these features only once a week or even less often.

An IUI does have its drawbacks. Users who process transactions many times a day through the UI can find an IUI cumbersome and sometimes in the way of their getting work done. They might prefer to see a seemingly complex transaction-specific screen that gives them all the options at once.

Sometimes IUIs and more advanced screens work together in the same application. You may implement obscure features as IUIs. Alternatively, you may have a simple or learning mode and then an advanced mode. Think of the tool WinZip. It has a *Wizard* mode that acts as an IUI and a *Classic* mode that is more like a standard Windows UI. The *Wizard* mode is nice for users just starting with this tool. The *Classic* mode works great for power users.

MORE INFO   Inductive user interfaces

There are a number of good white papers on the topic of IUIs. For more information, search the MSDN Library for the topic "Inductive User Interface."

Responsive   Once of the principal reasons for choosing a Windows UI is the performance of the user interface. This goal might also be assumed. However, users expect a Windows application to take advantage of the client machine; this means responsiveness and near-instant feedback when a user enters data, navigates between controls, clicks buttons, and generally interacts with the user interface. It's not acceptable, for instance, to create a Windows user interface that basically ignores the client and returns to the server as much or more than a Web application.

When your goal is to optimize for performance and create a responsive, interactive interface, you need to consider many implementation options. You might decide to cache data locally on the server to support faster access and paging through data. You might need to implement multithreading so that you can respond to user input events on the client, like mouse clicks and key presses, while data is being processed. You should consider using these events to restrict bad data access and provide client-side validation of input rules. You can process these rules and provide feedback in the form of graphics, text, and audio. These and similar items make the user feel as if the application is highly responsive; you want to limit users' wait times and increase feedback between them and the application.

Rich and Powerful   Users often indicate that they would like their application to have a rich Windows UI. What exactly *rich* means can be debatable. However, it often means responsive and powerful. Windows features are not the same as Web features. Users expect their Windows applications to have a rich feature set, for example. This can mean things like printing, status indication, progress bars, user customization of UI elements, toolbars, and so on. It can also mean a different implementation of features. For example, a Windows UI might implement autocomplete for search terms and data entry. When you hear users asking for a rich UI, you should think of a feature-packed, highly interactive interface.

Efficient   Data entry applications must consider efficiency for the users. This can come in many ways. You might be sure to define keyboard shortcuts for key commands, buttons, tab switching, and other actions. Users find that reaching for the mouse can often slow their progress. You also need to consider the layout of the controls on the form with respect to the user's workflow. You can save keystrokes and time by getting the UI aligned with the way users work. Finally, an efficient interface should always consider the cursor. When a user moves to a new form or tab, the cursor should automatically position.

All the terms that we've looked at with respect to user interface goals can be relative to the given situation and application. One person's definition of high performance, for example, might be another person's usability concern. It simply depends on the situation. For this reason, you need to spend time with the requirements, use cases, and the users themselves to make sure you understand how they wish to interact with their application. You should also consider creating mock-ups or showing examples to help build consensus on specific decisions.

Determine the Taxonomy of Your Application

An application's taxonomy is the definition of how you organize and group functionality to make the application easy to use and accessible. For example, you might define an *Orders* toolbar item to group all the features associated with order management. You might group all your user and data management under a section called *Administration*. You want to group the features of the application so they are logically and intuitively accessible to the users. These are simple examples. The key is you do not want users to jump around to perform common tasks. You want to consider their work, how they perform that work, and how often they have to do certain tasks. This will help you organize and group features in a way that's appropriate for the users' needs.

As an alternative example, suppose you create a customer service request application. This application might have an *Administration* module that allows for customer profile management. The primary interface might be designed to log customer service requests. Suppose you look at the use cases and user statistics and determine that nearly 85 percent of the calls require a customer service representative to edit the customer profile or change the customer's password. Logically, you might have already defined one area of the application for customer profile management and another area for logging all calls. However, forcing a customer service representative to log the call through one set of screens and then access a separate module to search for the customer and change the customer's profile can be cumbersome to the reps and cost the company time and money. If instead you put these features right on the call log screen, you might increase usability, cut down on call times, reduce costs, and increase customer satisfaction. The point is that the choices you make on taxonomy have real, important consequences.

Defining Your Taxonomy

Your taxonomy is often already at least partially defined for you by the business analysts. Look for natural groupings of requirements, use cases, and module definitions. These things typically indicate how the users think of the features in the application. You should usually embrace this natural ordering.

Features are usually grouped by a high-level concept. In productivity applications these concepts can be things like file management, document editing, managing the view of the user interface, the tools in the application, the help system, and other similar areas. Business applications might have similar groupings; however, they often also include the areas that define the application. A time-tracking application, for instance, should have a group for creating new timesheets, viewing old timesheets, accessing reports, administering data, and so on. These concepts most likely already group requirements, have related use cases, and define application modules.

Grouping functionality appropriately is the first step. Next you need to consider how users get work done. This is often defined by business cases and use cases. It is the workflow in the application. Features need to appear or be accessible in the application at the appropriate time or step in the process. If you read through a common use case, you should be able to easily recognize the way the application realized this use case. The application should not require the user to hunt for one feature and then another. Rather, the application should be aware of how users do work.

Evaluate User Navigation Needs

Users need to be able to find features in order to use them. This does not mean providing a single menu with a list of all possible actions. Most applications written these days are far too complex for this to work anyway. Instead, you need to consider how to lay out the application's navigation so as to meet the requirements of the application and stay true to how users view their work tasks.

Consider the User's Perspective

This last point is very important: you need to allow users to navigate the features of your application in a way similar to how they view their work. Users are getting their job done with the assistance of your software. They are not accessing features. You should therefore respect how they see their work and try to model it through your application's navigation.

As an example, consider an application that is built to allow users to manage their customer accounts and sales records. Suppose the features were grouped by common functionality, such as orders, contact management, invoicing, reports, and so on. Users log on to the application, navigate to one of these modules, select a task or feature within the module and find a customer, and finally begin to process work.

What this navigational layout does not consider is how users think about their work. Most users of applications like this do not set out to log onto the application and do "account maintenance" or a related feature. Instead, they use the application to perform a specific task on behalf of a specific customer. A better presentation might be to allow users to see all their associated customers and be able to navigate directly to one of those customers. From there they can decide what task they wish to perform on behalf of this customer. This is the way users typically think. They have a task in mind and want to be able to go directly to that task and not sort through the UI features. The job of the UI layout designer is to build this type of thought into the software through the definition of taxonomy and user navigation.

Navigation Tools and Controls

When defining the navigation of your Windows application, you need to be sure to use the many tools available to you. This includes obvious navigation controls such as the menu bar, the toolbar, context menus, and tabs. Application navigation, however, is more than just menus, toolbars, and tabbed dialog boxes. Navigation can be defined as any way in which you allow a user to move from one task to another. Navigation, then, can include things like buttons, action panes, keyboard controls, and even the mouse. Complex navigation such as hierarchical access to data might require other controls, such as a tree view (consider Outlook's access to e-mail folders). The following list explains some of the common navigational elements in a Windows application along with some things to consider when employing these items to satisfy specific requirements:

- **Menu**   Most Windows applications implement a menu across the top of the application. This menu provides access to the basic utilities and features of the application.

  For multiple-document interface (MDI) applications, you should use the standard File, Edit, View, Window, and Help menu items. You do not have to look far in Windows for examples. You should then consider creating menus that allow access to other key features.

  For a single-document interface (SDI) application you might create a set of menu items that allow access to various modules or categories in your application. For example, you might arrange an order management system with menus for Orders, Invoicing, Customers, Help, and so on.

- **Toolbar**   A Windows toolbar typically provides access to features of the application. A toolbar is often context-sensitive. It might categorize a group of features with which a user is working, or it might apply to a single document type. Users expect toolbars to provide quick navigation to features.

  Toolbars are sometimes also used to give users a means to navigate quickly to modules within the application. You should be careful with this; it can be seen as a nonstandard mechanism. It's often better to use the toolbars just for feature access and provide navigation to modules through a pane (a dockable window on the side of an application).

- **Context menus**   Users want the application to think like they do. If they are viewing data or a feature, they expect to have the obvious links and navigational items available from their mouse button. This means creating right-click (or context) menus that provide context-sensitive navigation that is meaningful to the user.

- **Tabs**   Tabs and the tab container control are great ways to categorize a set of elements that roll up to a given feature or module. This can cut down on the number of elements on a screen and still provide users with the feeling that they have instant access to these features.

  You do not want to overuse tabs. You want to try and avoid creating an application whose primary navigation is a large set of tabs and perhaps tab containers that contain other tab containers. You should use them when you wish to group a number of settings or property values for a particular object. A good example might be an Order form that contains tabs for shipping information, history, order items, tracking, and so on.

- **Buttons**   The buttons you put on your user interface can provide navigation and navigation cues. For example, a wizard allows a user to use the Next and Back (or Previous) buttons to navigate between steps. You should also enable and disable buttons based on what is possible and where they are in a given process.

- **Action panes**   Action panes give a user quick access to features or information with respect to the user's current context. An action pane might, for example, list all the application modules and submodules. Users can then use this hierarchical pane (think of Outlook) to quickly get to the information they are seeking. You might also consider action panes as similar to context menus. Navigation might appear in a portion of the pane based on what the user is doing or requesting (think Office Task Pane).

Lab: Choose an Appropriate Layout for the UI

This lab will help you understand the task of evaluating requirements and determining a layout for a user interface. The lab works through the goals of the interface, the taxonomy, and the navigational layout. In each exercise you will review content related to the given task. You will then use this information to execute the lab steps associated with each exercise. Each exercise builds on the previous exercise.

You are a senior developer for a commercial software products company. Your company intends to release a new version of its help desk management tool. You have been assigned to aid in the definition of the user interface layout.

▶ **Exercise 1: Review User Interviews and Determine UI Goals**

For this exercise, review the following user interviews. Then follow the steps listed below to determine the goals for the user interface and the actionable items for each goal. The following are the user interviews with which you will be working.

Interviews

You attend a meeting to brainstorm on the high-level requirements for the system and discuss the user interface. This meeting includes the business analyst, the product manager, and the sales manager. The following are statements made during the meeting:

- **Business analyst**   "The back-office users of the application are fairly technical people; they work the help desk and often fix computer-related issues. In addition, they work with the tool every day. They want fast and powerful.

  "Help desk personnel enter issues all day. However, more and more issues are coming right from the end users. These people only enter three to five issues per year. We need to make it really intuitive how to do it; this will cut down on help desk calls and can be a big selling point."

- **Product manager** "The application has many features that our current clients really like. They have become familiar with the way we do things; we can't change too much without a very good reason.

  "One complaint we do get is that the application requires too much jumping around to do things. When a user is working with a specific help desk issue, the application should know what can be done with that issue and provide the access right then and there. This would go a long way in making things easier."

- **Sales manager** "The application needs to work for the broadest possible audience. A number of customers have special requirements for things like large fonts and high-contrast; we need to have these features to compete.

  "One complaint we get from new customers is that it takes them a while to get new users up to speed. They have to go to the help file all the time at first. It would help if there was a way to turn on and off a 'help mode' for certain tasks."

Lab Steps

1. Document the goals for the application's user interface. Look for adjectives that describe how the user interface should operate. Create a list of these goals.

   As an example, the following might define the user interface goals for this application:

   a. G1–The user interface should give the back-office user a fast and powerful experience.

   b. G2–The user interface for logging issues by non–help desk users should be intuitive and inductive.

   c. G3–The user interface should be familiar to our existing clients; we can't discount the effort they have made with respect to training on our application.

   d. G4–The user interface should provide easy access to related features from anywhere within the application.

   e. G5–The user interface should have accessibility options. This is commercial software that runs on Windows; we should strive for the Windows logo.

   f. G6–The user interface should provide additional assistance for new users executing new tasks (at least until they become familiar with the interface).

2. Determine actionable items for each user interface goal. Ask, "How will we realize this goal through actual implementation of the user interface?" Document your results.

   As an example, the following might be actionable items based on the goals defined previously:

a. G1–Create a Windows user interface that caches data on the client to increase speed. Provide these technical trained users with many options on a single screen to increase their power.

b. G2–Create a wizard-like interface for logging issues. This interface should contain on-screen, step-by-step instruction.

c. G3–Use a lot of the current user interface. Do not change or move access to existing features. Keep a similar look and feel. For any drastic changes, consider providing a classic view along with the new interface.

d. G4–Create a context-sensitive menu system. When a user right-clicks a given entity in the system, the user should be able to access the actions (or features) for that entity based on the user's profile and the state of the entity.

e. G5–Implement the Windows XP (or Windows Vista) standards for user interfaces. This includes supporting large fonts, a high-contrast user interface, visual and audio cues, and full feature accessibility for both the keyboard and mouse.

f. G6–Create a task pane that walks a user through a new task. Users should be able to dismiss this task pane once they are familiar with a given task (and bring it back if they need it).

▶ **Exercise 2: Determine the Application's Taxonomy**

For this exercise, review the following lists that the business analyst has put together. Then follow the steps listed below to determine taxonomy for the application. The following are the user interviews with which you will be working.

Project Artifacts

The business analyst has already completed the requirements and use cases. These items (especially the use cases) represent how the users view their work and the application. In addition, the business workflow surrounding a help desk issue has also been documented. The highlights of these artifacts are as follows.

- **Key Use Cases**
  - ❑ Log an issue as a help desk user.
  - ❑ Log an issue as a user.
  - ❑ Triage and assign issues.
  - ❑ Find an issue.
  - ❑ View archived and closed issues.
  - ❑ Review stale issues.
  - ❑ Respond to an issue.
  - ❑ Verify and close an issue.
  - ❑ Manage my issue alert rules.

❑ Run an issue report.

❑ Get application help.

❑ Manage users, roles, and security.

❑ Administer common application data.

■ **Issue Management Business Workflow**

1. An issue is initially logged on to the system by either an end user or a help desk team member. Issue status should be set to NEW.

2. The issue is then triaged by the help desk manager. The triage typically assigns the issue to be worked on by a member of the support team. It also sets the issue's priority and expected completion date. Issue status should be set to TRIAGED.

3. The support team member is expected to read and confirm the issue within the appropriate time frame (based on priority). Once the issue is confirmed, its status is set to CHECKED OUT. If the issue is not checked out in the given time frame, it follows the notification rules until another support team member checks out the issue.

4. The support team member works on the issue. Once it's complete, the issue is marked RESOLVED.

5. Finally, the user who logged the issue is asked to verify the resolution. Once complete, the issue is marked as CLOSED. If a resolved issue is not marked CLOSED in the set duration, it automatically gets closed. If the issue is not verified, it is marked REJECTED and requires another triage by the help desk manager.

Lab Steps

1. Based on the use cases, define key groups (or categories) of features for the application.

   As an example, the following might define the application groups:

   ❑ User and Security Management

   ❑ Application Administration

   ❑ Issue Management

   ❑ Issue History and Reporting

   ❑ Help System

2. Consider the workflow of managing an issue through its completion. Define your application's taxonomy using this important workflow as the center of the application.

   As an example, you might consider making the following decisions:

   ❑ Active issue management is at the heart of the application. Therefore, users should be taken to this feature automatically when the application launches.

   ❑ Different users should see different issues, sorted by different fields. For example, when the help desk manager logs on to the application, the help manager should see all issues awaiting triage sorted by priority and date and time logged. When support team members log on they should see only the issues assigned to them sorted by priority and required completion date. They should also see a secondary list of issues they can "pick up" (or check out) if they have extra time.

❑ All other features support issues and issue management. These features should be made to seem secondary and related to the active issues.

Lesson Summary

■ The goals for the user interface of an application come from the requirements and use cases. You should look for comments that include adjectives like accessible, easy-to-use, familiar, intuitive, inductive, responsive, and rich. Each of these equates to something tangible in a successful Windows user interface. You need to get to the actionable items behind the adjectives so as to prioritize certain UI and layout decisions.

■ You want to organize the features of your application in a logical, accessible fashion. Users should not have to hunt for features or areas of an application. You need to consider how they view their work and then define the taxonomy of the application around these facts. Also, look for areas of the application where users think they should be able to access another feature. In these cases you can often increase productivity and user satisfaction.

■ Navigation is everywhere in a Windows user interface. Users have been trained to use menus for accessing common grouped features, toolbars for getting even quicker access to features, the context menu for finding features that relate to the current selection, and keyboard shortcuts for accessing areas of an application from an input device. Users are also becoming accustomed to task and action panes for navigation, buttons that move them backward and forward between items, and tab groupings within a form. You need to evaluate users' needs and use the navigational tools appropriately in order to meet these needs.

Lesson Review

You can use the following questions to test your knowledge of the information in Lesson 1, "Evaluate Requirements and Choose an Appropriate Layout for the Visual Interface." The questions are also available on the companion CD if you prefer to review them in electronic form.

NOTE   Answers

Answers to these questions and explanations of why each answer choice is right or wrong are located in the "Answers" section at the end of the book.

---

1. You have been asked to create an application feature that requires a user to set multiple complex groups of properties before executing a task. This feature will get little use. Which of the following approaches should you take?

    A. Create a form with multiple tabs. In each tab represent a group of properties. Name each tab based on the given group. Allow users to click a single Finish button on the form once they believe they are complete.

    B. Create a wizard that walks a user through each group of properties. Logically order the various property groups. Allow a user to go back and forth between the groups. Once all properties are completely set, enable the Finish button.

    C. Create a single powerful form that shows each property group as a group box. Allow the user to set the properties. Enable the Finish button once all properties are completely set.

    D. Automatically set each property to a commonly used default value. Display this list to the user. Allow users to right-click any property they wish to change. Allow users to hit a single Finish button on the form once they believe they are complete.

2. You have been asked to make the user interface highly accessible. To meet with other customer requirements, you have specified non-standard colors and fonts in your application. Which of the following will help you realize this goal? (Choose all that apply.)

    A. Use task panes to provide the user additional help on key tasks.

    B. Use both visual and audio cues to alert the user to items in the application.

    C. Allow the user to select an alternate, high-contrast color scheme for the application.

    D. Allow the user to change the application font size.

3. You are defining the taxonomy for your application. Because users have struggled with the current version, you want to create an intuitive layout. Which of the following should provide you the most input?

    A. The application requirements

    B. The current application

    C. The use cases

    D. The object role models (ORMs)

4.   You have an application that allows a user to go in and edit the properties and settings for a customer. Each user manages approximately 10 to 20 customers. Customers are organized by their primary location and then the offices under each location. Users have requested easy navigation to these customers. How should you implement this?

    A.   Create a Manage Customers menu item. Show a list of primary locations for customers on this menu. When a user selects a primary location, launch a dialog box to ask them to select a suboffice. When users select a suboffice they will be taken to the details of that office.

    B.   Create a Manage Customers menu item. Show a list of primary locations for customers on this menu. Under each primary location create a fan-out menu to list all the suboffice locations under the selected primary. When users select a suboffice, they will be taken to the details of that office.

    C.   Create a task pane (or panel) that contains a *TreeView* control. List each primary customer as a branch and each suboffice as a leaf under the branch. When users select a suboffice, they will be taken to the details of that office.

    D.   Create a set of toolbar buttons, one for each primary location. When a user selects a toolbar button, list each location's suboffice as a menu under the toolbar button. When users select a suboffice, they will be taken to the details of that office.

Lesson 2: Define a Strategy to Implement a Common UI Layout

Users want a consistent user interface. They do not want controls appearing in strange places or text not aligned properly. Instead, they want each feature and each form to look and feel the same—as if each piece is part of a single application. To make this work, you need to define an application container, agree on UI standards for control layout, and define a standard means of grouping functionality. This lesson helps you define the physical layout options for your application and the standards that determine these choices.

After this lesson, you will be able to:
- Define an appropriate application container based on the needs of users.
- Define layout standards used to implement a common consistent user interface.
- Pick the appropriate method to lay out groups of features and controls.

Estimated lesson time: 60 minutes

Define an Application Container

The term *application container* represents the host for the forms and navigation of the application. Consider it the outer shell that provides support for the development of working forms with which users interact. It's the application container that is responsible for loading and unloading working (or child) forms appropriately, providing a set of base services such as window management, menus, navigation, and the like.

You should define your application container first, before actual application screens are created. The container sets the tone for the user interface. It dictates how users perceive and work with your application. Most application containers have a few common elements, such as menus, toolbars, a base set of services, and a place to host (or contain) application screens. When you select an application container, you need to consider these elements. You also need to be able to choose between an SDI and an MDI. Let's discuss the merits of each.

Single-Document Interface (SDI)

The term *single-document interface* (SDI) represents an interface construct (typically a single form) that is used to contain application screens that are unique unto themselves. That is, each screen in an SDI application contains a set of controls and features bound to that screen. For instance, the SDI container does not manage multiple instances of a given document (as with an MDI application). Rather, the container provides a host for loading and unloading different forms (and user controls) based on user requests. An SDI application is the most standard Windows application written by professional developers.

SDI applications are useful for working with data, setting properties, viewing information, and doing related user tasks surrounding a business application. They are typically not thought of as productivity applications like a drawing tool or a spreadsheet might be. Instead, an SDI interface typically focuses a user on a core set of modules or data elements.

Let's consider an example of an SDI application. Imagine a customer order management system that allows users to set customer details, enter orders, and view information. You might create an SDI interface to allow users to work with the customer and order data in the system. This interface should have a file menu, a toolbar, and a status indicator. You might also provide a customer navigation pane to allow users to select customers. Finally, you might create another pane to show customer details when a user selects a given customer. Figure 4-1 shows a screen shot of just such an example.

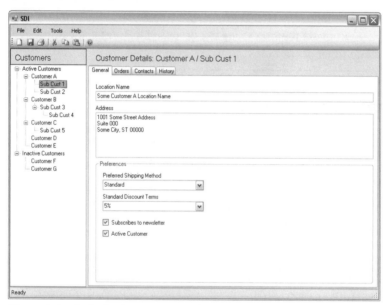

Figure 4-1   A single-document interface (SDI) application container.

Notice that with this layout, users are working with only a single customer record (or document) at any given time. There is no need to manage multiple instances of a customer. Therefore, an SDI interface works nicely.

Multiple-Document Interface (MDI)

The term *multiple-document interface* (MDI) refers to an application container that is designed to host multiple instances of a single document type. That is, each new document in an MDI application is the same type of document. Think of a word processor or graphics program. In both cases the application works with one or more similar documents.

MDI applications are great when you are asking users to work with actual documents (and not simply data that simulates a document). The MDI application should be centered on the document type. As a container, the MDI provides a number of base services for working with the document. These include operations like opening, saving, and creating new versions of the document type. The container also manages the open windows (or documents) with which a user is working. The features of an MDI application typically involve creating tools to help work with the contents of the document. You might create an image editor or the ability to manipulate selected text, for instance.

Exam Tip

It's important to know how MDI containers are created and how they work. For instance, you can set the *MdiWindowListItem* property of a *MenuStrip* control to a particular menu item that you want the container to use for showing and providing access to multiple windows. You should also know that an MDI child form with a menu component will merge its menu items with the parent MDI container's menu items. If this doesn't sound familiar or you haven't created MDI applications previously, it makes sense to go through the lab at the end of this lesson.

As an example of an MDI container, consider a tool that allows users to create, save, and open simple text documents. This application should have a parent MDI form that contains a menu, toolbar, and status bar. You then should create another form to act as the document. On this form you might add a rich text box. When a user adds a new document, you create a new instance of the form and manage that instance. Figure 4-2 shows an example.

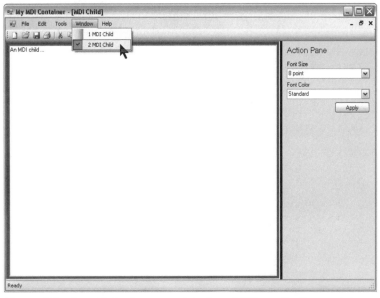

Figure 4-2   A multiple-document interface (MDI) application container.

NOTE SDIs that work like MDIs

Recent versions of traditional MDI applications have begun to behave like SDIs. Think of how Office applications like Word and Excel now behave. Each instance of your document is treated like an SDI in the way it shows up in the taskbar. However, you can still access other instances of the document type from any given instance. These interfaces are more advanced and go beyond the scope of this book. If, however, you are considering an interface that blends SDI and MDI, you can find a series of technical articles on MSDN on this subject. Search for "Adding SDI, Single Instance, and a Forms Collection to Windows Forms" for more information.

Layout Standards for the UI

A professional application should have a professional look and feel. One step to ensuring this is to define a standard for the layout of controls and enforce this standard to create consistent and cohesive forms. The controls you place on a screen should have proper and precise placement relative to one another, they should line up appropriately, and they should be used consistently. For example, labels should align with other similar labels, text boxes and their descriptions should align, buttons should have proper spacing between one another, and so on. Visual Studio 2005 provides a number of tools to help make this work. This section takes a look at how you can use them to create clean, cohesive, professional user interfaces.

Margin

The *Margin* property of a control defines the amount of space that surrounds the outside of the control. This is not unlike the margin of a document. It's the space that surrounds the contents of the control. Figure 4-3 shows a *GroupBox* control with a margin value of 10. Notice that as it is sized toward the form (or container) the margin is indicated by the designer with the line between the *GroupBox* control and the outer edge of the form.

Controls are spaced out on the form based on their margin value. For example, consider the two buttons placed on the form in Figure 4-3. They each have a margin value of 3. When aligned to each other, the space between them is the sum of their margins (or 6).

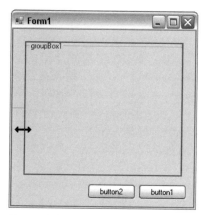

Figure 4-3   An example of a control's margin.

Padding

The *Padding* property of a control defines the spacing between items inside the control. For example, Figure 4-4 shows a *GroupBox* control with a *Padding* property value of 12. When the *RadioButton* control is added to the *GroupBox*, the padding is enforced on the interior of the *GroupBox*. You can think of padding as an interior margin.

Padding applies to more than just the interior of containers. For example, the text within a control is also spaced relative to the *Padding* property. A button's text, for instance, is surrounded by padding. If you increase the padding, the button will become larger to accommodate this padding.

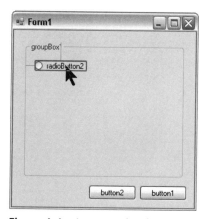

Figure 4-4   An example of a control's padding.

NOTE   Form padding

By default, a form's *Padding* property is set to zero for all sides of the form. However, Visual Studio interprets this zero as the default setting and actually applies a padding of 9 for all sides of a form. You can override this behavior by assigning a nonzero value to the form's *Padding* property.

Visual Studio 2005 defines a default margin and padding setting for all controls placed on a form. These values are set based on Windows user interface design guidelines. For most applications this should be sufficient. You should not have to modify many of the margin or padding settings. However, some applications might call for more space between controls to create a specific look. If you intend to override the default settings to achieve such a look, you need to make sure you do it consistently on every form and for all controls that apply. This can be a fair amount of work.

Snaplines

Snaplines are tools inside the Windows Forms designer that allow you to visually align controls to one another quickly. Snaplines respect the margin and padding settings defined on the form. They give you a visual indication when you have reached the bounds of these items. In addition, snaplines show alignment. They indicate when controls are aligned to one another and when the text inside the controls is aligned.

Figure 4-5 shows an example of snaplines. You can see that a line is under the text of each button indicating that the two buttons are properly aligned. Using snaplines, you can quickly create standard UIs with proper spacing and alignment.

Figure 4-5   An example of snaplines in the designer.

Automatic Sizing

You can use the *AutoSize* property of a control to indicate that a control should size to its contents. This can be very useful if you don't know the data in the control at design time. For example, you might be getting labels from a resource file in a multilingual application, or you might drive control data from the database. In either case you can set the *AutoSize* property of a control to *True* to allow the control to automatically grow based on its contents.

Not all controls support the *AutoSize* property. It's best used for controls like *Button*, *Label*, *CheckBox*, *RadioButton*, and *Panel*. For example, the text assigned to a *Button* control instance at run time might require the control to expand to fit the length of text. If *AutoSize* is set to *True*, this will happen. However, it's possible that the control can expand in such a way as to overlay another control. The best way to prevent this is to lay out these controls using a *FlowLayout-Panel* or a *TableLayoutPanel* control (more on these in a moment).

Many controls also allow you to set an *AutoSizeMode* property. This property has two values: *GrowOnly* and *GrowAndShrink*. The *GrowOnly* property indicates that the control can grow as much as required to fill its contents. However, as a user shrinks a form, the control will not be reduced to a size smaller than the control's *Size* property allows. The *GrowAndShrink* setting allows a control to both grow and shrink. You use this in conjunction with the *MinimumSize* and *MaximumSize* properties to indicate how much you want to allow the control to grow or to shrink.

Docking

Docking allows you to position containers and other controls on a form (or within another container) in such a way that they align to the edge of the item to which they are docked. You can dock to the left, right, top, or bottom of a container. You can also fill a container with the contents of the docked item. Figure 4-6 shows docking a *RichTextBox* control to a form. Notice the value is set to *Fill*. In this case the control docks to fill the form's space, minus the padding. The form's padding value is set to 5 so as to create a border effect around the control.

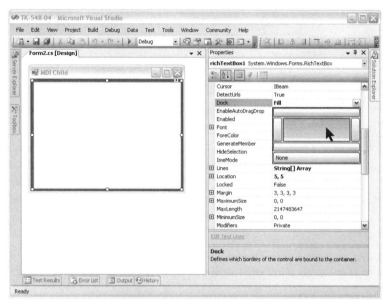

Figure 4-6   An example of docking through the integrated development environment (IDE).

Anchoring

When you lay out resizable forms, you need to consider sizing, docking, and anchoring. Anchoring allows a control to maintain its layout position. It's anchored to its spot. It might stay the same size or might resize depending on your settings. However, you typically want controls to stay in relatively the same place with respect to one another during a resize.

You can anchor a control's top, bottom, right, or left (and any combination thereof). Figure 4-7 shows an example of setting these values. When you set the control's anchor and the control's container is resized, the control maintains its position and distance with respect to its anchor. For example, if you want the buttons on your form to stay in the bottom left of the form and maintain their size when the form is scaled (or resized), then you set the button's anchor property value to right, bottom.

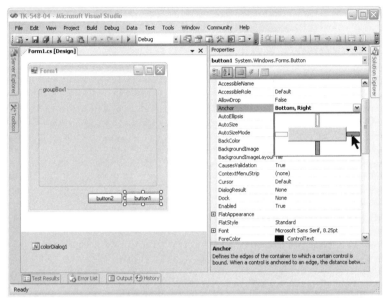

Figure 4-7   An example of anchoring through the IDE.

NOTE Putting it all together

You typically use a combination of multiple containers (like a *Panel* control), the *Splitter* control, docking, anchoring, and sizing to create advanced layouts for your UI.

Tab Order

Another important layout consideration is tab order. *Tab order* represents the order in which controls are activated as a user hits the tab key on the form. This is a common data entry technique. Users expect professional UIs to have a consistent, intuitive tab order.

Visual Studio 2005 provides a tool to help you set tab order on a form. With the form open, select the *Tab Order* option from the View menu. This will overlay your form with the values for the tab index order that are defined for your form. Figure 4-8 shows an example. You can use the cursor to click each control in a sequence to define the intended tab order for your form. When you are finished, reselect the *Tab Order* option from the View menu to turn this tool off.

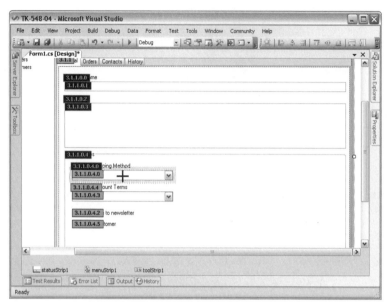

Figure 4-8   Setting a form's tab order.

Table and Flow Layout

Visual Studio 2005 provides the *FlowLayoutPanel* and *TableLayoutPanel* controls for situations that require additional layout features as content affects the size of controls or forms get resized. The *FlowLayoutPanel* allows you to define a horizontal or vertical flow direction for the layout of controls. You can use this control to allow groups of controls to be wrapped onto new lines or be separated into columns.

The *TableLayoutPanel* control provides the ability to arrange controls on a Windows form in a manner similar to that you would use on a Web page. For example, Web developers are accustomed to using the *<table>* element inside of Hypertext Markup Language (HTML) to define forms that grow and size based on content. The *TableLayoutPanel* offers similar features of rows, columns, cells, cell padding, cell merging, resizing, and so on.

The *TableLayoutPanel* is useful for creating forms that automatically adjust for localization. For example, if you are reading the value for the *Text* property for a set of *Label* controls at run time from a resource file, you need the form and the related input boxes to adjust themselves to this content. You can use the features of the *TableLayoutPanel* control, the *AutoSize* property, and additional panels to lay out forms for this purpose.

Lab: Define UI Layouts for SDI and MDI Applications

In this lab you will use the Windows Forms designer to create both an SDI and an MDI user interface. You will not be creating an entire working application. Rather, the intent is to lay out the user interface and become familiar with creating standard Windows user interfaces. You will also cover the details behind the Windows Forms designer.

▶ **Exercise 1: Create an SDI UI Layout**

In this exercise you will create a new Visual Studio Windows application. You can create this application in either C# or Visual Basic. You will then use the form designer to lay out an SDI application similar to the one previously shown in Figure 4-1.

1. Open Visual Studio 2005 and create a new Windows application (File | New | Project). Select the Windows Application template in your preferred language, give the project a name, and click OK. The Windows project template will add a new form called Form1 to your project. We will use this as the basis for your SDI container.

2. Using the Toolbox, add a *MenuStrip* control to the top of Form1. This control should automatically dock to the top of the form.

3. Click the task smart tag connected to the *MenuStrip* control (small arrow in the top-right corner) and then click Insert Standard Items. This will add the standard menu items to the *MenuStrip* control, set their icons, and define the quick-access keys for these items. Right-click the Open menu item under File and choose Delete.

4. Use the Toolbox to add a *ToolStrip* control to the top of the form (under the *MenuStrip*). This control should also dock to the top of the form (under the *MenuStrip*).

5. Click the smart tag associated with the *ToolStrip* and then click Insert Standard Items. This will add the standard tool bar icons to the control. Right-click the Open icon and then click Delete to remove this item.

6. Add a *StatusStrip* control to the bottom of the form. This control should automatically dock to the bottom of the form. Click the icon in the lower left of the control. Click *StatusLabel* to add a new label to indicate status. Set the *Text* property of this item to **Ready**.

7. Add a *SplitContainer* control to the middle of the form. This control should automatically dock to fill the remaining space on the form. You will use this control to define a container on the left for navigation and a container on the right for content. These containers are automatically split by a splitter bar. This allows users to resize these panels.

8. Add a *Panel* control to *Panel1* (left side of the *SplitContainer*). Name this panel panelTitle. This will be used to dock a title at the top of the left panel and create a border around it. Set the *Dock* property to *Top* and resize the height of panelTitle appropriately to contain a label. Set the *BorderStyle* property of this panelTitle to *FixedSingle*. Finally, set the *Padding* value of panelTitle to **9** for all sides.

9. Add a *Label* control to panelTitle and set its *Text* property to **Customers**. Align this control inside the panel based on the padding snaplines.

10. Add a *TreeView* control to the middle of Panel1 (under panelTitle). This will be used to house the hierarchical list of customers. Users will use this list to navigate between customers. Set the *Dock* property of the *TreeView* control to *Fill*. This should fill the rest of the space in Panel1. You might also wish to add a few nodes to the tree as visual cues.

11. Add a *Panel* control to Panel2 (right side of the *SplitContainer*). Name this panel panel2Title. This will be used to dock a title at the top of the right panel (similar to the one you created on the left). Set the *Dock* property to *Top*. Resize the height of panel2Title to align with the bottom of *panelTitle* (using snaplines). Set the *BorderStyle* property of panel2Title to *FixedSingle*. Set the *Padding* value of panel2Title to **9** for all sides.

12. Add a *Label* control to panel2Title and set its *Text* property to **Customer Details**. Align this control inside the panel based on the padding and alignment snaplines.

13. Add a *TabControl* to the middle of Panel2 (under panel2Title). Set the *Dock* property of the *TabControl* to *Fill*. This control will house the details related to the selected customer (from the left navigation).

14. Use the *TabPages* property (and resulting dialog box) of the *TabControl* to create the following tabs: General, Orders, Contacts, History. We will not fill in all the tabs. Instead we will add a few controls to the General tab. Click the General tab and set its *Padding* property to **9** for all sides.

15. Add a *Label* control to the General tab. Align this label to the top left of the screen using the padding snaplines. Set the control's *Text* property to **Location Name**. Next, add a *TextBox* control under the *Label* control. Align this control to the edge of the form. Extend the control to the right edge of the padding for the tab. Set the *Anchor* property of this *TextBox* to Top, Left, Right, and Bottom. Finally, set the *MaximumSize* property to a width of 400 and a height of 20 and the *MinimumSize* property to a width of 100 and a height of 20. This will prevent the control from growing too large or too small.

16. Repeat the steps outlined previously for an address label and related text box. Make sure to set the proper alignment and anchoring. Set the *Multiline* property of the address text box to *True*. Set its maximum height to 100 and its minimum height to 20. Expand its height to the maximum value using the designer.

17. Run the application. You should notice that the all controls work together during a resize and that the form looks proportioned.

▶ **Exercise 2: Create an MDI UI Layout**

In this exercise you will create a new Visual Studio Windows application. You can define this application in either C# or Visual Basic. You will then use the form designer to lay out an MDI application similar to the one previously shown in Figure 4-2.

1. Open Visual Studio 2005 and create a new Windows application (File | New | Project). Select the Windows Application template in your preferred language, give the project a name, and click OK. The Windows project template will add a new form called *Form1* to your project. We will use this as the basis for your MDI container.

2. Set the *IsMdiContainer* property of Form1 to *True*. This will indicate Form1 as an MDI container.

3. Using the Toolbox, add a *MenuStrip* control to the top of *Form1*. This control should automatically dock to the top of the form. Click the task smart tag connected to the *MenuStrip* control (small arrow in the top-right corner) and then click *Insert Standard Items*. This will add the standard menu items to the *MenuStrip* control, set their icons, and define the quick-access keys for these items.

4. Click the *MenuStrip* control and add a new menu item in the space provided. Title this item **Window**. This menu will be used to allow a user to track and access the MDI child windows. Select the *MenuStrip* control again. Set its *MdiWindowListItem* property to this new menu item (windowToolStripMenuItem).

5. Use the Toolbox to add a *ToolStrip* control to the top of the form (under the *MenuStrip*). This control should also dock to the top of the form (under the *MenuStrip*). Click the smart tag associated with the *ToolStrip* and then click Insert Standard Items. This will add the standard tool bar icons to the control.

6. Add a *StatusStrip* control to the bottom of the form. This control should automatically dock to the bottom of the form. Click the icon in the lower left of the control. Select *StatusLabel* to add a new label to indicate status. Set the *Text* property of this item to **Ready**.

7. Create a task pane by adding a *Panel* control to the MDI form. Set its *Padding* property to **9** for all sides. Set the *Dock* property of this *Panel* control to *Right*. Size the *Panel* control to take up approximately one-fourth of the width of the MDI container.

8. Add a *Splitter* control to the MDI container. Set its *Dock* property to *Right* and its *Width* property to **5**. This should enable users to resize the task pane as they see fit.

9. Add a *Label* control to the task pane (*Panel* control). Set the *Text* property of the control to **Action Pane**. Increase the font size to 10 points. Align the *Label* control to the upper-left side of the *Panel* using the Snaplines. Set the *Margin, Bottom* property of the *Label* control to **12**.

10. This task pane will allow a user to set the font and font size for the MDI child. Add a *Label* to the task pane. Set its *Text* property to **Font Size**. Align the *Label* control to the left of the *Panel* and under the previous *Label* title Action Pane (with respect to its bottom margin snapline).

11. Add a *ComboBox* control to the task pane. Align it to the left of the Font Size label text. Stretch the control to the right side of the panel using the snapline. Anchor the control to the top, left, and right side of the pane.

12. Repeat steps 10 and 11 to add another *ComboBox* and *Label* control under the previously created items. These controls should be used to set the Font Name.

13. Add a *Button* control to the task pane. Align the control to the right side of the *Panel* and under the Font Name *ComboBox*. Set the *Text* property of the *Button* control to **Apply**. Anchor this control to the top and right.

14. Add a new Windows form to the project. Use the default name for this form (Form2). This form will act as our MDI child form or document.

15. Set the *Padding* property of Form2 to **10** for all sides. This will create a border inside the form.

16. Add a *RichTextBox* control to Form2. Set its *Dock* property to *Fill*. This control will act as our document.

17. Return to the MDI parent form (Form1). Add code to the *Click* event for the *newTool-StripMenuItem*. The code should create a new instance of Form2 as follows:

```
' VB
Dim newMDIChild As Form2 = New Form2()
newMDIChild.MdiParent = Me
newMDIChild.Show()
```

```
// C#
Form2 newMDIChild = new Form2();
newMDIChild.MdiParent = this;
newMDIChild.Show();
```

18. Run the application. You should notice that the all controls work together during a resize and that the form looks proportioned. In addition, the Window menu should keep track of the open document in the MDI container.

Lesson Summary

- An application container represents the host for the forms (or screens) in an application. Defining this container is a very important decision. The container influences user perception about the UI. It also provides base services for developers, including navigation, window and form management, status indication, and more. Most Windows applications are either single-document interface (SDI), where all screens are somewhat unique in the system, or multiple-document interface (MDI), where the application is centered on a specific document type.

- Professional applications should have a professional look and feel. You can go a long way toward creating such an interface by defining and enforcing a UI layout standard. Visual Studio 2005 gives you many tools to do that. These include control margins, padding, and automatic sizing. You can also use snaplines in the Windows Forms designer to help you easily create screens that meet these standards. Finally, each control can be laid out on a form using anchoring and docking to allow for consistent resizing and scaling.

Lesson Review

You can use the following questions to test your knowledge of the information in Lesson 2, "Define a Strategy to Implement a Common UI Layout." The questions are also available on the companion CD if you prefer to review them in electronic form.

NOTE Answers

Answers to these questions and explanations of why each answer choice is right or wrong are located in the "Answers" section at the end of the book.

---

1. In which of the following scenarios would you create an MDI container? (Choose all that apply.)

    A. A contract management application that allows a user to create new contracts and edit existing ones.

    B. A role-based, user administration tool that allows a user to manage application roles and users in the database.

    C. An issue management system that contains the following modules: issue management, project setup, administration, and reports.

    D. A tool used by end users for securely capturing important notes and then encrypting this data as it is stored in the file system.

2. You add a *GroupBox* control to a Windows form named Form1. You want the space between the *GroupBox* and the edge of *Form1* to be 20 pixels. What should you do? (Choose all that apply.)

    A. Set the *Padding* property of *Form1* to **20**; set the *Margin* property of the *GroupBox* to **0**.

    B. Set the *Padding* property of the *GroupBox* to **10**; set the *Padding* property of Form1 to **10**.

    C. Set the *Margin* property of the *GroupBox* to **10**; set the *Padding* property of Form1 to **10**.

    D. Set the *Margin* property of the *GroupBox* to **20**; set the *Padding* property of Form1 to **0**.

3.   You need to add a number of labels to a form. Each label defines the content of an associated text box. The labels all align on the left side of the form; the text boxes align on the right. The content of the labels is determined at run time. You want to design your form in such a way as to allow the form to resize at run time to fit the content. What actions should you take? (Each item represents part of the solution. Choose two.)

   A.   Add a *TableLayoutPanel* control to the form and add two columns, one for the *Label* controls and another for the *TextBox* controls. Set each column's *SizeType* to *AutoSize*.

   B.   Add a *Panel* control to each column in the *TableLayoutPanel* control. Add each label control to the left column's panel. Add each text box to the right panel control's text box. Align all controls with respect to one another. Set the *AutoSize* property of each *Panel* control to True. Set the *AutoSizeMode* for each *Panel* control to *GrowAndShrink*.

   C.   Set the *Dock* property of the *Label* controls to *Left, Right*. Set the *Dock* property of the *TextBox* controls to *Left, Right, Top*.

   D.   Add two *Panel* controls to the form. Add the *Label* controls to one *Panel* control; add the *TextBox* controls to the other *Panel* control. Align each *Panel* control. Set the *AutoSizeMode* of the *Panel* control that contains the labels to *GrowOnly*. Set the *AutoSizeMode* of the other *Panel* control to *GrowAndShrink*.

4.   You are creating an SDI application. You need to define a menu, toolbar, and status bar on the form. You also need to create a left pane that covers the entire form, top to bottom. The right side of the form should be split between a bottom pane and a main content pane. The left pane should include a splitter that divides the form vertically. The right pane should include a splitter that divides that portion of the form horizontally. In what order should you add these controls to the form in order to dock them properly?

   A.   Left *Panel*, vertical *Splitter*, bottom *Panel*, horizontal *Splitter*, content *Panel*, *MenuStrip*, *ToolStrip*, *StatusStrip*

   B.   *MenuStrip*, *ToolStrip*, *StatusStrip*, bottom *Panel*, horizontal *Splitter*, left *Panel*, vertical *Splitter*, content *Panel*

   C.   *MenuStrip*, *ToolStrip*, *StatusStrip*, vertical *Splitter*, left *Panel*, horizontal *Splitter*, bottom *Panel*, content *Panel*

   D.   *MenuStrip*, *ToolStrip*, *StatusStrip*, left *Panel*, vertical *Splitter*, bottom *Panel*, horizontal *Splitter*, content *Panel*

Lesson 3: Understand and Standardize Control Usage

When you define your user interface you need to be aware of the tools you have available. In terms of today's Windows user interface, this means controls. You need to understand each control and standardize your usage around them. You want your users to know what to expect and how to work with an interface based on a consistent use of your controls. Visual Studio provides a full suite of controls to help you define UIs. In this lesson we will examine most of these controls and provide the usage scenario for each one.

After this lesson, you will be able to:
- Understand the purpose of the many controls that ship with Visual Studio 2005 to define a Windows user interface.
- Pick the appropriate Windows user interface control for a given situation.

Estimated lesson time: 15 minutes

Real World

Mike Snell

Know your control set. Controls are everywhere these days. You need to know the controls in Visual Studio. You also need to consider any user or custom controls that might exist in your company. I've found that the more you can standardize on these data entry elements, the more your users will feel they are working in a single environment.

I recommend that all UI designers spend some time looking at third-party controls for particular situations. Often these can offer a lot of complex functionality for a very low price or development impact. You might choose to create some of these controls yourself. However, this typically does not result in the same amount of features or polish that a third-party control provides—not to mention that most developers are not given the time to finish these type of projects. In the end, your users might thank you for the decision to use third-party controls.

Finally, before you select controls for a UI layout, I suggest you evaluate how controls are implemented in previous or ongoing applications in your environment. You can bet that users have been accustomed to these implementations. Therefore, you should consider either sticking with some of these layouts or doing a wholesale change. If you create a hodgepodge of new layout constructs with the old, the users will know—and you will most likely hear about it.

Evaluate User Needs and Select Controls

When you select controls, you need to have two things in mind: a good understanding of the controls available to you and the task the user is trying to accomplish with the control. The first item we will cover in a moment. The second item we will consider here. When you think about using a control, think about the user (and not how easy or difficult it might make your development effort).

The user is trying to accomplish a specific task with a given control or set of controls. You need to consider how easy the control will make the task and how familiar the user is with the control. For example, if your users use the keyboard a lot and require fast data entry, you might consider using *TextBox* controls and *AutoComplete* features instead of allowing users to select data from a list. This will speed their data entry. A list selection will slow them down. On the other hand, if users are not familiar with your application and require simple, can't-get-it-wrong data entry, then a list selection might be in order. You need to know the behavior and demographics of the users and create the right controls based on this information.

Creating Containers for Other Controls

We have already discussed many of the container controls. You should use these controls to group and contain other controls. Getting the right container can make the user interface work better in terms of sizing and resizing. Table 4-1 lists the common container controls in Visual Studio, along with their usage.

Table 4-1   Container Controls

Control	Usage
Panel	Use the *Panel* control to group a set of other controls. *Panels* are useful for defining dockable panes on a form. You can combine a *Panel* with a *Splitter* to allow a user to resize screen real estate.
GroupBox	The *GroupBox* control should be used sparingly to group a set of like controls. *RadioButtons* are often grouped with a *GroupBox* control.
TabControl	Use the *TabControl* to provide a series of forms and related controls on a given subject or data element. For example, you might use a *TabControl* to lay out the many groups of options related to a user managing an order in an order management system.
SplitContainer	The *SplitContainer* control is a useful combination of the common two panels and a splitter layout.
TableLayoutPanel	Use the *TableLayoutPanel* control when you need to dynamically resize portions of a form based on run-time content. The *TableLayoutPanel* helps in localization situations where label and button sizes change.
FlowLayoutPanel	The *FlowLayoutPanel* control should be used for managing complex layouts of a series of controls either horizontally or vertically.

User Commands and Navigation

The command and navigation controls are some of the most common controls a developer works with. They allow a user to gain access to the features of the application and provide decisive actions or requests. Table 4-2 lists the common command and navigation controls in Visual Studio along with their usage.

Table 4-2   Command and Navigation Controls

Control	Usage
Button	Use a *Button* control to allow a user to perform or cancel an action. Common actions for buttons include actions like new, save, cancel, close, apply, and so on.
ToolStrip	Use the *ToolStrip* control to provide a toolbar for users of your application. Toolbars should include quick access to common features (and not navigation). You should also use icons to represent these common features.
MenuStrip	Use the *MenuStrip* control to create application menus that allow a user to access important features.
ContextMenuStrip	The *ContextMenuStrip* control should be used to provide context-sensitive right-click menu items to users. If a user is working with data and can think of a common action, you should try to make that action available through a *ContextMenuStrip*.

Create Controls for Users to Enter Data

Most professional business applications have to do with users entering and updating data. This means you will spend a lot of time with the controls that allow this to happen. In this section we break down these controls into three types based on user needs: entering text values, selecting data from a list, and setting property values.

Entering Text Values

There are many ways for users to get text into your application. They may enter it through a text box, edit data in a grid, or provide formatted data through a Rich Text Format (RTF) control. You want to make this process easy for users. This means helping them enter and format data appropriately without being over-restricting. Table 4-3 lists the controls and their usage scenarios for the basic text entry controls in Visual Studio 2005.

Table 4-3   Text Entry Controls

Control	Usage
TextBox	Use the *TextBox* control to allow a user to enter or edit text. The *TextBox* control has a number of features that can help users, including the ability to automatically complete their data entries.

Table 4-3   Text Entry Controls

Control	Usage
RichTextBox	Use the *RichTextBox* control for situations that require a user to enter and format text data.
MaskedTextBox	Use the *MaskedTextBox* control when you need to constrain the data a user can enter in a given *TextBox*. The *MaskedTextBox* can also help users by automatically inserting items like hyphens in a phone number.

Selecting Data from a List

A common activity for a user is to select from a list of options. The most common example is a drop-down list. Lists are also useful to developers in that they restrict user input to valid elements. Table 4-4 represents the set of list controls in Visual Studio 2005.

Table 4-4   Data Selection Controls

Control	Usage
CheckedListBox	Use the *CheckedListBox* control to display a list of options for which a user can make multiple selections. Users can scroll through the list of options and select those that pertain to the situation. For example, you might be editing a user's profile and select the roles to which they belong from a *CheckedListBox*.
ComboBox	Use the *ComboBox* to display a single-column list of items for a user to select. A *ComboBox* presents a drop-down list. Do not overuse the *ComboBox*. If there are hundreds of items, a user might prefer to enter these items through a custom find or a *ListBox* or *ListView*.
ListBox	Use the *ListBox* to display a list of items for a user to select. A *ListBox* can show the item along with a graphic to represent the item.
ListView	Use the *ListView* control when you wish to give users the option to redisplay a list in multiple formats (small icons, large icons, and details view).
NumericUpDown	Use the *NumericUpDown* controls sparingly. Users typically don't like to scroll up and down to set a numeric value unless the numeric range is very small.
TreeView	The *TreeView* control is useful for displaying hierarchical data in a list for user selection. Users can expand and close nodes. In addition, the *TreeView* control can have icons and check boxes for selection.

Setting Specific Property Values

Most applications give users a lot of options. These options need to be presented in a standard way so as to help users understand their choices. Visual Studio 2005 provides a number of controls used for setting options (or properties). Table 4-5 lists these controls and their usage.

Table 4-5 Specifying Data Values

Control	Usage
CheckBox	The *CheckBox* control is used to allow a user to set (turn on or off) options.
RadioButton	Use the *RadioButton* control when you're asking a user to choose from a mutually exclusive set of options. These options should be few in number—otherwise you should consider a list control.
TrackBar	A *TrackBar* control (also called a slider) should be used in special situations where users can enter values by sliding an indicator up and down a scale. The *TrackBar* control is best used when a user doesn't care about the exact value but is more interested in the effect. In these cases you should show the effect as the user slides the bar. As an example, consider changing the brightness of a picture using a *TrackBar*.
DateTimePicker	Use the *DateTimePicker* when requesting a user to select a valid date. The control presents as a drop-down list that shows a calendar.
MonthCalendar	Use the *MonthCalendar* control when you need to display a calendar on a form. This can be useful for allowing a user to select a series of dates.

Displaying Data and Application Information

You need to keep users informed. Most applications will have a large amount of read-only text or report-like data. You need to standardize how this data gets to users. You also need to keep them updated on what the application is doing. You do not want them wondering if your application has crashed. Table 4-6 lists the controls in Visual Studio for keeping the user informed.

Table 4-6 Controls to Display Data and Information

Control	Usage
DataGridView	Use the *DataGridView* control to show users multiple columns and rows of data. This control is useful for allowing a user to sort, page, and work with this data.
Label	A *Label* control is used to display textual, read-only information to users.

Table 4-6 Controls to Display Data and Information

Control	Usage
LinkLabel	Use a *LinkLabel* to show a Web-style action button. The *LinkLabel* should be used to open Web pages. Using the *LinkLabel* to replace buttons can be confusing to users unless it is done consistently across an entire UI. Even in these cases you should consider *LinkLabels* for accessing external items or connecting to read-only data. Buttons should still be used for real user actions (just like on a Web page).
StatusStrip	Use the *StatusStrip* control to show information about the current state of the application. This can include text information, as well as progress bars for short, simple actions like saving or opening data.
ProgressBar	Use the *ProgressBar* control to provide status to the user for long-running operations.

Displaying and Graphics and Using Audio

A professional application should have a good use of visuals to display information and not just use simple text. In addition, sound at the appropriate times can help alert users. Table 4-7 discusses the use of the graphics and sound controls in Visual Studio.

Table 4-7 Working with Graphics and Sound

Control	Usage
PictureBox	Use the *PictureBox* control to show graphics and icons on your forms to users.
ImageList	Use the *ImageList* control to manage the images in your application.
SoundPlayer	Use the *SoundPlayer* control to provide audio cues to your users. This can be helpful at the end of a long- running transaction, for example.

Displaying Common Dialog Boxes

The use of the common dialog boxes for Windows in your application will promote familiarity and consistency for users. They already use these dialog boxes in other applications and throughout Windows itself. In addition, these dialog boxes can cut down on your development time. Visual Studio provides a number of these dialog boxes for your use. Table 4-8 lists these dialog boxes and their usage.

Table 4-8 Common Dialog Boxes

Control	Usage
ColorDialog	Use this dialog box to allow a user to select a color for a specific purpose.
FontDialog	Use this dialog box to allow users to select a font.

Table 4-8 **Common Dialog Boxes**

Control	Usage
OpenFileDialog	This dialog box should be used to allow a user to find and select a file.
PrintDialog	Use this dialog box to allow a user to select a printer, configure print options, and print application contents.
PrintPreviewDialog	Use this dialog box to provide a preview of a print job to a user.
FolderBrowserDialog	Use this dialog box when you need a user to select a folder from a list.
SaveFileDialog	Use this dialog box to help a user create a file name and save a file to the file system.

Displaying User Help

A professional application should come with some level of help. Users expect context-sensitive help and tool-tip help. Table 4-9 lists the controls that you can use to make this happen.

Table 4-9 **Showing Help to Users**

Control	Usage
HelpProvider	Use the HelpProvider control to provide context-sensitive (F1) access to help content.
ToolTip	Use the ToolTip control to provide pop-up help for specific controls when a user's mouse hovers over the control. Be careful in using it. Users like these at first but can quickly find them annoying. Therefore, you might consider providing a means to turn them off or creating a long delay before showing them.

Lab: Document Standard Usage for Controls

In this lab you will define and document how you intend to use controls within your organization for an upcoming application. Use the guidance provided in this chapter to consider and decide on key control usage scenarios. Each step listed below represents an action you should take to define your control usage standards.

1. Consider the users of the system. Document their familiarity with software, their usage patterns, and their needs. Take some time to look at the software your users are currently running on their machines. Document any commonalities that your software should align with.

2. Read through the set of user scenarios and requirements on the last few applications (or an upcoming application). Consider each scenario in terms of the controls available to you. Spend some time white-boarding how you might solve these scenarios with the controls.

3. Document common practices for providing text input controls to users. Consider each control available to you and decide in what scenario it makes sense to use the control and some of its key features (like autocomplete for a text box).

4. Consider the practice of showing data in a list to users. Determine what works and what does not. Ask the users if there are ways in which they would prefer to work with this list data (like find or sort). Document your standards and practices for showing data in a list.

5. Consider how you plan to make help available to users. Document your decisions and best practices in such a way that developers know how to implement this key feature.

6. Look for places in the usage scenarios that could benefit from additional graphics or sound. Document how you expect these items to be added to the UI and how they should behave.

7. Consider places where the common dialog boxes might be used. Document your decision on when, how, and if developers should use these controls. Also consider any places where a new common dialog box might be required to aid developers and provide consistency to users.

Lesson Summary

You need to select the right control for the given user task. This means considering standard control usage, the use case, and the user demographic to select the proper control for the job.

Visual Studio 2005 provides a lot of controls to help with data display, data entry, and common actions that require standard dialog boxes. You need to know the best practice for use of these controls in order to promote consistency with your users.

Lesson Review

You can use the following questions to test your knowledge of the information in Lesson 3, "Understand and Standardize Control Usage." The questions are also available on the companion CD if you prefer to review them in electronic form.

NOTE Answers

Answers to these questions and explanations of why each answer choice is right or wrong are located in the "Answers" section at the end of the book.

---

1. You wish to present the user with four distinct options for selection. A user can select only one option. Which controls would you use?

   A. *Panel* and *ListView*

   B. *GroupBox* and *CheckedListBox*

   C. *Panel* and *ListBox*

   D. *GroupBox* and *RadioButton*

2. Your design indicates that users must select one or more options from a list. Each option has an associated image and a set of descriptive data. You wish to allow a user to view the list by the image icon or in a detailed list. Which control should you choose?

   A. *ComboBox*

   B. *ListBox*

   C. *ListView*

   D. *TreeView*

3. Your requirement is to provide a user with a viewing pane for documents stored as graphics. Users want the ability to scale the contents of this pane based on their screen resolution and current viewing needs. They require fine-grained control over the scaling. Which control would you use to allow users to set the magnification percent for this pane?

   A. *Splitter*

   B. *TrackBar*

   C. *ComboBox*

   D. *SplitContainer*

4. You need to allow a user to select a series of dates on a calendar. These dates are sequential in nature (from and to) and fall within a single month. All of the following options will work for this task. Which represents the best, most intuitive choice?

   A. Create one *MaskedTextBox* control for users to select the "from" date. Create another for users to select the "to" date.

   B. Create one *DateTimePicker* control for users to select the "from" date. Create another for users to select the "to" date.

   C. Create a single *MonthCalendar* control.

   D. Create three *NumericUpDown* controls for users to select the "from" date. Create another set of controls for users to select the "to" date.

Chapter Review

To further practice and reinforce the skills you learned in this chapter, you can perform the following tasks:

- Review the chapter summary.
- Review the list of key terms introduced in this chapter.
- Complete the case scenario. These scenarios set up real-world situations involving the topics of this chapter and ask you to create a solution.
- Complete the suggested practices.
- Take a practice test.

Chapter Summary

- Getting your UI layout right can make a big difference in user satisfaction. User comments that include adjectives like accessible, easy-to-use, familiar, intuitive, inductive, responsive, and rich result in goals for your user interface. It's important to decide on actionable steps around UI decisions that will realize these goals. These steps should help define layouts that are logical and accessible to users. Your UI layout should be based on the activities of your users and the taxonomy of their business domain. Finally, consider the ways that make sense for users to navigate to and find features in your application. This should be intuitive. Users want access to features in a logical manner; they should not have to hunt for them.

- The application container choices you have for a Windows UI include single-document interface (SDI), where all screens are somewhat unique in the system, and multiple-document interface (MDI), where the application is centered on a specific document type. An application container should provide a set of base services to the development team such as navigation, window and form management, status indication, and more.

- Visual Studio 2005 provides layout tools to help you create professional, standard user interfaces. These tools include control margins, padding, and automatic sizing. Snaplines help you align controls to adhere to these standards. Anchoring and docking facilitates consistent resizing and scaling of controls on forms.

- Controls need to be used consistently and for the right task. You should evaluate the standard control usage, the application use cases, and the user demographics to select the proper control for the job.

Key Terms

Do you know what these key terms mean? You can check your answers by looking up the terms in the glossary at the end of the book.

- application container
- margin
- multiple-document interface (MDI)
- padding
- single-document interface (SDI)
- snapline

Case Scenario

In the following case scenario, you will apply what you've learned about defining a common user interface layout. You can find answers to these questions in the "Answers" section at the end of this book.

Case Scenario: Define a Common User Interface

You work as a senior developer for a company that processes loan applications for customers. You have an existing application with which users are pretty familiar. You have been asked to help redesign the user interface layout to help increase productivity and meet the new demands of the business.

Interviews

You attend a meeting to discuss the current user interface, the new demands of the business, and ideas on what might work. This meeting is facilitated by the business analyst and yourself. The meeting includes the trainer for new users, the manager of the loan consultants (who are responsible for processing loan applications), a user interface designer, and one of the loan officers. The following are statements made during this meeting:

- **User trainer** "Some of the loan consultants are advanced users of the system. They do not want the application to slow them down. They want speed when entering data. The application should help them enter data faster and not be a hindrance. These users would prefer to never reach for the mouse. This is a problem with the current system. Today they have to click around too much between screens. There idea is to have as many common features as possible right there on the screen. Of course, when they get the occasional anomaly in the loan process, they will want fast access to those features as well.

  "We have a lot of turnover with loan consultants. This means we are training new consultants at least twice a month. There is also a steady state of novice users who either slowly migrate to advanced, seasoned users of the system or leave the company. It would be nice to reduce the training and follow-up time required to work with these users without slowing down the advanced users."

- **Loan consultant manager**   "We average three loan contracts per loan consultant per day. Some users crank out more; others less. It would be nice to increase this productivity. Right now it seems the application gets in the way. The interface is very much centered on doing data entry. It would be nice if the application treated a loan application like the document that it creates. This would be more intuitive to the users.

  "A loan application is pretty simple at its base: you gather the customer information on name, address, phone, Social Security, and so on. You then get data for the type of loan, like a home, boat, or personal loan. Then you process a credit check, do some calculations, and submit the loan to the approval process. Of course there are other pieces, like reports and administration, but these aren't central to the processing application."

- **Business analyst**   "Users have indicated that they are constantly working on partial loans. They would like a quick and easy way to look up a loan and get working on it. Right now this is all based on telephone number, which can be problematic."

- **Loan officer**   "I review a lot of loans and have to make comments and edits before approving. Loan consultants often come to me or send me e-mails wondering what the status of a given loan might be. I need to know when loans are waiting my approval. In addition, the loan consultants should know the status of their active loans."

- **UI designer**   "The current interface looks cluttered; things are everywhere, and nothing seems to be lined up correctly. We need a clean, consistent user interface that makes use of white space to help improve usage."

Questions

While thinking about your response to the test plan, answer the following questions.

1. What are the primary goals for the user interface?
2. How should the user interface goals be implemented?
3. How would you define the application's taxonomy?
4. What navigational elements would you use to help users understand the system?
5. What type of container would you define for this application?

Suggested Practices

To help you successfully master the exam objectives presented in this chapter, complete the following tasks.

Evaluate Requirements and Choose an Appropriate Layout

The following practices will help you if you have never worked from requirements to user interface design. Consider Practice 1 if you have little experience in this regard. You should do

Practice 2 if you're not familiar with the guidelines for Windows. Finally, Practice 3 is something a UI developer should be doing all the time: staying on the lookout for a good layout.

- **Practice 1**   Look through past project requirements and use cases. Consider green-field user interfaces that would support these requirements. Do you have enough information in the requirements and use cases to come up with a design? If not, what are you missing? Fold this information into your next requirements or use a case-gathering session.

- **Practice 2**   Read through and familiarize yourself with the Windows XP design guidelines. Also, begin looking at the Vista interface design choices. Determine the differences between the two and work to understand the choices behind these changes.

- **Practice 3**   Consider how some existing applications that you like make your life easier. Consider applications that you don't like. Try to understand what might improve these applications.

Understand and Standardize Control Usage

If you need more practice defining good standard user interfaces, consider the following practices. These will help you to master this objective.

- **Practice 1**   Spend some time with the users of your application. Ask them what they like about the interface and what they would change. After all, they use the interface daily. They can provide a wealth of information on things like better navigation, better control usage, and simple fixes that can increase productivity.

- **Practice 2**   If you have a visual interface designer on staff, spend some time with that person. Get to know what the designer considers good UI design. Designers often have a different eye than developers. You might also consider a book or white paper on the topic. You shouldn't have to look hard for information on user interface design.

Take a Practice Test

The practice tests on this book's companion CD offer many options. For example, you can test yourself on just the content covered in this chapter, or you can test yourself on all the 70-548 certification exam content. You can set up the test so that it closely simulates the experience of taking a certification exam, or you can set it up in study mode so that you can look at the correct answers and explanations after you answer each question.

MORE INFO   **Practice tests**

For details about all the practice test options available, see the section titled "How to Use the Practice Tests" in this book's Introduction.

Chapter 5
Validation and User Feedback

One of the seminal works on how to create great user interfaces is *About Face: The Essentials of User Interface Design* (John Wiley & Sons, 1995) by Alan Cooper. The book lists some of the goals of software users. Two of them that are pertinent to this chapter are keeping the user from making big mistakes and keeping the user from looking stupid. So when it comes to designing the validation and feedback mechanisms in Microsoft Windows-based applications, these are the key aspects to keep in mind.

Exam objectives in this chapter:
- Choose an appropriate data validation method at the UI layer.
  - Choose a validation method based on the data type provided.
  - Decide how to report the feedback. Considerations include callbacks, exceptions, and writing to an event log.
  - Identify the source of invalid data.
  - Identify the cause of an invalid entry.
  - Evaluate whether invalid date can be prevented.
  - Evaluate whether an exception must be thrown.
  - Evaluate whether an exception must be logged.
  - Evaluate whether visual feedback, such as a message box or color, is required.
- Choose appropriate user assistance and application status feedback techniques.
  - Design a user assistance mechanism.
  - Choose an appropriate application status feedback technique based on available control types.
  - Choose an appropriate application status feedback technique to support accessibility.
  - Design an application status feedback mechanism.

Lessons in this chapter:

Before You Begin

To complete the lessons in this chapter, you should be familiar with Microsoft Visual Basic or C# and be comfortable performing the following task:

- Using the Accessibility Accessories (that is, Magnifier, Narrator).

Real World

Bruce Johnson

My interest in creating a good user experience goes back a long way. My background includes many years writing green screen applications, and I recall watching proficient users move through the data entry screens with a speed that astounded me. What I learned is that it's very important to take two groups of people into consideration when designing the validation and feedback mechanisms for any application. The first group contains new users. People who are not familiar with the application should have ways to get information about what needs to be done as easily as possible. However, it's the second group of users, the experts, that really matters for most business applications. They want to use your application to do their jobs as efficiently as possible. And woe to any developer that designs a validation or feedback system that gets in their way. For this reason, one of the themes of this lesson is to validate data as unobtrusively as possible while still providing the level of validation that the business requirements demand.

Lesson 1: Validating Data

Validating the data provided by the users at run time is one of the main tasks for any application. To be fair, validation has two components. The first, and the topic for this lesson, is where the best place is to perform the validation. The dilemma arises from the need to balance letting users enter anything they want versus the application's wanting complete control over the type and range of acceptable data. The second component, which is the topic for the second lesson in this chapter, is how to let the user know when the application has sensed that the data is bad.

After this lesson, you will be able to:
- Identify the different types of validation that can be used.
- Distinguish between the options available for validation in the .NET Framework.
- Understand the locations where validation can be performed and when one should be used over the others.
- Implement validation in bound *DataSets* and business objects.

Estimated lesson time: 50 minutes

Types of Validation

The first step in evaluating (or designing) a validation mechanism is to be aware of the basic types of validation that are normally present in an application. The distinction is necessary because the location and method for validation differ greatly depending on the validation type.

- **Data-Format Validation** The underlying assumption for any type of data validation is that the input from the user can't be trusted. As such, the first step in validating data is to make sure that it's in the correct format. Naturally "correct" will have different meanings depending on what data the application expects. If the expected data is an integer, the input should contain only numbers. If the expected data is a date, the input should be one of the recognized date formats. This level of validation is known as *data-format validation*. Also included in data-format validation is the need to have input fall within a given range. So enforcing the rule that the input is an integer between 1 and 100 is also considered a data-format validation.

- **Business Rule Validation** The other type of validation found in applications is associated with business rules. Examples of *business rule validations* abound in the real world: ensuring that an entered value is really a product number in a database; ensuring that the credit card has been authorized for the purchase; ensuring that the city and state are correct for the provided postal code. All these validations require processing over and above simply what the data looks like. And they all fall into the realm of business rule validation.

It is important, when architecting an application, to be aware of which type of validation is being performed. Mixing the different types within a single method call, whether unintentionally or by design, can result in a poorly designed class structure that makes it difficult to extend functionality as the need arises.

Location of Validation Code

The reason for paying attention to the types of validation is that the type has everything to do with where the validation code should be located. In general, the rule goes as follows: the more the validation deals with data formatting, the closer it should be to the client. So ensuring that data is a number or a date should fall to the client. Ensuring that the number represents a current customer or that the ordered products can be manufactured and delivered by the specified date falls to the server.

Exam Tip   Data-format validations are almost always those associated with the controls placed onto the form. Business rule validations are typically performed in a different class than the form so that the code can be reused.

One further element to this applies if you are creating a distributed application. Distributed applications, as are being considered here, include smart client applications, Web applications, and Windows Forms applications that use .NET remoting or Web services. For these applications it's important that validation takes place on any data that is submitted across a boundary. So even though validations might be performed in the browser or Windows application, the same validations should be performed by the server on the incoming requests. This prevents nefarious people from successfully submitting update requests that include invalid data.

Data-Format Validation

The easiest way to perform data-format validation in a Windows-based application is by using some of the controls that Microsoft has graciously provided. This includes using specialized controls, such as the *MaskedTextBox* control, and writing code to handle the *Validating* and *Validated* events. Developers can even create their own custom controls that support special validations. But because it's an important part of any control, extended or not, let's look at the event handlers.

Validating Event

The *Validating* event gets raised whenever a control needs to be validated. The "need" in this case is determined by whether the control that is about to gain focus has its *CauseValidation* property set to *True*. Any logic that is required to ensure that the entered data is correct is placed in the *Validating* event handler. In the case where the data is incorrect, the developer has the option to stop the movement of focus by setting the *Cancel* property to *True*. The *Cancel* property is found on the *CancelEventArgs* object that is passed into the handler. Let's look at an example.

A simple Windows forms application has a text box control on it. The data in the text box represents a full name so the input will be considered valid only if the *Text* property is not an empty string. The following code in the *Validating* event handler performs the appropriate processing.

```vb
' VB
Private Sub textBox1_Validating(ByVal sender As Object, _
   ByVal e As CancelEventArgs)
   If String.IsNullOrEmpty(textBox1.Text) Then
      e.Cancel = True
   End If
End Sub
```

```csharp
// C#
private void textBox1_Validating(object sender, CancelEventArgs e)
{
   if (String.IsNullOrEmpty(textBox1.Text))
      e.Cancel = true;
}
```

Although the *Validating* event is a convenient place to put data-format validation logic, it has a couple of problems:

- **The field must lose focus**   For the *Validating* event handler for a particular control to be executed, the control has to gain and lose focus. In a Windows form with many fields, it's possible that the user never enters one of the controls that needs validation and so validation never occurs.

- **Canceling takes the user out of the flow**   One of the premises of the *Validating* event is that, if the input is in error, moving to the next field is aborted. As has already been mentioned, this is done by setting *Cancel* to *True*. However, if a user is entering data in a heads-down mode, the user won't notice that the cancel occurred. So the user will continue typing until finally the error is noticed. At this point the user will curse at the application for wasting keystrokes. And adding a beep to the failure doesn't help. It just lets everyone else in the room know that the user made a mistake.

- **Validating event fires at awkward times**   If the *Validating* event includes code that sets *Cancel* to *True*, there are a number of situations where the results are not desirable. For example, if the user tries to close the form by clicking in the top-right corner, the *Validating* event for the current field gets raised. So if that field is invalid, the user is unable to close the form, a decidedly unexpected result. The same thing happens if the user presses F1 to get the context-sensitive help to display. As a result, it actually takes a lot of work to get the *Validating* event coded properly.

MORE INFO   Closing forms while data is invalid

It is still possible to handle the situation where setting *Cancel* to *True* prevents the closure of the form. This is accomplished by creating a handler for the *FormClosing* event and setting the *Cancel* property on the *FormClosingEventArgs* parameter to *False*.

If the *Validating* event is being used in your applications, a number of changes at .NET 2.0 help to alleviate some of these problems. The first is the *AutoValidate* property that can be set on the form itself. Actually, it can be set for any container control, but for this discussion the focus will be just on the form.

The purpose of *AutoValidate* is to control how data will be validated when focus is moved away from a control. Table 5-1 shows the possible values for this property.

Table 5-1   The Possible Values for *AutoValidate*

Name	Description
Disable	The *Validating* event won't be raised when focus leaves a control.
EnableAllowFocusChange	The *Validating* event is raised when focus changes, but setting *Cancel* to *True* doesn't prevent focus from moving to the next control.
EnablePreventFocusChange	The *Validating* event is raised when focus changes. If *Cancel* is set to *True*, focus is returned to the original control.
Inherit	This default value tells the container to inherit the *AutoValidate* property from its parent. If there is no container control, it defaults to *EnablePreventFocusChange*.

The *EnablePreventFocusChange* value is the default setting at a form level. This is what produces the already described behavior of returning focus to the invalid control. The interesting possibilities are created by the *Disable* and *EnableAllowFocusChange* values. When you set *AutoValidate* to *EnableAllowFocusChanged*, the *Validating* event is raised and all validation processing takes place. However, focus change is not prevented if there is a problem. This is almost (but not quite) like removing the logic for setting the *Cancel* property from the event handler. The reason for the "almost" qualifier is that the problem with closing the form using the top-right button still exists, even when *AutoValidate* is set to *EnableAllowFocusChange*.

Setting *AutoValidate* to *Disable* eliminates the raising of the *Validating* event. And without the *Validating* event being raised, the user can close the form as expected. But if the *Validating* event isn't raised, what's the purpose of putting any logic into the *Validating* event handler? Well, there is a reason. By using the *ValidateChildren* method, the *Validating* event handlers can be invoked on the form manually.

The *ValidateChildren* method iterates through all the controls in the form (or any other container control) and raises the *Validating* event. If the *Cancel* property is set to *True* in any of the *Validating* event handlers, *ValidateChildren* returns a *False*. But having *Cancel* set to *False* in one handler doesn't prevent all of the *Validating* events from being raised. *ValidateChildren* will raise the *Validating* event on every control even if one of them sets *Cancel* to *True*.

MaskedTextBox Control

In certain situations it would provide a better user experience if invalid data could be prevented before a *Validating* event gets raised. A good example of this is the *DateTimePicker* control. The control itself can easily validate that the input is not in a correct format. And there are user interface controls (such as a pop-up calendar) that can help the user provide properly formatted input. A second example of proactively preventing invalid data can be found in the *ComboBox* control. And the drop-down portion of the control provides the same visual clues to valid input.

Both the *DateTimePicker* and *ComboBox* control deal with the specific cases of date/time and data table validations. For the more generic case, the *MaskedTextBox* control can be used to force the input to match a particular pattern.

Any developer coming from a Visual Basic 6 or Microsoft Access background will recognize the functionality provided by *MaskedTextBox*. The heart of the *MaskedTextBox*'s capabilities is found in the *Mask* property. Using the *Mask* property, it's possible to restrict or require certain characters at certain points in the input. This would be like ensuring that a phone number contains only digits or that the fourth and eighth characters are dashes. As well, special conversions, such as from lowercase to uppercase, can be defined.

From the user's perspective, the *MaskedTextBox* also gives useful feedback about what input is expected. The display is a set of prompt and literal characters. The prompt character is indicative of the type of expected input (a number sign [#] would represent a digit, for example). And when an invalid character is provided, the *MaskedTextBox* control doesn't allow it to be entered. Whether a beep sounds or not is controlled by the *BeepOnError* property. For less intrusive or visual notification techniques, the *MaskInputRejected* event gets raised on bad input characters as well.

Two other seldom-mentioned elements of a *MaskedTextBox* can be used to solve some interesting problems. First, the *MaskedTextBox* control exposes a property called *MaskedTextProvider*. Although the property can't be set directly, an instance of a custom *MaskedTextProvider* can be included in the constructor. The purpose of the *MaskedTextProvider* is to define a set of custom mask characters. So instead of a number sign (#) representing a required digit, you could create a *MaskedTextProvider* that interprets an "n" the same way. Also, with a complete implementation of the *MaskedTextProvider* class, it's possible to limit the characters (like, for example, to only 0–9 and A–F for hex values) that can be used as input.

The second feature of the *MaskedTextBox* is there to solve an occasional problem with any masked control. Sometimes the mask is not sufficient to guarantee that the input is valid. The canonical example is a date. The mask for a date is normally something like "99/99/9999."

But based on this mask, a value of 50/50/2000 would be accepted. It's obvious that this is not a valid date, yet it passed through the mask.

The solution is found in the *ValidatingType* property of the *MaskedTextBox* control. This property can be assigned a data type. When control loses focus, the content will be validated by the assigned type. In the example described above, a *DateTime* type would be assigned to the property. When the control loses focus and the *MaskCompleted* property is *True*, the *DateTime* type parses the input. The results of the validation are made available through the *TypeValidationCompleted* event.

Naturally, since you have an enquiring mind, the first question will be "How does the type perform the validation? It's just a data type!" The answer is that the data type assigned to *ValidatingType* must expose a *Parse* method. The *Parse* method takes either a string alone or both a string and an *IFormatProvider* object and returns an object of the appropriate data type. Or a *FormatException* is thrown if the string can't be converted to the type. The *MaskedTextBox* control would catch the exception and indicate the failure in the *TypeValidationCompleted* control.

Exam Tip   Keep in mind that the *ValidatingType* can provide a great deal of format-style validation over and above the pattern matching provided through the *Mask* property.

Business Rule Validation

As the rules for "correctness" move out of the realm of formatting and into relationships with other data, the location for the validation code moves further away from the client application—at least in terms of the processing that must be done. The feedback mechanism still needs to be in the client, but, again, that's a topic for the next lesson.

For business rule validation, the logic should be placed into business classes. In the past it would have been embedded within Active Server Pages (ASP) or Windows forms, but it's pretty clear by now that that type of architecture is not maintainable. Nor, in many instances, is it secure or scalable. By placing such logic into classes, it is easily used in other situations that demand it. And it's easily locatable. And reviewable by peers. And testable. And so on, and so on.

So now that agreement has been reached that the implementation of the business rules should be in a class, the question remains as to how to connect the user interface to the business rules. And the answer, in the .NET world, is data binding.

Conceptually, data binding is the defining of a link between a user interface control and a backing data store. The data store can be a database, a *DataSet*, or a business object. As the data is changed in the control, the data store is updated. The timing of the update is not necessarily immediately. In .NET, the update takes place after the *Validating* event has been processed without the *Cancel* property being set to *True*. Once the update occurs, the business rules are invoked and the data is determined to be valid or invalid. If invalid, then the user interface is notified and the failure notification is delivered to the user.

Exam Tip   The mechanism used to bind to business objects has been greatly improved in .NET 2.0 and is likely to be the subject of some questions.

> ## Quick Check
> 1. What type of validation would be used to ensure that the user selects from one of five options?
> 2. What type of validation would be used to ensure that the value of an order is less than the credit limit for a customer?
>
> ### Quick Check Answers
> 1. Making sure that the user's input is from a list of choices is really a data-format validation. There could be instances where it might be a business rules validation, but that would be only if the list of choices changes and is data-driven.
> 2. Ensuring that a combination of fields is validated against a calculation is a very good example of a business rule validation. First, the validation belongs to more than one field. Second, the calculation falls well outside the range of data-format validation as the limits on what is allowable depends on outside forces.

Business Object vs. *DataSet*

There is an ongoing debate as to whether the data source used in the data binding process should be a business object or a *DataSet*. This is an area where there is no clear winner. Each of the choices has pros and cons, and successful applications have been developed using both options.

In order for a business object to be used in a data-binding scenario, it needs to implement the *IBindingList* interface. Or, if the entire interface is too much to handle (and some of the interactions between the binding list, the *IEditableObject*, and the *CurrencyManager* that rules over them can be interesting to deal with), the *BindingList* generic class can be used. A third option, the one that most business object developers will actually use, is the *BindingSource* object.

The *DataSet* class is already a natural source for data binding. It implements the *IListSource* interface, an interface which returns an object that can be bound to a data source. It provides a set of objects (*DataTable*, *DataRow*, and so on) that allows for the storing of data in a manner that is familiar to developers. It exposes a set of events that allows for the insertion of business rule logic at the appropriate place in the processing.

So where are the differences between these two approaches? Well, the first is found in the realm of object-orientation. The *DataSet* is designed to be a repository for data, specifically data stored in a tabular format. In this area it outshines any competition. There are also events that get raised as the most important data-binding actions take place. Column changes and row changes all raise events, allowing the validation rules to be conveniently added to the class at the appropriate time.

However, the tabular layout of the data means that it's very difficult to use a *DataSet* in a class hierarchy. It is rare to find a workable scenario where you can create a class hierarchy using a *DataSet* as the base class. Part of the reason for the difficulty is that the *DataSet* isn't designed to represent data but to contain it. The *DataSet* (even a typed *DataSet*) doesn't encapsulate the implementation details sufficiently to allow for effective representation without knowledge of the tabular structure. The same is not true for a business class. Business classes can be more easily designed to be extensible and therefore can be placed into a class hierarchy.

What business classes have a tougher time with, however, is maintaining data history. As a value gets changed, the validation logic will, on occasion, need to know both the old and the new value for a particular property. Although business classes can easily do that on a property-by-property level, it is a manual process. There is no support built in to *System.Object* (the base class for any business class) to provide old and new values support across the entire set of properties. There are a lot of times, even beyond straight data validation, when both the old and new value are needed.

MORE INFO   *DataSets* as Data Transfer Objects

There is a lot of information about using *DataSets* as the data store for a business class. In this case they are actually Data Transfer Objects (DTOs) and the resulting business classes are a hybrid of *DataSets* and business objects. For more information, see *http://msdn.microsoft.com/library/en-us/ dnpatterns/html/ImpDTODataSet.asp*.

Data Binding and Validation With *DataSets*

Using *DataSets* as the source for data binding is quite easy. The validation process is almost as easy. The main event to handle field-level validation is the *ColumnChanging* event in a *DataTable*. This event is raised any time that the value of a column in the *DataTable* is changed. The *DataColumnChangeEventArgs* parameter includes a number of properties that are of interest to a developer writing validation routines. The properties are shown in Table 5-2.

Table 5-2   The Public Properties of *DataColumnChangeEventArgs*

Property	Description
Column	Contains the *DataColumn* that contains the changing value
ProposedValue	The value that the column is being changed to
Row	Contains the *DataRow* in which the column is being changed

Each of the three properties in Table 5-2 is commonly used in validation. Naturally, the *ProposedValue* property will be the one that is most used. But along with seeing what the value of the column will become, it can also be used to change the value. That is to say that if you change *ProposedValue* as part of processing the *ColumnChanging* event, the new value will be assigned to the column.

The *Column* and *Row* properties are used to get contextual information for the change. The *DataColumn* represented by the *Column* property contains the data type and constraints for the change. The *DataRow* represented by the *Row* property contains, among other things, the values of the other columns in the same row as the one being changed. These values would be used if the validation includes calculations that involved other fields in the same row.

The big question when using the *ColumnChanged* event is how to indicate when invalid data has been provided. There are two possible approaches. The first is to raise an exception. The second involves using the *RowError* property or *SetColumnError* method. Both techniques have their places, with the user feedback mechanism being the determining factor as to which one to use.

There is one other event that can occasionally come in handy when it comes to validating data binding. Specifically, the *RowChanging* event gets fired when the editing of a *DataRow* is complete. This event is most frequently used when the data is displayed in a multirecord format, such as a *DataGrid* control. In that case, moving from one row to the next raises the *RowChanging* event. When you are looking at information in a form view (one record per form), the *RowChanging* event is still fired, but only when all the changes to the row have been made. And that is usually initiated by the user performing some action, like clicking a Save button. As a result, there is less incentive to use the built-in *RowChanging* event when only one record is being viewed at a time.

Data Binding and Validation with Business Objects

Validation using business objects is a little more natural than using *DataSets*. In *DataSets* the notification that a value was being changed came through the *ColumnChanged* event. In business objects the property methods are invoked directly, so the validation code can be placed into the *Set* portion of the method.

```
' VB
Public Property Name() As String
    Get
        Return _Name
    End Get

    Set
        ' Called when property is updated in the user interface
        If String.IsNullOrEmpty(Value) Then
            Throw New ArgumentOutOfRangeException("The name cannot be empty")
        Else
            _Name = Value
```

```
      End If
   End Set
End Property

// C#
public string Name()
{
   get { return name; }

   set
   {
      // Called when property is updated in the user interface
      if (String.IsNullOrEmpty(value))
         throw new ArgumentOutOfRangeException("The name cannot be empty");
      else
         name = value;
   }
}
```

Also, business objects that are used in binding should implement a couple of interfaces that allow for more integrated interactions with the Windows forms client.

- *IDataErrorInfo* Interface   This interface is used to provide information about the errors in a business object to the client interface.
- *INotifyPropertyChanged* Interface   This interface provides for the raising of an event when a property on a business object has been changed. This allows the user interface to react appropriately when the values in the object are updated.

From a validation perspective, the *IDataErrorInfo* interface is more pertinent. But *INotifyPropertyChanged* is useful if the validation process results in an entered value being changed to something that fits within the business rules. Still, let's focus on *IDataErrorInfo*.

The *IDataErrorInfo* interface supports two members—a string property named *Error* and an *Item*. The *Error* property returns a string indicating (in a single message) what's wrong with the object. The *Item* takes the name of a property and returns the error associated with that property or an empty string if there is no error.

The typical implementation of *IDataErrorInfo* in a business object would have a private property containing a *Hashtable* of error messages. When an error occurs within a property setter, the *Hashtable* is updated with a message using the property name as the key. If the property setter executes successfully, then any entry with that property is removed. Finally, the *Error* property builds a message out of the items that are in the *Hashtable*.

Lab: Common Validation Scenarios

In this lab a number of different techniques used to validate data will be explored. In each exercise a separate approach will be demonstrated so that the pros and cons can be more easily identified.

▶ **Exercise 1: Validating Event**

In the first exercise, validating data using the *Validating* event will be explored. The starting point is a form that contains a full name and a phone number. The full name is a required field, while each character in the phone number must be either a number or a dash.

1. Launch Visual Studio 2005.
2. Open a solution using File | Open | Project/Solution.
3. Navigate to the Chapter5/Lesson1/<language>/Exercise1-Before directory. Select the Exercise1 solution and click Open.
4. In the Solution Explorer, double-click the Form1 file to display the form designer.
5. Click the fullNameTextBox and then open the Property Sheet. Click the Events button to display a list of the events for the control. Double-click the *Validating* event to create the fullNameTextBox_Validating event handler.
6. Add code to the event handler to ensure that the *Text* property on fullnameTextBox is not blank. If it is, the change of focus will be canceled. Add the following code to the *Validating* event handler:

```
' VB
If String.IsNullOrEmpty(fullNameTextBox.Text) Then
    e.Cancel = True
End If
```

```
// C#
if (String.IsNullOrEmpty(fullNameTextBox.Text))
    e.Cancel = true;
```

7. Back in the form designer, click the phoneNumberTextBox and then open the Property Sheet. Click the Events button to display a list of the events for the control. Double-click the *Validating* event to create the phoneNumberTextBox_Validating event handler.
8. Add code to the event handler to ensure that the *Text* property on phoneNumberText-Box contains only numbers and dashes. If it doesn't, the change of focus will be canceled. Add the following code to the *Validating* event handler for the phoneNumberTextBox:

```
' VB
Dim c As Char
For Each c in phoneNumberTextBox.Text.ToCharArray()
    If Not (Char.IsDigit(c) Or c.ToString() = "-") Then
        e.Cancel = True
    End If
Next
```

```
// C#
foreach (char c in phoneNumberTextBox.Text.ToCharArray())
    if (!(Char.IsDigit(c) || c.ToString() == "-"))
    {
```

```
        e.Cancel = true;
        break;
   }
```

9. In the form designer, double-click the validateButton control to create a *Click* event handler.

    Add code to the *Click* event handler to display a simple message box. Add the following code to the handler procedure:

    ```
    ' VB
    MessageBox.Show("Validate clicked")
    ```

    ```
    // C#
    MessageBox.Show("Validate clicked");
    ```

10. Run the application using F5. Notice that you can't tab away from the Full Name field unless a value is in place. Neither can you tab away from the Phone Number field if it is invalid. Nor does the Validate button respond when clicked if the focus is on one of the invalid fields.

11. Stop running the application.

12. In the form designer, click the validateButton control. In the Property Sheet, set the *CausesValidation* property to False.

13. Run the application using F5. Notice that even when one of the fields is invalid, you can still click the Validate button.

▶ **Exercise 2: *MaskedTextBox* Control**

Next up is the *MaskedTextBox* control. The starting point is the ending point for the last exercise, except that over the course of the exercise the phoneNumberTextBox will be replaced by a *MaskedTextBox* control. The *Mask* property will be set so that the user is forced to enter data in a valid phone number format.

1. Launch Visual Studio 2005.

2. Open a solution using File | Open | Project/Solution.

3. Navigate to the Chapter5/Lesson1/<language>/Exercise2-Before directory. Select the Exercise2 solution and click Open.

4. In the Solution Explorer, double-click the Form1 file to display the form designer.

5. Click the phoneNumberTextBox control and then delete it.

6. From the Toolbox, add a *MaskedTextBox* control and add it to the form where the phoneNumberTextBox used to be.

7. Open the Property Sheet and change the name of the control to **phoneNumberTextBox**.

8. Still in the Property Sheet, click the button associated with the *Mask* property. The screen shown in Figure 5-1 appears. Select the Phone Number pattern and click OK.

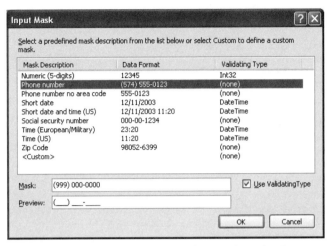

Figure 5-1 Selecting from the list of canned *Mask* values

9. Run the application and notice that the *MaskedTextBox* control has the appropriate mask and restricts the accepted keys to just numbers.

▶ **Exercise 3: *DataSet* Binding**

In the realm of business rule validations *DataSets* are one of the natural options. In this exercise we will configure a *DataSet* to allow for the validation of input data against a business rule. The form contains a product number and quantity field. Business rule is that the quantity needs to be greater or equal to 0 and less than 100. The validation for this rule will be implemented in the *ColumnChanged* event in the *DataSet*.

1. Launch Visual Studio 2005.
2. Open a solution using File | Open | Project/Solution.
3. Navigate to the Chapter5/Lesson1/<language>/Exercise3-Before directory. Select the Exercise3 solution and click Open.
4. In the Solution Explorer, double-click the Form1 file to display the form designer.
5. Double-click the form's surface to create a *Form.Load* event handler.
6. To start, we will be creating the *ColumnChanging* event handler for the productData *DataSet*. This handler will be invoked whenever the value of one of the bound columns is changed. Add the following code to the *Load* procedure:

```
' VB
AddHandler productData.Tables("Product").ColumnChanging, _
    New DataColumnChangeEventHandler(AddressOf validateProductData)
```

```
// C#
productData.Tables["Product"].ColumnChanging +=
    new DataColumnChangeEventHandler(validateProductData);
```

7. In order to have the binding validation take place, either an existing row or a new row needs to be active in the *DataSet*. To do this for the exercise, add the following line of code to the bottom of the *Load* procedure:

```
' VB
productBindingSource.AddNew()
```

```
// C#
productBindingSource.AddNew();
```

8. Next, the event handler for the *ColumnChanging* event needs to be created. The parameters include the sender and a *DataColumnChangeEventArgs* object. Add the following procedure below the *Load* procedure:

```
' VB
Private Sub validateProductData(ByVal sender as Object, _\
    ByVal e As DataColumnChangeEventArgs
End Sub
```

```
// C#
private void validateProductData(object sender,
    DataColumnChangeEventArgs e)
{
}
```

9. The *ColumnChanging* event gets raised every time any column in the *DataTable* is updated. For the validation we care only about the Quantity column. So the first element is to create an conditional block based on the name of the changed column. Add the following code to the *validateProductData* method:

```
' VB
If e.Column.ColumnName = "Quantity" Then
End If
```

```
// C#
if (e.Column.ColumnName == "Quantity")
{
}
```

10. Within this conditional block, the ProposedValue will be verified to be an integer between 0 and 100 inclusive. Add the following logic to the just-added *if* block:

```
' VB
Dim proposedValue as Integer
If Integer.TryParse(e.ProposedValue.ToString(), out proposedValue) Then
    If proposedValue < 0 Or proposedValue > 100 Then
        e.Row.SetColumnError(e.Column, _
            "The quantity must be between 0 and 100")
    Else
        e.Row.SetColumnError(e.Column, "")
    End If
Else
    e.Row.SetColumnError(e.Column, "The quantity must be numeric")
End If
```

```csharp
// C#
int proposedValue;
if (int.TryParse(e.ProposedValue.ToString(), out proposedValue))
   if (proposedValue < 0 || proposedValue > 100)
      e.Row.SetColumnError(e.Column,
         "The quantity must be between 0 and 100");
   else
      e.Row.SetColumnError(e.Column, "");
else
   e.Row.SetColumnError(e.Column, "The quantity must be numeric");
```

11. To report the value of the column error, add the following code to the bottom of the *validateProductData* method:

```vbnet
' VB
MessageBox.Show(String.Format("The message associated with {0} is {1}", _
   e.Column.ColumnName, e.Row.GetColumnError(e.Column)))
```

```csharp
// C#
MessageBox.Show(String.Format("The message associated with {0} is {1}",
   e.Column.ColumnName, e.Row.GetColumnError(e.Column)));
```

12. Launch the application using the F5 key. Set focus to the Quantity field and type **1111**. When you tab away from the field, a message appears indicating that the value is not in the correct range. Change the Quantity value to 75 and tab away again. Now the dialog box shows that the message is empty.

Lesson Summary

- Most validations can be grouped into two categories—data format validations and business rule validations.
- The category for a particular validation will have an impact on where the code to perform the validation should be placed.
- Business rule validation can be implemented in a normal class (or at least one that represents a business object) or in a strongly typed *DataSet*. There are pros and cons associated with both choices, so the "correct" way will depend on your specific environment.

Lesson Review

You can use the following questions to test your knowledge of the information in Lesson 1, "Validating Data." The questions are also available on the companion CD if you prefer to review them in electronic form.

NOTE Answers

Answers to these questions and explanations of why each answer choice is right or wrong are located in the "Answers" section at the end of the book.

---

1. You have a *TextBox* control that implements the *Validating* event to perform some validation. If the data is not valid, the *Cancel* property on the *CancelEventArgs* parameter is set
   to *True*. The form also has a Help button on the form. After deployment, a user indicates
   that clicking the Help button doesn't work. You determine that the *Click* event on the
   Help button is not processed if invalid data is in the *TextBox*. What is the solution?

   A. Set the *CausesValidation* property on the text box to *False*.

   B. Set the *CausesValidation* property on the text box to *True*.

   C. Set the *CausesValidation* property on the Help button to *False*.

   D. Set the *CausesValidation* property on the Help button to *True*.

2. You need a control that ensures the user's input is a valid postal code. The control needs
   to be aware of different formats for the postal code (such as five digits for the United
   States and six alphanumeric characters for Canada) based on an external list. How
   should you approach the validation problem?

   A. Use a drop-down–style *ComboBox* control.

   B. Use a *TextBox* control with a *Validating* event handler.

   C. Use a *MaskedTextBox* control.

   D. Use a *TextBox* control bound to a *DataSet* that has an event handler defined for the
   ColumnChanging event in the *DataTable*.

3. You want a control that validates the user input against the value of two other text boxes
   on the form. Which approach should you use?

   A. Use a composite control that contains all three *TextBox* controls, including the necessary *Validating* event handlers.

   B. Use *TextBox* controls with *Validating* event handlers.

   C. Use *MaskedTextBox* controls.

   D. Use *TextBox* controls bound to a *DataSet* that has an event handler defined for the
   ColumnChanging event in the *DataTable*.

Lesson 2: Providing Feedback

The issues associated with providing feedback to a user when invalid data is found are many. The starting point should be a philosophical one—how do you want to treat your users? Most developers like to think of their applications as needing to hold their users' hands. However, most applications should endeavor to let users do their jobs as efficiently as possible. And this approach leads to the basic ideas behind an effective user feedback mechanism.

1. Keep users from making mistakes, whenever feasible.
2. Let the user know in an unobtrusive manner when bad data has been entered.
3. Don't allow the user to save until all bad data has been corrected.

By following these three basic rules, you can ensure that users can use your application efficiently while maintaining data integrity. The goal of this lesson is to discuss the techniques that can be used to achieve this end.

After this lesson, you will be able to:

- ■ Itemize the most commonly used feedback techniques in Windows-based .NET applications.
- ■ Decide on the best way to provide feedback for invalid data.
- ■ Ensure that feedback is appropriate for all levels of users, including new users and those who use the accessibility aids.

Estimated lesson time: 30 minutes

Real World

Bruce Johnson

My ancient background comes from the green screen world, when I created applications on UNIX for VT100 terminals. At that time the only options available for catching the user's attention were bold versus dim lettering and reverse video (or, more likely, flashing reverse video). To suggest that these choices were inadequate for providing feedback is like saying that babies are cute—it's pretty obvious to everyone.

Back when I start creating Windows applications (this would be in Visual Basic 3), I was excited about the ability to use more colors than just green. So naturally I went wild, using every color in my palette and then some. But after I was sued for blinding users, I went with a more subdued approach. The judicious use of color can contribute greatly to the design rules outlined above. If you keep the number of colors on the form down to a minimum, the appearance of a bright color (such as red) will naturally attract the user's eyes. And, when you get down to it, attracting the user's attention is the goal of any feedback mechanism.

Available Feedback Options

To start the lesson, let's talk about the feedback options that fit within the initial design rules. This does mean that certain feedback choices will not be covered in detail, mostly because they don't fit within the philosophy. These would be message boxes and modal dialog boxes.

To be fair, there are instances where these feedback devices are absolutely required. Specifically, if the action initiated by the user is about to do something destructive, the application needs to have confirmation. And to get confirmation, message boxes and modal dialog boxes are the best solution. However, to be true to the chapter's title, getting confirmation is not part of the feedback mechanism for data validation. And in the realm of validation, there is no place for a mechanism that causes a user to break out of the flow of data entry.

Status Bar

When talking with developers inexperienced in creating a usable user interface, one of the first suggestions for notification is the status bar. Probably the main reason for its popularity is that it's used in a lot of "real" applications. Microsoft Word uses it to indicate the current page, line, and column. Microsoft Internet Explorer says Done when the page is ... er ... done loading. Since all these commercial-grade applications use it, why shouldn't a home-grown one?

The answer is that the status bar is almost completely useless for providing important information. There is a illustrative story related by a large number of people, including Paul Vick, who at the time of this writing was working with the Visual Basic .NET team at Microsoft. The story goes that, as part of a usability test for Microsoft Access, while the users were occupied on some other task the status bar message was changed to read "If you notice this message and tell the usability lead, we will give you $15." After none of the users claimed the $15 prize, it was decided never to put critical information into the status bar. And since the reason why a field is incorrect would certainly qualify as "critical," the status bar should never be used as the only place to display error messages.

Tool Tips

Another commonly suggested option for user feedback is the tool tip. And there are certainly some reasons why the tool tip is superior to the status bar. First of all, the message is now much closer to where the actual problem lies. Whereas a status bar can feedback on any control, it's immediately apparent which control is associated with a particular tool tip.

There are a couple of reasons, however, why tool tips aren't a good feedback choice. The first is that, in a well-designed application, the tool tip is already being used. For every field there should be a tool tip that contains a brief description of what the data is supposed to be. Replacing that value with an error message means that at the exact moment when it's likely that the user wants some additional information about what the field is (because, after all, there is a problem with it), an error message has replaced the information.

The second issue is one of notification. There is no way to tell by looking at a form which field has an error and which doesn't if the only place where the error message is recorded is the tool tip. Which is a nice segue into the next feedback mechanism.

Color

For many developers adding color is the solution to the problem of letting users know when the data in a field is invalid. A common color scheme is to make required fields yellow and fields that are in error red. In Figure 5-2, the light-colored box represents a yellow field, and the dark-colored box represents red.

Figure 5-2   Using color to indicate invalid data

For many developers this seems like a good solution. As has already been mentioned, color is a great way to automatically attract the attention of users. The problem is that only most users are attracted.

The use of color is not a good choice when the application that you're creating needs to support accessibility. Some people are colorblind, which reduces their ability to discern the different colors used to indicate status. Also, depending on the color, some people with a certain level of visual impairment will not be able to see the black text on the red background seen in Figure 5-2. And if the user is blind, the colors are useless.

ErrorProvider Control

All the feedback mechanisms mentioned so far have one problem or another. The *ErrorProvider* control was designed specifically to provide feedback to the user when invalid input is detected and, as such, avoids all the problems that have been identified.

First, the *ErrorProvider* control is not a control in the manner that's normally thought of. It's an *extender control*, which means that it provides a particular service to other controls. In this case the service is to add an error notification icon to the supported control.

At the most basic level, the *ErrorProvider* control displays an icon, usually flashing, to the right of a control when the *Error* property on the control is set. If you're thinking that the *TextBox* control doesn't have an *ErrorMessage* property, you'd be right. It doesn't ... until the *ErrorProvider* control is added to the form. The *ErrorProvider* control adds a number of properties to each supported control, as can be seen in Table 5-3.

Table 5-3   Properties Added by *ErrorProvider* Control

Property	Description
Error	This is the error message that describes what is invalid about the data currently in the control. If there is no error, this property should be set to an empty string.
IconAlignment	Indicates where the error icon should appear in relation to the control when the *Error* property is not empty.
IconPadding	Used to adjust the distance placed between the control and the error icon.

Turning the error icon on is a simple process. The *SetError* method on the *ErrorProvider* control takes a control and a string as parameters. It sets the *Error* property for the specified control to the string parameter.

' VB
```
errorProvider1.SetError(fullNameTextBox, "The name is required")
```

// C#
```
errorProvider1.SetError(fullNameTextBox, "The name is required");
```

This code (which would normally be placed in the *Validating* event handler for a control) causes the error icon to appear next to the *fullNameTextBox* control. Also, if the user hovers over the error icon, the tool tip for the icon would read "The name is required." So the problem of notifying the user that invalid data has been entered can be addressed without interrupting the flow of user entry. Also, the specifics of the problem can be easily determined through the error icon's tool tip.

Quick Check

- Explain the difference between the feedback offered by the *ErrorProvider* control and the status bar.

Quick Check Answer

- Although in both cases information about the error can be displayed, the *ErrorProvider* control places the notification feedback (the flashing icon) close to the area that is in error, while the status bar information is placed at the bottom of the screen where users won't look for it unless they are forced to.

The use of the *ErrorProvider* control doesn't eliminate some of the issues associated with control-level validation using the *Validating* event. Specifically, the error icon isn't set unless the *Validating* handler is invoked, which means that the control needs to gain focus at some point or the *ValidateChildren* method is invoked on the form. And once the validations have been performed, it is still necessary to ensure that none of the controls have the *Error* property set to a nonempty string. This functionality, unfortunately, isn't built into the standard form. However, the following code implements a mechanism for checking if all of the controls are valid:

```vb
' VB
Function IsContainerValid(ByVal container As Control, _
    ByVal errorProvider As ErrorProvider) As Boolean

    Dim ctl As Control
    Dim Result As Boolean
    For Each ctl In GetAllControls(container)
      If ctl.HasChildren() Then
         Result = IsContainerValid(ctl, errorProvider)
      Else
         Result = String.IsNullOrEmpty(errorProvider.GetError(ctl))
      End If

      If Not Result Then
         Exit For
      End If
    Next

    Return Result
End Function
```

```csharp
// C#
private bool isContainerValid(Control container,
    ErrorProvider errorProvider)
{
    Control ctl;
    bool result = false;
    foreach (Control ctl in GetAllControls(container))
    {
       if (ctl.HasChildren())
          result = IsContainerValid(ctl, errorProvider);
       else
          result =
             String.IsNullOrEmpty(errorProvider.GetError(ctl));

       if (!result)
          continue;
    }

    return result;
}
```

The *ErrorProvider* control also supports one further bit of cool functionality. As mentioned in the first lesson in the chapter, two of the choices for validating data using business rules are to bind controls to a *DataSet* or to a business object. If a control is bound to a *DataSet*, it's possible to have the *ErrorProvider* detect when an error occurs within the *DataSet* and use that information to trigger the display of the error icon, as well as the error message that gets displayed.

To connect an *ErrorProvider* to a *DataSet*, use the *DataSource* and *DataMember* properties. The *DataSource* is set to the *DataSet*, while the *DataMember* is set to the name of the *DataTable*.

Now when the *RowError* gets set, that information is propagated to the *ErrorProvider*, which displays the error icon and sets the *Error* property appropriately.

Connecting an *ErrorProvider* to a business object is a similar process. First, the business object needs to implement the *IDataErrorInfo* interface. If it does, the object can be assigned to the *DataSource* property on the *ErrorProvider* control. For business objects, the *DataMember* property doesn't have any meaning, so it can remain unset. Once the link between business object and *ErrorProvider* is made, the *IDataErrorInfo* and *INotifyPropertyChanged* interfaces work in concert to keep the error icon and *Error* property in sync with the values defined within the business object.

Exam Tip   Although the *ErrorProvider* control has been around for a couple of versions, the ability to integrate with business objects is new to .NET 2.0.

Helpful Feedback

Not every feedback mechanism deals with presenting the information about errors after the fact. In order to help prevent errors, as well as help users correct them, the help system that is built into Windows can be used to great effect. But to understand what needs to be done, let's take a brief look at the standard help features that are available to users.

Tool Tips

Tool tips is a function that every developer of Visual Studio 2005 (if not every Windows user) is familiar with. Hover your mouse over one of the buttons on a tool bar and you get the name of the control. This is a tool tip. Tool tips are used during debugging to display the current value of a variable. And tool tips can be just as useful to end users, assuming that you bother to set them up in your applications.

Tool tips are enabled through the *ToolTip* control. This is a provider control similar to the *ErrorProvider* control described in the last section. As a control, it has nothing that is visible to the user at run time. Instead, it adds a *ToolTip* property to the controls on a form at design time. Before execution, the property can be set through the property sheet. Or at run time the *SetToolTip* method on the *ToolTip* control can be used.

From a design perspective there is no reason not to use tool tips. They are simple to implement and, for any application that claims to be commercial quality, users will expect them. However, you should pay attention to the information that gets placed into the tool tip. Long tool tips are not welcome, and the caption should be descriptive of what the control contains in words the user will understand. In general, there is not enough room to describe what valid data might look like. This isn't always the case, but it's true most of the time.

For non-entry fields (like a picture box), the tool tip can be used to provide some status information so the user can get quick details without having to perform another action. Think about how useful it is to hover over a variable in Visual Studio 2005 debug mode and see the current value, even though seeing the value in a Quick View was never more than a keystroke away. Put that sort of thought into how you can use tool tips in your own application and you will go a long way toward making your users happy.

Context-Sensitive Help

Configuring the help that is available to your application is a little more complicated than setting up tool tips. The starting point is the *HelpProvider* control. It sounds like a broken record by this point, but the *HelpProvider* is yet one more example of a extender control. It adds a number of properties to controls on the form that can be used to provide help in a number of different ways.

The *HelpString* is the easiest property to use. This string property contains the value that is displayed when the F1 key is hit on a particular field. If you think of this functionality as an advanced tool tip, you're pretty close to understanding it. When the F1 key is used, the value of the *HelpString* is displayed as a Help tool tip for the field.

The second way to get *context-sensitive help* is to use the *HelpNamespace* and *HelpKeyword* properties in conjunction. The *HelpNamespace* property is set to the file that contains the source for the help information. The *HelpKeyword* property is set to the keyword within the help file that is associated with a particular control. Now when the F1 key is used, the help topic represented by the keyword is displayed as the Help tool tip. If no *HelpKeyword* is specified, then the entire help file is shown when the F1 key is used.

At the form level a *HelpButton* property is available. If it's set to *True*, a Help button appears at the top left of the form, near the minimize/maximize/close buttons. When the Help button is clicked, the cursor turns into an arrow with a question mark (by default). Then when a field is clicked, the context-sensitive help is displayed. Or, an event handler for the *HelpRequested* event can be defined on the form. This allows the developer to customize the handling of the help request as needed.

Accessibility

For many developers, accessibility is a bit of an afterthought to the coding process. It is frequently added after all the other work has been done. Fortunately, adding most of the information needed for accessibility can be easily done at the end of the project. However, a couple of twists, especially in the area of validation feedback, need to be considered.

At a basic level, all controls have three properties that control most of the accessibility features that are required. The list of properties can be found in Table 5-4.

Table 5-4   Accessibility Properties

Property Name	Description
AccessibleDescription	The long-form description of the control as it will be reported to the accessibility aids
AccessibleName	The name of the control as it will be reported to the accessibility aids
AccessibleRole	The role the control plays within the application

Notice that two of the three descriptions in Table 5-4 include the term *accessibility aid*. Packaged with Windows are a number of applications that allow accessibility features from a properly implemented Windows application to be accessed. The applications include the following:

- **Magnifier**   Used to magnify a portion of the screen
- **Narrator**   Reads on-screen text and descriptions and describes how to interact with the control
- **OnScreen Keyboard**   Displays a keyboard that can be controlled using a mouse

There is also an Accessibility Wizard that will optimize the Windows settings to meet common hearing, visual, and mobility needs. Thus the combination of defining the accessibility properties for each control, along with the availability of the accessibility aids (and third-party applications as well) go a long way toward creating accessible applications.

But other conventions should be followed to maximize the availability of a Windows application. Specifically, the following points are among the characteristics required for an application to receive the Certified for Windows logo.

- Provide support for the size, color, font, and input settings as defined within the Control Panel. As the user changes the settings in the control panels, visual elements on the form (menu bar, title, bar, borders, and status bar) will adjust their size to match the settings.
- Provide support for High Contrast mode.
- Provide keyboard access (and document it) to all features.
- Ensure that the location of the keyboard focus is available both visually and programmatically.
- Whenever possible (and it should be possible in most cases), don't use sound to convey important information.

To help meet these requirements, some conventions should be applied to other properties in a Windows-based application.

- Ensure that the *TabIndex* on the form is set properly. Specifically, make sure that the controls that don't have a built-in label (for example, *TextBox*, *ComboBox*) have their associated label immediately before the control in the tab order.

- Use the ampersand (&) in the *Text* property to define keyboard accessors.
- Unless the Font Size can be changed within the application, make sure that the smallest font used is 10 pt.
- Make sure that the *Foreground* and *Background* on controls is set to the default. This allows the control panel settings to modify the color scheme used by the application.
- Don't use a background image on the form because doing so can affect the visibility of the contents on the form.

MORE INFO   Accessibility implementation details

For details on how to implement these suggestions, see Chapter 5, "User Interface Fundamentals of the Application Specification for Microsoft Windows 2000 for Desktop Applications" at *http:// msdn.microsoft.com/library/default.asp?url=/library/en-us/dnw2kcli/html/W2Kcli_chapter5.asp*.

Accessibility and Validation Feedback

Although the *ErrorProvider* control described earlier in this chapter provides a good mechanism for sending information about the validity of data to the user, it's not an accessible solution. In order to see the error message, the mouse must be used to hover over the error icon. The lack of keyboard access to the error message violates one of the principles of accessibility.

The trick to creating a validation feedback mechanism that supports accessibility is to focus on two areas. First, it needs to be usable through the keyboard. This means that a keystroke or two should cause error information to be displayed. Second, the mechanism needs to display the validation messages in a form that the Narrator can process, so that visually impaired users are supported.

Although there are a number of solutions, one of the most complete ones (in terms of satisfying accessibility requirements) is to add a Validation Summary text box on each form. By default, the text box is invisible but can be made visible through a Show Validation Summary menu option. That menu option is made accessible using a keyboard accessor. As for populating the text box with information, the contents can be created by looping through the controls on the form and building a large text string containing the control that contains invalid data and the corresponding error message.

The final challenge is to detect when the contents need to be updated. The simple solution is to update it every time focus is set to the text box. A more complicated approach is to create an event handler for the *PropertyChanged* event that is exposed by the data source. Then, when a property has been changed, the contents can be rebuilt or, using an even more responsive technique, detect if the changed property has had an error added or removed.

Lab: Giving Feedback to the User

There are three exercises in this lab, concentrating on the three areas of user feedback covered in the lesson. To start with, the use of the *ErrorProvider* control as a means to indicate invalid data is demonstrated. Next, the use of tool tips and a help string to give users more details of the expected range of data is covered. Finally, there is a walk-through of a couple of accessibility features.

▶ **Exercise 1: Using the *ErrorProvider* Control**

The starting point for this exercise is the end of Exercise 3 from the previous lesson. The controls on a form have been bound to a *DataTable*. The validation code for the data is placed in the *ColumnChanging* event handler. What this exercise adds is the *ErrorProvider* to display any issues to the user rather than popping up a message dialog box.

1. Launch Visual Studio 2005.

    Open a solution using File | Open | Project/Solution.

    Navigate to the Chapter5/Lesson2/<language>/Exercise1-Before directory. Select the Exercise1 solution and click Open.

    In the Solution Explorer, right-click the Form1 file and select the View Code menu option. Locate the *validateProductData* method and delete the last line of code, the call to the *MessageBox.Show* method.

    Right-click in the code window and select the View Designer menu option.

    From the Toolbox, drag the *ErrorProvider* control onto the form's surface. You can find the *ErrorProvider* in the Components section of the Toolbox. And when dropped, the provider does not appear on the form but in the bottom portion of the designer.

2. Select the errorProvider1 control in the designer and open the Property Sheet.

3. For the *DataSource* property, click the drop-down button and select productBinding-Source.

4. Launch the application using the F5 key. Click the Quantity field and type **1111**. Then tab away from the field. Notice that the error provider icon is flashing. If you hover your mouse over the icon, you will see the error message.

5. Click the Quantity field again and change the value to **75**. Now when you tab away from the field, the error icon disappears.

▶ **Exercise 2: Providing Helpful Information**

In this exercise we continue from the end of the last exercise. We will be adding support for tool tips, as well as a help message for the Quantity field.

1. Launch Visual Studio 2005.

2. Open a solution using File | Open | Project/Solution.

3. Navigate to the Chapter5/Lesson2/<language>/Exercise2-Before directory. Select the Exercise2 solution and click Open.

4. In the Solution Explorer, double-click the Form1 file to display the form's designer.

5. From the Toolbox, drag the *ToopTip* control onto the form. When it has been dropped, the *ToolTip* control does not appear on the form but in the bottom portion of the designer.

6. Click the productNoTextBox and open the Property Sheet. Set the ToolTip on toolTip1 property to **The product number that is being entered**.

7. In the form designer, click the quantityTextBox control. Then back in the Property Sheet, set the ToolTip on toolTip1 property to **The quantity that is being entered**.

8. In the form designer, drag the HelpProvider control onto the form. Like the ErrorProvider control, you can find HelpProvider in the Components section in the Toolbox.

9. Click the quantityTextBox control and open the Property Sheet. Set the HelpString on helpProvider1 property to **The quantity being entered must be between 0 and 100 inclusive**.

10. Launch the application using the F5 key. Hover your mouse over the Product No and Quantity text boxes. Notice that the tool tip appears.

11. Click the Quantity text box and press the F1 key for context-sensitive help. Notice that a tool tip–like box appears containing the help string.

▶ **Exercise 3: Providing More Helpful Information**

In this exercise two of the accessibility aids will be demonstrated—the Magnifier and the Narrator. Some properties on the forms developed in Exercise 2 and earlier will be modified to support these functions.

1. Launch Visual Studio 2005.

2. Open a solution using File | Open | Project/Solution.

3. Navigate to the Chapter5/Lesson2/<language>/Exercise3-Before directory. Select the Exercise3 solution and click Open.

4. In the Solution Explorer, double-click the Form1 file to display the form's designer.

5. Click the productNoTextBox control and open the Property Sheet. Set the *Accessible-Name* property to **Product Number**. Set the *AccessibleDescription* property to **The number of the product being entered**.

6. In the form designer, click the quantityTextBox control and open the Property Sheet. Set the *AccessibleName* to **Quantity**. Set the *AccessibleDescription* to **The quantity for the product being entered**.

7. Launch the application using the F5 key.

8. Start the Magnifier application using Start | All Programs | Accessories | Accessibility | Magnifier.

9. Once Magnifier is running, an expanded view of where the mouse cursor is appears at the top of the screen. By default, the magnified area follows the mouse cursor, but that is configurable by the user. Bring the Magnifier screen to the top and click the Exit button.

10. Start the Narrator application using Start | All Programs | Accessories | Accessibility | Narrator.

11. If your machine has a speaker, make sure that it's turned on and the volume is turned up. If necessary, select the Announce Events On Screen check box.

12. Start to cursor around the application. Notice that when a tool tip appears, the narrator converts the text to speech. Also, when invalid data is entered, the narrator says so and, when hovering over the icon, describes the error.

Lesson Summary

- It is important to provide feedback to the user in a manner that is not obtrusive (that is, not a message box). The feedback should let users discover the problems with the input when they want to, not when the application wants to.

- The basic help functionality (tool tips and help messages) are easy to implement and should be a part of any Windows-based application.

- A lot of accessibility features are included with Windows and Visual Studio 2005. They are easy to implement, but it's important to test the results.

Lesson Review

You can use the following questions to test your knowledge of the information in Lesson 2, "Providing Feedback." The questions are also available on the companion CD if you prefer to review them in electronic form.

NOTE Answers

Answers to these questions and explanations of why each answer choice is right or wrong are located in the "Answers" section at the end of the book.

---

1. You are developing an application that is going to delete a record. You would like to let the user know that the deletions are permanent. What user feedback mechanism should you use?

    A. Status bar

    B. Message box

    C. Change the color of the form's background to yellow

    D. Display a warning icon using the *ErrorProvider* control

2. You are developing an application that is going to perform a long-running action in the background. You would like to let the user know the progress of the action. What user feedback mechanism should you use?

    A. Status bar.

    B. Display a nonmodal dialog box containing a progress bar.

    C. Change the color of the form's background to progressively brighter shades of yellow.

    D. Display a modal dialog box containing a progress bar.

3. You would like to provide the user with hints on the sort of content that is expected to go into a *TextBox* control. Which mechanism should you use?

    A. Narrator

    B. Magnifier

    C. Context-sensitive help

    D. Tool tips

Chapter Review

To further practice and reinforce the skills you learned in this chapter, you can perform the following tasks:

- Review the chapter summary.
- Review the list of key terms introduced in this chapter.
- Complete the case scenarios. These scenarios set up real-world situations involving the topics of this chapter and ask you to create a solution.
- Complete the suggested practices.
- Take a practice test.

Chapter Summary

- The goal of user validation is to ensure that valid data is entered while minimizing the impact of invalid data on the user experience.
- The less generic the validation gets, the more likely validation rules are to be implemented in a business rule.
- The feedback mechanism has the greatest impact on the user's experience with an application. Selecting the appropriate feedback mechanism is going to be based on the needs of the application combined with the desire for users not to be bothered.
- For applications that are widely distributed, care needs to be take to ensure that the design choices allow the accessibility features to be activated.

Key Terms

Do you know what these key terms mean? You can check your answers by looking up the terms in the glossary at the end of the book.

- accessibility aid
- business rule validation
- context-sensitive help
- data-format validation
- Data Transfer Object
- extender class

Case Scenarios

In the following case scenarios, you will apply what you've learned about delivering multimedia in a distributed environment. You can find answers to these questions in the "Answers" section at the end of the book.

Case Scenario 1: Choosing the Validation Mechanism

You are a corporate developer creating a Windows forms application that is used to enter contact information. This includes the contact's first and last name, the phone number, and e-mail address. You need to define the validations that will be performed on these fields.

Your challenge is to decide which validations will be performed on the fields.

Questions

Answer the following questions for your manager:

1. How should the first and last names of the contact be validated?
2. How should the phone number of the contact be validated?
3. How should the e-mail address of the contact be validated?

Case Scenario 2: Choosing the Feedback Mechanism

You are a corporate developer creating a Windows Forms application that is used to enter contact information. There are a number of places within the functionality of the application where different types of feedback are required. Your challenge is to decide which feedback mechanism is most appropriate.

Questions

Answer the following questions for your manager:

1. How should hints about the valid contents of a control be provided?
2. How should hints about the valid contents of a control be provided when the hint is longer than a line of text?
3. How should messages describing invalid input be displayed?

Suggested Practices

To help you successfully master the objectives presented in this chapter, complete the following tasks.

Validate Data

For this task, you should complete both practices.

- ■ **Practice 1**   Take a form from an application that has already been developed. Create a duplicate form that uses *DataSets* to provide the data. Define the *ColumnChanging* event handler to provide the appropriate validation.

- ■ **Practice 2**   Take a form from an application that has already been developed. Create a duplicate form that uses a business object to provide the data. Ensure that the business class implements the *INotifyPropertyChanged* and *IDataErrorInfo* events. Demonstrate how to display a message box when a changed property creates an error condition.

Providing Feedback

For this task, you should complete both practices.

- ■ **Practice 1**   Take a form from an application that has already been developed. Add an *ErrorProvider* control to the form. Integrate the display of the error icon with the validation of the controls on the form, whether performed on the form or in the business layer.

- ■ **Practice 2**   Take a form from an application that has already been developed. Add the necessary information to the accessibility properties. Evaluate the application's status and validation feedback mechanisms for suitability in an accessible application. Test the form using the Magnifier and Narrator accessibility aids to ensure that it works reasonably well.

Take a Practice Test

The practice tests on this book's companion CD offer many options. For example, you can test yourself on just one exam objective or you can test yourself on all the 70-548 certification exam content. You can set up the test so that it closely simulates the experience of taking a certification exam, or you can set it up in study mode so that you can look at the correct answers and explanations after you answer each question.

MORE INFO   **Practice tests**

For details about all the practice test options available, see the "How to Use the Practice Tests" section in this book's Introduction.

Chapter 6
Component Design

As your Microsoft Windows-based project is developed, you will be charged with designing individual pieces of the larger system. In particular, components will be required to perform specific tasks. Creating that design correctly is crucial to the success of any project.

Exam objectives in this chapter:

- Evaluate the design of a database.
    - Recommend a database schema.
    - Identify the stored procedures that are required for an application.
- Establish the required characteristics of a component.
    - Decide when to create a single component or multiple components.
    - Decide in which tier of the application a component should be located.
    - Decide which type of object to build.
- Create the high-level design of a component.
    - Establish the life cycle of a component.
    - Decide whether to use established design patterns for the component.
    - Decide whether to create a prototype for the component.
    - Document the design of a component by using pseudo code, class diagrams, sequence diagrams, activity diagrams, and state diagrams.
    - Evaluate tradeoff decisions. Considerations include security versus performance, performance versus maintainability, and so on.
- Develop the public API of a component.
    - Decide the types of clients that can consume a component.
    - Establish the required component interfaces.
    - Decide whether to require constructor input.

> **Real World**
>
> *Shawn Wildermuth*
>
> Designing components is one of the most important tasks of any professional developer. The key to any design is experience. You can't learn design from this or any book. It's a matter of designing components, reviewing them with other people, and finding out what mistakes you make ... rinse and repeat. The most important part of that process is that you review the design with *other people*. Software development is a collaborative process.

Lessons in this chapter:

Before You Begin

To complete the lessons in this chapter, you should be familiar with VB or C# and be comfortable with the following tasks:

- Using Visio to create Unified Modeling Language (UML) diagrams.
- Using Visual Studio 2005 to create class diagrams.

Lesson 1: Database Design

Before you can get data to the user, you will need a good design for storing your data. Storing your data in a database requires that you define the schema for that data. By building on the Object Role Model (ORM) discussed in Chapter 2, "Decompose Specifications for Developers," you will build a database schema in which to store that data.

After this lesson, you will be able to:
- Define data requirements from Object Role Model (ORM).
- Recommend a data schema.
- Identify correct use of stored procedures.

Estimated lesson time: 40 minutes

Database Design Basics

Designing databases is easy to do, but difficult to do well. The difficulty in designing databases lies in the apparent simplicity in slapping together tables in a database designer. The problems of bad database design are more obvious in the longer term. Databases are rarely seen as problematic when they are initially created. They exhibit problems like poor performance, lack of data consistency, and difficulty evolving the data model the longer they are in use.

In order to create a good database design, you should design the database to be normalized to at least the third normal form (3NF). The third normal form simply states that the data has adhered to a level of consistency and was designed according to the principles detailed in Table 6-1.

Table 6-1 Database Design Principles

Name	Description
Atomicity	Each entity in a database should be indivisible. An entity in a database should consist of a single logical entity.
PK Dependence	Every entity should have a primary key. For cases where the primary key is a single column, this is not a problem. For multiple-part keys, the entire key should relate to the entire entity.
Attribute Independence	Every attribute should be part of the entity and only the entity. This means that every attribute for an entity should belong to a single entity and only that entity.

In general, normalizing your database design simply ensures that each of the entities in the database will be independent of one another. These design principles are meant to ensure that your database design can mature and adapt to different requirements over time as well as ensure that the data in your database is as clean and consistent as possible.

MORE INFO   Normalization

Examining normalization in detail is outside the scope of this lesson. For more information on database design and normalization schemes please see the following texts:

The Art of SQL, Stephane Faroult (with Peter Robson), O'Reilly Media, 2006.

"Database Normalization in Wikipedia," *http://en.wikipedia.org/wiki/Database_normalization.*

Data Entities

In Chapter 2, you reviewed the requirements to determine what objects are required for your Windows-based project. As part of this review, you created an Object Role Model (ORM) to determine what sorts of entities the system needed. Now we need to examine the ORM to determine what data entities you need to store in the database.

Data entities define containers for data that we need to store in the database. Typically, a data entity is represented in the database as a single table, although there are exceptions where a single entity is better represented by multiple tables.

For example, the model shown in Figure 6-1 describes a simple project that will manage customers, salespeople, and orders.

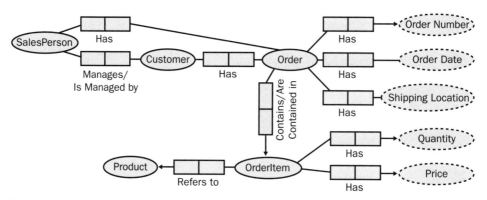

Figure 6-1   Example Object Role Model.

By reviewing this model, we can confidently take each of the defined entities and create a simple database design, as shown in an entity relationship diagram in Figure 6-2. Note that we have not yet designed the relationships, so the tables are not currently connected.

SalesPerson	Customer	Order	OrderItem	Product

Figure 6-2   Initial database design.

In this first pass of the database design, it is important to focus on the entities to be stored. You will have time to delve into the attributes of each entity as you complete the database design.

Figure 6-2 is a good first attempt at a database design, but do not accept the ORM diagrams as the final arbiter of what the database ultimately needs to look like. For example, if you look at Figure 6-1 you will see that it defines a shipping location for an order. It's obvious to me that we need a shipping location for an order, but, taking the long-term view of the design, I have to ask myself whether other types of locations will be required as the product matures. In other words, should we normalize locations throughout the database schema into a single table?

For example, will the customer have a location (that is, the company address for billing)? In addition, I could envision that the salesperson might have to have a location associated with a particular office the salesperson is working on. We could certainly embed this information in the *Customer* and *SalesPerson* entities, but wouldn't it be better to abstract the idea of a location and store all locations as a single entity in our system? On the other hand, it might be simpler to just embed this information into each of our entities because the retrieval of the entities will be faster and it will typically be easier to write queries.

So how do you decide how much normalization is the right amount? Normalizing all of your entities to at least the third normal form is almost always the right approach. But be aware that breaking out every type of common data and creating a new entity will invariably cause problems in your database. There is a middle ground between overuse and underuse of reusable entities.

Real World

Shawn Wildermuth

I have seen both sides of the data normalization problem. In some projects I have seen, no formal normalization has occurred and the tables were created without the benefit of keys or segmentation of data. On the other hand, I have actually seen overzealous use of abstracting in database designs. One of the more famous examples of this appeared on The Daily WTF Web site (*http://thedailywtf.com/forums/thread/75982.aspx*), where the database was designed to abstract out the notion of a date in the system into a single entity. Because of this, every table in the system had a foreign key constraint to this table. Writing even the most basic of queries was a nightmare.

In this case the right answer is to abstract out the location, because that is a sizable entity that will likely appear in different places throughout the schema. Making this change in the schema will likely also necessitate a change in the ORM diagram. Figure 6-3 shows an updated ORM diagram based on the abstraction of the location entity.

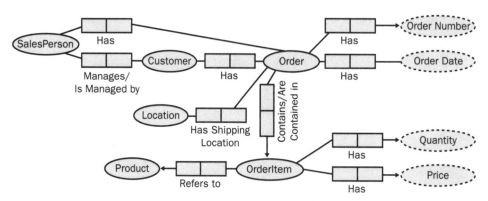

Figure 6-3   Updated Object Role Model.

Note that we changed the *ShippingLocation* attribute to a *Location* entity. The new diagram does not define locations for customers and salespeople because no requirement dictates that. If a new requirement for locations for either of those entities surfaces, our database design will make that change simple, but we should not include relationships in our database design for requirements that do not exist. In Figure 6-4 we can see the addition of this new *Location* entity.

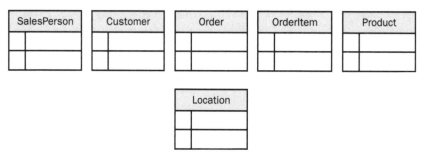

Figure 6-4   Updated database design.

Now that we have identified our database entities, we need to determine how to identify each of the entities.

Primary Keys

Once you have defined your entities to be stored in the database, the next step is to define how you want to uniquely identify entities within each database table. Inside the database this is referred to as a primary key. Every table in your database design needs to have a primary key defined. Being able to distinguish a specific row within a table inside the database is crucial to practically all database operations. Therefore it is critically important that you define a primary key for every table.

Although there are several rules of thought to entity identity, it is important to create an identity that is not only unique for each row in a table but also will not change over time. For example, it might be tempting to have a salesperson number that you use for the primary key. This is fine, except that if this salesperson number is visible to users within the resulting system, inevitably there will be a need to change that numbering system. The numbering system could need to change when data is added to a warehouse or data-mart or when merging two disparate systems. Therefore, I recommend that you always use a primary key that is not exposed to users directly. In the case of a salesperson number, I would store that as an attribute in the database table but make the primary key a different, machine-generated number. For example, if we take the earlier table layout for our entities and add primary keys, they would look like Figure 6-5.

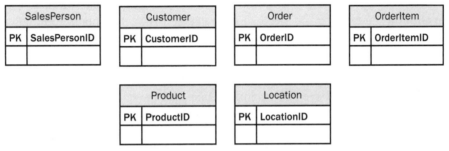

Figure 6-5 Database design with primary keys.

In this example I have used a simple integer to specify a special number associated with each of our entities to specify their primary key. In general, using numbers is preferable to other types of primary keys to reduce index fragmentation. Depending on your specific need, you can choose nonnumeric primary keys as long as you understand that performance and maintenance issues might result.

Quick Check

- Should you always use the same types of primary keys for different entities?

Quick Check Answer

- Although there are exceptions to this rule, in general you should always use the same kinds of primary keys for different entities. If you use an autoincrementing number for the primary key of your customer's table, you should also use an autoincrementing number for the other entities in the data model.

In order to create identifiers for each entity in your database design, take the following steps:

1. Start with any entity in the ORM diagram.

2. Create a new column (or more than one column if you determine you need a multipart key) in the database design for that entity to hold the identifier for that entity.

3. Ensure that the identifier is both marked required and is part of the primary key for that table.

4. Move onto the next entity in the ORM diagram and return to step 2 for that new entity.

Data Warehousing and Primary Keys

One consideration to make when defining your primary keys is how your data will be used in large systems. In the case of data warehousing it might be useful to create truly unique keys. For example, let's assume you were creating an e-commerce application where you expected to deploy separate databases for each customer who bought your e-commerce application. If you had a particularly big customer who bought several instances of your application, the customer might find the need to merge or warehouse data in each of these instances. If you use a simple numeric primary key, multiple databases will have the same key value that points at different logical entities.

In those cases you have two options: remapping primary keys or using universally unique keys. Remapping primary keys is the process of reassigning keys as you merge databases. This can be labor-intensive and processor-intensive, but it's often the right decision because of the few instances where this occurs or if the performance of the original system is more important than the processing time during merge. Alternatively, you can use universally unique keys (for example, globally unique identifier [GUID] or other uniqueness). The problem with using universally unique keys is that they generally perform worse than simple unique keys.

The rule of thumb is to remap primary keys by default and use universally unique keys only when you know that merging or data warehousing of data across databases is likely to occur.

A special type of entity deserves special attention: a mapping entity. A mapping entity is used to create a many-to-many relationship in some schema designs. More often than not you can define the primary key for these entities to be a multipart key made up of the primary keys of each of the entities. For example, let's assume that we need a vendor table in our design to know whom to buy our products from. But since we might buy products from more than one vendor, we need a way to "map" vendors to products. Our resulting table will look like Figure 6-6.

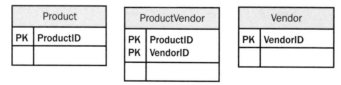

Figure 6-6   Mapping entity example.

Once we have settled on our identity fields we can move on to determining how the different entities are related.

Entity Relationships

When defining your database schema, it is important to define those relationships between entities so that the database can ensure that the data stored in the database is consistent and integral. To identify these relationships, you will go back to the ORM diagram for the first indication of what relationships are required. If you look back at Figure 6-3, you will see that specific entities have relationships to other entities. For example, the *Salesperson* entity shows two relationships: the *Customer* entity and the *Order* entity.

Using the ORM diagram as your guide to determining these relationships is a good first step. But be careful not to treat the ORM diagrams as a final arbiter. There might be relationships in the diagram that are either implied in the ORM diagram and not obvious—or simply missing.

The ORM diagram is also where you will determine parentage of a relationship. In general, one of the entities needs to be the parent of the relationship. You can determine this by looking at the description of the relationship in the ORM diagram. For example, because a Salesperson manages Customers in the ORM diagram, we can assume that the Salesperson is the parent in the relationship. When one entity is the parent in a relationship, that means that the child will need to store the key of the parent. To extend the parent-child example, we would need to add an attribute to the *Customer* entity to hold on to the Salesperson identifier so that we can determine which Salesperson is the parent of this particular Customer.

Relationships are defined in database schema as foreign-key constraints. The term foreign-key constraint indicates that a column in a table uses a key that was defined elsewhere (that is, is foreign). Therefore, to create a relationship in the schema you need two things: a new attribute (or more for multipart keys) in a table and a foreign-key constraint to ensure the integrity of the relationship. For example, if we create the relationship between the Salesperson and the Customer as we discussed in the previous paragraph, we will need not only to add a SalespersonID column to the Customer table but also to create a foreign key to make sure that only Salespersons currently in the Salesperson table can be used as a Customer's Salesperson. Figure 6-7 shows the foreign key and new attribute.

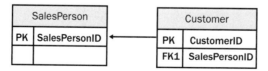

Figure 6-7   Foreign key and new attribute.

To identify all the entity relationships, take the following steps:

1. Start with any entity in the ORM diagram.

2. Look for relationships from that entity to another entity. You can ignore relationships to attributes at this point.

3. Determine from the type of relationship (for example, unary, binary, ternary, and so on) and the description of the relationship who the owner of the relationship is.

4. Create attributes in the child of the relationship to hold the key of the relationship parent.

5. Create a foreign-key constraint from the child table to the parent table on the new attribute(s) in the child table.

6. If you have more relationships in the ORM to review, pick a relationship and go back to step 3 for that new relationship.

Using these steps, we can add the relationships to our schema to come up with the schema seen in Figure 6-8.

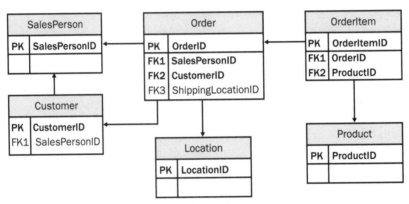

Figure 6-8   Database design with relationships.

Typically, when you create relationships you will also need to determine how you want to propagate changes down a relationship. For example, if an Order is deleted, should all of OrderItems associated with that Order also be deleted? In most cases the answer is yes because we think of an Order and its OrderItems as a logical unit. But on the other hand, if an OrderItem is deleted, should the Product that was in the OrderItem also be deleted?

When you create a foreign key, you have the opportunity to specify how to propagate that change. Foreign keys allow you to specify a referential action on both the delete and the update of the parent entity. For example, you could specify that when an Order is deleted the child is also deleted. But you could specify that, if the primary key of a Product was changed, the change would propagate down to the OrderItem. In most database engines, the referential actions that are detailed in Table 6-2 are supported for both deletes and updates.

Table 6-2   Referential Actions

Name	Description
No action	Nothing changes in the child.
Cascade	Changes are propagated to the child. For deletions that means the child is also deleted. For updates the change is propagated to the child.
Set NULL	When the parent changes or is deleted, the child's foreign key is set to *NULL*.
Set Default	When the parent changes or is deleted, the child's foreign key is replaced with the column's default value.

Now that we have entities, identifiers, and relationships created, all that is left to do is add the rest of the attributes to our entities.

Entity Attributes

Ultimately the goal for defining the database data is usually to store data. Once you have your entities and their keys defined, you can go through the process of determining what data is required for the particular project. The ORM diagrams can indicate data that is required for each entity but will likely not include every piece of information you will need.

In our ORM diagram (Figure 6-3) several entities actually have attributes associated with them. The *Order* entity has *Order Number* and *Order Date* attributes. In addition, other entities do not have any nonrelationship attributes defined. For example, the *Salesperson* entity has relationships only to *Order* and *Customer* entities. This ORM diagram is indicative of a common problem in ORM diagrams: lack of complete detail on entity attributes. Your role is to take these entities and determine the real data requirements for each entity.

The task of gathering attribute information about your entities is a fact-finding mission. It is part common sense and part detective work. It's your job to determine what attributes belong, but it's also important not to attempt to add every piece of data you think you might need one day.

To outline the task of gathering this attribute information, let's look at the *Order* entity. Currently the ORM diagram dictates that we have an *Order Number* and an *Order Date*. In addition, we have *Shipping Location*, *Salesperson*, and *Customer*. Although these are foreign keys, they are also attributes. It is likely that an order is a common e-commerce application that will need more attributes about an order. Using common sense, you could assume that there will be a need for some more information about an order. For example, we are going to want to store information about when an order was filled, when it shipped, and perhaps even a tracking number. We could also talk with the people responsible for fulfilling, shipping, and paying orders to see what other information they're going to need. After discussing it with them, you might find that you need to store payment information as part of an order as well. This process not only might determine what attributes are necessary but also might highlight new entities.

You might find that after discussing orders with the accounting people, you will want to store payment information as a separate entity entirely.

When defining attributes, you must also determine whether you should support the notion of *null* for each attribute. Using *null* in the database indicates that there is no value for a particular attribute. In general, supporting *null* is a recommended practice because it will lessen your database storage requirements and make indexing more efficient.

In addition to specifying the attributes for each entity, we must also determine what kind of data a particular attribute can store. Depending on the particular database engine you are using, you will want to make informed decisions about how to store each type of data within the database. You need four main types of data in order to determine how to store in your specific schema: strings, numeric values, date/time values, and Boolean values.

Strings

There are usually three decisions here: whether to use fixed length strings, what length to allow, and whether to use Unicode versions. Each of these decisions has implications for the database design.

Fixed length strings indicate how the database server will be storing the strings. If you use fixed length strings (for example, *CHAR* or *NCHAR*), the size of the fixed length string will be taken up regardless of how big the actual string is. So if you have a *CHAR(10)* but store "Hi" in it, it will still be taking ten characters of memory in the database. Variable length strings store only the actual string length in them. In that case, a *VARCHAR(10)* with "Hi" stored in it takes only the memory of two characters instead of ten. In general, if your data is fixed length (for example, a two-character status field), use fixed length strings. If your data will vary (for example, an address), use variable length.

There are different approaches to determining the right length for strings in the database. It is almost always the wrong approach to just make all the strings as long as possible. Limitations to the size of a row (which is different for different database engines) will likely not allow you to just make all strings huge. Discussing the requirements with the invested parties will almost always yield the right decision about string length. When you think about string sizes, consider strings in a database to be no longer than 250 or so characters in length. Anything longer should go into a special type of string that can store huge strings. These are referred to as large object blocks. In SQL Server 2005 you would refer to this large string data type as *VARCHAR(MAX)* or *NVARCHAR(MAX)*. Other databases might refer to these large strings as *CLOB* (Character Large OBject) or *Memo* fields. These special types of strings are not stored at the row level so they can store huge strings (some up to several GB in size). They are a good solution for large, unbounded fields.

You also must determine whether to use Unicode strings in your database. Since Unicode strings can store extended character sets to deal with globalized data, it is almost always the right decision to use Unicode strings by default. Unicode strings take two bytes per character, so choosing all Unicode strings will make all your strings take twice as much memory as non-Unicode strings. The only reason not to use Unicode strings is when you run into row size issues. For example, a row in SQL Server 2005 can be only 8000 bytes in size. If you start to run into row size issues, moving back to non-Unicode strings is an option.

Numbers

Storing numeric values in the database is more basic. The decision you have to make is what kind of numbers you need to store. For whole numbers only, using an integer-based number is an obvious choice. But when storing numbers like money values, percentages, or large scientific numeric values, you will need to carefully consider the types of data you want to store.

In our schema we need to store several types of number. In the *OrderItem* entity we will need quantity and price attributes. Because we don't know what kind of sales items our product needs, using a floating point value for the quantity makes more sense. This allows for non-whole numbers. For example, we could sell items per pound. Also, in *OrderItem* we need to store a price. Some databases have a data type called *Money* to specify that we are dealing with a monetary number. If you do not have a *Money* data type, you can specify either a floating point number or more likely a fixed point number (for example, NUMERIC(10,2) to mean a 10-digit number with two decimal places).

Date and Time Values

In general, if you need dates or time values, or both, most database engines have specific data types associated with dates and times. Usually there is a data type called *DATETIME* that will store both a date and a time. You will need to be aware that if you store just dates or just times in a *DATETIME* value you will need to manually ignore the other part of that value.

Boolean Values

Storing Boolean (that is, True/False) values directly in your schema is a common approach. Since standard SQL does not support Boolean values, some databases do not have specific Boolean data types. For example, SQL Server does not have a Boolean data type but instead has a bit data type that's essentially the same. But a bit is not a true/false indicator; instead it's a numeric value that can store only zero or one (though it can be null, as well). Generally, zero indicates false and one indicates true. If your database engine does not support Boolean as a data type, you should use a small numeric data type (*BIT*, *BYTE*, and so on) to indicate the true or false data you require.

You will often find that you do not actually need to store Boolean values in the database if other data implies it. For example, in the *Order* entity we could have a Boolean value for *Has-Shipped* as well as a *ShippedDate*. But the existence of the *ShippedDate* indicates that an order shipped just as easily as having a second field that could get out of sync with the *ShippedDate* field. In those cases do not create the Boolean attribute if other data in the entity can discern it.

Putting It Together

With this newly gathered information, we can fill in the attributes and new entities into our database design. Our new schema might look something like Figure 6-9.

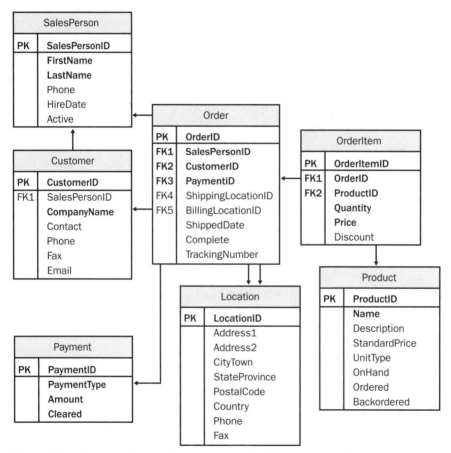

Figure 6-9   Database design with attributes added (required attributes are marked as bold).

Recommend a Data Schema

Now that we have defined all our attributes, a couple of tasks are still left before we can recommend our schema for use in a project. These tasks include defining secondary indexes, adding data constraints, and determining an effective concurrency management strategy.

Secondary Indexing

Secondary indexing is simply the task of determining other indexes to add to a database to make queries more efficient. It is called secondary indexing because when you defined the identifiers earlier in this chapter, every table in your schema got a primary key index to make searching by primary key very efficient. There is a cost for indexing in that as new values are added to your tables, the indexes must be updated with any new values that must be indexed. With this in mind, you will want to create as few indexes per table as possible but add indexes judiciously where necessary.

You are probably responsible for making sure that indexing is efficient when you recommend a data schema. That doesn't mean that you can't elicit advice. If your company employs database administrators, you should use them to help you make smart indexing decisions.

When you want to determine what secondary indexes you need, you will want to look at what types of data in the schema are likely to cause searches that do not use the primary key. For example, you might choose to add an index on the Order table's *OrderNumber* field so that searching for an order by its order number is a fast search.

Adding secondary indexes during the design mode can only get you so far. Typically, indexes will need to be tweaked once a project is delivered to help make real-world searches perform better. Using tools like SQL Server Profiler and SQL Server Database Tuning Wizard will help improve the performance of a running database.

Data Consistency

You need your database to help you make your data better. Other parts of the schema recommendation should include any constraints that are necessary to keep your data clean and consistent. For example, you might choose to make the e-mail address in your Customer table uniquely constrained to ensure that a customer is not entered twice. You might also find that adding check constraints to make sure that data that violates perceived consistency can't be added to the database. For example, the OrderItem table's Discount column should probably have a check clause to ensure that you can't add a discount greater than 100 percent.

Concurrency Management

When you design a database schema for an application, you will be forced to think a bit about the actual day-to-day use of the data in the database. In general, .NET database access uses disconnected concurrency to deal with sharing data in the database. This means there must be a way to ensure that data in a particular row has not changed since the data was retrieved.

There are several approaches to dealing with concurrency, but most of them do not require changes to the schema recommendation. If you are using a non-SQL Server platform, you will need to implement data comparison to do the disconnected concurrency. These types of data comparison techniques do not require that you change your database schema.

On the other hand, if you're using SQL Server, there's a common method that's highly effi-cient: timestamps. In SQL Server you can use a timestamp field to support concurrency. A SQL Server timestamp field is not a time field at all but an eight-byte number that is automatically updated every time the row is updated. You can't change this number directly, but every update to a row will increase the value of a timestamp field. This means you can use the times-tamp to ensure that the row is still in the same state as it was when you first retrieved the data. If you are using SQL Server as your database platform, it's suggested that you use timestamp fields to allow this concurrency management. This means adding a timestamp field to each of the schema tables that require concurrency management, as shown in Figure 6-10.

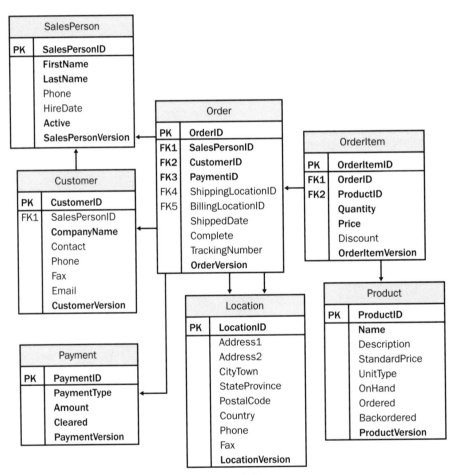

Figure 6-10 Database design with currency fields.

Identify Data Procedures

The last step in finalizing your schema design is to identify procedural code that will be required by the schema. Procedural code is simply stored procedures to perform most tasks that the database requires. Although stored procedures typically are created to perform many common database tasks, for the purpose of the schema design you should be concerned only with the Create, Read, Update, and Delete (CRUD) operations. This typically means creating a stored procedure for each one of the CRUD operations. For example:

- spCreateCustomer: stored procedure to create a new customer
- spGetCustomer: stored procedure to read a customer from the database
- spUpdateCustomer: stored procedure to update a customer
- spDeleteCustomer: stored procedure to delete a customer from the database

You should create stored procedures for each of these operations as part of your design of the database.

Exam Tip   On the exam you will want to be sure and note that stored procedures are expected for most, if not all, database operations. Although in the real world it's often a mix of parameterized queries and stored procedures, in the exam's simplified examples stored procedures are the right answer.

Lab: Defining Entity Relationships

In this lab, you will review an ORM diagram and identify what relationships are required between the entities.

▶ **Exercise: Defining Entity Relationships**

In this exercise, you will review an ORM diagram for relationships and identify them.

1. Open the Lesson1_ORM.pdf file (or look at Figure 6-3) to view the ORM diagram.
2. Open an instance of SQL Server Management Studio.
3. Attach the 70548_3.1.mdf database file. This database file (and its log) is located in the Chapter6\Labs\Lesson 1\Before directory on the DVD.
4. Open the newly attached instance of the database and look at the Lesson 6-1 database diagram.
5. Review the ORM diagram to determine what relationships are required and add them to the database diagram.
6. Save the new diagram to ensure that it's correct. Your resulting diagram should look something like Figure 6-11.

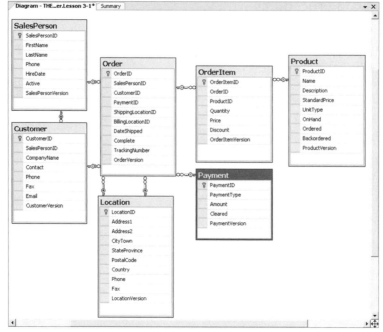

Figure 6-11   Database diagram after adding relationships.

Lesson Summary

- Using the ORM diagram, you can determine the entity requirements for a database schema.

- The ORM diagram is a good starting place to determine the data requirements, but a re-review with stakeholders and a survey of the requirements using common sense are both useful to complete real requirements.

- Every data entity in a database schema must have a primary key associated with it that is unique.

- Relationships between entities can be identified by referring to the data requirements.

- Finalizing a database schema includes adding obvious indexing, ensuring data consistency with constraints, adding concurrency columns if necessary, and identifying stored procedures for use with the schema.

Lesson Review

You can use the following questions to test your knowledge of the information in Lesson 1, "Database Design." The questions are also available on the companion CD if you prefer to review them in electronic form.

NOTE Answers

Answers to these questions and explanations of why each answer choice is right or wrong are located in the "Answers" section at the end of the book.

1. Primary keys provide what functionality? (Choose all that apply.)
   A. To provide unique identifiers for each row in a table.
   B. To provide a mechanism to propagate changes between related entities.
   C. To provide an efficient lookup for each table.
   D. To provide a relationship between two entities in the database.

2. What is the purpose of secondary indexing?
   A. To ensure that data is correct in a table.
   B. To improve performance of nonprimary key searches.
   C. To enforce type safety in the table.
   D. To provide a mechanism for propagating changes across tables.

3. Attributes in the Object Role Model (ORM) should become what in the database design?
   A. Primary keys
   B. Columns
   C. Foreign keys
   D. Stored procedures

Lesson 2: Designing a Component

Your Windows-based application needs functionality. That functionality will come in the form of a set of components that work together to fulfill a project's potential. Instead of just coding what you think the component needs to look like, you will want to actually design that component. In designing an individual component you will want to do a high-level design as well as determine the right characteristics for the component. In this lesson you will learn the different aspects of completing the design of a component.

After this lesson, you will be able to:
- Determine the correct characteristics for a component.
- Create a high-level design of a component.

Estimated lesson time: 35 minutes

Component Characteristics

For each component that you are going to need to design for your Windows-based application, you will have to review the requirements to plan for the component's requirements. This process involves three decisions: how to package the component, where to host the component, and what type of component to build.

Packaging

When reviewing the component you need to build, it's important to determine how the component will be packaged. Creating a single component is often the right decision, but as part of your design criteria you need to evaluate whether the new component is a single discrete component or a series of related components. For example, an Invoice component might involve creating components for an Invoice, an Invoice collection, and other components for parts of invoices (for example, Line Items, Payment information).

When determining how many components are necessary, you should make sure each component is not trying to be too many things to too many people. Typically this means that a component should contain a single logical facility.

In addition, you will want to determine how the actual containers for your components will need to be handled. In .NET, components are contained within assemblies. Determining the exact packaging of your components into assemblies has a lot to do with how you want to reuse and deploy your code. You might choose to use a single assembly with most of your components because deploying a single assembly is simpler and you don't have many applications on a single machine that use the code. On the other hand, you might choose a more granular method because you have a larger number of applications, each of which uses only a subset of the total number of components.

For example, if we know we need to build a component to store our customer information in the database, we could start by assuming that we need a single Customer component. This component will be responsible for reading and writing data to the database for a customer. To start out, we can assume a single component, as shown in Figure 6-12.

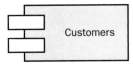

Figure 6-12   Customers component.

Our customer might have related components to deal with different objects that the customer owns (for example, Invoices, Payments, and so on), but in this case a single Customers component is useful. But if the requirement were to store Customers and their Invoices, you would have to assume that you really needed two separate components, as shown in Figure 6-13.

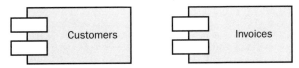

Figure 6-13   Customers and Invoices components.

Both of these components could have their own assembly (or package), but because they are so interrelated it's probably more useful to have them live in a single package. However, instead of thinking about what assemblies to create as you design your components, it's more useful to think of packaging throughout an application. This means developing logical assemblies for different types of code. For example, in a typical Windows-based application your packaging might be as simple as a main executable (for the user interface), a security package, a data package, and the database. An example of this structure can be seen in Figure 6-14.

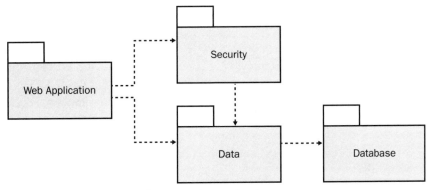

Figure 6-14   Packaging throughout the application.

You might find more packages more effective, but in general separating your user interface from the data is expected in all but the most primitive applications. Now that we have an idea of general packaging throughout our application, we can see clearly that our Customers and Invoices components belong in the Data package, and we can show that as seen in Figure 6-15.

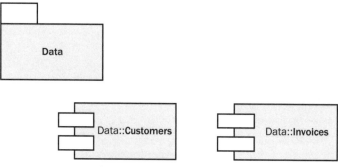

Figure 6-15   Packaged components.

Location

When determining the characteristics of your component, you will also need to determine where a component belongs in the architecture. Whether or not you have designed your architecture to have a physical middle (or data) tier, it should have a logical middle tier to contain data components. So when developing a component, it's important to determine where in the logical tier the component belongs. For example, if we go back to our Customers and Invoices components, they belong in the middle tier.

But you might have a component that performs other tasks, like graphing. That component will more than likely belong in the user interface tier. Determining that location will help you determine the correct high-level design and what a component interface should look like. This is because if components are to be used across an architecture tier, it will probably affect the design of the interface of a component.

Type

As the designer of a component, you will be challenged with how to capture the functionality of the component while making it accessible to other parts of the application. Your component could be a library of code, a custom control, or a design-time component. Deciding how to share the functionality with the clients of the component requires that you know how it's going to be used. For example, if your component is going to be used to show graphs of data, creating a custom control makes the most sense. But, on the other hand, if your component's job is to store information about a specific customer as stored in the database, a custom library makes a lot more sense.

There are no hard and fast rules about how to determine the right type of component to create, but there are some rough guidelines:

- If the component is going to show a user interface, it should be a custom or user control.
- If your component should be usable through the user interface but doesn't show a user interface (for example, the *Timer* component), a design-time component is appropriate.
- If your code does not have any user interface or design-time experience, it most likely should be a library for consumers of the component to use.

High-Level Design

Once you have the characteristics of your component, you will be ready to create the design of the component. The process of doing the high-level design is not about writing code but about providing the parameters around which code will be created. High-level design requires that you look at your component's role in the bigger picture of the architecture. Doing the high-level design requires a look at the component with consistency, life cycle, and design patterns in mind.

Life Cycle

The life cycle of a component involves simply taking into account the construction, lifespan, and destruction of the functionality you need. There are components that are created and live for long durations and others that perform functional tasks where they have little or no lifespan at all. Determining the component's life cycle is critical to the design of a component.

For example, in a simple Windows-based application, we might create an instance of a component and have it do some work for us, as shown in Figure 6-16.

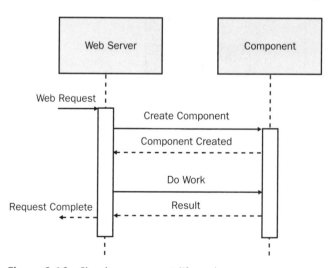

Figure 6-16   Simple component life cycle.

In this case the life cycle is very clear-cut: we create it, we have it do some work, and it is released for garbage collection. In this case, our class skeleton might look something like this:

```vb
' VB
Public Class SomeComponent
  Public Sub New()
  End Sub

  Public Function DoWork() As Integer
    Return -1
  End Function
End Class
```

```csharp
// C#
public class SomeComponent
{
  public SomeComponent()
  {
  }

  public int DoWork()
  {
    return -1;
  }
}
```

Depending on the construction and any state that the component has, this might be overkill. If you need a component that is stateless and contains functionality that simply processes inputs and returns some sort of data, then a static (or shared in VB.NET) method might be a better solution. The sequence diagram of that life cycle is more basic, as seen in Figure 6-17.

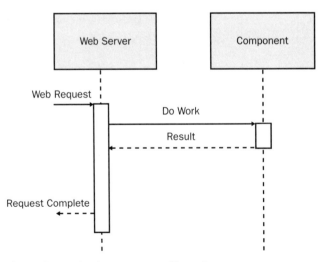

Figure 6-17   Static component life cycle.

When we create a skeleton of the code, it might look something like this:

```vb
' VB
Public Class SomeComponent
  ' Prevent Creation
  Private Sub New()
  End Sub

  Public Shared Function DoWork() As Integer
    Return -1
  End Function
End Class
```

```csharp
// C#
public class SomeComponent
{
  // Prevent Creation
  private SomeComponent() {}

  static public int DoWork()
  {
    return -1;
  }
}
```

Because you are developing for a Windows-based application, you might find that you do not need to worry as much about life cycle as for other types of applications (for example, Web applications), but that is not true. If your application is long-lived (for example, Windows Messenger), then keeping instances of classes will cause your application to take more and more memory over time. Typically you should try and minimize the use of long-lived objects unless you absolutely must have them. It is the rare application that can consume all the resources of a machine, so a well-behaved application should be designed from the start.

In order to be well-behaved, your component should plan on having a simple life cycle. A simple life cycle implies that the data associated with it should exist for a single instance of the component. In general, this means that hiding static data in order to cache data or attempt to improve performance is not encouraged. By storing instance data at the instance level, you allow the application to control the life cycle of the component. This is important because the nature of the application that uses your component might need to deal with the life cycle differently than you can currently envision its use. If the data needs to be cached, let the application deal with that possibility because it can better understand the use case for system resources.

Design Patterns

Rarely do we, as developers, run into problems that are completely unique to programming. This is where design patterns come in. In short, design patterns are commonly used frameworks for solving common problems in software development. Design patterns are typically structural solutions for common object-oriented concepts.

While designing your component, it's important to leverage design patterns as common solutions to your component structure. For example, one of the most common design patterns is the singleton. In some instances you will need to design a class where only a single instance of the class is appropriate. This is a classic place to use the singleton pattern. The design pattern for a singleton provides a framework for creating a singleton. For example, a skeleton class using the singleton design pattern would look like this:

```vb
' VB
Public Class Singleton
  ' Prevent Construction outside the class
  Private Sub New()
  End Sub

  ' The single Instance
  Private Shared theSingleton As Singleton = Nothing

  ' The static property to get the instance
  Public Shared Function Instance() As Singleton

    If theSingleton Is Nothing Then
      theSingleton = New Singleton()
    End If

    Return theSingleton
  End Function
End Class
```

```csharp
// C#
public class Singleton
{
  // Prevent Construction outside the class
  private Singleton() {}

  // The single Instance
  private static Singleton theSingleton = null;

  // The static property to get the instance
  public static Singleton Instance()
  {
    if (theSingleton == null)
    {
      theSingleton = new Singleton();
    }

    return theSingleton;
  }
}
```

This pattern of creating a class that exposes a single instance is a tried-and-true method that has been around for years. Leveraging this pattern will help you solve common problems with your design.

There are many, many design patterns that you can use to design your component. You could spend hours every time you design a component combing through books, Web sites, and blogs to find the right pattern. In general, it's a best practice to start with the "Gang of Four" design patterns as outlined in the book *Design Patterns*, by Erich Gamma, Richard Helm, Ralph Johnson, and John M. Vlissides. The "Gang of Four" refers to the book's four authors. See the "More Info" box for more information on this book and other useful links on design patterns.

MORE INFO   **Design patterns**

For more information and other useful links about design patterns, see *Design Patterns: Elements of Reusable Object-Oriented Software*, by Gamma, Helm, Johnson, and Vlissides (Addison Wesley, 1995) and "Design Patterns: Solidify Your C# Application Architecture with Design Patterns" at *http://msdn.microsoft.com/msdnmag/issues/01/07/patterns/*.

To Prototype or Not to Prototype

At this point you should have a good idea of what the design of your component might look like, even if it's only in your head. You now have an important decision to make: "Do I need to prototype the design?"

The decision about whether to prototype comes down to an assessment of the risks of not prototyping. You will need to look at the technological risks to help you make a decision about whether to prototype or not. If the component you're developing is particularly unusual or is using unproved or unfamiliar technology, you are better off going ahead and creating a prototype to test your design.

Another situation in which prototyping a component is needed is when there are needs to see the component design before the system design is complete. This can include a requirement that the project's proof of concept might need a prototype of your component to ensure that the project is feasible. There also might be situations in which it's more expedient to have a prototype of the component to satisfy eventual clients of the component.

Expressing the Design

Once you have an idea of what the design of your component design will be, you need to be able to capture that design in a way that it can be communicated to others. This includes creating activity, sequence, and class diagrams of your component, as well as possibly pseudo code to represent examples of how the component will be used.

For example, let's document the design of a fictional component called *ProductFactory* whose job it is to get the information about a specific product from the database and cache products for faster retrieval. We can document our new component in a number of UML diagrams. First of all, we could create a simple activity diagram like that seen in Figure 6-18 to show the primary flow of the component.

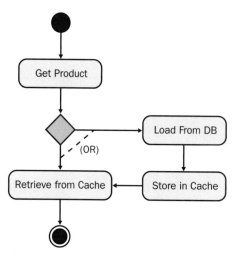

Figure 6-18 ProductFactory component activity diagram.

Next we will create a sequence diagram to show how we expect clients to use the component. The sequence is used to show not only the timeline flow of work but also the interaction between different components. In Figure 6-19 we can see that our *ProductFactory* component is using the database to get product information.

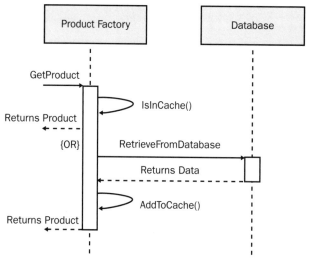

Figure 6-19 ProductFactory component sequence diagram.

Lastly, we need a class diagram to show the data and operations of our component. In the case of the UML diagrams, using Visio to do our diagrams is required because Visual Studio 2005 can't do our activity and sequence diagrams, but for our class diagrams the Visual Studio 2005 class diagram is a richer tool for creating real class diagrams. For example, we can use Visual Studio 2005 to create a *ProductFactory* class diagram to show the basics of our new class, as seen in Figure 6-20.

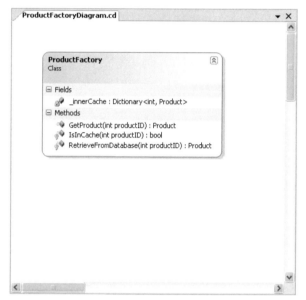

Figure 6-20 ProductFactory component class diagram.

MORE INFO Creating class diagrams

For more information on how to create class diagrams in Visual Studio 2005, see the MSDN Documentation at *http://msdn2.microsoft.com/en-us/library/ms304194.aspx*.

BEST PRACTICES Reviewing the design

Design is a very iterative process. As soon as we have our design documented, it is a good time to review the design to make sure we have made the best decisions possible for our component. This design, document, and review iteration cycle is important to get the right design. Reviewing a design might take the form of a self-analysis of the design or something more formal, like a peer review of the design. No matter how long you have designed software or how smart you think you are, the more people who critique the design, the better it is apt to become.

Design Tradeoffs

There is no such thing as a perfect design. If there were always a single "best" way to do something, you would not need to design your components. As you design any component you are going to have to make design tradeoffs. This means prioritizing performance, security, and maintainability. Depending on the scenario of your project, any of these priorities might be most important to you. For example, if your application requires that it be accessible from outside your company over a slow network connection, then your application would need to cache data to increase performance. Caching the data is likely going to be less secure, but it will allow performance to be acceptable. In this example, performance would take higher priority than security. This does not mean that security is not important; it simply means that it takes a back seat to performance.

In the example of an analytical application, we might choose to have more of our back-end data in an unencrypted form to make processing of the data smooth and more effective. But this might mean that if a nefarious employee breaks into our data center, the intruder might have more of a chance to access dangerous data (for example, payroll information). But since we are analyzing data that might not be sensitive, the data might not be worth protecting that much.

In contrast, if we had a payroll system, we would want to keep much of the data encrypted and use strong authentication to ensure that our employees' personal data was well protected. In this case we would likely make security the highest priority, even at the expense of performance or maintainability.

There are no hard and fast rules about which is the most important for a particular component. Only your experience and domain-specific knowledge about the project you are designing will allow you to make design tradeoff decisions.

Lesson Summary

- When designing a component, it's crucial to determine the component's initial characteristics, including packaging, location, and component type.
- While designing a component, following styles of other components in the system, as well as understanding its life cycle, is crucial to getting a solid design.
- Most designs can be advanced by reviewing common design patterns to see if the component to be designed can use an established software solution instead of your inventing something completely new.
- Determining whether to prototype a component depends on the complexity of the component, client requirements, and any technological risk factors.
- Using UML to express your design will allow you to communicate the design to a larger audience.

- Reviewing your design tradeoffs will allow you to make sure that decisions made in the design agree with the overall goals of the project.

Lesson Review

You can use the following questions to test your knowledge of the information in Lesson 2, "Designing a Component." The questions are also available on the companion CD if you prefer to review them in electronic form.

NOTE Answers

Answers to these questions and explanations of why each answer choice is right or wrong are located in the "Answers" section at the end of the book.

---

1. What are good reasons to create a prototype for a component that you are designing? (Choose all that apply.)
   A. Technological risks (for example, new technology or a new application of an old technology).
   B. Client request for a prototype.
   C. To get agreement on the component interface.
   D. It's required to complete a proof of concept for the project.

2. If you are creating a component that stores and retrieves data from the database, to which tier of the architecture does it belong?
   A. User Interface tier
   B. Data tier
   C. Database tier

3. Should all the criteria for designing your component (for example, security, performance, maintainability) be given equal weight in your component's design?
   A. Yes
   B. No

Lesson 3: Component Features

Designing the component involves more than determining what the component looks like; it also requires you to define how the component is called, what existing classes are used to implement features, and other component features. In this lesson, you will learn how to complete the design of the component by making these decisions.

***

After this lesson, you will be able to:
- Develop component interfaces.
- Determine the correct features for a component.
- Decide whether to implement or inherit functionality.
- Understand the decisions made with respect to working with unmanaged resources.

Estimated lesson time: 35 minutes

***

Component Interfaces

Working with components is simply a conversation between two objects inside the .NET run time. For components to be able to have the conversation, a common language must be decided on. That language is the component interface. In other words, the interface for a component includes the constructor, methods, properties, and events of a component. These are the ways that a conversation can take place between a client and a component.

The interface for a component is not necessarily an *Interface* in the .NET sense. The interface of a component might be a simple .NET class or as complicated as using interfaces, abstract (or *MustInherit* in VB.NET) classes, or even a Web service.

Consumers of the Component

Before you design the interface to your component, it's crucial that you understand the consumer of your component. The code that will consume your component should provide you with key information about what kind of interface you will need. Consumers of the component might expect to use the component as a simple class, in which case a simple class interface makes the most sense.

In contrast, you might have clients that might use the component through remoting. If your component will be accessed as a remote object, you will need to take that into account when defining the interface for your component. Why does remoting a component affect its interface? Remoting assumes that the actual object is across some expensive transport (for example, not in the current AppDomain). Because of this you will want to allow the consumer to do as many of the operations of the component as possible without lots of traffic across the transport. In other words, if you expect your object to be remoted, you will want to define the interface to avoid being chatty.

In addition, you might be developing a component that is expected to be called through a Web service. If your component is expected to be exposed as a Web service, it's important that your interface be as atomic and stateless as possible. A Web service is more than just another transport layer; it is a disconnected transport. In general, the best practice for using Web services in your components is to make the interface to the component message-based. In other words, a single operation should be able to take a payload that allows as much of the job as possible to be done in a single call. Trying to expose an object across Web services can be a nightmare if you try and have a stateful, chatty component.

You must also consider that, since you are writing components for a Windows Forms application, your component might take the form of a control or design-time component. When you consider who will consume your component, you should try and create components that are easily consumed. This means you might need to create wrappers for special needs or, in the case of creating controls and Web parts, you will likely need to create design-time features like preview of the control's ultimate UI output.

Component Lifetime Interface

Before we start with the rest of the interface for your component, one of the first decisions you will need to make is how the interface will handle the lifetime of the component. This includes both the construction and garbage collection of your component.

When deciding on how to handle construction of your object, you have several choices. If your component does not have any state, but instead will perform some specific task, you might want to consider using a static class (or a singleton design pattern). This pattern means that no one will generally create an instance of your class but instead just call methods on your type. Although this is a powerful pattern, it's practical only in a very narrow use case.

For most components you will need to decide how to create your objects. In general, asking for initialization data in the constructor is perfectly acceptable. Two-phase construction (for example, empty constructors plus an "initialization" method) is not considered a best practice. There are always exceptions to this best practice, but, in general, accepting initialization data in the constructor is the right thing to do. For example, here is an example of the one-phase versus two-phase interface design:

```vb
' VB
' Prefer single phase construction over two phase construction
Public Class OnePhase
   Public Sub New(ByVal someInit As String, ByVal moreInit As Integer)
      ' ...
   End Sub

   ' ...
End Class

' Don't use two phase construction unless you
```

```vb
' have a compelling reason to use it
Public Class TwoPhase
  Public Sub New()
  End Sub

  Public Sub Initialize(ByVal someInit As String, _
                        ByVal moreInit As Integer)
    ' ...
  End Sub

  ' ...
End Class
```

```csharp
// C#
// Prefer single phase construction over two phase construction
public class OnePhase
{
  public OnePhase(string someInit, int moreInit)
  {
    // ...
  }

  // ...
}

// Don't use two phase construction unless you have a
// compelling reason to use it
public class TwoPhase
{
  public TwoPhase()
  {
  }

  public void Initialize(string someInit, int moreInit)
  {
    // ...
  }

  // ...
}
```

Passing initialization data in the constructor avoids confusing the users of the component. There is a single way to initialize your new component and that should provide clarity of interface. Passing the initialization data in the constructor also prevents the unexpected side effects of users calling the initialization code twice.

Once you determine what you are going to do with a constructor, you have to look at how you are going to handle the end of a component's life. There are three ways of dealing with the end of the life of your component, as shown in the following table.

Life Cycle Type	Description
Stack-based object	Value types are stored on the stack and are not garbage collected because they are destroyed when the stack is destroyed. This life cycle is very fast and should be used for lightweight objects that are not kept around for longer than a method call.
Heap-based object	Objects are garbage collected. Garbage collection occurs when the system is not under load. Most components will fall into this category.
Objects with Unmanaged Resources	When you need to determine when an object is released, you can implement the *IDisposable* pattern. This is for resources that are not garbage collected (for example, database connections, IO completion ports, and so on).

In general, you should not use finalizers in your component designs at all. Finalizers allow you to perform clean-up code just before garbage collection occurs. Objects with finalizers are slower to garbage collect, and in almost every case you should be using the *IDisposable* pattern if you need control over your clean-up code instead of creating a finalizer.

Design the Interface

Once you understand the life cycle of your component, all that is left is to actually design the methods, properties, and events. You must look not only at how your component will fulfill its duties, but also at how homogenous the component is as it relates to the rest of the project. Homogeny is as important as consistency in how the way components work will make the development of client components or applications easier for developers.

In this case, homogeny means similarity of interface, naming, and workflow. For example, if the style of the interface of other components in your system is to have overloads for different types of operations, then yours should as well. For example, you might have this *Log* class in your system already:

```vb
' VB
Public Class Log
  Public Sub Write(ByVal message As String)
    ' ...
  End Sub

  Public Sub Write(ByVal message As String, ByVal ex As Exception)
    ' ...
  End Sub

  Public Sub Write(ByVal message As String, _
              ByVal ParamArray args As Object())
    ' ...
  End Sub
End Class
```

```csharp
// C#
public class Log
{
  public void Write(string message)
  {
    // ...
  }

  public void Write(string message, Exception ex)
  {
    // ...
  }

  public void Write(string message, params object[] args)
  {
    // ...
  }
}
```

Because this other class creates overloads for different types of messages, you might consider creating multiple methods that take different overloads to follow this stylistic pattern.

Lesson Summary

- Determining a component's interface is a matter of understanding the consumers of a component, what kind of lifetime the component has, and what the style of interface on other components in the system is.
- Determining how to implement features of a component depends on what functionality is needed. Extending an existing component, composing a new component by mixing other components, or writing a component from scratch are the three options from which to choose.

Lesson Review

You can use the following questions to test your knowledge of the information in Lesson 3, "Component Features." The questions are also available on the companion CD if you prefer to review them in electronic form.

NOTE   Answers

Answers to these questions and explanations of why each answer choice is right or wrong are located in the "Answers" section at the end of the book.

---

1. How should initialization data be passed to a component?
   A. In the constructor during construction of an instance of the component.
   B. In an initialization method after construction of the component.
   C. Using properties after construction of a component.
   D. It doesn't matter.

2. How should unmanaged resources be handled in your design?
   A. Nothing, they will be garbage collected by the common language runtime (CLR).
   B. Ensure that the callers of my component properly close the component.
   C. Implement the *IDisposable* interface to allow for handling of the unmanaged resources.
   D. Expose the unmanaged resources directly to the caller to manage.

3. When should you implement a finalizer for your component?
   A. When your component holds on to unmanaged resources.
   B. When your component needs to perform clean-up code.
   C. You should never implement a finalizer.
   D. When your component holds on to other components that implement the *IDisposable* interface.

Chapter Review

To further practice and reinforce the skills you learned in this chapter, you can perform the following tasks:

- Review the chapter summary.
- Review the list of key terms introduced in this chapter.
- Complete the case scenarios. These scenarios set up real-world situations involving the topics of this chapter and ask you to create a solution.
- Complete the suggested practices.
- Take a practice test.

Chapter Summary

- You can map entities in your design to tables in the database design.
- Creating a complete database schema is crucial to a successful Windows-based application design.
- Designing a component requires that you understand both the environment that a component will be used in as well as where the component fits into the architecture.
- Doing a high-level design of your component is the first step to completing your component design.
- Reviewing the design for possible uses of design patterns will help your design be that much better in the end.
- Expressing your design in UML diagrams will help you communicate the design to stakeholders and peers for review to make sure your design meets their needs.
- Designing a well thought-out interface requires that you understand who will use the component, what kind of lifetime the component will have, and what the stylistic preference for interfaces is within the entire architecture.

Key Terms

Do you know what these key terms mean? You can check your answers by looking up the terms in the glossary at the end of the book.

- consumer
- database schema
- design patterns
- foreign key
- primary key
- UML

Case Scenarios

In the following case scenarios you will apply what you've learned about how to design components. You can find answers to these questions in the "Answers" section at the end of this book.

Case Scenario 1: Design a Tax Collection Component

You work for a small company that has a point of sale (POS) application. You need to be able to calculate taxes for purchases that take place in the state in which the purchase is made.

Interviews

Following is a company manager's statement:

- **Engineering Manager** "Our developer who is responsible for our POS application needs to calculate taxes for customers as required by law. Please create a component that will do that calculation for them."

Questions

Answer the following questions for the POS application developer.

1. How should I package the tax system for the POS system?
2. How will you return me the tax information?

Case Scenario 2: Design a Database for a Company Library

You are working for a large technology company. They have decided to allow their employees to check out technical books from their internal library, but they want to require that they use a small Windows-based application to do that.

Interviews

Following is a company manager's statement:

- **Engineering Manager** "We need a database design for a simple library. Each employee can check out up to two books at a time."

Questions

Answer the following questions for the developer working on the Windows-based application code.

1. How many tables do you expect to have?
2. How are the tables related?

Suggested Practices

To successfully master the objectives covered in this chapter, complete the following tasks.

Create a Database Schema

For this task, you should complete at least Practices 1 and 2. You can do Practice 3 for a more in-depth understanding of data design.

- **Practice 1**   Create a database design for a CD collection. Include information on the title, artist, and year of release of each CD. Also store each song in a separate table.
- **Practice 2**   Create constraints to ensure that each song belongs to a CD.
- **Practice 3**   Add indexes on a commonly used column (for example, title) to see how adding indexes can improve the performance of queries.

Design Components

For this task, you should complete at least Practices 1 and 2. You can do Practice 3 for a more in-depth understanding of component design.

- **Practice 1**   Design a component that will show the date and time in separate user interface controls. Make up minimum requirements for the simple component.
- **Practice 2**   Review the design with peers to see if the design meets minimum requirements.
- **Practice 3**   Implement the design to ensure that it still meets the requirements.

Take a Practice Test

The practice tests on this book's companion CD offer many options. For example, you can test yourself on just one exam objective or you can test yourself on all the 70-548 certification exam content. You can set up the test so that it closely simulates the experience of taking a certification exam, or you can set it up in study mode so that you can look at the correct answers and explanations after you answer each question.

MORE INFO   **Practice tests**

For details about all the practice test options available, see the "How to Use the Practice Tests" section in this book's Introduction.

Chapter 7
Component Development

Now that you have the design for your component that you created in Chapter 6, "Component Design," you can move on implementing the functionality of your component. In this chapter we will discuss the many decisions you need to make in actually implementing features. These decisions include how to handle data, how to implement required features, and how to add common infrastructure to your component.

Exam objectives in this chapter:
- Develop the features of a component.
  - Decide whether existing functionality can be implemented or inherited.
  - Decide how to handle unmanaged and managed resources.
  - Decide which extensibility features are required.
  - Decide whether a component must be multithreaded.
  - Decide which functions to implement in the base class, abstract class, or sealed class.
- Develop the data access and data handling features of a component.
  - Analyze data relationships.
  - Analyze the data handling requirements of a component.
- Develop an exception handling mechanism.
  - Decide when it is appropriate to raise an exception.
  - Decide how a component will handle exceptions. Considerations include catching and throwing a new exception; catching, wrapping, and throwing the wrapped exception; catching and terminating, and so on.
- Develop a component to include profiling requirements.
  - Identify potential issues, such as resource leaks and performance gaps, by profiling a component.
  - Decide when to stop profiling on a component.
  - Decide whether to redesign a component after analyzing the profiling results.

Lessons in this chapter:

Before You Begin

- To complete the lessons in this chapter, you should be familiar with Microsoft Visual Basic or C#.

Real World

Shawn Wildermuth

Component development has been the heart and soul of my development life for the past decade or so. In particular, developing components for .NET has required that I pay particular attention to reusing other components. The .NET Framework is a vast library of functionality and at times it becomes easy to want to just reimplement some functionality. I have learned that investing the time to find the right parts of the .NET Framework to extend for my particular need is worth the effort.

Lesson 1: Implementing Component Features

Once the design of a specific component is complete, you will need to determine how to implement the features of a component.

After this lesson, you will be able to:

- Determine whether you need to extend, compose, or implement your component's specific features.
- Understand the decision on whether to make a component stateful or stateless.
- Make decisions about whether to support multithreaded environments.
- Know how to deal with unmanaged resources in components.

Estimated lesson time: 30 minutes

Extend, Compose, or Implement?

Before you can implement your component you will need to review the requirements for the component and determine how you are going to fulfill the feature requirements of the component. You need to determine what needs to be written and what can be built upon. Whether you use the expansive .NET Framework, third-party controls, or even other in-house development, you will need to decide what features your component needs that should be built and what features can be reused from other components. There are three real choices here for any component: extend, compose, or implement.

You might find that a particular class or control is close to what you need in your component but that you need to customize for your particular need. In this case you should extend the class or control by inheriting from it and adding your customization. For example, you might find that the best way to create a logging component is to extend a *FileStream* class instead of writing the files yourself. In that case you can use the same interface as the *FileStream* class but extend it to do the specific logging that you need. It is important that you can think of the new component as a type of the class or control that you are deriving from. In this example we really want a *LogStream*, not just a log class. Because we want a stream that will write only to a text log, extending the *FileStream* is the right approach. Our *LogStream* class would have a class diagram that looks something like Figure 7-1.

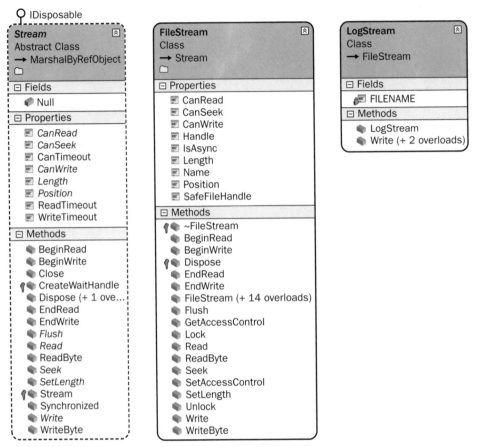

Figure 7-1 *LogStream* component class diagram.

You might find that your component needs the functionality from a number of different classes or controls. In this case you should choose to use composition to compose a new component that includes the functionality of all the different classes or controls. A very visual way of thinking of this is in the world of controls. You might decide that you need a control that allows users to enter a date and a time as separate pieces of data. You might find that creating a component that's composed of a calendar control and a textbox is the best solution. The new component is not necessarily a calendar control or a textbox, but a new type of component that includes both. That is the essence of composition.

Lastly, you might find that your component's features do not fit into either extending or composing existing components. For example, you might have a component that needs to perform some calculations that are specific to your project. In this case the only real option is implementing this logic in your own code.

All component implementations will always lean on other code, even if that code is just the *Object* class. But choosing the right approach to extending, composing, or implementing functionality is crucial to a well-designed and implemented component.

Building Class Hierarchies

Sometimes you decide that you need a hierarchy of classes that make up a component. You might need a class hierarchy when you need a variety of different types of components to share common functionality. This common functionality class is referred to as a base class. The *Stream* class in the .NET Framework is a classic example of this design. The *Stream* class itself is a base class that not only exemplifies the interface that the derived classes will follow but also supports basic functionality that all *Stream*-derived classes will share. Derived classes will specialize the stream for specific purposes. For example, the *FileStream* class is a *Stream* class that writes to a file. There are a number of different streams that are specialized versions of the *Stream* class, including *FileStream*, *MemoryStream*, and *DeflateStream*.

The *Stream* class is also an example of another decision to make. Do you need the base class to be abstract or not? Abstract classes (also referred to as *MustInherit* classes in VB) are classes you can't create an instance of. Specifically, only classes that inherit from the abstract class can be instantiated. For example, you might have an *Animal* base class from which a *Cat* class and a *Dog* class inherits. Although cats and dogs are both animals, you can't have an *Animal* itself. It is always a specialization of the animal concept. That is the canonical example of the abstract class. In that case the *Animal* class would be abstract.

The core concepts of abstract classes and interfaces can be seen as very similar. Although the two concepts seem similar, they are actually different. An abstract class is used to share not only interface and implementation, but also identity. An abstract class is an "is-a" relationship. A cat is an animal. A dog is an animal. Interfaces, on the other hand, define a calling convention or behavior. You might have an *IFeed* interface that defines that you can feed an object. That interface would probably exist on an *Animal* class. But that same interface could also exist on a *ParkingMeter* class. Although you feed an animal and a parking meter differently, the interface in this fictitious *IFeed* interface might define that they both need to be fed.

Stateful or Stateless

One of the most important decisions you will make in developing a component is whether it will be stateful or stateless. Making this judgment is simply a matter of determining whether your component needs to maintain data across multiple calls to a component. In this context, state usually refers to any data that is not consumed during a single method call in a component. The decision about whether to be stateful or stateless is not about whether your component needs data to accomplish its task; instead it's a decision about where that data is going to exist.

The general rule of thumb is that stateless components will scale out better, but at the cost of working without local state. Let's assume you needed a component that would create an e-mail for a customer to remind her of a payment that is due. You might have a stateful component that contains all the data for a customer (as is common with data access layers). You could decide to add the functionality to the existing customer component, which is stateful. When you issue a request for one of these e-mails, you would need to get the customer's component and then ask that the e-mail be sent. As your customer base expands, you might find that reading so many customers out of the database just to routinely send them an e-mail is slow because of all the user objects that are being created (that is, it does not scale out well). Instead you could create a component that was stateless that was passed the customer identifier and issued the e-mail. Internally, this e-mailing component might use data (for example, the identifier you passed it and the data it retrieved from the database) during the completion of the operation. But this component could scale out faster because it could be reused over and over for different customers. The additional scaling out of the component is accomplished in two ways: no extraneous data is being loaded that the component does not need, and you are avoiding a construction/destruction cycle for every e-mail creation. You can usually tell that a component takes state if it either has a constructor that takes data or includes a secondary initialization method (for example, *Create* or *Init*).

Stateful objects are not a bad idea. Most components that are created are stateful. Generally, they are quicker to develop and are required for many components that you will need in your development, but isolating key components to make stateless for the purposes of scaling out can be a real boon to most development projects.

Multithreading

You need to deal with two issues when working with multithreading in your component: thread safety and using multithreading in your component. Thread safety involves determining whether your component will be called from multiple threads simultaneously. Using multithreading means deciding whether you should be using threads in your component to improve your throughput.

Thread Safety

Assuming that your component is going to be stateful, you will need to determine whether the component will need to support thread safety. Thread safety is simply protecting data within a component from simultaneous access from multiple threads. But thread safety comes at a cost. No matter what locking scheme you pick to protect your data from multithreaded access, there is a cost. This cost is in development time, performance of the component, and testing of the component, as well as debugging difficulties.

It is important to know whether it must be valid to use any stateful component you create in a multithreaded environment. If it's valid to call the component from multiple threads, you must protect that data. There are components that never need to be thread-safe in that they're always used from a single thread. Typically, you should add thread safety only if your component specifically needs it.

Using Threads

As you implement your component's features you will need to determine whether to use threads. Introducing threading can dramatically improve the performance of a component by allowing multiple threads to do work at once. At the same time, introducing threading will increase the complexity of your component, both in implementation and in debugging.

So how do you decide whether to use threading or not? You should introduce threading only when you need it. Not every type of operation will benefit from multithreaded code. Typically, multithreading can help a component when the component has an operation that spends much of its time waiting. For example, you might have a component that's used to retrieve stock prices using a Web service. Because the retrieval of that information over the Internet might take some time, your component might just be waiting for the results to return. You could introduce threading to that component to allow you to fire off several threads to retrieve different stock results all at the same time so that you can have requests to the Web service being made while other requests are pending.

The benefit of adding threading must outweigh the additional complexity introduced to the process. There is no black-and-white rule that you can measure that decision against. You will have to rely on your experience to understand the risk-versus-reward decision.

MORE INFO   Multithreaded access

To learn more about the concepts of threading and the classes used to create multithreaded applications, read Chapter 7, "Threading," of *MCTS Self-Paced Training Kit (Exam 70-536): Microsoft .NET Framework 2.0 Application Development Foundation,* by Tony Northrup and Shawn Wildermuth, with Bill Ryan (Microsoft Press, 2006).

Unmanaged Resources

The Common Language Runtime (CLR) is an environment in which the memory is managed. By managed I mean that heap-based objects (that is, reference objects) are garbage collected. Once they go out of scope they are eligible to be reclaimed by the system when the garbage collector cleans up the environment. The garbage collector manages memory. There are other resources that are unmanaged. For example, database connections are an unmanaged resource. Even though the local memory that is associated with a database collection is managed by the CLR, the actual connect is not. If you open a database connection and wait until the garbage collection fires on the connection to have it close, the database will end up with many unclosed database connections and impede the basic performance of the database.

In the .NET Framework the *IDisposable* interface was created to support unmanaged resources. If you write a component that has unmanaged resources, you must allow for those resources to be cleaned up by the users of your component. You do this by supporting the *IDisposable* interface.

In addition, if you use objects that implement the *IDisposable* interface, you must call the object's *IDisposable.Dispose()* method to clean up their unmanaged resources. This means that if you use an object that supports *IDisposable* within a single call, you should wrap it with a using statement to call the *IDisposable* interface. If you hold on to an object that supports *IDisposable* for longer than a single call (for example, is a member of your component), you must support the *IDisposable* interface so that in your implementation of the *IDisposable.Dispose()* method you call your member's *IDisposable* implementation.

In addition to working with members that support *IDisposable*, you should also be aware of other unmanaged resources. Typically this is when you are holding on to resources that are outside the .NET Framework. For example, you might be using an external dynamic-link library (DLL) through interop. Because the external DLL is being used through interop, the DLL is not a .NET component and, therefore, is unmanaged. You will need to be able to release any resources that you use from that DLL, and by supporting the *IDisposable* interface you have a convenient place to do that.

Real World

Shawn Wildermuth

Understanding the implications of unmanaged resources is a crucial skill for every developer, of whatever level, to have. In my experience in doing a lot of code reviews, not handling unmanaged resources is one of the most common errors in projects. As you create components that use different parts of the .NET Framework, you will need to learn which types of objects support the *IDisposable* interface and which do not. For example, almost all of ADO.NET supports this interface. All classes that derive from *Component* also support this interface. This means that a large chunk of the .NET Framework should be dealt with as unmanaged resources. I've learned to tell people to look long and hard for this interface.

Lab: Add Handling of Unmanaged Resources

In this lab, you will add support to handle unmanaged resources in an existing component.

▶ **Exercise: Add Support for Unmanaged Resources**

In this exercise, you will take a partially completed class and add support for handling unmanaged resources.

1. Open the Exercise 1 "Before" project in Lesson 1 in your preferred language (C# and VB are included).

2. Open the *Logger* class code-file.

3. Identify the unmanaged resources (the *FileStream* and *StreamWriter* members).

4. Add the *IDisposable* interface to the *Logger* class.

5. Add the *IDisposable*'s *Dispose* method to the *Logger* class.

6. Inside the *Dispose* method, call the *FileStream* and *StreamWriter*'s *Dispose* methods.

7. The new *Logger* class might look like the following (changes from the starting project are in bold):

```vb
' VB
Imports System
Imports System.Collections.Generic
Imports System.Text
Imports System.IO


''' <summary>
''' A class for writing information to a standard log file.
''' </summary>
Public Class Logger
  Implements IDisposable

  Private Const logFileName As String = "logfile.txt"
  Private logFile As FileStream = Nothing
  Private writer As StreamWriter = Nothing

  ''' <summary>
  ''' Initializes a new instance of the <see cref="T:Logger"/> class.
  ''' </summary>
  Public Sub New()
    MyBase.New()
    logFile = File.Open(logFileName, FileMode.OpenOrCreate, _
      FileAccess.Write, FileShare.ReadWrite)
    writer = New StreamWriter(logFile)
  End Sub

  ''' <summary>
  ''' Adds the specified message.
  ''' </summary>
  ''' <param name="message">The message.</param>
  Public Overloads Sub Add(ByVal message As String)
    writer.WriteLine(message)
  End Sub

  ''' <summary>
  ''' Adds the specified message.
  ''' </summary>
  ''' <param name="message">The message.</param>
  ''' <param name="args">The args.</param>
  Public Overloads Sub Add(ByVal message As String, _
```

```
    ByVal ParamArray args() As Object)
      writer.WriteLine(message, args)
    End Sub

    ''' <summary>
    ''' Performs application-defined tasks associated with
    ''' freeing, releasing, or resetting
    ''' unmanaged resources. Implements the Dispose() method
    ''' of the IDisposable interface
    ''' </summary>
    Public Sub Dispose() Implements IDisposable.Dispose
      writer.Dispose()
      logFile.Dispose()
    End Sub

End Class

// C#
using System;
using System.Collections.Generic;
using System.Text;
using System.IO;

/// <summary>
/// A class for writing information to a standard log file.
/// </summary>
public class Logger : IDisposable
{
  const string logFileName = "logfile.txt";
  FileStream logFile = null;
  StreamWriter writer = null;

  /// <summary>
  /// Initializes a new instance of
  /// the <see cref="T:Logger"/> class.
  /// </summary>
  public Logger()
  {
    logFile = File.Open(logFileName, FileMode.OpenOrCreate,
                         FileAccess.Write, FileShare.ReadWrite);
    writer = new StreamWriter(logFile);
  }

  /// <summary>
  /// Adds the specified message.
  /// </summary>
  /// <param name="message">The message.</param>
  public void Add(string message)
  {
    writer.WriteLine(message);
  }

  /// <summary>
```

```
/// Adds the specified message.
/// </summary>
/// <param name="message">The message.</param>
/// <param name="args">The args.</param>
public void Add(string message,
params object[] args)
{
  writer.WriteLine(message, args);
}

/// <summary>
/// Performs application-defined tasks associated with
/// freeing, releasing, or resetting
/// unmanaged resources. Implements the Dispose() method
/// of the IDisposable interface
/// </summary>
public void Dispose()
{
  writer.Dispose();
  logFile.Dispose();
}
}
```

8. Open the *Program* class in the project.

9. Modify the code that creates the instance of the *Logger* class and use it to support auto-matic calling of the *IDisposable* interface.

10. The *Program* class might look like the following:

```
' VB
Class Program
  Public Overloads Shared Sub Main()
    Using theLog As New Logger()
      theLog.Add("Hello Mom")
    End Using
  End Sub
End Class

// C#
class Program
{
  static void Main(string[] args)
  {
    using (Logger theLog = new Logger())
    {
      theLog.Add("Hello Mom");
    }
  }
}
```

11. Compile the program and fix any coding errors found. Run the program and, once it's complete, find the logfile.txt file in the same directory as the executable to ensure that the code worked as expected.

Lesson Summary

- By reviewing existing classes both inside and outside the .NET Framework, you can determine whether to extend an existing class, composite an existing class, or implement an entirely new class to meet your functional needs.
- Determining whether to make the component stateful or stateless can be done by reviewing its requirements.
- Weighing the benefits of providing thread-safe data against the costs of implementing thread safety will allow you to decide whether to include thread safety in your own components.
- You must support the *IDisposable* interface if any of the data in your component is not managed.

Lesson Review

You can use the following questions to test your knowledge of the information in Lesson 1, "Implementing Component Features." The questions are also available on the companion CD if you prefer to review them in electronic form.

1. In what cases must you implement the *IDisposable* interface? (Choose all that apply.)
   A. Anytime you have a stateful component.
   B. If any of the component's data support the *IDisposable* interface.
   C. If the component has any unmanaged resources.
   D. If the component is stateless.

2. What is a base class used for? (Choose all that apply.)
   A. To specify a naming convention.
   B. To define a common interface for specialized classes.
   C. To hide implementation details from inheritors.
   D. To define common functionality to be shared by inherited classes.

3. When should you make your component thread-safe? (Choose one.)
   A. Always.
   B. Never.
   C. Only when the component is going to be used in a multithreaded environment.

Lesson 2: Developing Data Access Components

Data access is central to almost every project that is developed today. Whether you are working with a small Microsoft SQL Server Express database or working with a data center full of SQL Server, Oracle, DB2, and other legacy database servers, you will need to know how to create components that can consume that data.

After this lesson, you will be able to:
- Review project requirements to determine the correct data access method.
- Add business logic to your components.

Estimated lesson time: 10 minutes

Data Access

As we trudge through the development of our Microsoft Windows-based application, we will likely run into situations in which you need components that need to consume, create, or change database data. Data access is the code that allows you to communicate with the database. Data access simply consists of four operations: create, read, update, and delete. These four operations are often referred to as CRUD operations. Adding any (or all) of these operations to a component is what data access is.

Implementing data access in your own components involves reviewing several methods to pick the correct one. These include typed *DataSets*, untyped *DataSets*, *DataReaders*, and Web services.

Real World

Shawn Wildermuth

This lesson explains data access using the .NET Framework alone, but data access in the real world is a very different animal. Depending on the requirements of your project, the skill sets of your team, and other factors, you will find that many tools will help you accomplish data access. These tools range from simple object-relational mapping products to complex frameworks for building your business objects. As you decide on a strategy for your Windows-based applications, you should become familiar with solutions (both Microsoft and non-Microsoft) and how they match up to your requirements.

When you build components that consume data, the most obvious approach is to access the data using ADO.NET to implement the CRUD functionality. Typically, this means using *DataReaders* to get data from the database and using *Commands* when you insert, update, or delete. This approach can be very efficient (assuming your SQL code is efficient). *DataReaders* are essentially forward-only fire hoses of data to fill in your component data, so they get data from the database very quickly. Additionally, using *Commands* (in conjunction with stored procedures) to make changes works very efficiently because you are working with the database at a very basic level.

Exam Tip   If performance is the most important requirement, then using *DataReaders* in conjunction with *Commands* is the method of choice.

Using *DataReaders* and *Commands* is very efficient at run time, but at a cost: development time. For example, let's assume a simple business object that can do all the CRUD functions for contacts. Coding your component using *DataReaders* and *Commands* might end up with a class design like that shown in Figure 7-2.

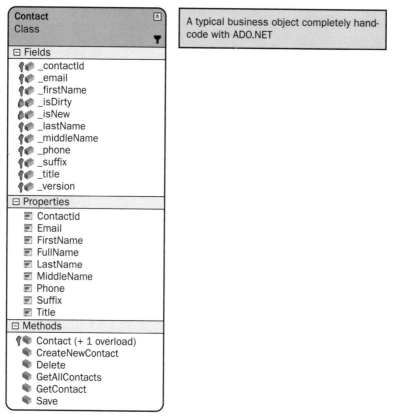

Figure 7-2   Contact component.

Much of this class's interface is composed of constructors and methods to get, create, save, and delete a contact (or a list of contacts). The component contains fields to manage if a contact is a new contact (*_isNew*) and if the contact has changes that need to be saved (*_isDirty*). Implementing this class means writing ADO.NET code in each of the data methods (for example, *GetContact*, *Save*, and *Delete*). Although this is not difficult, it is labor-intensive. For example, here is the *GetContact* method:

```vb
' VB
Public Shared Function GetContact(ByVal contactID As Integer) _
  As Contact

  ' Get the connection from configuration
  Dim connInfo As ConnectionStringSettings = _
    ConfigurationManager.ConnectionStrings("AdventureWorks")
  Dim factory As DbProviderFactory = _
    DbProviderFactories.GetFactory(connInfo.ProviderName)

  ' Create the ADO.NET Objects
  Using conn As DbConnection = factory.CreateConnection
    Using cmd As DbCommand = conn.CreateCommand

      ' Setup command to use a stored procedure to  get all the customers data
      cmd.CommandText = "Person.uspGetContact"
      cmd.CommandType = CommandType.StoredProcedure

      ' Add the input parameter
      Dim idParam As DbParameter = factory.CreateParameter
      idParam.ParameterName = "contactID"
      idParam.DbType = DbType.Int32
      idParam.Direction = ParameterDirection.Input
      idParam.Value = contactID
      cmd.Parameters.Add(idParam)
      Try
        ' Open the connection
        conn.ConnectionString = connInfo.ConnectionString
        conn.Open()

        ' Get the data
        Using reader As DbDataReader = _
          cmd.ExecuteReader(CommandBehavior.CloseConnection)

          ' Assuming only one record. If multiple are returned they are ignored
          If reader.Read Then
            Return New Contact(reader)
          End If
        End Using
      Finally

        If (conn.State <> ConnectionState.Closed) Then
          conn.Close()
        End If
      End Try
    End Using
  End Using
End Using
```

```
' Contact was not found, we return null
  Return Nothing
End Function

// C#
public static Contact GetContact(int contactID)
{
  // Get the connection from configuration
  ConnectionStringSettings connInfo =
    ConfigurationManager.ConnectionStrings["AdventureWorks"];
  DbProviderFactory factory =
    DbProviderFactories.GetFactory(connInfo.ProviderName);

  // Create the ADO.NET Objects
  using (DbConnection conn = factory.CreateConnection())
  using (DbCommand cmd = conn.CreateCommand())
  {
    // Setup command to use a stored procedure to
    // get all the customers data
    cmd.CommandText = "Person.uspGetContact";
    cmd.CommandType = CommandType.StoredProcedure;

    // Add the input parameter
    DbParameter idParam = factory.CreateParameter();
    idParam.ParameterName = "contactID";
    idParam.DbType = DbType.Int32;
    idParam.Direction = ParameterDirection.Input;
    idParam.Value = contactID;
    cmd.Parameters.Add(idParam);

    try
    {
      // Open the connection
      conn.ConnectionString = connInfo.ConnectionString;
      conn.Open();

      // Get the data
      using (DbDataReader reader =
             cmd.ExecuteReader(CommandBehavior.CloseConnection))
      {
        // Assuming only one record.
        // If multiple are returned they are ignored
        if (reader.Read())
        {
          return new Contact(reader);
        }
      }
    }
    finally
    {
      if (conn.State != ConnectionState.Closed)
      {
```

```
        conn.Close();
      }
    }
  }

  // Contact was not found, we return null
  return null;
}
```

In addition to the simple component that just needs to load itself up with data, you will need related entities. For example, if you had an Order component that had related Order Items, you would want an efficient way to just load up an order and have all the related data in the database be loaded at the same time. It's not intuitive to expect the user of the Order component to then load all the Order Items when that user needs them. Understanding these relationships and modeling them in your components and the database is crucial to creating smart data access components. You can do this by writing related classes that compose the relationships, but this requires even more hand-coded ADO.NET to efficiently load related data.

As you scale out your solution, you can safely remote these objects (or refactor the factory methods into remotable objects), so there is a clear upgrade path as your Windows-based application needs additional scalability. This method of handcrafting your data access components is preferable when run-time performance and maintainability are high on the list of requirements for your components.

Another solution for doing your data access is to use *DataSets*. The *DataSet* class is a container for related data. The *DataSet* has the advantage over raw ADO.NET code in that some of the common data access functionality that you require is built into the *DataSet*. This functionality includes support for related entities, data binding support in ASP.NET, standard mechanism for change handling, and support for database-type schema to ensure validation of data before going to the database. In developing your data access components, you can compose your components using a *DataSet* internally to be able to use built-in functionality instead of having to invent it all yourself. In addition, the use of *DataAdapters* can simplify retrieval of multiple entity types as well as provide efficient ways of updating *DataSet* data.

The problem with *DataSets* is that they are not as efficient as hand-crafted ADO.NET solutions and are not as agile at evolving into solutions involving remoting.

In addition to using *DataSets* in your code, Visual Studio includes support for using *Typed DataSets*. *Typed DataSets* are essentially a tool-based solution for generating compile-time type-safe wrappers around *DataSets*. *Typed DataSets* in themselves can help you create data access layers very quickly. Instead of using *DataAdapters* to actually do the data access, *Typed DataSets* use a set of created classes called *TableAdapters*. In some cases you can use *Typed DataSets* out of the box as your components. The *Typed DataSet* designer supports a partial class solution for adding your own functionality to the generated classes.

Although the *Typed DataSet* solution is the quickest one to develop, there are major problems with an upgrade path for *Typed DataSets*. If you need to move from *Typed DataSets* into real data access components, you will end up throwing away the *Typed DataSet* code and starting from scratch.

Each of these solutions has its own pros and cons. How do you pick which one is acceptable for your requirements? Table 7-1 outlines the general guidelines for which to pick when.

Table 7-1   Data Access Methodology Guidelines

Data Access Method	Requirements
DataReaders and *Commands*	Where performance and scalability are most important and development cost is least important.
DataSets	For good mix of scalability and development cost with some loss of run-time performance.
Typed DataSets	For rapid application design (RAD) or prototyping. No good, clear upgrade path from *TableAdapters* to other data access methodologies.

Business Logic

Inside your components you will need to handle working with the validation and rules that are associated with almost any application. This data-related logic is called business logic. This might include anything from ensuring that strings are not too big to fit into the database to more complex interactions like not allowing new order creation if no credit is available for a particular customer.

Adding this logic to your components requires understanding both the explicit requirements and the implicit requirements. Explicit requirements include logic that's required to implement specific business processes. For example, your requirements might state that when an invoice is finalized, you must calculate the sales tax only for customers who are in certain states. Implicit requirements are requirements that are more technical in nature, such as validating that data can be stored within the constraints of the database schema and that relationships are maintained. When implementing your data components, you must include functionality for both types of requirements.

Depending on the data access method, you will need to determine the correct way to add your business logic. For example, if you are using *DataSets* inside your component, you could use the *DataSet* to validate the data against the schema (for example, field length validation, foreign key validation) and use custom code in your component to perform the more complex business rules.

Case Scenario

In the following case scenario, you will apply what you've learned in this lesson.

Case Scenario: Pick a Data Access Method

In this case scenario, you will review the requirements for a Windows-based project and pick a data access method that fulfills the requirements.

1. You are presented with the following requirements for a Windows-based project:
   - ❑ This project must be delivered by the end of December in order to be complete in this fiscal year.
   - ❑ This project must handle being deployed to a large number of users. The application it is replacing has more than 1000 concurrent users.
   - ❑ The data the project must deal with is a complex relational database, and the component should be created with the expectation that the data structures will change over time.

2. Based on these requirements, you review using ADO.NET with *DataReaders* and *Commands*, using *DataSets* and using *Typed DataSets*.

3. Based on the need to deliver the project quickly, but with an eye to scaling up, you choose to use *DataSets* inside your components.

Lesson Summary

- Depending on the performance, development cost, and maintainability requirements of your project, you should be able to pick a suitable data access method among *DataReaders*, *DataSets*, and *Typed DataSets*.
- By leveraging the data access method, you can add business logic in the appropriate way in your components.

Lesson Review

You can use the following questions to test your knowledge of the information in Lesson 2, "Developing Data Access Components." The questions are also available on the companion CD if you prefer to review them in electronic form.

NOTE Answers

Answers to these questions and explanations of why each answer choice is right or wrong are located in the "Answers" section at the end of the book.

1. Which of the following data access methods will perform best? (Choose one.)
   - **A.** *DataReaders* and *Commands*
   - **B.** *DataSets*
   - **C.** *Typed DataSets*

2. How should you add business logic and data validation if you are using *Typed DataSets*? (Choose all that apply.)

    A. Write custom code in the generated code.

    B. Write custom code in partial class.

    C. Use *DataSet* schema.

    D. Use *DataSet* events.

3. What type of data access method should you choose for quickly prototyping a component? (Choose one.)

    A. *DataReaders* and *Commands*

    B. *DataSets*

    C. *Typed DataSets*

Lesson 3: Component Infrastructure

Unfortunately, developing your component's base features is often not enough for real-world systems. Most components should include common infrastructure requirements. These requirements include exception handling and profiling support. In this lesson we will discuss how to plan for this infrastructure.

After this lesson, you will be able to:
- Develop an exception handling mechanism.
- Support profiling in your component.

Estimated lesson time: 10 minutes

Exceptions

As you develop your component, you will need to plan for when the unexpected happens. Your component needs to deal with exceptions. You need to determine when it is appropriate to throw an exception as well as what course of action to take if an exception is thrown during your component's execution. We will deal with these two decisions separately.

Throwing Exceptions

Exceptions are about exceptional events. You should ask yourself, "Is this an exceptional case?" It might be perfectly valid to return a value that is indicative of failure without it being an exceptional case. For example, let's assume you have a Customer component that allows you to retrieve a customer based on the name of the company. If you attempt to find the customer but there's no customer with the specified name, should you throw an exception to indicate the customer was not found? No, you should return a null (or nothing in VB.NET) to indicate that the customer was not found.

You should avoid using exceptions for process flow. Exceptions are too heavy for process flow. For example, avoid this sort of code:

```
' VB
Try
  yourComponent.SubmitInvoice()
Catch re As InvoiceRejectedException
  ' ...
Catch ae As InvoiceApprovedException
  ' ...
Catch pe As InvoicePendingException
  ' ...
End Try
```

```
// C#
try
{
  yourComponent.SubmitInvoice();
}
catch (InvoiceRejectedException re)
{
  // ...
}
catch (InvoiceApprovedException ae)
{
  // ...
}
catch (InvoicePendingException pe)
{
  // ...
}
```

Instead, create a return value that you can use to indicate the results, like so:

```
' VB
Enum SubmissionResult
  Approved
  Rejected
  Pending
End Enum
```

```
// C#
enum SubmissionResult
{
  Approved,
  Rejected,
  Pending
}
```

Then you can use the return value to do the same process flow without using exceptions:

```
' VB
Dim result As SubmissionResult = yourComponent.SubmitInvoice()

Select Case result
  Case SubmissionResult.Approved
    ' ...
    break
  Case SubmissionResult.Rejected
    ' ...
    break
  Case SubmissionResult.Pending
    ' ...
    break
End Select
```

```csharp
// C#
SubmissionResult result = yourComponent.SubmitInvoice();

switch (result)
{
  case SubmissionResult.Approved:
  {
    // ...
    break;
  }
  case SubmissionResult.Rejected:
  {
    // ...
    break;
  }
  case SubmissionResult.Pending:
  {
    // ...
    break;
  }
}
```

MORE INFO   **Avoiding exceptions as process flow**

To fully understand why you should not use exceptions for process flow, please see *Improving .NET Application Performance and Scalability (Patterns and Practices)*, Microsoft Press, 2004, pp. 320–322.

When should you throw an exception? You should throw an exception only when something exceptional occurs. You should throw your own exceptions whenever something happens in your code that is unexpected. For example, if you attempt to submit an invoice and find that the invoice is invalid in an unexpected way, you should throw an exception. If there is a .NET Framework exception that's indicative of the problem (for example, *ArgumentException*), you should throw that exception. If one does not exist, you should create your own exception class that derives from *System.Exception*.

BEST PRACTICES   **Custom exceptions**

Prior to the .NET Framework 2.0, it was common advice to have all application exceptions derive from *System.ApplicationException*, but that provided a level of isolation with no real purpose. Deriving your own exceptions from *System.Exception* is now the accepted best practice.

Handling Exceptions

When the code inside your component causes an exception to be thrown (that is, not an exception you have explicitly thrown), you must determine whether to allow the exception to propagate or to attempt to recover from the exceptional case. Consider the Customer component example from earlier in the lesson. What happens if the database is not available? If the database is not available, the ADO.NET managed provider will throw a *DbException* alerting you that it could not locate the database server. At this point you have two choices: propagate the exception up the call stack or attempt to recover from the error.

When propagating an exception to the caller, you might find it useful to include contextual information about when an error happened. This is most often done by throwing a new exception and including the current exception as the inner exception. For example:

```vb
' VB
Try
  Dim result As InvoiceResult = yourComponent.SubmitInvoice()
  ' ...
Catch ex As Exception
  Throw New InvoiceException("Exception thrown while submitting invoice.", ex)
End Try
```

```csharp
// C#
try
{
  InvoiceResult result = yourComponent.SubmitInvoice();
  // ...
}
catch (Exception ex)
{
  throw new InvoiceException("Exception thrown while submitting invoice.", ex);
}
```

If you can't provide any additional information to help determine the source of the exception, you can choose not to catch the exception at all and simply let it flow up to the caller. Often this is the right approach for exceptions that you have no control over (for example, *OutOfMemoryException*).

Instead of propagating the exception, you have the choice of attempting to recover from the exception or exiting gracefully. In the case of the database not being available, you might decide to try and recover by retrying the database after a small delay. If the recovery fails, you can either propagate the exception to the caller or attempt to exit gracefully. Both are valid options in different circumstances.

Profiling

As part of the requirements for any component you develop, you should expect to profile that component in order to identify performance issues and resource leaks. Profiling a component entails using one of a number of profiling tools to test the effectiveness of the component. Profiling tools are listed in Table 7-2.

Table 7-2 Profiling Tools

Tool	Description
Visual Studio Performance Wizard	Monitors the run-time behavior of your component in order to report on the effective performance of code. Allows for either sampling or instrumentation. Sampling is useful for testing the effectiveness of a whole system, while instrumentation allows you to test the performance of individual components.
CLR Profiler	Allows you to create memory allocation scenarios under which to test your component or application. Allows you to see how well your application works in a variety of scenarios.
SQL Profiler	Allows you to profile operations inside SQL Server. Can help identify inefficient queries, stored procedure compilation issues, and deadlocks.

Before you can use the data in a profile, you must understand the requirements for your component:

- Do you have performance metrics for your component?
- What resource usage is acceptable for your component?
- Under what load scenarios do you need to test the component?

Quick Check

- What is profiling used for?

Quick Check Answer

- To test performance of a component against requirements and to isolate resource leaks.

Simply profiling your component to see how well it behaves will tell you only how it is working, not if it's working well enough to meet the requirements. Understanding these requirements (or creating them) is crucial to profiling your component.

At times you can go overboard trying to eke out every bit of performance from a component. By being mindful of the schedule and real-world use of a component, you should be able to determine when to stop profiling a component. Since there are two sides to profiling components you should be careful to continue profiling and fixing a component if it continues to have resource or memory leaks, but fulfilling the performance requirements of a component should dictate that you can stop profiling a component.

There are also times when the profiling of a component yields such poor results that you need to revisit not only the implementation but also the design of the component. This is especially pertinent in situations where you have profiled a component over several revisions to the implementation in attempts to solve the problems. If you have gone through more than a handful of revisions without any impact on the performance of the component, it is likely time to start redesigning the component.

Profiling your component is often the key to its success, both for your application and for its long-term ability to be reused in other projects. Taking the time to profile your component is necessary and should be part of any component's design and development plan.

Lab: Propagating an Exception with Context

In this lab, you will create a new exception class and then use it to wrap an exception that occurs with context.

▶ **Exercise: Propagating the Exception**

For this exercise, create a new exception class and use it to propagate context with your exception.

1. Open the "Before" project in Lesson 3 on the CD.

2. Run the project as is. You will notice that an exception is thrown when the invoice is submitted.

3. Add a new class to the project called *InvoiceException* that we will use to propagate the context information.

4. Derive this new class from the *System.Exception* class and create a constructor that takes a string for the message and an exception.

5. In the new constructor, call the base class's constructor with the string and exception arguments. The new *InvoiceException* class might look something like this:

```vb
' VB
Public Class InvoiceException
  Inherits Exception

  Public Sub New(ByVal message As String, ByVal innerException As Exception)
    MyBase.New(message, innerException)
  End Sub

End Class
```

```csharp
// C#
public class InvoiceException : Exception
{
  public InvoiceException(string message, Exception innerException)
    : base(message, innerException)
  {
  }
}
```

6. Go to the *Submit* method of the *Invoice* class and create a try-catch block around the method body.

7. In the catch portion of the try-catch block, catch an *Exception* type and throw your new *InvoiceException*, passing in an informative message and the caught exception. The method might look something like this:

```vb
' VB
Public Function Submit() As SubmissionResult

   Try
      Dim s As String = Nothing

      ' Exception will be thrown here
      Dim length As Integer = s.Length

      Return SubmissionResult.Success

   Catch ex As Exception
      Throw New InvoiceException("Failure during Invoice Submission.", ex)
   End Try

End Function
```

```csharp
// C#
public SubmissionResult Submit()
{
   try
   {
      string s = null;

      // Exception will be thrown here
      int length = s.Length;

      return SubmissionResult.Success;
   }
   catch (Exception ex)
   {
      throw new InvoiceException("Failure during Invoice Submission.", ex);
   }
}
```

8. Compile the program and fix any coding errors found. Run the program under the debugger and, when the exception happens, notice the new exception with the informative message. Also look at the inner exception of the new exception to find the original exception that was thrown.

Lesson Summary

- You should throw exceptions only in exceptional cases; do not use exceptions for program flow.

- When you propagate exceptions, you should include contextual information by wrapping it with a more descriptive exception.
- All components should be profiled to isolate performance problems and resource leaks.

Lesson Review

You can use the following questions to test your knowledge of the information in Lesson 3, "Component Infrastructure." The questions are also available on the companion CD if you prefer to review them in electronic form.

NOTE Answers

Answers to these questions and explanations of why each answer choice is right or wrong are located in the "Answers" section at the end of the book.

---

1. In which of the following examples should you throw an exception from a component? (Choose all that apply.)

    A. An invalid argument is sent to a method.

    B. While searching for a particular piece of data, it returns with no results.

    C. The system runs out of memory.

    D. The database is not available.

2. If you propagate an exception to the caller of a method, should you always wrap that exception to include context? (Choose one.)

    A. True

    B. False

3. What are the goals of profiling a component? (Choose all that apply.)

    A. To ensure that the component meets all functional requirements.

    B. To measure the performance of the component against any performance requirements.

    C. To isolate resource leaks.

    D. To ensure that the component will compile.

Chapter Review

To further practice and reinforce the skills you learned in this chapter, you can perform the following tasks:

- Review the chapter summary.
- Review the list of key terms introduced in this chapter.
- Complete the case scenarios. These scenarios set up real-world situations involving the topics of this chapter and ask you to create a solution.
- Complete the suggested practices.
- Take a practice test.

Chapter Summary

- Implementing component features includes decisions about how to create the desired functionality, including whether to extend, compose, or implement the functionality; whether to build it as a stateless or stateful component; determining where and how to use threads in the component; and how to deal with unmanaged resources.
- Creating data access components requires an understanding of which data access method to pick for your component.
- Adding business logic to a data access component can be accomplished a number of ways based on the data access method chosen for the component.
- Dealing with component infrastructure includes deciding when and how to deal with exceptions.
- All components should be profiled to ensure that they meet performance metrics, as well as to isolate any resource leaks.

Key Terms

Do you know what these key terms mean? You can check your answers by looking up the terms in the glossary at the end of the book.

- business logic
- profiling
- stateless
- thread-safe

Case Scenarios

In the following case scenarios you will apply what you've learned about how to design components. You can find answers to these questions in the "Answers" section at the end of this book.

Case Scenario 1: Choose a Data Access Method

Your company needs data access components created for a new application.

Interviews

Following is a company manager's statement:

- **Engineering Manager**   "We have a new application that needs to be brought up to allow employees of the company to request vacation time. The Accounting department expected this to be completed already, so we have a severe time constraint on completing this to make them happy."

Questions

Answer the following questions for the developer:

1. Which data access technique should we use?
2. How can I add business logic needed to ensure that each employee has only one request pending at a time?

Case Scenario 2: Locate a Resource Leak

The insurance company that you work for has an application that was released about five days ago. There is a problem with the application because it's consuming lots of memory. Your manager needs your help in locating the problem.

Interviews

Following is a company manager's statement:

- **Your Manager**   "We are under the gun. The system was not profiled before it went live and now the system is performing badly and is just eating memory. We need you to find out why it is consuming so much memory."

Questions

Answer the following questions for your manager:

1. How do you propose to find the memory problems?
2. Can you isolate the problems to which components are causing the problems?

Suggested Practices

To successfully master the objectives covered in this chapter, complete the following tasks.

Create a New Logging Component

For this task, you should complete at least Practices 1 and 2. You can do Practice 3 for a more in-depth understanding of "Implementing Component Features."

- **Practice 1** Determine how to implement a logging component by deciding whether to extend, compose, or implement the features for a component that will log data.
- **Practice 2** Decide whether you can create the component as stateless or stateful.
- **Practice 3** Make the component thread-safe.

Create a Data Access Component

For this task, you should complete at least Practices 1 and 2. You can do Practices 3 and 4 for a more in-depth understanding of "Developing Data Access Components."

- **Practice 1** Create a new class that exposes data from a database table.
- **Practice 2** Implement the features using a *Typed DataSet*.
- **Practice 3** Reengineer the component to use a *DataSet* and *DataAdapters*.
- **Practice 4** Reengineer the component to use *DataReaders* and *Commands*.

Take a Practice Test

The practice tests on this book's companion CD offer many options. For example, you can test yourself on just one exam objective, or you can test yourself on all the 70-548 certification exam content. You can set up the test so that it closely simulates the experience of taking a certification exam, or you can set it up in study mode so that you can look at the correct answers and explanations after you answer each question.

MORE INFO   **Practice tests**

For details about all the practice test options available, see the "How to Use the Practice Tests" section in this book's Introduction.

Chapter 8

Instrumenting Your Application

If you develop applications for a corporate environment, at some point the application will need to grow up. By "grow up," I mean that the application needs to communicate with operations staff about what it's doing, events that have caught its attention, and any problems it has encountered. It's not enough for the application to wave its hands wildly. A well-behaved application can be told where and how to deliver all types of messages—and even change the types and delivery while the application is running. The process of setting up your application to "grow up"—to work well in the enterprise—is called instrumentation. The goal of this chapter is to describe some techniques that you can use to instrument an application.

Exam objectives in this chapter:
- Choose an appropriate event logging method for the application
  - ❏ Decide whether to log data. Considerations include policies, security, requirements, and debugging.
  - ❏ Choose a storage mechanism for logged events; for example, database, flat file, event log, or XML file.
  - ❏ Choose a systemwide event logging method; for example, centralized logging, distributed logging, and so on.
  - ❏ Decide logging levels based upon severity and priority.
- Monitor specific characteristics or aspects of an application.
  - ❏ Decide whether to monitor data. Considerations include administration, auditing, and application support.
  - ❏ Decide which characteristics to monitor; for example, application performance, memory consumption, security auditing, usability metrics, and possible bugs.
  - ❏ Choose event monitoring mechanisms, such as System Monitor and logs.
  - ❏ Decide monitoring levels based on requirements.
  - ❏ Choose a systemwide monitoring method from the available monitoring mechanisms.

Lessons in this chapter:

Before You Begin

To complete the lessons in this chapter, you should be familiar with Microsoft Visual Basic or C# and must have:

■ The Enterprise Library application (January 2006 version) installed on the computer. Enterprise Library can be downloaded from *http://msdn.microsoft.com/library/en-us/dnpag2/html/EntLib2.asp*.

Real World

Bruce Johnson

For many developers instrumenting an application is an afterthought. Once the functionality has been completed, some arbitrary status message might be sent to a log file. Or, in more sophisticated cases, a trace listener. But that's not an application that's ready for use in an enterprise.

The problem is that enterprise-level operations expect more than the occasional message. Well-instrumented applications need to keep any interested parties informed of what they're doing. This includes successes as well as failures. More important, the operations staff should be able to "turn up the volume" on an application when needed. And that means that some thought needs to be given to the logging and messaging that gets put into an application. After feature completion is too late.

Lesson 1: When Should an Application Be Instrumented?

As might have been clear from the introduction to this chapter, it is a relatively common occurrence to need to instrument an application that is going to be used in a corporate environment. Still, following rules with no understanding of the nuances is not how to go through life. And the fact that you're reading this book says that black and white is not what you're interested in. So let's consider the rationale for instrumenting an application, as well as the level of complexity required by the environment in which it's running.

After this lesson, you will be able to:
- Decide whether data should be logged or monitored.
- Identify the expected audience for logged data.
- Determine the business requirements for logging and monitoring.

Estimated lesson time: 50 minutes

Logging vs. Monitoring

Two forces generally drive the need to instrument an application. And both forces emanate from the same group: operations.

Logging means that as interesting things happen while an application is running, information about those interesting things are published. *Monitoring*, on the other hand, involves exposing information about an application to interested parties.

To a certain extent, the difference is a matter of perspective. Logging is done when something interesting happens, regardless of whether anyone is there to hear it. Monitoring is useful only when some application is paying attention. But within those subtle differences of definition, logging and monitoring can be considered fundamentally the same from the application's perspective. And certainly the mechanics of providing logging and monitoring details is the same.

Who Wants Logging or Monitoring?

Given that there is little mechanical difference, the question of whether an application should implement logging or monitoring capabilities depends on the audience for the information. And whether, in the context in which the application will run, someone will care. The groups who are interested in logging are as follows.

Operations

Operations are the people who are responsible for ensuring that the corporate computing infrastructure continues to run; not just continues to run at all but continues to meet the users' expectations for performance and reliability. As a result, logging and monitoring are important to this group. In particular, they want to be able to "see" what an application is doing so that they can identify potential problems before they become serious problems. As a result of this focus, operations is really looking for two things: errors and performance metrics.

Auditors

For certain types of applications, it is necessary to keep track of all the functions that were performed. Consider an application that calculated the interest for all of the accounts in a bank. The transaction being performed causes money to be transferred from the bank's account to the consumer's. And a problem will cost the bank money, the consumer aggravation, or both.

For transactions such as this, the corporate auditors are going to want detailed information about which value was put where. But financial auditing isn't the end of the auditing function. Laws such as HIPAA and Sarbanes-Oxley mandate auditing of certain types of transactions. And although these laws apply only to the United States, there might be a need to comply if you plan on doing business in the United States. Not to mention that a growing number of other countries are introducing their own legislation that covers the same area.

Administrative Support

For certain types of businesses, information found in individual transactions becomes part of what goes into additional calculations within the business. Salespeople might be bonused on the transactions per month. Departmental budgets might be allocated using activity-based metrics. In both of these cases, there is a need to log information at the necessary level of granularity to provide meaningful input into the business process.

Developers

It might be hard to accept that developers need (or want) to read through log files. But the class of developers that this title encompasses are those who are responsible for identifying the reason why an application isn't working as expected. They can't step through the application in the same manner that the original developer could. After all, the application is running in production and people might depend on it. So instead of setting breakpoints, the log information becomes critical to helping them do their test. They need to have information logged at a detailed enough level that the cause of a particular problem can be isolated to a single method or less. And if you've ever been in the position of looking at a running application to try and determine why it's not working and cursing at the lack of detailed logging information, you'll understand the mindset necessary to define the appropriate logging statements.

Security

For many companies, logging and monitoring also fall hand-in-hand with security concerns. On both sides of the fence, as it turns out.

If your company is concerned about the security of your application infrastructure, there will be some point at the beginning of the process where a set of credentials will be requested from the user. The request might be explicit, such as when a user ID and password screen is displayed. It might also be implicit, such as when the identity of the already logged-in Microsoft Windows user is used to determine roles and functionality. But regardless of the source, the user's identity is verified.

But there are at least two occasions where logging and monitoring of this process is useful. First, when a pattern of failed logon attempts indicates that someone is trying to gain unauthorized access to the system. And second, when an attempt is made to access functionality that the user isn't authorized to use. In both cases, the fact that an attempt was made and failed should be logged.

Now these aren't the only two instances when logging of security information should take place. It might be that successful logons and function access is desired as well. But from a security perspective, the least amount of logging is the set of failed attempts.

But security cuts both ways with logging. When an application logs successful access to a function, there needs to be some awareness of the potential for privacy violations. If an application logs when a particular function is accessed, it creates a trail that might be used to determine who accessed it. Even if the name of the user isn't included in the log information, it might be possible to deduce the information based on the list of currently logged-on users. For certain types of functions, keeping this information might violate a privacy law. And given the complexity of privacy laws, especially once national boundaries have been crossed, it is something that management needs to be made aware of.

Exam Tip   Keep in mind which groups of users require logging and which require monitoring. Specifically, operations and security will be interested in the immediacy of monitoring, while auditors, developers, and administrative personnel will be happy with logs.

Real World

Bruce Johnson

To get an idea of the possible impact of security on logging, consider two incidents that made headlines in the United States. Late in 2005 the U.S. government sued Google to turn over logs related to some searches that were being performed using objectionable words. Because the detailed logs were available, the government was able to go to a judge and request that they be turned over. This is an instance where, if less detailed logs were maintained, the government's ability to request them would have been severely curtailed.

The second example involves the use of telephone call log information by the U.S. National Security Agency. In this particular case the telephone companies faced a conundrum. The information that was logged—the originating call number, the destination number, and the length—is required to generate billing information. And, naturally, that information needs to be maintained. But it also contained information that some people might have expected to remain private, or at least kept between themselves and the phone companies. It is these competing requirements that make the question of logging and monitoring an application more complex than might have originally been thought.

What Data Is Required?

Once the audience for the data has been identified, the question of what data needs to be captured becomes a lot easier to answer. But even if I know that auditors or accountants are going to read the logs, a few issues still need to be addressed.

Granularity

The *granularity* of logged data is broken down into two categories based on the amount of data that is stored.

- **Coarsely grained**   Coarsely grained data is a high-level, general type of data. The focus of this type of data is at an application or a computer level. It does not include detailed information about individual transactions but instead uses averages and aggregation to reduce the volume of data collected. And that is, ultimately, the reason for using coarsely grained data. Less information is collected and is therefore easier to process. And although any conclusions or patterns taken from this information are not precise, they can be more than adequate for the intended purpose.

- **Finely grained**   Finely grained data is pretty much the opposite of coarse-grained. Rather than being concerned with the "big picture," finely grained monitoring records the details of individual transactions. This is the information that will be used to generating billing details or track the effectiveness of a Web-based marketing plan. But, as you would expect, the volume of logged data can be large to the point of overwhelming. The processing of transaction level logs typically requires specialized applications because the level of detail is beyond what most people can deal with.

Naturally, there will be times when both types of logging are required. Or, more accurately, the coarsely grained logging is acceptable right up to the time when finely grained logging is needed. For example, coarse-grained logging might be sufficient while the application's performance falls within certain bounds. However, if the application becomes sluggish, the finely grained detail might be necessary to pinpoint the cause of the problem.

Quick Check

- What level of detail is an auditor likely to require? Operations? Security?

Quick Check Answer

- For an audit, they are probably going to require finely grained instrumentation information. They might not always want to see everything, but they will want the option. Both operations and security need more coarsely grained logging. Both operations and security do need, however, to be able to change the logging level on demand.

Operations Monitoring

The needs of operations demands some additional description of the capabilities that are provided through tools such as the Microsoft Operations Manager (MOM) and how they can be facilitated through the design of the logging and monitoring mechanisms. There are two main elements to most monitoring tools (including MOM). On each system being monitored, an agent is installed. This agent is responsible for checking on status and events originating from a number of sources on the system. When an interesting event occurs, the agent forwards a message to a central server. This central server makes up the second element in the monitoring tool.

The real power of tools such as MOM is on display in the server component. First, the notifications from different agents are collected in a single location. This certainly eases the workload of keeping track of many computers in different locations. But more important, MOM allows the operations staff to define filters on the incoming events–filters that will cause the operations staff to be notified only after one or more criteria associated with the incoming events are met. Too many events within a five-minute period? Too little free space on a machine? MOM will recognize this situation and raise a flag for operations to see.

MOM actually goes a step beyond this. In certain situations, MOM can be configured to be proactive when certain notifications are detected such as trying to free up some disk space on a machine when the "disk space low" message arrives. In this situation the operations staff might be notified only when the initial remedial action (freeing disk space) fails.

These possibilities can have an impact on the design of the logging and monitoring within an application. A balance in the granularity of the events must be struck to ensure that operations is notified in a timely manner when it matters. Yet at the same time, the number of false positives must be kept to a minimum. For this reason, the design of the logging/monitoring granularity is not only important but also should be done in conjunction with the operations people. Making sure that they get the type of information that they need when they need it should be one of the main design goals of the infrastructure.

Logging/Monitoring Levels

This schizophrenic requirement for both finely and coarsely grained logs leads to the idea of levels. A log level is a setting that becomes associated with each log statement to indicate the relative level of importance. Although the names of log levels are arbitrary, the *Windows Event Log* includes the following levels. You can use them as is or just as a guideline.

- **Error**   A significant problem with the application. It usually indicates a loss of data or functionality that needs to be addressed immediately.
- **Warning**   A less significant problem than the Error. Although there is no immediate concern, warnings could foreshadow future problems.
- **Information**   Used to indicate that a successful operation of interest has occurred.
- **FailureAudit**   An audit entry for a failed attempt to access a secured resource. It could be an invalid logon or attempting to read a file that isn't in an accessible directory.
- **SuccessAudit**   An audit entry for a successful attempt to access a secured resource.

The purpose of a log level is to indicate the level of interest that the audience for the logging and monitoring data has for the information. If the application runs with a log level of Warning, the implication is that only those log messages with a severity of Warning or higher should be logged. Any lower-level messages should be ignored. This implies that definition of the log levels also includes a hierarchy of severity, or multiple hierarchies, as is the case in the list shown above. For this list there are two hierarchies. The first three items are listed in order of decreasing severity, and the last two are in their own (again, decreasing in severity) order.

Once you have defined the log levels, you need to be able to adjust the levels within a running application. The application's configuration file normally contains the level of logging interest. For example, the following config element could be used to configure the application to log all messages of Warning or higher.

```
<appSettings>
   <add key='LogLevel' value='Warning'/>
</appSettings>
```

Please realize that the name of the configuration value (LogLevel) is arbitrary. You could name it whatever you'd like for your application. It is up to the logging mechanism that your application uses to evaluate the LogLevel setting and determine whether to include a particular message or not.

Exam Tip   Remembering the specific names of the log levels is not as important as being aware that different log levels can produce different instrumentation results.

Changing Log Levels in a Windows Application

The problem with changing log levels in a Windows application is exactly the opposite of a Web application. Whereas a change to web.config is automatically detected and picked up, a change to an application configuration file is not detected until the next time the application starts. So changing the App.config file does nothing to the level of log messages currently being generated.

App.config does not contain a mechanism for addressing this issue. As a result, the logging mechanism used in your application needs to take things into its own hands. Specifically, the *FileSystemWatcher* class can be used to monitor the App.config file for changes. Once a change is detected, the log level settings can be reloaded, and subsequent log attempts will respond accordingly.

The *System.IO.FileSystemWatcher* class includes three properties that are used to control what gets watched and when events are raised. First, the *Path* property indicates the directory to be watched. Then the *Filter* property is used to indicate which files are to have events raised for. Finally, the *NotifyFilter* determines which types of file system events (such as file addition, deletions, renames, and so on) cause an event to be raised.

```vb
' VB
Dim fsw as New FileSystemWatcher()
fsw.Path = Environment.CurrentDirectory
fsw.Filter = "*.config"
fsw.NotifyFilter = NotifyFilters.LastWrite
AddHandler fsw.Changed, AddressOf AppConfigChangeHandler
fsw.EnableRaisingEvents = True
```

```csharp
// C#
FileSystemWatcher fsw = new FileSystemWatcher();
fsw.Path = Environment.CurrentDirectory;
fsw.Filter = "*.config";
fsw.NotifyFilter = NotifyFilters.LastWrite;
```

```
fsw.Changed += new FileSystemEventHandler(AppConfigChangeHandler);
fsw.EnableRaisingEvents = true;
```

Once the file has been set up, an event handler needs to be defined. This event handler will be notified when the config file is changed. Within the event handler, the *RefreshSection* method on *System.Configuration.ConfigurationManager* is used to mark the section so that it is reread from disk the next time it is accessed.

```
' VB
Private Sub AppConfigEventHandler(ByVal sender As Object, ByVal e As FileSystemEventArgs)
   ConfigurationManager.RefreshSection("appSettings")
End Sub
```

```
// C#
private void AppConfigChangeHandler(object sender, FileSystemEventArgs e)
{
   ConfigurationManager.RefreshSection("appSettings");
}
```

Two potential issues need to be addressed before leaving this topic. First off, the *RefreshSection* method works correctly only if the configuration file being changed is external to the main App.config. This means that the section being refreshed needs to be defined using the *config-Source* attribute.

The second potential is a little less troublesome. The *FileSystemWatcher* does not respond with absolute accuracy to every single file system event. It is possible that if a large number of files were changed in a short time, the buffer that holds the change information would get overrun and a change might be missed. However, this is really only a hypothetical issue. It is very unlikely, given the filters being used, that a large enough number of changes would be made so as to cause this problem.

The Interesting Data

Now we're down to the data that each log should capture. To accurately identify this, the logging focus for the application needs to be identified. It could be one of the following areas:

- General application health
- Performance
- Availability
- Transactional auditing
- Security auditing

Regardless of which area or areas require the logging, identifying the intended audience is the first step in the data identification process. Doing this keeps the logging from being too narrow (which prevents useful data from being left out) or too broad (which prevents unnecessary data from being included).

A good way to start down this path is to make a prioritized list of the logging needs. With each item, include details on who should get the information, how much information they need, and how quickly they should receive it. Table 8-1 is an example of this type of list.

Table 8-1   Prioritized Logging Needs

Situation	Details
Run Time Exception	Deliver immediately to operations. Store in a persisted location. Include message, inner exception, stack trace, current user, and current request.
Failed Logon	Deliver to operations on demand. Store in a persisted location. Include originating Internet Protocol (IP) address, invalid user ID, date, and time.
Completed Order	Deliver to sales staff on demand. Include customer, order number, value, date, and time.
Delayed Order	Deliver to sales staff immediately. Store in a persisted location. Include customer, order number, value, and reason for delay.

The items in this list are simply examples of the types of situations that might use logging. The specifics of the application and the organization will dictate which areas need to be included and what the priorities are.

Part of the process of determining the data to be logged and monitored is to compare the requirements as indicated in the list of interesting events and match them against the options for logging and monitor. In some instances the match will be obvious. In others, finding the right storage and recording mechanism will be challenging. But in all cases, the needs of the audience for the data will be preeminent in tilting the design surface to its final resting place.

Lab: Changing Log Levels

The purpose of this lab is to demonstrate a technique that can be used to implement log levels in a Windows application.

▶ **Exercise: Log Levels in a Windows Application**

As has already been discussed, the technique to allow log levels to be modified in a running application is a little different for Windows applications. In this lab an easily implemented technique that allows for configuration files to be reloaded is demonstrated. The starting point is a simple Windows Forms application with a button that displays the log level as retrieved from the config file. With the initial implementation, changing the App.config file will not affect the displayed value. In other words, successive button clicks display the same log level even after it has been changed and saved. Feel free to prove this for yourself before getting started.

1.   Launch Visual Studio 2005.
2.   Open a solution using File | Open | Project/Solution.

3. Navigate to the Chapter8\Lesson1\<*language*>\Exercise-Before directory. Select the Exercise1 solution and click Open.

4. In the Solution Explorer, right-click GetConfigValue and select View Designer to display the design surface. Then double-click the form to create the *Load* event handler procedure.

5. In the *Load* event handler, add code to create the *FileSystemWatcher* object. The Path is set to the current directory. The *Filter* is set to be any file with a config extension. And the *NotifyFilter* is set to raise events when a file is updated.

```
' VB
Dim fsw As New FileSystemWatcher
fsw.Path = Environment.CurrentDirectory
fsw.Filter = "*.config"
fsw.NotifyFilter = NotifyFilters.LastWrite
```

```
// C#
FileSystemWatcher fsw = new FileSystemWatcher();
fsw.Path = Environment.CurrentDirectory;
fsw.Filter = "*.config";
fsw.NotifyFilter = NotifyFilters.LastWrite;
```

6. In the same *Load* event handler procedure, a handler for the *Changed* event needs to be added. This procedure gets called when a file system event that matches the *NotifyFilter* happens to the file (or files) indicated by the *Path* and *Filter* properties. Also, the *EnableRaiseEvents* property on the *FileSystemWatcher* object is set to true. Add the following code to the end of the *Load* event handler procedure:

```
' VB
AddHandler fsw.Changed, AddressOf AppConfigChangeHandler
fsw.EnableRaisingEvents = True
```

```
// C#
fsw.Changed += new FileSystemEventHandler(AppConfigChangeHandler);
fsw.EnableRaisingEvents = true;
```

7. The *Changed* event handler procedure needs to be created. From the code added in step 6, the name of this procedure is *AppConfigChangeHandler*. In this procedure, the *AppSettings* section of the configuration file is refreshed. Add the following procedure to the *GetConfigValue* class:

```
' VB
Private Sub AppConfigChangeHandler(ByVal sender As Object, ByVal e As
FileSystemEventArgs)
   ConfigurationManager.RefreshSection("appSettings")
End Sub
```

```
// C#
private void AppConfigChangeHandler(object sender, FileSystemEventArgs e)
{
```

```
ConfigurationManager.RefreshSection("appSettings");
}
```

8. Because the "official" App.config file can't be refreshed once the application has started, the *appSettings* element must be moved to an external configuration file. In the Solution Explorer, right-click the project and select Add | New Item from the context menu. Then select a template of Application Configuration File and give it a name of external.config.

9. Replace the contents of external.config that were generated automatically with the following Extensible Markup Language (XML) document:

```
<?xml version="1.0" encoding="utf-8" ?>
<appSettings>
<add key="logLevel" value="Information"/>
</appSettings>
```

10. So that the external.config file gets moved to the directory in which the application will be executed, a property needs to be set. Specifically, right-click the external.config file in Solution Explorer and select Properties. In the Property Sheet, change the value of Copy To Output Directory to Copy If Newer. If you're using the Visual Basic version of the project, this is the default for a newly added config file.

11. Open the App.config file. Find the *appSettings* element and replace the entire element (including the opening and closing tags) with the following. The newly added element references the just-created configuration file.

```
<appSettings configSource="external.config"></appSettings>
```

12. Launch the application using F5. Click the Get Config Value button and note the log level.

13. Without shutting down the application, use Microsoft Notepad to open the external.config file in the running directory (this is the bin\Debug directory underneath your project's path). Change the value of the *logLevel* attribute to *Warning*. Save the change.

14. Return to the running application. Click the Get Config Value button again and note that the displayed log level is now Warning.

Lesson Summary

- Instrumentation should be a part of most nontrivial applications.
- The audience for the logging and monitoring output needs to be considered when determining the granularity of the messages.
- Allowing both Windows Forms and Web applications to detect changing in log level configuration requires some thought beyond simply adding a value to a configuration file.

Lesson Review

You can use the following questions to test your knowledge of the information in Lesson 1, "When Should an Application Be Instrumented?" The questions are also available on the companion CD if you prefer to review them in electronic form.

NOTE   Answers

Answers to these questions and explanations of why each answer choice is right or wrong are located in the "Answers" section at the end of the book.

---

1. Your company's applications need to be kept running 24 hours a day. To help notify operations of problems, you will be instrumenting your application. But operations doesn't want to be notified of all monitoring messages. Which of the Windows Event Log levels should operations be looking for? (Choose all that apply.)

    A. Error

    B. Warning

    C. Information

    D. SuccessAudit

    E. FailureAudit

2. Which of the following audiences are more likely to be interested in logged information, as opposed to real-time metrics? (Choose all that apply.)

    A. Operations

    B. Developers

    C. Fast-response security personnel

    D. Auditors

Lesson 2: Storing the Data

Once the data of interest has been identified, the mechanics of getting the data into the appropriate store needs to be addressed. A number of alternatives are available, each of which has its pros and cons. Sometimes a database is overkill for a log entry that happens once a day. And the Windows Event Log isn't appropriate for continuous logging activity. So the idea is to look at the characteristics of the logging data, its frequency, and how the logged data will be used to determine which data store should be targeted. The purpose of this lesson is to outline the options and describe the scenarios in which each storage type could be used effectively.

After this lesson, you will be able to:

- Decide whether data should be logged or monitored.
- Identify the expected audience for logged data.
- Determine the business requirements for logging and monitoring.

Estimated lesson time: 35 minutes

Logging vs. Monitoring

When it came to the interesting data, the differences between logging and monitoring were minimal. The same techniques could be used with both goals to identify the data that needed to be reported. However, once we get to data storage, there is a big difference. Or at least there can be. And the "best" answer is directly related to how and when the audience expects to use the data.

Generally speaking, the differences between logging and monitoring have to do with the immediacy with which the data is required. If you're monitoring an application, there is an implicit requirement that the people doing the monitoring are notified of important events quickly. This element of immediacy affects where the monitoring information will be stored.

Along with immediate notifications, monitoring also includes the idea that an ongoing status of the application is available. It could be a running count of the transactions, a heartbeat that indicates the health of the application, or a graph of the CPU cycles being consumed. But regardless of how the information is visualized, there is real-time (or near real-time) feedback on the application.

Logging brings with it the connotation of much less immediacy. Instead of seeing transactions displayed on a screen, logs are stored in a dark, dusty corner of the server. Only when weekly or monthly reports are required do these files get pulled out and processed. So rather than being real-time, log files are historical archives of what has transpired in an application.

One other implied attribute of log files is the volume of data that is stored. Log files are frequently detailed transaction records. They can contain reams of data that need to be processed and analyzed by specially created applications. And rather than displaying the details, the visualization of a log file usually includes aggregations and summaries because there is too much information to be useful to people in an unfiltered manner.

Data Storage Choices

Let's start the discussion of which data storage choices are available for collecting instrumentation details. And, for each choice, the characteristics will be considered only within the context of instrumentation and using the gathered information.

Flat Files

For many developers, *flat files* are almost inextricably bound to the concept of a log file. For pure simplicity, none of the other choices come close. But none of the other choices come close to the lack of intrinsic functionality either.

The idea of a flat file log is that each line in the file contains the information for one interesting event. For each event a number of fields containing information about the event (date, time, type, description, source, and so on) are written to the line. The structure of each line usually falls into one of three categories:

- **Comma-separated**   Each field is separated by a comma. This is a common file format, enough so that Microsoft Excel can open a comma-separated values (CSV) file without conversion. The biggest drawback of the format is that the field information can itself contain a comma. And that extra comma throws off the format for the remainder of the line. The solution is to surround fields that contain a comma with single or double quotation marks, which in turn restricts the content of the field so that it can't contain a single or double quotation mark. You can see how this can go round and round, although in practice the solution is adequate for the vast majority of situations.

- **Tab-separated**   Tab-separated files use the same concept as a comma-separated file but use a less common character as the separator. As a result, the need for single or double quotation marks is usually avoided. All the other characteristics of comma-separated files still apply, including Excel's ability to read them with no conversion.

- **Fixed-length**   The number of characters allocated to each field is fixed. This means that the need for field delimiters is removed, along with the single/double quotation mark question. It does introduce a couple of other issues, however. First, the fixed length means that the space allocated to each field can't be changed, even if the amount of information in the event is greater than the field length. As a result, some information can be lost. If, however, the field sizes are set to the maximum available information, each record will be much longer than would be needed (assuming that fields only occasionally contain the maximum size). This means the log file takes up more space, with no additional information being provided.

Naturally, not all flat files need to be in one of these formats. The fact that flat files are simply text files means that the format of the line can be whatever the situation requires. Also, the format of each line could be different depending on the type of event. But both of these alternatives result in flat files that are more challenging to process automatically.

The simplicity of a flat file is one of its main benefits. It is simple to create and can be easily viewed using any text editor. Well, the viewing itself is easy. But sometimes the understanding of the content is challenging without some intervening process. The human brain isn't really equipped to deal with raw information presented in the flat file format.

One of the drawbacks of using a flat file is that it's a local-only mechanism. Although it's certainly possible to create a flat file on network share, it is rarely done. The processing time required to push the information across a network is significant (in computer scale). Not to mention that you have now introduced the possibility that a log entry can't be created because the network isn't available. So the normal usage of a flat file is to keep it local to the application that is updating it.

Event Log

Unlike a flat file format, the event log contains a fixed list of fields. When an event is posted to the log, the application has the ability to fill in some or all of the fields. The fields are listed in Table 8-2.

Table 8-2   Event Log Fields

Field Name	Description
Source	The name of the application that is the source for the event log. It must be registered on the computer before it can be used.
Message	The string that is the message for the log entry.
Type	The type of log entry. It must be one of the EventLogEntryType values.
Event Id	An application-specific identifier for the event.
Category	An application-specific subcategory that is associated with the log entry.
Raw Data	A set of binary data that is associated with the log entry.

In addition to the list of fields, three logs are also created by default. They are Application, Security, and System. These logs are intended to segregate the log entries to help with the searching and reporting process. In general, the System log contains entries associated with the operating system and its related processes. The Security log contains successful and failed resource access events. And the Application log contains entries associated with other nonoperating system applications. For the most part, the Application log will be the one used by most developers. It is also possible to create a new event log if the segregation of events to an even further degree is required.

The event log solves some of the problems associated with a flat file. For example, it does provide a slightly more centralized location for log information over a flat file. Instead of individual applications having their own log file, all the information is placed into a common repository. However, the cost of this centralization is a lessening of flexibility. Although a flat file can define whatever fields it wants, the event log has a set list of fields.

That having been said, there is a technique that can increase the flexibility. One of the fields in the log is a message, which can be arbitrary text. If you wanted to add fields to the information stored in the log, you could create a .NET class that contains the desired fields and then serialize an instance of the object into an XML or binary format and place that information into the message field. In this way, you can add whatever fields you want to the log. You would, however, need to write your own tool to process the messages because the Windows Event Viewer will display only a textual representation of the message.

The permissions necessary to write to the event log is also a topic worth covering. In .NET 1.0 and 1.1, the caller of the *WriteEntry* method (which, as you will see shortly, is used to create event log entries from within .NET) had to have full trust. In .NET 2.0, the actual caller of the *WriteEntry* method needs to run as full trust, but the *AllowPartiallyTrustedCallers* attribute can be used on the assembly to allow lower-privileged assemblies to invoke the necessary methods (that is, the one that calls *WriteEntry*).

The mechanics of writing an entry to the event log are fairly straightforward. The *System.Diagnostics.EventLog* class contains a static method called *WriteEntry*. In its simplest form, the method is used to post a string as the message portion of a log entry with an entry type of Information.

```
' VB
System.Diagnostics.EventLog.WriteEntry("This is the log message")
```

```
// C#
System.Diagnostics.EventLog.WriteEntry("This is the log message");
```

In more complicated overloads, you can specify additional information, including the log to which it will be written (such as Application, System, and Security), the event log type, the event identifier, the event category, and an array of bytes, to be included with the entry.

Exam Tip   The permissions required to add entries to the event log are an important consideration when Web applications are used. They also need to be considered when a Windows Forms application is deployed using Smart Client technology.

Database

With the first two sources, we moved from simple to slightly more complicated but didn't really address the problem of centralized accessibility. Not to mention that, in the first two cases, generating reports are difficult. If these two attributes (centralization and reporting) are a requirement, then using a database as storage is the destination you might want to consider. But there are, of course, other reasons for using a database. In fact, if you look at the reasons for using a database in the normal course of business, they apply equally well to using it as a logging or monitoring data store. Databases are reliable, scalable, capable of supporting simultaneous requests, and transactable.

This last feature is of particular importance for auditors interested in log files. The fact that a database server can operate within a transaction means that the developer can guarantee that an entry will be added to the log table only if the rest of the database updates are made. In other words, the creation of a log entry can be part of the same transaction as the business updates. From an auditing perspective, this functionality can be critical. It is also not something that can be accomplished using flat files or the Windows Event Log because neither of these supports transactions.

As with the event log, the layout of each entry is fixed. That takes place as the schema for the table into which the entries will be put are defined. However, unlike the event log (and more like the flat file), the fields that are included in the table are completely up to the developer. The limits on what can be stored in a database for a log entry are the same limits that apply to application data.

If reporting is important, the use of a database is an almost perfect choice. Not only are databases designed to facilitate reporting, but also tools are available for reporting. If SQL Server 2000 or 2005 is the database being used, SQL Reporting Services not only can generate professional looking reports but also can automate their delivery and retention. In other words, using a database makes it easy to retain, analyze, report on, and manage logging information.

There are two main downsides to using a database. One is that, well, you need a database engine. Both the flat file and event log storage type are built into the operating system. There is no way that a flat file or the event log will be unavailable unless the logging application doesn't have permissions. But a database engine needs to be installed. Not only installed, but the tables used to store the logged information must be defined. Because of these requirements, an application that uses a database can't use a pure XCOPY deployment technique. Unless, of course, the database engine and the necessary table are already installed on a separate server—which brings us to the second drawback.

One of the benefits of flat files and event logs is that they are local to the application that is performing the logging. So (absent any permission problems) they are always accessible. A database, especially a centralized one, needs to be running, and the network needs to be up. So using the database as a logging mechanism introduces one additional point of failure to the application. And, more important, it is one that might cause important information to be unavailable. For example, assume the database used for logging is the same one used by the application itself. If the database is unavailable, then the application will try to log that event.

However, because the database is unavailable, it won't be able to. So the application will fail without any pertinent logging information being stored.

No suggestion is being made here that there isn't a solution to this scenario. Of course there is. Log file aggregation, when the information is initially stored locally and then regularly moved to a central database, is one. Creating a fallback log where events that don't get successfully written to the central database are written to a local data store is another. The point is that you need to consider these possibilities if the data store has the potential to be one of the points of failure in the application.

The technique for placing logging data into a database is the same as that used for any data. It means (for a .NET application, anyway) that ADO.NET is likely to be involved. Given that ADO.NET is well understood by most developers and that detailed coverage is outside of the scope of this book, the sample code will be simple.

```vb
' VB
Dim cn As New SqlConnection(connectionString)
Dim cmd As New SqlCommand("INSERT INTO LogTable VALUES " & _
   "(GetDate(), @LogType, @LogMessage)"
cmd.Parameters.AddWithValue("@LogType", logType)
cmd.Parameters.AddWithValue("@LogMessage"md.Parameters.Add("changes to clarifyt a bye as
being blatantly slanted in a particular direction.th making the effort to answ, logMessage)
cmd.CommandType = CommandType.Text
cn.Open()
cmd.ExecuteNonQuery()
cn.Close()
```

```csharp
// C#
SqlConnection cn = new SqlConnection(connectionString)
SqlCommand cmd = new SqlCommand("INSERT INTO LogTable VALUES " +
   "(GetDate(), @LogType, @LogMessage)";
cmd.Parameters.AddWithValue("@LogType", logType);
cmd.Parameters.AddWithValue("@LogMessage"md.Parameters.AddWithValue(", logMessage);
cmd.CommandType = CommandType.Text;
cn.Open();
cmd.ExecuteNonQuery();
cn.Close();
```

E-mail

One of the drawbacks of using the event log, a flat file, or a database for logging and monitoring is the lack of immediate notification. Sure, information gets put to those sources immediately. But unless someone is watching for it, they won't see the newly created entries.

Now an argument can be made that the delivery of notifications falls outside the purview of the development staff. Tools are available to the operations staff to monitor the various data stores mentioned to this point and provide notification appropriately. But there are still situations in which people outside of operations staff need to receive immediate notifications, and for these times the three storage mechanisms mentioned so far aren't appropriate. Or not without some additional effort. It is this immediate notification ability that sets e-mail apart.

As many of you are probably aware, e-mail can be sent and received almost anytime, and almost certainly more often then many of us want. Our inability to get away from our inboxes is what makes e-mail good for those events that are of critical importance. If the database has gone down and the call center can't take orders, this needs to be recognized and addressed immediately. Waiting for someone to look in a log file isn't an option.

Also, e-mail has the ability to "reach out" beyond the corporate infrastructure. E-mail can be sent and received anywhere in the world. Blackberrys, cell phones, and Personal Digital Assistants (PDAs) are all options for receiving e-mail messages. For the other data storage mechanisms, you need to be logged onto the network to access the information.

The downside to e-mail is that it really isn't a data storage mechanism. You can't report on the logging information sent by e-mail directly. It's not possible (or at least, not easy) for developers to review the e-mail log files to see if they can identify the cause of a problem.

In fact, because of e-mail's immediacy, it's not a good idea to send finely grained log messages. Receiving too many messages of lesser importance will cause the really important ones to be ignored. See the fable "The Boy Who Cried Wolf" for an object lesson. Because e-mail really isn't a storage medium, it is more typical to find e-mail used in conjunction with other mechanisms. In this way, notification of critical events can take place in near real-time, but the detailed log files are placed in a more useful location.

In order to send e-mail, .NET 2.0 introduced a new class called *SmtpClient* as part of the *System.Net.Mail* namespace. The basic steps are relatively easy to follow. A new *MailMessage* object is created. The *MailMessage* contains the subject, the body, and the from and to addresses for the message. The *SmtpClient* is responsible for sending the message to the mail server. After the mail server is identified by name, the *Send* method is used to submit the *MailMessage* for processing.

Although this process is simple, it doesn't handle one of the most common requirements for sending e-mails—authentication. Many mail servers require that you specify a user ID and password before you can send an e-mail message. To do this, the *NetworkCredential* class is used in conjunction with the *Credentials* property on the *SmtpClient* object.

The *NetworkCredential* class is part of the *System.Net* namespace. A new *NetworkCredential* object is created with the necessary user ID and password. This instance is then assigned to the *Credentials* property. Also, *SmtpClient* needs to be told that the default credentials should not be sent. Otherwise, the Windows identity for the current user will be transmitted. The following code sends an e-mail message to an authenticated mail server:

```
' VB
Dim message As New MailMessage(fromAddress, toAddress, subject, messageBody)
Dim emailClient As New SmtpClient(mailServerName)
```

```
Dim smtpUserInfo = New System.Net.NetworkCredential(txtSMTPUser.Text, txtSMTPPass.Text)
emailClient.UseDefaultCredentials = False
emailClient.Credentials = smtpUserInfo
emailClient.Send(message)
```

```
// C#
MailMessage message = new MailMessage(fromAddress, toAddress, subject, messageBody);
SmtpClient emailClient = new SmtpClient(mailServerName);
System.Net.NetworkCredential smtpUserInfo = new
    System.Net.NetworkCredential(txtSMTPUser.Text, txtSMTPPass.Text);
emailClient.UseDefaultCredentials = false;
emailClient.Credentials = smtpUserInfo;
emailClient.Send(message);
```

System Monitor

Although e-mail provides immediate notification, as has already been noted, it is not a good repository for log information. Nor is it really good for keeping track of the system's health on an ongoing basis—the messages are too sporadic. For this reason, using the System Monitor is a nice compromise between log files/flat files and databases and the immediacy of e-mail.

The System Monitor is part of the Performance console for the Microsoft Management Console. System Monitor can be used to track a large number of counters from different aspects of the operating system. The counters are retrieved on a recurring basis and displayed as a graph. Figure 8-1 shows the System Monitor with the standard counters included.

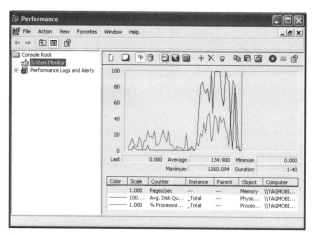

Figure 8-1   A sample display for System Monitor.

Although System Monitor comes with a large number of counters, it is possible for applications to add their own. And once added, the counters are capable of being captured and viewed using the same interface shown in Figure 8-1. We will demonstrate how to create and use the counters later in this section.

Although the main benefit of using System Monitor is the ability to observe the moment-to-moment status of an application, there are some drawbacks to its use. All of the techniques described so far allow for text information to be included in the log message. It could be a stack trace or a set of correlated fields. But regardless of the details, the log message contains additional information. The performance counter, on the other hand, is just that ... a counter. It might count the number of transactions or the number of failed logons. But it is just a numeric value that can be manipulated by the application over time. No additional information is available from the log entry. As a result, the System Monitor is good for monitoring the health and progress of an application but not good for capturing information that could be used to help solve a problem.

Using a performance counter from within a .NET application is not complicated. But before diving into the details, we need to look at the types of counters that are available. The counters can be divided into five basic categories.

- **Average**   Measures the counter value over a period of time. The displayed value is the average of the last two measurements. An average is actually a combination of two counters: a base counter that tracks the number of samples and a regular counter that tracks the values.
- **Difference**   Displays the difference between two successive measurements. This particular counter can't be negative, so if the second measurement is less than the first, a value of zero is displayed.
- **Instantaneous**   The displayed value is the counter value at that point in time.
- **Percentage**   The displayed value is the counter value as a percentage. This is different from instantaneous only in the way it is displayed.
- **Rate**   The displayed value is the change in counter value divided by the change in time; in other words, the rate of change of the counter over time.

You can create new performance counters either programmatically or directly through Visual Studio. Because it is more likely that the counters will be created programmatically, that's the technique we'll demonstrate.

The first step is to work on the category. The *PerformanceCounterCategory* class has a static method named *Exists*. This method is used to determine if a particular category has already been defined. If it hasn't, the *Create* method can be used to create the category.

Along with creating the category, the *Create* method can also be used to add new counters at the same time. And, as it turns out, this is the only way to add counters programmatically. They can't be added to existing categories. Instead, the category would have to be deleted and then recreated with the appropriate counters.

The creation of a counter involves two classes. The first, named *CounterCreationData*, is used to define the information about an individual counter. The second, named *CounterCreationDataCollection*, is a collection of (wait for it) *CounterCreationData* objects. And instances of this second class, populated with the counters to be added, are passed into an overloaded *Create* method.

```vb
' VB
Dim CounterDatas As New CounterCreationDataCollection()
Dim cntr1 As New CounterCreationData()
Dim cntr2 As New CounterCreationData()

cntr1.CounterName = "DemoCounter1"
cntr1.CounterHelp = "A description of DemoCounter1"
cntr1.CounterType = PerformanceCounterType.NumberOfItems64
cntr2.CounterName = "DemoCounter2"
cntr2.CounterHelp = "A description of DemoCounter2"
cntr2.CounterType = PerformanceCounterType.NumberOfItems64

CounterDatas.Add(cntr1)
CounterDatas.Add(cntr2)

PerformanceCounterCategory.Create("Demo Category", "A help message for the category", _
    PerformanceCounterCategoryType.SingleInstance, CounterDatas)
```

```csharp
// C#
System.Diagnostics.CounterCreationDataCollection CounterDatas =
    new System.Diagnostics.CounterCreationDataCollection();

System.Diagnostics.CounterCreationData cntr1 = new System.Diagnostics.CounterCreationData();
System.Diagnostics.CounterCreationData cntr2 = new System.Diagnostics.CounterCreationData();

cntr1.CounterName = "DemoCounter1";
cntr1.CounterHelp = "A description of DemoCounter1";
cntr1.CounterType = PerformanceCounterType.NumberOfItems64;
cntr2.CounterName = "DemoCounter2";
cntr2.CounterHelp = "A description of DemoCounter2";
cntr2.CounterType = PerformanceCounterType.NumberOfItems64;

CounterDatas.Add(cntr1);
CounterDatas.Add(cntr2);

PerformanceCounterCategory.Create("Demo Category",  "A help message for the category",
    PerformanceCounterCategoryType.SingleInstance, CounterDatas);
```

NOTE   **Performance counters and permissions**

Although most accounts can read and update performance counters, the creation of a performance counter category and the counters themselves require a higher level of permissions. The only default groups that are able to create categories and counters are Administrators and Power Users.

Accessing and updating the performance counters is relatively simple. The *Performance-Counter* class contains all the necessary methods and properties. First, a *PerformanceCounter* instance is created by specifying the category and counter name in the constructor.

```
' VB
Dim pc as New PerformanceCounter("Category", "CounterName")
```

```
// C#
PerformanceCounter pc = new PerformanceCounter("Category", "CounterName");
```

Once instantiated, the counter can be updated using the methods shown in Table 8-3.

Table 8-3 Performance Counter Update Methods

Method/Property	Description
Decrement	Reduces the value of the counter by one.
Increment	Increases the value of the counter by one.
IncrementBy	Increases the value of the counter by the specified amount.
RawValue	Sets the value directly through a simple assignment.

Quick Check

- If you are a member of the operations staff tasked with ensuring that the transactions per second performance of an application stays above a certain level, which data storage mechanisms are you most likely to need?

Quick Check Answer

- The use of a log file is not likely to give the operations staff the immediacy of notification that is required. Although additional tools can be used to do so, they add overhead to the process that isn't really required. The same applies to the Windows Event Log. However, database updates, performance counters, and e-mail are more timely in terms of providing information that would be useful.

Common Scenarios

Just to complete our journey, let's consider some common scenarios and consider which data storage alternative is likely to be the best choice.

24 by 7 Support

The overriding concern of a department that provides 24 by 7 support is almost certainly going to be immediacy of notification—at least for serious problems. For this reason, integrating e-mail messaging into the monitoring functionality is vital.

However, the needs of this department don't stop there. Knowing that a problem exists allows the support team to fly into action as quickly as possible. But being told that a problem exists is only part of the process of solving it. For this, the application will need to have logging functionality. Now the needs are a little different. The lack of reporting needs means that using a database will probably be overkill. So the choice comes down to the event log and a flat file. Because both can be centrally accessible, the choice is up to the developer.

Service Level Agreement Monitoring

A service level agreement (SLA) is a contract that states that the provider of a service (or an entire server) will maintain access to that service at or above a certain level. The "level" in this case could be measured in transactions per second, up-time, or any other measurable quantity. The requirement in this situation is to be able to determine if the agreed-to level was met over a period of time.

As you might deduce, the ability to report on the watched system is the most important criterion, which means that using a database as the data store will most likely be the way to go. But the monitoring need doesn't stop there. Since there is usually a financial penalty to not meeting an SLA, as soon as one of the monitored values go below a certain level, immediate notification is needed. This allows technicians to address the problem before it starts to cost money.

Application Monitoring

For most companies, keeping track of the health and ongoing operation of an application is the overriding purpose for logging and monitoring. This definitely eliminates e-mail as a logging/monitoring data store. The needs of application monitoring means finding a way to notify operations of a problem in a reasonably quick manner and then being able to determine the source of the problem.

The lack of criticality for notification means that working with a performance counter, which can in turn be monitored by System Monitor or MOM, should be sufficient. Also, creating a flat file that contains the status information should satisfy the need for after-the-fact problem isolation.

One of the more interesting aspects of this process is that in none of the three scenarios is a single type of logging/monitoring adequate to meet all of the needs. And, in an ideal world, it would be nice to turn up the amount of information available to the data source when a problem is detected through other means. This combination of requirements means that defining a centralized logging/monitoring mechanism would be useful in order to avoid having to continuously write the code to handle this level of complexity. All of this is covered in Lesson 3.

Lab: Manipulating a Performance Counter

In this lab, we demonstrate the technique used to add and update performance counters in an application.

▶ **Exercise: Adding and Using Categories and Counters**

In this exercise, we will add a category named Training Kit Counters. Into that category, we will create a counter called Counter1. In subsequent executions of the program, the counter will be incremented by a random number.

The steps are easily mastered, but there is one aspect to be aware of, that being permissions. In order to create a performance counter, you need to have full control on the following registry key:

```
HKEY_LOCAL_MACHINE\SOFTWARE\Microsoft\Windows NT\CurrentVersion\Perflib
```

Since providing full control to this registry key is not something that should be done lightly, the creation of performance counters and their corresponding categories is usually done at installation time. It becomes a lot more palatable to say that the application needs to be installed by an administrator than to say that the application needs to be run by an administrator every time.

1. Launch Visual Studio 2005.

2. Open a solution using File | Open | Project/Solution.

3. Navigate to the Chapter8\Lesson2*<language>*\Exercise-Before directory. Select the Lab1 solution and click Open.

4. In the Solution Explorer, double-click the Module1.vb file or the Program.cs file to display the coding editor. Since this is a Console application, the Main procedure will be shown and, at the moment, it's empty.

5. The first step is to determine if the counter category already exists. In this manner we can simply run the same application multiple times and not attempt to create the category each time. The *Exists* method on the *PerformanceCounterCategory* class is used for this purpose. Add the following code to the Main procedure:

```vb
' VB
If Not PerformanceCounterCategory.Exists( _
   "Training Kit Counters") Then
End If
```

```csharp
// C#
if (!PerformanceCounterCategory.Exists("Training Kit Counters"))
{
}
```

6. To add counters to this category, a *CounterCreationDataCollection* object is used. Into this collection, *CounterCreationData* objects are added. Then the collection is passed to the *Create* method. Add the following code to the *If* block created in the previous step:

```
' VB
Dim counterCollection As New CounterCreationDataCollection()

Dim newCounter As New CounterCreationData("Counter1", _
    "This is a demonstration counter", PerformanceCounterType.NumberOfItems64)
counterCollection.Add(newCounter)

PerformanceCounterCategory.Create("Training Kit Counters", "This is a demonstration
category", _
    PerformanceCounterCategoryType.SingleInstance, counterCollection)
```

```
// C#
CounterCreationDataCollection counterCollection = new CounterCreationDataCollection();
CounterCreationData newCounter = new CounterCreationData("Counter1",
    "This is a demonstration counter", PerformanceCounterType.NumberOfItems64);
counterCollection.Add(newCounter);

PerformanceCounterCategory.Create("Training Kit Counters", "This is a demonstration
category",
    PerformanceCounterCategoryType.SingleInstance, counterCollection);
```

7. Once we can be certain that the counters have been created, we can turn to using them. Start by declaring a *PerformanceCounter* variable. The following code is added below the *If* block created in step 5:

```
' VB
Dim counter As New PerformanceCounter("Training Kit Counters", _
    "Counter1", False)
```

```
// C#
PerformanceCounter counter = new
    PerformanceCounter("Training Kit Counters", "Counter1", false);
```

8. For this counter, use the *Increment* method (and the *Random* class) to update the counter's value.

```
' VB
Dim rand As New Random(Convert.ToInt32(DateTime.Now.TimeOfDay.TotalMilliseconds))
Dim incrementValue As Integer = rand.Next(1, 10)
counter.IncrementBy(incrementValue)
```

```
// C#
Random rand = new Random(Convert.ToInt32( DateTime.Now.TimeOfDay.TotalMilliseconds));
int incrementValue = rand.Next(1, 10);
counter.IncrementBy(incrementValue);
```

9. The coding for the application is now complete. All that remains is to ensure that it's doing what it's supposed to. Start by running the application using the F5 key. This

needs to be done before using System Monitor so that the category and counter can be created.

10. Once the application has been run successfully, start System Monitor using the Start | Run | Perfmon.exe command.

11. In System Monitor, click the Add button or use Ctrl+I to reveal the Add Counters dialog box (see Figure 8-2).

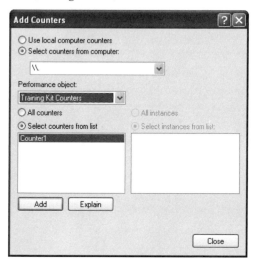

Figure 8-2   Adding counters in System Monitor.

12. Select a *Performance* object of Training Kit Counters. Then select Counter1 and click Add.

13. Click the Close button. The newly added counter is now displayed on the main chart for Performance console. Note the value of the Counter1 counter.

14. Run the lab application once more, using F5. Check that the value of Counter1 has been increased.

Lesson Summary

■ The list of possible data stores is varied, from a simple flat file to a full scalability and redundancy of a database.

■ The driving factor for selecting a data store is how the information will be used after it has been recorded. Application health monitoring requires a much more immediate feedback mechanism than application debugging does, for example.

■ In many real-world situations, a single logging or monitoring mechanism isn't sufficient. Competing needs from operations, debugging, and auditing mean that more than one type of data store is necessary to keep everyone happy.

Lesson Review

You can use the following questions to test your knowledge of the information in Lesson 2, "Storing the Data." The questions are also available on the companion CD if you prefer to review them in electronic form.

NOTE Answers

Answers to these questions and explanations of why each answer choice is right or wrong are located in the "Answers" section at the end of the book.

---

1. The application that you're creating is critical to the operation of your company. What mechanism should you use to notify administrators of a serious error?

   A. Flat file

   B. System Monitor

   C. Database

   D. E-mail

2. The application that you're creating needs to keep track of the date and time that sales orders were created for reporting purposes. What data store should be used for logging the sales order transactions?

   A. Flat file

   B. System Monitor

   C. Database

   D. E-mail

3. The application that you're creating will be deployed onto a large number of different systems outside of your company. You would like to receive notification when a serious error occurs. Which data store is most appropriate for this scenario?

   A. Flat file

   B. System Monitor

   C. Database

   D. E-mail

Lesson 3: Using an Instrumentation Framework

As was mentioned at the end of the last lesson, it is quite common for an application to have to support multiple logging and monitoring mechanisms. For most developers, this implies that the easiest implementation will be to centralize the logging process in a single method. That method can then be called in all circumstances and the destination for the log message will be determined either by parameters or by configuration information. The aim of this lesson is to discuss some of the attributes and functionality required by centralized log processing.

After this lesson, you will be able to:
- Decide whether an instrumentation framework is appropriate.
- Determine whether instrumentation as defined in the Enterprise Library is appropriate for your application.
- Configure the Enterprise Library instrumentation component.

Estimated lesson time: 35 minutes

Real World

Bruce Johnson

There is no question that developers appreciate well-instrumented code. There is nothing like the joy of finding the exact message needed to identify what went wrong in the exact place in the log file. However, developers appreciate well-instrumented code even more when they didn't instrument it. Which is one of the reasons why it's not done as often as it should be.

But there are more reasons for not adding code to your application that only *might* be useful. Some of the more common excuses ... er ... reasons are as follows:

- There is no good centralized instrumentation module.
- Adding instrumentation to an application increases "clutter" in the code, reducing readability.
- The development schedule for the application is too aggressive to justify the effort of instrumentation of the application.
- Any instrumentation messages are not nearly detailed enough to allow developers to debug the application.
- The instrumentation code causes the performance of the application to worsen.

None of these reasons qualify as acceptable for not instrumenting a truly enterprise-level application. However, they do indicate that the decision to instrument an application is not blindly "yes," a question that will be addressed in this lesson.

When Is a Framework Worth the Effort?

This is actually the second instrumentation question asked by developers. The first is "Do we need to instrument our application at all?" The main reasons for not doing so have already been outlined, so let's take a quick look at how they really apply.

Centralizing the Instrumentation

The evolution for instrumentation typically goes like this. The first time you write some code to log an error message, you write the code by hand. By the fifth time you've written the same code, you decide that creating a method to log the information would be much easier than writing the code out each time. So you create a class that exposes the *WriteEntry* method and refactor the application. At this point you have centralized instrumentation.

What centralized instrumentation means is that, going forward, additional functionality can be added to the *WriteEntry* method and get used by all callers. Yes, some additional parameters or overloads might need to be added. But the centralization is simple to do and a powerful way to implement and extend the instrumentation piece.

Code Clutter

There is no question that instrumentation code adds to the clutter and reduces the readability of a code module. There are, however, techniques that can be used to minimize this impact. For example, placing the instrumentation code into regions allows them to be collapsed when viewing is not needed. But there is one area that can greatly affect code clutter reduction—proper exception handling.

The number of methods that include try/catch blocks around the entire procedure is staggering. The sole function of the catch is to list out the method in which the exception took place. To be fair, many of these methods are upgrade code that was just compiled and not truly "upgraded." But in the world of .NET, this type of exception handling is a bane to readable code and the addition of instrumentation doesn't help.

Instead of using procedure-wide exception handling, well-organized applications have an unhandled exception handler. This handler gets invoked if an exception occurs that is not handled further down the call stack. The key is to *never* handle exceptions unless you can do something useful for the exception; "useful" means fix the problem, change an approach, or add useful, contextual information to the exception. This last choice implies that the exception will be rethrown. If you follow this advice, much of the clutter associated with instrumentation is cleared up.

Not Enough Room in the Schedule

Again, the addition of instrumentation adds to the development schedule. Even with a centralized module, code still needs to be added at the appropriate points. In fact, there is effort involved with determining where the appropriate points are, and tests need to be written to ensure that the code is called properly.

However, the cost of development is only a small percentage of the lifetime cost of an application. Spending time upfront to create an application that is more easily administered and where problems in the running application are more easily identified is worth the additional cost. Sure, you might need to convince your superiors of such an situation, but centralizing functionality and reducing the effort involved in adding instrumentation can help.

Useless Log Messages

To be fair, this is the weakest of the excuses. If insufficient detail is placed in the log messages, that's really the developer's fault. The solution is to put better information into the message.

There is a question of what information is most likely to be useful. In particular, what we care about is the information that will be useful for developers debugging a problem with a production application. For most other situations, the content of the message is easily determined beforehand (auditors have specific requirements) or allows users to drill into the information themselves (users can find out more information about an order with just the order number). Developers, on the other hand, are looking to have more information provided at the exact point where they need it.

Naturally, the first critical piece of information is the exception message. This describes what the exception actually is and will be needed to help narrow down the list of possible culprits naturally. But beyond that, the stack trace is the most important detail. The stack trace lists the methods that were called within the application to get to where the exception was thrown. Frequently, just knowing this information allows a developer to be able to identify what the application was doing when the problem occurred.

Beyond these two items, it falls to the developer to decide what might be pertinent. Parameter and loop variable values might help, for example, as might the SQL statement that is about to be executed against the data store. The trick is to balance the right information with clutter in the log file. And that is as much art as it is science.

Impact on Performance

There is a trade-off between adequate logging and monitoring and performance. It's usually possible to reduce the impact of logging to nothing by using a compiler flag and redeploying when logging is required. However, this is not a realistic choice. For most companies, the steps and approvals required to move code into production make the marginal gains not worth the effort. Not to mention that it becomes impossible to turn logging "on" while the application is running.

So if we assume that we're not going to redeploy to turn logging on, let's consider the real impact of logging. Every call to the logging method will check to see if logging is enabled. This check involves examining a configuration setting, which has already been loaded into memory. If logging is not enabled, the call returns immediately. In other words, if there is no logging to be done, the overhead of logging is minimal. Now if logging is turned on, the performance impact will definitely exist. Writing to a flat file or a database takes CPU cycles. But the idea behind being able to turn logging on and off in the configuration file is that the performance is affected only when it needs to be.

Given that most of the reasons that developers avoid adding logging code have been addressed, let's consider whether a framework is worth the effort. First of all, the difference between a framework and a centralized logging mechanism is relatively minimal. Theoretically, a framework has been designed to be extensible, both in terms of data stores and functionality. A centralized logging mechanism expands more organically. In fact, the people who design a framework have probably created a number of centralized logging mechanisms before, so they know where the hard edges and sharp corners in the process are.

But the question of whether a framework should be used also goes to the effort involved in configuring and using it. Frameworks have more generic functionality exposed. They support multiple data stores and different log levels. As a result of needing to support different calling protocols, the method calls tend to be more complicated. As a result, getting the framework properly configured can be challenging—certainly more complicated than adding an Enable Logging value to the AppSettings section in the configuration file.

So the answer to the "Is a framework worth the effort?" question comes down to the types of functionality that are needed and how flexible the logging needs to be. In the Enterprise Library that we'll be discussing shortly, the *Write* method can be configured to route messages to multiple data stores under different conditions, including the severity level and the message source. Each message can be sent to more than one destination. The destination for each message can be modified on the fly and changes detected immediately. It is truly (as the name suggests) enterprise-level in terms of functionality.

However, using and configuring the logging portion of Enterprise Library can be difficult. The method calls are not as simple as might be desired because of the functionality that is supported. Configuration involves multiple levels of indirect references. Using the Enterprise Library is worthwhile only if your application needs enterprise levels of logging functionality.

And that is really the answer to the question. A framework is worth including in your application if your corporate environment needs the flexibility that is offered. If not, then focus on creating a centralized logging mechanism that does exactly what you need it to do. You can always revert to a framework if the needs of your application infrastructure change.

Logging Application Block

The Logging Application Block is part of the Enterprise Library that is published by the Prescriptive Architecture Group at Microsoft. The Enterprise Library is a set of functional groups that allow for enterprise functionality to be easily added to applications that need it. This includes Caching, Cryptography, Data Access, Logging, and Security.

Two pieces of the Logging Application Block need to be understood in order to properly use it. The first is how it gets called. The second is how to configure the destinations. Since it's easier to understand configuration once the calling protocol has been defined, we'll begin with that.

Creating a Log Entry

The creation of a log entry for the Logging Application Block is done through the *Logger* class and, more specifically, through the *Write* method on the *Logger* class. A number of overloads are available that provide some default functionality, but a couple are used more frequently.

The *LogEntry* class is defined within the *Microsoft.Practices.EnterpriseLibrary.Logging* namespace. It contains properties such as *Categories*, *ActivityId*, *Severity*, *Priority*, and *EventId* that can be associated with each log entry, not to mention the *Message* property, which contains the logged message. Note that the *TraceEventType* class is located in the *System.Diagnostics* namespace. Also, in order to use the *LogEntry* class, a reference to the Microsoft.Practices.EnterpriseLibrary.Logging dynamic-link library (DLL) must be manually added to the project. This DLL can be found in the bin directory underneath the installation directory for Enterprise Library.

```vb
' VB
Dim log as New LogEntry()
log.Categories.Add("MyCategory1")
log.Message = "My message body"
log.Severity = TraceEventType.Error
log.Priority = 100
Logger.Write(log)
```

```csharp
// C#
LogEntry log = new LogEntry();
log.Categories.Add("MyCategory1");
log.Message = "My message body";
log.Severity = TraceEventType.Error;
log.Priority = 100;
Logger.Write(log);
```

Another property of *LogEntry* that can be quite useful is *ExtendedProperties*. This is a dictionary of name/value pairs included in the log entry. This property allows the developer to send any information that is desired into the logging mechanism. When the actual logging takes place, the collection is iterated and the name and value displayed/printed/included in the log.

It is also possible to use a *Write* overload to include the most common properties of the *LogEntry* class.

```
' VB
Logger.Write(message, category, priority, eventId, severity, title, properties)
```

```
// C#
Logger.Write(message, category, priority, eventId, severity, title, properties);
```

Configuring the Block

All of the configuration for the Logging Application Block is available in the App.config file for the application being logged. This means that it's possible to be able to define and modify the configuration by hand, just like it's also possible to develop enterprise-level applications using Notepad and the command-line compiler. Just because something is possible doesn't mean that it's a good idea.

To configure logging for an application, the Enterprise Library Configuration utility is the way to go. It provides a handy user interface to define the settings of interest. It can be launched from the Start | All Programs | Microsoft patterns & practices Enterprise Library – January 2006 | Enterprise Library Configuration menu option. Figure 8-3 illustrates the configuration utilities interface.

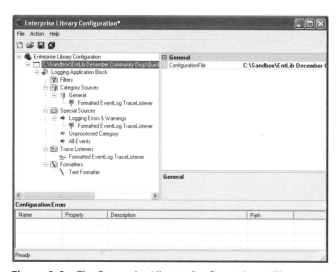

Figure 8-3   The Enterprise Library Configuration utility.

Once the application has launched, use the File | Open Application menu option to open the App.config file that needs to be modified. If this config file hasn't been set up for logging yet, right-click the configuration file on the left side and select New | Logging Application Block from the context menu.

To route a particular message, three elements need to be defined: a category source, a trace listener, and a formatter.

- **Category source**   The name of a category to which a message is posted. Along with the name, which is just a string value, there is also a source level that indicates the severity associated with this category.
- **Trace listener**   This is a reference to a class that monitors trace and debug output. Consider this to be the receiver of the log messages.
- **Formatter**   This is a reference to a class that formats the log entry for output. This is the class that makes the log output pretty, or at least appropriate for the ultimate destination.

When building up the logging configuration, you start with formatters. Included in the installation of Enterprise Library are binary and text formatters. Or you can create a custom formatter by defining a class that implements the *ILogFormatter* interface. The goal of the formatter is to convert a log entry into a format that can be delivered to the trace listener. For this reason, there is a direct correlation between a particular instance of a formatter and the trace listener.

Once the formatter has been defined, it gets associated with a trace listener. A number of trace listeners are provided with the installation, including database, e-mail, flat file, and the event log. Creating a specific trace listener means specifying a formatter to be used and then defining the properties associated with the specific destination. So, for example, an e-mail trace listener would have Simple Mail Transfer Protocol (SMTP) details, and a database trace listener would include a connection string.

The final step in the configuration process is to define the category. Here you specify the category name and severity level, as well as indicate which trace listener to use.

So now, when a log message is posted through the *Write* method, the category associated with the message is used to identify the trace listener to use. Then the formatter associated with the trace listener is used to format the log message into the appropriate string value. The listener then uses that string value when directing the output to the appropriate destination. If the listener is associated with a database, for example, the formatter will convert the log message into an INSERT statement, which the trace listener will then execute against the appropriate database.

It is also important to be aware that each category can have more than one listener associated with it. In other words, each log message can be directed to one or more listeners. This satisfies one of the characteristics that was identified at the end of Lesson 2, that being that most real-world scenarios require logging to have more than one destination.

Lab: The Logging Application Block

The Logging Application Block provides a lot of functionality. This unfortunately means that the configuration of the block can be challenging—a good reason to provide a lab.

▶ **Exercise: Basic Configuration**

In this exercise, we'll reduce the process of configuring the Logging Application Block for use in an application to the simplest level. We will create a Console application that does nothing by calling the *Logger.Write* method. We will then use the Enterprise Library Configuration utility to direct the output of the log message to multiple destinations, that being a flat file and the Event Log.

1. Launch Visual Studio 2005.

2. Open a solution using File | Open | Project/Solution.

3. Navigate to the Chapter8\Lesson3\<*language*>\Exercise-Before directory. Select the Lab1 solution and click Open.

4. In the Solution Explorer, right-click References and then click Add Reference. In the Add Reference dialog box, click the Browse tab. Select the Microsoft.Practices.EnterpriseLibrary.Logging file, which is located in the C:\Program Files\Microsoft Enterprise Library January 2006\bin\ folder by default. Click OK.

5. In the Solution Explorer, double-click Module1 or Program.cs to display the code view.

6. The sole purpose of the Main procedure is to create a log message and submit it to the Logging Application Block through the *Write* method. As such, we will declare a *LogEntry* class and populate some of the properties. A category of "Training Kit Category" will be added, as well as two extended properties. Add the following code to the Main procedure:

```
' VB
Dim log As New LogEntry()
log.Message = "This is a demonstration log entry"
log.Severity = TraceEventType.Information
log.Categories.Add("Training Kit Category")
log.ExtendedProperties.Add("First Property", "This is the value of the first property")
log.ExtendedProperties.Add("Second Property", "This is the second property's value")

Logger.Write(log)
```

```
// C#
LogEntry log = new LogEntry();
log.Message = "This is a demonstration log entry";
log.Severity = TraceEventType.Information;
log.Categories.Add("Training Kit Category");
log.ExtendedProperties.Add("First Property", "This is the value of the first property");
log.ExtendedProperties.Add("Second Property", "This is the second property's value");

Logger.Write(log);
```

7. Now that the coding is complete, we can go about configuring the application for logging. Start by launching the Enterprise Library Configuration utility with the Start | All Programs | Microsoft patterns & practices Enterprise Library – January 2006 | Enterprise Library Configuration menu option.

8. Open the App.config file associated with the Console application. Use the File | Open Application menu option and open the Chapter8/Lesson3/Lab1/<language>/Before/App.config file.

9. Add the Logging Application Block portion of the config file by right-clicking the just-opened application and selecting New | Logging Application Block from the context menu. A Logging Application Block section should be added to the application that has been opened.

10. For convenience, we will be using the existing text formatter. So create a new trace listener by right-clicking the Trace Listeners node underneath the Logging Application Block and selecting New | Flat File Trace Listener from the context menu. We will be leading the default values along, but notice that the name of the file into which the output will be placed is trace.log.

11. Finally, we add a new category. Right-click the Category Sources node and select New | Category from the context menu.

12. Change the name of the category to Training Kit Category. And change the SourceLevels property to Information.

13. Add the listeners. Right-click the Training Kit Category node and select the New | Trace Listener Reference context menu item.

14. In the created item, set the ReferencedTraceListener to FlatFile TraceListener.

15. To add the second listener, right-click the Training Kit Category node and again select the New | Trace Listener Reference context menu item.

16. In the created item, set the ReferencedTraceListener to Formatted EventLog TraceListener.

17. Save the configuration changes with File | Save Application.

18. All the configurations are now in place. So, back in Visual Studio 2005, run the application using F5. The application will run for only a few seconds.

19. Open up the newly created trace.log file in Chapter8/Lesson3/<language>/Exercise1-Before/bin/Debug. Notice that all of the information provided as LogEntry properties in the Main procedure have been recorded, including the extended properties.

20. Open up the Event Viewer using Start | Run | **eventvwr.msc**.

21. Look at the Application log. Note that an Information-type entry with a source of Enterprise Library Logging has been created. If you double-click the entry, the message includes the same information seen in the trace.log file.

Lesson Summary

- Most developers don't properly instrument their applications for reasons that are not, generally speaking, valid.
- Although a centralized logging mechanism is useful for most applications, using a framework makes sense only if you need it to save time or to provide advanced functionality.

■ The Logging Application Block provides a useful and extensible set of functionality. Also, it eliminates some of the challenges of configuration through the use of a utility application.

Lesson Review

You can use the following question to test your knowledge of the information in Lesson 3, "Using an Instrumentation Framework." The question is also available on the companion CD if you prefer to review it in electronic form.

Answers   Answers to this question and explanations of why each answer choice is right or wrong are located in the "Answers" section at the end of the book.

---

1. The application that you're creating needs to place debug messages into a flat file to assist with debugging any problems that occur. There is no need for immediate notification of any problems because the application is not mission-critical. Nor will the logged information be used in any reporting. Which is the more effective (in terms of programming effort) way to implement this logging functionality?

   A. The application that needs to log a message should open the flat file, add the log entry, and close the file.

   B. Create a centralized method to put the log message into the flat file.

   C. Create an extensible framework to support logging.

   D. Add the Logging Application Block to the application and use the *Write* method to update the flat file.

Chapter Review

To further practice and reinforce the skills you learned in this chapter, you can perform the following tasks:

- Review the chapter summary.
- Review the list of key terms introduced in this chapter.
- Complete the case scenarios. These scenarios set up real-world situations involving the topics of this chapter and ask you to create a solution.
- Complete the suggested practices.
- Take a practice test.

Chapter Summary

- The audience for the logging or monitoring information needs to be considered when determining all of the other factors associated with recording the information. It is important to provide the correct level of detail to ensure that valuable information isn't missed or overlooked.
- Data stores are available to support all of the most common logging and monitoring requirements. And how the information gets pushed into the store means that if a particular requirement isn't supported out of the box, creating the necessary store should be pretty easy.
- Although there are many convenient excuses for not instrumenting an application, in the vast majority of cases the benefits outweigh the costs.

Key Terms

Do you know what these key terms mean? You can check your answers by looking up the terms in the glossary at the end of the book.

- flat file
- granularity
- *ILogFormatter* interface
- instrumentation
- logging
- monitoring
- performance monitor
- Windows Event Log

Case Scenarios

In the following case scenarios, you will apply what you've learned about delivering multimedia in a distributed environment. You can find answers to these questions in the "Answers" section at the end of the book.

Case Scenario 1: Instrumenting an Application for Monitoring

You are a corporate developer creating a Windows Forms application that will be available to users within your company. The operations group within your company needs to be able to watch the ongoing performance of the application in order to identify usage patterns as well as to address performance issues as soon as they are noticed. Also, to help out with debugging problems, you would like to place tracing messages at strategic points within the code.

Your challenge is to determine which instrumentation technique should be used to address each of these situations.

Questions

Answer the following questions for your manager:

1. Where should the information used to determine usage patterns be stored?
2. Where should the information about the current health of the Windows application be stored?
3. Where should the tracing information be stored?

Case Scenario 2: Instrumenting a Smart Client Application

You are a corporate developer creating a Windows Forms application that will be available to users on the corporate intranet. The application will be deployed on a central server and downloaded to the client machines using Smart Client technologies. The operations group within your company needs to be able to watch the ongoing performance of the application on the client in order to identify usage patterns.

Your challenge is to determine which instrumentation technique should be used to address this situation.

Questions

Answer the following question for your manager:

- Where should the information about the current health of the application be stored?

Suggested Practices

To help you successfully master the objectives presented in this chapter, complete the following tasks.

Choose an Appropriate Event Logging Method for the Application

For this task, you should perform the following practices from the perspective of the most appropriate techniques to use.

- **Practice 1**   For an application that is already developed (or that is still under development), evaluate the audience for any logging or monitoring information. Identify the groups within the company that will want to see logs from the application. Determine if there is any group that will need to monitor the application's status on an ongoing basis.
- **Practice 2**   Using the same application used in Practice 1, identify the method that should be used to give each interested group of users the information they require.

Monitor Specific Characteristics or Aspects of an Application

For this task, you should complete both practices, concentrating on the specifics of the techniques used to provide the described functionality.

- **Practice 1**   Create a Windows service that monitors a directory for the addition of files and moves them to a different directory based on the file extension. The arrival and dispatch of the files should be logged to a flat file, and the number of files of each type processed per minute should be made available to the System Monitor.
- **Practice 2**   Create a Web service that delivers stock quotations. The method takes a stock symbol and returns the price of the last trade. Instrument the Web service so that the number of requests per second are available to System Monitor and the number of requests for each symbol can be determined by operations on a historical basis.

Take a Practice Test

The practice tests on this book's companion CD offer many options. For example, you can test yourself on just one exam objective or you can test yourself on all the 70-548 certification exam content. You can set up the test so that it closely simulates the experience of taking a certification exam, or you can set it up in study mode so that you can look at the correct answers and explanations after you answer each question.

MORE INFO   Practice tests

For details about all the practice test options available, see the "How to Use the Practice Tests" section in this book's Introduction.

Chapter 9
Building Components

The component is the building block of a .NET application. Some components are built in-house, some are purchased from third-party companies, and some are a combination of the two—extensions built in-house from purchased components. All of this sounds not only simple but also familiar. Developers have been given these choices for years, going back to at least the early days of Visual Basic and beyond.

But there is still a choice to be made. Make, buy, or extend are still issues that need to be addressed. And if you choose to make, what needs to be done to make sure that you can extend later on, as need be? The goal of this chapter is to consider not only the reasons for making the build, buy, or extend choice, but also how to design your own components to be part of future decisions of the same nature.

Exam objectives in this chapter:
- Consume a reusable software component.
  - Identify a reusable software component from available components to meet the requirements.
  - Identify whether the reusable software component needs to be extended.
  - Identify whether the reusable software component needs to be wrapped.
  - Identify whether any existing functionality needs to be hidden.
- Choose an appropriate implementation approach for the application design logic.
  - Choose an appropriate data storage mechanism.
  - Choose an appropriate data flow structure.
  - Choose an appropriate decision flow structure.

Lessons in this chapter:

Before You Begin

To complete the lessons in this chapter, you must have:

- A computer that meets or exceeds the minimum hardware requirements listed in this book's Introduction.
- Visual Studio 2005 installed on the computer, with either Visual Basic .NET or C# installed.
- Visual Studio Team System installed on the computer. Specifically, the Tester or Developer version is required to be able to run the unit tests in the lab for Lesson 2, "Implementation Practices."

Real World

Bruce Johnson

The decision to make or buy a component is always a conundrum for developers. On one hand, they like new and challenging work. And almost always, making a component from scratch falls into that category. But then again, if the problem has been solved, much of the challenge falls away. And many developers hate to work on problems that already have a readily available solution. On the other hand, how can a component created by someone else be better than the precise area that you would focus on?

Almost every developer has wrestled with this dilemma. The real challenge is to come up with a systematic way to evaluate whether a component should be purchased or constructed and to identify the risks and costs associated with each choice. In this lesson we describe just such a system.

Lesson 1: Make, Buy, or Extend

The application's requirements have been gathered and approved. The architectural design has been conceived and vetted by experts. The elements of the application have been identified. Now it's time to estimate the project.

Part of the estimation process for any development effort involves identifying not only the components that are involved but also how those components are going to come into being. Some will be purchased from third parties. Some will be written from scratch. Others might be a combination of the two approaches, taking the good parts of existing components and adding enough new stuff to fill the bill. The purpose of this lesson is to outline the criteria that are used to decide which one of these paths to take.

After this lesson, you will be able to:

- Understand the factors that lead to the decision to make, buy, or extend components.
- Evaluate components for suitability.
- Extend, where appropriate and possible, existing components to fit your needs.

Estimated lesson time: 40 minutes

The Make or Buy Decision

At the lowest level, the decision of whether to build or buy a component is an economic one. The choice is between the costs associated with purchasing, learning, and integrating a component created by a third party and the costs associated with building a component from scratch. But even with these elements as the foundation, the values that go into this calculation are not nearly as simple as might be assumed. Because the overall costs of buying or building a component go far beyond the actual cost of ... er ... buying or building one. The "costs" are not as obvious as might be hoped.

Development Costs

This is the first and most expected of the costs associated with the decision. And it is easy to say that building a component from scratch will cost more than buying an existing component. But does it really? It actually depends on what the component is supposed to do.

For example, let's consider the need to create a Web control that allows users to pick dates. The basic functionality involves providing two options: letting a user enter a date or displaying a calendar control and letting the date be selected by clicking the desired day. Are there components out there that provide this functionality? Of course there are. But do the components provide exactly the functionality that is desired? Not necessarily. It could be that the mechanism for selecting the date doesn't fit with the user's needs. Or the months don't align with the

13 months (of four weeks each) that make up the corporate calendar. In other words, when comparing development costs, you need to make sure that you're comparing the costs of developing exactly what the application requires against the purchased component and not what it would cost to redevelop the component from scratch.

Just to avert criticism, please realize that for a component such as a date/time picker, it will almost never be worthwhile to develop the functionality from scratch. Most variations on what can be done are already implemented in some off-the-shelf product. The component was simply used as an example. It's not until the components get larger and more (or overly) complicated that custom development might make sense.

Post-Development Costs

A less frequently considered cost is the one associated with supporting components after the first version has been deployed. For components that were created by in-house staff, management has complete control over which changes are made and when they are released. They can update the component on a monthly basis, enhance it as business demands, or simply leave it without further modification.

With third-party components, management doesn't have quite that much flexibility. New versions arrive at the whim of the component's vendor. Desired features might or might not be added. And, at some point, support for older versions of the component is withdrawn, forcing management to upgrade to a possibly unneeded new version or to include an unsupported piece of software in a production environment, neither of which is an optimal option.

Time-to-Market Costs

As with development costs, there is little debate that using a third-party component will get the needed functionality into production in less time than custom development. There is the minimal impact of learning the interface for the component and making sure that the component fits well within the application being developed. But unless the size of the project is significant (and the contribution of the component relatively small), there is little question that the third-party component will be faster to get into place.

Support Costs

Although it might not be readily apparent, third-party components from reputable vendors do decrease support costs. After all, look at the current code-to-bug ratio within your development staff (you have the statistic memorized, right?). For commercial software, the standard metric is in the neighborhood of 20–30 bugs per 1000 lines. So, if you assume that the code your team writes is just as good as that written by the third-party's development staff, there should be no difference in support costs and bug fixes.

Yes, there is a "but" coming. The "but" is that the third-party component is being run in hundreds of applications in other companies, each of which has the opportunity to try out the functionality and report bugs so that they get fixed before you see them. There are a lot more eyes looking to find some (never all) of the bugs in each third-party component. Compare that to the custom development model, where only one company is using the component. The result is a much higher possibility that a new bug will catch the application unaware when the component has been built in-house.

Risk Costs

A couple of other areas need to be considered in the realm of component costs—all of them dealing with less frequently considered but still very real risks. For example, there is the risk that a third-party component won't be able to meet your needs even after evaluation. How can this happen? Mostly through shifting requirements. Although it's nice to believe that the complete set of requirements can be defined beforehand, that's not always possible. User needs change, as do business requirements. So it is possible that, even after careful evaluation and purchase, the third-party component will not fit the bill.

Another risk associated with third-party components is backward compatibility. Depending on the vendor, it sometimes happens that the newest version is not completely compatible with the older version. Which means that any new functionality (including bug fixes) might not be available unless some redevelopment takes place.

In a similar vein is the risk of untimely upgrades. Say you have deployed a third-party component into an ASP.NET 1.1 Web application. The time comes to upgrade to ASP.NET 2.0. But you find out that you can't run .NET Framework 1.1 (required by the old component) and 2.0 (for the upgraded pages) in the same virtual directory. If the vendor of the component doesn't have a 2.0 version of the component available, you will have to jump through some hoops to get the component operational. And there is no guarantee that you'll succeed.

A less frequently considered risk with third-party components is security. Because hackers like to maximize their efforts, they are much more likely to target third-party components instead of custom-built applications. In fact, the higher the profile of the component, the more likely that it will be targeted. When you bring third-party components into your application, you add one more potential security vulnerability. Or maybe not, depending on the relative skills of your development staff with respect to security. The size of this risk depends entirely on the attack surface presented by the component and the priority given to defending that surface by the component's authors.

These last few risks has been focused on third-party components. But custom development has some additional risks, too. And, it could be argued, the risks are more likely to actually occur. Like having the schedule for the custom development slip. Sure, the developers say they can write the component in five days. But can they really? Fortunately, you (as their manager) will already have information about their estimating capability. But even with accurate estimations, things happen. And those things increase the cost of the custom development, which can throw off the economic comparison.

Political Costs

The one cost to which an actual value can't be attached is the political cost of the decision. Some development teams suffer from the "Not Invented Here" syndrome. Others companies use the creation of a custom component as incentive to motivate the staff. In other words, it's a break from mundane maintenance tasks. The political costs of not using custom components in this situation can be significant. Fallout can range from lowered productivity to a passive/aggressive approach to implementation. Although there are no associated numbers, the possibility needs to be included in the calculations.

If it's possible to sum up these choices in a simple sentence or two, it would be the following. If you are evaluating a component that automates a commodity function or process, buy it rather than make it. If the component will increase your competitive advantage or provide an incremental improvement in one of your company's core competencies, build it. Although this doesn't hold in every single situation, it's true often enough that deciding against this truism should be done only with eyes open and blinders off.

Evaluating Components

Since, in many cases, third-party components are a legitimate option in the creation of a component-based .NET application, the process of evaluating components is an important one. What follows is a list of seven criteria for making such a selection. Naturally, the weight given to each criterion will depend on the strengths and weaknesses of the environment into which it will be deployed. But it is a good exercise to evaluate components using a list such as this one to ensure that each point is being given due consideration.

Ease of Use

Keep in mind that one of the main reasons for buying a component over building it is developer productivity. The sooner that a developer can put the component into production (and we're talking about the production of code by the developer here), the sooner the benefits of buying start accruing. But the ease of use we're talking about takes two forms.

First, a good component should be easily installed and configured. It should, out of the box, do what the developer is looking for. There should be no need to read through manuals or help pages to find out how to use the component. The best scenario is for the component to come with a sample application that demonstrates the technique that the developer requires.

The second element of "ease of use" has to do with the steps that the developer needs to take to accomplish the desired functionality. Is a single method call sufficient? Or are multiple method calls interspersed with property assignments needed? As you might guess, the former contributes to a high ease of use rating while the latter contributes to the overall graying of the hair among the developer population.

In some instances the ease of use consideration will be judged on how easily developers can take advantage of its features. For many tools, this means tight integration with Visual Studio. Does the component work with the existing designers? Does it have its own designer? Does it fit seamlessly with the various patterns used by the .NET Framework? If the answer to these questions are appropriate, then not only will developers find the component easy to use, but they also will strive to find places to use it. If not, the component is more likely to languish on the virtual shelf.

Ease of Customization

Although customization seems related to ease of use, it fits into a slightly different category because of the potential for dynamism. Some components require that their properties be set programmatically instead of associating important values with a configuration setting. Or, once properties are set, it is difficult to change them on the fly. Components that exhibit this behavior lose out on the customizability score. In an ideal world, the source for property assignment and the ability to make changes while the application is running means that design and configuration decisions can be put off. And in most instances, the later a decision can be made, the better.

Performance

The weighting for this criterion varies widely, depending on what the component does. For some, it will be critical. For others, it will be a moderate afterthought. But regardless of where the component being considered falls within this range, it will need to perform well enough to meet expectations. For example, although the performance of a drop-down list box isn't an important factor in the decision-making process, it will become one if the delay between clicking the component and the appearance of the data is longer than a couple of seconds.

Another consideration is the ease with which performance can be measured. This really comes into play only if the performance of the component is critical. But if it is, the developer needs to be able to isolate the component's function so that an appropriate measurement of the component's performance can be obtained.

Documentation

Even if the component's interface consists of a single method call, the level of documentation provided with a component is important. At the very least, two pieces need to be considered. The first is that the component needs to have a help manual, preferably in the form of an online, searchable help file. The second is that the component should have sample code demonstrating its functionality. For a large number of developers, the second type of documentation is much more important than the first.

To go beyond just the basics, a component will provide more in-depth information. For example, samples that show more than the simple exercising of the component's functionality can be invaluable. Also, a description of some of the inner workings of the component can be greatly appreciated, especially if there are integration issues that need to be resolved. The more information that can be provided to the developer, the more comfortable the developer will feel using the component in critical situations.

Technical Support

In the past, technical support would consist of people who were available on the phone to receive calls from stumped developers. Today this is no longer the case. Instead, technical support consists of basically two areas: e-mail and online forums.

E-mail support is important to help ease the mind of developers. When implemented properly, the availability of someone who can be sent an urgent e-mail is a useful release valve for a developer under pressure. Of course, to implement this properly implies that someone will be available to read and respond to these e-mails. A response within some reasonable time frame is necessary to get high marks. And, when evaluating the component, make sure that you don't take the word of the vendor that all e-mail is responded to within 24 hours. Test it out multiple times at different times of the day and week, just to make sure that the claim isn't all marketing fluff.

Online forums are the dynamic equivalent to the frequently asked questions (FAQs) or knowledge base that many component developers provide. The nice thing, from everyone's perspective, is that a much wider range of experience is available to draw knowledge from than with e-mail support. Hopefully, people who have real-world experience using the component will be providing answers, and the more active the forums are for the component, the more useful this line of technical support becomes.

Evaluation Versions

The number of readily available components that don't have a trial version of some type is rapidly decreasing. In fact, if there is no trial version of a component, the possibility of a sale is greatly diminished. But because of its ubiquity, having a trial version is no longer sufficient. Instead, pay attention to what is disabled in the trial. Are there critical functions that have been disabled—functions that you need to know must work to meet the requirements? Or is it a time-limited or nag-screen enabled component that has all features enabled but can be used only for a short period of time? This second approach is the better way to go because developers want to be certain of the completeness of a component's functionality.

There is a risk associated with using an evaluation version of software as the development process moves through the typical stages until the inevitable deployment to production, that being that the component is not converted to a nonevaluation version prior to production. Although it certainly can have a larger impact on Web applications or server-based components where there is no user interface (ever see a modal dialog box increase the response time of a service to infinity?), a surprising number of applications released for internal company use require the users to regularly click a dialog box so that the application works. Not a happy user experience, to be sure, and all for the want of a few hundred dollars in licensing fees.

Future Enhancements

This criterion relates to the ability of the component to support the future plans for the application where it is going to be used. The last thing a company needs is to have its path to the future or the schedule for following that path dictated by a third-party vendor. And that can happen when the functionality offered by a component doesn't allow for that desired growth path. From an evaluation perspective, you would look at both the current and planned feature set of the component. This set would then be compared against the functionality that your application requires from the component both now and in the next release cycle. Ideally, all of the required application functionality would already be in the component. But if not, then you need to evaluate the risk that the needed feature won't be added or won't be released when you need it.

Once these criteria have been identified, they need to be assigned a weighting consistent with your goals for the project. Implicit in that last statement is that the weighting could very well be different for each project. This is to be expected. In fact, you will find that the set of criteria that you consider and the weight assigned to each will depend on three factors: the primary goal of the project (speed to market, budget, functionality), the skill set of the development team, and the requirements of the application (flexibility, functionality). But whatever criteria and weight are ultimately used, a consistent application across all of the alternatives will go a long way toward ensuring a successful implementation.

Extending Components

When it comes to extending components, two questions need to be asked: what can be extended and what should be extended. The answer to the first is almost always easier than the second. And the starting point for both is *inheritance*.

Inheritance is a relationship between two classes. Specifically, when class *B* is inherited from class *A*, then class *B* is given the public method and property definitions of *A* without requiring that any coding is performed. If class *A* has a method called *Method1*, then any instance of class *B* will be able to have the *Method1* method called. And when *Method1* on a class *B* object is called, the code in class *A* is what is actually called.

The main benefit of this relationship is the easy reuse of code. And the main purpose of inheritance is to extend the functionality of the *base class*. In our example, that means that class *B* will contain all of the functionality of *A*, as well as any new and exciting functionality that is added specifically to class *B*.

In order to participate in an inheritance relationship, the base class must be designed to do so. This actually requires that decisions be made on what methods to expose and how to expose them. As a result, some components simply can't be extended using inheritance. If you are developing custom components and don't want them to be a base class, you can use the *NotInheritable* (VB) or *sealed* (C#) keywords.

```
' VB
Public NotInheritable Class ClassA
   ' Class definition
End Class
```

```
// C#
public sealed ClassA {
   // Class definition
}
```

So assuming from here on (for this section, anyway) that the class we're talking about can be a base class, there is a question of accessibility. In the .NET world, properties and methods can be defined with various levels of exposure:

- **Public**   Any method decorated as being public is completely accessible to any derived classes, as well as to any class that wishes to call the derived class.
- **Private**   At the opposite end of the spectrum, private methods are not accessible to any other class, whether it is derived or not.
- **Protected**   This indicates a method that's in between public and private. It is accessible to the derived class but can't be used by any class not in the *inheritance hierarchy*.

Given these three accessibility levels, the focus for inheritance will be the public methods, for the simple reason that the private and protected methods can't be accessed outside of the inheritance hierarchy.

At its most basic, inheritance simply takes the functionality of the base class and adds to it. The inheritance relationship is set up by using the *Inherits* keyword in Visual Basic or the colon in C#.

```
' VB
Public Class ClassA
  Sub Method1)
    ' implementation
  End Sub
End Class

Public Class ClassB : Inherits ClassA
```

```
  Sub Method2()
    ' implementation
  End Sub
End Class
```

```
// C#
public class ClassA {
   public void Method1() {
      // implementation
   }
}

public class ClassB : ClassA {
   public void Method2() {
      // implementation
   }
}
```

Once a ClassB has been defined as above, the following statements are valid:

```
' VB
Dim o as New ClassB()
o.Method1()
o.Method2()
```

```
// C#
ClassB o = new ClassB();
o.Method1();
o.Method2();
```

As we have already mentioned, the author of a component has the ability to enable or disable inheritance. But authors can get even more granular in their choice by limiting the methods that can be *overridden*. In fact, the choice is actually the opposite, in that the author needs to explicitly allow the implementation of a method to be overridden using the *Overridable* (VB) or *virtual* (C#) keyword.

```
' VB
Public Class ClassA
  Overridable Sub Method1()
    ' implementation
  End Sub
End Class

Public Class ClassB : Inherits ClassA
  Overrides Sub Method1()
    ' new implementation
  End Sub
End Class
```

```
// C#
public class ClassA {
   public virtual void Method1() {
```

```
        // implementation
    }
}

public class ClassB : ClassA {
    public override void Method1() {
        // implementation
    }
}
```

One more aspect to component extension needs to be considered before we leave the subject. That is whether the third-party component has any licensing restrictions. For the most part, there are no extra licensing requirements when deriving from a third-party component. All of the normal licensing is required, of course, but nothing extra. You will, of course, need to have the assemblies required by the third-party component, and those assemblies must abide by whatever licensing requirements the vendor has. For licensing consideration, the responsibility falls to the developer to ensure that extending the component is valid within the vendor's licensing scheme.

If you decide to extend open-source components, you need to be aware of the license under which it has been made available. Some open-source licenses, such as the GNU General Public License (GPL), require that the rights provided to you with the original component must be passed on to any derived work. And your extended component could qualify as such a derived work. The important aspect of this point is not to keep you from using open-source components. Using these components can often save your company time and money. But you do need to make sure that you examine the details of the license requirements for any externally created software that you use within your application. You don't want to find out that the use of a GPL component has invalidated the licensing for your current application after you have spent time integrating the two.

Wrapping Components

Sometimes extending a component is not a possibility. One of the more common cases is if the base component is a COM object. Another situation where extending a component is not possible arises if the base component has been sealed yet you would still like to extend it. Although the two situations are different, the technique used to address them is the same.

A wrapped component is implemented through a class that contains a private variable of the type that is being wrapped. For example, if you have a component called *CantBeBase*, you could create a class called *Wrapped*. In the definition for *Wrapped*, there could be a private variable with a type of *CantBeBase*. The *Wrapped* class could expose all of the methods of the *CantBeBase* class (or at least those that need to be accessible). In the implementation of these methods in the *Wrapped* class, the actual functionality will be delegated to the base class. The code below demonstrates the premise and shows how the second situation can be implemented.

```vb
' VB
Public Class CantBeBase
  Public Sub Method1()
    ' implementation
  End Sub
End Class

Public Class Wrapped
  Private baseClass As New CantBeBase()
  Public Sub Method1()
    baseClass.Method1()
  End Sub
End Class
```

```csharp
// C#
public class CantBeBase {
   public void Method1() {
      // implementation
   }
}

public class Wrapped {
   CantBeBase baseClass = new CantBeBase();
   public void Method1() {
      baseClass.Method1();
   }
}
```

One of the ironies of the wrapping scenario for the COM object is that a form of wrapping is used to create the interoperability layer between .NET and the target object. As you add a reference to a COM object in a Visual Studio project, a proxy object is actually generated. This proxy class exposes the same set of methods that the COM object does. All calls to the COM object go through the proxy, which is responsible for converting the parameter data types on the inbound and outbound side as well as trapping any exceptions or error that occurred. This is, ultimately, a wrapped component, albeit a highly sophisticated one.

Another form of wrapping occurs within the traditional class inheritance scenario. In this situation a method in the base class that has not been marked as being overridable/virtual is actually overriden. This technique is called *method hiding*, and in the real world the need to use this technique arises only very rarely. The keyword to accomplish method hiding is *Overloads* (VB) or *new* (C#).

```vb
' VB
Public Class ClassA
  Overridable Sub Method1()
    ' implementation
  End Sub
End Class

Public Class ClassB : Inherits ClassA
```

```
   Overloads Sub Method1()
      ' new implementation
   End Sub
End Class

// C#
public class ClassA {
   public virtual void Method1() {
      // implementation
   }
}

public class ClassB : ClassA {
   public new void Method1() {
      // implementation
   }
}
```

A method needs to be hidden when developers inherit from base classes that are not under their control. Let's say you have purchased a *DateTimePicker* control. You extend the control by adding a method called *Parse*. You test the new method, deploy the extended component, and all is well in the world.

However, in the next version of *DateTimePicker*, the vendor decides to implement a method called *Parse* as well. What happens to your code when the vendor's *Parse* doesn't do the same thing as your *Parse*? Without the ability to hide this new method in the base class, your application would break. So the real purpose of *Overloads*/*new* is to allow you to ensure that future versions of a base class can't break your derived class. And if you really want to expose the functionality offered by the vendor's *Parse* method, you would create a method on the derived class named *VendorParse*, for example. The *VendorParse* method would, in its implementation, invoke the *Parse* method on the base class.

Lab: Identifying Test Scenarios

In this lab, we will be adding some functionality to the Microsoft Windows Forms *TextBox* control. The new *TextBox* (called *AutoCompleteTextBox*) will keep track of a set of options. If you encounter a problem completing an exercise, the completed projects are available on the companion CD in the Code folder.

▶ **Exercise: Adding Functionality to the Windows Forms TextBox Control**

As characters are entered into the *TextBox*, the current value of the *Text* property is compared to a list of string values. If there is a partial match, the *Text* property is automatically completed with the full value from the list. To support this, a property of *PossibleValues* will be added to the extended control. Also, code will be added to the *OnTextChanged* procedure to perform the look-up in the list of choices.

    1. Launch Visual Studio 2005.

2. Open a solution using File | Open | Project/Solution.

3. Navigate to the Chapter9/Lesson1/Lab1/<language>/Before directory. Select the Lab1 solution and click Open.

4. In the Solution Explorer, double-click the AutoCompleteTextBox file in the Extended-Controls project.

5. The control needs to be derived from the *TextBox* control in the *System.Windows.Forms* namespace. So modify the class declaration to the following:

```
' VB
Public Class AutoCompleteTextBox
    Inherits TextBox
End Class
```

```
// C#
public class AutoCompleteTextBox : TextBox
{
}
```

6. From a functional perspective, four elements need to be addressed. The first one that we'll tackle is the creation of the list of options for the automatic completion. Externally, we'll use a property called *PossibleValues* with a type of an array of strings. Internally, however, we'll store the values in an *ArrayList*. The reason for not exposing the *ArrayList* directly is to avoid letting the client add or remove items on the fly. Although we could support such functionality, it's much easier not to. And, for a lab exercise, simpler is better (unless it relates to the topic at hand). The following code should be added to the *AutoCompleteTextBox* class.

```
' VB
Private _possibleValues As New ArrayList()
Public Property PossibleValues() As String()
    Get
        Return CType(_possibleValues.ToArray(GetType(String)), String())
    End Get
    Set(ByVal value As String())
        _possibleValues = New ArrayList(value)
    End Set
End Property
```

```
// C#
private ArrayList possibleValues = new ArrayList();
public string[] PossibleValues
{
get
{
    return (string[])possibleValues.ToArray(typeof(string));
}
set
{
```

```
            possibleValues = new ArrayList(value);
    }
}
```

7. Next up in our list of functions to implement is the handler for the *TextChanged* event. This is a method that is overridden from the base class, so the declaration needs to be marked accordingly. The following code should be added to the *AutoCompletionTextBox* class:

```
' VB
Protected Overrides Sub OnTextChanged(ByVal e As EventArgs)
End Sub
```

```
// C#
protected override void OnTextChanged(EventArgs e)
{
}
```

8. To minimize the number of bad interactions with the control, there are a number of times when the autocompletion functionality should be avoided. Specifically, we will not automatically complete when there are no items in the list, when the text to compare is empty, and when we are updating the text manually. This last condition requires the creation of a control-level variable, so add the following code above the OnTextChanged declaration:

```
' VB
Private updatingTextDirectly As Boolean = False
```

```
// C#
private bool updatingTextDirectly = false;
```

9. And within the OnTextChanged procedure, add the following code:

```
' VB
If _possibleValues.Count = 0 Or String.IsNullOrEmpty(Me.Text) Or updatingTextDirectly
Then
    MyBase.OnTextChanged(e)
Else
End If
```

```
// C#
if (possibleValues.Count == 0 || String.IsNullOrEmpty(this.Text) ||
updatingTextDirectly)
    base.OnTextChanged(e);
else
{
}
```

10. In the *else* clause for that last added *if* statement, we need to find out if the *Text* property of the control can be found at the start of any of the possible values. So we get the enumerator for the *ArrayList* and loop through the values, checking to see if we should automatically complete the text. Add the following code to the *else* clause that was added in step 9:

```vb
' VB
Dim valueList As IEnumerator = _possibleValues.GetEnumerator()
Dim found As Boolean = False
Dim currentValue As String = Me.Text.ToUpper()

While valueList.MoveNext() And Not found
   Dim testValue As String = valueList.Current.ToString()
   If testValue.ToUpper().IndexOf(currentValue) = 0 Then
   End If
End While
```

```csharp
// C#
IEnumerator valueList = possibleValues.GetEnumerator();
bool found = false;
string currentValue = this.Text.ToUpper();
while ((valueList.MoveNext()) && (!found))
{
    string testValue = (string)valueList.Current;
    if (testValue.ToUpper().IndexOf(currentValue) == 0)
    {
    }
}
```

11. If a match is found, the matching value will be put into the *Text* property and the unmatched value is selected. Also, because the *Text* property is being assigned to directly, the updatingTextDirectly is set to *True* before the assignment and back to *False* afterward. This eliminates the loop that could otherwise occur. The following code is added to the *if* statement within the *while* loop:

```vb
' VB
updatingTextDirectly = True
Me.Text = testValue
Me.SelectionStart = currentValue.Length()
Me.SelectionLength = testValue.Length - currentValue.Length
found = True
updatingTextDirectly = False
```

```csharp
// C#
updatingTextDirectly = true;
this.Text = testValue;
this.SelectionStart = currentValue.Length;
this.SelectionLength = testValue.Length - currentValue.Length;
found = true;
updatingTextDirectly = false;
```

12. The last piece of this handler is to call the *OnTextChanged* event in the base class. The following code is added below the *while* loop:

```
' VB
MyBase.OnTextChanged(e)
```

```
// C#
base.OnTextChanged(e);
```

13. Only two more pieces of functionality to create. And these last two are very similar. The idea is that when a Delete or a Backspace key is hit, we don't want to perform a match. Although this is a little arbitrary, experience has shown that performing the automatic completion when backspacing is a little off-putting for the user. The following code should be added below the *OnTextChanged* handler:

```
' VB
Protected Overrides Sub OnKeyDown(ByVal e As System.Windows.Forms.KeyEventArgs)
    If e.KeyValue = 8 Or e.KeyValue = 46 Then
        updatingTextDirectly = True
    End If
    MyBase.OnKeyDown(e)
End Sub

Protected Overrides Sub OnKeyUp(ByVal e As System.Windows.Forms.KeyEventArgs)
    If e.KeyValue = 8 Or e.KeyValue = 46 Then
        updatingTextDirectly = False
    End If
    MyBase.OnKeyDown(e)
End Sub
// C#
protected override void OnKeyDown(KeyEventArgs e)
{
    if (e.KeyValue == 8 || e.KeyValue == 46)
        updatingTextDirectly = true;
    base.OnKeyDown(e);
}

protected override void OnKeyUp(KeyEventArgs e)
{
    if (e.KeyValue == 8 || e.KeyValue == 46)
        updatingTextDirectly = false;
    base.OnKeyUp(e);
}
```

14. Now that we have the derived component in place, we need to demonstrate the functionality. First, build your project. Then, in the Solution Explorer, double-click the Form1 file to open the form designer.

15. Open the toolbox. Drag the *AutoCompleteTextBox* control onto the form.

16. Double-click the form to create an event handler for the form's *Load* event. In this handler we want to initialize the *PossibleValues* property on the control. Add the following code to the *Load* event handler:

```vb
' VB
Dim possibleValues As String() = {"Jacob", "Emily", "Emma", "Michael", "Joshua",
"Madison"}
AutoCompleteTextBox1.PossibleValues = possibleValues
```

```csharp
// C#
string[] possibleValues = { "Jacob", "Emily", "Emma", "Michael", "Joshua", "Madison" };
autoCompleteTextBox1.PossibleValues = possibleValues;
```

17. Build your application. Then, use Explorer to run the DemoContainer.exe file from the project's Bin directory. When the form is displayed, try typing values into the text box. An "M" automatically completes to "Michael," for example.

Lesson Summary

- The costs associated with building or buying a component can be more complicated than it might appear at first glance.

- When evaluating a third-party component, other factors get applied to the process once the hurdle of "does it do when I need?" has been passed.

- Extending a component can be a relatively simple process, assuming that the component has been designed for extensibility. However, not all components have been designed for that purpose.

Lesson Review

You can use the following questions to test your knowledge of the information in Lesson 1, "Make, Buy, or Extend." The questions are also available on the companion CD if you prefer to review them in electronic form.

NOTE   Answers

Answers to these questions and explanations of why each answer choice is right or wrong are located in the "Answers" section at the end of the book.

---

1. You have been charged with the job of evaluating third-party components for use in an application that is being built. The application is a line-of-business system that is critical for the ongoing operation of the company. The part of the application where the component will go is the notification to the shipping department that manufacturing is finished and that an order is ready to ship. Of the following criteria, which will be given the least weight in evaluating the components?

   A. Evaluation version

   B. Technical support

   C. Performance

   D. Future enhancements

2. While creating a class hierarchy, you would like to define a method that can be overridden by any derived class but is accessible only from within a derived class. Which modifier(s) should be used? (Choose all that apply.)

   A. *Public*

   B. *Private*

   C. *Protected*

   D. *Overridable*(VB)/*virtual* (C#)

3. In which of the following scenarios are you likely to choose the techniques for wrapping components instead of extending components? (Choose all that apply.)

   A. Inheriting from a COM object

   B. Inheriting from a class that, in turn, is derived from *ComponentServices*

   C. Inheriting from a class that, in turn, is derived from another class

   D. Inheriting from a sealed class

Lesson 2: Implementation Practices

Even if the application being developed includes a large number of third-party components, some custom components will need to be created. The design has been created by an architect and approved by the user, and now you're ready to code. A wide variety of common situations will arise for which there are "best practices." And although "best practice" is an overused term, there are instances where, through empirical evidence, a certain programming pattern is found to be better than the others. In this lesson we look at a couple of common patterns that fit this mold.

After this lesson, you will be able to:
- Build a string using the most efficient technique for the situation.
- Decide the best way to create and persist connection information.
- Determine the most appropriate way to access SQL data from within your application.

Estimated lesson time: 35 minutes

Real World

Bruce Johnson

How can such seemingly simple things be so complicated? How to create a string? Access data? These are fundamentals that every programmer learns while still in diapers (relatively speaking). But here is a lesson devoted to the best way to approach these simple things. Has the world gone mad?

Well, no, it hasn't. But the complexity of the systems that we write and the demands placed upon us by financial auditors, security experts, and users who demand subsecond response times mean that we need to pay more attention to the minutiae than we would like. The good news is that once you have used the techniques for a short time, you won't forget them. The bad news is that to learn the techniques, you need to start by reading this lesson. Sorry there isn't a better way.

Working with Strings

In the .NET world, data types break down into two general categories: value types and reference types. Value types consist of most of the intrinsic data types: integers, floats, Booleans. Reference types are the more complex object: hashtables, *DataSets*, database connections, and so on. There are some fundamental differences between the two data types regarding where values are stored and how they get passed around.

NOTE Stack vs. heap

Although the details are beyond the scope of this book, a big difference between value and reference types is where the memory for them gets allocated. Value types are defined on the *stack*. The stack, which is also used for parameter passing, is a very fast reference place that is not subject to garbage collection. For this reason, the creation and destruction of integers, Booleans, and so on are very fast.

Reference types are allocated on the *heap*. As well as taking up space in the heap, a reference to the newly allocated space is made on the stack. So accessing a reference type takes slightly (and I do mean a very, very small amount) longer than a value type.

Sitting in the middle of these two types is the *String* object. For most people the *String* object is considered intrinsic and therefore is expected to be a value type. However, the implementation of string in .NET makes it a reference type. What's more, it's *immutable*, which in the object-oriented world is an object whose state can't be modified after it has been initially created. Concatenate a value to the end of a string? A new *String* object gets created. Use the *Replace* method on the contents of a string? A new *String* object gets created. The constant (relatively speaking) creation and destruction of *String* objects is one of the reasons why we care about how strings are manipulated.

StringBuilder

Much has been published about *StringBuilder*, in both the MSDN documentation and various blogs. The basic information is as follows.

The *StringBuilder* class is used to construct strings. It should be used in place of a series of string concatenation operations. So, for example, instead of the following:

```
' VB
Dim s As String
S = "abc"
S += "def"
S += "ghi"
S += "jkl"
```

```
// C#
String s = "abc";
S += "def";
S += "ghi";
S += "jkl";
```

you should instead write:

```
' VB
Dim s As New StringBuilder
s = "abc"
s.Append("def")
```

```
    s.Append("ghi")
    s.Append("jkl")

// C#
StringBuilder s = new StringBuilder();
s = "abc";
s.Append("def");
s.Append("ghi");
s.Append("jkl");
```

The reason for making this choice is that each concatenation operation causes a *String* object to be destroyed and then recreated. The *StringBuilder*, on the other hand, is instantiated only once. Although the *StringBuilder* is a larger object (in terms of overhead) than a *String*, once enough *String* objects have been created and destroyed, it is more efficient to use *StringBuilder*.

When to Use *StringBuilder*

There are some mild differences of opinion on when to convert from using string concatenation to using the *StringBuilder* object; the general rule of thumb is once you get past the fourth concatenation or are working with strings longer than 256 bytes. But there are instances where, even though it looks like you're using concatenation, what's happening under the covers might not be what you expect.

```
' VB
Dim s as String
Dim a as Integer = 5
Dim b as Integer = 10

s = "A" & a & "B" & b & "C"

// C#
String s;
int a = 5;
int b = 10;

s = "A" + a + "B" + b + "C";
```

In this case, the compiler optimizes to use the *Concat* method on the *String* object. From a performance perspective, the optimal way to code the string assignment is as follows:

```
' VB
s = String.Concat(New Object() { "A", a, "B", b, "C" }).ToString

// C#
s = string.Concat(new object[] { "A", a, "B", b, "C" }).ToString();
```

And, lucky for us developers, this is what the compiler produces.

Another commonly used string building pattern is to use the *Format* method on the *String* class, like the following:

```
' VB
s = String.Format("A{0}B{1}C", a, b)
```

```
// C#
s = String.Format("A{0}B{1}C", a, b);
```

What happens behind the scenes is that the implementation of *String.Format* includes the creation of a *StringBuilder* object. So there are no worries that concatenation is being used under the covers.

Working with Connection Strings

Moving up from strings, the next thing to talk about is connection strings. Yes, the segue is weak, but what can we do?

.NET Framework 2.0 has made some changes to how connection strings can be worked with. To understand why the features were necessary, consider the issues with connection strings that older applications had to deal with.

Sensitive Information   Many connection strings have an embedded plaintext user ID and password. Having credentials that are modified for each user negates any connection pooling that could take place, so this is the norm for ASP.NET applications. But storing user IDs and passwords in a file that is easily accessible through the file system is a serious breach of security.

Inconsistent Naming   So when you create a connection string in your configuration file, what name do you give the element? *ConnectionString*? *ConnectionStr*? *ConStr*? Or some other variation? Although variety is the spice of life, it's the bane of maintainability.

Confusing Syntax   The syntax of a connection string is a frequent source of errors. And once the application is in production, mistakes in the options can have serious repercussions.

In the face of this, Microsoft added three features to the .NET Framework to make working with connection strings easier and more secure.

connectionStrings Section

In the configuration file, there is now support for a *connectionStrings* element. Within this element, connection string information can be added or removed through the <add>, <remove>, and <clear> nodes. For example, the following element defines a connection string called *ConnStr1* that connects to a SQL Server database called *AdventureWorks* on the local machine:

```
<configuration>
   <connectionStrings>
      <add name="ConnStr1" connectionString="LocalSqlServer: data
         source=127.0.0.1;Integrated Security=SSPI;
         Initial Catalog=AdventureWorks"
```

```
        providerName="System.Data.SqlClient" />
    </connectionStrings>
</configuration>
```

Once the connection string has been defined in the *connectionStrings* section, it can easily be accessed from within the application. This is accomplished with the *System.Configuration.ConnectionManager.ConnectionStrings* property on the *ConnectionManager* class. *ConnectionStrings* is a collection of the *connectionStrings* elements in the configuration file. As a result, individual connections can be accessed by name.

```
' VB
ConnectionManager.ConnectionStrings("ConnStr1").ConnectionString
```

```
// C#
ConnectionManager.ConnectionStrings["ConnStr1"].ConnectionString
```

In Visual Basic, the name of the *connectionString* element can actually improve its accessibility. Start by naming your *connectionString* as follows:

```
project.My.MySettings.connectionName
```

where *project* is the name of your project and *connectionName* is the name you want to give to the connection string. If you do this, the connection string can be accessed using the following statement:

```
' VB
My.Settings.connectionName
```

Securing Sensitive Information

Although the *connectionStrings* section makes persisting and retrieving connection strings more consistent, it doesn't solve the nagging problems of exposing sensitive information. That is solved by a new option to the aspnet_regiis command. The aspnet_regiis command is normally used to register ASP.NET 2.0 with a particular instance of IIS. But in this case it also provides some command-line options that allow sections of the configuration file to be encrypted. The details of how aspnet_regiis is used can be found in Chapter 11, "Application Configuration."

Building Connection Strings

The last piece of this puzzle is the *ConnectionStringBuilder* classes. The challenge with a connection string is making sure that the attribute names within the string are correct. Is it *Initial Catalog*, *InitialCatalog*, or *InitCat*? Although it might seem like a small thing to keep track of (and remember) this sort of detail, things like this actually reduce developer productivity. And it's also where the *ConnectionStringBuilder* classes takes over.

The *DbConnectionStringBuilder* class is an abstract class that provides support for a number of data provider–specific classes. The underlying functionality is to collect a number of name/value pairs and then transform those pairs into a properly formatted connection string. But that's not the stuff that really matters to developers. Instead, it is the data provider–specific classes that provide the useful functionality; for example, *SqlConnectionStringBuilder*. This class exposes properties such as *UserID*, *Password*, and *InitialCatalog*. Programmatically, these properties get assigned values. Then, when it comes time to establish the connection to the data source, the *ConnectionString* property on the class combines the properties into the appropriate connection string.

Also, the data provider–specific classes expose other properties consistent with the underlying data source's capabilities. So the *SqlConnectionStringBuilder* class includes *ConnectTimeout*, *FailoverPartner*, and *Encrypt*. And the *OracleConnectionStringBuilder* and *OleDbConnectionStringBuilder* have similar properties that apply uniquely to the underlying data source.

```
' VB
Dim builder As New SqlConnectionStringBuilder()
builder.DataSource = "(local)"
builder.IntegratedSecurity  = True
builder.InitialCatalog = "AdventureWorks"
Console.WriteLine(builder.ConnectionString)
```

```
// C#
SqlConnectionStringBuilder builder = new SqlConnectionStringBuilder();
builder.DataSource = "(local)";
builder.IntegratedSecurity  = true;
builder.InitialCatalog = "AdventureWorks";
Console.WriteLine(builder.ConnectionString);
```

Passing Data Around

One of the more common questions asked at the architecture level is how complex data should be passed around. To be clear, this type of question is relevant only in distributed applications. If the data is being passed within a single process, the content is rarely passed. Instead a reference gets passed and the data is accessed through that reference.

The question of complex parameter passing is also relatively moot when working with .NET Remoting. The automatic serialization that occurs means that objects are (basically) passed by value—at least in the mechanism that moves the data across the component boundaries.

This leaves the question of Web services. And, more explicitly, the question of Extensible Markup Language (XML) versus *DataSets* comes into play. From a versioning perspective, it is clear that the structure of the parameters passed into a Web service needs to be flexible. But should the mechanics of passing the data be XML or *DataSets*?

NOTE RPC vs. document style in versioning

Remote Procedure Call (RPC) messaging is a style of designing a Web service interface that closely resembles the calling of methods on classes. This is different from a document style of messaging, where all the information is placed in the body of the Simple Object Access Protocol (SOAP) envelope and it is left up to the Web service to determine what should be done with it.

RPC-style messaging suffers from the same versioning problem that any parameter-based interface does. If the parameters need to change, backward compatibility is lost. Document-style messaging is based on a schema. And the schema can be extended as future changes require. For this reason, in Web services where versioning is expected to be a concern, it's frequently worth implementing document-style messaging, even though it's more complicated to put into place.

The difference between XML and *DataSet*s is a little misleading. The reason is that *DataSet*s are serialized into XML by default when they are used in a Web service method. This isn't to say that there aren't techniques that can be employed to use binary serialization of *DataSet*s. There are, assuming that both ends of the connection are .NET. However, the most common usage of *DataSet*s in Web services uses XML as the wire format.

As it turns out, the serialization of *DataSet*s isn't necessarily into the XML form that might be expected. What is generated (by default) is an XML *Diffgram*. This form goes beyond the current value for each row and column. It also tracks the original values for the columns, as well as the state (Added, Deleted, or Modified) of each row. By storing this information, it allows for not just the raw data to be transmitted but also the changes made to the data. The result is the functional equivalent of a remote batch update.

Naturally, a typical XML document doesn't have this capability, not unless it is explicitly included in the underlying schema. However, the XML document requires less space to convey the current state information than does a *DataSet*. What this means to the *DataSet* versus XML decision is that the purpose of the document is really the ultimate factor in deciding which format to use.

If the message is intended to convey a set of information with no historical context, then XML is a better choice. It provides all of the needed capabilities with much less overhead. If, on the other hand, the message needs to include current values and updates that had been applied to the data, then the *DataSet* is the better choice.

Real World

Bruce Johnson

Lest you think that the *DataSet* is too big for your data updating situation, allow me to relate some real-world experience. Many of the people we talk to believe that *DataSets* are too bulky and do not perform well enough to satisfy their requirements. They believe that they can create a "lightweight" format that gives them the *DataSet*'s functionality without all of its excesses. So off they go to design and build "*DataSet*-Lite."

After a couple of weeks they come back with an implementation that they claim is ready to go. So we start to put it into some screens and quickly run up against a snag. Some scenario comes up that hasn't been addressed in the design. Back they go for a few more days before a new version is released. Again, it gets used in a real-world Web page and is lacking in some other functionality. At this point the developer gets that frazzled look as he or she realizes that the masterpiece is not as elegant (or as functional) as had been hoped. This is also about the time that the developer takes another look at the *DataSet* because the benchmarks on performance for the new component have been abysmal.

The point here is two-fold. *DataSets* are designed to do exactly what they do. Although there might be a little bit of baggage in the exposed functionality, most of what is in the class is there for a reason. Also, *DataSets* perform surprisingly well. But this should be expected because dozens of developers looked at the code for performance (and other) improvements before it was released.

Data Storage

When it comes to storing data, a number of choices are available. The "right" choice will naturally depend on the level of functionality that you need from the storage mechanism. The reasons for picking one over the other must be based on your needs. Below is a basic list of the options and when they are appropriate.

Physical Files

Yes, there is a physical file element to every persisted data storage mechanism. The idea here is to store information in some format that is amenable to retrieval. Almost anything goes here, from comma-delimited to tab-separated. Even a binary format is fine, not to mention the configuration files that are commonplace in .NET applications.

The problem with physical files is the access mechanism. There are no transaction capabilities, which means that only one application can access a file at a time. And there is no ability to roll back partial changes if something goes wrong. So a physical file is good for only simple data storage.

Isolated Storage

When an application uses isolated storage, you open the logical equivalent of a file system for your application in the current user's private area. Within that file system any type of file can be written or retrieved. Consider this to be a private version of the physical files just mentioned. Details on how to access isolated storage can be found in Chapter 11.

Database

For many developers a database is the assumed data storage mechanism. And, yes, the vast majority of databases provide a wonderful mechanism for being able to persist data, complete with transactional support, isolated access (from other users), and centralization.

The real danger with using a database is that it's overkill in a lot of situations. And given some of the issues associated with deployment and the dependencies that it introduces, make sure that the capabilities of the database are required before making use of it.

Stored Procedures vs. Dynamic SQL

First off, it is important to realize the passions that can be raised by having this discussion. Whether stored procedures or dynamically created SQL should be used to access data is a touchy topic that doesn't have a truly clear winner. The terminology in use can also be a little confusing, so let's set out a clear definition. A stored procedure is a set of SQL statements defined in the database that can be invoked though a single request. Dynamic SQL is the creation of the SQL that is to be executed against the database while the application is running.

One other clarification about what dynamic SQL is needs to be made. The following is *not* legitimate dynamic SQL:

```
' VB
Dim s As String = "SELECT * FROM Orders WHERE CustNo = " & value
```

```
// C#
string s = "SELECT * FROM Orders WHERE CustNo = " + value;
```

It's not that these statements don't dynamically build a SQL statement; it's just that they demonstrate two problems that are quite common in coders who work with in-line SQL. First, and less dangerous, is the use of the wildcard in the SELECT clause. Good dynamic SQL should be explicit in the fields that need to be retrieved. Allowing everything that is defined in the table to be retrieved should be done only if the application really wants everything back. And it is rarer than you might think that an application wants to deal with fields that were added after the last deployment.

The second issue is the injection of a value directly into the SQL statement. Instead of just appending the value, it should be inserted through a parameter in the SQL. Creating a statement in the manner illustrated above leaves the application open to injection attacks, especially if the value included in the WHERE clause is taken from user input.

Now that the basics are out of the way, let's consider the areas of contention for the stored procedures versus dynamic SQL argument.

Performance

The basic thesis here is that stored procedures are precompiled and therefore execute faster than dynamic SQL. Unfortunately, as a blanket statement, that is completely incorrect. From the SQL Server Books Online document:

> *SQL Server 2000 and SQL Server version 7.0 incorporate a number of changes to statement processing that extend many of the performance benefits of stored procedures to all SQL statements. SQL Server 2000 and SQL Server 7.0 do not save a partially compiled plan for stored procedures when they are created. A stored procedure is compiled at execution time, like any other Transact-SQL statement. SQL Server 2000 and SQL Server 7.0 retain execution plans for all SQL statements in the procedure cache, not just stored procedure execution plans.*

And just so there is no confusion, the same information also applies to SQL Server 2005. What this says is that stored procedures and dynamic SQL have the same opportunity for performance gains, at least when it comes to reusing execution plans. There is no precompilation. The first time a stored procedure or statement gets executed, an execution plan is generated and cached. Subsequent executions will reuse the cached plan, if possible. Although stored procedures might be more likely to use a cache, the fact that dynamic SQL is generated (as opposed to being hand-typed) reduces that advantage significantly.

The other opportunity for performance is in network traffic. And the gains that can be made in this area depend greatly on the types and volume of SQL that are required. While a single stored procedure and a single dynamic query produce similar amounts of network traffic, you can realize performance benefits by adding some business logic to a stored procedure and replacing multiple dynamic queries. Now a single request (the stored procedure name) replaces not only multiple statements but also the requisite transfer of data back and forth between the client and the database server.

Security

One of the most quoted reasons against the use of dynamic SQL is the inability to properly secure the database. By using stored procedures, administrators can allow access to the needed stored procedures and deny access to the individual tables. Also, through the use of views, access to individual columns can be controlled at a very granular level.

The reality is that the importance of this particular factor depends greatly on your environment. Some companies demand that stored procedures be used for all data access. In other words, users are not given access to individual tables and no dynamically generated SQL is allowed at all. However, this really isn't the security savior that is expected. Role-based security provides the same level of security that stored procedures do, especially when combined with views. So long as the application uses the view, the database is secure, whether SQL statements are generated dynamically or run in a stored procedure.

Stored Procedures as an Abstraction Layer

For many people, the justification for using stored procedures is to abstract the physical data model from the application. This means that the actual tables in which the data is stored can be changed as needed without needing to modify the code. And this is certainly true. By using stored procedures, the developer or database administrator has defined an API (a set of exposed methods) through which data is accessed. The implementation details, including the data schema, is irrelevant to the calling program.

The only question is—how often does this happen in a real database? Specifically, how often does the underlying database schema change without some modification to the functionality offered by the application itself? If a column is added to a table, the application needs to be modified to recognize the new column. Yes, it is certainly possible to create an application that dynamically recognizes the addition of a new field. But you don't often find that level of sophistication in your typical business application. More common is the situation where the addition of a field results in the current application, or even other applications, breaking. The benefits that might be gained by using stored procedures as an application layer are rarely realized to the extent that was originally envisioned.

Although the database schema might not change, there are certainly times when having the data access code in a stored procedure is useful. For example, it allows changes to be made to improve performance without diving into the application code, not to mention avoiding the challenge of finding all the places where the SQL is put together within the code.

The conclusion to this debate ends pretty much as it started. There really is no obvious answer to whether stored procedures or dynamic SQL is a better choice, certainly not one that can be considered true every single time. Much of what works best depends on the application that is being developed, the other applications that are already in place, and the skill set of the development team.

Data Flow and Decision Flow

Data has qualities that make it of importance to the entire enterprise. The metaphor that data is the lifeblood of a company is not a bad one. Data flows in from many sources and is transformed and combined as it moves from person to person, process to process. The efficiency with which this transformation takes place is a good measure of the overall success of the company.

Here are some things to consider when you're looking at enterprise data flow:

- What data is needed for the ongoing operations of the organization?
- What data is needed for the reporting of all styles, including both historical and business intelligence?
- What data do the individual departments need to make the decisions that are expected of them?
- What types of transformations does the data need to go through?
- Who makes the decisions about data transformation, data storage, and enterprise data flow?

The goal of the data flow is to support business operations, which is ultimately the flow of decision making. The traditional uses of data can be summarized as follows:

- Effective customer response, including information about their orders, requests, questions, and other needs.
- Efficient use of corporate resources: not just what the resources are, but where they are stored and when they are needed in the process. This data improves the decision-making capabilities of the organization.
- Improvement of process efficiency. The processes that are used in the business are those of the corporate resources, even though they might not appear on the balance sheet. The data generated by each business process can be captured and analyzed to find opportunities for improvement.
- Finding competitive advantages. In today's global business environment, finding competitive advantages is not a luxury. It is something that needs to be done in order to stay in business. If you can use your data more effectively than your competitors, you can gain an advantage over them. If other companies are using their data to improve their business processes and you are not, you will start slipping behind.

The structure used to make decisions is actually one of the less-documented parts of many companies. The answers to common questions, such as which customer gets a scarce product and which discounts to offer to whom, are not always written down with great precision. Instead, this incredibly valuable corporate asset is kept in the heads of the employees who make the decisions. So any mechanism that can be found to document the decision flow, or even automate it, is frequently worth the cost and effort. In the .NET world, there are two main ways to document and automate common business decisions:

- **BizTalk Server** This is the old guard for decision-flow automation. It provides a mechanism that allows for inputs to be taken from various sources. Once it's captured by the system, the information can be used to make decisions, change program flow, and generate outputs in many shapes and formats. This is the high end of decision flow in the .NET world.

- **Windows Workflow Foundation**   This is the newcomer to the Windows world. As part of .NET 3.0, this component allows for the graphical representation of the decision flow within a component. Also, the workflow can control not only the movement of data but also the decision points about which processes get executed.

Both of these tools can greatly improve the automation of the decision making and the efficiency of the data flow. And, as has already been noted, this is critical to the success of the corporation.

Lab: Accessing Connection Information

In this lab, we demonstrate the ease with which connection string information can be extracted from the configuration file. If you encounter a problem completing an exercise, the completed projects are available on the companion CD in the Code folder.

▶ **Exercise: Extracting Connection String Information from the Configuration File**

Storing connection strings in a configuration file is something that a large number of applications have in common. And being able to retrieve that information from the configuration file is critical. In this exercise a technique to retrieve this information will be covered.

1. Launch Visual Studio 2005.
2. Open a solution using File | Open | Project/Solution.
3. Navigate to the Chapter9/Lesson2/Lab1/<language>/Before directory. Select the Lab1 solution and click Open.
4. In the Solution Explorer, double-click the Program.cs or Module1.vb to gain access to the *Main* method. All we're going to do is display the connection string from the App.config file. This is done through the *ConnectionManager.ConnectionStrings* collection. Once the named *ConnectionString* has been accessed, the *ConnectionString* property is used to retrieve the connection information. Add the following code to the *Main* method:

```
' VB
Console.WriteLine(ConfigurationManager.ConnectionStrings("ConnStr1").ConnectionString)
Console.ReadLine()
```

```
// C#
Console.WriteLine(ConfigurationManager.ConnectionStrings["ConnStr1"].ConnectionString)
;
Console.ReadLine();
```

5. Of course, to retrieve the connection string from the config file, it needs to be in the config file. In the Solution Explorer, double-click the App.config file. Add the following block inside the *<configuration>* element:

```
<connectionStrings>
  <add name="ConnStr1" connectionString="LocalSqlServer: data
source=127.0.0.1;Integrated Security=SSPI; Initial Catalog=AdventureWorks"
    providerName="System.Data.SqlClient" />
</connectionStrings>
```

6. Once this has been done, launch the application using F5. The connection string information associated with the ConnStr1 connection is displayed.

7. If you're not using Visual Basic, you're done. But if you choose Visual Basic, there is a little extra joy in this lab. Go back into the App.config file and add the following element to the connectionStrings section:

```
<add name="ConnectionDemo.My.MySettings.DemoConn"
    connectionString="LocalSqlServer: data source=127.0.0.1;Integrated
    Security=SSPI; Initial Catalog=Northwind"
  providerName="System.Data.SqlClient" />
```

8. This by itself doesn't modify the My.Settings section, so save the changes to the App.config file using the File | Save App.config menu option.

9. Right-click the project in the Solution Explorer and select Properties. In the properties pages, select Settings on the left side. You will see a message indicating that the App.config has changed. Click OK and then save the updated settings with a File | Save ConnectionDemo menu option.

10. Back in the Module1.vb file, we're going to add another WriteLine. This WriteLine will use the My.Settings object. Add the following line of code to the *Main* method above the Console.ReadLine statement:

```
' VB
Console.WriteLine(My.Settings.DemoConn)
```

11. Run the application once more using F5. Notice that now two connection strings are produced.

Lesson Summary

- *StringBuilder* should be used when frequent concatenations are expected to build a string.
- The .NET Framework has introduced a number of features that help developers work with and secure connection strings more easily.

- The debate between stored procedures and dynamically generated SQL does not have a clear-cut winner. The details of the development environment contribute to the "correct" answer.

Lesson Review

You can use the following questions to test your knowledge of the information in Lesson 2, "Implementation Practices." The questions are also available on the companion CD if you prefer to review them in electronic form.

NOTE Answers

Answers to these questions and explanations of why each answer choice is right or wrong are located in the "Answers" section at the end of the book.

---

1. You need to build a string that represents a single row in a tab-delimited file. The string contains 15 fields. If readability is not an issue (that is, optimizing performance is more important than maintenance), which technique should be used?

   A. Use a *StringBuilder* class. Add the fields as calls to the *Append* method.

   B. Use a single *String.Concat* method.

   C. Use a single *String.Format* method.

   D. Use the self-concatenation operator (&= or +=) for each field.

2. You are storing a connection string in a configuration file. Which class provides the easiest mechanism to access the persisted strings?

   A. *AppSettings*

   B. *ConnectionStrings*

   C. *ConnectionStringsSection*

   D. *DbConnectionStringBuilder*

3. You are trying to decide on the format to be used for the parameters in a method. The method will be called both remotely (through a Web service) and locally to the client application. The method modifies some of the parameters, and the calling application needs to easily determine which parameters were modified. Which style of parameter passing is most appropriate?

   A. Use individual parameters.

   B. Use a *DataSet*.

   C. Use an XML document.

   D. Use an XML document formatted as a SOAP message.

Chapter Review

To further practice and reinforce the skills you learned in this chapter, you can perform the following tasks:

- Review the chapter summary.
- Review the list of key terms introduced in this chapter.
- Complete the case scenarios. These scenarios set up real-world situations involving the topics of this chapter and ask you to create a solution.
- Complete the suggested practices.
- Take a practice test.

Chapter Summary

- The decision to make or buy a component will depend on a large number of factors. The criteria to select which way to go will ultimately be based on whether commodity functionality is appropriate for the application, as opposed to the competitive advantage that can be gained through custom development.
- Some seemingly straightforward programming practices actually have some complexities when it comes to optimal performance.
- Improvements in .NET Framework 2.0 make previously challenging tasks (like encrypting connection information) much easier to implement.

Key Terms

Do you know what these key terms mean? You can check your answers by looking up the terms in the glossary at the end of the book.

- base class
- derived class
- Diffgram
- heap
- immutable
- inheritance
- inheritance hierarchy
- override
- stack

Case Scenarios

In the following case scenarios, you will apply what you've learned about delivering multimedia in a distributed environment. You can find answers to these questions in the "Answers" section at the end of the book.

Case Scenario 1: Evaluating a Component

You are a corporate developer creating a Windows service application that processes flat files. Each flat file contains lead information that needs to be converted into database records. The flat file can contain anywhere from 1000 to more than 1,000,000 leads.

One of the tasks needed by the process is to validate e-mail addresses. Three steps are involved in determining that a user's input is a valid e-mail address.

- Does the user's input match the regular expression for an e-mail address?
- Does the domain in the user's input have a mail server?
- Does the domain's mail server verify the account portion of the user's input?

The last two validations involve sending a request to a mail server across the Internet. Your challenge is to decide whether the component should be purchased or built.

Questions

Answer the following question for your manager:

- Which are the two most important criteria that will go into the make-versus-buy decision?

Case Scenario 2: Evaluating Data Abstraction

You are a corporate developer at the beginning of designing a Windows Forms application. One of the choices you have to make is how to access the data. In other words, should you use dynamic SQL or stored procedures? The factors that weigh into this decision include the speed of the clients (slower than average), the bandwidth of the network connection (less than 100 KB), and the existence of some existing stored procedures to perform some business logic

Questions

Answer the following questions for your manager:

1. Which style of data access should be the default for use in the application?
2. Under which conditions would the alternative access technique be appropriate?

Suggested Practices

To help successfully master the objectives covered in this chapter, complete the following task.

Make, Buy, or Extend

For this task, you should complete both practices.

- **Practice 1**   Using one of the projects that are currently under development, identify a component that could be purchased. Define the criteria that should be used to evaluate the component, including the weightings. Compare at least two third-party components against the effort involved with custom building.

- **Practice 2**   Using an application that is currently being developed, analyze the performance of the string-processing logic. Are too many concatenations being used? Are there places where *StringBuilder* would make for a more efficient application?

Take a Practice Test

The practice tests on this book's companion CD offer many options. For example, you can test yourself on just one exam objective, or you can test yourself on all the 70-548 certification exam content. You can set up the test so that it closely simulates the experience of taking a certification exam, or you can set it up in study mode so that you can look at the correct answers and explanations after you answer each question.

MORE INFO   Practice tests

For details about all the practice test options available, see the "How to Use the Practice Tests" section in this book's Introduction.

Chapter 10
Handling Exceptions

Every application needs to be able to handle exceptions as they occur. How the exception gets handled will very much depend on the context in which the exception occurs, but there is no reason a user should ever see an exception unless it's included as part of a nice, friendly message that lets the user know what can be done to help the situation. In this chapter we look at the techniques that are used to ensure that users always get the pretty message instead of an ugly, unintelligible message followed by the application aborting unceremoniously.

Exam objectives in this chapter:
- Choose an appropriate exception handling mechanism.
  - Evaluate the current exception handling mechanism.
  - Design a new exception handling technique.

Lessons in this chapter:

Before You Begin

To complete the lessons in this chapter, you should be familiar with Microsoft Visual Basic or C# and be comfortable with the following task:

- Throwing and catching exceptions using Visual Basic .NET or C#.

Also, to complete the exercises, the following additional software needs to be installed on your computer:

- The Enterprise Library application (January 2006 version). Enterprise Library can be downloaded from *http://msdn.microsoft.com/library/en-us/dnpag2/html/EntLib2.asp*. The Enterprise Library must have been compiled and the assemblies copied to the c:\Program Files\Microsoft Enterprise Library January 2006\bin directory. The Build-Library.bat command file can be used to build the application, and the CopyAssemblies.bat command file moves the assemblies to the bin directory.

Real World

Bruce Johnson

Applications that don't handle exceptions properly are a pet peeve of mine. Usually developers code their applications in one of two ways, and I'm still trying to decide which is worse.

In one case, the application has no code at all that deals with exceptions. So if anything unexpected happens, the application is terminated with, at most, the Microsoft Windows default unhandled exception dialog box. In the second case, the application catches every single exception that the operating system could possibly throw. Now, regardless of what might happen on the computer, there is no way that the application will ever shut down unexpectedly. This also means that the application continues to assume that everything is working properly even as the memory chips are sizzling and flames are lapping at the hard drive.

The best applications take a middle path. They find ways to handle exceptions that can be anticipated while providing a graceful exit mechanism for cases that have no immediate resolution. This chapter discusses the attributes of this more appropriate exception handling mechanism so that you can more easily integrate one into your application.

Lesson 1: The Goals of Exception Handling

Ask a developer what an exception is and the answer will frequently be "when something unexpected happens." Go further and ask about what sort of problem isn't expected and the developer's answer usually becomes a little less certain. The reason is that there is some confusion between unexpected and unanticipated. These two words are at the heart of what the goal of exception handling should be.

After this lesson, you will be able to:

- Recognize what "bad" exception handling looks like.
- Identify the purpose of good exception handling.
- Construct a mechanism to handle exceptions that are not anticipated by the application.

Estimated lesson time: 40 minutes

Hand the following block of code to your favorite developer and ask for an opinion. The answer reveals a lot about the developer's level of experience.

```vb
' VB
Try
    ' Code goes here
Catch ex As Exception
    ' More code goes here
End Try
```

```csharp
// C#
try {
    // Code goes here
}
catch (Exception ex) {
    // More code goes here
}
```

In case your favorite developer doesn't have any complaints, these code blocks are examples of the most despicable pattern in .NET. There are two reasons for making this statement. First, catching every exception betrays a philosophy that is dangerous—that being that every exception is created equal and all of them can safely be ignored. The second reason is that once an application heads down this road, there is a high cost involved with fixing it. It takes a lot of work to handle exceptions properly when you first write some code. After the code is written, the challenges are multiplied.

The Four Outcomes Of Synchronous Requests

When a method in .NET (or any other language) is called synchronously, there are four possible outcomes.

- **Synchronous success**   This is the normal "happy path" outcome of the request. The method completes and everything works as expected.

- **Asynchronous success**   Some requests can't be satisfied immediately. Due to a delay in accessing some necessary resource, the requestor must be kept waiting before completing the request. Think of this as waiting in line to make a purchase at a clothing store. Eventually the request will be completed successfully before processing continues. It just takes a little longer than normal.

- **Optimistic success**   This outcome is a little strange. It involves assuming success on the part of the requestor with the actual final completion delayed for a period of time. Optimistic success is best described with an example. Back in the clothing store, you pay for your purchase with a check. At the time you write the check, there isn't enough money in your bank account to pay for it. But you know that you'll be able to deposit the necessary funds before the check clears the bank. In this case, the cashier who accepted the check will have experienced optimistic success. The requestor assumed success that didn't actually take place until later.

- **Abject failure**   This is the worst-case scenario. Either immediately or after some delay, the request fails for whatever reason. In this case the most important thing for the method to do is let someone know that a failure has occurred. Without this notification, the application could continue to process requests with unpredictable consequences. Consider the clothing store example. If your credit card payment wasn't processed successfully but you weren't notified before you walked out of the store, you would likely be arrested for shoplifting. This would qualify as a bad outcome.

When designing a class, it is very important that every method call results in one of those four outcomes. Most important, if a method call fails, it must fail with notification. The notification can take one of two forms—an exception being thrown or a return value that distinguishably indicates the failure. An example of the latter would be the return code that anyone familiar with the Win32 application programming interface (API) functions will recognize.

Exceptions vs. Return Codes

Given that any method that fails must do so with notification, let's examine the difference between return codes and exceptions; specifically, why an exception is almost always better than a return code for managing failure notification.

Code Cleanliness

If return codes are used, the code that handles the error needs to be placed near the method being called. This leads to patterns such as the following pseudo code.

```
returnValue = obj.Method()
If returnValue <> 0 Then
    Handle the error
```

Multiply this by every statement that involves calling a method and checking a return value and the code can quickly become cluttered. The use of exceptions eliminate this clutter, not to mention the fact that in the real world developers don't check for return codes after each method, even if the method might fail.

There is a downside to using exceptions in this sort of situation. With return values, it is very easy to see where the handling is taking place. When exceptions are used, it can be very challenging to find the handler for a particular exception by simply looking at the code. The *Catch* block for an exception can be multiple levels up in the call stack, and the viewer of the method doesn't have a good way to trace this flow at design time. This leaves the possibility of bugs being introduced by forgetfulness.

Channel Reduction

The use of a return code eliminates what is frequently a natural way to return information from a method. More important, it opens up the possibility for convenience to overtake good design and good judgment. Say you have a small method that performs a calculation. There is no way that the method can fail, so you simply return the calculated value instead of a return code.

After a few more iterations of development, the calculation becomes more complicated. It calls a few other methods and extracts some information from a database. Now it's possible for the method to fail. But the method already returns a value, so it can't be "converted" to return a status code. Instead, the developer creates a "dummy" return code, say a −1, to indicate failure. And, of course, every place where the method is being called needs to be updated to recognize that a return value of −1 is a failure. This problem is eliminated through the use of exceptions.

Content-Rich Information

A return value from a method is quite limited in the information that can be conveyed. Say the problem is that a file can't be opened in the file system. This might be a return code of −101. So now the caller knows that a file can't be opened. But why? Was the file not there? Was the directory missing? Did the user have insufficient access rights? There is a lot of information that would be nice to know about the failure that can't be conveyed with a return code.

Because the exception is an object in its own right, it can contain a lot of additional information over and above a basic description of the problem. Also, you have the ability to create your own classes that are derived from *System.Exception* and that are therefore capable of being thrown and caught as if they were native .NET exception objects.

Handling Exceptions

There are two places within an application where exceptions should be handled—not specific places (only two would be too much to ask for), but places in general. The distinction between the two relates to the reasons why exceptions should be handled in the first place. So let's first consider when an exception should be handled. And there are only four instances where an exception should be caught within any method.

Gather Information for Logging

Sometimes information that is necessary for logging is available only around the lines of code that caused the exception. If this is the case, then the exception should be caught and the information collected. Where the information goes at this point depends on the organization's standards. In some cases it might get added to a custom exception that is then rethrown. Or logging could take place right at the point where the exception is detected so that the information is available to interested parties at a later time.

However, it should be made clear that the following code block is absolutely *not* a good practice.

```
' VB
Try
    ' Code goes here
Catch ex As Exception
    Logger.Log(ex)
End Try
```

```
// C#
try {
    // Code goes here
}
catch (Exception ex) {
    Logger.Log(ex);
}
```

The problem is that the exception, every exception, has been handled. Once the exception has been logged, the application continues processing as before. This is rarely a good thing. Instead, the exception should be rethrown with a *Throw* statement from within the *Catch* block. The term applied to catching an exception without rethrowing the original exception or a new one is called *swallowing the exception*.

Add Details to the Exception

Similar to the previous reason, adding details to an exception involves taking the local information that might be useful to identify the cause of an exception and associating it with the exception. The process for doing this is similar to the code shown in the previous section. However, instead of calling Logger.Log, a new instance of an exception is created. This exception would normally be a *custom exception* and would contain the properties that need to be propagated to the next exception handler.

If a new exception is created, the original exception should be placed in the *InnerException* property of the new exception. This allows the handler of the exception to see the original information about the exception, along with the details that are being added.

```vb
' VB
Try
    ' Code goes here
Catch ex As Exception
    Throw new CustomException("Message", ex)
End Try
```

```csharp
// C#
try {
    // Code goes here
}
catch (Exception ex) {
    throw new CustomException("Message", ex);
}
```

Clean Up Resources

This is the most common reason to catch an exception. And, if coded properly, there isn't a *Catch* block, but a *Finally* block. The basic pattern is as follows.

```vb
' VB
Try
    ' Code goes here
Finally
    ' Clean up resources
End Try
```

```csharp
// C#
try {
    // Code goes here
}
finally {
    // Clean up resources
}
```

In the *Finally* block all of the clean-up of unmanaged resources takes place. In particular, the clean-up code should address any resource that needs to be released before garbage collection (such as a lock on a file or database record) or that requires a call to a different method to perform the proper clean-up, such as the *Close* method on a *SqlConnection* object.

Attempt to Recover

This is the least likely scenario for catching an exception. The idea is that the method that catches the exception has anticipated that this exception is possible. So it attempts to resolve the issue that caused the exception to be thrown.

Say, for example, a call is made to a Web service method. The call fails because the Web service is unavailable. So the calling method catches that exception and instead changes the Uniform Resource Locator (URL) property to direct the method to a backup Web service. The calling method has recovered from the exception and is able to move forward as if nothing happened.

Quick Check

1. A class contains a method that opens a file and processes the contents. The path to the file is specified as a parameter. Should the method catch a *FileNotFoundException* exception?

2. A class contains a method that uses a Web service to validate e-mail addresses. The method has two possible Web service endpoints to choose from in order to perform the validation. Should the method catch a *WebException* exception?

Quick Check Answers

1. No. The caller to the method might want to catch it, but the method that actually throws the exception can't do any of the four actions mentioned as the reason for catching an exception. The greatest temptation is to "recover" from the problem. But within the context of this method there is no recovery that can be done. This is the reason that the exception should be allowed to propagate up to the caller.

2. Yes. In this case the logic associated with determining which Web service endpoint to use and the fact that they are interchangeable is encapsulated within the called method. So catching a *WebException* and trying the second endpoint is quite reasonable. And if the second endpoint fails as well, the method should return a different exception (that is, not a *WebException*), indicating that the validation couldn't take place.

What Should Exception Handling Accomplish?

All this talk of not catching exceptions leads to the question of when, where, and which exceptions should be caught. As a lead-up to this discussion, let's look at what the real goals of exception handling are.

Application Integrity

One of the first goals of exception handling is to ensure that the integrity of the application remains intact. Conceptually, the idea is that any method call should ensure that there are no side effects if a failure happens during processing. This is where the *Finally* block is useful. Any clean-up code gets placed in the *Finally* block and there is a guarantee that the *Finally* block will be executed, whether an exception occurs or not.

Another element of exception handling and application integrity is the outright swallowing of all exceptions. This is what happens when the *Catch* block catches the general exception type. By doing so, you are acting as if the application can continue functioning regardless of what else might be going on. So picture the fan on the computer bursting out in flames. Smoke is billowing out of the drive bays. And your application is asking the user whether to save the changes before continuing. Unless you really expect your application to operate under these conditions, it doesn't make sense to catch every exception that an application can throw.

Corporate Requirements

Sometimes corporate standards require exceptions to be handled in a certain way. For example, operations might want to be notified when something unusual happens within the application. This allows them to respond in a timely and proactive manner, rather than having to clean up after applications that have left databases and other resources in an inconsistent state.

Troubleshooting

For the developer, the ability to troubleshoot problems is a leading rationale for the "correct" handling of exceptions. And, unfortunately, to many developers "correct" handling means catching the exception as soon as it is thrown. This is a tradition that has deep roots in Visual Basic and Active Server Pages (ASP) history. But it is no longer necessary in the .NET world.

One of the reasons for not requiring that catching take place at the point of detection is that the *Exception* class includes a *StackTrace* property. This property contains a list of the calls that occurred to get to the point where the exception was thrown. This provides most of the information that developers require to pinpoint the source of the exception.

The only concern that a developer truly faces is ensuring that caught exceptions are rethrown properly. The worst case scenario is having an exception caught and then a new exception thrown, losing the *StackTrace* information.

```
' VB
Try
    ' Code goes here
Catch ex As Exception
    Throw new ApplicationException("details")
```

```
End Try
```

```
// C#
try {
   // Code goes here
}
catch (Exception ex) {
   throw new ApplicationException("details");
}
```

The *StackTrace* property in the new exception will have only the call stack down to the throw statement for the new exception. The stack trace that contains the location of the original exception will be lost, unless it is included as the *InnerException* on the new exception. This is one of the reasons for using the *InnerException* property.

If the only action in a catch is to log some information, then instead of creating a new instance of an *Exception* object, the original object should be propagated with a throw statement.

```
' VB
Try
   ' Code goes here
Catch ex As Exception
   Throw
End Try
```

```
// C#
try {
   // Code goes here
}
catch (Exception ex) {
   throw;
}
```

This technique keeps the information in the original exception, including the *StackTrace* property, intact.

Exception Filtering

Given these goals for exception handling, there is still the outstanding question of which exceptions should be caught. That question really isn't worded clearly. As the preceding examples have shown, the *Catch* portion of the statement can include an *Exception* variable. In particular, it includes a variable that can be any type (so long as the type is derived from the *Exception* class). Consider the following code.

```
' VB
Try
   ' Code goes here
Catch ex As ArgumentException
   Throw
End Try
```

```csharp
// C#
try {
    // Code goes here
}
catch (ArgumentException ex) {
    throw;
}
```

In this example the code in the *Catch* block will be executed only if the exception is of the *ArgumentException* type. Any other type of exception will be processed as if it were unhandled. It is also possible to have multiple *Catch* blocks for a single *Try* statement.

```vb
' VB
Try
    ' Code goes here
Catch nex As ArgumentNullException
    Throw
Catch ex As ArgumentException
    Throw
End Try
```

```csharp
// C#
try {
    // Code goes here
}
catch (ArgumentNullException nex) {
    throw;
}
catch (ArgumentException ex) {
    throw;
}
```

With this code, the first *Catch* block is executed only if the exception is an *ArgumentNullException* exception. The second *Catch* block is executed only for *ArgumentException* exceptions. Any other exception is left unhandled. Also, notice that the *ArgumentNullException* class is actually derived from the *ArgumentException* class. That means that if the first *Catch* block weren't present, an *ArgumentNullException* exception would have been handled in the second *Catch* block.

This is exception filtering in practice–the idea that by ordering the *Catch* blocks and specifying the appropriate exception types, you can be very specific about which exceptions are handled and when, even within the same *Try* block. And when using exception filters, keep in mind that the order is important. Once an exception is handled by a *Catch* block, it will not be handled by any subsequent ones. So keep the most restrictive exceptions (when the class is most specific) at the top of the list.

The rationale for using exception filtering is a strong one. For any of the instances where an exception really does need to be handled, the exception is quite specific. If you plan on trying to recover from a specific exception, for example, you should use that specific exception type in the *Catch* block. Any exceptions that can't be recovered shouldn't be caught.

Handling Unhandled Exceptions

To this point, the idea that exceptions should not be unilaterally caught has been stressed. The question of where exceptions *should* be caught remains. At no time has it been suggested that exceptions should be left uncaught. If they were, the user would see an ugly message that would not likely be understood. Nor would the user be likely to convey the information to the support line. Well-behaved applications don't expose their users to ugly, meaningless (to them) messages.

So instead of allowing the default exception message to appear, any exception that hasn't been handled needs to be caught and processed before it bubbles up to the user. This is done by using one of the unhandled exception handler techniques. The appropriate technique depends on the type of application.

Windows Forms Applications

The key to handling unhandled exceptions in Windows Forms applications is the *Thread-Exception* event that is exposed by the *Application* object. If you look at the *Main* method that is used to launch a Windows Forms application, you will see code that looks like the following.

```vb
' VB
Public Shared Sub Main()
    Application.Run(New Form1())
End Sub
```

```csharp
// C#
static void Main()
{
    Application.Run(new Form1());
}
```

The *Run* method starts the message loop that is the heart of all Windows applications on the current thread. It then displays the Form that is passed in as a parameter.

The *Application* object exposes a *ThreadException* event. This event gets raised when an exception is allowed to propagate to the top of a thread's call stack. In other words, it is the unhandled exception event. So to protect users from the unhandled exception dialog box, a handler for *ThreadException* needs to be added to the event. The following code accomplishes this.

```vb
' VB
Public Shared Sub Main()
    AddHandler Application.ThreadException, AddressOf unhandledExceptionHandler
    Application.Run(New Form1())
End Sub
```

```csharp
// C#
static void Main()
{
    Application.ThreadException += new ThreadExceptionEventHandler(
```

```
        unhandledExceptionHandler);
    Application.Run(new Form1());
}
```

Of course, in order to compile properly the *unhandledExceptionHandler* method needs to have the appropriate signature, such as the following:

```
' VB
Private Sub UnhandledExceptionHandler(ByVal sender As Object, _
    ByVal args As ThreadExceptionEventArgs)
End Sub
```

```
// C#
private void unhandledExceptionHandler(object sender, ThreadExceptionEventArgs e)
{
}
```

Now, within the *unhandledExceptionHandler* method, what needs to be done? Normally, it would involve the launching of a form that contains the information about the exception, or sending an e-mail message to support indicating that a particular exception had occurred. In every case, something should be done to capture the information and convey to the user (in a friendly manner) that the application did something unanticipated. But the specifics can be left up to the developer or the corporate standards.

Console Applications

Conceptually, a console application gets an unexpected event handler in the same manner as a Windows Forms application. That is, an event gets raised when an unhandled exception propagates to the top of the call stack. Prior to launching the application, a handler is associated with the event so that the unhandled exception gets recognized and the appropriate information can be displayed. The only real difference between the processing performed by these two application types is the details.

For a console application, the *UnhandledException* event raised on the current *AppDomain* object is what needs to be handled. The current *AppDomain* is associated with the current thread, so the easiest way to access it is through the *Thread.GetDomain* method. So the code to hook the event is as follows:

```
' VB
Public Shared Sub Main()
    AddHandler Thread.GetDomain().UnhandledException, AddressOf unhandledExceptionHandler);
End Sub
```

```
// C#
static void Main()
{
    Thread.GetDomain().UnhandledException += new
        UnhandledExceptionEventHandler(unhandledExceptionHandler);
}
```

The signature of the method that handles the event is almost the same as with the Windows Forms application.

```vb
' VB
Private Sub UnhandledExceptionHandler(ByVal sender As Object, _
   ByVal args As UnhandledExceptionEventArgs)
End Sub
```

```csharp
// C#
private void unhandledExceptionHandler(object sender, UnhandledExceptionEventArgs e)
{
}
```

There are two caveats to be aware of when handling unhandled exceptions in a console application. The first is that every thread needs to have an unhandled exception handler if it wants to trap such a situation. Unhandled exceptions don't get marshalled across thread boundaries, so the process that created the thread doesn't automatically get notified if the thread fails.

Also, the *UnhandledException* event isn't really a place to handle unhandled exceptions. It is a notification that an unhandled exception has made its way to the top of the call stack. The event enables the developer to clean up any resources allocated on the thread, but it does not provide a mechanism to prevent the thread from terminating. So even if you write an *UnhandledException* handler, the thread that threw the exception will terminate as soon as the handler has done its job. This is different from the *ThreadException* event available on the *Application* object.

From the perspective of processing an *UnhandledException*, .NET console applications are lacking a key feature that limits the options for display. Console applications don't have the Windows Forms message pump available. As a result, it can't display a dialog box or a Windows form containing the exception information. Thus, the information about the exception is simply dumped to the output channel to be read by the user.

Lab: Handling Unhandled Exceptions

Having just covered the topic of how exceptions should be handled, this lab is intended to give you a working knowledge of how it works in practice.

▶ **Exercise 1: Configuring a Windows Application**

The starting point is a project that has an existing exception information form. This form will display the details of a particular exception. In the lab, you will arrange to connect the *ThreadException* event to a method that displays the form containing the exception details.

1. Launch Visual Studio 2005.
2. Open a solution using File | Open | Project/Solution.
3. Navigate to the Chapter10\Lesson1\<language>\Exercise1-Before directory. Select the Lab1 solution and click Open.

4. In the Solution Explorer, double-click *Main* (for VB.NET) or *Program* (for C#) class to display the code designer.

5. Note that the class contains a shared/static public method called *Main*. This is the method that is used to launch the application. The *Application.Run* method call is used to start the Windows message loop, displaying the Form1 instance.

6. Prior to calling *Application.Run*, a handler method needs to be associated with the *ThreadException* event. Insert the following code immediately before the *Application.Run* statement:

```vb
' VB
AddHandler Application.ThreadException, _
   AddressOf UnhandledExceptionHandler
```

```csharp
// C#
Application.ThreadException +=
   new ThreadExceptionEventHandler(UnhandledExceptionHandler);
```

7. Naturally, the *UnhandledExceptionHandler* method needs to be created. This is the event handler that will get invoked when the exception bubbles to the top of the stack. In this handler a new instance of the ExceptionDialogForm form will be created and displayed. Add the following code below the end of the *Main* method:

```vb
' VB
Shared Sub UnhandledExceptionHandler(ByVal sender As Object, _
   ByVal args As ThreadExceptionEventArgs)
   Dim form As New ExceptionDialogForm(args.Exception)
   form.ShowDialog()
End Sub
```

```csharp
// C#
static void UnhandledExceptionHandler(object sender,
   ThreadExceptionEventArgs args) {
   ExceptionDialogForm form = new ExceptionDialogForm(args.Exception);
   form.ShowDialog();
}
```

8. Build the solution using the Build | Build UnhandledExceptionDemo menu option.

9. Unfortunately, it isn't easy to test this from within Visual Studio. The reason is that Visual Studio traps the unhandled error without letting the *ThreadException* event get raised. As a result, the way to test is to run the application from outside of Visual Studio. In Windows Explorer, navigate to the Chapter10/Lesson1/Lab1/<language>/Before/ bin/debug directory. Double-click UnhandledExceptionDemo.exe.

10. Click Throw UnhandledException. Notice that, after a brief moment, the dialog box shown in Figure 10-1 appears.

Figure 10-1   The Unhandled Exception dialog box.

▶ **Exercise 2: Configuring a Console Application**

The starting point is a project that has an existing exception information form. This form will display the details of a particular exception. In the lab, you will arrange to connect the *Thread-Exception* event to a method that displays the form containing the exception details.

1. Launch Visual Studio 2005.

2. Open a solution using File | Open | Project/Solution.

3. Navigate to the Chapter10\Lesson1\<*language*>\Exercise2-Before directory. Select the Lab2 solution and click Open.

4. In the Solution Explorer, double-click *Module1* (for VB.NET) or *Program* (for C#) class to display the code designer.

5. In the *Main* method, the event handler for the *UnhandledException* event exposed by Thread.GetDomain needs to be hooked up. Add the following code to the *Main* method:

```
' VB
AddHandler Thread.GetDomain().UnhandledException, _
    AddressOf UnhandledExceptionHandler
```

```
// C#
Thread.GetDomain().UnhandledException += new
    UnhandledExceptionEventHandler(UnhandledExceptionHandler);
```

6. Now the *UnhandledExceptionHandler* method needs to be created. Unlike the previous exercise in which a Windows form was displayed, this method will send the exception information to the console. Add the following method below the *Main* method:

```
' VB
Private Sub UnhandledExceptionHandler(ByVal sender As Object, _
    ByVal e As UnhandledExceptionEventArgs)
    Console.WriteLine("An unhandled exception({0}) occurred.", _
```

```
      e.ExceptionObject.GetType().FullName)
   Console.WriteLine("Message: {0}", CType(e.ExceptionObject, _
      Exception).Message)
   Console.WriteLine("Stack Trace: {0}", CType(e.ExceptionObject, _
      Exception).StackTrace)
   Console.ReadLine()
End Sub
```

```
// C#
static void UnhandledExceptionHandler(object sender,
   UnhandledExceptionEventArgs e)
{
   Console.WriteLine("An unhandled exception({0}) occurred.",
      e.ExceptionObject.GetType().FullName);
   Console.WriteLine("Message: {0}",
      ((Exception)e.ExceptionObject).Message);
   Console.WriteLine("Stack Trace: {0}",
      ((Exception)e.ExceptionObject).StackTrace);
   Console.ReadLine();
}
```

7. Back in the *Main* method, the code to throw the exception needs to be added. The following statements are placed below the statement that adds the event handler:

```
' VB
Dim demo As New DemoClass()
demo.ThrowException()
```

```
// C#
DemoClass demo = new DemoClass();
demo.ThrowException();
```

8. Build the solution using the Build | Build UnhandledExceptionDemo menu option.

9. As with the previous exercise, Visual Studio gets in the way of demonstrating the functionality as a deployed application would see it. So instead of running the application from within Visual Studio, use Windows Explorer to navigate to the Chapter10/Lesson1/Lab2/<language>/Before/bin/Debug directory.

10. Double-click UnhandledExceptionDemo.exe. Note that the information about the exception appears in the console screen. Press Enter to exit the screen.

11. Depending on how your system is configured, you might next see the default Microsoft Unhandled Exception Handler dialog box. If you do, click Don't Send.

NOTE Configuring the default unhandled exception handler dialog box

The standard installation configures Windows to show Microsoft's unhandled exception handler dialog box. To remove this dialog box or modify it when it appears, right-click My Computer and select the Properties menu option. Select the Advanced tab. Click Error Reporting. In the dialog box that appears, select the desired option. To eliminate it for *all* applications, select Disable Error Reporting. However, that is extreme and should be done only with due consideration.

Lesson Summary

- Exceptions have a number of advantages over return values when notifying calling applications of an error.

- Before catching an exception, a method should be ready to perform one of four actions. Otherwise, the exception should not be caught.

- The goal of well-designed exception handling is to assist operations and developers in troubleshooting and to ensure that application integrity is maintained.

Lesson Review

You can use the following questions to test your knowledge of the information in Lesson 1, "The Goals of Exception Handling." The questions are also available on the companion CD if you prefer to review them in electronic form.

NOTE   Answers

Answers to these questions and explanations of why each answer choice is right or wrong are located in the "Answers" section at the end of the book.

---

1. You are the chief architect for a Windows Forms application that will eventually be deployed to more than 100 users in the company. The users will be geographically dispersed in offices around the country. Much of the data updating takes place using Web services that are called asynchronously.

   As part of the exception handling design process, the type of outcome expected for each method is being documented. For a method that calls the Web service asynchronously, which outcomes can be expected? (Choose all that apply.)

   A. Synchronous success

   B. Asynchronous success

   C. Optimistic success

   D. Abject failure

2. You are developing a Windows Forms application that invokes a Web service to validate some information. There are three possible endpoints for the Web service, each of which provides identical validation functionality. You decide to wrap the call to the Web service in a *Try-Catch* block where the *WebException* type is the only type that is caught. Which of the four reasons for catching an exception can be applied to this situation?

   A. Gather information for logging.

   B. Add details to the exception.

   C. Clean up resources.

   D. Attempt to recover.

3. You are designing the exception handling mechanism for a Windows Forms application. The exception handling mechanism needs to send information about any unexpected exceptions to the operations staff. Which technique should you use?

    A. Wrap every method in a *Try-Catch* block. The *Catch* block should catch the generic *Exception* object and log the information.

    B. Place a *Try-Catch* block around the *Application.Run* statement in the *Main* method.

    C. Create a procedure to log the exception information and associate the procedure with the *Application.ThreadException* event.

    D. Create a procedure to log the exception information and associate the procedure with the *UnhandledException* event for the current *AppDomain*.

Lesson 2: Application-Wide Exception Handling

As developers work on more and more applications, some commonality of code becomes apparent. One of them is the type of processing that needs to be done when an exception occurs. It becomes obvious that moving logging functionality, the sending of e-mail warnings, and other notifications should be placed in globally available classes and methods.

But once exception handling logic has been centralized, another need becomes apparent. If the globally available methods are coded directly into the application, the ability to change the type of notification on the fly is affected. It could be that sending information to the Windows Event Log is sufficient most of the time but that during a debugging session the details need to go to a text file. Or that certain types of exceptions should result in sending immediate notifications to operations while others can just be logged. Adding this logic into each *Catch* block is tedious and prone to error. And every time some new functionality is required, all the *Catch* blocks need to be updated. Sounds like a perfect place for a framework to be useful.

After this lesson, you will be able to:

- Identify where an exception handling framework might be useful.
- Configure and use the Exception Handling Application Block properly.

Estimated lesson time: 25 minutes

How Can a Framework Help?

The goal of an exception framework is to provide common functionality to all exception handlers while maintaining the flexibility to change the routing used by any specific exception at run time. Some of the information used to modify the routing could include the severity of the error, the source of the error, or the type. That's a lot to accomplish, so let's start by looking at the requirements in more detail.

Routing Options

There are a number of choices for where information about an exception can be sent. The obvious choices are the Windows Event Log, a text file, or a database. Not so obvious choices include e-mail messages or text messages. But the details of the destination are not important. What really matters is the ability to route different exceptions to different destinations.

Exception Type

One of the more obvious determinants for routing exceptions is the type of exception. This is the most distinguishing characteristic of an exception because it provides the first level of detail about what actually went wrong. So an exception handling framework will need to be able to recognize different types of exceptions and react accordingly.

Error Severity

Being able to send exception information to different destinations is important only if there is information available to distinguish between different types of exceptions. One of the most common is the severity of the exception. Yes, by definition an exception is exceptional. But even with that, there are still differences between types of exceptions. A database row being locked is not likely to be as important as an out-of-disk-space exception. In one case, waiting a little longer might be sufficient. In the other, some manual intervention will be required to continue processing. So a good exception handling framework will need to provide the ability to indicate the relative severity of exceptions.

Exception Source

Another potential determining factor for routing exception information is the source. As with severity, the source for an exception can indicate who might be interested in hearing that an exception occurred. It can be used to provide some context for the exception that might be pertinent in determining the routing. For example, if a row-locked event is raised in a batch updating process it's not as important as if the same exception occurred within a Web application. In the first case, the batch can be reprocessed. In the second, a real person talking to your Web site is being affected.

Configurability

All the functionality that has been mentioned so far can easily be incorporated into an application using a common set of classes and methods. However, as has already been noted, that really isn't sufficient for an enterprise-class application. What needs to be implemented is the ability to configure and modify as easily as possible the routing of exception information based on the factors mentioned. For a .NET application, this means that an element of configurability needs to be available. And this is where a framework is important.

A well-designed framework will collect the information about the exception, such as the type, the severity, and the source. That information will then be used to look up the desired destination (or destinations) in a separate location, such as a configuration file. If this is implemented, then not only does the exception handling framework eliminate common code, but also it provides functionality that allows operations to adjust the workings of the exception routing process as they need to, even while the application continues running.

Quick Check

- What is the main reason for wanting to use an exception handling framework?

Quick Check Answer

- It is a combination of reusing existing code and providing a consistent mechanism for processing exceptions.

Real World

Bruce Johnson

I'm a big fan of frameworks. When used properly, they can add a lot of functionality to an application, functionality that is useful but that would be onerous to create more than once, or even once, if an adequate, already-developed framework can be "borrowed" from someplace else. In the case of an exception handling framework, it can be.

The Prescriptive Architecture Group at Microsoft has made available the Enterprise Library. This library includes a number of functions that are typically found in enterprise-scale applications. This includes logging, exception handling, caching, and cryptography. Naturally, for this chapter the exception handling portion is of greatest interest. But if your application requires any of the functionality implemented in the Enterprise Library, you should take a close look at it. In some specific cases it might seem like some of the functionality is overkill. And indeed it might be. But if you need even some of the functionality of a particular block, it's worth using the already-tested, well-documented, and extensible framework. After all, the less code you have to write, the fewer bugs you introduce into an application.

The Exception Handling Application Block

As part of the Enterprise Library toolkit, the Exception Handling Application Block provides the framework functionality that has already been discussed. Specifically, the scenarios addressed by the block are as follows:

- **Exception wrapping**   In some cases an exception needs to be wrapped by another type of exception. In this situation the original exception is assigned to the *InnerException* property of the new exception. The new exception is usually of a type that the callers further upstream expect and can handle.

- **Exception replacement**   Unlike exception wrapping, this goal involves the outright replacement of the original application with a new application.

■ **Exception logging**   It is quite common for a developer to want to log an exception at the point that it happened. To satisfy this requirement, the application block provides a method that will log the exception and then indicate whether it needs to be propagate further up the call stack. Also, through the logging mechanism, the different routing options (log file, Event Log, database, and so on) become available.

Exception Handling Design

The Exception Handling Application Block is designed to be as extensible as possible. There are two main points of extensibility—exception handlers and exception formatters. The basic flow of an exception is illustrated in Figure 10-2.

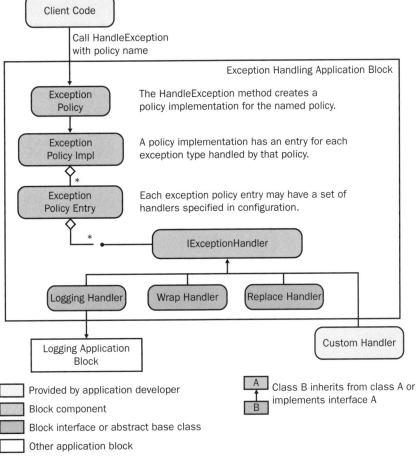

Figure 10-2   The design of the Exception Handling Application Block.

The processing of the exception starts with an exception policy. The policy determines the type of processing that will be performed based on the exception type, severity, and source. It is purely a configuration artifact in that, without a particular policy, the exception is not handled and (assuming proper coding on the part of the developer) will be propagated up the call stack.

The exception policy maps an exception to a specific exception handler. An exception handler is a class that implements the *IExceptionHandler* interface. The handler is invoked, based on the exception policy, and performs some type of action on the exception. Included with the application block are logging, wrapping, and replacing exception handlers. Also, you could easily create your own exception handler to support custom functionality.

The other point of extensibility is the format of the exception as the handler processes it. This is implemented in a class that is derived from the *ExceptionFormatter* class. The various virtual and overridable methods exposed by a formatter get invoked as the handler is building the information about an exception.

Exception Handling Configuration

The configuration information for the Exception Handling Application Block is stored in a configuration file. However, due to the complexity associated with manipulating Extensible Markup Language (XML) manually, the Enterprise Library also includes a configuration utility. This is by far the easiest way to configure exception handling.

Within the Enterprise Library Configuration tool, the starting point is to open the configuration file for an existing application. Then a new application block is added through the Action | New | Exception Handling Application Block menu option. Once the application block is added, a new Exception Policy is added with the Action | New | Exception Policy menu option. Finally (at least as the startup configuration), a new exception type is added to the exception policy using the Action | New | Exception Type menu option. At this point, you are presented with a list of the currently loaded data types that have *System.Exception* as a base class. These are the types that the application block recognizes and can act on.

The base level of configuration for an exception type includes a single value that indicates what should happen after the exception has been processed. The options are shown in Table 10-1.

Table 10-1   Post Handling Actions

Action	Description
None	The exception is assumed to have been handled completely and will not be propagated.
NotifyRethrow	Tells the caller that the original exception should be rethrown.
ThrowNewException	Throws the new or wrapped exception.

For a particular exception type, the handler or handlers that are to be used are not defined. Through the Action | New menu option, there is a choice of Custom Handler, Logging Handler, Replace Handler, and Wrap Handler. The logging handler allows the administrator to specify the information about the logging component that will be used. Chapter 8, "Instrumenting Your Application," goes into detail about how the logging application block is configured.

For the replace and wrap handlers, two properties need to be defined. The first is the *ExceptionMessage*. This is the string that will be placed in the *Message* property for the newly created exception. The second is the *ReplaceExceptionType* or the *WrapExceptionType*. Even though the properties have different names, the basic purpose is the same. The property indicates the exception type that gets created when the original exception is replaced or wrapped.

The custom handler option is used when you need to provide some nonstandard functionality to the exception handling process. For example, the message associated with the exception could be localized using a custom handler that is a variant on the *Replace* handler. Because the functionality, and therefore the necessary properties, are left up to the developers, the information that needs to be provided in the property section will depend on the details of the handler.

Handling Exceptions Using the Block

Once the block has been configured, the pattern by which it gets used needs to be understood. One of the most common misunderstandings is that the Exception Handling Application Block handles exceptions. Actually, it doesn't. What it does do is allow for the configurability of exception processing. But let's hold this discussion until the code has been covered.

```vb
' VB
Try
  ' Code goes here
Catch ex As Exception
  Dim rethrow As Boolean = ExceptionPolicy.HandleException(ex, "Demo Policy")
  If (rethrow) Then
    Throw
  End If
End Try
```

```csharp
// C#
try {
  // Code goes here
}
catch(Exception ex) {
  bool rethrow = ExceptionPolicy.HandleException(ex, "Demo Policy");
  if (rethrow)
    throw;
}
```

All of the processing of the application block takes place in the *HandleException* method. The second parameter passed in is the name of the exception policy to be applied to the exception that is passed as the first parameter. So *HandleException* looks at the exception types configured in the policy and routes, wraps, or converts the information as required. The return value for *HandleException* is a Boolean value that indicates whether the original exception should be rethrown.

Notice that, in the preceding sample code, the exception is not really handled. Assuming, that is, that "handled" means that the problem that caused the exception to be thrown has been addressed. All that *HandleException* does is log the exception or perform some conversion to another type of exception. Even if you create a custom exception handler, there is no assumption that the exception is handled, only that it has been processed. Developers still need to write any code to truly handle the exception on their own.

Lab: Using an Exception Handling Framework

Since the purpose of the lab is to get your hands dirty in code for the real world, let's spend this lab on how the Exception Handling Application Block in the Enterprise Library gets used. There are two exercises: one that demonstrates how to process an exception within the application block and one that configures different handlers.

▶ Exercise 1: Processing Exceptions

The starting point for this exercise will be an existing Windows Forms application. The form has two buttons on it, both of which call a method on a class that throws an *ApplicationException*. The difference between the two will be the exception policy that is used to process the caught exception.

1. Launch Visual Studio 2005.
2. Open a solution using File | Open | Project/Solution.
3. Navigate to the Chapter10\Lesson2\<*language*>\Exercise1-Before directory. Select the Lab1 solution and click Open.
4. Add a reference to the Microsoft.Practices.EnterpriseLibrary.ExceptionHandling dll. By default, this is located in the C:\Program Files\Microsoft Enterprise Library January 2006\bin\ folder.
5. In the Solution Explorer, right-click the Form1 file and select View Code from the context menu.
6. In the *firstExceptionButton_Click* method, code will be added to call the *ThrowException* method on the DemoClass. As you might expect, this method throws an exception, specifically an *ApplicationException* exception. We will catch the exception and then use the Exception Handling Application Block to process it. Start by adding the following code to the *firstExceptionButton_Click* method:

```vb
' VB
Try
    Dim demo As New DemoClass()
    demo.ThrowException()
Catch ex As Exception
End Try
```

```csharp
// C#
try
{
    DemoClass demo = new DemoClass();
    demo.ThrowException();
}
catch (Exception ex)
{
}
```

7. Now that the exception processing structure is in place, it's time to add the actual code. The *HandleException* method on the *ExceptionPolicy* class is called, passing the exception and the name of the policy. Add the following code to the *Catch* block that was just added:

```vb
' VB
Dim rethrow As Boolean
rethrow = ExceptionPolicy.HandleException(ex, "First Exception")
If rethrow Then
    Throw
End If
```

```csharp
// C#
bool rethrow = ExceptionPolicy.HandleException(ex, "First Exception");
if (rethrow)
    throw;
```

8. The same functionality needs to be given to the *secondExceptionButton_Click* method. The only difference between the two methods is the name of the exception policy. Add the following to the *secondExceptionButton_Click* method:

```vb
' VB
Try
    Dim demo As New DemoClass()
    demo.ThrowException()
Catch ex As Exception
    Dim rethrow As Boolean
    rethrow = ExceptionPolicy.HandleException(ex, "Second Exception")
    If rethrow Then
        Throw
    End If
End Try
```

```csharp
// C#
try
{
```

```
        DemoClass demo = new DemoClass();
        demo.ThrowException();
    }
    catch (Exception ex)
    {
        bool rethrow = ExceptionPolicy.HandleException(ex, "Second Exception");
        if (rethrow)
            throw;
    }
```

9. At this point the application should build successfully. You can make sure of this by using the Build | Build ExceptionHandlingDemo menu option. However, the application will not run without error until Exercise 2 is complete.

▶ **Exercise 2: Configuring the Application**

The starting point for this exercise is the project as it was left at the end of Exercise 1. In this exercise, the configuration information for the exception handling is added to the configuration file and then demonstrated.

1. Launch Visual Studio 2005.

2. Open a solution using File | Open | Project/Solution.

3. Navigate to the Chapter10\Lesson2\<language>\Exercise2-Before directory. Select the Lab2 solution and click Open.

4. Add a reference to the Microsoft.Practices.EnterpriseLibrary.ExceptionHandling, Microsoft.Practices.EnterpriseLibrary.Common, and Microosft.Practices.ObjectBuilder dlls. By default, these are located in the C:\Program Files\Microsoft Enterprise Library January 2006\bin\ folder.

5. In the Solution Explorer, right-click the ExceptionHandlingDemo project and select the Add | New Item... menu option. In the New Item dialog box, select Application Configuration File and click Add.

6. The configuration of the App.config file is most easily accomplished using the Enterprise Library Configuration tool. Use the Start | All Programs | Microsoft Patterns & Practices | Enterprise Library - January 2006 | Enterprise Library Configuration menu option.

7. Use the File | Open Application menu option and then navigate to the just-added App.config file (found in the Chapter10/Lesson2/Lab2/<language>/Before directory). Click Open.

8. In the left pane, right-click the App.config node and select New | Exception Handling Application Block from the context menu.

9. Right-click the just-added application block and select New | Exception Policy from the context menu.

10. On the right pane, change the name of the policy to First Exception.

11. Back on the left pane, right-click the First Exception exception policy and select New | Exception Type from the context menu.

12. In the dialog box that appears, select ApplicationException (under mscorlib.System) and click OK. This adds a new exception type to the policy.

13. For this exception type, change the PostHandlingAction on the right side of the form to ThrowNewException.

14. Right-click the ApplicationException on the left pane and select the New | Replace Handler menu option.

15. On the right side of the form, change the ExceptionMessage property to This Is A Replacement Exception. Change the ReplaceExceptionType to System.ArgumentException.

16. Next, we add the second exception policy. You begin by right-clicking the Exception Handling Application Block on the left pane and choosing the New | Exception Policy menu option. Change the name of the new exception policy to Second Exception.

17. Back on the left pane, right-click the Second Exception exception policy and select New | Exception Type from the context menu.

18. In the dialog box that appears, select ApplicationException and click OK.

19. For this exception type, change the PostHandlingAction on the right side of the form to ThrowNewException.

20. Right-click the ApplicationException underneath the Second Exception exception policy on the left pane and select the New | Wrap Handler menu option.

21. On the right pane, change the ExceptionMessage property to This Is A Wrapped Exception. Change the WrappedExceptionType to System.ArgumentException.

22. Save the configuration changes using the File | Save Application menu option.

23. In order to easily see that the exception has been wrapped and replaced, a minor change will be made to the *Catch* blocks. Keep in mind that this is strictly because we are demonstrating some functionality. We would never see this particular code pattern in a real application. Start by going back to Visual Studio and right-clicking Form1 in the Solution Explorer. Select View Code from the context menu.

24. Wrap the code in the *Catch* block in a *Try-Catch* block of its own. The catch here will display the exception's message, as well as the inner exception's message, if one exists. Change the code in the *Catch* block for the *firstExceptionButton_Click* procedure to the following:

```vb
' VB
Try
    Dim rethrow As Boolean
    rethrow = ExceptionPolicy.HandleException(ex, "First Exception")
    If rethrow Then
        Throw
    End If
Catch newEx As Exception
    MessageBox.Show(newEx.Message)
    If newEx.InnerException IsNot Nothing Then
```

```
      MessageBox.Show(newEx.InnerException.Message)
   End If
End Try
```

```
// C#
try
{
   bool rethrow = ExceptionPolicy.HandleException(ex, "First Exception");
   if (rethrow)
      throw;
}
catch (Exception newEx)
{
   MessageBox.Show(newEx.Message);
   if (newEx.InnerException != null)
      MessageBox.Show(newEx.InnerException.Message);
}
```

25. Change the code in the *Catch* block for the *secondExceptionButton_Click* procedure to the following. Note that the only difference between the code in step 23 and this one is the name of the exception policy in the third line.

```
' VB
Try
   Dim rethrow As Boolean
   rethrow = ExceptionPolicy.HandleException(ex, "Second Exception")
   If rethrow Then
      Throw
   End If
Catch newEx As Exception
   MessageBox.Show(newEx.Message)
   If newEx.InnerException IsNot Nothing Then
      MessageBox.Show(newEx.InnerException.Message)
   End If
End Try
```

```
// C#
try
{
   bool rethrow = ExceptionPolicy.HandleException(ex, "Second Exception");
   if (rethrow)
      throw;
}
catch (Exception newEx)
{
   MessageBox.Show(newEx.Message);
   if (newEx.InnerException != null)
      MessageBox.Show(newEx.InnerException.Message);
}
```

26. Launch the application using the F5 key.

27. Click Throw First Exception. Notice that a message box appears containing the text This Is The Replacement Exception. After clicking OK, click Throw Second Exception. Now the message box display reads This Is A Wrapped Exception. After clicking OK, a second message is displayed that says This Is A Demonstration Message.

Lesson Summary

- Application-wide exception handling relates to the centralization of routing and processing options.
- For any significant application, an exception handling mechanism can help standardize exception routing as well as reduce the amount of code required to process exceptions.
- The Enterprise Library application provides a flexible and extensible framework on which exception handling can be built.

Lesson Review

You can use the following questions to test your knowledge of the information in Lesson 2, "Application-Wide Exception Handling." The questions are also available on the companion CD if you prefer to review them in electronic form.

NOTE Answers

Answers to these questions and explanations of why each answer choice is right or wrong are located in the "Answers" section at the end of the book.

1. You are starting to develop a .NET application and are trying to determine whether an exception handling framework is going to be appropriate. In which of the following scenarios is a framework likely to be worth the effort? (Choose all that apply.)

   A. A Smart Client application deployed to over 100 geographically dispersed users.

   B. A Windows Forms application that contains 10 forms running on a single user's computer.

   C. A Windows service that routes incoming fax documents to the appropriate addressee.

   D. A Windows console application that is automatically invoked every time the user logs in. The application scans a number of known directories looking for application updates to apply.

2. You have noticed that an exception raised by your application includes some sensitive information about the database and table names. This information is included in the *Message* property, which is displayed by the application's unhandled exception handler. You need to modify the configuration of the Exception Handling Application Block so that this information is not displayed. Which type of handler would address this problem in the simplest manner while allowing the exception information to be available if it's needed?

    A. Custom handler
    B. Logging handler
    C. Replace handler
    D. Wrapping handler

3. You have noticed that an exception raised by your application is falling through to the unhandled exception handler. It should be possible to recover from the exception, but the code in the application didn't anticipate this particular exception type. You need to modify the configuration of the Exception Handling Application Block to address this problem in the simplest manner possible. Which type of handler should you use? (Choose all that apply.)

    A. Custom handler
    B. Logging handler
    C. Replace handler
    D. Wrapping handler

Chapter Review

To further practice and reinforce the skills you learned in this chapter, you can perform the following tasks:

- Review the chapter summary.
- Review the list of key terms introduced in this chapter.
- Complete the case scenarios. These scenarios set up real-world situations involving the topics of this chapter and ask you to create a solution.
- Complete the suggested practices.
- Take a practice test.

Chapter Summary

- One of the goals of exception handling is to ensure application integrity. For this reason it is very important that an application not swallow an exception without notification or correction.
- A method should not catch an exception except in four situations: logging, providing addition details, resource clean-up, or recovery. Any other behavior is potentially dangerous to the application's integrity.
- An exception handling framework can assist with the process of standardizing how exceptions are dealt with in an enterprise-class application—or even in smaller ones where flexibility and standards warrant.

Key Terms

Do you know what these key terms mean? You can check your answers by looking up the terms in the glossary at the end of the book.

- AppDomain
- custom exception
- InnerException property
- replacing an exception
- swallowing the exception
- wrapping an exception

Case Scenarios

In the following case scenarios, you will apply what you've learned about delivering multimedia in a distributed environment. You can find answers to these questions in the "Answers" section at the end of the book.

Case Scenario 1: Appropriate Exception Handling

You are a corporate developer reviewing the code of an application that has already passed its unit tests. You notice that the following pattern is used in a number of places in the code. The example shown is taken from the *GetData* method.

```vb
' VB
Try
    ' Code goes here
Catch ex As Exception
    Throw New ApplicationException("An unexpected exception has " & _
        "occurred in the GetData method.", ex)
End Try
```

```csharp
// C#
try {
    // Code goes here
}
catch (Exception ex) {
    throw new ApplicationException("An unexpected exception has " +
        "occurred in the GetData method.", ex);
}
```

Your challenge is to decide if this is an appropriate use of exception handling and to provide alternatives, if necessary.

Questions

Answer the following questions for your manager:

1. Is this an appropriate use of exception handling?
2. If it is not appropriate, what would be a better approach?

Case Scenario 2: Appropriate Exception Handling—The Sequel

You are a corporate developer reviewing the code of an application that has already passed its unit tests. You notice that the following pattern is used in a number of places in the code. The example shown is taken from the *GetData* method.

```vb
' VB
Try
    ' Code goes here
Catch ex As Exception
```

```
    Dim rethrow As Boolean
    rethrow = ExceptionPolicy.HandleException(ex, "First Exception")
    If rethrow Then
        Throw
    End If
End Try

// C#
try {
    // Code goes here
}
catch (Exception ex) {
    bool rethrow = ExceptionPolicy.HandleException(ex, "First Exception");
    if (rethrow)
        throw;
}
```

The Exception Policy named First Exception is configured to match any exception with a type of *System.Exception* and replace it with an *ApplicationException* exception.

Your challenge is to decide if this is an appropriate use of the Exception Handling Application Block and to provide alternatives, if necessary.

Questions

Answer the following question for your manager:

1. Is this an appropriate use of exception handling?

Suggested Practices

To help successfully master the objectives covered in this chapter, complete the following task.

Choose an Appropriate Exception Handling Mechanism

For this task, you should complete both practices.

- **Practice 1** Take an application that is currently under development or that has recently been deployed. Scan the code looking for *Try-Catch* blocks. For each block, evaluate which of the four reasons for catching the exception has been satisfied.

- **Practice 2** Take an application that is currently under development or that has recently been deployed. Scan the code looking for *Try-Catch* blocks. For each block, determine if the functionality that is in the block can be refactored into a common class/method. Also, evaluate the common functionality to see if the Exception Handling Application Block might be appropriate.

Take a Practice Test

The practice tests on this book's companion CD offer many options. For example, you can test yourself on just one exam objective, or you can test yourself on all the 70-548 certification exam content. You can set up the test so that it closely simulates the experience of taking a certification exam, or you can set it up in study mode so that you can look at the correct answers and explanations after you answer each question.

MORE INFO   Practice tests

For details about all the practice test options available, see the "How to Use the Practice Tests" section in this book's Introduction.

Chapter 11
Application Configuration

Adding configuration information to an application is a frequent resident on the developer task list. This type of requirement has been part of applications for years. For Microsoft Windows Forms applications, the trend has gone from .ini files to the registry to config files. Fortunately, over time the tools to support configuration settings have greatly improved. And .NET 2.0 has gone so far as to include a whole assembly devoted to application configuration. The goal of this chapter is to explore the possibilities, demonstrate the reality, and enjoy the freedom from having to write tedious configuration-related code that is a part of all but the most trivial applications.

Exam objectives in this chapter:
- Evaluate the application configuration architecture.
  - Decide which configuration attributes to store.
  - Choose the physical storage location for the configuration attributes.
  - Decide in which format to store the configuration attributes.

Lessons in this chapter:

Before You Begin

To complete the lessons in this chapter, you must have:

- A computer that meets or exceeds the minimum hardware requirements listed in this book's Introduction.
- Visual Studio 2005 installed on the computer, with either Visual Basic .NET or C# installed.

Real World

Bruce Johnson

In my work as a developer, the saving and retrieving application configuration mechanism is a daily part of life. Has been for (I hesitate to say it) decades. And although earlier versions of .NET included some help, there have been areas of configuration that .NET just didn't address. It was quite easy to shy away from these areas and do less than you could to create a customizable, usable Windows application. After all, no user really expects noncommercial applications to "remember" where they left off the next time they started.

But no more. Between binding control properties to configuration files, updating configuration files, and a wide variety of persistence mechanisms, .NET 2.0 makes it a lot easier to bring your corporate applications up to the standards that users expect. All without extraordinary programming effort.

Lesson 1: What Should Be Stored?

On the surface, deciding which applications should be persisted between invocations sounds like it should be easy. But the flexibility offered by .NET 2.0 provides options that hadn't been available in the past without a great deal of effort. And anytime developers are given new options, they need to rethink their standard approach. The purpose of this lesson is to explore the available choices.

> **After this lesson, you will be able to:**
> - Decide which configuration attributes to store.
> - Identify the proper scope for configuration information.
> - Locate the configuration file for each configuration scope.
>
> **Estimated lesson time: 25 minutes**

Application-Level Settings

Traditionally, managed code applications saved only application-level information in an application configuration file. Actually, "saved" isn't quite correct. Information could be retrieved from the application configuration file. The actual "saving" process was an awkward one that involved manual editing or the creation of a custom application to modify the config file. There was no built-in capability to save application-level data from within the application itself.

Also, there was no scoping of the configuration settings. All of the settings were in a single file that was accessible to anyone who ran the application—not the greatest situation from a security perspective. And certainly not a good place to store user-level preferences.

Although .NET 2.0 has added a lot of functionality to the *System.Configuration* namespace, this base application setting's functionality is still in place. What has changed, however, is the focus of application settings. Rather than being a catch-all for anything that should be parameterized, *application settings* now fills its intended purpose—being a repository for information that is required for the application to run, regardless of who is using it.

That last phrase is the important distinction for experienced developers to understand. Application settings contain information that is to be used across all users of the application. So database connections, queue names, and log file directories would be appropriate. The screen location to which the user had last dragged the main form should not be; at least, not any more.

From an architectural perspective, the values that are stored in application-level configuration files are those that are common across all instances of the application. In other words, pretty much anything that isn't specific to a particular user can be put there. But even with those fairly obvious boundaries, the application architect needs to be aware of some issues in order to ensure that only appropriate information is stored there.

Don't Update Application-Level Settings

Application-level settings should not be updated. This isn't to say that the capability doesn't exist to update application-level settings. Only that it opens the door to subtle problems with the proper functioning of the application. A couple of examples will help clarify the potential issues.

Simultaneous Usage

The configuration file is not a database. That sounds like an obvious statement, but it should also be apparent that the *System.Configuration* namespace doesn't have the trappings of a database. Important functionality, like record locking and transactions, doesn't exist (nor should it). For the majority of Windows Forms applications, this isn't a problem. After all, there is normally only one user working on a machine at a time.

But what if the Windows Forms application gets deployed onto a server that is acting as a Terminal Services host? And more than one user logs onto the host at a time, each of them running your application? Now, all of a sudden, simultaneous updates to the application-level settings are a possibility. And nothing in the *System.Configuration* namespace prevents it from happening.

Keep in mind that this isn't a likely scenario for most applications. But in those instances where you're faced with this situation, the effort of trying to track down the cause of a misconfigured configuration file will be significant—roughly akin to finding threading issues in an application where multiple threads are not expected.

Security

The other potential issue associated with updating application-level settings has to do with security. Again, in many situations this isn't a problem. If the application is run from the local hard drive, it runs in the Trusted zone. The default rights for the application allows write access to the directory from which the application is being run.

However, if the application is running as a click-once deployment or if it has been launched from a network share, then it isn't (by default) running with full trust. And without full trust, the application might not be able to write to the application's directory and, therefore, the configuration file.

You can address both these situations by changing the security policy under which the application is running—a relatively simple task. The issue being raised is not that the security concern can't be addressed, but that application architects need to be aware of it. Because if your developers are not testing the application in a non-full trust environment, this is the type of problem that is found only when the application gets deployed.

Encryption

Since the application-level settings are available to every user of the application, the config file itself must be visible to every user. This can be a problem if the information stored in the configuration file is sensitive (a connection string that contains a password, for example). Fortunately, the Internet Information Services (IIS) web.config file includes a concept called *protected configuration*. With protected configuration, the aspnet_regiis command can be used to encrypt all or part of a configuration file.

A number of options are available on aspnet_regiis that can be used to encrypt and decrypt sections of the web.config file. These same commands can be used to encrypt traditional app.config files as well. The encryption options are shown in Table 11-1.

Table 11-1   Encryption Options

-pd *section*	Decrypts the configuration section. Additional options used by the –pd option are: -app *virtualPath* – Specifies that decryption should occur at the level of the included path. -location *subPath* – Specifies the subdirectory to decrypt. -pkm – Specifies that the Machine.config file should be decrypted instead of the Web.config file.
-pdf *section path*	Decrypts the specified configuration section of the Web.config file in the specified physical (not virtual) directory.
-pe *section*	Encrypts the specified configuration section. Additional options used by the –pe option are: -prov *provider* – Specifies the encryption provider to use. -app *virtualPath* – Specifies that encryption should occur at the level of the included path. -location *subPath* – Specifies the subdirectory to encrypt. -pkm – Specifies that the Machine.config file should be encrypted instead of the Web.config file.
-pef *section path*	Encrypts the specified configuration section of the Web.config file in the specified physical (not virtual) directory.

The result of encrypting a section within a configuration file will be a fragment like the following:

```
<connectionStrings
  configProtectionProvider="DataProtectionConfigurationProvider">
  <EncryptedData>
    <CipherData>
      <CipherValue>AQAAANCMnd8BFdERjHoAwE/Cl+sBAAAAH2... </CipherValue>
```

```
    </CipherData>
  </EncryptedData>
</connectionStrings>
```

Notice that the *configProtectionProvider* attribute has been added. This identifies the encryption mechanism that was used.

CAUTION   **Encrypted data isn't completely secure**

It should be made clear that, even though the data is encrypted, this does not make it completely secure. The fact that any user has access to the configuration file means that a determined hacker could take a copy of the file and break the encryption using any one of a number of techniques. Also, the config file is decrypted as it is loaded into memory, which means that if memory is breached, the plaintext version of the config file will be accessible.

Also, depending on the configuration provider being used, the location of the decryption key could also be a point of concern. For the Data Protection API (DPAPI), the machine key is found at %windir%\system32\Microsoft\Protect\S-1-5-18. For RSA, the machine keys are stored in the \Documents and Settings\All Users\Application Data\Microsoft\Crypto\RSA\MachineKeys folder.

Locating the Configuration File

For most applications, the configuration file is called *app.exe*.config, where *app.exe* is the complete name of the application that is running. And "complete" means that the file extension is included in the name as well. Along with having a name that includes the executable, the config file must also exist in the same directory as the executable.

There are a number of scenarios where the default location for the configuration file is not the running directory for the application. For example, if an application is installed through Click-Once, the config file will be found in %InstallRoot%\Documents and Settings*username*\Local Settings.

Even taking ClickOnce into consideration, the idea that the config file must exist in a particular directory in the executable is a simple concept most of the time. There are, however, some situations in which there are challenges with finding the correct config file. These are the cases in which the process that's running is not the same as the application being configured.

For example, if you have created a server-style COM+ application, the actual running process is called dllhost.exe and can be found in the System32 directory. Based on our previously gained knowledge, you might guess that the config file is actually called dllhost.exe.config. And you'd be right. But every COM+ application is run by the same process, a situation that introduces the possibility of conflicting configuration settings.

In this scenario locating the "real" config file involves two steps. First, the COM+ application needs to have an Application Root Directory defined. The actual directory isn't important. What matters is that the directory is different for every COM+ application. You can set the

Application Root Directory by running the Component Service Microsoft Management Console (MMC) snap-in (Start | All Programs | Administrative Tools | Component Services) and navigating to the desired COM+ application. Right-click the COM+ application and then click Properties. In the properties dialog box, click the Activation tab. The dialog box shown in Figure 11-1 appears.

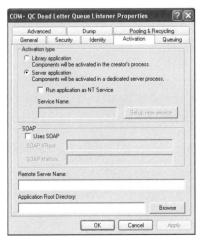

Figure 11-1   Setting the Application Root Directory for a COM+ application.

Once you have created the Application Root Directory, you need to add two files to the directory. The first is a file called *application.manifest.* This file is intended to describe the dependencies that a particular application requires. However, for this situation, describing dependencies is not so much the concern as the mere presence of the file. The following Extensible Markup Language (XML) document is sufficient for our purpose:

```
<?xml version="1.0" encoding="UTF-8" standalone="yes"?>
<assembly xmlns="urn:schemas-microsoft-com:asm.v1"
    manifestVersion="1.0">
</assembly>
```

The second file, also placed in the Application Root Directory, is called *application.config.* The contents of this file is the normal config file. When these two files are in place, the COM+ application can access its own configuration information through the regular mechanism (for example, the *ConfigurationManager* class). If the COM+ application had already been running, be sure to restart it to pick up the application definition changes.

User-Level Settings

In the past, managed code applications were able to retrieve only application-level configuration settings. But sometimes it's necessary to keep track of settings that are associated with a particular user. These are called *user preferences* in Microsoft parlance because they reserve the term *settings* as application-level values.

The most common situation for using user preferences is when the application wants to capture its state (for example, form size and location, most recently opened files, toolbar settings) at the time of closing so that the state can be reset when the application is next launched. This is the sort of thoughtfulness that makes an application successful with users.

The *System.Configuration* namespace provides the capability for both retrieving and, more important, saving configurations at a user level. This is the functional equivalent of giving each user his or her own configuration file. Specifically, each user gets a file called *user*.config where *user* is the Windows logon ID. And, unlike the application configuration file, user configuration files are stored in the user's Application Data directory. By default, the full location is:

```
%InstallRoot%\Documents and Settings\user\Local Settings\Application Data\productpath
```

As before, *user* in the above path is the current Windows logon ID and *productpath* is the application-specific path segment, *companyname\productname\productversion*, where

- **Companyname**   is the name of the company that wrote the application
- **Productname**   is the name of the application; and
- **Productversion**   is the version of the application.

Each of these values can be set through the Properties page for the product. In Visual Studio, right-click the project and select Properties. In the Application section, click Assembly Information. In the Assembly Information dialog box that appears, the *Company*, *Product*, and *Assembly Version* fields correlate to the *companyname*, *productname*, and *productversion* values.

NOTE The location of the user configuration file

As with application-level settings, the location of the user configuration file is different if the application is run through the ClickOnce mechanism. In that case, the config file can be found in the same directory as the application configuration file, %InstallRoot%\Documents and Settings\user\Local Settings.

The application architect needs to have an understanding of what's going on "under the covers" to ensure that the technology meets all the requirements and to be aware of any potential for pitfalls.

Updatable Data

User-level settings do not run into the same updating issues that application-level settings do. By their very nature, they are specific to a user. Which means that, unless the same user ID is being used simultaneously on the same machine, updating is danger-free. And, in fact, a number of features in the .NET Framework make updating user settings automatic.

Property Binding

One of the more useful additions to the configuration framework at .NET 2.0 was the ability to bind properties on controls to configuration settings. Also, at least in Visual Basic .NET, it's possible to configure the application to perform automatic two-way binding. That is, properties are set when the form launches and saved when the form closes.

The mechanism to bind properties to configuration settings is found in the Property Sheet for a control. At the top of the list of properties for the selected control (assuming that they are sorted alphabetically), is a selection called Property Bindings. When expanded, you can see one or two commonly bound properties and an option for (PropertyBinding). Click the ellipsis button to the right of (PropertyBinding) to see the form shown in Figure 11-2.

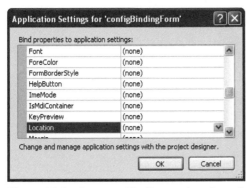

Figure 11-2 Property Binding options for a form.

From this dialog box, select the property to be bound and then click the drop-down button. At this point you can select from any existing settings or create new ones. If you select the New link in the bottom-left corner, you are presented with a dialog box (Figure 11-3) where you can specify the name of the setting, the data type, the scope (application-level or user-level), and the default value. Clicking OK in this dialog box completes the property binding process.

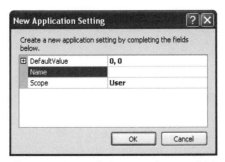

Figure 11-3 Defining a setting to which a property will be bound.

Binding properties in this manner results in the initial value of the property being taken from the appropriate configuration file when the form is initialized. At this point, the difference between the Visual Basic .NET and C# IDE becomes apparent. For Visual Basic .NET, no additional code is required to cause the configuration setting to be updated when the form is closed. There is an option in the Project Properties dialog box (see Figure 11-4) on the Application tab to indicate whether My Settings should be saved when the form closes.

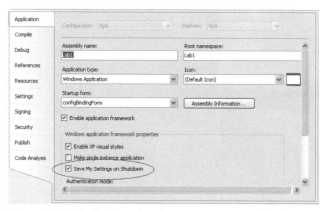

Figure 11-4   Indicating that the current settings should be saved to the configuration file.

For C#, however, the following line of code needs to be executed before the form has closed in order to save the settings. Typically, it would go into the *FormClosing* event handler.

```
Properties.Settings.Default.Save();
```

Although the binding that has just been defined works quietly behind the scenes, it is not the only way to bind configuration settings to control properties. Simple assignment can be used to retrieve and update the setting information. And if the settings are defined properly, the *Properties.Settings* class will be automatically extended so that newly created settings show up as properties on the *Properties.Settings* class. For example, if a setting called demoFormPosition has been created, you would access with the following code:

```
' VB
My.Settings.demoFormPosition
```

```
// C#
Properties.Settings.demoFormPosition
```

Although creating these bindings is easy to do, there are instances where the automatic binding can't be used. For example, the *Size* property on a form can't be bound to in this manner. Technically, the reason has to do with when the size of the form is determined during the form initialization process relative to when the binding assignment takes place. But regardless, a few properties can't be bound automatically and have to be assigned manually. However, most of them can be bound with no problem.

Lab: Binding Configuration Information

In this lab, the techniques used to bind form properties to user preferences will be demonstrated. The ability to easily connect the properties on Windows Forms controls to configuration attributes is not new to .NET 2.0. However, the ability to automatically save values back to the configuration file is new and, when used properly, quite powerful.

▶ **Exercise: Automatic Binding of User Preferences**

This exercise demonstrates the two-way binding of properties to configuration attributes. By the end of the exercise, you will be able to move and resize a form and have the next launch of the application "remember" the last values for these properties.

1. Launch Visual Studio 2005.

2. Open a solution using File | Open | Project/Solution.

3. Navigate to the Chapter11\Lesson1\<language>\Exercise-Before directory. Select the Lab1 solution and click Open.

4. In the Solution Explorer, double-click Form1 to show the form in design view.

5. We'll start by binding the form's location to the user-level settings. Right-click the form and select Properties. At the top of the list of properties in the Property Sheet (when in alphabetical order), expand (ApplicationSettings). Click Location and then click the drop-down button at the right of the property's value. Click the New link to create a new binding.

6. In the dialog box that appears, provide a name of configBindingFormLocation. The DefaultValue is 0, 0 and the scope is User. Click OK to complete the binding process.

    Only if you are working in C# do you need to complete the following steps to save the form location on exit.

7. In the Property Sheet, click Events to display the events. Then double-click the *FormClosing* event. This creates the event handler for the *FormClosing* event.

8. Within the event handler, add the following line of code to save the form's location (and, indeed, any other bound settings) to the configuration file.

    ```
    Properties.Settings.Default.Save();
    ```

    At this point, all the Visual Basic .NET users can stop smirking and start following the steps again.

9. If you run the application at this point, the form will now remember its location between executions. So run the application. Move the form to a different position on the screen. Then shut down the application. Start the application one more time and the form will appear right where it had been previously.

10. Next, we're going to bind the form's *Size* property to the user configuration settings manually. Right-click the Lab1 project and select Properties. Select the Settings tab to display the defined settings for the project. Notice that there is already one there for configBindingFormLocation.

11. In the line immediately below configBindingFormLocation, click the Name cell. Enter **configBindingFormSize**. Select a Type (the next column) of System.Drawing.Size. The Scope should be user and the Value should be 500, 500.

12. Back in the form's design view tab, right-click the form and select Properties. Click Events to display the events for the form. Double-click the *Load* property to create the form's *Load* event handler.

13. In the *Load* event handler, add the following line of code, which assigns the saved value for the *Size* property to the form's *Size* property:

```
' VB
Me.Size = My.Settings.configBindingFormSize
```

```
// C#
this.Size = Properties.Settings.Default.configBindingFormSize;
```

14. Next, we'll add the code to save the form's *Size* property into the user preferences when the form is shut down. For Visual Basic .NET users, go back to the Property Sheet for the form and double-click the *FormClosing* event to create an event handler. C# users created this event handler a couple of steps ago. They should right-click the form and select View Code.

15. Inside the *FormClosing* event handler, add the following line of code:

```
' VB
My.Settings.configBindingFormSize = Me.Size
```

```
// C#
// Add this line BEFORE the call to Properties.Settings.Default.Save()
Properties.Settings.Default.configBindingFormSize = this.Size;
```

16. At this point, the configBindingFormSize configuration value has been manually linked to the form's Size property. If you run the application now, the size of the form will be set to 500, 500. Resize the form and then shut down the application. Restart the application and notice that the form's size has been "remembered."

Lesson Summary

- Configuration settings can be scoped at both the application and user levels.
- Although both types of settings can be updated, usually only user-scoped settings should be.
- In .NET 2.0, control properties can be bound to configuration settings. The property values can be easily saved to the configuration file.

Lesson Review

You can use the following questions to test your knowledge of the information in Lesson 1, "What Should Be Stored?" The questions are also available on the companion CD if you prefer to review them in electronic form.

NOTE Answers

Answers to these questions and explanations of why each answer choice is right or wrong are located in the "Answers" section at the end of the book.

---

1. As part of the functionality of your log-viewing application, users select files to be opened from within your application (called *logviewer.exe*). You need to remember the last four files opened by each user so that you can present a "last opened" list on the menu. In which type of configuration file should you store the list of files?

   A. logviewer.exe.config in the same directory as the executable

   B. user.config in the %InstallRoot%\Documents and Settings*username*\Local Settings\ logviewer\1.0 directory

   C. application.config file in the Application Root Directory

   D. I:\Shared\logviewer.exe.config, where the I: drive is a directory shared by everyone in the company

2. Within your Windows Forms application (called db.exe), each user is allowed to specify the database to which he or she wants to connect. You would like to store the connection string for the last selected database. In which file would you place the connection string information?

   A. db.exe.config in the same directory as the executable

   B. user.config in the %InstallRoot\Documents and Settings*username*\Local Settings\ db\1.0\Settings directory

   C. application.config file in the Application Root Directory

   D. I:\Shared\db.exe.config, where the I: drive is a directory shared by everyone in the company

3. Your Windows Forms application uses a database to retrieve a list of orders to display for the users. The same database is used for all users. The application is being deployed using ClickOnce. You would like to store the connection string information in a configuration file. Which location should you choose?

   A. logviewer.exe.config in the same directory as the executable

   B. logviewer.exe.config in the %InstallRoot\Documents and Settings*username*\Local Settings directory

   C. application.config file in the application's root directory

   D. I:\Shared\logviewer.exe.config, where the I: drive is a directory shared by everyone in the company

Lesson 2: The Choices for Persistence

The *System.Configuration* namespace offers a great deal of flexibility regarding the location for the configuration information. And, to be clear, the "location" under consideration isn't the specific directory in which the configuration file can be found. That was covered earlier in the chapter. What's really being considered is the type of data repository that can and should be used.

> **After this lesson, you will be able to:**
> - Decide where application configuration information should be stored.
> - Direct configuration data to different types of data stores.
>
> **Estimated lesson time: 15 minutes**

Physical Files

This is the default repository for configuration settings. It's also the one that most developers think about when "config file" is used in architecture or specification documents. There are certainly some benefits of storing a configuration file in this manner.

Ease of Deployment

The file can easily be moved about with the rest of the application. In fact, all that is required is that a copy of the file be given the correct name and placed into the appropriate directory.

Ease of Maintenance

The physical config file is just an XML document, which means that it's in a text format and can easily be modified using Microsoft Notepad, Wordpad, or any one of your favorite text editors.

Of course, this is also a bit of a negative, in that the configuration can be modified by anyone who has access to the file. And if the running application modifies the settings (which means that the user needs to have write access to the config file), then anyone who can run the application can also do what they want to the file.

Also, because it is so easy to modify the file, specialized editors aren't commonly used. So it is possible that a well-intentioned user can forget to add a quotation mark to one of the attribute values and the entire application fails because the config file can't be successfully parsed.

Isolated Storage

Isolated storage is a mechanism that allows data to be directly associated with code. When you use isolated storage, you open the logical equivalent of a file system for your application in the current user's private area. Within that file system you can read and write files (of any format) to your heart's content. And the files being saved can be segregated by user, by application, or even by AppDomain. Other users and other applications don't (by default) have access to this isolated file system.

Access to isolated storage is made through the *IsolatedStorageFile* class. This class exposes a static method called *GetStore* that retrieves a reference to an isolated store. The specific store is determined by the parameters.

```vb
' VB
Dim store As IsolatedStorageFile
store = IsolatedStorageFile.GetStore(IsolatedStorageScope.User _
    Or IsolatedStorageScope.Assembly, Nothing, Nothing)
```

```csharp
// C#
IsolatedStorageFile store = GetStore(IsolatedStorageScope.User |
    IsolatedStorageScope.Assembly, null, null);
```

Reading and writing to the isolated store becomes a matter of instantiating an *IsolatedStorage-FileStream* and using the standard input/output methods to manipulate it.

```vb
' VB
Dim writer As New StreamWriter(New IsolatedStorageFileStream("IsolatedFileName.txt", _
    FileMode.CreateNew, store))
writer.WriteLine("Hello Isolated Storage")
writer.Close()
```

```csharp
// C#
StreamWriter writer = null;
writer = new StreamWriter(new IsolatedStorageFileStream("IsolatedFileName.txt",
    FileMode.CreateNew,store));
writer.WriteLine("Hello Isolated Storage");
writer.Close();
```

Isolated storage fills a need in several situations:

- **ClickOnce deployment**   Isolated storage requires only that partial trust be granted, which is the default permission in a click-once environment. By using isolated storage, you have a file system that is writable, something that the regular file system is not (by default).
- **Roaming**   If you have a group of users who move from machine to machine and you would like their application settings to move with them, isolated storage can help. Isolated storage follows users from machine to machine, allowing their most recent application settings to travel with them.
- **Shared configuration**   Isolated storage can be accessed based on an assembly. If the same assembly is shared between different applications, it's possible to have one set of configuration settings be used by both applications.

There are also situations in which isolated storage should definitely not be used:

- **Storing sensitive data** Although the actual location of the isolated storage file is obfuscated, the file is not completely hidden. If you know what you're looking for, you can find it. Nor are the contents of the file automatically encrypted, which means that storing sensitive information in isolated storage is only slightly better than storing it in plain text. You can, however, use isolated storage to write encrypted data.

- **Application-level settings** Isolated storage is not shareable across users. Each user gets his or her own. This means that you don't want to use it to store information (like application-level settings) that's applicable to all users of an application.

Database

Storing configuration information in a database is a natural extension of local config files and isolated storage. After all, configuration settings are data, and databases just love storing data. Also, the mechanics of retrieving and updating information from a database are well understood.

The benefits of using a database to store configuration information are fairly obvious. It provides the ability to support roaming users. There is transactional support, so the configuration information will never become invalid as a result of an interrupted update.

As an added benefit, if user preference information is stored in a database, administrators have access to be able to modify it as necessary. This is a feature that the other repositories don't provide. And, even though the information is in a database, there are many simple and commonly used mechanisms to update the information if necessary. Query Analyzer, SQL Management Studio, and the osql command are three that spring to mind, but many others could be used.

The biggest drawback to using a database is the need to have a network presence to retrieve application settings. Sure, it's possible to have a local database to store the settings, but then some of the pros (roaming, administrator access) are lost. So, assuming that a central database is being used, the user needs to be connected to the database to retrieve and update the settings. Depending on the needs of the application (such as when you expect users to be able to work offline), the always available network presence might not be something to be counted on.

Also, in an ironic twist, using a database as the data store for configuration information is rarely sufficient. Part of the configuration information is typically the connection string to various databases, including, it is reasonable to assume, the configuration database. So even if a database is used, another configuration data store would be required to support the connection string.

Registry

The *Windows Registry* is what many developers who created Windows applications prior to .NET first think of when application settings come to mind. The registry is basically a database of Windows configuration information as well as a repository for the configuration data of many third-party applications.

It is still possible to use the registry to store and retrieve application settings. It's even possible to store user preference information (that is, user-level settings) in the registry. However, the need to use the registry has been pretty much eliminated by improvements to *System.Configuration*. Prior to .NET 2.0, the registry was the repository for connection strings that had been encrypted using the DPAPI functions. But in .NET 2.0, the ability the encrypt all or part of a config file has eliminated even that use. At the moment, the only reason to look at using the registry is if you need to support older application components.

Custom Providers

Among the choices for the configuration settings repository, only the physical file option (that is, the config file) provides the property binding and strongly typed support (through *My.Settings* or *Properties.Settings*) that were described in the first lesson. For the other locations, the mechanics of retrieving and updating the settings must take place within the classes and methods that support it (*IsolatedStorageFile, SqlConnection, Registry*).

Until, that is, you look at *SettingsProvider* and *ApplicationSettingsBase* classes. By using both of these classes, it is possible to, if necessary, completely rewrite the configuration subsystem to provide whatever functionality you require.

ApplicationSettingsBase Class

The purpose of the *ApplicationSettingsBase* class is to provide a concrete wrapper for implementing application settings. To access a group of settings, you create a class derived from *ApplicationSettingsBase*. This class, a wrapper for a group of related settings, exposes each of the settings as a public, strongly typed property. The ability to access the setting values through properties makes for cleaner, less bug-prone code. It also emulates the *My.Settings* and *Properties.Settings* classes that are part of the .NET Framework.

Also associated with each of the settings properties is a set of attributes that identify the scoping level and the default value for the setting. A typical setting property looks like the following:

```
' VB
<UserScopedSetting()> _
<DefaultSettingValue("0, 0")> _
Public Property FormLocation() As Point
Get
Return CType(Me("FormLocation"), Point)
End Get
```

```
Set
Me("FormLocation") = Value
End Set
End Property

// C#
[UserScopedSetting()]
[DefaultSettingValueAttribute("0, 0")]
public Point FormLocation
{
    get { return (Point)(this["FormLocation"]); }
    set { this["FormLocation"] = value; }
}
```

The wrapper class is also responsible for implementing *Save* and *Reload* methods. However, this implementation does *not* include the details of how the settings are to be persisted, only which settings are to be saved and retrieved and the configuration repository into which they will be placed (application or user). The actual saving of the settings is done through a settings provider.

SettingsProvider Class

The actual work of saving and retrieving settings data falls to classes derived from the *Settings-Provider* class. This abstract class defines the mechanism through which the *ApplicationSettingsBase*-derived wrapper class can access and update the data. Any class deriving from *SettingsProvider* must expose the following three members:

- *ApplicationName*   The name of the currently running application.
- *GetProperties*   Retrieves a collection of property values for a given application.
- *SetProperties*   Saves a collection of property values for a given application.

So the methods that implement the persistence mechanism, whatever form that takes, are *GetProperties* and *SetProperties*. If the repository is a database, then *GetProperties* and *SetProperties* will depend heavily on the database provider. If the repository is isolated storage, then *IsolatedStorageFile* will be used. This encapsulation of the data access logic to these two methods frees the application settings mechanism from worrying about the "where" and "how" of saving in order to concentrate on the "what" (as in what configuration settings are important).

Lesson Summary

- The default storage location is a config file. The name and location of the file depend on the name and type of application that is running.
- .NET 2.0 supports both old and new methods of saving configuration information.
- Through the *ApplicationSettingsBase* and *SettingsProvider*, architects have the flexibility to design and implement any configuration framework that suits their needs.

Lesson Review

You can use the following questions to test your knowledge of the information in Lesson 2, "The Choices for Persistence." The questions are also available on the companion CD if you prefer to review them in electronic form.

Answers Answers to these questions and explanations of why each answer choice is right or wrong are located in the "Answers" section at the end of the book.

---

1. Your application uses an application-level setting that identifies the current version of a Web service to use. You need to be able to modify the version number from a central location, whether the client machines are turned on or not. Where should the version information be stored?

   A. Physical file (config file)

   B. Isolated storage

   C. A network database

   D. Registry

2. You are creating two independent Windows Forms applications. The applications share an assembly, which retrieves a DataSet from a Web service call. The applications are deployed using ClickOnce and are normally executed by users who are not connected to your corporate network. You need to be able to share the results of the Web service call between the two applications. Where can the result of the Web service call be stored? (Choose all that apply.)

   A. Physical file (config file)

   B. Isolated storage

   C. A network database

   D. Registry

3. Your Windows Forms application will be deployed using ClickOnce technology. Traveling salespeople who work without being connected to the corporate network might use the application. You need to both retrieve and update settings associated with the application. What type of data store should be used?

   A. Physical file (config file)

   B. Isolated storage

   C. A network database

   D. Registry

Lesson 3: Formatting Settings in Storage

It's all about choice. For the longest time, the options available for persisting settings in Windows applications were very limited. The Windows Registry supported only the most basic data types. INI files allowed only name/value pairs where the value had to be a string. Even the initial versions of configuration files in .NET 1.0 leaned very heavily on the name/value pair model, in which value had to be a string.

Fortunately, the situation has improved. In .NET 2.0 it's possible to save pretty much any type of object into configuration files that can be stored in quite a wide variety of formats. In this lesson we look at the choices for persisting in terms of the format of the data.

After this lesson, you will be able to:
- Decide where application configuration information should be stored.
- Direct configuration data to different types of data stores.

Estimated lesson time: 24 minutes

Real World

Bruce Johnson

The ability to go beyond storing simple strings in the configuration files is one of the more underused capabilities in .NET. I suspect that part of the reason is the expected difficulty in getting an object into and out of a configuration file. What is frequently overlooked is the ease with which this can be done given the tools available in the .NET Framework.

Once developers get over that mental hurdle, it's often like a dam has broken. In fact, more often than not, I need to pull back on how often it's used. For reasons such as this, it is very important for developers and architects to gain an understanding of how the persistence mechanism works and when it makes the most sense.

String-Formatted

The default format for storing data in the .NET configuration framework is a string. Specifically, the *LocalFileSettingsProvider* performs the following steps as it is saving the settings:

1. Using reflection, all of the properties on the wrapper class are examined. Those that are decorated with the *UserScopedSetting* or *ApplicationScopedSetting* attribute are processed for saving.

NOTE Wrapper class

If you have used the Visual Studio 2005 IDE to create the settings, you have actually created a class that derives from *ApplicationSettingsBase* behind the scenes. So these steps are followed even if you don't explicitly create a wrapper class for your settings.

---

2. The *ConvertToString* method (or *ConvertFromString*, for retrieval) is invoked on the *Type-Converter* associated with the property's data type. If this succeeds, the string value is stored.

3. If the value can't be converted to a string (because, for example, the property is a nonintrinsic data type), then the value of the property is serialized into its XML format.

XML-Formatted

At a conceptual level, the serialization of an object into its XML representation is straightforward. The value of each public, readable, and writable property is placed into an XML document. Exactly where in that document the value goes depends on some attributes that will be discussed shortly. But in the absence of any additional information, each property value is placed in its own XML element. The XML representation of a simple *Contact* class can be seen below.

```xml
<?xml version='1.0' />
<Contact>
   <Address>
      <Street>One Microsoft Way</Street>
      <City>Redmond</City>
      <State>WA</State>
      <ZipCode>98052</ZipCode>
   </Address>
   <PhoneNumber>
      <LongDistanceCode>1</LongDistanceCode>
      <AreaCode>425</AreaCode>
      <LocalNumber>882-8080</LocalNumber>
   </PhoneNumber>
</Contact>
```

In this case, the *Contact* class has two public properties: *Address* and *PhoneNumber*. Each of these properties is itself a class. *Address* contains the properties *Address*, *City*, *State*, and *ZipCode*. The *PhoneNumber* class contains *LongDistanceCode*, *AreaCode*, and *LocalNumber*. As can be seen in the example, the hierarchy defined in the class is walked in order to generate the serialized version of the object.

Attributes That Control XML Formatting

The attributes described in Table 11-2 can be applied to class and property declarations to modify the XML representation of a class.

Table 11-2   Attributes That Control XML Formatting

Attribute	Description
XmlAnyAttribute	Allows any attributes that do not have a corresponding member in the object to be returned as an array of *XmlAttribute* objects.
XmlAnyElements	Allows any elements that do not have a corresponding member in the object to be returned as an array of *XmlElement* objects.
XmlArray	Provides greater control over how an array of elements is serialized. The default is to serialize an object as a nested XML segment. With *XmlArray*, you override the default to specify a different structure or name.
XmlArrayItems	Specifies the type that can be placed into an array within the XML document. Frequently, this element is used in conjunction with the *XmlArray* attribute to specify the data type that can be contained within the array.
XmlAttribute	Any property marked with *XmlAttribute* becomes an attribute of the root element, as opposed to the default behavior of being an element within the root document.
XmlChoiceIdentifier	Identifies a property that is serialized as an xsi:choice element.
XmlDefaultValue	Sets the default value for the XML element if the associated property doesn't have a value.
XmlElements	Defines the information associated with the elements serialized into the XML document.
XmlEnum	Indicates how a enumerated property will be serialized.
XmlIgnore	Causes the value for the associated property not to be placed into the serialization stream.
Xmlns	Specifies whether to keep all namespace declarations. It is used in conjunction with the *XmlSerializerNamespaces* class to control the namespaces associated with the XML document.
XmlRoot	Provides details on how the root element of the XML document is constructed.
XmlText	Instructs the serialization process to render the value of the attributed property as XML text.
XmlType	Specifies the type name and namespace that are used to serialize a class or property.

In order to affect the generation of the serialized version of an object, these attributes decorate the class and property declarations of the class. When an instance of the class is serialized, the *XmlSerializer* class examines the attributes and changes the generated XML document appropriately. The same steps are taken in reverse when an XML document is deserialized.

IXmlSerializable Interface

Even with this wide variety of attributes available to control XML serialization, there will be times when they are not sufficient. This is one of the reasons that the *IXmlSerializable* interface was created. It allows developers to have finely grained control over how an object gets serialized into XML.

The *IXmlSerializable* interface is simple to implement because it contains only three methods.

- *ReadXml* Creates an instance of an object using an XML document as the starting point
- *WriteXml* Converts the current state of an object into an XML representation
- *GetSchema* Returns the schema for the XML representation as implemented by the interface

In a nutshell, the *WriteXml* method is used to generate the XML. If you are implementing *IXmlSerializable*, then in *WriteXml* the code that creates an *XmlDocument* object based on the current state would be found. That *XmlDocument* becomes the XML representation. The *ReadXml* method takes an XML representation and recreates the object's state. Because, as a developer, you have complete control over the XML that is generated, you can cause the object to be serialized into any form that is desired.

It is important to realize that the *WriteXml* and the *ReadXml* need to be paired. Although nothing stops the *ReadXml* from understanding a format that is different from what the *WriteXml* would generate, that would be completely unexpected by any future developer who is looking at the code.

NOTE *IXMLSerializable* and .NET 1.1

The *IXmlSerializable* interface existed prior to .NET 2.0 as an unsupported interface. That is to say, the interface was used to serialize/deserialize objects passed across Web service boundaries, but it wasn't part of the official product and, as such, could have been changed in a future version. Fortunately, it is now officially part of the .NET Framework.

The mechanics of serializing an object to XML are not complicated. The *XmlSerializer* class includes a *Serialize* method that takes an instance of the object to serialize and places the XML representation into a stream.

```vb
' VB
Dim itemToSerialize as New Contact()
Dim serializer as New XmlSerializer(itemToSerialize.GetType())

Dim writer as TextWriter
writer = New StreamWriter("configfile.xml")
serializer.Serialize(writer, itemToSerialize)
writer.Close()
```

```csharp
// C#
Contact itemToSerialize = new Contact();
XmlSerializer serializer = new XmlSerializer( typeof(Contact) );

TextWriter writer = new StreamWriter("configfile.xml" );
serializer.Serialize( writer, itemToSerialize );
writer.Close();
```

The deserialization process is just as straightforward. Again, the *XmlSerializer* class is used. But this time, the *Deserialize* method is used. It takes a stream of XML data as a parameter and creates a object of that type. The object is then cast into a strongly typed variable and can be used normally.

```vb
' VB
Dim stream as Stream
Stream = new FileStream("configfile.xml", FileMode.Open)

Dim serializer as New XmlSerializer()
Dim deserializedItem As Contact
deserializedItem = CType(serializer.Deserialize(stream), Contact)
stream.Close()
```

```csharp
// C#
Stream stream = new FileStream( "configfile.xml", FileMode.Open );

XmlSerializer serializer = new XmlSerializer();
Contact deserializedItem = (Contact)serializer.Deserialize( stream );

stream.Close();
```

NOTE Serializing private variables

Only the public, readable, and writable properties are serialized as part of what *XmlSerializer* does. The reason has to do with how the serializer interacts with the object. Because private properties can't be directly assigned from outside the class, there is no way for the serializer to assign those values as part of the deserialization. If it is absolutely necessary to serialize private variables, you will need to implement *IXmlSerializable* on the class.

Binary-Formatted

If there is no requirement to be able to modify the configuration settings manually, using a binary format to store the information might be an option. Although the settings are no longer human-readable, it is more efficient to save and restore data in a binary format than to convert to and from XML.

As with XML serialization, the conversion of an object into its binary format is easily accomplished. Instead of *XmlSerializer*, the *BinaryFormatter* class is used. But, other than that, the steps remain the same.

```
' VB
Dim itemToSerialize as New Contact()
Dim formatter as New BinaryFormatter()

Dim stream as New FileStream("configfile.dat", FileMode.OpenOrCreate)
serializer.Serialize(stream, itemToSerialize)
stream.Close()
```

```
// C#
Contact itemToSerialize = new Contact();
BinaryFormatter formatter = new BinaryFormatter();

Stream stream = new FileStream("configfile.dat", FileMode.OpenOrCreate);
formatter.Serialize( stream, itemToSerialize );
stream.Close();
```

And, for the deserialization:

```
' VB
Dim stream as Stream
Stream = new FileStream("configfile.dat", FileMode.Open)

Dim formatter as New BinaryFormatter()
Dim deserializedItem As Contact
deserializedItem = CType(formatter.Deserialize(stream), Contact)
stream.Close()
```

```
// C#
Stream stream = new FileStream( "configfile.dat", FileMode.Open );

BinaryFormatter formatter = new BinaryFormatter();
Contact deserializedItem = (Contact)formatter.Deserialize( stream );
stream.Close();
```

Lab: XML Serialization

XML serialization has an impact on many parts of the .NET Framework, even beyond saving configuration attributes. This lab covers some of the techniques that you can use to customize serialization.

▶ **Exercise: Changing the Default XML Serialization**

In this exercise the default XML serialization for class will be modified. The starting point is a *Contact* class that contains a list of addresses and a phone number. The list of addresses is implemented as a generic *List*. The phone number is actually an instance of a *PhoneNumber* class. The resulting serialization will look like the following:

```
<?xml version="1.0" encoding="utf-8" ?>
<DemoContact xmlns:xsi="http://www.w3.org/2001/XMLSchema-instance"
  xmlns:xsd="http://www.w3.org/2001/XMLSchema">
  <Addresses>
    <Address>
      <StreetAddress>One Microsoft Way</StreetAddress>
      <City>Redmond</City>
      <State>WA</State>
      <ZipCode>98052</ZipCode>
    </Address>
    <Address>
      <StreetAddress>1950 Meadowvale Blvd</StreetAddress>
      <City>Mississauga</City>
      <State>ON</State>
      <ZipCode>L5M 8L9</ZipCode>
    </Address>
  </Addresses>
  <Phone LongDistanceCode="1" AreaCode="425" LocalNumber="882-8080" />
</DemoContact>
```

1. Launch Visual Studio 2005.
2. Open a solution using File | Open | Project/Solution.
3. Navigate to the Chapter11\Lesson3\<*language*>\Exercise-Before directory. Select the Lab1 solution and click Open.
4. In the Solution Explorer, double-click serializationDemoForm to show the form in design view.
5. We'll start by setting up the serialization process. Double-click Serialize to create the *Click* event handler. Add the code to serialize an instance of the Contact object into a file called demo.xml. Once the object has been serialized, use the webBrowser1 control to navigate to the file.

```vb
' VB
Dim itemToSerialize as Contact = PopulateContact()
Dim serializer As New XmlSerializer(itemToSerialize.GetType())

Dim writer As TextWriter = New StreamWriter("demo.xml")
serializer.Serialize(writer, itemToSerialize)
writer.Close()

WebBrowser1.Navigate(String.Format("file://{0}/demo.xml",
Environment.CurrentDirectory))
```

```
// C#
Contact itemToSerialize = PopulateContact();
XmlSerializer serializer = new XmlSerializer(typeof(Contact));

TextWriter writer = new StreamWriter("demo.xml");
serializer.Serialize(writer, itemToSerialize);
writer.Close();

webBrowser1.Navigate(String.Format("file://{0}/demo.xml",
Environment.CurrentDirectory));
```

6. Add the following lines to the top of the serializationDemoForm code file:

```
' VB
Imports System.IO
```

```
// C#
using System.Xml.Serialization;
using System.IO;
```

7. Run the application and click Serialize. You should see a screen that looks like Figure 11-5.

Figure 11-5 The default XML serialization for the Contact object.

8. Start by modifying the *PhoneNumber* class to put the property values as attributes in the element. This is done by decorating the property with an *XmlAttribute* attribute. Open the PhoneNumber file through the Solution Explorer and add the attribute to each of the properties.

```
' VB
<XmlAttribute()> _
Public Property LongDistanceCode() As String
…
<XmlAttribute()> _
Public Property AreaCode() As String
```

```
...
<XmlAttribute()> _
Public Property LocalNumber() As String
...
```

```
// C#
[XmlAttribute()]
public string LongDistanceCode

[XmlAttribute()]
public string AreaCode
...
[XmlAttribute()]
public string LocalNumber
...
```

9. Run the application and click Serialize. Notice that the PhoneNumber element now contains attributes for LongDistanceCode, AreaCode, and LocalNumber.

10. Next we change the elements names for the serialization. Use the *XmlElement* attribute on the *ContactPhone* property. Open the Contact file through the Solution Explorer and add the *XmlElement* to the *ContactPhone* property.

```
' VB
<XmlElement("Phone")> _
Public Property ContactPhone() As PhoneNumber
...
```

```
// C#
[XmlElement(ElementName="Phone")]
public PhoneNumber ContactPhone
...
```

11. To change the name of the Contact element to DemoContact, use the *XmlRoot* attribute on the *Contact* class. Add the attribute to the Contact declaration.

```
' VB
<XmlRoot("DemoContact")> _
Public Class Contact
...
```

```
// C#
[XmlRoot(ElementName="DemoContact")]
public class Contact
...
```

12. Finally, change the name of the element contained in the array using the *XmlArray* attribute. Add the attribute to the *ContactAddresses* property.

```
' VB
<XmlArray("Addresses")> _
Public Property ContactAddresses As List(Of Contact)
...
```

```
// C#
[XmlArray(ElementName="Addresses")]
public List<Address> ContactAddresses
...
```

13. Run the application and click Serialize to see the final result (Figure 11-6).

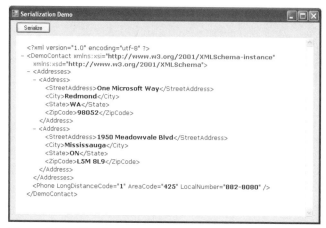

Figure 11-6   The final XML serialization after the *Contact* and *PhoneNumber* classes have been decorated.

Lesson Summary

- The default format for storing configuration information is as a string. However, if the data type can't be converted to a string, the XML representation is used.

- The format of the XML can be controlled using a series of attributes that decorate the class and property declarations.

- If the configuration information is to be stored in a binary format, you have to handle the serialization/deserialization process manually.

Lesson Review

You can use the following questions to test your knowledge of the information in Lesson 3, "Formatting Settings in Storage." The questions are also available on the companion CD if you prefer to review them in electronic form.

NOTE   Answers

Answers to these questions and explanations of why each answer choice is right or wrong are located in the "Answers" section at the end of the book.

1. You have a Windows Forms application for which performance is critical. The application uses complex objects to store application settings. You need to ensure that the retrieval of configuration information is as fast as possible. Which format should you use?

   A. Strings

   B. XML

   C. Binary

   D. MIME-encoded

2. You have a class that you would like to store in the configuration file. The class contains a number of read-only properties, as well as a property that is a recursive reference to the classes, all of which need to be included in the storage. Also, you would like to work with only the standard providers. Which format should you use?

   A. Strings

   B. XML

   C. Binary

   D. MIME-encoded

3. You have a class that you would like to save in the configuration information for an application. The class contains only intrinsic data types and properties that are both readable and writable. Also, although the class has been serialized into the configuration file, the user should be able to make changes to the values. Finally, only the native providers should be considered. Which format should you use? (Choose all that apply.)

   A. Strings

   B. XML

   C. Binary

   D. MIME-encoded

Chapter Review

To further practice and reinforce the skills you learned in this chapter, you can perform the following tasks:

- Review the chapter summary.
- Review the list of key terms introduced in this chapter.
- Complete the case scenarios. These scenarios set up real-world situations involving the topics of this chapter and ask you to create a solution.
- Complete the suggested practices.
- Take a practice test.

Chapter Summary

- The .NET 2.0 Framework provides a wide range of options for saving and retrieving configuration information. The addition of built-in support for updating is a big step forward for creating effective applications.
- Configuration data can be segregated into the application-level settings, which are available to every user running the application, and user-level settings, which are available to each individual user.
- The format for the configuration can vary from strings to XML documents to a pure binary format, depending on the speed and maintainability requirements.

Key Terms

Do you know what these key terms mean? You can check your answers by looking up the terms in the glossary at the end of the book.

- application settings
- isolated storage
- protected configuration
- roaming
- user preferences
- Windows Registry

Case Scenarios

In the following case scenarios, you will apply what you've learned about delivering multimedia in a distributed environment. You can find answers to these questions in the "Answers" section at the end of the book.

Case Scenario 1: Sharing Configuration Information

You are a developer in a company that has both Java and .NET applications. Although the applications are independent, they both have to interact with a legacy mainframe application that is responsible for processing all of the business rules on any data. Communication with the mainframe is accomplished through a message queue. The specific message queue is configured at run time. For the Java application, the configuration values are stored in a MySQL database. For the .NET application, they are stored in various application config files.

A problem occurred when the appropriate message queue was changed. The MySQL database was updated properly, but some of the application config files were missed. As you can imagine, the fallout from this mistake took a significant amount of effort to correct. Your challenge is to design a mechanism that will prevent this from reoccurring.

Answer the following questions for your manager:

1.   What mechanism should be used to integrate the configuration information? One of the key criteria for the choice should be the minimization of the risk of the configuration data getting out of sync and the need for corporate memory to "remember" to perform simultaneous changes.

2.   What are the potential drawbacks to the proposed solution? Are there ways to mitigate the most likely issues?

Case Scenario 2: Securing Configuration Information

You are a developer of a Windows Forms application that will be installed on a number of "hotel" workstations in your company. A "hotel" workstation is one where itinerant employees (such as salespeople) can work at on an occasional basis. The application stores configuration information about the user. However, because the workstation is basically a public one, it's necessary to have the configuration kept independently of each user.

Answer the following questions for your manager:

- 1.   What mechanism should be used to isolate the configuration information? One of the key criteria for the choice should be to minimize the risk of a different user viewing and using each user's configuration information.

- 2.   What mechanism should be used to secure the configuration information?

Suggested Practices

To help successfully master the objectives covered in this chapter, complete the following task.

Improving the User's Experience with Configuration Information

For this task, you should complete both practices.

- **Practice 1** Create a Windows Form that contains a connection string to a database. Use the aspnet_regiis.exe command to encrypt just the connection string section.
- **Practice 2** Create a Windows Forms application that uses the user's identity to keep track of the menu items that have been used. The menu item tracker is implemented as a collection of *UsedMenuItem* objects, where each object represents a particular menu item that has been used. The goal of this practice is to persist this collection in the user-scoped configuration file.

Take a Practice Test

The practice tests on this book's companion CD offer many options. For example, you can test yourself on just one exam objective, or you can test yourself on all the 70-548 certification exam content. You can set up the test so that it closely simulates the experience of taking a certification exam, or you can set it up in study mode so that you can look at the correct answers and explanations after you answer each question.

MORE INFO Practice tests

For details about all the practice test options available, see the "How to Use the Practice Tests" section in this book's Introduction.

Chapter 12

Define and Evaluate a Testing Strategy

No one deliberately sets out to build buggy, low-quality software. However, as projects move through the schedule, bugs slide by and the right testing does not always get done. The result might be a great application, but if it has a lot of bugs, no one will notice. Your project's overall quality is often in direct proportion to the strength of your testing strategy. A well-defined and thorough testing strategy will lead to a solid, problem-free user experience. If you rely on the team to define the strategy as they create tests, you will get software that is poorly tested and riddled with problems upon release. A good testing strategy, along with good testing and tracking tools, will help you to release the high-quality software you intended to write all along.

This chapter covers creating and evaluating testing strategies that measure the quality of your application. We will first look at creating an effective unit testing strategy. This strategy is typically owned and created by developers. We will then cover how, as a developer, you can evaluate and provide input into the integration, stress, and performance testing plans created by the test team. Finally, we will also explore the feedback that a developer is expected to give relative to the test lab hardware, software, and data used for testing.

Each of these testing strategies—unit, integration, stress, and performance—measures an application from a specific angle. For example, unit tests measure the quality of the code (objects and their methods) that defines the behavior of your application in terms of business rules and data interaction. Integration testing confirms that individual components work together to make a cohesive solution. Stress testing indicates how your application will scale and respond to increased or fluctuating demand. Performance testing allows you to understand whether your application meets the benchmarks set forth for the project and helps you identify any related gaps. Taking a disciplined, planned approach to testing your application from each of these angles will ensure that you always release a high-quality software product.

Exam objectives in this chapter:
- Design a unit test.
    - ❏ Decide coverage requirements.
    - ❏ Evaluate when to use boundary condition testing.
- Evaluate the testing strategy.
    - ❏ Create the unit testing strategy.
    - ❏ Evaluate the integration testing strategy.
    - ❏ Evaluate the stress testing strategy.
    - ❏ Evaluate the performance testing strategy.
    - ❏ Evaluate the test environment specification.

Lessons in this chapter:

Before You Begin

To complete the lessons in this chapter, you should be familiar with developing Microsoft Windows applications with Microsoft Visual Studio 2005 using Visual Basic or C#. In addition, you should be comfortable with both of the following tasks:

- Creating a Windows Form-based application. This includes an understanding of the Windows controls and the programming model and methods associated with Windows Form-based applications.
- Working with object-oriented programming, including developing business objects (classes) that contain domain-specific properties and methods.

Real World

Mike Snell

There is no substitute for quality. If you have ever worked with the famed resource triangle from the Microsoft Solutions Framework (MSF), you might have found yourself trying to explain this to a customer or colleague. The resource triangle dictates three points: features, time, and resources. The idea is that you can't move one of these points without having an effect on the others.

You can use this triangle to demonstrate to project sponsors that they can constrain only two items on the triangle (not all three). The third item will have to fluctuate to support the two constraints. For example, if the project sponsor determines that you must have a certain set of features and that you will be given only three resources, then the project team controls the time point. Features and resources are nonnegotiable, and therefore your only management tool is the schedule; you will have to extend it to support every feature with your allotted resources.

Notice that quality is not a point on the triangle. This is because quality should be nonnegotiable. I have been on projects where developers, architects, and project managers were often asked (sometimes forced) to "give a little" in order to meet the schedule or cost (resource) constraint. This is like adding a fourth leg to a triangle. It doesn't work. You might fool yourself or the project sponsors for a time, but the quality (or lack thereof) always comes through.

Over the years I have come to learn firsthand that project sponsors will complain about costs and schedules. However, they never forget buggy, difficult-to-use software—no matter how many features you packed in, how cheap it was, or how many days ahead of schedule you delivered. Your project's success depends on quality. I have made it my job to help customers understand that quality can't be compromised and that quality software comes at a cost. If you take the time to do this, you'll find that customers do not wish to deliberately compromise on quality. Rather, they will begin to be your biggest quality advocate; after all, they have the most to gain from high-quality software.

Lesson 1: Creating a Unit Testing Strategy

An effective unit testing strategy can lead to higher quality code, increased productivity, and easier application maintenance. This lesson examines what goes into creating an effective unit testing strategy. We will first look at an overview of developer unit testing. We will then discuss defining an approach for managing and creating unit tests. Finally, we will cover the best practices that support a good unit testing strategy.

MORE INFO   Creating unit tests

This lesson focuses squarely on defining a unit testing strategy. For information on creating a unit test, see Lesson 1, "Creating Effective Unit Tests" of Chapter 13, "Creating Development Tests."

After this lesson, you will be able to:
- Determine where, in your solution, to manage unit tests.
- Determine an approach for creating unit tests.
- Determine the conditions that should be tested as part of a unit test.
- Understand best practices for defining a unit test.
- Establish metrics for unit test code coverage.

Estimated lesson time: 20 minutes

Unit Testing Overview

Developers are responsible for testing their code prior to its alpha or beta release. Traditionally, this has meant that you walk through your code line-by-line inside a debugger. To do so, developers often create a crude user interface (or test harness) that can be used to simulate standard user interaction, edge cases, and error conditions. This approach is problematic for a number of reasons. First, it relies on the developer to re-execute tests after each change. Along the same lines, it is not automated and repeatable by other developers or testers. Last, it relies on the developer to confirm that all code gets tested. The result of following this approach is a lower quality product released to the test team.

What was needed was a more formal process for developer testing. As a result, the concept of a unit test evolved. A *unit test* is a test that isolates a portion of your application and tests all conditions (typically one-by-one) of that "unit." Unit tests can be manual or automated. A manual unit test is one that is documented and then executed by a developer. Manual unit tests have many of the same problems mentioned previously. However, automated unit tests seek to solve these problems.

An automated unit test is a piece of test code that you write to exercise a portion of your application code. These automated unit tests exist inside a unit test framework. This framework is responsible for running the tests and communicating the results. The first such framework for .NET was nUnit. This was written as an open-source project for .NET 1.0/1.1. A similar unit-testing framework was then built into .NET 2.0. With it, you can create unit tests that can be automatically run inside of Visual Studio and then reported on to give visibility into the code's quality.

Benefits of Automated Unit Testing

The principal benefit of defining an automated unit test is that you can create a complete, repeatable test for a given unit of your code. This test ensures that that unit of code works as developed. Once created, it can be run over and over to make sure the code continues to operate as designed. In addition, new conditions can be added to the test as they arise (or are thought of). In this way the tests grow stronger over time. This seemingly simple goal of creating a repeatable test for a unit of code has a number of ancillary benefits as well. Let's take a look.

Confirm Code Is Tested   The unit testing framework in .NET tracks which code gets tested by the unit tests and which code does not. It then reports this information. In this way you get real metrics on exactly what code (and what percentage of code) is tested. A developer can use this information to make changes that increase the unit test code coverage.

Build a Set of Regression Tests   You create unit tests one at a time. However, as you continue to build unit tests the cumulative result is that you have a set of tests that exercise a major portion (if not all) of your application. This set of tests often becomes a large portion of your regression test. A *regression test* is a test that represents a baseline to exercise the entire application. Often your regression test is known to have worked at one time and can therefore be used after changes are made to determine if things still work.

Make Changes with Confidence   Having a set of unit tests allows you to more confidently make changes to an existing application. This can be great if you are a new developer and wish to change someone else's code. In addition, if you are doing a code review and wish to refactor some portion of the code late in the cycle, you can do so with a higher degree of confidence. The unit tests can be run after the change. The tests should then identify any problems that resulted from the change.

Aid in Understanding   Developers can use unit tests to walk through and understand the intention of existing code. The unit tests serve as a sort of documentation of what should and shouldn't be possible for a given method or property. By reading through the unit test code and watching it execute inside the integrated development environment (IDE), a developer can more quickly understand the intent of the code.

Unit Testing Limits

Unit testing is just one piece of the testing puzzle. It helps developers ensure that each unit of their code works as intended. However, testers still need to do their part. Unit testing does not cover integration, user interface, stress, or performance testing. Testers still need to execute these types of tests to ensure that the application is tested from all angles.

Quick Check

1. What is the definition of a unit test?
2. What is the primary purpose of a unit test?
3. What are the benefits of coding a set of unit tests using a unit test framework?

Quick Check Answers

1. Strictly speaking, a unit test is a test that isolates a portion of code and tests it for expected behavior and outputs based on a certain set of inputs. An automated unit test in Visual Studio 2005 is a piece of code that is written to call an isolated segment of the application (typically a single method or property). The unit test asserts a set of truths about the expected results after the application code has been called. The unit test framework built into Visual Studio then runs this automated unit test.

2. The primary purpose of a unit test is to help the developer ensure that the code works as intended. The unit test isolates it and tests it for a specific condition. A single piece of application code may be tested for many conditions using many unit tests.

3. Writing automated unit tests as part of a unit test framework has all of the following benefits: it builds up a set of regression tests for the application, it confirms that each method works as intended, it helps identify dependency issues between bits of code when changes are made to the application, and it aids in understanding the intent of a given piece of code.

Managing and Storing Unit Tests

You have a number of options available for storing and managing the unit tests you create for your application. It is helpful to define a single strategy in this regard, communicate it, and stick to it. In doing so, it is important to remember that unit tests are the developer's domain. Developers create them initially and run them the most often. Testers may use them, but developers must take ownership. You want to make sure they have the best experience when working with these tests. Therefore, it is advisable that you do not embed your unit tests in the middle of a large testing project that contains the test team's many additional tests. Your developers will most likely be running a version of Visual Studio that does not have access to these other tests. In addition, these other tests might get in the way of the development team and the testers. You should therefore segment your unit tests into a test project separate from other tests. You have a number of options for doing so. The following are the two most common options:

- **Create a single test project within your solution.**   This strategy involves defining a single unit testing project inside your solution. Developers will add their unit tests to this project. The result is a centralized store for all unit tests on the project. When you run the unit tests, you typically run all tests in the project. This approach can, therefore, be good if you wish each developer to run the full set of tests each time.
- **Create one test project per application project.**   With this strategy you define a one-to-one relationship between class library or project and unit test project. This can be helpful if you wish your developers to focus on a single piece of the application at one time. It's also great if you are developing reusable components because the component and the component's tests are discrete. However, it becomes difficult to run the full set of unit tests for the entire solution using this method.

Naming Unit Test Files

It is advisable that you have a single unit testing file for each file you intend to unit test. This creates a one-to-one relationship between items in your application and your tests. For example, if you have both *Product.cs* and *Order.cs* class files, you should also have two separate unit test files (one for each class file). In addition, you should name your unit test files after the class they test. In the previous example you would create the files *ProductTest.cs* and *OrderTest.cs*.

Defining an Approach to Creating Unit Tests

There are two primary ways to create unit tests for your project: automatically generated and manually crafted. Each method has its advantages in a particular situation. It is important to base your decision on how you will employ one of these methods in a disciplined approach. This will ensure that your team builds a full set of tests for your application. Let's take a look at each option.

Manually Create Unit Tests

You can create your unit tests from a standard class file without any help from Visual Studio. Typically you employ this strategy in test-first, or test-driven, development. This approach is conceptually different from the typical development process of writing code and then testing that code. Test-driven development demands the opposite approach. You create your tests first; you then write application code to satisfy those tests. The idea is that you want to see a test fail before you write code. In fact, if you add a new feature to your application, you start by defining that feature's tests. You then write the code around those tests.

A test-driven approach can help you ensure two things. First, the only code that will get written is just enough to pass the tests. Developers should not be writing extra code that is not intended by the tests; if more code is required, more tests will also be needed. Secondly, your unit tests should end up being of a high caliber, with high code and condition coverage. This is a result of coding (and thinking about) the tests before writing the application code.

A test-driven strategy requires a switch in mindset for most developers. It is just not how developers have been trained to work or think. In addition, to be effective it requires a total buy-in from the team and a disciplined approach. It is also not always practical. Many applications exist today with few or no unit tests. It would not be practical to try and rewrite these applications test-first.

Generate Unit Tests

Visual Studio 2005 allows you to generate a set of unit tests from existing code. You can run the Unit Test Wizard and select the classes and their members for which you want unit tests generated. Visual Studio will then create a test file that contains a number of unit tests that are stubbed out and in many cases have the beginning of your unit test.

This strategy can be very effective when you're working with an existing class or library that does not already have unit tests defined. You can generate the unit tests and begin to fill in the details around them. This offers more productivity than creating unit tests by hand. In addition, many developers who are accustomed to creating code and then doing their testing will find this approach more in line with their experience. In this way they can code a class or set of features and then work to write appropriate unit tests from the head start provided by Visual Studio.

Quick Check

1. What is test-driven development?
2. In what ways can you define a unit test?

Quick Check Answers

1. Test-driven development demands that you write tests before you write application code. You write application code only to satisfy broken tests. This ensures that your tests and code stay in full sync. It also makes sure you do not write a lot of extra code. However, it requires a different discipline and approach for most developers.

2. You can create a unit test using a test project and a class file. You can also select an existing set of application code (class) and have Visual Studio generate your unit tests for you.

Define What Needs to Be Unit Tested

A good unit testing strategy defines exactly what in the application will be unit tested and exactly how it should get unit tested. This ensures that developers understand where and when to employ various unit test types as well as test for all conditions. This section looks at the various types of unit tests and the many conditions that should be tested.

When to Use a Unit Test

Unit tests are created mostly to test the class libraries of your Windows application. They work best when they call the members of a given class, pass a set of parameters, and make assertions based on the results. They are typically not written to exercise your user interface or to validate the structure and content of your database. Other tests can do these things. Unit tests should be focused on testing developer code in terms of classes, fields, and properties.

NOTE   Bind a unit test to data

You can create a data-driven unit test that is bound to a data source. In this case your test is typically run once for each row in the data source. You will want to create data-driven unit tests for methods that take a wide variety of input. In these cases, instead of writing a number of separate, common unit tests or creating a looping structure, you can define one test and bind it to a data source that contains sample data.

Unit Test Conditions

A good unit test should single out a piece of code (method or property) in your application and test a single condition. You might need to make multiple assertions in the test, but the overall test should be focused on a given condition, such as a success condition, error condition, null values, and so on. The condition should either fail or pass. You do not want to test multiple conditions in a single unit test. The following list describes some of the conditions and scenarios for which you will want to write tests:

- **Success baseline**   You will want to start by defining a unit test that represents a common, successful path through your code. This test should represent the most likely scenario for executing your code.
- **Parameter value mix**   You should create one or more unit tests that provide a varied mixture of parameters for a given method. This will ensure that more than just the success baseline works effectively. You might consider creating this test as a data-driven unit test. The data would have the varied mix of parameter values.

- **Bounds checking**   You will want to create one or more unit tests that test the upper and lower limits of your code. That is, if your method takes a numeric value, you will want to test that method with values that represent both the upper and lower range of the data type.

- **Null values**   You need to make sure your unit tests measure what happens when null values are passed to a given method or property.

- **Error conditions**   You want to create unit tests that trigger error conditions in your code. You can tell the unit test that you expect a certain error as a result. If that error is not thrown, the test will fail.

- **Code coverage scenarios**   You need to make sure that all the code in your method gets called by one or more unit tests. You do not want untested code sitting inside of conditional statements. If this happens, you want to write tests that hit those conditions inside your application code.

Define Code Coverage Metrics

Your unit testing strategy should define a metric for code coverage. *Code coverage* refers to the percentage of code that is exercised by the unit tests. Prior to Visual Studio 2005 this metric was difficult to obtain. Now this information is readily available from the tool. This gives you a measurable understanding of what portion of your code is tested. The measurement is based on the code executed by the tests relative to the total logic in the application.

Typically, you want to strive for 70 percent code coverage or better. You can use this metric to measure the effectiveness of your unit tests and the quality of a given build. For example, it means something completely different if a given build has all unit tests pass but has a unit test code coverage of only 20 percent versus a build with 90 percent coverage.

Developers can also use code coverage analysis to identify code that is not covered by unit tests. They can turn on code coverage for a given library from the .testrunconfig file. They can then view test results and see low-coverage areas in their code. The results window will allow them to jump straight to those areas and then create tests to increase their coverage.

NOTE   **Prevent check-in for poorly covered code**

You can create a policy that prevents code check-in that does not meet your measure for unit test code coverage.

Quick Check

1. What are some common unit test types or scenarios in which unit tests work well?
2. What conditions should you make sure to test with your unit tests?

Quick Check Answers

1. Unit tests are best suited to test methods and properties of your classes. You can also use the unit test framework to bind data to test methods that create tests based on a wide variety of parameter input.
2. Many conditions can be tested with unit tests. You will want to start by ensuring that you test the common, successful scenario. You will also want to make sure your application behaves appropriately under error conditions. You will want to check your inputs with null values and values that verify the upper and lower bounds of a given data type. Finally, you want to make sure your unit tests cover all the lines of code in your application.

Unit Testing Best Practices

As with most things, the more you do it, the better you get. The same is true for writing unit tests. As you create more and more, you start to see patterns, and best practices emerge. Your unit testing strategy should take into account these best practices. The following list describes some of the best practices that have been established for writing effective unit tests:

- **Write one test for each condition or scenario**   You should test each outcome or scenario independently. If your method has a number of expected outcomes, you should write a test for each scenario.
- **Create atomic unit tests**   Your unit tests should not require others tests (or a sequence of tests) to be run prior to its execution or as part of its execution.
- **Cover all conditions**   Your unit tests should cover all cases. An effective set of unit tests covers every possible condition for a given method, including bounds checks, null values, exceptions, and conditional logic.
- **Run without configuration**   Your unit tests should be easy to run (and rerun). They should not require setup or configuration. You do not want to define tests that require a specific environment every time you run your tests (or they will not get run). If setup is required, you will want to code that into a test initialize script.
- **Test a common application state**   Your unit tests should be run against a common, standard, good state. For example, if your application works with data, this data should be set to common state prior to the execution of each unit test. This ensures that one test is not causing an error in another test.

Lab: Define a Unit Testing Strategy

The best way to ensure that you understand this material is to create an actual unit testing strategy. You can use this practice section as an aid to define a unit testing strategy for your organization or your next project.

▶ **Exercise: Document Your Unit Testing Strategy**

In this exercise you will define and document a unit testing strategy. You will want to apply the guidance provided in this chapter to your real-world conditions. Each step represents a section that you should define for your strategy.

1. Determine where you intend unit tests to be stored and managed in your application. Document your reasoning relative to your specific project, process, or situation.

2. Define and document how you intend to create unit tests on your project. Consider the trade-off between test-first development and the ability to generate tests from existing code.

3. Indicate what, in your application, will get unit tested. Set boundaries between the various elements of the application and unit tests. You should also define when you intend to use data-driven unit tests.

4. Document the conditions you expect to see for each unit test in your application. You might also define the bounds for each data type (such as a date range) as an aid for developers.

5. Indicate an acceptable metric for unit test code coverage.

6. Consider creating a reference implementation of a set of unit tests for a given class. This reference implementation should follow your standards. It will serve as an example for developers when they implement their own tests.

7. Finally, present your strategy to your organization or project team. Get their feedback and understand their acceptance criteria for your strategy. Not only will this refine your strategy, but also it should serve to solidify these concepts for you.

Lesson Summary

■ Unit tests are the responsibility of developers (not testers). Therefore, the unit testing strategy should come from the technical lead or a senior developer on the team. The team should document and review the strategy.

■ An automated unit test is a piece of code you write that isolates a specific method or property in your application and executes it for a given condition.

■ Unit tests are now part of the .NET Framework 2.0. Prior to this, the open-source nUnit framework was available for .NET developers.

■ Unit tests have their limits. They are best used for testing class libraries. They do not work well for ensuring the user interface or doing integration testing.

- You add unit tests to a test project in Visual Studio. You can create a single, centralized unit test project or solution. Alternatively, you can define a single unit test project per application project.
- Visual Studio can automatically generate unit tests for your project. This is useful for existing code that has no unit tests already developed.
- Test-first development involves creating tests prior to writing application code. You write a test and then write application code to make those tests pass.
- You can bind a unit test to a database or data source. This is useful for calling the test for each item in the data source. In this way you can feed the test with multiple sets of parameters.
- Your unit tests should test all conditions for a given unit. This includes both success and error conditions. It should also include bounds-checking various parameters.
- Visual Studio can provide you with statistics on what code was tested by your unit tests. These statistics are referred to as code coverage analysis. You can get a percentage of code that is covered and uncovered. You can also jump straight to uncovered code in the IDE.
- Your unit tests should not require configuration; they should be atomic in nature, and they should test a common application state.

Lesson Review

You can use the following questions to test your knowledge of the information in Lesson 1, "Creating a Unit Testing Strategy." The questions are also available on the companion CD if you prefer to review them in electronic form.

NOTE Answers

Answers to these questions and explanations of why each answer choice is right or wrong are located in the "Answers" section at the end of the book.

---

1. You intend to assign each developer on your team an entire set of classes to write. That is, they will not share the burden of writing any one class. Rather, they will be fully responsible for writing their assigned classes. You want to define a strategy that isolates the unit tests into groups so that developers can focus on just writing and executing their unit tests. What action should you take?

    A. Define separate unit testing projects for each project in your application.

    B. Create a single class file inside your Windows user interface project directory. Mark the class file as a test class. Define all your tests within this class file.

    C. Add a class to each project in your application. Mark each of these classes as a test class. Define the tests for the given project inside of each class file.

    D. Create a single test project for your application. Add classes to this project. Mark each class as a test class.

2. Which of the following are characteristics of unit tests? (Choose all that apply.)

    A. Unit tests help to confirm the execution of your user interface.

    B. Unit tests should be used for integration-testing your code.

    C. Unit tests help to document your code.

    D. A full set of unit tests result in the ability to do smoke (or regression) testing.

3. You need to define the items that you intend to test with unit tests. Which of the following items are good candidates for testing with unit tests? (Choose all that apply.)

    A. A business object

    B. Windows Forms usability

    C. Database access code

    D. Database table relationships

4. You have just delivered a new build of your application. Nearly all of the unit tests pass. You need to decide if the build is of a high enough quality to pass to the test team. What action should you take?

    A. Check the ratio of passing tests to failed tests. If this ratio is high, pass the build to the test team.

    B. Check the ratio of code tested to total logic. If this ratio is high, pass the build to the test team.

    C. Check the ratio of new code relative to existing code. If this ratio is low, pass the build to the test team.

    D. Check the ratio of code churn relative to stabilized code. If this ratio is low, pass the build to the test team.

5. You have a method that takes a short (Int16) for a parameter. The method uses this value in a calculation. You need to define a boundary check unit test for this method. Which of the following values should you use in your test? (Choose all that apply.)

    A. −32,768 and 32,767

    B. 0 and −1

    C. −32,769 and 32,768

    D. 1 and 9999

Lesson 2: Evaluating the Integration, Stress, and Performance Test Strategies

Once you have completed your unit tests and are satisfied with your code coverage, it is time to turn the code over to the test team. At this point the testers should verify that all the components work as a cohesive system. They need to determine the amount of stress that can be applied to the system before it breaks. And they should measure the application's performance. These test types fall inside the domain of testers. However, given their proximity to the application, developers and architects should give their input into these test plans. You should help define how these tests are created and what to expect in terms of results.

This lesson examines the input developers should provide to the application's testing strategy. We will first take a look at how to help with integration testing input. We will then cover both stress testing and performance testing. Finally, we will look at the test lab setup.

> **After this lesson, you will be able to:**
> - Define developer responsibilities relative to the integration testing strategy.
> - Provide feedback and guidance on the appropriate stress levels for your application.
> - Define key performance metrics that should be monitored during performance testing.
> - Provide feedback on the test lab setup used for load testing your application.
>
> **Estimated lesson time: 25 minutes**

Developer Responsibilities for Integration Testing

The primary goal of integration testing is the find and fix issues that are discovered when individual components are brought together to form a single cohesive solution. Typically, each module or component gets developed by one or more different developers. These developers write their components, unit test them, and rely on the overall application design to know that they are building toward a cohesive application. It is only when their components are integrated with the other components that this design will be fully tested and confirmed.

Exam Tip

The exam focuses on the responsibility of the developer (and not the tester). You need to be aware of this delineation of roles and focus your study efforts proportionately. This means spending more time on unit testing. Be aware of developer inputs to load, performance, stress, and integration testing.

When to Perform Integration Testing

Integration testing happens after unit testing is considered complete or nearly complete. Many testing methodologies suggest that integration testing, like unit testing, be a continuous process. Application components should be integrated as they are developed and unit tested. This is referred to as *continuous integration*.

An integration testing strategy that stresses continuous integration helps find bugs related to integration early in the software development life cycle. Integration tests found early in the process are easier (and cheaper) to fix. You invite big surprises in your project when you wait until the end to begin integration testing. These surprises come in the form of missed requirements, bad design, bad assumptions, and so on. The surprises are magnified because of their timing. If you wait until all code is complete there is typically a general feeling that you are nearly done. In this case, any surprise is big.

Big surprises cause schedule overruns and extra costs. In addition, if you had found the issue earlier, you would be less likely to repeat the root-cause issues that are causing the integration problems. All bugs, especially integration-related bugs, tend to cluster in specific areas of the application. They also tend to look alike. For example, if you find a bug related to calling a specific method, chances are good that this bug can be found over and over in the application—that is, unless this issue is found early and reported to the development team. This allows the team to take corrective action and not repeat the same mistake. This has the effect of reducing costs and increasing overall quality.

NOTE **Integration tests should always call real code (not stubs)**

A unit test may call an application stub or a simple interface. This allows a developer to continue working on his or her code while another developer finishes the interface stub. This is acceptable for unit testing. However, integration tests should always call the real code being tested through integration.

Integration testing leads to system testing. These two types of tests are often combined as the same, or similar, tests. This difference is that with continuous integration, each block or module of the application gets added to the overall system test. In this way, you end up testing the system as you build it. You add new modules or components to the already tested and verified system. Once you are code-complete with the system you should then have a full set of unit tests and a complete set of integration tests. You can run these integration tests as a group in order to verify the entire system (system testing).

IMPORTANT   System test against a production environment

Your final system test should be a comprehensive integration test that is performed in a testing environment that is identical to your production environment. In addition, once your code has been moved to the production environment, it is wise to perform this same test again (if possible) to ensure that the deployment was complete and successful.

Real World

Mike Snell

All process and risk management has its roots in someone getting burned. I recall a time not too long ago when testing was considered something that should be done at the end of a project. This was the standard waterfall approach. We would do envisioning and design followed by development of the entire system. At some time just before release, we would turn the code over to the testing team for their review.

This invariably led to the testing team finding things that went beyond simple bugs. This included issues with integration, problems related to the interpretation of requirements, and more. These issues often led to design changes that rippled through the code, which was meant to be complete. It also pitted the test team against the development team and made for big surprises when all along everyone thought things were running smoothly. As you can imagine, this caused a lot of pain and led to schedule delays and a lack of confidence in the process, team, and project.

We, like everyone else, got tired of this. Nowadays we have test plans at the start of the project, we do developer unit testing, we have continuous integration testing, we do iterative development with multiple user-acceptance tests along the way, and we leverage automated testing tools and test case management to help us deliver quality throughout the project. Too many people got burned, which forced the industry to change. The result should be better software in a more reliable, predictable process.

Black Box Testing

Integration testing is considered functional, or black box, testing. That is, testers write test cases that indicate a given input into the application. Based on this input, they make assumptions about the output of the application. The testers then execute these integration tests as a "black box." That is, they don't care about what happens inside the box (the code); they simply care that they get the expected results based on the given input.

Developers typically help the test team understand the expected black box behavior of their code. They do so by reviewing the test cases and providing example input and output. As an example, a test case might indicate that if a user executes a credit card transaction that fails, the user should be visually notified of the failure. When a developer reviews this test case, the developer may add to the test case that failed transactions get logged by the system. The tester may then add to the test case to verify this logging behavior.

NOTE   White box vs. black box testing

White box (or glass box) testing refers to testing that works with the application's internals (or code). White box testing is typically done by developers using the IDE, debugger, and unit tests. Black box testing is typically how testers interact with the application. They provide input to the box (through the application interfaces) and verify the output.

Quick Check

1. What is the definition and purpose of integration testing?
2. When should you perform integration testing?

Quick Check Answers

1. Integration testing is the process of testing various application elements together as a single solution that performs a business function. The purpose of integration testing is to ensure that the individual units of an application work together to form a complete solution.
2. Integration testing should be done continuously. As units are made ready by developers, they should be integrated into the build and tested with the other application elements.

Defining an Integration Test Plan

The integration test plan is typically the responsibility of the test team. They work to understand the system as a sum of its constituent parts. They then define test cases that will verify each of these parts as they are brought together to form bigger and bigger portions of the overall application. A *test case* represents a series of steps that a tester can execute (through manual or automated testing) to verify the proper application response based on input. Test cases work to verify the integration of components as well as the requirements of the system.

Developers play a role with the creation of the integration test plan. Specifically, they should help to verify the test cases. They should make sure that the test cases cover the many possible integration points, that they test the application on multiple levels, and that the test cases consider all aspects of the application. Finally, developers should provide details on the expected metrics and outputs of the various test cases. The following checklist should be applied to the test cases during developer review:

- Verify that the test cases include scenarios that test application communications. This includes communication from the user interface to the other layers of the application, communication from one application to another (application integration), communication between processes, communication to the database, and all other communication points.

- Ensure that the test cases define a series of inputs to the application interfaces along with expected outputs. This includes inputs and expected results for the user interface, the public methods, and any component or programming layer in your application.

- Verify that expected performance levels relative to application output response are set. This is not performance testing. Rather, it is meant to help testers understand when they encounter areas of the application that are not performing to anticipated metrics. These metrics might indicate a response time for a method's execution or the amount of time it takes to receive confirmation of an order or credit card, for example.

- Check that the test cases will be run several times to verify that the results are always consistent. This helps test for reliability.

- Verify that the test cases define specific bounds testing relative to integration. The test cases should cover a common or normal scenario. However, they should also define inputs that are at, or just outside, the boundaries of the expected input. It has been proven that errors often happen at these boundary levels.

- Verify that the plan is to test the components in a simulated production environment. Most unit tests are executed on a developer's machine. An integration test should run the application on real servers that mimic the production environment.

NOTE Finding similar integration defects

Developers should work closely with the test team, especially when defects are found. When an integration issue is identified, a developer can research a fix for the issue. The developer can also often search the rest of the code for similar defects. It is very likely that if you find one integration defect, the same or a very similar defect will be found in other places in the code.

Developer Responsibilities for Stress and Performance Testing

Stress and performance testing are all interrelated. In fact, they are often grouped together as a single test. This is because they each are meant to exercise a system through the simulation of user load. Stress and performance testing are derivatives of load testing. The goal of a load test is to ensure that your application behaves as required given the anticipated load. Stress testing tries to find the application's breaking point by applying additional load or stress until the application no longer behaves as intended. Performance, of course, is a key indicator in each of these tests. However, the primary goal of performance testing is to find the areas in the application that do not perform according to the required standards. This includes verifying your performance under normal load and during stress conditions.

The test team is responsible for conducting these tests. They define the application's test plan (including the load, stress, and performance test strategy) at the onset of the project. They then work to define test cases that simulate user interaction with the system. These test cases can be used to represent virtual users applying load to the system.

Developers and architects help to review the load test strategy and provide proper guidance. Some of this guidance is provided during requirement definition and system specification. For example, developers should be involved with defining what is reasonable with respect to performance metrics for the application. Developers should also verify that the test plans realistically simulate the actual user load for the application.

Testers should begin executing load tests as soon as complete modules of the application are available. In a Windows application, this usually means that a screen in the user interface is working as expected (connects to the middle tier, writes data to the database, and so on). This ensures continuous load testing as the application builds. The tests should be run in an environment that approximates the production infrastructure. The tests should again be performed as a group once the application reaches a release point like beta release. Visual Studio 2005 Team Test lets you automate these tests so they can be easily run over and over as the application evolves.

Load Testing

The goal of load testing is to make sure your application works under the expected concurrent user load. This expected load is typically defined at the beginning of the project. For example, you might have a requirement that your application be able to support up to 100 concurrent users. The test team needs to verify that the code deployed into the environment meets this requirement.

Testers can create automated load tests for the application. In a Windows application they can define a load based on a set of unit tests. This is the only means of creating automated load testing for Windows applications using the Visual Studio tools. Web developers, on the other hand, can create a Web test that is driven by the user interface. No similar tool exists inside of Visual Studio for Windows for developers (there are third-party solutions). Instead, you can use the unit test framework to define a special set of unit tests that can simulate user interaction with your system. These unit tests might not follow the standards described earlier. Instead, each test might perform an entire business function. You can then use the unit test framework to determine whether that business function succeeded. You can also use the load testing tools to execute that function to simulate user load.

Let's look at an example. Suppose you have a form in your application that allows a user to view and edit product detail information in your system. This form might instantiate multiple objects and call many of the methods associated with those objects. You would want to write a unit test for each business function exposed by this form. You might have one for all of the following: get a list of products, get product details, update product, and delete product. You might already have these unit tests or you might be able to wrap existing unit tests to define these business transaction–type tests. Once created, the tester can use these unit tests to define a load test. They might distribute this load by indicating that for every five times the product list is viewed, a product is updated. In addition, the load tests can be bound to data to help simulate varying user load.

NOTE   Application layering and Windows load testing

If you work to layer your application between user interface and presentation code, you should have an easier time creating these business transaction–type unit tests. Your user interface code in this case would not create objects directly. Instead it would defer to presentation code that knows how to respond when a user is requesting an action. This presentation code could then simply be unit-tested and would simulate the user load.

Again, in a Windows application you create load tests from one or more unit tests that represent the application's business functions, or test cases. The load tests define what test cases will be tested and how the user load will be simulated. The load test simulates multiple users making multiple requests of your application. Developers should review the load tests and provide their feedback. When reviewing a load test, you should consider all of the following:

- Make sure the load tests use test cases that simulate user load. This requires special attention when working with unit tests. You do not want to just load-test your unit tests. Rather, you want to create special-case unit tests that simulate a business transaction. This business transaction should have a similar representation from the user interface.

- The standard load test should be set to approximate the required number of concurrent users. It should not step up the user load. A stepped load adds more and more users to the application over time. This is great for stress testing. However, the standard load test should verify that the application works with the required user load.

- Ensure that the test cases are distributed to various sections of the application based on real user behavior. For example, if your users log 20 calls to get a single order, you should define a unit test for logging a call and another for taking an order. You should then set the test distribution ratio of the log call test to 95 percent and set the take order distribution to 5 percent.

- Verify that the load tests assume a standard set of think times. *Think time* represents the time a user spends thinking between requests. You can use recorded think times or a standard set. However, you do not want to turn off think times because this does not approximate real user load.

Stress Testing

The goal of stress testing is to discover the breaking point of your application in its current environment. Load testing confirms that the application meets the required safe working load. Stress testing pushes the application beyond this safe load and determines where and when it might fall down.

IMPORTANT   Stress testing for peak load

Stress testing can also be used to make sure your application can perform at a peak load. This is typically set to 1.5 times the expected load. Therefore, if you expect to support up to 1000 concurrent users, you should stress test for a peak load of 1500 concurrent users. The application should not break under this peak load. It might behave slightly poorer than expected, but it should continue to operate.

Stress testing should be performed by the test team. Load tests are leveraged for this purpose. A tester might simply copy a load test and apply a different concurrent load to simulate additional stress. When you review the stress tests you should follow the guidelines outlined in the load test section. In addition, developers should also consider how user load is stepped.

User load should be stepped up throughout the stress test. That is, the tests should start with a set of concurrent users. As time progresses, additional concurrent users should be added in steps. Each step should be run for a realistic duration (enough time for each user in the step to get through his or her activities at least once). Additional stress is applied to the application as load is stepped. It stands to reason that at some point, the application will be stressed to its maximum capacity and will either break or begin to respond too slowly. This breaking point might be defined as a combination of the number of rejected requests, the threshold for response times, a threshold for processor usage on the server, and so on.

Once you become aware of your application's stress levels, you can work to either modify the software or hardware to increase your capacity, or you can simply publish these levels to the support team. The support team should then monitor the application to make sure they take appropriate action if the load begins to trend up toward the breaking point.

Performance Testing

Performance testing is meant to verify that the application performs to the metrics defined during the requirements phase. For example, you might have a requirement that all business transactions are completed in less than four seconds. The performance testing can verify this metric and report on transactions that do not meet the requirement.

Testers execute the performance testing strategy. They do so again through the load tests. There are typically three levels of performance testing: single-user performance, performance under normal load, and performance at peak stress points. The first step allows the tester to ensure that the application behaves correctly for an individual user. Testers should expect this test to have the best performance. They then must verify that the application still performs as expected under normal load conditions. Finally, they should record how the application performs under a spike in load (typically 1.5 times the normal load). It might be acceptable to be 20 percent outside the bounds of the expected performance metrics under these peak conditions.

Developers should help the testers understand which performance indicators to monitor and what the acceptable range of results is. In most Windows applications you will want to monitor the load on the machine in terms of process and memory. You will also want to monitor the unit test itself in terms of average test execution time, failed tests, and so on. Finally, if you are testing against a database, you might want to monitor the processing performance of the database.

NOTE   **Define notification thresholds**

The Visual Studio tools allow a tester to define thresholds and receive warnings and errors when the application nears or surpasses these thresholds. This can save testers the eyestrain of looking over the many performance indicators on the output graphs.

> ## Quick Check
> - Explain the differences between load, stress, and performance testing.
>
> ## Quick Check Answer
> - Load testing tests that an application works as expected based on a target, concurrent user load pattern. Stress testing is meant to increase user load to find where, when, and how an application breaks under extreme stress. Performance testing is meant to verify performance metrics for the application in terms of execution and response times.

Evaluate the Test Lab Hardware and Software

When executing your load, stress, and performance tests, it's important to configure a proper testing lab so as not to interrupt normal business and to ensure the validity of your tests. Ideally, your tests should be executed on hardware identical to that of the production environment and on a quiet network. A *quiet network* is one that is dedicated to the test lab only. Business users don't rely on it, and it doesn't transmit their traffic (and thus potentially skew your test results). This lab needs to be instrumented to output the proper metrics. You also need a machine(s) to execute the tests and a machine to capture and report on the collected data.

The test lab setup should be the responsibility of the infrastructure team. Both the test team and the developers should provide input into the setup of this test lab. You should have a general understanding of how this lab should be set up so as to provide proper feedback into the plan.

Agents, Clients, and Controllers

A load test that requires the simulation of a large number of concurrent users requires a more complex setup. This is generally the case for Windows applications that are of a client-server or service-oriented nature. You can use Visual Studio Team Test to accomplish the setup and execution of large load scenarios.

In these scenarios there are four types of machines: clients, servers, agents, and a controller. These items are collectively known as the *rig* or *test rig*. You set up this rig in the test environment and use it to manage the load testing of your application. The following list gives details on each of the machine types in the rig:

- **Clients**   The client represents the machine of one or more testers. Testers use the client to create and edit tests and to view published test results.
- **Servers**   The server represents the test environment in which your application is deployed. This environment might include one or more application servers, a database server, a load balancer, and so on.
- **Agents**   Agents are computers that run your tests. Agents listen for commands from the controller. They then execute the intended test and pass their results back to the controller. Each agent can have only one controller at a given time. Agents execute load tests on multiple threads concurrently. Each thread represents a user. In addition, a typical load test will leverage multiple agents.
- **Controller**   The controller is a single, central computer that administers the agents and collects their results. The test lab typically has one controller. The controller passes the test to the agents for execution. It then tells them when to start and when to stop. The controller can apply a weight to various agents to help distribute the load. Agents with more horsepower should have a higher weight because they can handle a higher user load.

Test Lab Data

Most applications connect to one or more data sources. It's important that you consider these data sources when testing your application. For example, your performance results will vary if you run your tests against a test database with just a few thousand rows when you expect millions of rows in production. It's therefore imperative that you test your application using a realistic version of your production data. This can present a challenge to the test team. When reviewing the test lab setup, you should consider all of the following aspects of test lab data:

- Tests should be run against a test version of the database. They should not be run against your production database servers.

- Your test data should be of the same nature and size as the data in your production server. This includes tables, their relationships, their indexes, and their data. If, for example, you have a table with millions of rows, it is important to test your application against a similar table with the same number of rows.

- You should test a steady state of the database. This ensures that tests are all testing against a stationary target. They might run and change this steady state, but when they are rerun they should be rerun against the initial state of the database. This also helps you to compare results between tests.

- You should create an automated means to initialize your test database. Your tests should be easily executed and re-executed. Having this automation ensures that tests can easily set up and reinitialize the database, as required.

- Test data should not typically be an exact copy of your production data. Most databases store some sort of personal or confidential data, such as credit card information, user names and addresses, Social Security numbers, and so on. You should write a data extraction algorithm that either replaces this data with scrambled versions or removes it. Tools are available that can help you with this process.

Lab: Create a Test Plan

Testers are responsible for creating the test plan. However, if you really want to understand what should go into the test plan, it can be beneficial to create one yourself. Alternatively, you can work with the test manager on your team to create a test plan. You can use this lab section as an aid in defining a test plan that takes into account integration, stress, and performance testing.

▶ **Exercise: Define Your Project's Test Plan**

In this exercise you will define and document a test plan. You will want to apply the guidance provided in this chapter to an actual project with which you are working. Each step listed below describes an action you should take to define the test plan.

1. Determine how your project will be integration tested. Make sure you consider testing the communication between components and any third-party systems. Also, define a plan that includes continuous integration. This plan should define a process by which developers pass their complete, unit-tested components to the test team on a daily basis.

2. Help to write one or more test cases. When writing a test case, consider the requirements of the application. If you have previously defined use cases (or user scenarios), these will help greatly. You can take a user scenario and define a test that takes a common path through the system to enable a common user activity. You then define the input and

expected output from executing the test. The test cases should also define alternative scenarios, such as those that should generate errors.

3. Determine and document the expected load for the application in terms of concurrent users. If your application typically has peak load times, use the figure that represents the concurrent users whom you expect during these spikes.

4. Define a load test plan for the application. This load test plan should indicate test case, think time, and network distributions. These distributions should simulate the anticipated load.

5. Define a stress test plan that leverages the load tests to determine a breaking point in your application. Define a stepped user load that can be applied to the application in chunks of time. You should also define a threshold by which you determine the application to be broken (such as average transaction response time exceeds seven seconds).

6. Define an acceptable set of performance metrics for the application under load. For example, you might indicate that transactions return in under four seconds. You might also point out the transactions in the system that are allowed to take a little longer, such as processing an order or retrieving a report.

7. Define the test lab that should be used for load testing. This lab should identify hardware that approximates production. In addition, you should plan for a dedicated machine as a test controller. Finally, you should also plan to install test agents on multiple computers that can be used to simulate load.

8. Present the test plan to the project team. Get their feedback on your testing strategy. Presenting the strategy will really help to solidify these concepts in your mind.

Lesson Summary

- Integration tests verify that the application's parts work together as a cohesive solution.
- Load testing verifies that the application works as expected when the target, concurrent user load is applied.
- Stress testing uses the load tests to find the application's breaking point in terms of concurrent users. It also verifies how the application might perform under spiked load conditions.
- Performance tests are used to find any performance problems with the application under the expected load. Testers look for responses that are outside of a set performance threshold.
- Integration, load, stress, and performance tests are the responsibility of the test team. Developers should understand how these tests are performed and should be expected to provide feedback on, and input into, the tests.

- Integration, load, stress, and performance tests should be done continuously throughout the project as modules become available. This reduces surprises that cause schedule and cost overruns.
- Integration, load, stress, and performance tests are built from the test cases. The full set of integration tests often suffices to form the final system test.
- Integration, load, stress, and performance tests are all examples of black box testing. Test cases are run and the output is verified. Testers do not look inside the application (or box).
- Integration, load, stress, and performance tests should be performed in a test environment that approximates the production environment.
- Load, stress, and performance testing should be done on a quiet network using hardware that simulates the production environment.

Lesson Review

You can use the following questions to test your knowledge of the information in Lesson 2, "Evaluating the Integration, Stress, and Performance Test Strategies." The questions are also available on the companion CD if you prefer to review them in electronic form.

NOTE Answers

Answers to these questions and explanations of why each answer choice is right or wrong are located in the "Answers" section at the end of the book.

---

1. You want to verify that your application can support the target number of concurrent users without becoming unusable. This is an example of what type of testing?

   A. Bounds testing

   B. Load testing

   C. Performance testing

   D. Stress testing

2. Which of the following are true statements about integration testing? (Choose all that apply.)

   A. Integration tests, like unit tests, are white box tests and thus the responsibility of developers.

   B. Integration tests should define a series of inputs and expected outputs for each test case.

    C. Testers are advised to wait until all code for the application is complete prior to executing integration testing. This ensures that the entire system can be integration tested as a unit.

    D. Each integration test should succeed multiple times before the test is considered passed.

3. You determine that your application must support approximately 500 concurrent users. Approximately 400 of them come in through the local area network (LAN) and 100 through a virtual private network (VPN) tunnel. In addition, users of the application process one transaction for every 10 read requests. Which of the following describes how you should configure your load test? (Choose all that apply.)

    A. Define a load test that steps users in increments of 50 to a maximum of 750 users (or 1.5 times your expected load).

    B. Set your network distribution to 80 percent LAN and 20 percent VPN.

    C. Create two unit tests, one that simulates the processing orders test case and one that represents a shopper. Configure your load test distribution to be 90 percent for the shopper test and 10 percent for the load test.

    D. Create one unit test that mimics a shopper browsing for 10 products before placing an order. Configure your load test to use this unit test.

4. Your testers plan to conduct performance testing of your application. They wish to make sure that each transaction executes within the expected performance window. Which performance indicator should be monitored?

    A. Client processor utilization

    B. Database server memory utilization

    C. Number of requests per second

    D. Request response time

5. Your test lab includes clients, servers, agents, and a controller. Which of the following are the responsibilities of the test agents? (Choose all that apply.)

    A. The test agents execute multiple tests on multiple threads.

    B. The test agents provide test data to the test controller.

    C. The test agents provide performance data to the test controller.

    D. The test agents are used by testers to write and edit tests.

Chapter Review

To further practice and reinforce the skills you learned in this chapter, you can perform the following tasks:

- Review the chapter summary.
- Review the list of key terms introduced in this chapter.
- Complete the case scenario. This scenario sets up real-world situations involving the topics of this chapter and asks you to create a solution.
- Complete the suggested practices.
- Take a practice test.

Chapter Summary

- Developers create unit tests to automate the testing of an isolated unit (method or property) in an application. A good unit test should not require configuration; it should be atomic in nature; it should test a common application state; and it should test all method conditions, including errors, null values, and boundary checks. You can verify the percentage of code that your unit tests cover. You should target at least 70 percent coverage for your unit tests.

- Integration, load, stress, and performance testing are all black box tests performed by the test team. Developers need to be aware of how these tests should be performed in order to provide feedback to the test team relative to testing their code. Integration tests verify that components work together to create a complete solution. Load tests are used to verify the application's performance under load. You can leverage load tests to stress test and performance test your application.

Key Terms

Do you know what these key terms mean? You can check your answers by looking up the terms in the glossary at the end of the book.

- agent
- black box testing
- bounds check
- code coverage
- controller
- integration test
- load test
- performance test

- rig
- stress test
- test case
- test-driven development
- test plan
- unit test
- white box testing

Case Scenario

In the following case scenario, you will apply what you've learned about definining and evaluating a testing strategy. You can find answers to these questions in the "Answers" section at the end of this book.

Case Scenario: Evaluating a Testing Strategy

You work as a senior developer for a company that builds large industrial-size equipment for use in the nation's ports. You have been assigned the job of lead developer for the upcoming quote management project. This application will allow sales representatives and bid managers to configure equipment, services, shipping, and travel to arrive at a bid for prospective customers. Users will log on to the system, select a piece of equipment, set its many parameters and options, and then calculate a cost for the customer. Shipping costs will also be calculated based on location of the customer, the equipment, its configuration, and available shipping channels. Finally, users will need to configure installation costs, training costs, and associated travel for service personnel.

Interviews

You attend a meeting to discuss testing scenarios with the project stakeholders. This meeting is facilitated by the test manager. The following is a list of the project stakeholders interviewed and their statements:

- **IT manager** "We will need to extract data from a number of disparate data sources. The latest product configuration data is inside our engineering database. You will have to connect to our shipping partner's data to get their information. I believe they have exposed a set of Web services for this. You will have to write an interface to house training and service rates. We will need an administrative interface to modify this data as required. Travel costs are sent to us in a daily feed from our corporate travel vendor. This is a file-based extract."

■ **Sales manager** "We have five sales reps now. We do about 10 quotes per week. Each quote requires a lot of product configuration knowledge. It would be nice to have this built into the system. I have been told that the product configuration data represents tens of thousands of rows of data. We need to find a way to ensure that this data is accurate because our customers are relying on it.

"When a bid is created, all relevant parties need to review it. This means that engineering, service, training, shipping, and I (sales manager) all need to review and approve the bid before a final copy can be sent to the customer. In addition, we all will be reviewing and reporting on these quotes on a weekly basis.

"The sales reps must be able to get a quote relatively quickly; sometimes a rough quote is given over the phone. The site should allow them to get in and retrieve this information with response times under five seconds."

■ **Project manager** "Management has their eye on this project. We need to show more than just status; we need to show quality measures as we build the application. This means we need to know which tests are passing and which are failing. We need to report on these tests every week."

■ **Development manager** "We have one senior developer on the project to bring everything together. This developer works in my department and reports to me. We are going to rely on the engineering support team to provide a developer for their work. We will be using our shipping vendor to build and help test their piece. Each of these developers will be working independently on his or her part of the system. These items need to get integrated at the end of the project.

"The architect has already stubbed out the integration interfaces. This will allow the developers to code against these dummy interfaces and get a response.

"We want to use automated unit testing on this project. It would be nice if developers were forced to have 75 percent or greater code coverage for their unit tests prior to checking in their code."

■ **Test manager** "We have only a single full-time tester at the moment. This resource has already been working with the business analysts to define test cases for the application. In addition, the tester was recently given training in Visual Studio Team Test."

■ **Application support manager** "Right now we get a lot of complaints about slow network traffic on Monday mornings when the weekly report updates come out. I hope this slowdown doesn't affect this application.

"Some of our users are working from home. Some of these users have a dial-up connection, some DSL, and some cable modems. I would say that 90 percent of the users are on the LAN and 10 percent are connected by other means."

Test Plan

After the test planning meeting the test manager sends you a draft copy of the test plan. You are supposed to provide your input and feedback. The following is a high-level overview (or summary) of the test plan's content:

- **Unit testing**   Each developer will be responsible for unit testing his or her code. We will ask developers in the weekly status meeting what percentage of their code is covered by unit tests. We plan to create a single central project for managing developer unit tests.

- **Integration testing**   We will leverage the use cases to define our test cases for integration. These use cases cover how a user successfully interacts with the application. An integration test should be considered successful if no error conditions are thrown.

- **Test case unit tests**   We will create a single transactional unit test that mimics a sales rep entering a bid in the system and that bid flowing through the review and approval process (sales manager, engineering, services, shipping, and training). We will then bind this unit test to a data source that contains customers, a set of related bid data, and approval information.

- **Load testing**   The application will be load tested through an automated load test that runs a steady load of users for one hour. The networking of these users will be set to LAN. Standard think times will be used between requests.

- **Stress testing**   The application will be stress tested using the load test defined in the load test plan. The stress test will be set to run overnight for four hours.

- **Performance testing**   We need to verify that the transactions executed by the sales reps return in under five seconds. To verify this information, we intend to monitor the average transaction time.

- **Test lab**   The test lab will be built on a quiet network. The test team's PCs will be used for running test agents. These agents should run only early in the morning, at lunch, or at night. The test controller will be put on a separate PC. The database schema will be built on a test database server. Real data will not be available until nearly the end of the project. Therefore, the tester will add at least 10 rows of data to each table. Once this initial data is loaded into the database, the testers and developers will be able to manipulate as they need to.

Questions

While thinking about your feedback to the test plan, answer the following questions.

1. What changes would you suggest to the unit test plan?
2. How many concurrent users should the test team target for load testing? For stress testing?
3. What are the advantages and disadvantages of the tester defining a single transactional unit test for the application?

4. How should the load test strategy be modified to better test the actual way in which users will use the application?

5. What thresholds should you suggest for testers when monitoring the server during load testing?

6. What improvements would you suggest relative to the integration test plan?

7. How would you suggest improving the test lab definition in order to better simulate your actual environment?

Suggested Practices

To help you successfully master the exam objectives presented in this chapter, complete the following tasks.

Evaluating a Unit Testing Strategy

If you have never written unit tests before, you should execute the tasks in Practice 1. This will help you better master this objective. If you have spent some time writing unit tests but want to make sure you understand them, try Practice 2. If you can demonstrate unit testing to another developer, you should be ready for this objective when it comes to the test.

- **Practice 1** Find some old code. You can use any code whose language you are familiar with. The important thing is that you are not up to speed on this code. Examine the methods in the code. Try to design unit tests as pseudo code for these old methods. Think about what tests you will want to create and how you will segment these tests.

- **Practice 2** Persuade a manager or another team member to consider unit testing. That person will have questions and wonder why unit testing is important. Sometimes explaining this to another person out loud helps you to solidify these concepts in your mind. This applies the adage "If you want to really learn something, try teaching it to someone else."

Evaluation of Integration, Stress, and Performance Testing Strategies

Most developers don't spend a lot of time testing. However, to become a professional developer it's important that you understand this key aspect of the software development life cycle. The following practices will help you master this objective.

- **Practice 1** Spend an hour with a tester for your application. Watch the tester work; understand the tester's process. This can help you better understand how to deliver input into the testing of your code.

- **Practice 2**   Create a set of transactional unit tests for your application. These unit tests should cover a business function and simulate a use case.
- **Practice 3**   Use the tests you created during Practice 2 to define load, stress, and performance tests using Visual Studio 2005 Team Test (you can download a trial version if you don't own it). Evaluate the results. Watch the tests perform against your application.

Take a Practice Test

The practice tests on this book's companion CD offer many options. For example, you can test yourself on just the content covered in this chapter, or you can test yourself on all the 70-548 certification exam content. You can set up the test so that it closely simulates the experience of taking a certification exam, or you can set it up in study mode so that you can look at the correct answers and explanations after you answer each question.

MORE INFO   Practice tests

For details about all the practice test options available, see the section titled "How to Use the Practice Tests" in this book's Introduction.

Chapter 13
Creating Development Tests

Software quality starts with software developers. They have the chance to make the largest impact on the overall quality of an application, the duration of the testing schedule, and the cost of finishing a product. Developers can be a key quality asset—provided they are given the time and tools to test their code as they write it. When developers deliver high-quality code to the test team, testing cycles are shrunk due to less verification and retesting, fewer builds are needed, and there is less rework. In addition, when testers aren't simply trying to get code to work, they are free to focus on a higher degree of application testing. For example, they can review the application for usability, requirements verification, user acceptance, load, performance, and more.

This chapter is the second chapter in this book on testing and stabilizing an application. The prior chapter, "Define and Evaluate a Testing Strategy," dealt primarily with testing strategies and plans. This chapter covers the tasks that developers undertake to create and perform development-specific tests. We will first examine how you design and implement good unit testing. We will then take a look at the process of doing a code review. Next, we will walk through how to perform integration testing of components. Finally, we will end the chapter by looking at how you should approach troubleshooting, evaluating, and fixing bugs in your application.

Exam objectives in this chapter:
- Design a unit test.
    - Describe the testing scenarios.
    - Decide the type of assertion tests to conduct.
- Perform integration testing.
    - Determine if the component works as intended in the target environment.
    - Identify component interactions and dependencies.
    - Verify results.
- Consume a reusable software component.
    - Test the identified component based on the requirements.
- Perform a code review.

■ Resolve a bug.

❑ Investigate a reported bug.

❑ Reproduce a bug.

❑ Evaluate the impact of the bug and the associated cost and timeline for fixing the bug.

❑ Fix a bug.

Lessons in this chapter:

■ Lesson 1: Creating Effective Unit Tests

■ Lesson 2: Performing a Code Review

■ Lesson 3: Evaluating and Fixing a Bug

Before You Begin

To complete the lessons in this chapter, you should be familiar with developing Microsoft Windows applications with Microsoft Visual Studio 2005 using Visual Basic or C#. In addition, you should be comfortable with all the following tasks:

■ Creating a Windows Form-based application. This includes an understanding of the Windows controls and the programming model and methods associated with Windows Form-based applications.

■ Understanding object-oriented development concepts.

■ Reading and working with class diagrams.

■ Developing a business object (class) that contains domain-specific properties and methods.

■ Working with attributes in your development.

■ Working with the unit testing framework in Visual Studio 2005 to write and execute tests.

IMPORTANT   To complete the practice exercises for Lesson 1, you will need to have Microsoft Visual Studio 2005 Team Edition for Software Developers installed on your computer. This is available as part of Visual Studio 2005 Team Suite. You can download a free 180-day trial version of Visual Studio 2005 Team Suite from *http://www.microsoft.com/downloads/details.aspx?FamilyId=5677DDC4-5035-401F-95C3-CC6F46F6D8F7&displaylang=en*. You will need to uninstall Visual Studio 2005 Professional to install Visual Studio Team Suite on the same computer.

Real World

Mike Snell

The release-to-testing milestone is more than just a date on a calendar—at least it should be. I have worked on a few projects where developers frantically wrapped up their code and made sure it compiled in order to get it to the test team by a target date. This typically made the project manager and some of the stakeholders happy. They were able to convince themselves that things were on time and okay. This happiness, however, was often short-lived.

The code got stuck in a seemingly endless testing cycle. Testers went back and forth with the developer. Each time, the developer added more and more code to the features under the guise of bug-fixing. The testing cycle stretched on and on and pressure was applied to get the code fixed and released. This process turned out to be more costly in terms of time and money than having the developer simply finish the code and ensure its quality before it was released to the test team. This was because the process interrupted the standard coding process that a developer would follow and instead interjected testers, users, build managers, releases, and more into the developer's coding process. It was a very frustrating experience for all involved; it wasted a lot of time and a lot of money.

In more recent years, we have tried to root out this problem. The way to do this is through tools like the unit testing framework, code coverage analysis, and the static code analyzer. Code reviews have also helped; it is one thing to get the status from a developer and another to actually verify this status. We no longer allow developers to code in a vacuum (or provide simple percent-complete status). Instead, they must periodically demo their code (typically weekly) in order to demonstrate status. This has helped create a culture of honest assessment of progress and quality. The result has allowed us to save money and reduce risks on our projects.

Lesson 1: Creating Effective Unit Tests

The unit test framework built into Visual Studio 2005 allows you to define tests for your code as you write your application (or, in the case of the test-driven approach, before you build it). The namespace *Microsoft.VisualStudio.TestTools.UnitTesting* provides the classes and features that make this possible. This lesson examines those features. We start by reviewing the basic structure of a unit test. We then look at some best practices for creating a unit test using test cases, requirements, and the unit test plan (see the previous chapter for more details on unit test plans). We also examine the developer's role in integration testing. We finish the lesson by walking through a detailed lab where you create a set of unit tests and verify key integration points for your code.

After this lesson, you will be able to:

- Understand how to read a use case to better write test cases.
- Understand the elements of a test case and why test cases help developers.
- Review and refine your unit tests based on the unit test plan and the test cases.
- Determine which unit test assertions to make.
- Write an effective set of unit tests for key methods in your application.
- Understand the developer's role with regard to integration testing.

Estimated lesson time: 60 minutes

The Basic Structure of a Unit Test

It makes sense to start by looking at an existing simple unit test. This will help you recall the makeup and structure of a unit test. Recall that a unit test is code that you write to call the methods and properties of your application. Inside the unit test you first make a call to a method or property; you then execute a number of assertions to confirm the results of your call. For example, you might assert that the return value of a given method be true based on the parameters you pass into the method. If this assertion fails, the unit test fails. Let's examine how this example looks as code.

An Example Application

In this chapter we will work with an application that tracks billing against projects executed for clients. We will call this application *Project Tracking and Billing*. It will help us illustrate our testing examples. The example application has a few straightforward classes that make up the domain model. Figure 13-1 illustrates these classes. The principal class here is *Invoice*. It represents the invoice or bill to a given client account for a project. Note that this class also exposes the *Account* that is being billed and the *Project* on the bill.

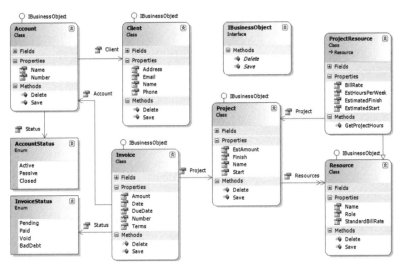

Figure 13-1   The sample business objects.

Now that we have established the domain model, we will define some user activity around creating an invoice. These actions will be contained in a separate static class that we will call *InvoiceManager*. Figure 13-2 shows this class and its methods. We have defined methods for retrieving the details of a given invoice, changing the status of the invoice, getting a list of invoices, and more. We will use a number of these methods and the domain model to illustrate example tests throughout this chapter.

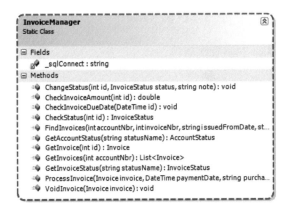

Figure 13-2   The *InvoiceManager* class.

An Example Unit Test

Let's start by looking at a pretty simple example. This will help you recall the basic structure of unit tests. In this example we are testing the *GetBooking* method of the *BookingManager* class. The code below shows our example test.

```vb
' VB
<TestMethod()> _
Public Sub GetInvoiceTest()
  Dim invoiceNumber As Integer = 123456
  Dim inv As Invoice = InvoiceManager.GetInvoice(invoiceNumber)
  Assert.AreEqual(invoiceNumber, inv.Number)
End Sub
```

```csharp
// C#
[TestMethod()]
public void GetInvoiceTest() {
  int invoiceNumber = 123456;
  Invoice inv = InvoiceManager.GetInvoice(invoiceNumber);
  Assert.AreEqual(invoiceNumber, inv.Number);
}
```

Notice that the test is decorated with the *TestMethod* attribute class. This indicates to the unit test framework that this method is a test and should be executed during a test run. Inside the actual test we simply retrieve a known invoice. We then use the *Assert* class to make sure the *Invoice* instance that is returned is what we requested. If this assertion and the test method succeed, the test succeeds. If anything fails, the test is considered to have failed. Of course this is a basic example. You might add a few more assertions to round out the test. You might also create a few additional tests for the *GetInvoice* method. However, this should serve as a basic review of a unit test. We will build on this in the coming sections as we examine a few approaches to writing effective unit tests.

A Primer on the Unit Test Framework

The classes and methods in the unit test framework can be found in the *Microsoft.VisualStudio.TestTools.UnitTesting* namespace. This includes key attribute classes that are used to decorate classes and methods for execution by the framework. Table 13-1 lists the common attribute classes you need for unit testing.

Table 13-1 The Attribute Classes in the *UnitTesting* Namespace

Attribute Class	Description
TestClass	Use this class to decorate an entire class as containing unit tests.
TestMethod	Use this class to indicate that a given method is a unit test. A test method must not return a value and can't take parameters. However, you may bind data to a test method.

Table 13-1   The Attribute Classes in the *UnitTesting* Namespace

Attribute Class	Description
TestInitialize	Use this class to indicate that the framework should run the decorated method prior to each unit test. This is useful if you need to reset the database between each test, for instance.
TestCleanup	Use this class to indicate that the decorated method should be run after each test.
ClassInitialize	Use this class to indicate that the decorated method should be run once prior to any tests being run.
ClassCleanup	Use this class to indicate that the decorated method should be run once after all tests have been executed.
ExpectedException	Use this class to indicate that the decorated method should expect a certain exception as the result.

The *Assert* class inside the *UnitTesting* namespace is another class that is used in nearly all of your unit tests. This class contains a number of methods that allow you to evaluate given conditions for true and false values. If the result of any assertion in your test is false, your unit test is considered failed. Table 13-2 lists the key assertion methods (all static) for unit testing.

Table 13-2   Assertion Methods of the *Assert* Class

Attribute Class	Description
AreEqual / AreNotEqual	Tests whether or not two values are equal to each other
AreSame / AreNotSame	Tests whether or not two objects are the same object
IsInstanceOfType / IsNotInstanceOfType	Tests whether or not an object is of a specified type (or class)
IsNull / IsNotNull	Tests whether or not an object contains a null reference
IsTrue / IsFalse	Tests whether or not a condition is true

Create Test Cases

Your unit tests will be more effective at finding problems with your code provided they are thought out and planned in the context of actual requirements and usage scenarios. In the previous chapter we worked to define the unit test strategy. Here we will look at creating effective unit tests based both on this strategy and on the requirements of the application.

It is helpful to think of the unit testing strategy as the guideline for how your company writes unit tests. What is not defined by this guideline is a method for ensuring that your unit tests cover the actual usage patterns of the application. That is the domain of the test case. This section explores how to write a test case to drive effective unit tests.

Evaluate Methods and Properties That Warrant More Testing

Most developers create a set of unit tests for every method and property in their application. This task is made easy by the *Generate Unit Test* feature of Visual Studio 2005. With this feature you can quickly set up unit tests to make sure your property "gets" and "sets" operate correctly. You also get a one-for-one set of test methods to application methods. This makes for a simple, straightforward approach to creating unit tests from existing code. It makes sure the majority of your code gets run, it serves as a good regression (or smoke) test, and it helps you meet your code-coverage requirements.

However, every application has a set of methods that really defines the functionality of the application. These principal methods typically result in the most bugs, the highest percentage of coding effort, and the most rework. Therefore it's important to identify these methods and plan additional testing around them. In addition, you need to understand how other developers might use them. You also need to explore how users will work with them to get their tasks accomplished. This additional planning, focused on a key set of methods, will result in a big benefit to the quality of the application.

Thankfully, these methods are typically easy to recognize in your application. They are usually the methods that do the principal work of the application, such as executing transactions and saving data. The following list presents an ordered overview of what methods to look for when identifying principal methods that require additional unit test focus (listed from highest importance to lowest):

1. Methods that execute transactions on behalf of the user or the system. These methods often have the most business logic built into them (and can therefore be very complex). Some examples include updating inventory, processing an order, and processing a credit card.

2. Methods that save or update data. Examples of these methods include saving a customer's profile or updating product information in your system. Again, these methods are usually full of business logic.

3. Methods that check, verify, and validate data. Often this logic is embedded in the methods mentioned previously. However, sometimes this logic is pulled out in order to allow many methods to access the same set of rules. Examples might include verifying a customer's credit limit, checking inventory on hand, or rejecting invalid input.

4. Methods that delete data or cancel a transaction. Examples include deleting a customer's shipping address or canceling a customer's order.

5. Methods that execute a search and retrieval of data. These methods have less business logic but can require special attention to make sure that the right data is retuned based on many, often varied, parameters. Some examples include retrieving orders based on a set of criteria or finding a set of customers with similar buying behaviors.

6. Other methods that retrieve data based on a set of parameters. Some examples include getting a customer's order, finding the customer's profile, or returning the customer's transaction history.

7. Lower on the list are methods that set and get specific properties or methods that do very simple tasks. Some examples include setting a customer's name, updating the customer's password, or calculating the tax on an order.

You can use this list to help score the methods in your application. Those methods that fall in the top three or four categories should be identified and targeted for additional unit testing based on usage scenarios.

For example, if we were to apply this list to the *InvoiceManager* class in our example (refer back to Figure 13-1 and Figure 13-2), then we should be able to identify those methods that require the most focus in terms of developing unit test cases. The methods would be categorized as follows (parentheses indicate the category number from the previous list): *ProcessInvoice* (1), *ChangeStatus* (1), the *Save* (2) methods on each business object, *CheckInvoiceAmount* (3), *CheckInvoiceDueDate* (3), *CheckStatus* (3), the *Delete* (4) methods on each business object, *VoidInvoice* (4), *GetInvoice* (6), and *GetInvoices* (6). From this information we can then determine that the methods *ProcessInvoice*, *ChangeStatus*, *Save*, *CheckInvoiceAmount*, *CheckInvoiceDueDate*, and *CheckStatus* most likely warrant additional focus in terms of unit testing and test case development. The other methods should still be tested. However, the further you move down this list, the more likely that the unit tests for these methods will be simple and straightforward and therefore will not require as much attention. Using this method allows you to concentrate your efforts where they will get the most results.

Understand How Your Code Will Be Consumed

You need to also consider how other developers might use your code. This information will factor into how you develop your tests cases for your unit tests. Developers might consume your code in many ways. For example, you might be writing a library or base class that other developers will rely on for their development. You might also be writing methods that will be called by other components out-of-process. You need to understand these and similar cases so that you can factor them into your test cases and thereby add tests to ensure these conditions.

Review (or Create) Use Case Scenarios

Another input to your test case is the use cases or user scenarios. A *use case* is a description of tasks centered on a common user goal. The use cases and related requirements directly influence the code you write. Use cases are often developed to support the requirements (before code gets written). They are typically created by a business analyst and reviewed by the user community (or their representatives). An application designer or architect then works with this information to design the system. Developers then code to this design.

It is important that your unit testing loops back to the original set of user scenarios to make sure the code meets the goals set forth by the user community. In addition, these use cases often describe how a bit of code will be used and thus tested. You can often drive your test cases directly from the use cases.

An Example Use Case Scenario

Let's take a look at a use case to help you better understand how use cases can provide input into your test cases. Our Invoice Manager sample application contains a use case that defines a standard user scenario for processing an invoice. This use case might look as follows:

1. User opens the application and logs in to the system as a member of the Accounts Payable group.
2. User selects the menu option Process Invoice.
3. The system presents the user with the Find Invoice screen.
4. User enters search details to find the invoice the user wishes to process. Search details might be the account number, invoice number, invoice date range, client name, or client phone number. User selects the Find Invoice option (button).
5. System searches for invoices that match the search criteria. System displays invoices that match the search criteria to the user.
6. User reviews the invoices and selects the invoice he or she intends to process.
7. System displays the full details of the invoice to the user in invoice print format.
8. User enters processing information for the invoice. Processing information includes payment date, purchase order (PO) number or check number, status (Paid or Paid Partial), and any processing notes. User selects the Process Invoice option (button).
9. System validates the user's input.
10. The system updates the Project Tracking and Billing application with the new information.
11. System records the invoice in the accounting system by calling a common interface to this third-party system. The accounting system returns a confirmation number.
12. System updates the invoice with the confirmation number.
13. System displays the invoice processing confirmation number to the user.

By examining this use case you can determine just how users will be working with your code. This will give you a better understanding of how you should approach defining your test cases and related unit tests. For example, you can see that from this use case users might execute a number of searches for an invoice prior to finding the one for which they are looking. For this reason, you might create a unit test for finding invoices and then decide to bind this unit test to a series of data that represents a number of search combinations. In addition, you will want to write test cases that define searching for invoices and then processing them according to this use case. We will look at writing the test cases in a moment.

Alternate (Edge) Cases

A good use case defines the standard path to the common user goal. It then defines a number of alternate paths or what are commonly called *edge cases*. Edge cases are alternate paths the user might take to reach the same goal, tasks they might do that are out of the ordinary success path, options they might have, and so on. A good use case writer (and, coincidentally, a good tester) knows how to look for, and find, edge cases. It is here, within these edge cases, where your unit tests can really benefit. The edge cases will define additional tests you might not have considered. Let's look at an example.

In our previous use case, a user has searched for invoices and then selected an invoice to process. However, it is possible that during the time it took to process the invoice it might have changed or already been processed by another user. The use case should account for this alternate path. Typically, alternate use cases might look like the following:

▶ **Alternate Case: Selected Invoice Has Changed (or Already Been Processed)**

1. Use case follows standard path through step 9.
2. System verifies that the invoice has not changed before processing.
3. If the invoice has changed, the system cancels the user's transaction.
4. System indicates to the user that the invoice has changed and presents the new details to the user.

You can see that this alternate path is a good edge case to think about as a developer and as a tester. A developer wants to plan for this occurrence with code; a tester wants to confirm how the system will react under such an edge case. If one or both don't do their job it will be the user who will eventually find out the consequences of double-processing an invoice. Therefore, you will want to be sure to write a unit test that simulates this edge case to confirm that you have accounted for it.

Let's look at another alternate case. This edge case examines what should happen if the system fails to finish processing the invoice. Recall that the invoice process also included the third-party accounting system. We want to make sure that this process is transactional; that is, the project tracking and billing system should be updated only if the accounting system is also updated. You will want to be sure to look for (or write) these important edge cases as well. The following is an example:

▶ **Alternate Case: Accounting System Transaction Fails**

1. Use case follows standard path to step 10.
2. The transaction to update the accounting system fails.
3. The system cancels the update to the project tracking and billing application (step 10).
4. System indicates the details of any failure to the user.

We should also consider an alternate case for when the confirmation number fails to write back to the invoice. An example of this follows:

▶ **Alternate Case: Confirmation Number Transaction Fails**

1. Use case follows standard path to step 11.

2. The transaction to update the invoice with the accounting system confirmation number fails.

3. This error is most likely the result of the database being down. If so, the transaction can't be committed or cancelled. In addition, the accounting system has already been updated. Therefore, the system should log this condition; a help desk ticket with the details of the problem should also be generated.

4. Finally, the system should show the details of the failure to the user, indicating that the data might be corrupt.

When you write these edge cases, it's important to remember that you're writing a use case and not a design specification. You can see from this last alternate use case that the author is trying to think through possible conditions that might arise and how they might get handled. The system could fail in the project system update, the accounting system update, or when the confirmation number is writing back to the invoice. You will want to write test cases to simulate each of these scenarios. This will ensure that you know exactly how your code will behave when these edge cases are encountered.

It can often be helpful to have your testers review the use cases to help develop error cases. Testers will dig up many potential error scenarios with your code. Of course, often it's not practical to define a use case for every potential error condition. In fact, your users might not see the benefits of reviewing, refining, and signing off on all of these use cases; they might only be confused by the many additions to the standard path. In this event you may opt to draw a line between real user scenarios and these alternate, error cases. You can then save the latter for the test cases. We will now look at just how use cases and test cases can work together to drive higher quality.

Define Test Cases from Use Case Scenarios

Test cases and use cases are very similar. For this reason you can usually derive one from the other. Use cases are written first, so it makes sense that you typically move from a use case to a test case. Recall that a use case describes a set of tasks focused on a common user goal. A test case is typically also focused on a common user goal. However, a *test case* describes a set of tasks (and related data) that a tester can execute to verify a use case, requirement, or feature of the system.

BEST PRACTICES **Developers should take advantage of test cases**

Testers write test cases. However, developers should use these test cases to help them write better unit tests. For this reason, developers should review, and provide their input for, the test cases. They should also consume them and use them to increase the quality of their code.

The Structure of a Test Case

A test case typically has many elements. It may define the state of the system prior to the beginning of the test case. It may also describe the inputs and expected outputs for the test case. A good test case includes explicit instructions on how to work with the system, what data to enter, and what to expect as the result. The following are all potential elements of a test case:

- **Name**   You should define a name for your test case. This is usually in relation to the use case or feature that is being tested by the test case. For example, "Process an Invoice" or "Check Invoice Status."

- **Description of the functionality tested**   You want to describe what features or use cases you intend to verify with the test case. You can use a reference here to an existing definition of requirements or use cases.

- **System state/dependency**   You should describe the system state prior to the test being run. For instance, if you need to reset the test data in the database prior to running the test, you would indicate that here. You may also define dependencies for the given test case (such as, another test case must execute first). You should try to minimize dependencies because they often block test cases from being executed.

- **Test case/steps**   You should describe the detailed steps for executing the test case. You want to indicate to the user how to launch the application, how to navigate to the feature, what data entry elements to use, and so on. You will also want to link these steps to the data input definitions (see below).

- **Data input**   You should define the data that should be used for the test. Here you define data that is relevant to your test. If you are defining a success-path test, you will want to define common data as input. If, on the other hand, you are writing a bounds-check test case, you will want to enter data at and outside the bounds of the expected input.

- **Expected result**   This is your hypothesis or desire for the test to succeed. For example, you might expect that no errors are thrown and that you can verify the data has been input, changed, or deleted. You might also have negative tests where the expected result is that a user can't complete an action such as logon or accessing secure data.

You might wish to define a standard, successful test case as you would with a use case; you can then define derivatives for each edge, or alternate test case. These variants might use the same tasks as those listed in the test case but require different data. They also typically reset the definition of your expected result.

A test case should also include execution information. The execution information should represent a running log of who ran the test case and the results. Of course, Visual Studio Team Foundation Server and Team Test provide this type of functionality. You can also keep a log manually, using a Microsoft Excel spreadsheet or similar application.

Quick Check

1. What attribute class is used to indicate to the testing framework that a given method is a unit test?
2. What is the purpose of the *Assert* class in the unit testing framework?
3. On what type of methods should you focus most of your unit test efforts?
4. What is a use case and why is it important to unit testing?

Quick Check Answers

1. The *TestMethod* attribute class is used to decorate methods as unit tests.
2. The *Assert* class exposes a number of static methods that are used to verify whether conditions evaluate to true or false (success or failure) for a unit test.
3. You should be sure to execute a number of varied unit tests on methods that execute important transactions on behalf of users. You should also consider those methods that save and update data.
4. A use case describes a series of actions a user may take around a common goal. Use cases feed test cases. Test cases can be used to write better unit tests.

An Example Test Case

Let's take a look at a sample test case. We will use the use case defined previously for booking an excursion as the basis for the test case. Recall that the test case will describe how the user interacts with the system to verify the use case and requirements. This means that some design (and possibly some code) has been done between use case and test case. We will assume this design for now; please don't think we are overlooking this important task. Rather, we are focusing on just the test case here. The Process an Invoice test case might look as follows:

- **Name**   Process an Invoice.
- **Description of functionality tested**   This test case verifies the requirements associated with a user processing an invoice through the Project Tracking and Billing system. These requirements are defined in the requirement set and the Process Invoice use case.
- **System state/dependency**   The database should be loaded with only the standard test data prior to test execution. The test data includes data rows for the following entities: account, project, invoice, resource, and client.

   This test case is also dependent on the logon test case. The logon test case should be executed prior to executing this test case.
- **Test case/steps**   To execute this test case, complete the following steps:

   Precondition: Tester has logged on to the system as a member of the Accounts Payable group.

1. Select the Process Invoice option on the main navigation menu.

2. Verify that you are now on the Find Invoice screen and that this screen lists the following data entry points for search: account number, invoice number, invoice date range, client name, and client phone number.

3. Enter parameter values as found in the data input file (see below) into the Find Invoice screen. You will want to repeat this step for each input and verify the search results.

4. Click Find Invoice.

5. Verify that you are now on the Select An Invoice screen and that it displays only invoices that match your search request (for the client, "Test Client"). Also verify that each invoice has the status of Pending.

6. Select one of the invoices from the data input and click Process Selected Invoice.

7. Verify that you are now on the Process Invoice screen and that you are being shown a copy of the invoice. The system should also be showing you the invoice processing data fields: Payment Date, PO/Check Number, Status, and Processing Notes.

8. Enter the data input details for the processing data fields: Payment Date, PO/Check Number, Status, and Processing Notes.

9. Click Process.

10. Verify that you are in now on the Invoice Processed screen. The invoice number should match the original invoice number and you should now have an invoice confirmation number.

11. Try to process the same invoice by following these steps again. Confirm that the invoice is not available for processing.

12. Execute an invoice search (see the Find Invoice test case) and confirm the status of the invoice as Paid.

13. Search the accounting application for the invoice and confirm that it is also paid in that system.

- **Data input**   The success-path test data can be found inside the Process Invoice Test Data.xls file. This data contains a variety of possible test invoices and data elements to try and execute.

- **Expected result**   This test case should execute without error. Each row listed in the test data should result in a processed invoice.

Alternate (Edge) Test Cases

The prior test case example defines the standard path to test the process invoice transaction. The tester also needs to consider alternate paths (or edge cases) that do not have such successful results. These alternate paths should have a different set of expectations to pass. The alternate paths might derive from the alternate paths defined for the use cases or might originate as error cases here in the test case. We will use our use case definition from earlier to create our alternate test cases. The following are examples of alternate test cases to our sample test case above:

■ **Alternate case**   Selected Invoice Changed.

■ **Description of functionality tested**   Tests that users can't process an invoice that has changed during their processing.

■ **System state/dependency**   The system should be initialized to the testing data prior to execution.

■ **Test case/steps**   To execute this test case, complete the following steps:

1. Begin processing an invoice. Stop before committing the processed invoice (step 9).
2. Open another instance of the application on another machine.
3. Find the same invoice.
4. Open the invoice for edit.
5. Change the invoice status to BadDebt.
6. Return to the first instance of the application and click Process.
7. Verify that the invoice did not successfully process. This information should be indicated on the screen. You should also be presented with an error message and be asked if you'd like to open the invoice as stored in the database for edit.

■ **Data input**   You can use the success-path test data as defined in the main test case.

■ **Expected result**   This test case should execute as described. The invoice should not successfully process.

Let's define another alternate test case. Remember the second edge case from the use cases? It examined what would happen if the system failed to finish processing the invoice by writing the confirmation number to the database. The tester should verify whether the entire process is a transactional unit or that data might possibly get out of sync between the two systems. The following is an example test case around this scenario:

■ **Alternate case**   Process Invoice Transaction Fails.

■ **Description of functionality tested**   Confirms that the update to the accounting system and the invoice update in the Project Tracking and Billing application are transactional and log appropriately when a failure occurs.

■ **System state/dependency**   The system should be initialized to the testing data prior to execution.

■ **Test case/steps**   To execute this test case, complete the following steps:

1. Begin processing the invoice as defined in the prior test case.
2. When entering the invoice number to test, use the bad accounting invoice test number (invoice not in the accounting system) as defined in the test data.
3. Finish processing the invoice as described previously.

4. Verify that the invoice processing failed. The status of the invoice should not have been updated in either system.

■ **Data input**   Use the bad invoice number data row.

■ **Expected result**   This test case should execute as described. The invoice should not process; an error should be logged to the event log.

We will use this test case and its alternates in the lab. You will build actual unit tests for a portion of the sample application. This will allow you to see how use cases fuel test cases and how good test cases make your unit tests strong and your code of higher quality.

Perform Integration Testing

Before you start the lab, let's first take a look at the developer's role in integration testing. As we discussed in the prior chapter, integration testing is not the responsibility of developers. Developers should write their code and their unit tests, perform code reviews, and fix bugs. All other tasks in the testing process are the primary responsibility of the test team. However, as you've seen with other parts of the testing process, some integration testing will naturally fall into your hands. The question is, Where do you draw the line between developer integration testing and the role of the tester? The following list will help you to draw that line. Each item defines an integration test task that falls to the developer.

■ **Verify your API**   Developers need to verify that the code they write that is intended for the consumption of other developers has an appropriate public application programming interface (API). This API will be used for communication and integration with other components in the system. You should therefore check your API against the published specification. If this is a new version or upgrade, you should verify that you have not broken compatibility with prior versions.

■ **Verify deployment**   Developers need to make sure the components they release to the build will operate as intended in the target environment. If, for instance, you write your code against version 2.0 of the .NET Framework and the target environment is running 1.1, you have a problem. The same holds true for other settings, such as the Web server's metabase. A good configuration management plan will help you define the target environment. You might then create a virtual PC that mimics this target. This will allow the developers to test-deploy in the target environment before breaking a build.

■ **Identify dependencies**   Developers need to check their code for dependent items. This includes items that might be used at the integration level, as well as dependent libraries running on the development machine. Your goal is to release your software to the build without breaking the build or another developer's code. Therefore, if your public interface requires an object you wrote that is not part of the test build, you can't release your code. In addition, if you depend on a third-party component, you need to make the build manager aware of this before releasing your code.

Developers should strive to run their code in a development environment that is similar to test and production. This will help confirm integration at the environment level. Once they verify the results, they can hand their code off to the test team for the full integration test. Taking this extra step will result in fewer broken builds and less rework for the team.

Exam Tip

The exam deals mostly with the developer's role in integration testing. It's not designed to test knowledge of the tester's process. In addition, when studying for the exam, you should focus mostly on integration tests that verify calls to external libraries.

Lab: The Test Case Translated to Unit Tests

The test case as described sounds like a set of manual tests to be executed by a tester sitting at a PC. If that tester has test tools, he or she might record these steps to build out an automated test; the tester might then bind the test to a data source. That is the principal intention behind a test case: to define a test for a tester. However, as you look through the test case with the eye of a developer looking to write unit tests, you see that the test case leads to unit tests that you should write. In this lab you will walk through each step of the test case and examine how the test case might influence the unit tests you write.

IMPORTANT   Beyond simple unit tests

The tests you write in this lab go beyond the standard tests you should write for each class and method in your application. You still need to write those. However, this lab assumes that those tests have been written and that you are now reviewing the test case for additional input into your unit tests.

Lab Setup

This lab builds a set of unit tests from exercise to exercise. You will want to start with Exercise 1 and move through each exercise in sequence. You can follow the steps below to set up the lab on your machine.

NOTE   Sample application

The application used in the lab is simply a sample designed to illustrate effective unit testing. You should not use this sample as a model to create production-ready applications. This sample takes shortcuts and makes assumptions that only sample applications should.

---

1. Use Windows Explorer to copy either the C# or VB version of this lab to your computer. The lab can be found in the following path: Chapter 13\Lesson1*<language>*\Exercise1-Before. Separate sample projects are provided for before and after each exercise; however, you can continue to work with your open project for all six exercises.

2. You will need SQL Express running on your machine for this lab. The lab contains two file-based SQL Express databases. One is called ProjectTracking.mdf; the other is TestData.mdf. These files are in the LessonDatabaseFiles folder. You will want to copy this folder to your machine as well. Note the path on your machine where you copied the folder. You will use this path to update the connection strings used by the projects in this application.

3. You need to reset the connection string in the testing project to point to the database file on your machine. You can do that by opening the App.config file in the InvoiceManagerUnitTests project. This class contains a configuration element called *InvoiceManagerConnectionString*. You should set the attribute *connectionString* to point to your copy of the database. This configuration element looks as follows (line breaks have been added to fit the format of the book, but you should put the *<add>* element on a single line):

```
<connectionStrings>
  <add name="InvoiceManagerConnectionString"
    connectionString="DataSource=.\SQLEXPRESS;AttachDbFilename=
    'C:\Chapter13\Lesson1\LessonDatabaseFiles\
    ProjectTracking.mdf';Integrated Security=True;User Instance=True" />
</connectionStrings>
```

4. You need to replace the "C:\..." in the prior example with the actual path to the .mdf file you copied to your machine as part of step 2.

5. Follow the same procedure (steps 3 and 4) for the App.config file in the SetupProjectTrackingDb project. Point this configuration to the TestData.mdf file.

6. If you are using any of the completed projects (and not just walking through the exercise), you will also have to modify another connection string. At the beginning of the Exercise 3 process, you define an attribute for the FindInvoicesTest method to bind the test to data. Modify the connection string in the InvoiceManagerUnitTests project for the FindInvoicesTest method to point to the same database file, TestData.mdf.

▶ **Exercise 1: Create a *ClassInitialize* Method to Load the Test Data**

In the System State/Dependency section of the test case, notice that the test case requires the database to have standard test data loaded prior to execution. You should consider doing the same thing prior to your unit tests executing. This will ensure that you are always running tests against the same standard view of the data. In this exercise you will write a method to reset the test database when the test class is initialized by the unit test framework.

1. Navigate to the test class called InvoiceManagerTests inside the InvoiceManagerUnitTests project. This file contains the unit tests for the methods in the InvoiceManager class (inside the BusinessDomain project).

2. Add a static method called *ClassInit* to the *InvoiceManagerTest* class. This will serve as your class-initialize method.

3. Add code to the *ClassInit* method to reset the ProjectTracking database. We have created a static method inside of the *ResetTestData* class (found in the SetupProjectTrackingDb project) to do so. This method parses the database script file ResetDbScript.sql and executes this script against the database. If you have never written a test file like this, you might want to peruse this code. The call to this method is as follows:

```
SetupProjectTrackingDb.ResetTestData.ResetTestDatabase()
```

4. Add the *ClassInitialize* attribute class to the *ClassInit* method. This will tell the testing framework to run this method prior to running tests. Your method should now look as follows:

```
' VB
<ClassInitialize()> _
Public Shared Sub ClassInit(ByVal testContext As TestContext)
  SetupProjectTrackingDb.ResetTestData.ResetTestDatabase ()
End Sub
```

```
// C#
[ClassInitialize()]
public static void ClassInit(TestContext testContext) {
  SetupProjectTrackingDb.ResetTestData.ResetTestDatabase ();
}
```

5. Run the test class a couple of times and verify the database to make sure everything is working as expected. You will have to add a simple test in order to run the *ClassInit* method. The following simple code should suffice:

```
' VB
<TestMethod()> _
Public Sub SomeTest()
End Sub
```

```
// C#
[TestMethod()]
public void SomeTest() {
}
```

▶ **Exercise 2: Create a Unit Test to Find Invoices**

In steps 2 through 4 of the sample test case the tester is being asked to enter search criteria to find invoices and verify the returned data as accurate. You should consider a unit test to do the same. In this exercise you will write a unit test to call the method that returns invoices based on search information; you will then test the data that is returned.

1. Navigate to the test class called InvoiceManagerTest inside the InvoiceManagerUnitTests project. This file contains the unit tests for the methods in the InvoiceManager class (inside the BusinessDomain project).

2. Open the InvoiceManagerTest file and create a new test method called *FindInvoicesTestEx2* as follows:

```
' VB
<TestMethod()> _
Public Sub FindInvoicesTestEx2()
End Sub
```

```
// C#
[TestMethod()]
public void FindInvoicesTestEx2() {
}
```

3. Add code to your unit test to call the *FindInvoices* method of the *InvoiceManager* class. This method returns a collection of Invoice objects based on a set of search criteria. The parameters for the method include (in order): accountNbr, invoiceNbr, issuedFromDate, issuedToDate, clientName, clientPhoneNumber. The code to call this method should look something like the following:

```
' VB
Dim invoices As List(Of Invoice)
Dim clientNameSearch As String = "Client B"
invoices = InvoiceManager.FindInvoices(0, 0, Nothing, Nothing, clientNameSearch,
Nothing)
```

```
// C#
List<Invoice> invoices;
string clientNameSearch = "Client B";invoices = InvoiceManager.FindInvoices(0, 0, null,
null, clientNameSearch, null);;
```

4. You now need to add code to the test method to verify the results of the call. This requires you to know something about the test data. You can then search through the results to verify what was returned. The following is an example of this unit test:

```
' VB
<TestMethod()> _
Public Sub FindInvoicesTestEx2()
  'find invoices
  Dim clientNameSearch As String = "Client B"
  Dim invoices As List(Of Invoice)

  invoices = InvoiceManager.FindInvoices(0, 0, Nothing, Nothing, clientNameSearch,
Nothing)

  'should only be 2 matching invoices in the database
  Assert.IsTrue(invoices.Count = 2, "Wrong number of invoices found in test data")

  'verify the details of each invoice
  For Each i As Invoice In invoices
    Assert.IsNotNull(i, "Invoice cannot be null")
    Assert.IsTrue(i.Number > 0, "Invoice number must be greater than zero")
    Assert.IsTrue(i.Account.Client.Name = clientNameSearch, "Client name must match
search")
```

```
          Next
        End Sub

        // C#
        [TestMethod()]
        public void FindInvoicesTestEx2() {

          //find invoices
          string clientNameSearch = "Client B";
          List<Invoice> invoices;
          invoices = InvoiceManager.FindInvoices(0, 0, null, null, clientNameSearch, null);

          //should only be 2 matching invoices in the database
          Assert.IsTrue(invoices.Count == 2, "Wrong number of invoices found in test data");

          //verify the details of each invoice
          foreach (Invoice i in invoices) {
            Assert.IsNotNull(i, "Invoice cannot be null");
            Assert.IsTrue(i.Number > 0, "Invoice number must be greater than zero");
            Assert.IsTrue(i.Account.Client.Name == clientNameSearch,
              "Client name must match search");
          }
        }
```

5. Run the test and verify that it passes. You can try to change an invoice in the database for the given client (or add a new one). This should cause the test to fail. This test validates both the code and the test data.

▶ **Exercise 3: Bind Data to a Unit Test**

Step 3 of the test case tells the tester to try multiple parameter values and verify the results. Both the use case and the test case indicate that this method will be called several times with varying parameters. You should therefore use this step as a trigger for binding data to the unit test you created in the previous exercise. In addition, you should verify that your test data includes bounds check data for each parameter.

1. Navigate to the test class called InvoiceManagerTest inside the InvoiceManagerUnitTests project. This file contains the unit tests for the methods in the InvoiceManager class (inside the BusinessDomain project).

2. Open the test method called FindInvoicesTest that you created previously.

3. Recall that the test case discussed verifying multiple search options. You should create another version of the test case and bind it to a set of test data. The test data should include input parameters and expected results. The lab has such test data already created for your use. This test data is found in the TestData.mdf file inside the folder Chapter 13\Lesson1\LessonDatabaseFiles. You can review this test data. It works with the database reset script to make sure you have the right assumptions. Figure 13-3 provides an overview of this test data.

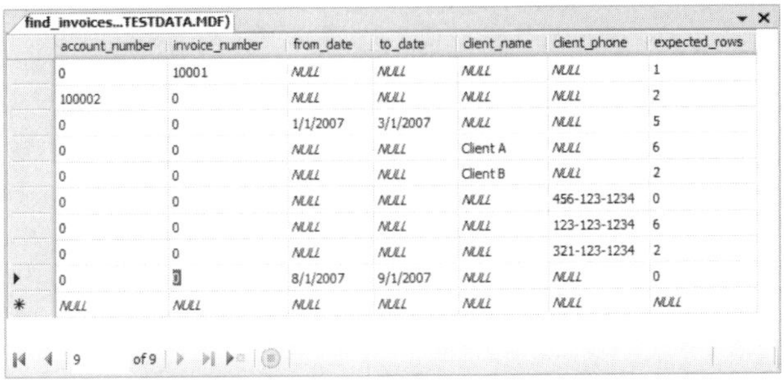

account_number	invoice_number	from_date	to_date	client_name	client_phone	expected_rows
0	10001	NULL	NULL	NULL	NULL	1
100002	0	NULL	NULL	NULL	NULL	2
0	0	1/1/2007	3/1/2007	NULL	NULL	5
0	0	NULL	NULL	Client A	NULL	6
0	0	NULL	NULL	Client B	NULL	2
0	0	NULL	NULL	NULL	456-123-1234	0
0	0	NULL	NULL	NULL	123-123-1234	6
0	0	NULL	NULL	NULL	321-123-1234	2
0	0	8/1/2007	9/1/2007	NULL	NULL	0
NULL	NULL	NULL	NULL	NULL	NULL	NULL

Figure 13-3   TestData.mdf.

4. You now need to modify your unit test definition to use this test data as a data source. You do so using the *DataSource* attribute class of the unit testing framework. This class takes a provider, connection string, default table, and access method. You will want to set the provider to *System.Data.SqlClient*, the connection string to the TestData.mdf file (with the correct path on your computer), the table name to find_invoices_unit_test_data, and the access method to *DataAccessMethod.Random*. The following is an example of this code (line breaks have been added to fit the format of the book, but you should put the *<TestMethod>* element on a single line):

```
' VB
<TestMethod(), DataSource("System.Data.SqlClient",
  "Data Source=.\SQLEXPRESS;AttachDbFilename=
  'C:\Chapter 13\Lesson1\LessonDatabaseFiles\TestData.mdf';
  Integrated Security=True;User Instance=True",
  "find_invoices_unit_test_data", DataAccessMethod.Random)> _
Public Sub FindInvoicesTest()
```

```
// C#
[TestMethod()]
[DataSource("System.Data.SqlClient",
  @"Data Source=.\SQLEXPRESS;AttachDbFilename=
  'C:\Chapter 13\Lesson1\LessonDatabaseFiles\TestData.mdf';
  Integrated Security=True;User Instance=True",
  "find_invoices_unit_test_data", DataAccessMethod.Random)]
public void FindInvoicesTest()
```

5. You should now connect the parameters to your unit test to the bound data. You can do so through the *DataRow* method of the TestContext object. The following code is one example of binding a variable to a data source element:

```
' VB
Dim acctNbr As Integer = _
  Integer.Parse(TestContext.DataRow("account_number").ToString())
```

```
// C#
int acctNbr = int.Parse(TestContext.DataRow["account_number"].ToString());
```

6. Finally, you should rework your assertions to use this new data. If, for example, a given search criterion is used, it should be verified in the results. In addition, it is a good idea to add messages to each assertion so you know you have more data when a test fails. Your final unit test should look as follows (line breaks have been added to fit the format of the book, but you should put the *<TestMethod>* element on a single line)::

```vb
' VB
<TestMethod(), DataSource("System.Data.SqlClient",
  "Data Source=.\SQLEXPRESS;AttachDbFilename=
  'C:\Chapter 13\Lesson1\LessonDatabaseFiles\TestData.mdf';
  Integrated Security=True;User Instance=True",
  "find_invoices_unit_test_data", DataAccessMethod.Random)> _
Public Sub FindInvoicesTest()
  'define parameters
  Dim acctNbr As Integer = Integer.Parse( _
    TestContext.DataRow("account_number").ToString())
  Dim invNbr As Integer = Integer.Parse( _
    TestContext.DataRow("invoice_number").ToString())

  Dim fromDate As String = Nothing
  If TestContext.DataRow("from_date").ToString() <> "" Then
    fromDate = TestContext.DataRow("from_date").ToString()
  End If

  Dim toDate As String = Nothing
  If TestContext.DataRow("to_date").ToString() <> "" Then
    toDate = TestContext.DataRow("to_date").ToString()
  End If

  Dim clientName As String = Nothing
  If TestContext.DataRow("client_name").ToString() <> "" Then
    clientName = TestContext.DataRow("client_name").ToString()
  End If

  Dim clientPhone As String = Nothing
    If TestContext.DataRow("client_phone").ToString() <> "" Then
    clientPhone = TestContext.DataRow("client_phone").ToString()
  End If

  Dim expectedRows As Integer = Integer.Parse( _
    TestContext.DataRow("expected_rows").ToString())

  'find invoices
  Dim invoices As List(Of Invoice)
  invoices = InvoiceManager.FindInvoices( _
    acctNbr, invNbr, fromDate, toDate, clientName, clientPhone)

  'checked the number of returned rows
  Assert.IsTrue(invoices.Count = expectedRows, _
    "Wrong number of invoices found. Expected: {0}, Found: {1}.", _
    expectedRows.ToString(), invoices.Count.ToString())
```

```vb
    'verify the details of each invoice against the search criteria
    For Each i As Invoice In invoices
      Assert.IsNotNull(i, "Invoice cannot be null")
      Assert.IsTrue(i.Number > 0, _
        "Invoice number must be greater than zero")

      If acctNbr > 0 Then
        Assert.IsTrue(i.Account.Number = acctNbr, _
          "Account number must match search")
      End If

      If (invNbr > 0) Then
        Assert.IsTrue(i.Number = invNbr, _
          "Invoice number must match search")
      End If

      If (fromDate <> Nothing) Then
        Assert.IsTrue(i.Date >= DateTime.Parse(fromDate), _
          "Invoice date must be greater than search date (from)")
      End If

      If (toDate <> Nothing) Then
        Assert.IsTrue(i.Date <= DateTime.Parse(toDate), _
          "Invoice date must be less than search date (to)")
      End If

      If (clientName <> Nothing) Then
        Assert.IsTrue(i.Account.Client.Name = clientName, _
          "Client name must match search")
      End If

      If (clientPhone <> Nothing) Then
        Assert.IsTrue(i.Account.Client.Phone = clientPhone, _
        "Client phone must match search")
      End If
    Next
End Sub
```

```csharp
// C#
[TestMethod()]
[DataSource("System.Data.SqlClient",
  @"Data Source=.\SQLEXPRESS;AttachDbFilename=
  'C:\Chapter 13\Lesson1\LessonDatabaseFiles\TestData.mdf';
  Integrated Security=True;User Instance=True",
  "find_invoices_unit_test_data", DataAccessMethod.Random)]
public void FindInvoicesTest() {
  //define parameters
  int acctNbr = int.Parse(
    TestContext.DataRow["account_number"].ToString());
  int invNbr = int.Parse(TestContext.DataRow["invoice_number"].ToString());
```

```
            string fromDate = null;
            if (TestContext.DataRow["from_date"].ToString() != "") {
              fromDate = TestContext.DataRow["from_date"].ToString();
            }
            string toDate = null;
            if (TestContext.DataRow["to_date"].ToString() != "") {
              toDate = TestContext.DataRow["to_date"].ToString();;
            }
            string clientName = null;
            if (TestContext.DataRow["client_name"].ToString() != "") {
              clientName = TestContext.DataRow["client_name"].ToString();
            }
            string clientPhone = null;
            if (TestContext.DataRow["client_phone"].ToString() != "") {
              clientPhone = TestContext.DataRow["client_phone"].ToString();
            }
            int expectedRows = int.Parse(
              TestContext.DataRow["expected_rows"].ToString());

            //find invoices
            List<Invoice> invoices;
            invoices = InvoiceManager.FindInvoices(
              acctNbr, invNbr, fromDate, toDate, clientName, clientPhone);

            //checked the number of returned rows
            Assert.IsTrue(invoices.Count == expectedRows,
              "Wrong number of invoices found. Expected: {0}, Found: {1}.",
              expectedRows.ToString(), invoices.Count.ToString());

            //verify the details of each invoice against the search criteria
            foreach (Invoice i in invoices) {
              Assert.IsNotNull(i, "Invoice cannot be null");
              Assert.IsTrue(i.Number > 0,
                "Invoice number must be greater than zero");

              if (acctNbr > 0) {
                Assert.IsTrue(i.Account.Number == acctNbr,
                  "Account number must match search");
              }
              if (invNbr > 0) {
                Assert.IsTrue(i.Number == invNbr,
                  "Invoice number must match search");
              }
              if (fromDate != null) {
                Assert.IsTrue(i.Date >= DateTime.Parse(fromDate),
                  "Invoice date must be greater than search date (from)");
              }
              if (toDate != null) {
                Assert.IsTrue(i.Date <= DateTime.Parse(toDate),
                  "Invoice date must be less than search date (to)");
              }
              if (clientName != null) {
                Assert.IsTrue(i.Account.Client.Name == clientName,
```

```
          "Client name must match search");
      }
      if (clientPhone != null) {
        Assert.IsTrue(i.Account.Client.Phone == clientPhone,
          "Client phone must match search");
      }
    }
  }
}
```

7. Run the unit test and view the results. The test should pass. You can view the details of the passed test to see how each bound data row behaved. To view test details, double-click the test in the Test Results pane of Visual Studio. Figure 13-4 shows an example of the test results.

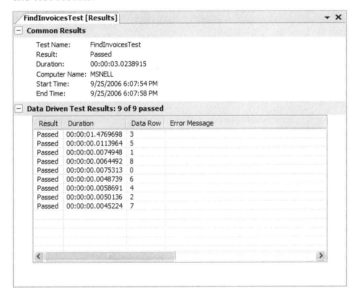

Figure 13-4   Data bound unit test results.

▶ Exercise 4: Verify Invoice Processing

Steps 8 through 10 of the test case represent the actual booking process. This process requires a set of processing information and executes a transaction. In this exercise, you will write a unit test to verify that the standard invoice processing works without exception and returns a confirmation number.

1. Navigate to the test class called *InvoiceManagerTest* class.

2. Create a new test method called *ProcessInvoiceTest* as follows:

```
' VB
<TestMethod()> _
Public Sub ProcessInvoiceTest ()
End Sub
```

```
// C#
[TestMethod()]
  public void ProcessInvoiceTest() {
}
```

3. Write a unit test to process a pending invoice and verify the results through assertions. Your unit test might look the following:

```
' VB
<TestMethod()> _
Public Sub ProcessInvoiceTest()

  'get a pending invoice to process
  Dim invoices As List(Of Invoice)
  invoices = InvoiceManager.FindInvoices( _
    0, 10008, Nothing, Nothing, Nothing, Nothing)
  Dim invoice As Invoice = invoices(0)

  'verify
  If invoice.Number <> 10008 AndAlso _
    invoice.Status <> InvoiceStatus.Pending Then
    Assert.Inconclusive("Bad invoice")
  End If

  'process the invoice
  Dim confirmation As String = InvoiceManager.ProcessInvoice( _
    invoice, New DateTime(2007, 2, 1), "POXCV678", InvoiceStatus.Paid, _
    "received payment", "msnell")
  Assert.IsNotNull(confirmation)
  Assert.IsTrue(confirmation.ToString().Length > 0)

  'get the invoice again and check its status
  invoices = InvoiceManager.FindInvoices(0, 10008, Nothing, _
    Nothing, Nothing, Nothing)
  Dim invoice2 As Invoice = invoices(0)
  Assert.IsTrue(invoice2.Number = 10008)
  Assert.IsTrue(invoice2.Status = InvoiceStatus.Paid)

End Sub
```

```
// C#
[TestMethod()]
public void ProcessInvoiceTest() {
  //get a pending invoice to process
  List<Invoice> invoices;
  invoices = InvoiceManager.FindInvoices(0, 10008, null, null, null, null);
  Invoice invoice = invoices[0];
  //verify
  if (invoice.Number != 10008 && invoice.Status != InvoiceStatus.Pending) {
    Assert.Inconclusive("Bad invoice");
  }
   //process the invoice
   string confirmation = InvoiceManager.ProcessInvoice(
```

```
        invoice, new DateTime(2007,2,1), "POXCV678", InvoiceStatus.Paid,
        "received payment", "msnell");

    Assert.IsNotNull(confirmation);
    Assert.IsTrue(confirmation.ToString().Length > 0);

    //get the invoice again and check its status
    invoices = InvoiceManager.FindInvoices(
        0, 10008, null, null, null, null);
    Invoice invoice2 = invoices[0];
    Assert.IsTrue(invoice2.Number == 10008);
    Assert.IsTrue(invoice2.Status == InvoiceStatus.Paid);
}
```

4. Run the unit test. The test should pass. We will build on this test in the next exercise.

▶ **Exercise 5: Process Invoice Accounting Transaction Fails**

In this exercise you will write a unit test similar to the one you wrote in Exercise 4. However, this unit test covers the second edge case, Process Invoice Transaction Fails. In this test case you will try to process an invoice that has the same invoice number as the bad accounting invoice test number. This test is part unit test and part integration test. You are testing the ProcessInvoice method, but you are making sure that its call to the external accounting system works as expected (even on error).

1. Navigate to the test class called InvoiceManagerTests.

2. Copy and paste the ProcessInvoiceTest.

3. Rename the second copy of the test ProcessInvoiceTestBadInvoiceNbr.

4. Modify all references to the good invoice number, 10008, to the bad invoice number: 10003.

5. When you run this test, it fails. However, it's doing what it's supposed to do—return an exception. You can tag the test method as expecting the exception. This will cause the test to pass. The following is an example:

```
' VB
<TestMethod(),
ExpectedException(GetType(AccountingSystemFailureException))> _
Public Sub ProcessInvoiceTestBadInvoiceNbr()
```

```
// C#
[TestMethod()]
[ExpectedException(typeof(AccountingSystemFailureException))]
public void ProcessInvoiceTestBadInvoiceNbr()
```

▶ **Exercise 6: Process the Same Invoice Twice**

Step 11 of the test case describes a situation in which an invoice might be processed twice. Your UI might not allow this, but you can't count solely on the UI. Chances are good you probably also would not typically consider this case in your unit tests. In this exercise you will write a unit test that verifies that the invoice can be processed only once.

1. Navigate to the test class called InvoiceManagerTest.
2. Copy and paste the ProcessInvoiceTest.
3. Rename the new copy of the test ProcessInvoiceTwiceTest.
4. Modify this test to process the same trip invoice twice. Also, set the *ExpectedException* attribute for the test method. The following code is an example:

```vb
' VB
<TestMethod(), ExpectedException(GetType(ApplicationException))> _
Public Sub ProcessInvoiceTwiceTest()

    'get a pending invoice to process
    Dim invoices As List(Of Invoice)
    invoices = InvoiceManager.FindInvoices(0, 10001, Nothing, _
      Nothing, Nothing, Nothing)
    Dim invoice As Invoice = invoices(0)

    'process the invoice once
    Dim confirmation As String = InvoiceManager.ProcessInvoice( _
    invoice, New DateTime(2007, 2, 1), "POXCV678", InvoiceStatus.Paid, _
      "received payment", "msnell")

    Assert.IsNotNull(confirmation)
    Assert.IsTrue(confirmation.ToString().Length > 0)

    'process the invoice a second time
    confirmation = InvoiceManager.ProcessInvoice( _
    invoice, New DateTime(2007, 2, 1), "POXCV678", InvoiceStatus.Paid, _
      "received payment", "msnell")

    Assert.IsNotNull(confirmation)
    Assert.IsTrue(confirmation.ToString().Length > 0)
End Sub

// C#
[TestMethod()]
[ExpectedException(typeof(ApplicationException))]
public void ProcessInvoiceTwiceTest() {

    //get a pending invoice to process
    List<Invoice> invoices;
    invoices = InvoiceManager.FindInvoices(0, 10001, null, null, null, null);
    Invoice invoice = invoices[0];

    //process the invoice once
    string confirmation = InvoiceManager.ProcessInvoice(
    invoice, new DateTime(2007, 2, 1), "POXCV678", InvoiceStatus.Paid,
      "received payment", "msnell");
    Assert.IsNotNull(confirmation);
    Assert.IsTrue(confirmation.ToString().Length > 0);

    //process the invoice a second time
```

```
confirmation = InvoiceManager.ProcessInvoice(
  invoice, new DateTime(2007, 2, 1), "POXCV678", InvoiceStatus.Paid,
  "received payment", "msnell");
Assert.IsNotNull(confirmation);
Assert.IsTrue(confirmation.ToString().Length > 0);
}
```

5. Run the test. Notice that it fails. It does not return an exception. This means we have not trapped for this condition in the code. You would now have to consider adding code to check for this condition. Figure 13-5 shows the failed test results.

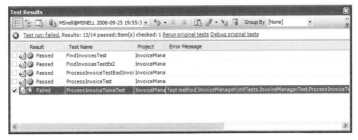

Figure 13-5   Failed test results.

Lesson Summary

- Visual Studio 2005 ships with the unit testing framework. The classes in this framework are defined inside the namespace Microsoft.VisualStudio.TestTools.UnitTesting.

- You define a unit test by marking methods with the *TestMethod* attribute class.

- You can define a method to execute prior to executing your tests using the *ClassInitialize* attribute. You can also create a method to run between each unit test using the *TestInitialize* method.

- The *ExpectedException* attribute class indicates that the unit test should result in a given exception in order to be considered a success.

- You use the static methods of the *Assert* class to determine success or failure of your unit test. This class has assertions for checking Boolean values (*IsTrue*, *IsFalse*), check for null values (*IsNull*, *IsNotNull*), verifying if objects are the same (*AreSame*, *AreNotSame*), and more.

- You should write one or more unit tests for every method and property in your application. However, for methods that are key transactions of the system you should spend time reviewing the use cases and test cases. You should then use this information to write additional unit tests for these methods.

- A use case is a set of tasks focused on a common user goal. Use cases are a great start to writing test cases. Pay special attention to the alternate, edge cases in the use case. These are things that you need to test that are always obvious.

- A test case is a set of steps, related data, and expected results centered on a common user goal. A tester uses a test case to verify the functionality of the system.
- Integration testing is the responsibility of testers. However, developers should verify their API, define their dependencies, and identify component interactions. They should run their code in a test environment. Once they have verified the results, they can hand off to the test team.

Lesson Review

You can use the following questions to test your knowledge of the information in Lesson 1, "Creating Effective Unit Tests." The questions are also available on the companion CD if you prefer to review them in electronic form.

NOTE Answers

Answers to these questions and explanations of why each answer choice is right or wrong are located in the "Answers" section at the end of the book.

---

1. You want to make sure the code you wrote to reset the database is run before each unit test is executed. What action should you take?
    A. Add the *TestCleanup* attribute to the database reset method.
    B. Add the *TestInitialize* attribute to the database reset method.
    C. Add the *ClassCleanup* attribute to the database reset method.
    D. Add the *ClassInitialize* attribute to the database reset method.

2. You need to write an assertion to verify that two objects are identical. Which of the following code segments should you choose?
    A. Assert.AreEqual(obj1, obj2)
    B. Assert.IsTrue(obj1, obj2.TosString())
    C. Assert.IsInstanceOfType(obj1, typeof(obj2))
    D. Assert.AreSame(obj1, obj2)

3. You have been given an extra couple of days to write some additional unit tests. Based on their description, which of the following methods should you consider for additional unit test work? (Choose all that apply.)
    A. A method to return the descriptive details of a product
    B. A method that updates inventory data after an order has been processed
    C. A set of properties that allows you to access configuration information for your application
    D. A method (used by multiple applications) that calculates the estimated shipping date and price for an order

4. Which of the following statements describe a test case? (Choose all that apply.)

    A. A test case is written to flush out the requirements of the system. It does so by describing a set of steps centered on a common user goal.

    B. A test case is typically written by a tester and derived from a use case.

    C. A test case is written to help developers write unit tests.

    D. A test case includes steps, data, and expected results.

5. Which of the following integration testing tasks is the responsibility of developers? (Choose all that apply.)

    A. Execute a test case to verify that all components work together as an integrated solution.

    B. Confirm that calls to external libraries work as intended.

    C. Verify that component deployment works in the test environment.

    D. Identify component dependencies against the configuration management plan.

Lesson 2: Performing a Code Review

Code reviews are another tool that developers can use to improve the quality of their code. Typically, code reviews are done on a peer-to-peer basis or by an application architect or technical lead. Code reviews should be performed before code is released into the test build. This lesson takes a look at how developers can help one another through the code review process.

After this lesson, you will be able to:
- Understand the process for performing a code review.
- Identify issues to look for when reviewing code.
- Understand the automated code review tools available to you.
- Propose improvements to help developers fix their code.

Estimated lesson time: 20 minutes

Real World

Mike Snell

You can make your development team better by tracking issues found during code reviews. When I was on a big project with a team that was somewhat new to .NET, we decided to share information found during code reviews in a central knowledge base. When we identified an issue, we spent about a half-hour writing up the issue and the resolution. This information was stored in a central database. The development team was sent an e-mail when new items were added. In addition, each new item became part of a checklist. We made this checklist part of the code review process. Before a developer could do a code review, the developer went through this checklist to verify that these issues did not exist in their code. This helped the entire team benefit from this process. In fact, developers started adding other best practices to the database outside of just code reviews.

The Code Review Process

A *code review* is simply the process of checking code to improve its quality and help ensure that the development team follows best practices. Many code review processes help reach this goal. Many development teams follow a peer-to-peer review process. This is where each developer checks the other developer's code and suggests improvements.

Other teams have a more formal process in which code reviews are made mandatory and tracked closely. For example, you might have a code review checklist and form. An architect or technical lead might review a portion of code and then fill out the checklist and form. The issues listed on the form must be resolved before the code goes on to test or production.

There are even code reviews that are done by third parties. You might, for instance, have your code reviewed by a company that acts as a testing center or certification house. You might even have your code audited by another company for compliance with security measures.

Each of these processes has a common set of steps for reviewing code and identifying issues. The following is a list of some of the standard steps involved in doing a code review.

- Define standards.
- Identify conformance to standards.
- Propose resolution and improvements.
- Refactor code.

This list represents the categories of a code review checklist. You can see that you start with standards. You then review the code against these standards. You can also verify the code with respect to best practices for things like error handling, security, and performance. Let's take a closer look at each of these code review steps.

Define Standards

It is impossible to review code without a baseline for standards. You need to know what the target is for the system before you can indicate that the code does not hit the target. For example, if your standard is to use Enterprise Library for writing errors to the error log, then you need to define that for the development team. There are naming standards, coding standards, architecture standards, and best practice standards. It's a good idea to get these standards on paper and make sure the team understands them. The following is a definition of each type of standard.

- **Naming standards**   You need to define how you name classes, variables, methods, and properties. Naming standards are important to make sure that the system is maintainable and readable. Most .NET applications these days follow the naming standards set forth by Microsoft for the .NET Framework. This is always a great place to start.
- **Coding standards**   Coding standards are a guide for developers on how they should and shouldn't write their code. These standards typically define things like the use of switch (C#) or select case (VB) statements, how to properly exit loops, how to handle exceptions and log errors, the use of reference parameters, the proper way to comment and document your code, and more.
- **Architecture standards**   You should create a solution architecture document for your application. This document is meant solely to define the application's overall architecture. It should cover things like application layers, state management, frameworks, the use of application blocks and third-party libraries, and more. In addition, a reference

implementation of this architecture is helpful to both solidify the architecture and serve as a model for developers.

■ **Best practice standards**   These standards represent generally accepted best practices for building .NET applications. These standards help with performance, maintainability, security, and much more. The standards exist in the .NET documentation, white papers, and the patterns-and-practices documentation. Senior developers and architects need to be aware of these standards in order to review code against them.

Identify Conformance to Standards

Once you define the standards by which your application should be reviewed, you can review it for compliance to these standards. You can verify most naming and coding standards and some best practices standards automatically using Code Analysis features of Visual Studio 2005 (see the following section, "Automated Code Reviews"). Of course you can still read through the code and check it for these things if you like.

Architecture standards are more difficult to verify. This requires a careful review. For example, if your architecture dictates that you put no UI logic or validation into the actual UI forms but instead into a UI layer, then you must go through the UI form code to verify that this is true.

MORE INFO   **Use templates to enforce standards**

Visual Studio 2005 provides a number of tools you can use to help enforce compliance with standards. You can write your own project templates that set up the project using your standards. You can also create your own item templates that you set up with your standards and your guidance.

Propose Resolution and Improvements

The next step in the process is to log the issue for tracking and provide guidance on resolving it and improving the code base. This task is typically the reviewer's responsibility. However, in some environments developers log their own issues.

It's often best to log the issue in terms of the library, class, and line number. You then need to label the issue. The label might be related to the standard that is out of compliance. You should then either point to the standard or write a brief paragraph that describes how the developer might resolve the issue. The following is an example of a logged issue in a formal review:

■ Reviewer: Some Reviewer, December 10, 2006

■ Build: December 9 Daily Build

■ Library: MyApplicationLibrary

■ Class/Method: SomeClass.SomeMethod

■ Line Number(s): 456–461

- Issue Name: Reliability Issue. Does not use *Dispose*.
- Issue Description: You need to dispose of objects before the application loses scope. Notice that the code potentially exits the method inside the *if* block without calling *Dispose*.
- Proposed Resolution: Suggest you use the *using* statement to ensure that the object is disposed.
- Resolved by: TBD
- Resolved date: TBD
- Resolution: TBD

MORE INFO **Use Team Foundation Server**

You can use Team Systems and Team Foundation Server to log and track code review issues. You create a new work as defined above. Developers can then be assigned these items, attach progress, and connect the issue with the code that resolves it.

Refactor Code

The final step in the code review process is to resolve any issues that were found during the code review. The good news is that Visual Studio 2005 now provides a number of tools to help make these changes. These tools are referred to as refactoring tools. They are available to C# developers through the *Refactor* menu. Visual Basic developers can download a version of these tools from a third party (see *http://msdn.microsoft.com/vbasic/downloads/tools/refactor/* for details).

The tools use the compiler to make sure your changes don't break other code in the system. This was always the worst part of code reviews. Just when things are working you have to go back and make changes that start breaking things. Thankfully, these tools help lessen this risk. In addition, a proper set of unit tests will help you find any areas affected by code review changes. Table 13-3 lists the refactoring tools inside Visual Studio 2005.

Table 13-3 Refactoring Tools Inside Visual Studio 2005 (C#)

Tool	Description
Rename	Used to rename fields, properties, methods, and variables
Extract Method	Used to create a new method using existing code within a different method or routine
Promote Local Variable to Parameter	Used to move a local member of a method to a parameter of the method
Reorder Parameters	Used to change the order of parameters for a given method

Table 13-3 Refactoring Tools Inside Visual Studio 2005 (C#)

Tool	Description
Remove Parameters	Used to remove a parameter from a method
Encapsulate Field	Used to quickly create a property from an existing field
Extract Interface	Used to create an interface from an existing class or structure

---

Quick Check

1. Describe the purpose of a code review.
2. What are three types of code review processes?
3. What types of standards should you define for your application?

Quick Check Answers

1. The purpose of a code review is to improve the quality of the application and help developers follow coding standards and best practices.
2. Code review processes include peer-to-peer, formal, and third-party reviews.
3. You should define naming standards (for classes, methods, and properties), coding standards (for exception handling, conditional statements, and so on), and architectural standards.

Automated Code Reviews

It is getting increasingly difficult (and costly) to review and check all of an application's code by hand. Code reviews can add weeks to development schedules. Thankfully, Visual Studio 2005 has provided an automated Code Analysis tool to help.

The Code Analysis tool is based on its precursor, FxCop. FxCop was a command-line tool that shipped with earlier versions of .NET. It checked code against a common set of rules. The new tool, called Code Analysis, has a common set of rules, standards, and best practices built into it. You can turn these rules on and off. You then run them against your code base and receive warnings when a rule is broken.

Figure 13-6 shows the Code Analysis tool in Visual Studio. You access this tool through the property pages of your application. You then select the Code Analysis tab down the left side. You must enable the Code Analysis feature for it to run. You can do so with the Enable Code Analysis check box.

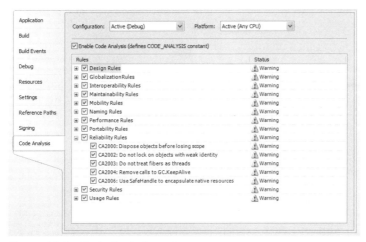

Figure 13-6   Code Analysis settings.

Notice that rules are grouped by category. There are rules for naming conventions, globaliza-tion, security, and so on. If you expand a group, you see a set of individual rules. Each rule has a description. You can turn various rules on and off for your application.

Each Code Analysis rule has an identification that starts with the letters CA. You can use this identification to look up the details of the rule inside the Microsoft Visual Studio 2005 docu-mentation. Each rule is documented in terms of cause, description, and how to fix.

Lab: Perform a Code Review

If you haven't worked on a team that does code reviews, you should give them a try. Code reviews can lead to better quality throughout your application. You can use this practice sec-tion to help you get started.

▶ **Exercise 1: Define Standards and Review Code**

In this exercise you will define your coding standards and execute a code review. Each step listed below represents input into your code review process.

1. Define your coding standards for your application. You might already be able to point to a set of standards. You should at least be able to point to your solution architecture. As an alternative, you can adopt the .NET naming standards and use the Code Analysis rules as your standards.

2. Create a code review checklist. This checklist should define the items that should be verified during the code review. The checklist is meant to provide mental triggers to the reviewer so as not to miss anything during the review.

3. Create a formal code review form or work item. This step is optional. However, if you are just getting started with code reviews, it can be helpful to formally document the first few rounds. If you use Team Systems and Microsoft Solutions Framework (MSF) for Capability Maturity Model Integration (CMMI), there is already a Review work item. If you are using MSF Agile, you should consider creating a code review work item.

4. Ask another developer to review your code. Sit with another developer (or group of developers) and get your code reviewed against the standards.

5. Put the shoe on the other foot. Try to review another developer's code.

6. Document the issues and propose resolutions. Document any issue you find during the code review. In addition, try to propose the resolution for each item.

7. Use the refactoring tools and unit tests to make changes to your code. The refactoring tools will make the changes easier. Your unit tests should confirm that things still work as intended.

▶ **Exercise 2: Run the Code Analysis Tool**

In this exercise you will use the Code Analysis tool to check your code against known rules.

1. Open some existing code inside of Visual Studio 2005. If you do not have code available, use the code from the lab in Lesson 1, "Creating Effective Unit Tests."

2. Right-click the project and choose Properties. On the Property page select the Code Analysis tab.

3. Choose the Enable Code Analysis option to turn on code analysis. Review the rules. Turn off any rules that you don't think apply to your situation.

4. Right-click your class library or executable and choose Run Code Analysis.

5. Review the results. Right-click a warning and get additional help on the warning item.

6. Fix the issues that make sense to fix. Turn the other issues off for future code analysis.

Lesson Summary

- A good code review process should improve the quality of the application and help developers follow coding standards and best practices.

- You should consider implementing either a peer-to-peer or formal code review process. Some applications require third-party reviews and audits.

- To be successful, a code review should start with a definition of standards. You should define naming standards (for classes, methods, and properties), coding standards (for exception handling, conditional statements, and so on), and architectural standards.

- You should track issues identified in the code review process. You should give each issue a name, description, and proposed resolution.

- You can use the refactoring tools inside Visual Studio 2005 to help you make changes identified during code reviews.

- Visual Studio provides an automated, static code analyzer called Code Analysis. This tool reviews code for known issues on security, globalization, performance, naming, and more.

Lesson Review

You can use the following questions to test your knowledge of the information in Lesson 2, "Performing a Code Review." The questions are also available on the companion CD if you prefer to review them in electronic form.

NOTE Answers

Answers to these questions and explanations of why each answer choice is right or wrong are located in the "Answers" section at the end of the book.

---

1. Which of the following are benefits to implementing code reviews? (Choose all that apply.)

    A. Ensure compliance to standards

    B. Higher-quality test cases

    C. Reduced bugs

    D. Ensure compliance to requirements

2. Which of the following items represent a coding standard? (Choose all that apply.)

    A. Data access methods should not trap exceptions. Rather, these exceptions should be raised up through the layers of the application, where the central error-handling mechanism will deal with them.

    B. Developers should not put data access code inside their business objects.

    C. Developers should avoid switch statements in their code.

    D. All variables should be camel case, as in *someVariable*.

3. Which of the following is a refactoring operation that allows you to define a new property from a private local variable in your code?

    A. Extract Field

    B. Encapsulate Field

    C. Promote Field

    D. Extract Property

4. Which of the following statements are true about the Code Analysis tool? (Choose all that apply.)

    A. The Code Analysis tool reviews executing code, in-process.

    B. You must run all the Code Analysis rules against your code.

    C. Issues found with Code Analysis are treated as warnings in your code.

    D. Each Code Analysis issue has an associated "how to fix" section.

Lesson 3: Evaluating and Fixing a Bug

The testing process will generate bugs. That is its goal: to find and fix as many bugs as possible. Developers do their best to ensure that their code has been properly unit tested and integrated into the build. However, issues will still arise during the testing phase. When they do, you need to be ready to investigate, reproduce, analyze, and fix these bugs.

This lesson describes how you should go about investigating bugs and fixing them. We will also look at how you can evaluate the impact of a bug and analyze trade-offs of potential actions.

After this lesson, you will be able to:
- Investigate the cause of a bug.
- Understand how the environment can be responsible for the bug.
- Work with testers to reproduce a bug.
- Evaluate the impact of a bug and analyze possible trade-offs.
- Understand the process for fixing a bug.

Estimated lesson time: 20 minutes

Investigate a Reported Bug

Testers report bugs. These bugs are typically triaged by a lead developer or project manager. During triage the bug is analyzed, its impact is assessed, and a decision is made to fix the bug, defer it to a later phase, or escalate it to the project stakeholders. Developers are assigned to fix bugs; they are also assigned to assess their impact so that a decision can be made.

Evaluate the Impact of the Bug

The triage process typically involves some assessment of the bug. It identifies its impact, sets the priority, categorizes it, and assigns a developer. The person doing the triage work will often assign the bug to a developer for further investigation. In fact, the workflow for the bug work item inside of Team System supports this step. Developers are often asked to assess the impact of a given bug. This assessment helps the person doing the triage make a decision on how to proceed. When assessing the impact of a bug, you should consider all of the following:

- **Time to fix**   Estimate the number of hours it will take to fix the bug.
- **Resources to fix**   Determine who can fix the bug. Understand how the bug might affect their schedule.
- **Bug risk**   Identify the risk the bug poses to the integrity of the application. This can be difficult to assess. It helps to think of this in terms of, "What would be the risk of not fixing the bug?"

■ **Impacts**   Identify the components, people, and other resources that are affected by the bug. Are your trading partners, for instance, affected by this bug? Will the marketing department by affected? Those affected most should help determine how to proceed with the bug.

You should pass this information back to the person doing the triage work to help with decision making. Ultimately, that person will have to decide whether to fix the bug, defer it, or escalate it to project stakeholders and key decision makers.

Prioritize a Bug

You need to be able to triage a bug relative to the other bugs in the system. This is an important step in making sure the right resources are applied to the right issues during testing. Priorities help developers know which items they need to fix first. A list of priorities might look as follows: Critical, High, Medium, and Low. Critical usually means that the bug breaks the build or is preventing testers from completing a test case. On the other end, low means the bug is more an annoyance than anything. You should expect to fix all bugs that are of Critical and High priority. These bugs typically also take the longest to troubleshoot and fix. Bugs lower on the priority scale can be assigned in batches to a junior developer. They typically involve making text changes or the like. Of course, the longer you test an application, the higher up the scale these bugs move. In the early days, only critical bugs are marked as such. When you are near release and have eliminated all the critical issues, noncritical bugs tend to move up the scale.

Like priority, bug categories are important to help the team understand where to focus their efforts. A typical set of bug categories might look like this: Change, Bug, Enhancement, User Interface, Data, and Validation. Bugs that are marked as Change or Enhancement might be pushed into the next release. Of course, bugs that are marked as a Bug need to get fixed. The other categories help define whether a given bug is a UI issue, an issue with the data, or an issue with validation and business rules. Categorizing bugs also helps you report on quality metrics in the system. It is one thing to report 50 bugs in your application and another to indicate that you have 10 bugs, 30 UI issues, 5 data issues, and 5 validation issues.

Quick Check

1. Which role in the development process should be responsible for triaging bugs?
2. Which role should be responsible for assessing the impact of a bug?

Quick Check Answers

1. The lead developer or a strong project manager is often the best choice for triaging bugs.
2. Developers should determine the impact of a bug in terms of schedule, resources, and risk.

Reproduce and Fix a Bug

When you are assigned a bug, you should first try to reproduce it. Hopefully, the tester has indicated the steps to reproduce the bug. You should try these steps in your environment with your version of the source code. If you see the bug the tester has described, you should begin stepping through the code and identifying possible fixes. If you can't reproduce the bug, you should sit with the tester and walk through the steps that produce the problem. Often you see the application through someone else's eyes and realize that person is using it differently than you had anticipated. This can be a good learning experience. Other times you determine that the bug is happening only in the test environment. In this case you need to re-create the bug environment.

Re-create the Bug Environment

You should first look for differences between the environments. You might have a good configuration management plan, but it might not have been followed. There might be differences among your development environment, staging (preproduction), and the production environment. Some of the more typical differences include security (authorization, authentication), the operating system, the framework, third-party tools, hardware configuration, and other similar issues. If you can identify the difference, you can usually either fix the bug by updating the test environment or re-create the bug by changing your environment.

Other things to look for include the version of the code and the data. It's possible that the data the tester is using is something you did not predict. Getting a copy of this data or pointing your code to the test database can help here. Of course you should also make sure that your code matches what is deployed in the test environment. It is possible that the bug was fixed and the fix not yet deployed. In this case you need to return to the branch of code that is on the test environment to verify the issue and the resolution.

Fix a Bug

All developers are familiar with the task of fixing a bug. You do it all the time. Sometimes it's in response to a unit test or your debugging effort. Other times fixing a bug is a more formal process in response to a bug that has been assigned. Team System, for example, makes the process of fixing a bug very structured. This structure should be in place for all professional development, whether or not you use Team System. The common procedure for fixing a bug is as follows:

1. The developer receives some notification that a bug has been assigned. This is typically an e-mail.
2. The developer might check out the given bug work item. This indicates the developer is working to resolve the bug.
3. The developer should then try to reproduce the bug.

4. Once identified, the developer should check out the code associated with the bug.

5. The developer should then work to fix the bug and update the unit test. The developer needs to verify the fix by running the code.

6. The developer should then check his or her code back into source control and comment it with respect to the bug information. If you are using Team System, you should associate the change set with the bug work item.

7. The developer should then add fix information to the deployment plan and release notes. This ensures that the developer's code will be deployed with the next build. It also tracks which bugs were fixed in the given build (Team System can do this for you).

8. Finally, the developer should update the bug tracking software to mark the bug as resolved. The developer can't close the bug; that's the role of the tester after the tester has verified the fix.

Lab: Assess and Triage Bugs

It's possible that you have never before had the opportunity to triage bugs. The process involves making decisions on which bugs should be fixed, by whom, and when. It is an important step in becoming a professional developer. You can use this practice section to better understand the process.

▶ **Exercise: Define Standards and Review Code**

In this exercise you will be presented with a number of bugs. Your task is to evaluate each one and determine how you would triage it. You should evaluate each bug against the following categories:

- **Impact**   Indicate whether the bug requires no additional impact assessment, requires an impact assessment, or requires stakeholder escalation.
- **Risk**   Define the risks associated with not fixing the bug.
- **Priority**   Define the bug's priority as Critical, High, Medium, or Low.
- **Category**   Determine a category for the bug, such as Bug, Enhancement, Specification Change, User Interface, Data, or Validation.
- **Bug list**
    - B1   When testing the view product screen, I noticed that products are being displayed with the wrong product information. The image looks right, the price is correct, the product name and number are right, but the product description does not match the product being shown.
    - B2   When testing the lease application process, I get to step three out of the six and the system returns me to the first page in the step. I have tried with several customers and get the same results.

B3 Marketing has requested that we modify the application's theme based on the new company colors and logo. The current version of the application is using the older color scheme.

B4 I was testing the system's globalization and noticed that a number of labels (over 100) on many pages weren't picking up the alternate language translation. I know this build won't be distributed to other cultures, but we did intend to prepare for a future build that supports multiple languages.

B5 I was reviewing the application with engineering, and they have decided that they would like to include a product configuration option. This feature should allow users to select the options they would like to receive on their ordered products.

Lesson Summary

- Testers find and document bugs. These bugs are typically triaged by a lead developer on the team. They are sometimes assigned to a developer to assess their impact before a decision on how to proceed is made.

- Developers should assess the impact of a bug in terms of hours to fix, resources required, the risk of not fixing the bug, and the impact the bug will have on the system and the users.

- Bugs should be prioritized according to their criticality. The most critical bugs are those that stop the testing from proceeding or break the build.

- Bugs should be categorized into groups such as enhancement, specification change, user interface, data, validation, and bug. This helps understand the nature of the items that the test team is logging.

- To fix a bug you must be able to re-create it. Code often works in one environment and not in another. If this is the case, you need to review the environment and find the differences.

- It is important that developers follow a structured process for fixing a bug. This includes updating code, updating unit tests, verifying the fix, updating the build plan, and updating the bug as fixed.

Lesson Review

You can use the following questions to test your knowledge of the information in Lesson 3, "Evaluating and Fixing a Bug." The questions are also available on the companion CD if you prefer to review them in electronic form.

NOTE Answers

Answers to these questions and explanations of why each answer choice is right or wrong are located in the "Answers" section at the end of the book.

---

1. You are late in the testing phase of your application. The code is complete and nearing a release. Based on the following bug synopses, which makes the most sense to escalate to project stakeholders prior to fixing?
   - A. Marketing has asked to lay out the product search results form again. The code is working right now. The development team has looked at the layout and has reported that it will take about two hours to accommodate the request.
   - B. The administrative console application is crashing when users try to save new products to the database. The development team believes this is a problem with the code that will take about four hours to fix.
   - C. The order management team indicated its request for an order tracking feature that wasn't in the current build. Upon further investigation, it seems that their requirements never made it into the specification. The development team has said this feature will take over 40 hours to code and unit-test.
   - D. The system is not validating user e-mail addresses. Instead, it allows any text to pass through. Developers have looked at the code and indicated that it is a bug. It should take about an hour to fix.

2. You are assigned a bug. You can't reproduce the bug in your environment. Which of the following should you look at to determine the reason? (Choose all that apply.)
   - A. A comparison of the version of the code between your environment and the test environment
   - B. The operating system and .NET Framework version
   - C. The user credentials for the executing code
   - D. The data in the test environment

3. Once you've fixed a bug and verified your fix, what additional steps should you take? (Choose all that apply.)
   - A. Branch your code to create a new build that isolates your fix.
   - B. Update the deployment plan and release notes to include your fix.
   - C. Update the bug item and mark it as fixed.
   - D. Add a comment to your code to associate it with the bug tracking system.

Chapter Review

To further practice and reinforce the skills you learned in this chapter, you can perform the following tasks:

- Review the chapter summary.
- Review the list of key terms introduced in this chapter.
- Complete the case scenarios. These scenarios set up real-world situations involving the topics of this chapter and ask you to create a solution.
- Complete the suggested practices.
- Take a practice test.

Chapter Summary

- The unit testing framework is built into Visual Studio 2005. The namespace *Microsoft.VisualStudio.TestTools.UnitTesting* provides the classes and methods that make up this framework. This includes attribute classes like *TestMethod*, *ClassInitialize*, and *ExpectedException*. The *TestMethod* class is used to mark a method as a unit test. The *ClassInitialize* class allows you to create a method to execute prior to executing your unit tests. The *ExpectedException* class indicates that a given unit test expects an exception to be raised as its result. In addition, the namespace includes the *Assert* class to help you to determine if a unit test succeeded or failed. This class has assertions for checking Boolean values (*IsTrue*, *IsFalse*), checking for null values (*IsNull*, *IsNotNull*, verifying if objects are the same (*AreSame*, *AreNotSame*), and more.

- Testers are responsible for integration testing. Developers need to play a part, however. They should verify their API, define their dependencies, and identify component interactions. They should run their code in a test environment. Once they have verified the results, they can hand off their code to the test team.

- Code reviews should start with a definition of standards. You should define naming standards (for classes, methods, and properties), coding standards (for exception handling, conditional statements, and so on), and architectural standards. Once these standards are in place, you should implement peer-to-peer or formal code reviews. The intent is to improve the quality of the application and help developers follow best practices.

- Developers should follow a structured process for fixing a bug. First, you need to be able to re-create the bug. Code often works in one environment and not in another. If this is the case, you need to review the environment and find the differences. Once you have identified the issue as a bug, you should update your code, update your unit tests, verify your fix, update the build plan, and update the bug as fixed in the tracking log.

Key Terms

Do you know what these key terms mean? You can check your answers by looking up the terms in the glossary at the end of the book.

- code analysis
- code review
- edge case
- test case
- use case

Case Scenarios

In the following case scenarios, you will apply what you've learned about the developer's responsibilities for creating tests. You can find answers to these questions in the "Answers" section at the end of this book.

Case Scenario 1: Defining Unit Tests from a Test Case

You are a senior developer at company that is rewriting its customer relationship management (CRM) application. You have been assigned the module Schedule Customer Meeting. You have written this code to specification and developed one basic unit test for every property and every method in the application. You've just been given the Schedule Customer Meeting test case for your review.

Test Case

The following represents the Schedule Customer Meeting test case:

- **Name**   Schedule Customer Meeting
- **Description of functionality tested**   This test case verifies the requirements associated with a CRM user scheduling a customer meeting. The user works with the application user interface to find a registered customer, enter the details of the meeting, and receive confirmation. This test case references the use case with the same name.
- **System state/dependency**   This test case requires that the test customer data be loaded into the test database.

  This test case requires connectivity to the site reservation system and the location mapping engine.

- **Test case/steps**   To execute this test case, complete the following steps:
  1. Open the CRM Windows client application from your desktop.
  2. Proceed as if logging a customer request. Find the customer, "Test Customer," and choose View Customer Information.
  3. Select the option to Schedule Meeting for the customer.
  4. Verify that you are now on step 1 of 5 for scheduling a customer meeting. This step should be to enter the details of the meeting. Verify that you are now on the Enter Meeting Details screen.
  5. Enter the test details for the meeting. This should include the following: purpose, attendees, agenda, date, start time, end time.
  6. Select Next to continue scheduling the meeting. Verify that you are now on the form Meeting Location Details (step 2 of 5).
  7. Select from the list of known meeting locations. You will also want to try and enter new meeting locations. Indicate that the meeting should include a map to the location. Also indicate that attending the meeting requires travel for some of the participants (indicate which participants require travel).
  8. Click Next to continue. Verify that you are now on the Site Reservation form (step 3 of 5).
  9. Select a hotel from the location list (it might be already be selected if there is only one option). Indicate the type of conference room required and the number of guest rooms required. Select the Check Hotel's Availability option. Verify that the hotel has availability for the selected meeting date and time and has returned a quote for booking.
  10. Select Book Meeting to continue. Verify that you received a confirmation number for the meeting from the hotel. Verify that you are now on the Send Meeting Details to Participants form (step 4 of 5).
  11. Confirm the meeting details. Click Send to complete the scheduling process.
  12. Verify that you are now on the Meeting Scheduled form (step 5 of 5). Verify that the test e-mail account received the meeting details.
- **Data input**   You should use a mix of data to properly test this module. The test data can be found in an Excel spreadsheet entitled "ScheduleCustomerMeetingTestData.xls". This test data includes customer information, meeting data, location options, and a set of expected results.
- **Expected result**   See each row in ScheduleCustomerMeetingTestData.xls to confirm the results of each instance of this test.

Alternate Case 1

The following represents an alternate test case:

- **Name**   Hotel unavailable.
- **Description of functionality tested**   Tests how the system behaves when the selected location has no hotel availability.
- **Test case/steps**   To execute this test case, complete the following steps:
  1. Follow the meeting scheduling process as indicated in the test case. However, select a bad hotel from the location data (see data below).
  2. Verify that the hotel scheduling fails and that the user is properly warned.
  3. Verify that the system returns the user to the Site Reservation page.
  4. Select a good location from the list and continue the process.
  5. Verify that that the transaction completes and the confirmation page is accurate.
- **Data input**   See the Bad-Locations tab in ScheduleCustomerMeetingTestData.xls for a list of hotel bookings that will fail.
- **Expected result**   Each use of a "bad-location" should fail. Subsequent schedules with a good hotel should succeed without a problem.

Questions

While thinking about your unit tests and the test cases above, answer the following questions.

1. What modifications might you make to your test cases based on the System State/ Dependency section of the use case?
2. What additional unit test might you consider for verifying the navigation of the system through the event registration wizard (from page to page)?
3. What changes might you make to your ScheduleMeeting unit test based on the Data Input and Expected Results sections of the test case?
4. What additional unit tests might you consider based on the alternate test case?

Case Scenario 2: Performing a Code Review

You are a senior developer hired to work at a consulting company. The last couple of projects this company did had a number of quality issues. These problems seemed to stem from the code being unnecessarily complex and disjointed. In addition, the development team is made up of several new developers with very little experience. Your company can't afford another quality issue and needs to track quality closely.

The development manager sets up a meeting with you to discuss this issue. During the meeting he mentions that they have very little in terms of documented coding process and standards. He then starts asking you questions about doing code reviews.

Questions

Answer the following questions for your development manager:

1. We want to set up a process for doing code reviews. Where should we start?
2. Who should do the code reviews? Should this be a peer-to-peer process?
3. How will code reviews help us improve quality?
4. How can we report on the effectiveness of the code reviews?

Suggested Practices

To help you successfully master the exam objectives presented in this chapter, complete the following tasks.

Creating Effective Unit Tests

If you have just started creating unit tests, you should consider completing both practices below. These will help you think through how you do more than just create simple unit tests. They will help you write effective unit tests that will make a significant improvement in quality.

-   **Practice 1**   If you are currently working on a project, you can use it for a basis. If not, find some old code that you wrote or download someone else's code. Think of this code from the user's perspective. Document the scenario that the user would use to describe his or her steps for working with the feature. Use this information to create an effective test case. Think through the alternate edge cases you would write to make sure the feature is sufficiently tested. If you have a tester on the team, ask that person to review your test case and give feedback.
-   **Practice 2**   Use the test case you created in Practice 1 to define a set of unit tests. Think about which methods will require the most unit tests. Think about how you can improve your unit tests to satisfy the test case and edge cases. If you already have unit tests for this code, compare them to what you came up with. Document the gaps. If you don't have unit tests, consider writing them. This will be good practice.

Performing a Code Review

To help master this objective, you should complete the following practices. If you already do code reviews, you might wish to skip this task section.

-   **Practice 1**   Talk to your development manager about defining a set of standards. This does not need to be a long process. Just work as a team to brainstorm ideas. Document them and post them in a central area. As the team writes code, they should add to the standards.

- **Practice 2**   Create a code review checklist. You can use the standards document from Practice 1 for a guide. You should also consider your architecture document and some of the items inside the Code Analysis tools as input. Review this checklist with the team and get their input.

- **Practice 3**   Perform peer-to-peer code reviews. You can start by working with another team member to spot-check each other's code. You might consider working with your development manager to formalize a code review process.

Evaluating and Fixing a Bug

Most developers process bugs all the time. However, you might not always think about these bugs in terms of management or impact. The following practices should give you a better understanding of how bugs affect the software development life cycle.

- **Practice 1**   The next time you are assigned a bug, think about it from an impact perspective. It might make sense to document the bug's impact in terms of estimated time to complete, risk of not fixing it, priority, and so on. This will help you understand the importance and cost of quality.

- **Practice 2**   If you do not have a formal bug management system, consider creating something in Excel to log and track these items. You can create simple graphs that report on the quality of the system. Use these graphs to help provide a window into the testing process and the current state of the application.

Take a Practice Test

The practice tests on this book's companion CD offer many options. For example, you can test yourself on just the content covered in this chapter, or you can test yourself on all the 70-548 certification exam content. You can set up the test so that it closely simulates the experience of taking a certification exam, or you can set it up in study mode so that you can look at the correct answers and explanations after you answer each question.

MORE INFO   **Practice tests**

For details about all the practice test options available, see the section titled "How to Use the Practice Tests" in this book's Introduction.

Chapter 14
Deploying an Application

Once an application has been completely developed, tested, and approved, it is ready to be deployed. Unfortunately, because it comes at the end of the development life cycle, the deployment of an application sometimes gets short shrift. For many applications, the only "deployment" question that gets asked prior to this point is, "Is this going to be a Web application or a Microsoft Windows application?" The only reason for the question is that Web applications are so much easier to deploy and the developer wants to know how much pain will have to be endured at the end of the development project.

But is it really true? Does the deployment of a Windows-based application have to be more onerous than a Web application? In many cases the answer is no. The purpose of this chapter is to give you enough information to be able to pick the deployment method that is most appropriate for your application, your audience, and your infrastructure, and to minimize (where possible) the pain endured by the developer.

Exam objectives in this chapter:
- Evaluate the deployment plan.
    - Identify component-level deployment dependencies.
    - Identify scripting requirements for deployment. Considerations include database scripting.
    - Evaluate available deployment methods.
- Validate the production configuration environment.
    - Verify networking settings.
    - Verify the deployment environment.

Lessons in this chapter:

Before You Begin

To complete the lessons in this chapter, you must have:

- A computer that meets or exceeds the minimum hardware requirements listed in this book's Introduction.
- Visual Studio 2005 installed on the computer, with either Visual Basic .NET or C# installed.
- Although it is not required, there is some mention of the application design tools found in Visual Studio Team System for Software Architects.

Real World

Bruce Johnson

I have been guilty of delaying deployment thoughts until the end of a project. I often depended on the kindness of wizards and third-party applications to ensure that all of my components were deployed and configured properly. And in more cases than I care to think about, the first attempt at deployment to a real client machine failed. Perhaps I forgot about a configuration setting. Or didn't deploy a needed file. In the real world these are almost unforgivable acts because they reduce the trust that a user has in the application before the user has even started using it. In software, as in relationships, first impressions are important and not deploying correctly is a bad way to start out.

The goal of this chapter is to make it easier to deploy without fear. This includes the identification of all of the components that need to be included in a deployment and the ability to ensure that deployment works correctly, including the starting of any required services.

Lesson 1: Deploying the Application

The starting point for deploying an application is the project in which it is running or, more likely, the entire solution for the project. In Visual Studio 2005, MSBuild uses the solution file to gather and compile the various components that make up the application. Assuming that the application compiles successfully (a minimum requirement for deployment), much of the dependency information about the components can be gleaned from there. But that is not sufficient. Additional files and settings might need to be included with the deployment. As part of this lesson, a list of the most common parts of a deployment will be considered, along with the ways that they can be loaded onto a user's machine.

After this lesson, you will be able to:
- Recognize the application elements that need to be deployed.
- Deploy application elements using the appropriate techniques.
- Understand the differences between the deployment methods and when each is appropriate.

Estimated lesson time: 35 minutes

The Elements of Deployment

When discussing a deployment strategy, it's important to know what needs to be deployed. This helps to determine the techniques that are viable and the privileges that the installer needs to have to ensure success. So the next few pages will focus on the elements that make up the vast majority of application deployments.

Assemblies

The most commonly deployed element in a .NET application is going to be an assembly, whether in the form of a dynamic-link library (DLL) or executable. Although it's not a requirement for assemblies that aren't deployed to the *global assembly cache* (GAC), there are a number of good reasons to strongly name any deployed assemblies. This includes both *private assemblies* and *shared assemblies*. The benefits of strong naming include the following:

- **Guaranteed uniqueness of name**   If an assembly is not strongly named, any search performed by the common language run time (CLR) (such as when an assembly is loaded into a process) uses only the name of the assembly. As a result, it's possible for someone to replace the correct assembly with another with the same name and to have that bogus assembly loaded into your application. If the assembly is strongly named, a digital signature is used to identify the assembly, ensuring that no such substitution can take place.

- **Guaranteed lineage of versions** With a strong name, the author of an assembly can ensure that no one else can create an newer version of an assembly. The version number of the assembly is included in the search criteria, so the wrong version can't be loaded without the author's "permission."

- **Guaranteed tamper-free** Included in the strong naming process is the generation of a hash based on the contents of the assembly. Any attempt to tamper with the assembly is detected and the loading of the assembly fails.

- **Side-by-side deployment of versions** Since nonstrongly named assemblies are distinguishable only by file name, it is not possible to have different versions of the assembly available at the same time. The information used to locate strongly named assemblies includes the version number, meaning that different versions can be installed simultaneously.

A discussion of strongly naming assemblies and deployment frequently includes the GAC. Specifically, the question of when to deploy assemblies into the GAC arises. A lot of developers think that every strongly named assembly should go into the GAC. Others think that no assemblies should be put into the GAC. Unfortunately, both extremes are incorrect.

To understand when it's appropriate to use the GAC requires an appreciation of life prior to the GAC–during a time known as "DLL Hell." A main characteristic of DLL Hell is that the updating of a DLL during the installation of one application would cause a separate unrelated application to fail. This is because only one version of a DLL could be registered at a time. So although the newly installed application might use version 1.1 of a DLL, existing applications were expecting version 1.0. And since backward compatibility is not guaranteed, the existing application was the one that suffered. And by "suffered" we mean "crashed."

One of the goals of the GAC was to provide a central repository for assemblies that are shared across multiple applications. Any assembly that might be shared across applications was expected to be placed into the GAC. Once it's there, additional information (such as the public token, version, assembly name, and culture) is used to uniquely identify the assembly. This allows multiple versions of the same assembly to be resident in the GAC simultaneously. Now both old and new applications have access to the assembly they require.

The problem is that placing assemblies into the GAC doesn't automatically eliminate the issues that caused DLL Hell in the first place–or, more accurately, that the GAC isn't necessary to eliminate the issues. Two examples clarify this statement.

Figure 14-1 illustrates the first situation. In the initial deployment, two applications share an assembly. After the shared assembly is upgraded, only one of the two applications is modified to use the new assembly.

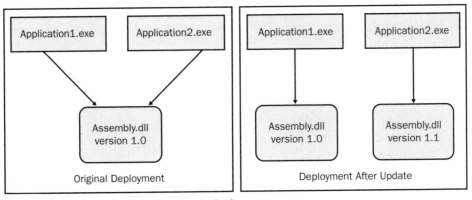

Figure 14-1   One example of assembly deployment.

In this particular situation there is no real reason to share the assembly. Each of the applications is really using its own copy of the assembly, even if initially it appeared as if there was some sharing going on. Unless the applications upgrade to the different version in sync, there is no reason to place it into the GAC.

The second situation involves the idea of using a *publisher policy* to upgrade all the applications that use a particular assembly to a new version. The problem with the publisher policy is that it is automatically applied to every single application that uses the assembly, including not just the two applications that you deployed but also any other application that might be using the assembly. This list has the potential to contain applications that you don't even know about, making it very challenging (that is to say, impossible) to test. In other words, it's dangerous to deploy an updated assembly using a publisher policy.

So in both of these situations (which the GAC was anticipated to address), the GAC really isn't necessary to address the problem. When, then, would it be useful? The following scenarios benefit greatly from the use of the GAC:

- Providing critical assembly updates without breaking any existing functionality. This is how Windows hot fixes and service packs work. It's unlikely to happen in the real world because of the onerous testing requirements.
- Sharing types between independent applications that require identical types; for example, the client and server portion of a .NET Remoting application that is deployed onto a single machine.

Dependent Assemblies

If the deployment executable for an application is created through a Visual Studio Setup Project, then the dependencies associated with each assembly area are automatically detected and included in the installation package. Although it's possible to include the dependencies manually, it's usually preferable to allow the automatic detection to take place. The automatic detection for managed code assemblies is completely accurate. The problems arise when the dependent assemblies lie outside of the managed code realm. And the exceptions fall into a couple of distinct categories, each with their own solution.

It's possible that an application references a DLL that is installed only as part of another product. An example of this is the Web Browser control in .NET 1.1 and its dependence on the shdocvw.dll file. This particular DLL is installed only with Microsoft Internet Explorer. The general solution is to include logic in the installation package to determine if the related product (Internet Explorer in this example) is present, and terminate the installation if it has not already been installed.

It's possible that the reference DLL is not part of a product (such as Internet Explorer) but is an external component. The dependency that System.Data.dll has on the Microsoft Data Access Component (MDAC) is an example. The difference with this example is that the external component could have a merge module that can be used as part of the installation of the application. In that way, not having the component available won't terminate the installation process.

In some cases the unmanaged dependent components might not expose all of its dependencies. If so, the automatic detection of Visual Studio 2005 won't include the dependency. An example is Microsoft Foundation Classes (MFC), which don't expose any localized satellite assemblies as dependencies. In cases such as this, the inclusion of the required assemblies must be done manually. This, in turn, means that the developer must manually determine the dependencies.

Along with unexposed dependencies, it's possible that a component uses late binding to load a needed assembly. In such a situation, Visual Studio 2005 might not automatically detect the dependency. Consider a case in which the name of the assembly to be loaded is included in the application's configuration file. Visual Studio 2005 doesn't examine the configuration file for the (potential) names of assemblies to include, and, as such, the automatic detection process would miss it. Again, the author of the installation package needs to include this sort of assembly manually.

Files and Folders

Naturally, the movement of files and folders to the target system is going to be a major part of any deployment. And although assemblies are files that frequently get copied as part of deployment, they aren't the only files that need to be moved. Also included in this category are configuration files, Extensible Markup Language (XML) files, Extensible Schema Definition (XSD) files, database files, and images. Of these, the configuration files really make up the group that requires more explanation.

Three types of configuration files can be deployed:

- **Application configuration** This is the file that most developers think of when configuration files are mentioned. It is an XML file that exists in the same directory as the executable and contains information used by the various components of an application.
- **Machine configuration** The machine configuration file is named machine.config and can be found in the Config directory of the .NET Runtime's installation directory. It contains settings used by a long list of applications, including the assembly bindings used across all .NET applications, .NET Remoting channels, and, if installed, ASP.NET.
- **Security configuration** The security configuration file (named security.config) is found in the same directory as machine.config and contains the code group hierarchy and permission sets. It's rarely modified directly, the preferred mechanism being to use the Code Access Security Policy (caspol.exe) tool or the .NET Framework Configuration (mscorcfg.exe) tool.

Installation Components

Windows applications regularly require some external resource to be installed as part of the deployment. Although there are any number of ways to perform such an installation, installation components provide a mechanism that's nicely integrated into the typical deployment mechanisms. An installation component is a small piece of functionality that allows application resources to be created and configured during installation. The installation components provided with the .NET Framework integrate with installutil (for Windows Services), .msi files (Windows Installer files), and the Windows Installer Service. Installation components come in two flavors: predefined components and installer classes.

There are five types of predefined installation components. Table 14-1 lists them, along with a brief description.

Table 14-1 Predefined Installation Components

Component Name	Description
EventLogInstaller	Installs and configures event logging.
MessageQueueInstaller	Installs and configures message queues.
PerformanceCounterInstaller	Installs and configures performance counters.
ServiceInstaller	Installs and configures a Windows service.
ServiceProcessInstaller	Installs the executables required by a Windows service. *ServiceInstaller* and *ServiceProcessInstaller* work in concert to install a Windows service.

If the predefined components are not adequate, it's possible to define a custom installer class. This custom class is created by defining a class that derives from the *System.Configuration.Install.Installer* class. Also, the class definition needs to be decorated with the *System.ComponentModel.RunInstaller* attribute.

```
' VB
<System.ComponentModel.RunInstaller(True)> _
Public Class DemoInstaller
    Inherits System.Configuration.Install.Installer
End Class
```

```
// C#
[System.ComponentModel.RunInstaller(true)]
public class DemoInstaller : Installer
{
}
```

In the custom installer class, two methods need to be overridden. The *Install* method is invoked when the installation is performed. The *Uninstall* method is invoked when the application is uninstalled. The code that goes into these methods is exactly what is required to install and uninstall the desired components. So if the external resource is a database, the *Install* method would include the code to create and populate the database, while the *Uninstall* method would remove the database. There are also *Commit* and *Rollback* methods that are available to be overridden, should the demands of the deployment require it.

NOTE Exceptions at installation time

If an exception occurs in any of these overridden methods, the exception text will be displayed to the user. This is not conducive to a good user experience, so within the methods, trap and log all exceptions and display a friendly message to the users instead.

Exam Tip The differences between the predefined installation components and what can be accomplished through a custom installer class provides an area where in-depth knowledge could be probed.

COM Components

Even through the .NET Framework has passed version 2.0 and is heading toward version 3.0, there are still instances where applications need to use COM components. Wherever this happens, the deployment of the application must consider the registration process for the COM components on the target system. If the COM component has been used as part of a Visual Studio 2005 solution, then creating a deployment project based on the solution will result in the COM component being installed and registered as needed.

Along with the COM component, there is also an *interop assembly* that needs to be deployed. The interop assembly doesn't contain any implementation code but instead contains a description of the data types that are implemented in the COM component with which it's related. There are two types of interop assemblies in .NET:

- **primary interop assembly (PIA)** This is the interop assembly that is created by the original author of the COM component. As such, it's the "official" source for interoperability information.
- **alternate interop assembly** This is any interop assembly that is not the primary one. As such, it isn't generated by the COM component's author. Although they still allow access to COM functionality, alternate interop assemblies don't have the weight of approval from the component's author.

For each COM component, one of these types of interop assemblies will be generated. The reason for distinguishing them is that the location of the assembly's deployment depends on the type. A COM component differs from a .NET assembly in that the COM component is accessible by any application on the machine by default. As a result, if your application includes the PIA, that assembly would best be deployed into the GAC. That way, other applications using the COM component will have the interop assembly available to it. If, on the other hand, your application is deploying an alternate interop assembly, then it should be installed as a private assembly so that other applications don't use it inadvertently.

Serviced Components

A *serviced component* is a .NET assembly that relies on COM+ to provide transaction management, object pooling, activation, and other related functionality. At an implementation level, it is a class that uses the *System.EnterpriseServices.ServicedComponent* class as a base class. Once installed, the component is hosted by a COM+ application. Access by any application to the types exposed by the service component is done through COM+. As a result, COM+ needs to have access to the assembly, which places a couple of demands on the deployment, specifically the following:

- The assembly must be strongly named.
- The assembly must be registered in the Windows Registry.
- The type library definitions for the assembly must be registered and installed into a specific COM+ application. The need to be in a specific COM+ application is important because that directly affects how callers will access the types.

There are three main ways to register a serviced component. The first, called *dynamic registration*, is the easiest. When a serviced component is first accessed, the CLR detects that the component has not been registered. It then reflects on the assembly to determine the characteristics of the COM+ application that is required and creates it. The assembly containing the serviced component is then installed into the application, where it is available for use immediately and for any future executions.

Although dynamic registration is the simplest installation mechanism for a serviced component, it also has the drawback of requiring the user of the application to have administrator rights. Only administrators are allowed to create the COM+ application that the assembly will be installed into. Thus the application now has the requirement of running as administrator, a level of privilege that might not be required for anything beyond the first execution.

As a result, the creation of the COM+ application and the registration of the assembly is frequently done at installation time. Yes, an administrator needs to run the installation, but that is a much less onerous requirement than having the application run at that permission level. To install the COM+ component during installation, there are two choices:

- **Regsvcs.exe utility**   The Regsvcs utility performs basically the same function as the dynamic registration. That is, it reflects on the assembly to determine the characteristics of the COM+ application, creates the application if required, and registers the assembly into the application.

- **System.EnterpriseServices.RegistrationHelper class**   In the *RegistrationHelper* class there is an *InstallAssembly* method that can be used to programmatically register .NET assemblies with COM+. This technique would normally be used in conjunction with an installer class.

Exam Tip   The main difference between dynamic and explicit registration has to do with the permissions required to run the application. This need to run an application in Administrator mode goes against the concept of "least privilege," which is a focus of the security initiatives within Microsoft.

Registry Settings

For most .NET applications, the need to use the Windows Registry directly has been greatly reduced. However, sometimes it's required, and when that happens the deployment process needs to be able to address it. Three techniques are commonly available:

- **Programmatic creation**   Registry keys, subkeys, and their values can be created programmatically using the *Microsoft.Win32.RegistryKey* class. The code to create (and destroy) can then be placed into a custom installer class.

- **Declarative definition**   The Setup and Deployment project in Visual Studio 2005 provides for the definition of registry keys that are then automatically created as part of the installation.

- **Registration Entries file**   Information about the registry keys and subkeys to create can be exported into a *Registration Entries file*. The file (denoted by a .reg extension) can then be installed using the following command:

```
Regedit /s <path to .reg file>
```

Scripts

Sometimes scripts are a necessary part of the deployment process. Although it's true that almost anything that can be done through scripts can be done programmatically, sometimes using scripts results in a more maintainable solution.

A good example is when a database needs to be created or modified. Although you could write C# or VB code to create and populate the tables, it's much easier to create the Data Definition Language (DDL) scripts to generate the database objects (using SQL Server Management Studio, if that is easiest) and then execute the scripts using the *osql.exe* command-line tool. No one would suggest that identifying the database elements and writing the C#/VB code to create them is not more tedious and error-prone than the scripting solution. Not to mention that the object generation scripts can be maintained much more easily than the corresponding code in terms of keeping up to date on schema changes. Areas where scripts are likely to provide a superior installation process include:

- IIS-based components, such as Web services
- Active Directory directory service
- Windows Management Interface (WMI)
- Database creation/schema updates

A number of scripting technologies are available to developers looking to include scripts within their deployment process. However, not all of them are included by default with the operating system. To avoid having to install a scripting engine along with your application, it's a good idea to use a scripting technology that already exists on the target machine, which usually means Windows Scripting (the latest version is 5.6). That means that the choices include VBScript, Jscript, and WScript. In each case, the script will be executed by the Windows Script Host (WSH).

The logistics of working with scripts during deployment means that the file containing the script needs to be deployed onto the target system. Once it has been moved to the target machine, the script gets launched using the appropriate command, which in the case of WSH is cscript.exe.

With respect to scripts in deployments, there are really only two additional issues to address. The first is whether the script file should remain on the target system after installation. This is more a matter of personal choice than anything else. The only real danger from leaving the script on the target system is if there is some information that could be used to attack the application. Because determining this is difficult and there is normally no reason to leave the script installed, it's usually better to delete it once the installation is complete.

The second issue is one that arises not during installation but during the uninstallation of the application. Depending on what the script is doing, it might or might not be possible to uninstall the changes made during installation. If the script creates a database, should the uninstall process delete the database? What about any changes the user made to the schema? Or any data that was added? If, in the face of these possibilities, the answer is "yes, it should be uninstalled," then a second "uninstall" script will be necessary. Although the Windows Installer is capable of automatically rolling back certain deployment tasks, those that are performed in a script are not in that list. This is true, by the way, if an installation gets cancelled or aborted part way through the process. If a script has run and then the installation is stopped, there are no transaction-like rollback capabilities. Yes, a *Rollback* method would be called, but, as with the uninstall, a script would need to be set up to handle this case.

Quick Check

1. Why should any deployed assembly be strongly named?
2. If you need to create a message queue as part of the installation of an application, which technique is easiest to use?
3. As part of the installation process, a script creating a database gets executed. If you wanted to remove the database when the application is uninstalled, would you place the code to execute the script in the *Uninstall* method in a custom installer class?

Quick Check Answer

1. Deployed assemblies should be strongly named to allow for side-by-side deployment, version checking on loading, and the ability to ensure that assemblies have not been tampered with.
2. There is a predefined installation component that can be used to create a message queue. This is the easiest option, although you could create a message queue using scripting as well.
3. No. The only way to uninstall those parts of an application installed using a script is to create a script that specifically performs the uninstallation. There is no mechanism to automatically uninstall scripted installation components.

Deployment Methods

In the .NET world there are basically three methods for deploying applications.

- File Copy (also called XCOPY deployment)
- Windows Installer package
- Click Once (also called No Touch, Zero Touch, and Smart Client)

File Copy

The simplest deployment method involves copying the files necessary to run an application to the target directory. More specifically, the output from the build process (assemblies, configuration files, graphics, and so on) is simply transferred to the target machine. This approach meets the basic definition of a deployment. It also satisfies some common requirements—it's easy to create, it's easy to perform, and it's easy to install upgrades.

For simple applications, copying the files is adequate. However, if your application needs more sophisticated configuration, File Copy is not adequate. For example, if your application requires one of the following, a different approach is required:

- An item on the Start menu
- Updates to the Windows Registry
- The installation of a Windows service
- Changes to security policy
- Customization of configuration files based on the target system (for example, if the database connection string needs to changed)

Although not every application has one or more of these deployment requirement, they are common enough that File Copy isn't sufficient in a significant number of applications.

Windows Installer Package

For most developers, "installation" means the creation of a Windows installer package. An installer package is capable of deploying all manner of Windows applications, from Windows Forms to Windows services to Web applications. It can also be used to install cabinet (CAB) files and merge modules. Distribution of the installer package can be in the form of a single file, whether it be an .exe or the familiar .msi. In other words, the installer package can be used across the full spectrum of Windows applications.

Using an installer package provides a number of benefits over and above the File Copy technique.

- The installation has a graphical interface and uses a wizard to walk the installer through the various choices.
- The installation is compatible with Add/Remove Programs in the Control Panel. This gives the user a consistent interface for deployment, as well as a place to go when an application needs to be removed.
- The installation can run in a silent mode, with the default for all options taken and requiring no interactions with the user once the installation has been started.
- The installation is performed as a transaction. If there is a problem with any part of the installation, the Rollback logic on the installation is performed. There are exceptions to this (see the discussion of scripts in the last section), but it is true in most cases.

- The installation can be done using Active Directory or System Management Server (SMS). In Active Directory environments, the Windows Installer (MSI) file can be deployed using Group Policy software distribution, which can automatically install applications on computers throughout a domain. SMS provides similar capabilities, but includes more features for managing software in large enterprises.

Click Once

Click Once technology is the newcomer of this group. It was first introduced as Zero Touch deployment in .NET 1.0, and although .NET 1.1 had some improvements, it has really come into its own with .NET 2.0. The aim of Click Once is to provide superior user experience of Windows Forms with the deployment of a Web application. So rather than force a user to execute a Windows installer package, the deployment package for Click Once is placed in a centrally accessible location (like a file server or a Web server). The user accesses the package through Microsoft Internet Explorer. As part of the execution process, any assemblies that are needed are downloaded from the same central location. All of the downloaded assemblies are stored in an isolated location, meaning that the installation of an application through Click Once has no impact on existing deployed applications.

In terms of the interest shown among the three deployment methods, Click Once is getting the most press by far. The reason is that the other approaches have some weaknesses, especially when it comes to deploying updates. Click Once was really designed to address three installation problems.

- **Updating applications**   To update a traditional application, you need to distribute an update throughout your organization.
- **Target system impact**   The installation of an application using XCOPY or Windows Installer results in permanent changes to the system. This introduces the possibility that the installation of one application affects others, however unintentionally. Click Once deployment keeps applications isolated from one another.
- **Installer permissions**   Windows Installer deployments often require Administrator permissions outside of Active Directory environments. Although XCOPY deployment doesn't have these issues, the limitations of XCOPY, as already discussed, mean that complex installations are normally installer packages. Smart Client deployment allows nonadministrative installation and grants only those permissions required by the application.

Click Once technology definitely fills a need. Although Web applications are a breeze to update, they do have some limitations in terms of the user interface. So being able to install and upgrade a Windows Forms application automatically is greatly desired. However, Click Once deployment is not suitable for every application. The main limitation comes from the fact that Click Once does not leave a permanent footprint on the target machine. If some element of the application requires a more permanent update, such as those in the following list, Click Once can't be used.

- Installation for multiple users
- Installation of shared files
- Installation of drivers
- Installation into the GAC
- Adding an application shortcut to the Startup group
- Updating the registry (in some cases, the registry can be updated, but it requires Full Trust permissions be given to the deployed application)

Lab: Application Deployment

A large portion of how applications get deployed has been automated with the Setup and Deployment Project Types that are available from within Visual Studio. Wizards are available to help with most of the common deployment techniques. So for this lab, the focus is on a technology that is used for custom deployment tasks. If you encounter a problem completing an exercise, the completed projects are available on the companion CD in the Code folder.

▶ **Exercise: Creating a Custom Installer**

In this exercise, we will be creating a custom installer to add an event log and source to the operation system. In addition to the installation functionality, we will also be implementing uninstall capability.

The starting point for the exercise is a Windows Forms application that displays a list of the event logs installed on the local machine. After the necessary install class has been added, the installutil function will be used to install the component. After installation, a new event log will be visible. And, after using installutil to remove the component, the event log will go away.

1. Launch Visual Studio 2005.
2. Open a solution using File | Open | Project/Solution.
3. Navigate to the Chapter14/Lesson1/<language>/Exercise1-Before directory. Select the Exercise1 solution and click Open.
4. In the Solution Explorer, right-click the project and select the Add References context menu item.
5. Find the *System.Configuration.Install* component and click it. Click OK.
6. In the Solution Explorer, right-click the project and select the Add | Class context menu item.
7. In the Add New Item dialog box, select Class. Change the name of the new class to **CustomInstaller** and click OK.

8. Before starting on the code, add a couple of *using/Imports* statements at the top of the class module. Specifically, add statements for *System.Configuration.Install*, *System.ComponentModel*, and *System.Diagnostics*.

9. In order for a class to be recognized as an installer class, it needs to be public, derived from the *Installer* class, and marked with the *RunInstaller* attribute. The following is the class definition:

    ```vb
    ' VB
    <RunInstaller(True)> _
    Public Class CustomInstaller
        Inherits Installer
    End Class
    ```

    ```csharp
    // C#
    [RunInstaller(true)]
    public class CustomInstaller : Installer
    {
    }
    ```

10. In the installer class, the *Install* and *Uninstall* methods must be overridden. We start with *Install*. First in *Install* is to call the base *Install* method. Then perform any custom installation functionality, which in this exercise is to create an event source.

    ```vb
    ' VB
    Public Overrides Sub Install(ByVal stateSaver As System.Collections.IDictionary)
        MyBase.Install(stateSaver)
        EventLog.CreateEventSource("Installer Demo", "548TK Demo Log")
    End Sub
    ```

    ```csharp
    // C#
    public override void Install(System.Collections.IDictionary stateSaver)
    {
        base.Install(stateSaver);
        EventLog.CreateEventSource("Installer Demo", "548TK Demo Log");
    }
    ```

11. Overriding the *Uninstall* method is quite similar except that, instead of creating the event source, it is deleted, along with the Event Log.

    ```vb
    ' VB
    Public Overrides Sub Uninstall(ByVal savedState As System.Collections.IDictionary)
        MyBase.Uninstall(savedState)
        EventLog.DeleteEventSource("Installer Demo")
        EventLog.Delete("548TK Demo Log")
    End Sub
    ```

```
// C#
public override void Uninstall(System.Collections.IDictionary savedState)
{
    base.Uninstall(savedState);
    EventLog.DeleteEventSource("Installer Demo");
    EventLog.Delete("548TK Demo Log");
}
```

12. At this point the application can be built and launched using the F5 key. When the form appears, click Get Sources. Notice that there is a list of event log sources. Once you have drunk in the beauty of the list, stop the application.

13. Launch the Visual Studio 2005 Command Prompt. The default steps to do this are Start | All Programs | Microsoft Visual Studio 2005 | Visual Studio Tools | Visual Studio 2005 Command Prompt.

14. In the command window, navigate to the directory containing the DisplayEventLogSource executable, namely Chapter14\Lesson1*<language>*\Exercise1-Before\DisplayEventLogSources\bin\Debug.

15. Execute the command to install the application.

```
Installutil DisplayEventLogSources.exe
```

16. After seeing a successful installation, rerun the application through Visual Studio 2005. Click Get Sources, and an event log source named 548TK Demo Log appears. Close the application.

17. Back in the command prompt, execute the following command to uninstall the application.

```
Installutil /u DisplayEventLogSources.exe
```

18. After seeing a successful uninstallation, rerun the application through Visual Studio. Click Get Sources. Notice that the previously existing log source, 548TK Demo Log, is no longer in the list.

Lesson Summary

- Different elements of a deployment require different techniques for accurate installation.
- There are three types of deployment methods in Windows—File Copy, installer packages, and Click Once.
- There is a deep relationship between the items being deployed and the available methods.

Lesson Review

You can use the following questions to test your knowledge of the information in Lesson 1, "Deploying the Application." The questions are also available on the companion CD if you prefer to review them in electronic form.

1. You have an application that uses a COM+ component. The application has no need to run with Administrator privileges. Which method should be used to deploy the application?

    A. File Copy

    B. Windows installer package

    C. Click Once

    D. Smart Client

2. You have an application that uses the *WebBrowser* control as part of its functionality. You create a Windows Installer deployment package for the application. While testing the deployment, you discover that the application will not execute once it has been installed. Specifically, a *FileNotFoundException* is detected. What is the likely source of the problem?

    A. One (or more) of the dependent files have not been copied to the target machine.

    B. One (or more) Windows Registry entries have not been made.

    C. The primary executable for the application has not been signed.

    D. An incorrect version of one of the dependent assemblies was installed.

3. You have an application that needs to be deployed using the Group Policy functionality enabled through Active Directory. Which of the following deployment techniques should you use?

    A. File copy

    B. Windows installer package

    C. Click Once

    D. Smart Client

Lesson 2: Making Sure It's Ready to Run

The installation phase is the first of two steps to getting your application successfully deployed. Once the necessary files have been moved to the target machine and the necessary configuration performed, it's a good idea to ensure that the application is ready to run. That the target machine has all of the necessary infrastructure, like network access. That the required services are running. And that all the needed Web services are accessible. Of course, the specifics of what is required will vary from application to application. But the goal of this lesson is to describe some of the techniques that you can use to verify that the application is ready to go.

After this lesson, you will be able to:
- Determine the dependencies that exist between components.
- Identify the tools available in Visual Studio Team Systems for Software Architects that can be used to document deployment details.
- Verify the correct installation of common application components.

Estimated lesson time: 35 minutes

Deployment Dependencies

One of the most challenging parts of designing the deployment of a significant application is to manage the dependencies. At a low level, most of the dependencies are handled for you automatically. For example, if you build a .NET application and then use the IL Disassembler (ILDASM) to view the manifest (see Figure 14-2), you can easily see the list of dependent assemblies.

The challenge is to manage the application dependencies at a higher level. As different projects are deployed, it can be difficult to track the relationships between them. Which Windows services need to be running? What is the Uniform Resource Locator (URL) for the required Web service? What is the .NET Remoting endpoint? All of these questions need to be answered for a successful implementation. But more important, the developer of the deployment needs to know which questions to ask.

```
 MANIFEST                                                        _ □ ✕
Find  Find Next
// Metadata version: v2.0.50727                                      ▲
.assembly extern mscorlib
{
    .publickeytoken = (B7 7A 5C 56 19 34 E0 89 )
    .ver 2:0:0:0
}
.assembly extern System.Windows.Forms
{
    .publickeytoken = (B7 7A 5C 56 19 34 E0 89 )
    .ver 2:0:0:0
}
.assembly extern System
{
    .publickeytoken = (B7 7A 5C 56 19 34 E0 89 )
    .ver 2:0:0:0
}
.assembly extern System.Configuration.Install
{
    .publickeytoken = (B0 3F 5F 7F 11 D5 0A 3A )
    .ver 2:0:0:0
}
.assembly extern System.Drawing
{
    .publickeytoken = (B0 3F 5F 7F 11 D5 0A 3A )
    .ver 2:0:0:0
}
.assembly DisplayEventLogSources                                     ▼
 ◄                                                           ►
```

Figure 14-2   Sample manifest as generated by IL Disassembler.

Real World

Bruce Johnson

The maintenance of deployment dependency information is an annoyance to many developers. Developers like to focus on the low-level details of class interaction without worrying about the movement of messages and information between individual components. For many companies it is left up to the architect to identify and maintain the information. And keeping the information up to date over the course of the project is not always done as promptly as it should be.

For those who balk at these chores, I suggest considering the following situation. Say you were a person who had no information about the application but were asked to deploy it. Or asked to maintain or support it. Would you want some sort of description of what the various parts are and how they fit together? Of course you would. And the dependency information would be quite useful in building that description.

Most developers, when you put it in these terms, are more willing to help create and maintain the dependency list.

Modeling Deployment

A *deployment model* is one choice for documenting the dependencies that exist within the components of an application. When you think about the dependencies of the components in terms of how they get deployed, you can more easily identify the interactions that exist between the components. Awareness of such interactions has increased in recent years with an upswing in the interest in service-oriented architectures. A great deal of information is available on how to identify the boundaries that messages must move across. And how to document them as well. One of the benefits of this activity is to move the consideration of deployment issues to earlier in the development process.

The thought process involved in deriving a deployment model starts with a few questions.

- What existing systems does the application integrate with?
- What existing systems integrate with the application?
- How robust does the application have to be?
- What communications channels or protocols are being used?
- What hardware or software on the client machine does the application interact with?
- How secure does the system need to be?

The reason for taking this relatively methodical approach is to help visualize overall design. Large systems are typically fragmented into many pieces with numerous interactions. Gathering all of that information into a coherent whole is difficult, but ultimately useful. The design of the application can be affected by the answers to the questions, so getting the necessary details as soon as possible allows you to make the right decisions.

Although this discussion has been theoretical, Visual Studio 2005 for Software Architects has a number of tools that help with creating and maintaining deployment and dependency diagrams. These include the following:

- **Application Connection Designer**   Defines a collection of applications that will be combined into a single system for deployment. The tool includes a number of predefined application prototypes, as well as the ability to create a custom prototype. The tool can also create a prototype by reverse engineering an existing project or solution.
- **Logical Datacenter Designer**   Creates a model of the interconnected logical servers that represent the infrastructure of a datacenter. This provides documentation of the target deployment environment. The information includes the number and types of servers, the types of interserver communication, the allowed communications pathways, and the enabled services.
- **System Designer**   Used to compose and configure systems using the applications defined in the Application Connection Designer. In the vernacular of Team Systems, a *system* is a unit of deployment and is composed of one or more applications.
- **Deployment Designer**   Used to map a system onto a logical datacenter so that the deployment steps can be defined. The applications that make up the system are bound to the logical servers in a datacenter. Once the bindings are complete, the deployment can be validated. The validation consists of ensuring that the connections, services, and capabilities of the logical servers can meet the requirements defined in the system.

Application Verification

The validation performed by the Team System tools works at a high level. It's not the same as ensuring that the individual components of an application are ready to go. The details of what constitutes "ready" depends on the details of the component. This section covers some techniques that verify some of the more common requirements.

Web Services

In a service-based world, making sure that a particular service is accepting requests is a common requirement. Two levels of verification can take place. One doesn't require the cooperation of the service; the other does.

At its heart, a Web service is a Web server that responds to requests. Send it a Hypertext Transfer Protocol (HTTP) request and you should get an HTTP response. So the first, and simplest, level of verification is to send the Web service endpoint a request. An active Web service will return a response. Because, as the developer, you know the methods that have been exposed by the Web service, you have the ability to select one that is reasonable to use. One that doesn't update any data would be best.

The problem is that just accessing the endpoint is not sufficient to determine if the Web service is ready to accept requests. There could be internal resources that are not available, yet the Web service returns a response. That would leave it up to the caller to parse the response to try and determine if the Web service was really ready. This is too much work and never 100 percent accurate. The ideal Web method is one that is designed specifically to be used to check on the health of the Web service, which is a nice segue to the second level of verification.

A properly designed Web service includes a method that has traditionally been called a *heartbeat method*. This method is called to verify not only that the endpoint is receiving requests but also that any internal resources required to respond to requests are operational. So, as part of the application verification process, the heartbeat method for any Web services gets called, providing a deep level of certainty on readiness.

MORE INFO   **Monitoring Web services using heartbeats**

The heartbeat method is an important part of the monitoring and instrumenting of a Web service. For more information on this topic, check out *http://msdn.microsoft.com/library/en-us/dnbda/html/MSArcSeriesMCS6.asp*.

Database

There are two ways to look at whether a database is accessible or not. The first is to determine whether the server is reachable and the database is running. The second is to ensure that all of the connection information is complete and correct. Although the SQL-DMO COM object can be used to verify that the database is operational, so can the connection information. So the readiness process for a database consists of establishing a connection using the information provided in the configuration file (or anyplace else a connection string is being stored).

Networks

Information about the network has changed at .NET 2.0 Framework. In earlier versions, the Win32_NetworkAdapter WMI object could be used to retrieve details on the network adapters on the machine. But .NET 2.0 added the *System.Net.NetworkInformation* namespace. As can easily be guessed, due to the wisdom of the class naming group at Microsoft, this namespace contains classes that provide information about the network—specifically, details about the available adapters, addresses that are in use, traffic, and status.

Consider the following as an example. As part of the verification process, the application needs to have at least one nonlocal network adapter. The following code retrieves all of the network adapters and searches for the first nonlocal one.

```vb
' VB
Dim nics() as NetworkInterface = NetworkInterface.GetAllNetworkInterfaces()
Dim adapter as NetworkInterface
For Each adapter in nics
   ' Check adapter information
```

```csharp
// C#
NetworkInterface[] nics = NetworkInterface.GetAllNetworkInterfaces();
foreach (NetworkInterface adapter in nics)
   // Check adapter information
```

Beyond ensuring that network adapters are available, it is sometimes good enough just to know that a particular server is available. For this, the *Ping* class can be used. More specifically, the *Send* method on the *Ping* class takes a host name or an Internet Protocol (IP) address and sends an Internet Control Message Protocol (ICMP) message. The results can be found in a *PingReply* object. The *Status* property on *PingReply* contains the information on the success or failure of the request.

```vb
' VB
Dim pinger As New Ping()
Dim reply As PingReply = pinger.Send("objectsharp.com")
If reply.Status = IPStatus.Success Then
   ' Valid domain name
End If
```

```csharp
// C#
Ping pinger = new Ping();
PingReply reply = pinger.Send("objectsharp.com");
if (reply.Status == IPStatus.Success)
   // Valid domain name
```

There is one potential limitation on the use of *Ping* to determine machine accessibility, one that can be fatal to *Ping's* success. *Ping* requires that the target system respond to the ICMP request. Although many systems running on internal networks do respond to pings, many systems that are exposed to the Internet do not, and many recent operating systems block ping requests by default. In particular, popular Web sites, such as microsoft.com, specifically ignore ICMP requests as part of their defenses against denial-of-service attacks. So inaccessibility through *Ping* is not a 100 percent guarantee that the system is truly unreachable.

Quick Check

■ Is there a way to determine a machine's availability with 100 percent certainty?

Quick Check Answers

■ In short, no. The *Ping* command is not perfect because the destination machine can refuse to process the request. The best that can be done is to access the machine using the same technologies that that application will use while it's running. But that doesn't guarantee that the tested software will exist when the application runs.

Windows Services

Determining if a Windows service is running is similar to determining if a Web service is running. At a superficial level, it is easy to see if the service is running. But depending on what the service is supposed to be doing, it might be difficult to determine (without help) whether the service is operating correctly.

To determine if a service is running, call the *GetServices* method on the *System.ServicePro-cess.ServiceController* class. In the example shown below, the list of all processes is scanned to find out whether a specific service (as determined by the service's name) has been installed..

```
' VB
Dim services As ServiceController() = ServiceController.GetServices()
Dim _service As ServiceController
For Each _service in services
    If _service.ServiceName = "Windows Service Name" Then
        ' Service has been installed
    End If
Next
```

```
// C#
ServiceController[] services = ServiceController.GetServices();
foreach (ServiceController service in services)
    if (service.ServiceName == "Windows Service Name")
        // service has been installed
```

But installed is not the same as running, because a Windows service might be stopped. And a Windows service needs to be running to perform its tasks. The *ServiceController* class includes a *Status* property that contains the current status of the service. A value of *StatusControllerStatus.Running* indicates a service that is ready to be used. Also, methods on the *ServiceController* class can be used to start, stop, pause, and continue the service.

Lab: Verifying Application Installation

Once the application is installed, it's necessary to ensure that the environment in which it has been placed is ready to run. In this lab we look at two methods that can be used to validate the application's installation. If you encounter a problem completing an exercise, the completed projects are available on the companion CD in the Code folder.

▶ **Exercise 1: Remote Machine Availability**

In this lab, we examine a technique that can be used to determine if a remote machine is available. The process has two steps. In the first, we ensure that the current system has a working network adapter. In the second, we use the *Ping* class to send an ICMP request to the destination machine.

1. Launch Visual Studio 2005.

2. Open a solution using File | Open | Project/Solution.

3. Navigate to the Chapter14/Lesson2/<language>/Exercise1-Before directory. Select the Exercise1 solution and click Open.

4. In the Solution Explorer, double-click the Program.cs or Module1.vb to gain access to the *Main* method. We'll start by retrieving all of the network interfaces on the machine. Add the following code to the *Main* method:

```
' VB
Dim nics() As NetworkInterface = NetworkInterface.GetAllNetworkInterfaces()
```

```
// C#
NetworkInterface[] nics = NetworkInterface.GetAllNetworkInterfaces();
```

5. Once the network interfaces are retrieved, we loop through them looking for at least one that is not a loopback adapter. Add the following code below the just added code:

```
' VB
Dim adapter As NetworkInterface
For Each adapter In nics
    If adapter.NetworkInterfaceType <> NetworkInterfaceType.Loopback And _
        adapter.OperationalStatus = OperationalStatus.Up Then
        Console.WriteLine("Adapter {0} is active", adapter.Name)
    End If
Next
```

```csharp
// C#
foreach (NetworkInterface adapter in nics)
    if (adapter.NetworkInterfaceType != NetworkInterfaceType.Loopback &&
        adapter.OperationalStatus == OperationalStatus.Up)
        Console.WriteLine("Adapter {0} is active", adapter.Name);
```

6. Next, we check to see if the remote machine is pingable. Create a *Ping* object and use the *Send* method to submit the ICMP request. Add the following code below the previously added code, changing the domain *contoso.com* to one that is active in your own network:

```vbnet
' VB
Dim pinger As New Ping()
Dim reply As PingReply = pinger.Send("contoso.com")
```

```csharp
// C#
Ping pinger = new Ping();
PingReply reply = pinger.Send("contoso.com");
```

7. The last bit of processing for the exercise is to check on the status returned by the *Send*. For this, the *Status* property needs to be *IPStatus.Success*. Add the following code after the just added lines:

```vbnet
' VB
If reply.Status = IPStatus.Success Then
    Console.WriteLine("The host could be pinged")
Else
    Console.WriteLine("The host could not be pinged ({0})", _
        reply.Status.ToString())
End If
Console.ReadLine()
```

```csharp
// C#
if (reply.Status == IPStatus.Success)
    Console.WriteLine("The host could be pinged");
else
    Console.WriteLine("The host could not be pinged ({0})",
        reply.Status.ToString());
Console.ReadLine();
```

8. Launch the application using the F5 key. If you are attached to a network, you will quickly see the network adapter name or names appear. And then, after a few seconds, the message appears that the ping request has timed out. That's because the *microsoft.com* domain doesn't process ICMP requests.

▶ **Exercise 2: Is a Windows Service Running?**

In this lab, we show how to determine if a Windows service is running. The important consideration is the name of the service that is running. Once the desired service is identified, the status of the service is checked to ensure that it is currently running.

1. Launch Visual Studio 2005.
2. Open a solution using File | Open | Project/Solution.
3. Navigate to the Chapter14/Lesson2/<*language*>/Exercise2-Before directory. Select the Exercise2 solution and click Open.
4. In the Solution Explorer, double-click the Program.cs or Module1.vb to gain access to the *Main* method. We'll start by retrieving all of the currently installed services. Add the following code to the *Main* method:

```
' VB
Dim services() As ServiceController = ServiceController.GetServices()
```

```
// C#
ServiceController[] services = ServiceController.GetServices();
```

5. Next, add the following code to the *Main* method:

```
' VB
Dim _service As ServiceController
For Each _service In services
    If _service.ServiceName = "Eventlog" AndAlso _
        _service.Status = ServiceControllerStatus.Running Then
        Console.WriteLine("The EventLog service is running")
    End If
Next
Console.ReadLine()
```

```
// C#
foreach (ServiceController service in services)
    if (service.ServiceName == "Eventlog" &&
        service.Status == ServiceControllerStatus.Running)
        Console.WriteLine("The EventLog service is running");
Console.ReadLine();
```

6. Launch the application by using the F5 key. Almost instantaneously, the message indicating that the event log process has been found will appear.

Lesson Summary

- Information about deployment dependencies can affect decisions made throughout the life of a project.
- The ability to verify the installation of individual components varies based on the technology.
- In some instances 100 percent verification is difficult to accomplish.

Lesson Review

You can use the following questions to test your knowledge of the information in Lesson 2, "Making Sure It's Ready to Run." The questions are also available on the companion CD if you prefer to review them in electronic form.

---

1. You are responsible for creating and maintaining the deployment model for a large development project. You want to talk to the architects of the project to identify the main components and the interactions that exist between them. Which of the following questions will *not* provide information that is pertinent to the creation of a deployment diagram?

    A. How robust does the application need to be?

    B. Is a factory pattern being used to establish connections to the data source?

    C. Are there plans to use a service-based architecture?

    D. What integration exists between existing corporate applications?

2. Which designer is used to create a model for the deployment of an application?

    A. Application Connection Designer

    B. Deployment Designer

    C. Logical Datacenter Designer

    D. System Designer

3. Which designer is used to create a model for the flow of information between the components of an application?

    A. Application Connection Designer

    B. Deployment Designer

    C. Logical Datacenter Designer

    D. System Designer

Chapter Review

To further practice and reinforce the skills you learned in this chapter, you can perform the following tasks:

- Review the chapter summary.
- Review the list of key terms introduced in this chapter.
- Complete the case scenarios. These scenarios set up real-world situations involving the topics of this chapter and ask you to create a solution.
- Complete the suggested practices.
- Take a practice test.

Chapter Summary

- Although the Setup And Deployment Wizard can help identify some of the artifacts that are part of the deployment, certain types of components require additional processing to install.
- The appropriate deployment method depends on both the complexity of the application and the technique that will be used to distribute upgrades.
- It can be challenging to maintain a deployment diagram throughout the life of the project. Things change as the project moves forward, and getting the developers to participate is like herding cats.

Key Terms

Do you know what these key terms mean? You can check your answers by looking up the terms in the glossary at the end of the book.

- deployment model
- global assembly cache (GAC)
- heartbeat method
- interop assemblies
- private assembly
- publisher policy
- Registration Entries file
- shared assembly

Case Scenarios

In the following case scenarios, you will apply what you've learned about delivering multimedia in a distributed environment. You can find answers to these questions in the "Answers" section at the end of the book.

Case Scenario 1: Choosing the Deployment Method

You are a corporate developer on a team that is creating a Windows Forms application. Your responsibility is to design the deployment method that will be used for the application.

The application consists of three main components. The Windows Forms application contains the user interface and business logic. It's expected to be deployed onto the users' machines. Regular updates are anticipated as additional features are added to the project.

Communication to the database will be through a COM+ component. This component will also be installed on the users' machines. However, unlike the Windows Forms application, it is not expected that any regular change to this component will be required.

The third tier of this application is the database. The data used by the application will be stored in a new database on an already installed SQL Server system.

Questions

Answer the following questions for your manager:

1. What deployment method should be used by the user portion of the application?
2. What deployment method should be used by the database tier?

Case Scenario 2: Verifying the Deployment

You are a corporate developer on a team that is creating a multi-tier Windows Forms application that uses a number of different components. Your responsibility is to prepare for deployment by modeling the components (with respect to the servers on which they will be deployed) and to ensure that the components are in a state in which the application can be executed.

Questions

Answer the following questions for your manager:

1. What tools should be used to model the component deployment strategy?
2. What types of verification should be performed?

Suggested Practices

To help successfully master the objectives covered in this chapter, complete the following tasks.

Deploying the Application

For this task, you should complete both practices.

■ **Practice 1**   Using a project that is currently under development, identify the artifacts that will need to be deployed. Then create a Setup and Deployment project for the project. Compare the list of items that actually get deployed by the Setup And Deployment Wizard to the list that you identified to ensure the completeness of your list and to see if the project contains any artifacts that the wizard missed.

■ **Practice 2**   For a project that is just starting the development phase, examine the deployment options that are available. For the project, identify any design areas that might be affected by each of the possible deployment technologies.

Making Sure It's Ready to Run

For this task, you should complete this practice.

■ **Practice 1**   For a project that is currently under development, create a deployment model. The model should include all of the components that are being created and the interactions that the components have. Also, map the identified components to the hardware platform on which the application will be deployed.

Take a Practice Test

The practice tests on this book's companion CD offer many options. For example, you can test yourself on just one exam objective, or you can test yourself on all the 70-548 certification exam content. You can set up the test so that it closely simulates the experience of taking a certification exam, or you can set it up in study mode so that you can look at the correct answers and explanations after you answer each question.

MORE INFO   Practice tests

For details about all the practice test options available, see the "How to Use the Practice Tests" section in this book's Introduction.

Chapter 15
Supporting an Application

There is a reason that only a fraction of the cost of an application is spent on the initial development effort. That reason is that applications (hopefully) live long and productive lives within the corporate infrastructure. And over that long life, there are groups of people (operations and maintenance developers mostly) whose job it is to see that not only does the application remain a part of the daily work process but also it doesn't fall down when employees need it the most.

For this reason, we have a chapter devoted to the elements of supporting applications. This includes monitoring production applications for performance issues and thresholds that might be approaching. Also, we discuss how to evaluate the complexity of components, with an eye to determining the potential issues associated with enhancing functionality.

Exam objectives in this chapter:
- Evaluate the performance of an application based on the performance analysis strategy.
  - Identify performance spikes.
  - Analyze performance trends.
  - Track logon times.
- Analyze the data received when monitoring an application.
  - Monitor and analyze resource usage.
  - Monitor and analyze security aspects.
  - Track bugs that result from customer activity.
- Create an application flow-logic diagram.
  - Evaluate the complexity of components.
  - Evaluate the complexity of interactions with other components.

Lessons in this chapter:

Before You Begin

To complete the lessons in this chapter, you must have:

- A computer that meets or exceeds the minimum hardware requirements listed in this book's Introduction.
- Visual Studio 2005 installed on the computer, with either Visual Basic .NET or C# installed.

Real World

Bruce Johnson

Evaluating an application for performance takes patience and diligence. Think CSI for the geeky set. Armed with only a magnifying glass (in the guise of the Performance Monitor), your job is to track down the areas where an application is not as efficient as it could be. Sometimes, even when the clues are all there, it's hard to see clearly. The clues can be (metaphorically) stacked on top of one another, each one obscuring the others. It's your job, using the experience of hundreds of hours of code writing, to discern what is really going on. Where the bodies (again, metaphorically...no developers need be harmed in the tuning of an application) can be found. And, most important, which part of the application is really to blame.

Personally, this is one of the facets of application development that I find most enjoyable. There is an element of "hunch" to the process of tuning that can look magical to the outsider. The source of a performance issue is often identified almost by "feel." As in, it "feels" like that piece of code is taking longer to run than it should. But, like most good detective work, the results must be proven. So although hunches might take you close to the source of the performance woes, you still need to be able to back up your hunches with data. And where you can find the data (and how to interpret it) is the topic of this lesson.

Lesson 1: You Can Tune an Application...

Tuning the performance of an application is as much art as science. The basic reason for this truism is because of the inevitable trade-offs involved. Reduce the input/output (I/O) bottleneck and CPU usage rises. Decrease the CPU and the memory footprint increases. Round and round you go trying to catch the brass ring of optimal performance. But in this game there is never a brass ring. There are always different ways to configure and rework the application to improve some part of its performance profile, usually at the expense of another part. It becomes a question of balancing the parts to reach the optimal conditions for the local environment.

There are actually two elements to tuning an application—discovery and mitigation. In this lesson we're going to focus on discovery—the identification of where a performance problem might exist. This means using clues that are made available through utilities such as the Performance Monitor. The second element, mitigation, involves making the changes in the application to eliminate the identified performance bottlenecks. This is left as an exercise for the reader.

After this lesson, you will be able to:

- Customize the views in Performance Monitor to capture information in the most desirable manner.
- Evaluate the performance counters associated with overall memory and CPU usage.
- Select the most appropriate counters to identify .NET Framework-specific performance issues.

Estimated lesson time: 25 minutes

Gathering Performance Information

When it comes to gathering performance information, developers have a number of options. However, once the application gets into production, the choices become much more limited. Limited, in fact, to information that the application provides directly or indirectly. The direct information includes any logging details or custom performance counters that have been built into the application. The indirect information takes the form of performance counters that are associated with the .NET Framework and other applications (SQL Server, MSMQ, and so on) that are installed on the production machine. You might have noticed a common thread between these two sources—performance counters.

When trying to identify the performance issues for an application running in production, the Performance Monitor is a critical tool. So the starting point for this lesson is a brief discussion of how you can use the Performance Monitor. There are actually four views for the Performance Monitor, each of which is described in the following sections.

Chart View

The first, and probably most familiar, is a pseudo–real time graph illustrating a number of settings. Figure 15-1 shows an example of this type of view.

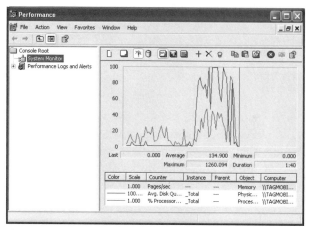

Figure 15-1   A sample display for the Performance Monitor.

Although this particular view is nice under certain situations (such as when monitoring an environment), it's not very useful for identifying trends that appear only over a period of time. The reason is that the collected information scrolls off the display every couple of minutes (or, more accurately, is overwritten). So long as what you are looking for appears within that couple of minutes (and assuming that you're staring at the screen), the view is good. But for the gathering of information over a longer period of time, this display is not effective.

Alert View

The Alert view displays a list of *performance alerts* that have been defined. A performance alert basically polls one or more counters at a regular interval and sends out a notification when the counters exceed (or fall below) a specified limit. For example, you could set up a performance alert so that an action is taken when the CPU usage is greater than 95 percent and the page faults per second are greater than 100. When the criterion, whatever it might be, is met, the Performance Monitor can take up to four actions:

- Add an entry to the application event log
- Send a network message a user ID
- Start logging the data for a named set of counters
- Launch a program, passing a defined argument on the command line

Although alerts can be useful, they are not perfect. The criteria are checked through polling. This means that thresholds can be momentarily crossed between polls without an alert being fired. Instead, the alert is only fired if the threshold is crossed at the moment of poll. Also, criteria can't include a time value. For example, you might want an alert raised only if the CPU usage is above 95 percent for 60 seconds. Performance alerts can't be configured to work with this type of criteria.

Report View

This view simply displays the values of the counters that have been specified. The values can be taken from current readings or use the data in a log file. From the perspective of analyzing performance, the report view is not very useful. For both current activity and log files, the view shows only a single data point for each counter. This is not a great tool for trend analysis.

Log View

The Log view isn't so much a view of information as a view of the counter sets that have been created and an interface to start them collecting information. An example of the Log view can be seen in Figure 15-2.

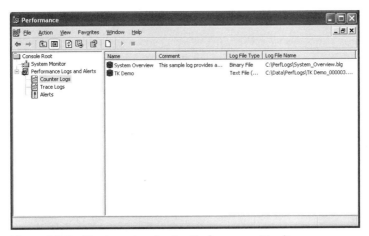

Figure 15-2   The Log view for the Performance Monitor.

To create a new log, right-click the panel on the right side of the screen. After providing a name for the log, you can select the counters that are to be included in the log. You can also specify the location and format for the log file. Once the log and counters have been defined, right-clicking on a particular log lets you start and stop the data collection processing using the Start and Stop options on the context menu.

Exam Tip   Be aware of the different view types for the Performance Monitor and when each type is likely to be useful in terms of providing support for a production application.

For analyzing the performance of an application, it's the Log view that is most useful. The information gets collected over a period of time and stored in a file. The file format can be as generic as a comma-delimited or tab-delimited file. This allows the log file to be opened and analyzed using other tools, such as Microsoft Excel. But even with the power of Excel, you still need to understand what the various counters are and how their values represent the various performance elements of your system. And that is what is covered in the next few sections.

Analyzing Performance Counters

At the heart of the Performance Monitor are the performance counters that are updated by the various components and applications installed on the system. Unfortunately, the number of available performance counters is quite large. And, except in unusual circumstances, most of them don't provide the type of information that you need to identify the cause of poor performance. Over the next few sections, the most generally useful counters will be covered, including how to interpret the values. For convenience, the counters will be broken down into the potential bottlenecks that they measure, that being CPU, Memory, and Other.

CPU Performance

A bottleneck on the CPU occurs when the processor is so busy doing work that requests for time can't be satisfied in a reasonable interval. From the perspective of users, this manifests itself as a sluggish response time on their applications. But from the analyst's point of view, it's a combination of processor use and the length of the request queue that indicates a problem in this area. More specifically, it's the request queue length that really matters. If a system has high processor usage but no queue of requests, the CPU is not the problem you think it is.

Given these goals, it should not be surprising that the counters on the System and Processor objects are going to be of most interest.

- **Processor – % Processor Time for _Total Instance**   This counter is well known to most developers as the CPU usage found in the Task Manager. The precise definition is that it's the percentage of elapsed time that the processor spends to execute a non-idle thread. This value is an average over the time interval, so any peaks and valleys are included. On a multiprocessor system, this value is the average % Processor Time for each processor. So on a dual-processor machine, having one CPU running at 100 percent and the second run at 50 percent, this counter will show as 75 percent. This becomes a consideration if any of the running applications are using processor affinity. A value of around 75 to 80 percent is considered normal. Anything more requires additional digging.

- **System – Processor Queue Length**   This counter contains the number of threads currently in the processor queue. This is not an average value but a "point-in-time" count. As a result, the trending on this counter is best viewed in a graph so that any anomalies become readily apparent. Also, there is only one processor queue, even if you're measuring a computer that has multiple processors. However, having more than one processor has an impact on the acceptable value. Each processor can adequately deal with a queue of around 5 to 10 items. So divide the reported value by the number of processors, and, if the number is greater than 10, it's likely that some process is chewing up too many CPU cycles.

- **Processor – % User Time for _Total Instance**   CPU time is spent in one of two modes. *User mode* is most typically associated with the standard user applications. Privileged or *kernel mode* is used when the CPU is performing operation system-level tasks. A low percentage of user time indicates that the machine is spending too much time on OS housekeeping tasks. This is indicative of an underpowered system in relation to the applications that are being run. Ideally, this value should be 80 percent or greater.

- **Process – % Processor Time for Individual Instances**   If you have identified that the CPU might be the bottleneck, you can drill down into the individual processes to see if there is a particular culprit. This is actually where the Processes tab on the Task Manager comes in handy because it lists all of the currently running processes and the % Processor Time for each. There is no particular threshold for this counter that is generically useful because the acceptable range is going to depend greatly on the types and numbers of applications running on the system.

- **Processor – Interrupts/Sec on the _Total Instance**   This last counter is really needed only if the source for apparent performance issues can't be nailed down using the techniques just described. This counter indicates the number of interrupts that have been processed per second, on average. A high number (and more than 4000 interrupts per second is considered "high") could be due to a faulty piece of hardware overwhelming the CPU with requests to be handled.

Memory

When it comes to identifying the counters that reveal memory problems, two areas actually need to be checked. The first set has to do with memory across all applications. The second set has to do with memory as allocated and released by .NET.

The basic concepts related to system-wide memory will be familiar to some. For the rest of you, memory in Microsoft Windows is divided up into *pages* that can contain either executable code or data. A *page fault* occurs when a program requests a page of memory that is not current in its *working set* (the set of pages visible to the program in physical memory). There are actually two types of page faults:

- **Soft page fault**   Occurs when a requested page is found elsewhere in physical memory.
- **Hard page fault**   Occurs when a requested page is not found in physical memory and therefore needs to be loaded from the disk.

In terms of their impact on performance, hard page faults are the ones to avoid. Soft page faults involve the moving or simply referencing of memory. There's not much computational effort involved there. Hard page faults involve physical file I/O and will always perform worse than rearranging memory. For this reason, the focus on the performance counters will be on detecting hard page faults.

- **Memory – Page Faults/sec**   This counter records the average number of pages faulted per second. This value includes both hard and soft faults. But, as has already been noted, hard faults are what we care about. So why bother with this counter? Because if this value isn't high, there's no reason to search any further for memory problems, at least in the system-wide measurements.

- **Memory – Pages Input/sec**   This counter is the average rate of hard page faults per second. Hard page faults occur when a process refers to a page in virtual memory that is not in its working set or elsewhere in physical memory and must be retrieved from disk. This value is used in conjunction with the Page Reads/sec counter to determine the average number of pages read into memory during each read operation.

- **Memory – Page Reads/sec**   In terms of an indicator of a memory shortage, this is one of the more important ones. This counter reflects the frequency that the system is reading from the pagefile on disk as a result of a hard page fault. More precisely, it's the number of disk reads performed to satisfy a hard page fault. When a page is faulted, the system tries to read multiple contiguous pages into memory to maximize the benefit of the read operation. As a result, there is not necessarily a one-to-one relationship between page faults and disk reads. However, for this counter, the magic number is 5. If there is a sustained (for multiple minutes) reading greater than 5, it's likely that the system is short on memory.

The counter that appears to be missing from this list is the working set that is associated with each process. After all, if you're trying to identify issues associated with memory, the working set seems like it should be critical. In fact, if you look at the Task Manager output, you'll see a Mem Usage category (which is actually the working set) listed beside each process.

The problem, at least for .NET applications, is that the working set is not an accurate representation of how much memory the application is consuming. If you launch a simple .NET application (even one as simple as a "Hello World" form), the working set appears to be around 12 MB. To many people, this is just one more example of how Microsoft doesn't care about getting its applications to run on lower-powered systems. But that's not the case here. The correct reason for this amount of memory being reporting actually has two elements.

First off, the .NET application isn't really using 12 MB of memory. That is just memory that has been allocated to the process. The vast majority of that 12 MB is completely available should another application request it. To prove this point, minimize the .NET application and see how much memory is now reported in the working set. It should be down to around 800 KB.

Along with overallocation, a second issue causes the working set counter to be incorrect. Some of the memory that's allocated to a particular process is actually part of the .NET Framework. Because of the Framework's design, this is actually memory that's shared among .NET applications. So if you have five .NET applications running on your system, the working set of each application will include this shared memory, resulting in a double counting of memory being reported in the working set.

To be fair, the 800 KB working set is also inaccurate, but in the opposite direction. When a .NET application is minimized, the working set is trimmed. This is the equivalent of executing the *SetProcessWorkingSetSize* application programming interface (API) with parameters of −1 and −1. The trimming of the working set includes moving any page that can be moved to the physical pagesys file. But once a page is in pagesys, it's no longer considered as part of the working set counter value, even though the page is required for the application to run and would get loaded back into memory shortly after the application gets maximized.

For .NET applications, the more appropriate counter to use is Private Bytes in the Process object. This counter contains the bytes allocated to a process that can't be shared with any other application. So for a .NET application, the shared .NET Framework memory is removed. Also, the pages that have been moved to pagesys are included because they can't be allocated to another process.

When it comes to analyzing memory-related issues specific to .NET applications, the focus of the performance counters is aimed more at memory allocation and the garbage collection mechanism.

MORE INFO   Garbage collection

In order to understand some of the interplays that are exposed by the Performance Monitor, a firm grasp of garbage collection, including the purpose behind the different generations, is required. Check out the article "Garbage Collection: Automatic Memory Management" in the Microsoft .NET Framework at *http://msdn.microsoft.com/msdnmag/issues/1100/gci*.

- **.NET CLR Memory – % Time in GC**   This counter is the percentage of elapsed time spent in garbage collection as compared to the total elapsed time since the last collection cycle. It indicates how much time is spent performing garbage collections, but unless there are specific calls to *GC.Collect*, it's also a representation of how frequently garbage collection takes place. And frequent garbage collection is an indication that objects are being rapidly created and destroyed. Generally, a value greater than 10 percent is an indication that objects are being allocated too frequently.

- **.NET CLR Memory – Allocated Bytes/sec**   Although it might appear obvious that this counter represents the number of bytes allocated each second, it's not that straightforward. Instead, the number of allocated bytes is calculated at the end of each garbage collection cycle. The result is that the value is not so much an average as it is the difference between the values observed at the beginning and the ending of the sample interval divided by the duration of the sample interval.

- **.NET CLR Memory – Gen 0 Heap Size, Gen 1 Heap Size, Gen 2 Heap Size**   Although these are three separate counters, the description of each one is quite similar. And the important value is the relationship between the counters, not the absolute value for any of them. First, the definition of the counters is the number of bytes in the heap currently marked as being in the corresponding generation. What's important here is to understand how objects are moving through the generations. From a memory perspective, the biggest concern is if a large number of objects move into Gen 2 heap. The reason is that these objects are not garbage collected unless a full collection is performed. And a full collection is an expensive and relatively rare occurrence. So if objects move into Gen 2 and then immediately become dereferenced, memory is being wasted. The pattern that indicates this situation is that of the ratio between Gen 0 and Gen 1 heap sizes staying roughly the same while the Gen 2 heap grows.

- **.NET CLR Memory – Large Object Heap**   In .NET, if an object is larger than 85 KB, it gets allocated on the large object heap instead of the regular heap. The reason is that mixing large objects with small objects can impair the efficiency of the garbage collection process. By placing the large objects onto a different heap and collecting them with a different frequency, the process can be made more efficient. However, if this counter steadily increases over time, the relative infrequency of collection means that memory can grow more quickly than is desirable. The absolute value of this counter is not as important as much as the trend. A continually increasing trend is not healthy for memory usage.

- **.NET CLR Memory – Finalization Survivors**   This counter is the number of garbage collected objects that survived the collection because they were waiting to be finalized. Also, although it is not included in this counter, objects that are referenced by the uncollected object can't be collected either. If this number gets high, it indicates that key objects are not being efficiently disposed of. Check on the finalization (that is, *Dispose*) method to ensure that there isn't code that executes in a nondeterministic time frame.

Underutilized CPU

Sometimes the .NET application is running slowly but the CPU does not appear to be maxed out. At those times there are a number of possible culprits, ranging from locking to too many exceptions. This set of counters is intended to help you identify which area to focus remediation on.

- **.NET CLR LocksAndThreads – Contention Rate/sec**   This counter contains the number of times that a .NET application has attempted to acquire a lock and failed. The technique used to acquire the lock (a lock statement, *System.Monitor.Enter*, and so on) is irrelevant. And the legitimacy of any value depends on the type of application. However, if a .NET application is performing sluggishly and this value is increasing (or increases dramatically as a particular function is exercised), examining the locking approach is probably worthwhile.

- **Thread – Context Switches/sec** A context switch occurs when the CPU changes the thread that's currently being executed. This counter displays the rate at which the context switches are being performed. By themselves, context switches are not bad things, of course. They allow the system to continue functioning while waiting for (relatively) long-running operations to take place. However, when this rate gets high, especially for a specific process, it indicates that the work being performed by the individual threads is too small. It might be worth increasing the scope of the parallelized elements to minimize the switches that are required.

- **.NET CLR Exceptions – # of Exceps Thrown/sec** It is common knowledge that using exceptions to control program flow (as opposed to signaling unexcepted situations) hurts performance. This counter contains the rate at which exceptions are being thrown. If this value is increasing, consider the places where exceptions are raised and find out if you can take a better approach. Realize that, in many cases, catching and rethrowing an exception might be the root cause for a high value for this counter.

- **.NET CLR Interop – # of Marshaling** This counter indicates the number of times that parameters need to be marshaled between managed and unmanaged code. What is considered a "high" value depends greatly on the type of application. Some applications will see no marshaling at all while others (such as ones that interact with old COM dynamic-link libraries [DLLs]) will see quite a high number. However, marshaling does have an impact on performance, and it might be possible to reduce the impact of marshaling by changing the types of parameters that are passed.

- **.NET CLR Security – % Time in RT Checks** This counter represents the time spent checking the *Code Access Security* (CAS) since the last time a check was performed. It's not an average but a point-in-time value, so don't evaluate it as a percentage over time. However, if this percentage becomes significant, it might be worth re-evaluating the demands that are being placed onto the security system so that the cost of CAS checks can be reduced.

- **.NET CLR Jit – % Time in Jit** Just-in-time (JIT) compilation occurs the first time that a method is executed. So as the various functions of an application are used, this value should get lower until it's almost zeroed out. If this value does not settle down to that level, it could be that dynamic code generation is being performed on an ongoing basis.

Quick Check

1. Your application is performing sluggishly while running on a system that you believe has insufficient memory. Which counters should you check to determine the validity of your belief?

2. Your application is running on a system that has sufficient memory and a fast CPU. After a while the application suddenly halts. You believe that the problem is that available memory has been exhausted. Which counters should you check to confirm or disprove this hypothesis?

Quick Check Answers

1. You can check lack of available memory by examining the Page Faults/sec, Pages Input/sec, and Page Reads/sec counters.

2. Monitor the Private Bytes counter for the .NET application. If it continually grows, then it's likely that the problem is caused by a memory leak in the .NET application.

Lab: Common Performance Metrics

In this lab, we will demonstrate how various coding behaviors can affect some of the Performance Monitor counters.

▶ **Exercise: Evaluating Memory Counters**

This exercise will focus on demonstrating some of the counters that are available to analyze the memory usage of an application. To accomplish this, we will start with a simple .NET application, the testing equivalent of "Hello world." On the form will be a couple of buttons. By clicking the appropriate button, some facet of memory usage will become visible through the Performance Monitor.

1. Launch Performance Monitor. You do this by using the Start | Run | perfmon command.

2. By default, the Performance Monitor has three counters automatically added. For this exercise they aren't needed. So click the top one in the list immediately below the graph and click the Delete button three times. This should remove all the counters.

3. In Windows Explorer, navigate to the Chapter15/Lesson1/<language>/Exercise1-After directory. Open, build, and run the solution to launch the demo form. The reason for launching first is that some of the counters we're going to add are specific for a process and the process needs to be running before they can be added.

4. To view the performance information, we're going to add four counters to the list. In Performance Monitor, click the Add button above the graph.

5. Select a Performance object of Process. Select the Working Set counter. Select the MemoryDemonstration instance. Click Add.

6. Select a Performance object of Process. Select a counter of Private Bytes. Select the MemoryDemonstration instance. Click Add.

7. Select a Performance object of .NET CLR Memory. Select a counter of Allocated Bytes/ sec. Select the MemoryDemonstration instance. Click Add.

8. Select a Performance object of .NET CLR Memory. Select a counter of Large Object Heap Size. Select the MemoryDemonstration instance. Click Add and then click Close.

9. Arrange the Performance Monitor and the Memory Demonstration form so that both are visible. In Performance Monitor, select the Working Set counter. Note the last value that appears. It should be about 12 MB to 20 MB.

10. Now minimize the Memory Demonstration form. Note that the Working Set counter plummeted in value.

11. Restore the Memory Demonstration form to its previous size. Note that although the Working Set value has gone up, it did not rise to its previous value. This is because only those pages that were required to display the form were pulled out of the paging file.

12. In Performance Monitor, click the Private Bytes counter. Minimize the Memory Demonstration form and then restore it. Note that the number of private bytes allocated to the application didn't change.

13. In Performance Monitor, click the Allocated Bytes/sec counter. Note the Last value.

14. In the Memory Demonstration form, click the Allocated Strings button. This button causes 1,000,000 strings to be allocated, assigned a value, and deallocated one after another. Notice the spike that appears in the Allocated Bytes/sec value.

15. Click the Private Bytes counter. Then click the Allocated Strings button again. Notice how the number of allocated bytes doesn't change. That's because the memory was already allocated to the process, so the number of allocated bytes didn't increase.

16. Click Garbage Collect. This button executes the *GC.Collect* method. Notice that the number of private bytes or the size of the working set didn't change.

17. In the Memory Demonstration form, click Allocate Large Objects. This button allocates 1000 byte arrays with a size of 100,000 elements. Notice that the Allocated Bytes/sec counter spiked and the size of the Private Bytes and Working Set counters increased.

18. Click Garbage Collect. This decreases the Private Bytes and Working Set counters back to roughly the level they were at before the large objects were allocated. The reason for this delay is that a full garbage collection has never been performed.

Lesson Summary

- Use the graph view of Performance Monitor to view short-term trends. Use the log view to gather more information over a longer period of time. The log view's data can easily analyzed by Excel or a third-party tool.

- To properly tune an application, a fairly in-depth understanding of the inner workings of the .NET Framework is required.

- Identifying the reason for a performance bottleneck requires both patience and deductive reasoning, which is the reason why the inner workings of .NET are so useful.

Lesson Review

You can use the following questions to test your knowledge of the information in Lesson 1, "You Can Tune An Application...." The questions are also available on the companion CD if you prefer to review them in electronic form.

NOTE   Answers

Answers to these questions and explanations of why each answer choice is right or wrong are located in the "Answers" section at the end of the book.

---

1. You have been tasked with the job of evaluating the performance of an application that is currently running in production. You need to come up with a strategy to track certain performance metrics so that they can be analyzed later. Which technique would be the most appropriate one to use?

    A. The default (graph) view on Performance Monitor

    B. Performance alerts

    C. The log view on Performance Monitor

    D. The report view on Performance Monitor

2. You have been tasked with the job of evaluating the performance of an application that is currently running in production. The application is running sluggishly, but an initial evaluation of the performance counters suggests that CPU is not being maxed out, nor is memory an issue. What are the likely causes for this behavior? (Choose all that apply.)

    A. Excessive exceptions being thrown

    B. Excessive allocation of strings

    C. Excessive allocation of large objects

    D. Inefficient locking mechanism

Lesson 2: Application Flow-Logic Diagrams

An application flow-logic diagram documents not only the components that an application uses but also the relationship between them—specifically, the interfaces that are used and the dependencies that exist. In this lesson we look at the basic elements of the diagram, as well as the steps to follow to create one.

After this lesson, you will be able to:
- Create an application flow-logic diagram.
- Evaluate the complexity of an application.
- Identify how complexity affects the ongoing support and maintenance of an application.

Estimated lesson time: 15 minutes

Real World

Bruce Johnson

Complexity is the enemy of solid development. The more complex the solution, the more likely that a bug will arise, either in the logic of the design or in the implementation. As an application moves from the development phase to support, the cost of complexity grows. The transfer of knowledge from the original developer to the maintenance group is rarely (okay...never) perfect.

The goal of an application flow-logic diagram (which is also called a component diagram in some circles) is to document the complex interplay between components. Although the utility of such a diagram can be argued, the reality is that any information that decreases (or documents) complexity should be both practiced and encouraged.

Application Flow-Logic vs. Class Diagrams

If you think of an application in terms of the components that comprise it, you are well along the way to creating an application flow-logic diagram. But as a refresher, let's consider the difference between components and classes and the corresponding diagrams.

A component is a piece of executable code. Typically, this definition also includes the idea that the component is a unit of deployment as well. It is self-contained (in a single DLL, for example) and can be deployed as a stand-alone unit (not that the stand-alone unit will be able to do anything on its own, but the same component could be replaced or reused individually). A class, on the other hand, is a functional structure. It contains data and methods that act on that data. It is not an executable code but is really defined by the implementation.

The difference between the diagrams is similar. A class diagram includes the relationships and aggregations that exist between various classes. Each link is bidirectional in that a class can, for example, access parental methods or be cast into a more specific derived type. The relationship between components, however, is unidirectional. If there is a dependency from component A to component B, there is no way for component B to also be dependent on component A. If component A calls a method exposed on component B's interface, there is no requirement that component B also call a method on component A's interface.

Elements of the Diagram

There are, as has already been mentioned, three elements in the application flow-logic diagram:

- **Component**   As has already been described, a component is executable code bundled as a single unit of deployment. In the application flow-logic diagram, it is typically modeled as a rectangle.
- **Interface**   An interface is a set of public available properties and methods that are exposed by a component. The fact that the interface is associated with a component is represented by the lollypop symbol.
- **Dependency**   A dependency is the requirement that a particular component have the interface for a different component available in order to function correctly. A dependency relationship is indicated by a dotted directional line from the component to the dependent component.

Based on these elements, Figure 15-3 contains a sample of an application flow-logic diagram.

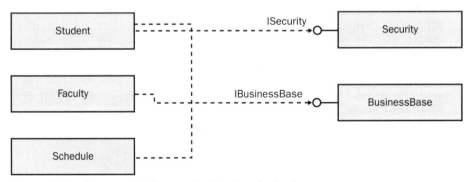

Figure 15-3   An example of an application flow-logic diagram.

Guidelines for Creation

When creating an application flow-logic diagram, you should follow a number of guidelines. These are not hard-and-fast rules, but if you follow them, the resulting diagram will be easier to understand.

- Use descriptive names for the components. These are not class names, nor are they used in code. As such, brevity is not necessarily a good thing. Proper naming, especially keeping the name as a noun, makes the discussion of the component design more natural.

- Avoid modeling data and user interface components. Although many applications do have components specifically related to data and user interface elements, they really don't affect the logic or flow of the application. As such, they shouldn't be included in this diagram.

- Interfaces should be represented by the lollypop notation even if no other component in the diagram uses the interface.

- Although it might appear contradictory, only relevant interfaces should be shown. An example of this would be the *IDisposable* interface. It is unlikely that the inclusion of the interface in the application flow-logic diagram will be necessary.

- Flow the dependencies from left to right and top to bottom on the diagram.

- Components should depend only on interfaces. This makes the implementation and deployment of a particular module much cleaner.

- Compilation dependencies should not be modeled. The relationship between components is about dependency, not the order in which components need to be compiled in order to have the latest changes available. Although the compilation dependencies might provide clues to the existence of a relationship, the compilation dependencies should not be included by themselves.

Quick Check

- What is the difference between an application flow-logic diagram and a class hierarchy diagram?

Quick Check Answer

- The relationship between components in the application flow-logic diagram is unidirectional, while the classes in a hierarchy have a bidirectional relationship.

Component Complexity

In the software world, complexity measures a number of elements associated with the software. Although a number of different algorithms can be used, for this lesson we'll concentrate on cyclomatic complexity because the algorithm ties nicely to the application flow-logic diagram and because of the analytical value that it adds to the support process.

Cyclomatic complexity is a broad measure of the soundness and confidence of a system. The premise behind the measure is that in any software application there are a number of independent paths and connections between the various elements. By measuring the connectedness of the elements, a single number can be reached. This single number then (generally) represents the complexity of the system. The less complex the system, the more confident a user or developer can be of its correctness. And, from a support perspective, less complex systems are much easier to maintain and enhance.

The algorithm used to calculate cyclomatic complexity is relatively straightforward. It is as follows:

```
C = E - N + p
```

The variables used in this equation are

- **E** The number of edges in the diagram. When applied to the application flow-logic diagram, this is the number of dotted lines.
- **N** The number of nodes in the diagram. Again, relating to the application flow-logic diagram, this is the number of components.
- **p** The number of connected components. Some components in a system can exist without external (to the component) dependencies. This value is the number that have dependencies.

Given that this formula results in a single number, it now comes down to how this value can be applied. Based on a large set of sample data, Table 15-1 contains the range of values and a general interpretation.

Table 15-1 Cyclomatic Complexity Ranges

Complexity	Interpretation
1–10	A simple, easy-to-comprehend system.
11–20	A moderately complicated system. Still reasonable to modify, but some care needs to be taken.
21–50	A complex system with many interactions to be considered. Changes can be made, but with a high risk of unplanned behavior.
> 50	A very complex system that qualifies as being almost untestable. Changes are almost certain to have unexpected side effects.

As can be seen in Table 15-1, the higher the cyclomatic complexity, the more difficult it is to maintain and test an application. Also, complexity tends to increase as enhancements are made to the application without a corresponding refactoring of components. The refactoring of components into smaller elements with fewer interactions would work to decrease complexity. However, without this refactoring, complexity increases as maintenance activities occur.

As well as identifying the risk associated with change, the complexity of a system is also a direct function of how much testing needs to take place. The higher the complexity, the more test cases that need to be created in order to capture not just the interactions but also the boundary cases associated with each interaction. So for a complex system, creating a comprehensive test suite becomes a prohibitive exercise.

One final note for this section. Although we used cyclomatic complexity as the example, any number of formulae can be used to calculate the complexity of a system. Although the specific results might vary, in general the rationale for complexity doesn't differ. And the conclusions with respect to the impact on maintenance activity and testability do not depend on the method used because both are directly related to the understandability of a system. And understandability is one of the features that complexity, in whatever form, is intended to measure.

Lesson Summary

- The application flow-logic diagram documents the dependency relationship between components.
- The complexity of a system has a direct impact on the understandability and maintainability of the system.

Lesson Review

You can use the following questions to test your knowledge of the information in Lesson 2, "Application Flow-Logic Diagrams." The questions are also available on the companion CD if you prefer to review them in electronic form.

NOTE Answers

Answers to these questions and explanations of why each answer choice is right or wrong are located in the "Answers" section at the end of the book.

---

1. Which of the following statements is not true about an application flow-logic diagram?
   A. It documents the dependencies that exist between components.
   B. Every component must have a one-to-one correlation to a class.
   C. The connections between the components must include an interface.
   D. The application flow-logic diagram can't have a circular reference.

2. Based on an analysis of your application, it is determined that the cyclomatic complexity is 15. Which of the following statements are true? (Choose all that apply.)

    A. Changes to the application can be made with low to moderate risk of introducing side-effect bugs.

    B. Adding a new component that contains some of the functionality of a current component will reduce the complexity of the application.

    C. Combining the functionality of two components will reduce the complexity of the application.

    D. It will be very difficult to change the application without creating new bugs.

3. Which of the following is not a component of an application flow-logic diagram?

    A. Class

    B. Component

    C. Dependency

    D. Interface

Chapter Review

To further practice and reinforce the skills you learned in this chapter, you can perform the following tasks:

- Review the chapter summary.
- Review the list of key terms introduced in this chapter.
- Complete the case scenarios. These scenarios set up real-world situations involving the topics of this chapter and ask you to create a solution.
- Complete the suggested practices.
- Take a practice test.

Chapter Summary

- Supporting an application that is running in production requires either that the application is proactive in providing details about its health or that external tools, such as Performance Monitor, have to be used to impute its status.
- Identifying the source of performance issues requires patience, attention to details, and an understanding of some of the inner workings of the .NET Framework.
- A system with a large number of component dependencies relative to the number of components will have a high complexity level. This in turn will make maintenance tasks more challenging to accomplish.

Key Terms

Do you know what these key terms mean? You can check your answers by looking up the terms in the glossary at the end of the book.

- complexity
- cyclomatic complexity
- kernel mode
- page
- page fault
- performance alert
- privileged mode
- user mode
- working set

Case Scenarios

In the following case scenarios, you will apply what you've learned about delivering multimedia in a distributed environment. You can find answers to these questions in the "Answers" section at the end of the book.

Case Scenario 1: Tuning an Application

You are a corporate developer who created a Windows application that processes flat files. Each flat file contains sales lead information that needs to be converted into database records. The flat file can contain anywhere from 1000 to more than 1,000,000 leads.

Now that the application has been released, you are getting reports that the performance, especially on large files, is slower than users would like to see.

Questions

Answer the following questions for your manager.

1. On the surface, which is the most likely source for a performance issue, CPU or memory? How would you make sure that your hunch was correct?
2. If the source is memory, which counters would you consider using to further identify the cause?
3. If the source is CPU, which counters would you consider using to further identify the cause?

Case Scenario 2: Diagramming an Application

You are a corporate developer who is creating some of the documentation that will be used to support the application after deployment. To help, you are creating an application flow-logic diagram.

Questions

Answer the following questions for your manager.

1. Which elements should be included in the diagram?
2. Should the diagram model the class hierarchy?
3. A number of data access components are in the application. Should they be included in the diagram?

Suggested Practices

To help successfully master the objectives covered in this chapter, complete the following tasks.

You Can Tune an Application...

For this task, you should complete both practices.

- **Practice 1**   Using a .NET application that has currently been deployed, use the Performance Monitor to track the CPU usage. Look for situations where there are spikes in the usage value and try to associate them with a particular function being performed by the application.

- **Practice 2**   Using a .NET application that has currently been deployed, use the Performance Monitor to track the allocation of memory. Use the Private Bytes and Allocated Bytes/sec counter to determine if an excessive number of objects is being created.

Application Flow-Logic Diagrams

For this task, you should complete both practices.

- **Practice 1**   Using a .NET application that is already deployed or is close to the deployment phase, create an application flow-logic diagram.

- **Practice 2**   Using the same .NET application used in Practice 1, calculate the complexity of the system. Use this value to identify the level of risk associated with making modifications to the application.

Take a Practice Test

The practice tests on this book's companion CD offer many options. For example, you can test yourself on just one exam objective, or you can test yourself on all the 70-548 certification exam content. You can set up the test so that it closely simulates the experience of taking a certification exam, or you can set it up in study mode so that you can look at the correct answers and explanations after you answer each question.

MORE INFO   Practice tests

For details about all the practice test options available, see the "How to Use the Practice Tests" section in this book's Introduction.

Chapter 16
Multimedia in Windows Applications

Developers have long shied away from the challenges of adding graphics to Microsoft Windows applications. The starting point for avoidance was the complexity associated with Graphics Device Interface (GDI). And, although vast improvements have been made (see GDI+ and DirectX), how to draw lines and circles onto a form is not familiar to a large number of developers.

To be fair, there has not been a large demand for adding "pretty pictures" to business applications; at least, not until recently. The networked world is now colorful, and an application that can sketch only in black and white will be frowned on. Multimedia is all over the Web. To avoid unfavorable comparisons to Web pages, the same functionality must be delivered to users who are using Windows Forms applications. The goal of this chapter is to examine the mechanisms you can use to modernize your user interface (and probably your user's day) by adding rich content to Windows applications.

Exam objectives in this chapter:
- Choose an appropriate mechanism to deliver multimedia data from an application.
  - ❑ Evaluate available multimedia delivery mechanisms. Considerations include bandwidth problems, file formats, frames per second, and streaming types.
  - ❑ Design a multimedia delivery mechanism.

Lessons in this chapter:

Before You Begin

To complete the lessons in this chapter, you must have:

- A computer that meets or exceeds the minimum hardware requirements listed in this book's Introduction.
- Visual Studio 2005 installed on the computer, with either Visual Basic .NET or C# installed.
- DirectX Software Development Kit (SDK) installed on the computer. The August 2006 SDK installation file can be downloaded from *http://www.microsoft.com/downloads/ details.aspx?familyid=C72D9F1E-53F3-4747-8490-6801D8E8B4EF*. Earlier versions of the SDK might also work.

Real World

Bruce Johnson

I'm very quick to admit that I lack the graphics gene. When it comes to creating compelling images, either still or moving, I'm not the person to turn to. And I'm not the leader in making music, either—perhaps it's not a tin ear, but certainly an inability to translate the music in my head to a more compatible format. In all cases, there are others who are much more capable of creating the pictures, videos, and sounds that can make applications more memorable.

Although there is little that Microsoft can do to help my multimedia-challenged mentality, the .NET Framework contains a number of classes that are aimed at allowing me to deliver rich content (created by others) to my users. The supported formats, along with the pros and cons, are the topics of this lesson.

Lesson 1: Choosing a Delivery Format

As with any technology that is on the leading edge (and, really, multimedia does fall into this category), a number of options are available. The toughest part for a developer is knowing what the trade-offs are so that the most appropriate approach can be selected. Multimedia makes this even more challenging because there are really two areas that need to be considered—audio and video. In this lesson, the formats (and the attributes that define them) will be considered separately.

After this lesson, you will be able to:

- Identify the different audio and video formats that are supported by the .NET Framework.
- Understand the different approaches that each format uses.
- Evaluate the requirements of your application to determine which format is most appropriate.

Estimated lesson time: 15 minutes

Audio Formats

In .NET 2.0 the *System.Media* is the namespace used to hold the classes associated with playing an audio file. Unfortunately, there is built-in support only for WAV files. Happily, by using the Windows Media Player SDK, you do have the capability to also play WMA and MP3 files, giving you the (questionably applied) option to launch your Windows application to the strains of "Funky Cold Medina."

Although there are a number of formats to choose from, what is the difference between them that makes one better than another? In general, the distinguishing characteristics fall into one of two categories, and both of them are related to the process of minimizing the size of the file so that it can be more easily delivered or distributed.

Sampling Rate

Unlike analog sound, in which the audio representation is a continuous wave, digital sound consists of a set of discrete tones. Only by playing the tones sequentially at high speeds can an approximation of the analog sound be achieved. The *sampling rate* is the frequency at which analog sound is converted to a digital representation. Consider it to be the number of datapoints taken per second that the analog sound is playing. A sampling rate is normally measured in hertz (Hz) and is the first determinant in the quality of the sound. CD-quality audio is typically 44.1 kHz, which is 44,100 samples per second.

As you might expect, there is a trade-off between sound quality (higher sampling rate) and file size. The higher the sampling rate, the more datapoints are required to reproduce the sound.

So why not have as high a sampling rate as possible? First, the quality of the original source might not justify a high sampling rate. A vinyl album or a microphone might not have the capability to capture CD-quality audio. Second, the destination of the sound might not be able to reproduce CD-quality sound with sufficient fidelity. In both cases it would be a waste of disk space or bandwidth to provide CD-quality audio if it's going to be played back on PC-quality speakers.

Audio Compression

There are two main ways to describe the mechanics of audio compression. The most common standard defines how some information about the sound is eliminated in order to reduce bandwidth requirements. This is known as audio data compression. The second type of compression (known as audio level compression) involves eliminating some of the dynamic range of the sound to the same effect, that being a reduction in the size of the file or stream.

From a developer's perspective, the main consideration for audio data compression is whether it is lossless or lossy. Lossless compression means that all of the information about the original sound is included in the compressed version. The most common format of this type is the Free Lossless Audio Codec (FLAC). Lossy compression makes use of the fact that we humans have limited hearing abilities. People are not capable of hearing all frequencies and volumes with the same effectiveness. Thus, by eliminating data points that represent sounds either outside or at the edge of our ability to perceive them, the size of the audio content can be reduced. MP3 and earlier versions of WMA take this approach. Since WMA 9.0 was released in 2003, a set of lossless codecs has been available.

A common file format for audio files is the WAV format. This is a standard developed by Microsoft and IBM. It's not normally a compressed format, although it's capable of stored compressed versions of the sound. Although it was a very popular format earlier in the age of multimedia, it has decreased in popularity as the growth of Internet-delivered audio has increased. WAV files are lossless, which results in a relatively large file system. The lack of compression also contributes to this large size. Its main appeal is the simplicity of the file format.

Quick Check

1. What is the difference between lossy and lossless compression algorithms?
2. What two techniques are used to compress audio files?

Quick Check Answers

1. Lossless compression algorithms keep all of the data associated with the sound. Lossy compression algorithms use the characteristics of the sound and the limitations of human aural capabilities to remove some of the data associated with the sound.
2. The two techniques are audio data compression and audio level compression.

Video Formats

Video formats face many of the same challenges that audio formats do when it comes to reducing content size. So although the terms might be different than in the audio formats, many of the concepts are the same—particularly in the area of trying to strike a balance between file size and quality.

Frame Rate

The *frame rate* is the equivalent of the sampling rate for video. The name comes from the number of still pictures on the reel of tape that was used by mechanical video projectors. Motion pictures typically run at 24 frames per second (fps), while digital images are closer to 60 fps. The actual number depends on the specific video format.

Resolution

Resolution is a concept most of us developers are familiar with due to our constant exposure to computer monitors. It's the number of pixels in the horizontal and vertical dimensions of an image. The range can be from 640 x 480 (standard definition television) to 1920 x 1080 (high-definition television, HDTV). Naturally, it can be higher (and probably will be someday), but this is the range for the hardware that is currently in common use.

For the developer, the resolution of the video and the resolution of the monitor need to be in sync. Not that they need to be identical, but certainly some understanding of the restrictions on the client hardware is necessary. After all, you don't want to deliver a 640 x 480 video stream to a hi-def television, nor a DVD-quality stream to a cell phone's screen. The desired resolution will depend on the target for the content. If you're streaming video to computer users, using a high-definition resolution will usually be a waste of bandwidth.

Compression

Video has the same need for compression that audio does; perhaps more so, given the amount of information that is required to serve up a single frame. And although the approach might seem similar to audio compression, video compression takes advantage of the fact that consecutive frames have a great deal of spatial and temporal redundancy. Compression techniques usually fall into one of two categories:

- **Intraframe** Registers the differences between parts of a single frame. This approaches uses the spatial redundancy on each frame, that being the idea that the individual data point on an image is similar to immediately adjacent points. This is conceptually the same as performing basic image compression on each individual frame.
- **Interframe** Registers the differences between contiguous frames. This technique takes advantage of the temporary redundancy by assuming that, for the most part, only a small percentage of each image changes from frame to frame.

The most common format for video compression is MPEG (Moving Pictures Experts Group), with MPEG-2 and MPEG-4 being the typical implementations. MPEG-2 is used for satellite television and DVDs. MPEG-4 is used for home videos. Microsoft has produced a format called Windows Media Video (WMV) that was originally based, in part, on some of the same principles as MPEG-4. Over time, some improvements were made and submitted for standardization. As of 2006, WMV version 9 is an approved standard and is no longer considered proprietary.

Quick Check

- What areas affect the quality of the video stream?

Quick Check Answer

- The frame rate, the resolution, and the compression affect the quality (and, by the same token, the size) of the video stream.

Challenges in Multimedia Delivery

When it comes to delivering multimedia, deciding which of the available formats to use is only part of the problem. Other potential issues include network capacity, client capabilities, and licensing.

Network Capacity

For all but the most trivially small files, multimedia content has an impact on network performance. Graphics images tend to be larger than text, and streaming video and audio provide a greater and potentially more protracted load. Unrestrained and unplanned multimedia delivery can easily bring a network to a crawl.

Planning a network is akin to designing the streets of a town. In order to figure out where the streets should go, you need to know where people start and where they end up. You need to know how many people travel over a period of time. All of this information is taken into consideration as the town planner designs and approves the various layouts. The challenge is to balance the joy of unlimited capacity (that is, roads everywhere) with the sorrow of paying for unlimited capacity (that is, no parks, houses, and so on).

Network planning requires the same basic inputs to arrive at an optimal design. A network engineer needs to know what the source and destination of packets are and how many are expected to be sent and when. The details of multimedia content distribution will naturally be of interest to the network engineer engaged in a capacity planning exercise. The engineer will want to know the types of content that are being delivered. The engineer will be interested in the patterns of usage for the content. The timing of the requests and their frequency are part of the analysis. All this information can be used to ensure that the network capacity is sufficient to support the planned application.

It should be made clear that the information about the demands made by the content on the network is only part of what a network engineer will consider. When it comes to network capacity, what's most important is the number of simultaneous users who will access the content. Assuming you're not targeting connections running through a 56-KB modem stage, almost every network can handle the delivery of a single content stream. What really matters is how the network will perform (and how it needs to perform) as the number of simultaneous users increases.

Quality of Service

With multimedia content, simply having available bandwidth isn't always sufficient. Instead, the latency, *jitter* (change in latency), and point-in-time throughput might be more important. This is especially true when the content is streamed audio or video. Network delays can cause client applications to pause, stutter, or just stop working. And for audio and video, this degradation is not only noticeable but could also cause the application to fail in the eyes of the users.

From a development perspective there is little you can do to control the quality or bandwidth of the network used by your application. This falls into the realm of the network experts who make up your operations staff—people to whom Quality of Service (QoS) has a special meaning.

MORE INFO   Quality of Service in Windows applications

The QoS for Windows applications can be configured on a per computer or per subnet basis. For more details on exactly what capabilities are available and how to activate them, check out the "Quality of Service" section of the TCP/IP Core Networking Guide at *http://www.microsoft.com /technet/prodtechnol/windows2000serv/reskit/cnet/cndc_qos_hrgn.mspx?mfr=true*.

When giving the engineers the needed information, make sure that you provide sufficient details. There are many facts to consider when calculating network bandwidth usage. It is rarely as simple as just adding up the size of the delivered files and comparing it to the size of the network pipes. Caching and peer networking can eliminate much of the drain on the network if they are configured properly. Providing the network engineers with the necessary details will go a long way toward ensuring a successful deployment.

Client Capabilities

If you are creating a Windows application that includes multimedia, one of the most annoying words you will hear is *codec*. A codec (short for compression/decompression or coder/ decoder, depending on whom you ask) is a piece of software that is responsible for handling the compression and decompression of a stream of content. Figure 16-1 illustrates the position of codecs within the content stream.

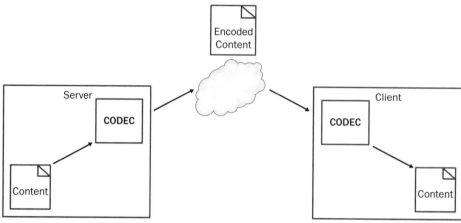

Figure 16-1   Codecs in the content stream.

For most formats, whether audio, video, or graphical, the main client requirement comes in the form of a codec. When consuming multimedia content, it's important to be aware of the codec requirements for the client. This is especially true for video streams because they have a history of being more dependent on the presence of specific codecs. Also, if you expect the video stream to have sound (a common situation), there will be a separate audio stream, complete with its own codec. There is no requirement that a particular video codec be paired with a specific audio codec. The result is that strange combinations of codecs can be required in order to play seemingly "simple" content.

The details of how to install the required codecs depend on the vendor of the codec. All vendors will have their own mechanisms and steps that need to be followed. Also, you need to be aware of the licensing restrictions associated with the codec. It's possible that the compression algorithm is proprietary. It's up to the developer to make sure that the licensing requirements are followed as the software gets deployed.

Digital Rights Management

Digital Rights Management (DRM) is a term that applies to a broad set of technologies associated with the management of the intellectual property rights of digital content. In most cases, DRM software handles the monitoring and enforcement of the usage of digital works through a copy protection or a technical protection mechanism.

In the Windows world one of the more common mechanisms with which to implement DRM is Windows Media Rights Manager (WM Rights Manager). This application helps administrators continually control access to protected information. For example, it's possible to require that a person accessing protected content have a license that is generated by WM Rights Manager before it can be played. Although WM Rights Manager isn't the only resource available to provide DRM functionality, it's certainly more than capable of supporting a large number of common scenarios.

> ## Quick Check
> - What trade-offs have to be made when determining which audio format to use? What about the video format?
>
> ### Quick Check Answers
> - In both cases the trade-off is speed and size of the delivered content versus quality of output. Providing high fidelity in both audio and video means that more data needs to be transmitted. And more data increases the bandwidth requirement, as well as the computational effort to decode the stream of bytes.

Lesson Summary

- The audio and video formats attempt to strike a balance between quality and size of content.
- The impact that multimedia content has on the network goes beyond the size of the binary data. In also encompasses the number and regularity of the requests for the data.
- If bandwidth considerations are an issue, make sure that you don't overdeliver the content. In other words, match the quality and compression to the expected target audience.

Lesson Review

You can use the following questions to test your knowledge of the information in Lesson 1, "Choosing a Delivery Format." The questions are also available on the companion CD if you prefer to review them in electronic form.

NOTE   Answers

Answers to these questions and explanations of why each answer choice is right or wrong are located in the "Answers" section at the end of the book.

---

1. You are writing a Windows Forms application. Part of the application plays a two-minute audio track downloaded on demand from a remote Web site. What factors go into choosing the appropriate format? (Choose all that apply.)

   A. The source of the audio track

   B. The compression level of the audio track

   C. The available bandwidth between the application and the remote Web site

   D. The sampling rate of the audio track

2. Your company has created a software application that will be sold to third parties. Part of the application includes the display of a number of videos. The videos are to be located on a server, while the application will be installed on each of the client computers. Your responsibility is to document the information that needs to be gathered before installation can take place. Which of the following topics is *not* an area that will be covered in your document?

   A. Network bandwidth requirements

   B. Content licensing requirements

   C. Codecs required on the client's computer

   D. Quality of Service requirements

Lesson 2: Building a Delivery Mechanism

Once you have selected the format to use, the next trick ... er ... step is to deliver the multimedia content to the desktop. In this lesson we talk about some of the classes in the .NET Framework that you can use to present audio and video to the user.

After this lesson, you will be able to:

- Play system sounds, as well as more complex audio formats, in Windows Forms applications.
- Identify the components of DirectShow that can be used to control the display of video content.
- Display video either in a separate application window or embedded within a Windows form.

Estimated lesson time: 30 minutes

Playing Audio

When it comes to playing sound in a .NET 2.0 application, the *System.Media* is the first namespace to look at. The sounds that can be played using the *System.Media* classes fall into two categories: system sounds and WAV files.

System Sounds

The system sounds that can be played for your application are available through the *System-Sounds* class. This class exposes five properties: *Asterisk*, *Beep*, *Exclamation*, *Hand*, and *Question*. Each of these properties is actually a *SystemSound* object. By invoking the *Play* method on these objects, the WAV file associated with each of these system sounds will be heard.

```
' VB
System.Media.SystemSounds.Exclamation.Play()
```

```
// C#
System.Media.SystemSounds.Exclamation.Play();
```

The reason for using these properties is to allow users to customize the sounds that emanate from your application. If a user decides to change the sounds on a computer from the default, your application picks up the changes and acts like a well-behaved citizen of the Microsoft Windows world.

WAV Files

Even with the wide variety (okay, five) of system sounds that can be played, sometimes additional sounds might be required. For these times, the *SoundPlayer* class (also part of the *System.Media* namespace) can be used.

First of all, the *SoundPlayer* class is limited in that only WAV files can be played. But within that limitation, the *SoundPlayer* class exposes a number of useful features. In terms of specifying the location of the WAV file, the *SoundLocation* property is used. This property can be assigned a file path, a Universal Naming Convention (UNC) path, or even a Uniform Resource Locator (URL).

Given the fact that the sound could be located on a URL (that is, on a remote Web site), the speed at which the file is available might have an impact on how the sound is delivered. To accommodate this, sound can be played in a number of ways.

If the location of the sound is close to the application playing the sound, then the *Play* method on the *SoundPlayer* class can be used. This simply loads the WAV file and plays it. One of the convenient (and unexpected) features of the *Play* method is that although it is synchronous, it does not block the current thread. Instead, a separate thread is created and the file is loaded and played on that thread. This keeps a large or slowly loading WAV file from blocking the application, which is an important consideration if the *SoundPlayer* were to be invoked from within a Windows Forms application because in that case blocking the main thread would result in the application appearing to hang.

```
' VB
Dim Player As New SoundPlayer
Player.SoundLocation = "C:\Program Files\Messenger\newemail.Wav"
Player.Play()
```

```
// C#
SoundPlayer player = new SoundPlayer();
player.SoundLocation = @"C:\Program Files\Messenger\newemail.Wav";
player.Play();
```

If the location of the file is further away, the loading of the WAV file can be performed asynchronously. Then once the file is loaded, it can be played synchronously.

```
' VB
Dim Player As New SoundPlayer
Player.SoundLocation = "C:\Program Files\Messenger\newemail.wav"
Player.LoadAsync()
If Player.IsLoadCompleted Then
    Player.Play()
End If
```

```
// C#
SoundPlayer  player = new SoundPlayer();
player.SoundLocation = @"C:\Program Files\Messenger\newemail.wav";
```

```
player.LoadAsync();
if (player.IsLoadCompleted)
    player.Play();
```

Rather than polling the *IsLoadCompleted* property, the *LoadCompleted* event could be used. *LoadCompleted* gets raised once the file has finished loading. This means that you could create a *LoadCompleted* event handler that includes the *Play* method. If the loading of the WAV file was unsuccessful for any reason, the *Error* property on the *AsyncCompletedEventArgs* parameter will be set to a non-null value.

If it is absolutely required that the WAV file be played on the current thread, the *PlaySync* method can be used.

```
' VB
Dim Player As New SoundPlayer
Player.SoundLocation = "C:\Program Files\Messenger\newemail.Wav"
Player.PlaySync()
```

```
// C#
SoundPlayer  player = new SoundPlayer();
player.SoundLocation = @"C:\Program Files\Messenger\newemail.Wav";
player.PlaySync();
```

The caveat here, of course, is that if the file is large or slow to retrieve, the application will appear to freeze until the WAV file has finished loading and playing.

One of the events exposed by the *SoundPlayer* is called *SoundLocationChanged*. It is raised every time that the *SoundLocation* property is assigned a different property. One of the reasons for interest in this property is that it might be appropriate for an application to load the sound as soon as the location has changed. Loading is actually a separate process from playing. The *Play* method performs a load (if necessary) followed by a play. But the purpose of the *Load* method is to allow the developer to separate these two steps. The *Load* retrieves the sound, but doesn't start playing. Then the next invocation of *Play* or *PlaySync* won't require the file to be loaded.

Exam Tip   There are subtle differences between *Play*, *PlaySync*, *Load*, and *LoadAsync*. These differences could make for some very interesting exam questions.

Other Audio Files

The main limitation of the *SoundPlayer* class is that it plays only WAV files. If you need to play MP3 or WMA files, another option is required. Although a number of third-party components accomplish this, there is nothing in the .NET Framework to accomplish this. If you want to use a Microsoft solution, the Windows Media Player SDK must be incorporated in the solution.

Install the Media Player SDK and add a reference to the libraries. Then you can used the *WindowsMediaPlayer* class to play any audio file supported by Windows Media Player using the following code:

```
' VB
Dim WMP As New WMPLib.WindowsMediaPlayer
WMP.URL = "C:\My Music\Funky Cold Medina.wma"
WMP.controls.play()
```

```
// C#
WMPLib.WindowsMediaPlayer WMP = new WMPLib.WindowsMediaPlayer();
WMP.URL = @"C:\My Music\Funky Cold Medina.wma";
WMP.controls.play();
```

MORE INFO   Interacting with the Windows Media Player

The Windows Media Player SDK can be downloaded from *http://www.microsoft.com/windows /windowsmedia/forpros/platform/sdk.aspx*.

Playing Video

There are no managed classes in .NET 2.0 Framework that support the playing of video. Instead, the developer is left to using COM Interop to carry out this apparently simple task. A number of options are available. Using the Media Control Interface (MCI) is one, but that application programming interface (API) is a string-based message to make functional requests. For example, in order to play a particular file, a string containing a "play" command followed by the name of the file is sent. Although MCI can be used, it is neither the easiest nor the most robust approach.

MORE INFO   Commands used in the Media Control Interface

A complete list of the commands used with MCI can be found in the "Classifications of MCI Commands" article at *http://windowssdk.msdn.microsoft.com/en-us/library/ms707311.aspx*.

Instead of looking at the MCI command, this section will concentrate on DirectShow. Direct-Show is a COM-based streaming media architecture. It provides a simplified interface to play media, convert from one format to another, and capture video from an available source.

In order to get a handle on DirectShow, it helps to understand the underlying architecture. It's a modular one where each stage of processing is performed by a *filter*. The implementation of a filter is as a COM object. The filters are strung together into a pipeline so that the stream of video can be retrieved, split, converted, and displayed as necessary. Figure 16-2 illustrates the filters that would be involved in the displaying of an AVI file.

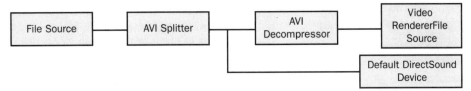

Figure 16-2 Filters used to display an AVI file.

A description of the individual steps is as follows:

- Raw data is read from the file system and presented to the next step as a byte stream.
- The AVI headers in the stream are examined. Two separate streams are created, one for video and one for audio.
- The video stream is decoded into individual video frames.
- The frames are displayed.
- In the second stream, the audio samples are sent to the default sound device.

DirectShow provides a large number of filters, but you do have the ability to write your own. However, the DirectShow architecture greatly depends on a multithreaded structure. When you combine that with the challenges of COM interoperability, creating a filter in managed code is not recommended.

In most scenarios the process of playing the video is more straightforward than this list of steps might suggest. The starting point is the *FilgraphManagerClass* class. This class is part of the quartz.dll that's installed in the %winroot%\System32 directory by default. This dynamic-link library (DLL) needs to be added as a reference to any project before starting. Because it's a COM DLL, an *Interop* class gets created when the reference is added. The name of the *Interop* class is *Interop.QuartzTypeLib*, and the exposed namespace is *QuartzTypeLib*. Although there are a number of open source wrappers for this DLL, the basic functionality implemented by the classes in *QuartzTypeLib* are easily accessible without further assistance. For more complicated functionality, using one of these wrappers is a productive approach to take.

There are two ways to use DirectShow to play video from within a Windows Forms application. The easiest way is to use a separate form. To accomplish this, two methods are called on a *FilgraphManagerClass* instance. The *RenderFile* method prepares a video file for showing, and the *Play* method launches a separate form to display the video.

```vb
' VB
Dim graphClass As New FilgraphManagerClass()
graphClass.RenderFile("configure_group_policy.avi")
graphClass.Play()
```

```csharp
// C#
FilgraphManagerClass graphClass = new FilgraphManagerClass();
graphClass.RenderFile("configure_group_policy.avi");
graphClass.Play();
```

Although this plays the video on a separate form, sometimes playing the video on an existing form is preferable. Programmatically, this is accomplished by using the *IVideoWindow* interface on the *FilgraphManagerClass* class. The owner of the *IVideoWindow* object is set to the handle of a container. The *WindowsStyle* and position of the *IVideoWindow* are then set to eliminate the border that would otherwise appear.

```vb
' VB
Dim graphClass As New FilgraphManagerClass()
graphClass.RenderFile("configure_group_policy.avi")
Dim videoWindow As IVideoWindow
videoWindow = CType(graphClass, IVideoWindow)
videoWindow.Owner = CType(Panel1.Handle, int)
videoWindow.WindowStyle = WS_CHILD Or WS_CLIPCHILDREN
videoWindow.SetWindowPosition(Panel1.ClientRectangle.Left, Panel1.ClientRectangle.Top, _
    Panel1.ClientRectangle.Width, Panel1.ClientRectangle.Height)
graphClass.Play()
```

```csharp
// C#
FilgraphManagerClass graphClass = new FilgraphManagerClass();
graphClass.RenderFile("configure_group_policy.avi");
IVideoWindow videoWindow = graphClass as IVideoWindow;
videoWindow.Owner = (int)Panel1.Handle;
videoWindow.WindowStyle = WS_CHILD | WS_CLIPCHILDREN;
videoWindow.SetWindowPosition(Panel1.ClientRectangle.Left, Panel1.ClientRectangle.Top,
    Panel1.ClientRectangle.Width, Panel1.ClientRectangle.Height);
graphClass.Play();
```

Although this code makes it appear that the image is being hosted in a *Panel* control, it's important to understand that is not what is actually happening. The *Play* method always causes a separate form to appear. By associating the form with a container control's handle, we cause the separate form to be displayed inside that panel. However, the form is still a form, complete with borders, title bars, and a control box. To remove those items from the image in the panel, you need to adjust the *WindowStyle* of the form appropriately. Specifically, the form that contains the video needs to be defined as a child form and to clip the contents to the size of the parent.

The *Play* method simply starts playing the video and moves on to the next statement. If you want the video to play through until completion, the *WaitForCompletion* method on the *FilgraphManagerClass* object is called. This method takes as parameters a timeout value and an output value representing the result code. The timeout value is the number of milliseconds before the *WaitForCompletion* returns, even if the video is not finished. This allows you to poll for completion without blocking on the main UI thread. A value of −1 for the timeout parameter results in waiting until the video is finished before continuing. This, naturally, blocks the UI thread and makes the application seem like it is hung, although the video continues playing.

To avoid this problem, it's usually a good idea to play the video on a background thread. A thread from the *ThreadPool* can be used, and then blocking on that thread by calling *Wait-ForCompletion* with an infinite timeout will provide the expected user experience while still allowing the video to play to completion.

It's important to make sure that the COM object gets released appropriately when the video has finished playing. To do this, the *Marshal.ReleaseComObject* method should be called.

```
' VB
While (Marshal.ReleaseComObject(graphClass) > 0)
Loop
```

```
// C#
while (Marshal.ReleaseComObject(graphClass) > 0) ;
```

MORE INFO   Exploring DirectShow's capabilities

As you might guess, there is a lot more functionality available through DirectShow, including the ability to capture video from an external source and create a single frame from a video. See the article "Fun with DVR-MS" at *http://msdn.microsoft.com/library/en-us/dnxpmce/html/dvr-ms.asp* for a description of some of these additional features.

Lab: Delivering Multimedia to the Desktop

In this lab we'll explore a couple of the mechanisms that can be used to provide audio and video content to Windows Forms applications. In both cases a local file will be retrieved and played. For the audio exercise, it will be a WAV file. For the video version, it will be an AVI file.

▶ **Exercise 1: Delivering Music**

In this exercise you will go through the steps to play a WAV file at the push of a button. The WAV file is already included in the project. Also, to eliminate the need to provide a full path, the WAV file is marked in the project as being always copied to the output directory.

1. Launch Visual Studio 2005.
2. Open a solution using File | Open | Project/Solution. Navigate to the Chapter16/ Lesson2/<language>/Exercise1-Before directory. Select the Exercise1 solution and click Open.
3. In the Solution Explorer, double-click Form1.
4. A small form appears in the designer. The form consists of a text box containing a file name, a button that displays a File Open dialog box, and a button labeled Play. The idea is that when the Play button is clicked, the file in the text box will be played. Double-click Play to open the *Click* event handler method.
5. Add an *If* statement to ensure that the text box has been populated. This is just a good coding practice.

```vb
' VB
If Not String.IsNullOrEmpty(soundFileTextBox.Text) Then
End If
```

```csharp
// C#
if (!String.IsNullOrEmpty(soundFileTextBox.Text))
{
}
```

6. Within the *If* block, instantiate a *SoundPlayer* object. Then set the *SoundLocation* to the value of the *Text* property of the *soundFileTextBox* control and play the sound.

```vb
' VB
Dim player as New System.Media.SoundPlayer()
player.SoundLocation = soundFileTextBox.Text
player.Play()
```

```csharp
// C#
System.Media.SoundPlayer player = new System.Media.SoundPlayer();
player.SoundLocation = soundFileTextBox.Text;
player.Play();
```

7. Launch the application using the F5 key.

8. Click Play (making sure that you have speakers and that the volume is turned up). You should hear the sound that Windows XP makes when you log on.

9. Terminate the running application.

10. Next, we'll set up the loading of the WAV file to take place asynchronously. In the *Click* event handler for the Play button, delete the player.Play() statement.

11. In the same method, add a procedure that will be invoked when the loading of the WAV file is completed. Add the following code in place of the just deleted statement:

```vb
' VB
AddHandler player.LoadCompleted, New _
    AsyncCompletedEventHandler(AddressOf player_LoadCompleted);
```

```csharp
// C#
player.LoadCompleted += new AsyncCompletedEventHandler(player_LoadCompleted);
```

12. Below the just added statement, add the following code to start the asynchronous load process:

```vb
' VB
player.LoadAsync()
```

```csharp
// C#
player.LoadAsync();
```

13. Now you need to add the method that gets invoked when the load is completed. In this method, the *Play* method on the *SoundPlayer* object is invoked. In the *LoadCompleted* handler, the *SoundPlayer* is the sender of the event. Add the following procedure below the *Click* event handling procedure:

```vb
' VB
Private Sub player_LoadCompleted(sender As Object, e As AsyncCompletedEventArgs)
    If e.Error Is Nothing Then
        CType(sender, System.Media.SoundPlayer).Play()
    End If
End Sub
```

```csharp
// C#
private void player_LoadCompleted(object sender, AsyncCompletedEventArgs e)
{
    if (e.Error == null)
        ((System.Media.SoundPlayer)sender).Play();
}
```

14. Launch the application using the F5 key.

15. Click Play (making sure that you have speakers and that the volume is turned up). You should hear the sound that Windows XP makes when you log on.

▶ **Exercise 2: Delivering Video**

In this exercise you will go through the steps to play an AVI file at the push of a button. The AVI file is already included in the project. Also, to eliminate the need to provide a full path, the AVI file is marked in the project as being always copied to the output directory.

1. Launch Visual Studio 2005.

2. Open a solution using File | Open | Project/Solution. Navigate to the Chapter16/ Lesson2/<language>/Exercise2-Before directory. Select the Exercise2 solution and click Open.

3. In the Solution Explorer, double-click Form1.

4. Double-click Play to create the *Click* event handler procedure.

5. Use the *FilgraphManagerClass* to render the file that is to be displayed. Once the file is rendered, play it in a separate window. Add the following code to the *Click* event handler procedure:

```vb
' VB
Dim graphClass As New FilgraphManagerClass()
graphClass.RenderFile("..\..\..\..\..\configure_group_policy.avi")
graphClass.Run()
```

```csharp
// C#
graphClass = new FilgraphManagerClass();
graphClass.RenderFile(@"..\..\..\..\..\configure_group_policy.avi");
graphClass.Run();
```

6. In order to be notified when the video is completed, the *WaitForCompletion* method must be used. Because this is a short video, set the wait period to infinite by adding the following code after to the call to the *Run* method:

```vb
' VB
Dim code as Integer
```

```
graphClass.WaitForCompletion(Timeout.Infinite, code)
graphClass.Stop()
```

```
// C#
int code;
graphClass.WaitForCompletion(Timeout.Infinite, out code);
graphClass.Stop();
```

7. Launch the application with the F5 key.

8. Click Play. Notice that the video starts running and it now runs through to completion. However, while running, the rest of the application is nonresponsive. When the video is finished, terminate the application.

9. To get the video to play on a separate thread (specifically, not the UI thread), the *Thread-Pool* is used. To start, remove all of the code immediately below the call to *RenderFile*. You don't want to delete it because it will be used momentarily, but it needs to be moved out of the current method. In its place, add a statement to call a method named *runVideo* using the *ThreadPool*.

```
' VB
ThreadPool.QueueUserWorkItem(New WaitCallback(AddressOf runVideo), graphClass)
```

```
// C#
ThreadPool.QueueUserWorkItem(new WaitCallback(runVideo), graphClass);
```

10. Next, the *runVideo* method needs to be created. Most of the statements are those that were mentioned in Step 9. The *runVideo* method, which should be added below the *Click* event handling procedure, will look like the following:

```
' VB
Private Sub runVideo(state as Object)
    Dim graphClass As FilgraphManagerClass
    graphClass = CType(state, FilgraphManagerClass)

    graphClass.Run()
    Dim code As Integer
    graphClass.WaitForCompletion(Timeout.Infinite, code)
    graphClass.Stop()
End Sub
```

```
// C#
private void runVideo(object state)
{
    FilgraphManagerClass graphClass = (FilgraphManagerClass)state;
    graphClass.Run();
    int code;
    graphClass.WaitForCompletion(Timeout.Infinite, out code);
    graphClass.Stop();
}
```

11. Launch the application with the F5 key.

12. Click Play. Notice that the video starts running and it now runs through to completion. And now, while it's running, the rest of the application is completely responsive. When the video is finished, terminate the application.

13. The last step is to place the video inside a panel on the form. To do this, the *Owner* of the *FilgraphManagerClass* is set to the *Handle* property of the panel. And the *WindowStyle* property on the *FilgraphManagerClass* object is set to eliminate those elements of the stand-alone form that don't look good when embedded in a panel. Add the following code prior to the call to the *QueueUserWorkItem* method:

```vb
' VB
Dim videoWindow As IVideoWindow
videoWindow = CType(graphClass, IVideoWindow)
videoWindow.Owner = Convert.ToInt32(videoDisplayPanel.Handle)
videoWindow.WindowStyle = WS_CHILD Or WS_CLIPCHILDREN
            videoWindow.SetWindowPosition(videoDisplayPanel.ClientRectangle.Left, _
    videoDisplayPanel.ClientRectangle.Top, _
    videoDisplayPanel.ClientRectangle.Width, _
    videoDisplayPanel.ClientRectangle.Height)
```

```csharp
// C#
IVideoWindow videoWindow = graphClass as IVideoWindow;
videoWindow.Owner = (int)videoDisplayPanel.Handle;
videoWindow.WindowStyle = WS_CHILD | WS_CLIPCHILDREN;
            videoWindow.SetWindowPosition(videoDisplayPanel.ClientRectangle.Left,
    videoDisplayPanel.ClientRectangle.Top,
    videoDisplayPanel.ClientRectangle.Width,
    videoDisplayPanel.ClientRectangle.Height);
```

14. Launch the application with the F5 key.

15. Click Play. Notice that the video starts running inside the panel on the form, and that there are no borders, titles, or control boxes.

Lesson Summary

- The only audio format supported by managed code classes is WAV. The *System.Media* namespace includes classes that can be used to play either WAV files directly or the sounds associated with various system events.

- There is no support for displaying video using managed code.

- The two main methods to display video in .NET application are to use the Media Control Interface (MCI) or the *DirectShow* class that is part of the DirectX family.

Lesson Review

You can use the following questions to test your knowledge of the information in Lesson 2, "Building a Delivery Mechanism." The questions are also available on the companion CD if you prefer to review them in electronic form.

NOTE   Answers

Answers to these questions and explanations of why each answer choice is right or wrong are located in the "Answers" section at the end of the book.

---

1. Which of the following statements is *not* true about displaying video in .NET applications?
   A. The .NET Framework provides support for AVI, MPG, and QuickTime formatted video files.
   B. DirectShow exposes methods that can be used to play video playback.
   C. Media Control Interface exposes methods that can be used to play video playback.
   D. There is no managed code class that is used to display video.

2. Which of the following techniques should be used to play MP3 files from within a .NET application?
   A. Call the *PlaySound* Win32 API function.
   B. Use the *SoundPlayer* class.
   C. Use the *SystemSound* class.
   D. Use the Windows Media Player's SDK functions.

3. The Windows Forms application that you're creating includes the playing of a video. You want to make sure that the user interface thread is not blocked while the video is playing. Which technique should you use?
   A. Create an *IVideoWindow* instance from the *FilgraphManagerClass* class and set the *AutoShow* property.
   B. Call the *RenderFile* method on the *FilgraphManagerClass* class.
   C. Call the *Run* method on the *FilgraphManagerClass* class.
   D. Call the *Run* method, followed by the *WaitForCompletion* method, both on the *FilgraphManagerClass* class.

Chapter Review

To further practice and reinforce the skills you learned in this chapter, you can perform the following tasks:

- Review the chapter summary.
- Review the list of key terms introduced in this chapter.
- Complete the case scenario. This scenario sets up real-world situations involving the topics of this chapter and asks you to create a solution.
- Complete the suggested practices.
- Take a practice test.

Chapter Summary

- Support for playing audio and video files in Windows Forms applications using .NET is relatively limited. Instead, external COM-based components are used to drive the functionality.
- The main focus of choosing among the different formats is to balance delivering the appropriate quality of content with using a reasonable time to do so.

Key Terms

Do you know what these key terms mean? You can check your answers by looking up the terms in the glossary at the end of the book.

- codec
- filter
- frame rate
- jitter
- sampling rate

Case Scenario

In the following case scenario, you will apply what you've learned about delivering multimedia in a distributed environment. You can find answers to these questions in the "Answers" section at the end of the book.

Case Scenario: Delivering Multimedia Content

You are a corporate developer who is creating a Windows application that uses both audio and video to enhance the user's experience. When deployed, the application will be run internally, both at a corporate headquarters and at 35 remote offices around the country. The remote offices have limited bandwidth available for data transfer.

The content of the audio and video are regularly changed. To make deployment of updates easier, it has been decided to place the content onto a drive that is shared by all users in the network.

Questions

Answer the following questions for your manager:

1. What format should be used for the audio files? Does making this choice require any changes to the deployment requirements for the application?

2. What format should be used for the video files? Does making this choice require any changes to the deployment requirements for the application?

Suggested Practices

To help successfully master the objectives covered in this chapter, complete the following tasks.

Choosing a Delivery Format

For this task, you should complete both practices.

- **Practice 1** Using a common source (such as a CD), create a WAV file and a WMA or MP3 file for the same sound. Compare the file sizes and audio quality of each format.

- **Practice 2** Using a common source (such as a digital camera), create an MPEG2 and MPEG4 file for the same video. Compare the file sizes and the quality of each format.

Building a Delivery Mechanism

For this task, you should complete both practices.

- **Practice 1** Using the Media Player SDK, create a Windows Forms application that plays a WAV file that is at least four minutes long. Place the file both locally and on a central server to compare the retrieve and playback performance.

- **Practice 2** Using DirectShow, create a Windows Forms application that plays an AVI file. Place the file both locally and on a central server to compare the retrieve and playback performance.

Take a Practice Test

The practice tests on this book's companion CD offer many options. For example, you can test yourself on just one exam objective, or you can test yourself on all the 70-548 certification exam content. You can set up the test so that it closely simulates the experience of taking a certification exam, or you can set it up in study mode so that you can look at the correct answers and explanations after you answer each question.

MORE INFO   **Practice tests**

For details about all the practice test options available, see the "How to Use the Practice Tests" section in this book's Introduction.

Answers

Chapter 1: Lesson Review Answers

Lesson 1

1. **Correct Answer: B**
   - A. **Incorrect:** A business requirement defines an actionable, measurable feature for the system from the business perspective.
   - B. **Correct:** This is a quality of service (QOS) requirement because it is talking about the desired application performance.
   - C. **Incorrect:** A user requirement defines a task the user needs to be able to perform to meet the objectives of the job.
   - D. **Incorrect:** A functional requirement is a specification for a developer.

2. **Correct Answers: A, C, and D**
   - A. **Correct:** Testers can trace the application back to the agreed-to set of requirements.
   - B. **Incorrect:** The process by which a user accomplishes a given task is a use case (or scenario) and not a requirement. Requirements are sometimes derived from use cases. However, these should be considered separate activities.
   - C. **Correct:** The principal benefit of documenting requirements is gaining a consensus on the business problem that is to be solved.
   - D. **Correct:** The requirements should feed the technology recommendations.

3. **Correct Answer: D**
   - A. **Incorrect:** The application is a data-entry application. It should be written as a forms-based user interface. There are no requirements that push this toward Excel.
   - B. **Incorrect:** A standard client is not easy to deploy, is not easily updatable, and doesn't provide offline access to users.
   - C. **Incorrect:** Users must access the application from their corporate machines.
   - D. **Correct:** A Smart Client will allow easy deployment through click-once and offline access through Smart Client Offline Application Block (SCOAB). Smart Clients also have a highly interactive user experience because they are rich Windows clients.

4. **Correct Answer: C**

    A. **Incorrect:** There is no justification for SQL Enterprise in this situation.

    B. **Incorrect:** SQL Express would work. However, it has a higher footprint than SQL Everywhere. In addition, it does not synchronize as easily.

    C. **Correct:** This offers a low-impact installation with the ability to work disconnected. Users have to get database updates only on a monthly basis.

    D. **Incorrect:** This is too big and too costly to install on each user's machine or device.

Lesson 2

1. **Correct Answer: A**

    A. **Correct:** A vertical prototype covers a vertical slice of the entire application through the layers. The questions all define how data will be managed between these layers.

    B. **Incorrect:** A horizontal prototype, also called a mockup prototype, fills in the gaps that exist in the understanding of the user interface.

    C. **Incorrect:** A database prototype considers only the database and not the layers of the system.

    D. **Incorrect:** A mockup prototype, also called a horizontal prototype, fills in the gaps that exist in the understanding of the user interface.

2. **Correct Answers: A, B, and C**

    A. **Correct:** A reference architecture will give you an understanding of the level of effort for the various layers in the system.

    B. **Correct:** You can help validate your estimates by getting an accurate picture of the screens, the screen types, and their complexities.

    C. **Correct:** A reference architecture takes a look across the layers. You should also look at unique elements in the UI and elsewhere to confirm your scope and the effort that will be required.

    D. **Incorrect:** You should update your requirements. However, this does not help you validate your estimates.

3. **Correct Answers: A, B, C, and D**

    A. **Correct:** You need to confirm your authentication mechanism (forms or Windows).

    B. **Correct:** You need to verify your approach to how users will be authorized to access features and data.

    C. **Correct:** You should evaluate how key resources, such as files or connection strings, will be secured.

    D. **Correct:** You should work with the infrastructure team to understand whether your recommendations are feasible in terms of firewall rules and the like.

4. **Correct Answers: A and C**

   A. **Correct:** The intent of a prototype is to uncover gaps. You know you've done your job when you see this happen.

   B. **Incorrect:** This might be true, but it does not indicate that the prototype was effective. It might indicate that either the prototype did not go far enough or it was not warranted.

   C. **Correct:** This is a good sign. You need to identify areas of high risk and work to reduce this risk.

   D. **Incorrect:** This rarely happens with new technology. You need to make sure the prototype went far enough. If it did, great. However, by itself it does not indicate effectiveness.

Chapter 1: Case Scenario Answers

Case Scenario: Evaluate Requirements and Propose an Application Design

1. The high-level user requirements of the system might be documented as follows:

   ❏ The system should track member profile data, such as name, address, phone, demographics, and health profile.

   ❏ A member should be tracked only once in any system.

   ❏ A member's health profile should include information about the family members with which the member lives as well as the member's family health history.

   ❏ Member representatives should be able to access and update member data.

   ❏ When a member representative speaks with a member or sends the member a correspondence, that contact should be recorded in the system for auditing purposes.

   ❏ The system should store information about member services. This information is in the form of documents and best practices. Member representatives should be able to access this data.

   ❏ Member representatives should be notified when new service information or process guidance is available.

   ❏ The system should allow member representatives to verify that they have read all new information before taking member calls.

   ❏ Member representatives should be able to search for member data using member profile information.

   ❏ The system should allow for a health management workflow application based on scoring questions.

❑ Malady specialists should be able to modify health-related questions and their scoring. They should also be able to modify the remedy steps associated with the actions based on a given profile. All modifications require an appropriate approval before going live.

❑ Members should be able to access and update their member profile data.

❑ A quarterly member data extract should be created for the analysis team. This data should be aggregated and scrubbed of any data that is private to any given member.

❑ A set of common reports should be created. Each report should be filtered by the user and department requesting the data.

❑ Ad hoc reports should be allowed for those with the appropriate rights.

2. The high-level business requirements of the system might be documented as follows:

❑ We need an application that centralizes member data and eliminates duplicate work and duplicate management.

❑ The application should reduce the training time for new hires.

❑ The application should promote best practices for managing the health needs of members.

❑ The organization should get on the same page using the same reports to verify effectiveness.

3. The high-level QOS requirements of the system might be documented as follows:

❑ The application should respond to user requests in less than 5 seconds.

❑ The application should have a clean user interface, be easy to use, be approachable, and reduce confusion on what needs to be done.

❑ The application should support up to 100 concurrent users.

❑ The application should expect to store the data from over 40,000 users.

4. The following are requirements from the interviews that are functional in nature:

❑ The application must support a Windows client that takes advantage of the user's desktop.

❑ Member data should be retrieved as XML from *http://contoso/members/member-service.asmx*. There are two Web service methods: *GetMembers(searchCriteria)* and *UpdateMember(memberData)*.

❑ The application will be built using .NET 2.0.

❑ The application should provide a scrubbed data extract to the statistical modeling tool. This extract should follow the MemberExtract schema and be in the format of CSV.

5. All the business requirements are ambiguous and not very actionable. For example, "the application should have a clean user interface, be easy to use, and approachable." These read like goals, not requirements. You might decide to turn these into goals and then

track the requirements that realize a goal back to the given goal. Or you might rewrite these in an unambiguous manner.

6. Your security model should leverage the fact that all users are in the Active Directory. You can, therefore, use Windows security.

7. The requirements indicate you should continue to use the analysis tool as part of the application. This is an offline process you simply need to support. You might consider SSIS to create your extracts. In addition, the requirement for reports and ad hoc reporting should lead you to examine a reporting tool such as SQL Reporting Services. You might also look at Windows Workflow Services to help with the updates and approval to questions and to manage the process steps and scoring.

8. You should recommend a standard version of SQL Server. You have a large number of users, a sizable scale, and a lot of information you need to store and protect.

9. You should create a mockup prototype to validate the requirements and define the interaction both a member services representative and a malady specialist will have with the system. In addition, your developers are new to .NET. Therefore, you should consider creating a reference architecture of key elements in the system. This includes screens, business objects, and data access code (a vertical implementation).

Chapter 2: Lesson Review Answers

Lesson 1

1. **Correct Answer: C**
   A. **Incorrect:** These items represent only some of the primary objects. The answer misses the other logical objects that are important to the ORM.
   B. **Incorrect:** These items represent only some of the primary objects. The answer misses the other logical objects that are important to the ORM.
   C. **Correct:** These are all objects from the statements. You can use these objects to begin building your ORM.
   D. **Incorrect:** These are not objects. They are actions.

2. **Correct Answer: C**
   A. **Incorrect:** Three objects make up the relationship (Corporate User, Support Request, and Application Access). Unary is a single object relationship to itself.
   B. **Incorrect:** A Support Request can't exist with just a Corporate User or just an Application Access definition. Therefore, two binary relationships would not really represent the relationship.

    C. **Correct:** A ternary relationship exists among Support Request, Corporate User, and Application Access as: Support Request has a Corporate User, Support Request defines Application Access.

    D. **Incorrect:** A quaternary relationship is among four objects. We have only three defined in this question.

3. **Correct Answers: A and C**

    A. **Correct:** This is the left-to-right reading of the relationship fact.

    B. **Incorrect:** This does not model the fact as defined. It assumes a new object, Approval.

    C. **Correct:** This is the right-to-left reading of the relationship fact.

    D. **Incorrect:** This does not model the fact. It too assumes a new object, Approval.

4. **Correct Answer: A**

    A. **Correct:** A Shipping Slip must have a single, Ship-to Address. Therefore, the Shipping Slip is mandatory to form the relationship. However, a Ship-to Address does not need a Shipping Slip. So the inverse part of the relationship is not mandatory (a Ship-to Address defines zero or more Shipping Slips). The arrow over the left side (Shipping Slip) indicates a many-to-one relationship. That is, each Ship-to Address can define many Shipping Slips.

    B. **Incorrect:** This indicates that Ship-to Address is mandatory to form this relationship. However, the relationship does not exist without a Shipping Slip. The arrow on the right indicates a one-to-many relationship. This would only be true if a Shipping Slip were allowed to ship to multiple locations.

    C. **Incorrect:** No circle indicates that neither item is required for the relationship. This is not true. Shipping Slip is required to form this relationship. The two arrows indicate a one-to-one relationship. That would only be true if Ship-to Address could exist only on a single Shipping Slip. That is, an address could only receive a single shipment.

    D. **Incorrect:** The mandatory part of the relationship is correct. However, the single, long arrow indicates a many-to-many relationship. This would be true if the Shipping Slip allowed multiple Ship-to Addresses. However, this would confuse the shipper.

Lesson 2

1. **Correct Answers: A, B, and D**

    A. **Correct:** Creating layers can increase reuse. A business logic–only layer, for example, might allow other systems to access this information. Other applications can leverage a database abstraction class or application services code.

B. **Correct:** Layers give developers a logical understanding of where their code should be written and what code is accessible (referenced) from that code. Layers provide guidelines and structure to code base.

C. **Incorrect:** Layers are logical. They do not dictate the physical packaging or deployment. The layers might influence some of your decision, but it is not a primary benefit.

D. **Correct:** By encapsulating code into layers you can more easily change individual pieces without affecting other code elements.

2. **Correct Answers: A and C**

A. **Correct:** The presentation layer abstracts the user interface layout code from the code that is used to transact (such as business object and database access code). Therefore, your Windows Form code would fit the definition of presentation.

B. **Incorrect:** The presentation code would not couple the business processing rules tightly. Rather, it would separate itself from these duties.

C. **Correct:** The use controls of the system are similar to forms. They abstract presentation from the business and transaction code.

D. **Incorrect:** The database access code should not be coupled in the presentation tier. The presentation tier should concern itself only with form layout and responding to user activity.

3. **Correct Answer: C**

A. **Incorrect:** This many layers are overkill based on the constraints. The application is simple and small. The layers should be few in number.

B. **Incorrect:** Separating the application into even three layers is not warranted based on the constraints. The simple business layer code can be embedded in the user interface.

C. **Correct:** The application is a throwaway, has a tight time frame and a small amount of users, is simple, and will be deployed on a single server. Therefore, the fastest solution here will be a Windows client-server application.

D. **Incorrect:** Nothing in the constraints indicates the use (or need) for application services.

Lesson 3

1. **Correct Answer: D**

A. **Incorrect:** The component diagram shows the logical grouping of classes. It is not a specification that can be implemented.

B. **Incorrect:** A collaboration diagram shows how objects work together through message calls. It does not define the specification for those objects.

C. **Incorrect:** Pseudo code illustrates a complex method using code-like terms.

    D. **Correct:** A class diagram is a static view of your classes and their relationships, properties, and methods. Developers can use this model to implement code. They use the other model to help understand how that code works as a solution.

2. **Correct Answers: B, C, and D**

    A. **Incorrect:** Both sequence and collaboration diagrams can show asynchronous messaging.

    B. **Correct:** A sequence diagram is read left-to-right, top-to-bottom. You must follow the numbers on the messages to read a collaboration diagram's order.

    C. **Correct:** A collaboration diagram does not show when objects get created and destroyed. This is left for interpretation.

    D. **Correct:** A collaboration diagram can be useful when you want to see objects laid out in a different manner.

3. **Correct Answers: B, C, and D**

    A. **Incorrect:** Class interactions are best defined through sequence diagrams. Class groupings are defined through component diagrams.

    B. **Correct:** An activity diagram is good for modeling the steps inside complex algorithms.

    C. **Correct:** An activity diagram allows you to indicate activities both in sequence and in parallel. It also shows where things fork and where they come back together (or join). Therefore, it is very good at showing workflow. This is not often a physical model, but it can be useful nonetheless.

    D. **Correct:** An activity diagram can show actions in parallel. For this reason it is often used to model multithreaded methods.

4. **Correct Answers: A, B, C, and D**

    A. **Correct:** A node in a component diagram illustrates where components will be deployed. This is typically a server or piece of hardware.

    B. **Correct:** You can define a dependency between nodes. You can label this node with a communication protocol.

    C. **Correct:** You can group your components into UML packages. These packages can be defined to represent your layers. Your component model will then show which components are part of which layer.

    D. **Correct:** The dependencies between components on the diagram illustrate references between objects.

Chapter 2: Case Scenario Answers

Case Scenario: Evaluate User Inputs and Create Physical Models

1. The two following figures present possible ORM diagrams for this use case (the ORM diagram is split into two figures in order to fit in this book). This ORM model was created by defining the objects in the system and their relationships from the use case.

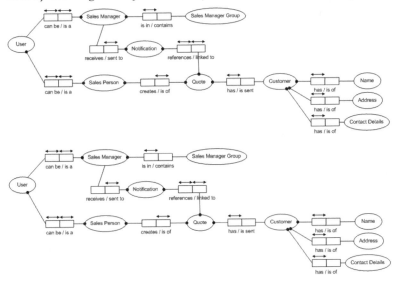

2. The following figure presents a possible application layers diagram based on the aforementioned design goals. The presentation tier is both a Windows UI and the e-mail client. The business objects should be their own layer, given that the business services will be reused across different user experiences. Each business object also accesses the database directly.

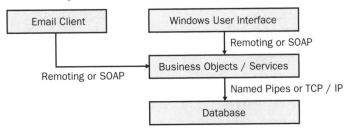

3. The following figure presents a possible object model for the solution. This model does not show the security model for the application or the additional details (properties and methods) not indicated by the use case. It also does not consider the user interface.

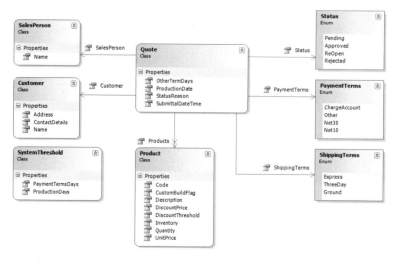

4. The following figure presents a possible sequence diagram for the use case listed above. This use case assumes the application layers defined as part of the model. The call to Get-Details() is illustrating the calls to return the properties of the quote for display to the user (by means of ApproveQuoteUI).

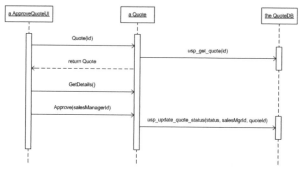

Chapter 3: Lesson Review Answers

Lesson 1

1. **Correct Answers: A, C, and D**

   A. **Correct:** Requiring authentication will reduce the possibility that unauthorized users will have access to data that is accessible only from within your Windows-based application.

    B. **Incorrect:** Although using a Web service is an option for getting data between an application and a database, it doesn't provide any implicit protection. It is easy to think you are isolating the application against direct database interaction by using a Web service, but it's easy to introduce other data holes (for example, like sending the data as plain text between the application and the Web server).

    C. **Correct:** Encrypting sensitive data protects against unscrupulous usage of that data.

    D. **Correct:** By not storing local caches of data on the client, you can reduce the surface area of data that can be accessed without proper authorization.

2. **Correct Answers: B, C, and D**

    A. **Incorrect:** Although using stored procedures in the database is a "best practice," stored procedures do not affect the availability or recoverability of a system.

    B. **Correct:** Reliable transactions will allow for integrity of data across a system, even in the event of catastrophic failure.

    C. **Correct:** The recoverability of an application should extend itself to rebuilding corrupted local files wherever possible.

    D. **Correct:** The availability of your application will be higher if you use database failover to deal with hardware failures in your data center.

3. **Correct Answer: A**

    A. **Correct:** A component in the logical design should be part of one, and only one, of the logical tiers. This separation ensures that the code is maintainable over the long term. A component may be used by more than one tier, but it can only be created in one tier.

    B. **Incorrect:** A component in the logical design should be part of one, and only one, of the logical tiers. This separation ensures that the code is maintainable over the long term.

    C. **Incorrect:** A component in the logical design should be part of one, and only one, of the logical tiers. This separation ensures that the code is maintainable over the long term.

    D. **Incorrect:** A component in the logical design should be part of one, and only one, of the logical tiers. This separation ensures that the code is maintainable over the long term.

Lesson 2

1. **Correct Answer: B**

   A. **Incorrect:** Physically separating your middle tier into a separate machine might increase performance in large applications and should always be an option for improved scalabilities, but for lower load applications it can be a drain on performance.

   B. **Correct:** Using the middle tier on the same machine as the client is a perfectly acceptable way to deploy the middle tier.

2. **Correct Answer: A**

   A. **Correct:** Enforcing the data integrity constraints outside the database allows you to help the user enter valid data without the overhead of going all the way to the database to find incorrect data.

   B. **Incorrect:** Enforcing the data integrity constraints outside the database allows you to help the user enter valid data without the overhead of going all the way to the database to find incorrect data.

3. **Correct Answer: A**

   A. **Correct:** Using a VPN ensures that any data that is communicated between your application and your servers is securely transmitted.

   B. **Incorrect:** Writing complex systems just to avoid using a VPN for external usage of internal servers is almost always an over-engineering of a project.

Chapter 3: Case Scenario Answers

Case Scenario 1: Review the Logical Design of a CRM Application

1. By reviewing the original requirements, I will compare them to the logical design to ensure that there are no gaps.

2. By ensuring that the design has kept the user interface and business logic tiers separate, I can ensure that the maintainability of the system is adequate for our needs.

Case Scenario 2: Review the Physical Design of a CRM Application

1. By reviewing the physical design to determine what kind of security is going to be used, we can evaluate the security model of the physical design.

2. The location of shared components and controls needs to be evaluated to make sure that updating individual shared elements will benefit other projects using those same controls.

Chapter 4: Lesson Review Answers

Lesson 1

1. **Correct Answer: B**
   - A. **Incorrect:** The feature is not used very often. Creating multiple tabs requires users to deduce what they need to do and in what order. In addition, they don't know when they're done (the button is always enabled).
   - B. **Correct:** A wizard will help guide users appropriately through this seldom-used feature. If they change their minds or make mistakes, they can also easily navigate backward and forward through the interface. Finally, they know when they're done by when the button enables.
   - C. **Incorrect:** This form would increase power but also increase the need for user training. A wizard is a better choice.
   - D. **Incorrect:** This approach requires a user to know something about each property and to find out how to interact with the form (through the context menu).

2. **Correct Answers: B, C, and D**
   - A. **Incorrect:** A task pane can be helpful. However, it does not affect accessibility.
   - B. **Correct:** Your application should not rely on one form of notification. You need visual cues for those without sound and audio cues for those who use the application and have limited vision.
   - C. **Correct:** A high-contrast user interface can help users who have a hard time seeing color depths or grayscale.
   - D. **Correct:** A larger font size can increase accessibility for those people who have a hard time reading small text on a computer screen.

3. **Correct Answer: C**
   - A. **Incorrect:** The requirements define what you are going to create. They typically do not offer much in the way of how you should create or lay out the UI.
   - B. **Incorrect:** It is stated that the current application is hard to use. It should not be considered as a good example of how to lay out the new version.
   - C. **Correct:** The use cases will tell you how users think about their work. You will want to align the application's layout with these concepts.
   - D. **Incorrect:** The ORMs provide the logical model of the system. They can help you see the principal perspectives and perhaps aid with defining key modules. However, they do not play as big a role as use cases when defining an intuitive layout.

4. **Correct Answer: C**

   A. **Incorrect:** There are too many items for a menu control. Also, users do not like having to select a portion of their selection from one interface and the rest from another (the dialog box). Finally, menus typically provide access to features (not customers).

   B. **Incorrect:** This is too many items for a menu. Also, users expect to access features from menus and not customers.

   C. **Correct:** This task pane and *TreeView* control will show the customers nicely and provide an intuitive means of access.

   D. **Incorrect:** Toolbar buttons should be reserved for access to common features. Also, all of these items will clutter the interface.

Lesson 2

1. **Correct Answers: A and D**

   A. **Correct:** This application would be a good use of an MDI container in that the application is centered on a single document type: a contract.

   B. **Incorrect:** This type of application is best implemented as an SDI, given that there are multiple data types (users and roles) and the application is database-driven.

   C. **Incorrect:** This application should be an SDI. It has multiple modules, each with its own data elements.

   D. **Correct:** This application should be implemented as an MDI because of its focus on a single document type. Users will expect to be able to work with multiple open documents at any given time.

2. **Correct Answers: A, C, and D**

   A. **Correct:** Setting the *Padding* property of the form to 20 will create a space of 20 pixels between the *GroupBox* and the edge of Form1.

   B. **Incorrect:** The *Padding* property of the *GroupBox* will affect only the interior controls added to the *GroupBox* control. These settings will create a space of only 10 pixels between the edge of Form1 and the *GroupBox*.

   C. **Correct:** The *Margin* property of the *GroupBox* will define 10 pixels. The *Padding* property of Form1 will set another 10 pixels. These will be added together to create a space of 20 pixels between the edge of Form1 and the *GroupBox* control.

   D. **Correct:** If the *Margin* property of the *GroupBox* is set to 20, it will create a space of 20 pixels between the edge of Form1 (with *Padding* set at 0) and the *GroupBox*.

3. **Correct Answers: A and B**
    A. **Correct:** A *TableLayoutPanel* will allow you to define a layout that can be sized based on the content of the controls it contains. In this scenario you don't need a row for each label and text box because you're not looking for the text boxes to grow vertically. You need growth only horizontally.
    B. **Correct:** The *Panel* controls will allow you to lay out the other controls and align them properly. In addition, the entire *Panel* will automatically size to the contents of the *Label* controls. Finally, the columns of the *TableLayoutPanel* will automatically size as well.
    C. **Incorrect:** The *Dock* property will not affect the automatic sizing of controls based on content. It only stretches or contracts based on a user resizing the form.
    D. **Incorrect:** This solution creates two *Panel* controls that will resize. However, if they are not in a layout control such as *TableLayoutPanel*, they will resize over the top of each other.

4. **Correct Answer: D**
    A. **Incorrect:** Adding the menu, toolbar, and status bar last will create a docking conflict with the panels. These items will all be docked to the edge of the form and not with respect to the panels.
    B. **Incorrect:** This will create a form that has a bottom panel docked across the entire form and not just the right side.
    C. **Incorrect:** This will not properly set the splitters. The splitters will be aligned to the edge of the forms and not to the edges of their respective panels.
    D. **Correct:** This will create the desired effect. Adding controls in the proper order will facilitate proper docking on the form.

Lesson 3

1. **Correct Answer: D**
    A. **Incorrect:** The *Panel* will contain the controls but not restrict input. The *ListView* shows data in a list but does not provide an intuitive means for users to know to select a single item.
    B. **Incorrect:** The *CheckedListBox* control will show each option with a check box. Users will expect that they can select multiple options from the list.
    C. **Incorrect:** The *Panel* will contain the controls but not restrict input. The *ListBox* shows data in a list but does not provide an intuitive means for users to know to select a single item.
    D. **Correct:** A *GroupBox* control will constrain the radio buttons to force users to select a single item. The *RadioButton* controls will present mutually exclusive options to users.

2. **Correct Answer: C**

    A. **Incorrect:** A *ComboBox* is good for showing data in a drop-down list. It is not good for allowing users to select multiple items or redisplay content in different views.

    B. **Incorrect:** The *ListBox* does not provide the feature of displaying a list in multiple views.

    C. **Correct:** The *ListView* control allows a user to view data by icon or by a detailed list of items.

    D. **Incorrect:** The *TreeView* control shows data in a hierarchical structure.

3. **Correct Answer: B**

    A. **Incorrect:** The *Splitter* control is used to size two panes with respect to each other. This would not be a good choice for setting magnification.

    B. **Correct:** The *TrackBar* provides a slider for a user to move left and right to get the size right for the document. You should use this control and magnify the pane as the user moves the control to provide real-time visual information to users.

    C. **Incorrect:** The *ComboBox* would be a nice choice given that users are familiar with setting view percentages this way. However, this case calls for fine-grained control based on specific situations. Users are not concerned about the actual percentage. They are concerned about getting the size the way they want it for their purpose. For this reason, the *TrackBar* is a much better choice.

    D. **Incorrect:** A *SplitContainer* provides two panels and a splitter bar. This would not be a useful set of controls for the purpose of setting the magnification of a document.

4. **Correct Answer: C**

    A. **Incorrect:** The *MaskedTextBox* will allow users to enter data in the specified format. However, users will still most likely have to look at a calendar to enter this information. They do not know in their head when certain days fall in the week, for instance.

    B. **Incorrect:** This requires users to select two options where they could select only one. In addition, it requires validation that the dates are not within the appropriate range ("to" date is less than "from").

    C. **Correct:** This will allow you to show a calendar on the form from which users can easily select their desired range of dates. You might also consider providing a label that displays their selection in a textual format.

    D. **Incorrect:** The *NumericUpDown* presents users with a difficult interface. They can't see a calendar, and they are expected to scroll through dates to pick their choices.

Chapter 4: Case Scenario Answers

Case Scenario: Define a Common User Interface

1. The goals for the user interface should be taken directly from the comments. These include the following: increase user productivity, provide fast data entry, lay out features and screen in an intuitive manner, and create a clean and consistent interface.

2. You need to define attainable items relative to the goals for the UI. These might include increasing productivity and data entry through features like AutoComplete and additional data caching on the client. You should also lay out controls in a logical fashion (the way in which users do their work). You should pay attention to control tabbing and quick-key access for users who consider the mouse an obstacle to performance. You should implement standards on padding and margins to create a clean and consistent UI.

3. The taxonomy for the application should include all the following modules: Loan Processing, Reports, Administration, and Loan Approval. You should consider using these groups to group features of the application.

4. The advanced users could benefit from context menus and smart tags right within the document or data with which they are working. This will provide relevant actions as soon as they need them.

   In addition, you should cut down on users having to search for common information. You might achieve this by creating a dashboard pane in the application. This pane might show users data that pertains to their roles. For example, loan officers would see loans waiting their approval. Loan consultants might see a list of active loans they are working on. This will reduce their need to navigate.

   You should also increase the ability to quickly find loans. You might add an item to the toolbar for simple searches. You could then create a button to access a more advanced search.

5. You should consider creating an MDI application centered on the loan document type. This will help users think of and work with loans as the documents that they are. You might jump out to an SDI application for administration or reporting.

Chapter 5: Lesson Review Answers

Lesson 1

1. **Correct Answer: C**
   A. **Incorrect:** Setting the *CausesValidation* property on the control that is losing focus has no impact on the raising of the *Validating* event.

B. **Incorrect:** Setting the *CausesValidation* property on the control that is losing focus has no impact on the raising of the *Validating* event.

C. **Correct:** In order for the *Validating* event to be raised, the destination control must have *CausesValidation* set to *True*. By setting it to *False*, you ensure that *Validating* will not be raised and therefore the invalid input doesn't prevent the clicking of the button.

D. **Incorrect:** Although setting *CausesValidation* on the destination field is the correct control, the value to disable the *Validating* event is *False*, not *True*.

2. **Correct Answer: B**

A. **Incorrect:** There are too many possibilities for a drop-down combo box to be effective.

B. **Correct:** The *Validating* event handler has the ability to retrieve the externally defined patterns and validate that the input matches one of the patterns.

C. **Incorrect:** The *MaskedTextBox* control doesn't allow for the definition of multiple patterns.

D. **Incorrect:** Although the input data would be validated using this technique, if any data retrieved from a database doesn't match the external patterns, an exception would be raised. The validation (at least from the accepted patterns perspective) should take place only in the client portion of the application.

3. **Correct Answer: D**

A. **Incorrect:** This option has two problems. First, the use of a composite control limits the placement of the three individual *TextBox* controls. Second, the *Validating* event handlers require that the individual fields lose focus in order to be fired.

B. **Incorrect:** The *Validating* event handler requires that the individual field lose focus in order to be fired. When multiple fields are involved, it becomes possible to change one field without entering the other related fields.

C. **Incorrect:** The *MaskedTextBox* control doesn't allow for multiple controls to be related in any way.

D. **Correct:** The relationship that exists between multiple fields is really a business requirement. As such, it makes more sense to encode it in the business class or the *DataSet*.

Lesson 2

1. **Correct Answer: B**

A. **Incorrect:** The information on the status bar is seldom, if ever, paid attention to. Using the status bar is roughly the same as not letting the user know at all.

B. **Correct:** For feedback on a destructive process, getting the user's attention is important. And it works for every accessibility aid as well.

C. **Incorrect:** Changing the color of the form might get some attention, but some people will not see the color change because of a visual impairment. So this is not a good choice.

D. **Incorrect:** The warning icon shown by the error provider suffers from the same problem, which is that it's not an accessible option. Not to mention that the icon was intended to be ignored until the user chooses to see it, while in this instance the application wants to demand immediate attention.

2. **Correct Answer: A**

A. **Correct:** In this situation the status bar is the best choice. It is unobtrusive yet visible when the user needs the status information. Also, it remains part of the application in that, if the main form is closed, the status information doesn't linger on the screen.

B. **Incorrect:** Of the incorrect choices, this is definitely the one closest to correct. In certain instances you could use a nonmodal dialog box to display the status. The reason for it not being completely correct is that it becomes a separate form in the application. The form takes up real estate on the screen, making it awkward to view the status when working with the rest of the application.

C. **Incorrect:** Although this would be an interesting (and by "interesting," I mean "annoying") status mechanism, it should never be used. Aside from the issues of usability by the visually impaired, it has the potential to distract and peeve the users.

D. **Incorrect:** The idea of using a modal dialog box flies in the face of the status information on a background process being unobtrusive. With a modal dialog box, there is no way the user could continue working on the rest of the application.

3. **Correct Answer: D**

A. **Incorrect:** The Narrator application is used to provide information to visually impaired users. It's not appropriate for quick hints about the contents of a field.

B. **Incorrect:** The Magnifier application is used to enlarge portions of the screen. This will not be useful in determining what should go into a particular field.

C. **Incorrect:** This is almost the correct answer. Context sensitivity helps in terms of providing pertinent information. However, the speed with which the information is provided through context-sensitive help makes this option incorrect.

D. **Correct:** The tool tip provides the most readily accessible option for displaying hints about the content of a control.

Chapter 5: Case Scenario Answers

Case Scenario 1: Choosing the Validation Mechanism

1. In general, the only validation that can be performed on free-form name input is whether or not they are required. If so, then this validation would be performed in the *Validating* event on the form.

2. The phone number of the contact should be initially validated using a *MaskedTextBox* with an appropriate pattern assigned to the *Mask* property. As a secondary validation, you could ensure that the area code is correct and that the exchange exists within the area code. This second validation would take place as part of the business rule validation.

3. The e-mail address of the contact should be validated (to start with) using a regular expression in the *Validating* event handler. Although it might seem that the *Mask* property could be used, the reality is that the patterns don't work well for arbitrarily long input. Once the format of the address has been validated, a second level of validation could take place, including verifying that the domain name exists.

Case Scenario 2: Choosing the Feedback Mechanism

1. Hints about content are best placed within a tool tip. This information is readily available to the user, should the user require it. However, if the hints aren't necessary, the user will not be inconvenienced. Also, the tool tip takes up no on-screen real estate, so the fields don't need to be repositioned in order to display the tip.

2. The limitation on tool tips is that they can't be more than a single line long. For more detailed hints, context-sensitive help is a better choice. The information is still easily retrievable, but the amount of room available is greatly increased.

3. In general, the best way to display error messages is to use an *ErrorProvider*. Although there might be instances where other feedback mechanisms are more appropriate, the consistency and functionality (such as accessibility) make it simpler to develop and easier to use the resulting application.

Chapter 6: Lesson Review Answers

Lesson 1

1. **Correct Answers: A and C**

   A. **Correct:** Unique identification is the job of primary keys.

   B. **Incorrect:** A foreign key, not a primary key, provides a way to specify how deletes and updates are propagated between entities.

C. **Correct:** A primary key is used to provide an efficient lookup for each table in the database. Usually this takes the form of a primary key's index.

D. **Incorrect:** A foreign key, not a primary key, indicates a relationship between entities.

2. **Correct Answer: B**

A. **Incorrect:** Secondary indexes do not provide any data integrity. See answer B.

B. **Correct:** Secondary indexing provides a way to improve nonprimary key searches.

C. **Incorrect:** Secondary indexes do not provide any type of safety. See answer B.

D. **Incorrect:** Foreign keys provide a mechanism for propagating changes across tables, not secondary indexes.

3. **Correct Answer: B**

A. **Incorrect:** Specific types of attributes can signify a primary key, but every attribute should become a column (or multiple columns) in the database design.

B. **Correct:** Each attribute in the ORM should become a column (or multiple columns) in the database design.

C. **Incorrect:** Specific types of attributes can signify a foreign key, but every attribute should become a column (or multiple columns) in the database design.

D. **Incorrect:** Attributes do not indicate stored procedures in the ORM.

Lesson 2

1. **Correct Answers: A, B, and D**

A. **Correct:** Technological risks can be lessened by a component prototype to ensure that assumptions made by the design can be achieved.

B. **Correct:** If a client requests a prototype, this is reason enough to have a prototype created. A client might be the user of the component or a stakeholder in the project.

C. **Incorrect:** You can get agreement on the component interface through the class diagram; a prototype is not required to get that agreement.

D. **Correct:** If a prototype of the component is needed to complete a project proof of concept, it's perfectly acceptable to create the prototype.

2. **Correct Answer: B**

A. **Incorrect:** Components that do data access do not belong in the User Interface tier.

B. **Correct:** Components that do data access should live in the Data tier of the architecture.

C. **Incorrect:** Even though the component does data access, it does not belong in the database. It belongs in the Data tier.

3. **Correct Answer: B**

    A. **Incorrect:** Every design requires tradeoffs between different criteria in order to create an effective design.

    B. **Correct:** Design tradeoffs are critical to an effective design.

Lesson 3

1. **Correct Answer: A**

    A. **Correct:** Initialization data should be passed as part of the construction of an object. There is no benefit to using a multiphase construction.

    B. **Incorrect:** Initialization data should be passed as part of the construction of an object. There is no benefit to using a multiphase construction. Single-phase construction prevents unexpected workflow patterns, such as if the initialization method is called multiple times.

    C. **Incorrect:** Initialization data should be passed as part of the construction of an object. There is no benefit to deferring it to property calls after the object is constructed.

    D. **Incorrect:** The best practice is to pass initialization data in the constructor.

2. **Correct Answer: C**

    A. **Incorrect:** The garbage collector will not manage unmanaged resources. Use the *IDisposable* interface to handle unmanaged resources.

    B. **Incorrect:** No, you should use the *IDisposable* interface to handle unmanaged resources.

    C. **Correct:** The *IDisposable* interface is used to handle unmanaged resources.

    D. **Incorrect:** No, you should use the *IDisposable* interface instead to manage the unmanaged resources.

3. **Correct Answer: C**

    A. **Incorrect:** Unmanaged resources should be handled with the *IDisposable* interface.

    B. **Incorrect:** Clean-up code should be handled using another facility (for example, *IDisposable* or a *Close* method.)

    C. **Correct:** Finalizers should not be used in your components.

    D. **Incorrect:** If your component holds on to objects that support *IDisposable*, you should also implement *IDisposable* to support calling their *Dispose* method.

Chapter 6: Case Scenario Answers

Case Scenario 1: Design a Tax Collection Component

1. Because this is a Windows-based application for doing on-site sales, I will package it as a library that will need to be installed on every POS machine.

2. I will return you the effective tax rate. You will be responsible for calculating the tax rate against what they are purchasing.

Case Scenario 2: Design a Database for a Company Library

1. There will be three tables: an *Employee* table, a *Book* table, and a *CheckOut* table to store which employees have checked out what books.

2. There will be a foreign key from the *CheckOut* table into the *Employee* table, as well as a foreign key from the *CheckOut* table to the *Book* table.

Chapter 7: Lesson Review Answers

Lesson 1

1. **Correct Answers: B and C**
   A. **Incorrect:** If you have state in your component but none of the state supports *IDisposable*, you do not have any unmanaged resources.
   B. **Correct:** The *IDisposable* interface is indicative of an unmanaged resource. Therefore, you must release this unmanaged resource in your class.
   C. **Correct:** If you have any unmanaged resources (which could include unmanaged resources that are not wrapped in .NET classes), you should implement the *IDisposable* interface.
   D. **Incorrect:** If the component is stateless, you have no resources and therefore no unmanaged resources.

2. **Correct Answers: B and D**
   A. **Incorrect:** Base classes are not used to define naming conventions.
   B. **Correct:** A base class can be used to define a common interface for derived classes.
   C. **Incorrect:** Base classes are not used to hide implementation details from inherited classes.
   D. **Correct:** A base class can be used to create common functionality that is used by inherited classes.

3. **Correct Answer: C**

   A. **Incorrect:** Making all components thread-safe is unnecessary and a waste of effort, both in development time as well as in performance.

   B. **Incorrect:** Some components need to be thread-safe to allow them to safely be used in multithreaded code.

   C. **Correct:** Adding thread safety is crucial to components that will be used in multi-threaded code, but the cost of thread safety is not worth it if the component will not be used from multiple threads.

Lesson 2

1. **Correct Answer: A**

   A. **Correct:** *DataReaders* in combination with *Commands* is the best performing of all the methods.

   B. **Incorrect:** *DataSets* require more overhead for maintaining state about changes and indexing, so from a purely performance-based standpoint, they perform more poorly.

   C. **Incorrect:** *Typed DataSets* require more overhead for maintaining state about changes and indexing, so from a purely performance-based standpoint, they perform more poorly. They are marginally better than untyped *DataSets* but still slower than *DataReaders*.

2. **Correct Answers: B, C, and D**

   A. **Incorrect:** You should never change the generated code in a *Typed DataSet*.

   B. **Correct:** You can write custom code in the partial class to add business logic.

   C. **Correct:** The *DataSet* schema is good for data validation.

   D. **Correct:** Additional business logic can be added to event handlers for *DataSets* to ensure that all code paths lead to the business logic being tested.

3. **Correct Answer: C**

   A. **Incorrect:** *DataReaders* in combination with *Commands* is the most labor intensive; therefore, you should be using *Typed DataSets* to prototype a project.

   B. **Incorrect:** No, *Typed DataSets* will allow you to prototype your project the quickest.

   C. **Correct:** *Typed DataSets* are the quickest at developing data access and therefore should be used for prototyping.

Lesson 3

1. **Correct Answers: A, C, and D**

   A. **Correct:** Sending a method an invalid argument is an exceptional case and should result in an exception being thrown.

B. **Incorrect:** Executing a search and finding no results is not exceptional but is a valid result; therefore, you should not throw an exception.

C. **Correct:** Running out of memory is exceptional and should result in an exception being thrown.

D. **Correct:** The database not being available is exceptional and should result in an exception being thrown.

2. **Correct Answer: B**

A. **Incorrect:** You should include contextual information only if it's helpful in correcting exceptional cases. For systemic issues (for example, *OutOfMemoryException*), just allowing exceptions to propagate without context is acceptable.

B. **Correct:** You should include contextual information only if it's helpful in correcting exceptional cases. For systemic issues (for example, *OutOfMemoryException*), just allowing exceptions to propagate without context is acceptable.

3. **Correct Answers: B and C**

A. **Incorrect:** Profiling is performed to ensure that a component meets performance requirements and to find resource leaks.

B. **Correct:** Profiling is performed to ensure that a component meets performance requirements and to find resource leaks.

C. **Correct:** Profiling is performed to ensure that a component meets performance requirements and to find resource leaks.

D. **Incorrect:** Profiling is performed to ensure that a component meets performance requirements and to find resource leaks.

Chapter 7: Case Scenario Answers

Case Scenario 1: Choose a Data Access Method

1. We should use *Typed DataSets* because we need to complete this project very quickly. It might mean that we have to re-engineer part of this project again later, but because time is the most important factor, we should use *Typed DataSets*.

2. Put any business logic in the partial class that can be generated with the *Typed DataSet*. Do not put any code in the generated classes.

Case Scenario 2: Locate a Resource Leak

1. We should profile the system in two phases: first, we should use the CLR profiler to see what components are consuming the most memory; second, we should instrument the targeted components to see why they are eating up the memory.

2. We can isolate the problem by using a variety of profiling tools, although the CLR Profiler and the Visual Studio Performance Wizard are probably the best tools for the job.

Chapter 8: Lesson Review Answers

Lesson 1

1. **Correct Answers: A and E**

   A. **Correct:** The Error level is intended for critical, application-threatening situations—certainly something that operations would like to see immediately.

   B. **Incorrect:** The Warning level is intended to be not as critical as an error. Although operations might want to see warnings, they won't want to monitor for it because the number of "false positive" log entries might obscure serious problems.

   C. **Incorrect:** The Information level is purely for informational messages and should not be directed to the operations monitoring application.

   D. **Incorrect:** Accessing a resource successfully is not something that operations should be alerted to.

   E. **Correct:** If someone attempts to access a resource to which they haven't been given access, operations should be notified immediately. Operations might need to specify thresholds that alert them only if multiple failures occur. Otherwise, they might be notified each time a user mistypes a password.

2. **Correct Answers: B and D**

   A. **Incorrect:** Operations is much more likely to care about the moment-to-moment status of the system. As such, logged data is not likely to be of immediate interest.

   B. **Correct:** Although developers are occasionally interested in messages as they happen, they will usually be looking at the logged information generated by the application.

   C. **Incorrect:** Although security personnel might be interested in logged information, a fast-response team wants to know immediately when there are any security violations.

   D. **Correct:** Auditors are more interested in the record of the transactions that took place. For this reason, they are likely to be interested in the saved data so that it can be analyzed later.

Lesson 2

1. **Correct Answer: D**

   A. **Incorrect:** Without some overly complicated programming (and, in reality, even then), placing log entries into a flat file is not going to get them noticed immediately.

  B. **Incorrect:** The System Monitor is not really an appropriate place to indicate error conditions. Although a counter could be set up and there are tools that "watch" the counters, the solution is fragile and overly complex.

  C. **Incorrect:** Like the flat file solution, placing log entries into a database does not normally get them noticed immediately.

  D. **Correct:** Sending an e-mail message is the most immediate way to get notification to a person.

2. **Correct Answer: C**

  A. **Incorrect:** Yes, it's technically possible to generate reports using a flat file as the data source. But the reality is that no one would dream of doing so in the real world.

  B. **Incorrect:** The System Monitor measures point-in-time and average-over-time values. It is not suitable for generating reports of the time identified in the question.

  C. **Correct:** Placing the sales order information into a database is by far the easiest way to allow it to be used to generate reports. Also, the database supports transactional updates, allowing the developer to be certain that the correlation between log entries and sales is completely accurate.

  D. **Incorrect:** Using e-mails to send sales order information does not place it into a location that can easily be used to generate reports.

3. **Correct Answer: D**

  A. **Incorrect:** Updating a flat file on the system where the error occurs will not help get that information to you. And because the flat file exists on the user's system, it is unlikely that you would be able to access it remotely.

  B. **Incorrect:** The System Monitor is not normally the appropriate store for tracking serious errors, unless all you're interested in is counting how many. Serious errors usually include exception details and other text-based information, so other data stores are better suited for the task.

  C. **Incorrect:** Although placing the log information into a database would certainly ensure that the logged data is available, additional functionality would be required to get the information out of the remote sites.

  D. **Correct:** Of all the data stores described in this chapter, e-mail is the one that is best suited to deliver log and notification messages outside the corporate network.

Lesson 3

1. **Correct Answer: B**

  A. **Incorrect:** Too much code needs to be added at each logging location.

  B. **Correct:** Centralizing the logging mechanism means that creating a log message is just a matter of making a method call.

C. **Incorrect:** Creating a framework of any kind is very challenging. And for the described application, the effort isn't required to provide the unnecessary functionality.

D. **Incorrect:** Although the Logging Application Block will do what is required, for the described application it is overkill.

Chapter 8: Case Scenario Answers

Case Scenario 1: Instrumenting an Application for Monitoring

1. The ability to process usage pattern information will hinge on how easy it is to visualize the large volume of data that could be generated. The conversion of data into a visual format (such as a report) is best accomplished by retrieving information from a data store designed for reporting. This means that the usage log messages should be stored in a database.

2. The application status information should be made available through a number of counters in System Monitor. This mechanism allows for monitoring applications through a common repository. The fact that it's common means that third-party tools designed to hook into the performance counter system will be able to interact with the application you're creating in the same manner as any other Windows application.

3. For tracing information, it might seem that a flat file is the most appropriate choice. And in many situations it is. However, the fact that the application is running on many computers makes flat files less practical. If the flat file is stored locally, operations will need to find a way to aggregate the data. If the flat file is placed in a central location, the problems of having multiple users attempting to update the file simultaneously must be addressed. As a result, the tracing information should be stored in a central repository, which in this case would be a database.

Case Scenario 2: Instrumenting a Smart Client Application

1. Performance counters, by their nature, maintain information about the local system and applications. What they are not really appropriate for is to provide information for a number of remote sensors back to a central location. As a result, performance counters should not be used to monitor remote application status. Instead, a storage mechanism that allows remote transmission should be used. This would be databases or e-mail, with a database being the more natural choice for gathering information together for central reporting.

Chapter 9: Lesson Review Answers

Lesson 1

1. **Correct Answer: D**

    A. **Incorrect:** Because the application being built is a critical one for the company, good project managers won't let a component be introduced without knowing that it will do what is required. It might be only a proof-of-concept application, but an evaluation version is an absolute requirement.

    B. **Incorrect:** Although being given less weight than having an evaluation version, the ability to contact technical support in the case of problems, especially during production, is still important. And this is one instance where being able to talk to a live person will add points in the evaluation process.

    C. **Incorrect:** Again, performance is further down the weighting scale from having an evaluation version and technical support. But the performance of the component needs to be reasonable in order to support operations. Excessive latency could result in a less than optimal production environment; this can easily be addressed during the component selection process.

    D. **Correct:** It seems unlikely that a component such as this will be subject to a great number of future enhancements. Typically in the manufacturing sector, once a process is in place, changes to that process are rare and would involve much more than just upgrading a single component.

2. **Correct Answers: C and D**

    A. **Incorrect:** The *Public* modifier gives access to the method to any class, not just those in the inheritance hierarchy.

    B. **Incorrect:** A *Private* method is not accessible to any class outside of the class it is contained within.

    C. **Correct:** The *Protected* keyword indicates that a method can be accessed only be classes that are derived from the containing class.

    D. **Correct:** The *virtual* or *Overridable* keyword indicates that any class that inherits from the containing class can implement its own version of the method.

3. **Correct Answers: A and D**

    A. **Correct:** A .NET class can't be directly inherited from a COM object. The only way to emulate inheritance is to wrap the COM object and expose the COM's interface through methods in the .NET class.

    B. **Incorrect:** Although the *ComponentService* is the class used to access COM+ services from within .NET, there is nothing stopping a developer from deriving from a class that is derived from *ComponentServices*.

C.   **Incorrect:** There is no reason to use a wrapping technique in the described scenario. .NET components are designed to be inherited even through multiple levels of derived classes.

D.   **Correct:** A sealed class, by definition, is one that can't be the base class in an inheritance hierarchy. So if the need arises to extend or inherit a sealed class, the wrapping technique is the only one available.

Lesson 2

1.   **Correct Answer: B**

A.   **Incorrect:** Although using a *StringBuilder* iteratively produces the most maintainable code, it is not as efficient as *String.Concat*.

B.   **Correct:** *String.Concat* doesn't create any addition objects as overhead to the string-building process.

C.   **Incorrect:** *String.Format* uses a *StringBuilder* object under the covers, which will make it less efficient than *String.Concat*.

D.   **Incorrect:** This is the style of building strings that *StringBuilder* was created to replace. It is the least efficient of the options.

2.   **Correct Answer: B**

A.   **Incorrect:** Although the *AppSettings* class can be used to access connection string information, it is not the most efficient class to use.

B.   **Correct:** The *ConnectionStrings* class contains the connection strings that are in the application's configuration file.

C.   **Incorrect:** The *ConnectionStringsSection* class defines the section in the application configuration file where the connection strings are stored. It can't be used to access the configuration strings themselves.

D.   **Incorrect:** The *DbConfigurationStringBuilder* class is used to build a connection string. It is not, however, used to persist or retrieve connection strings from the application configuration file.

3.   **Correct Answer: B**

A.   **Incorrect:** If individual parameters are used, the client becomes responsible for determining when the parameter values are changed. Although it's possible, it's certainly not the easiest way to go.

B.   **Correct:** Using a *DataSet* as a parameter allows information of all types to be passed into the method. More important, the *DataSet* class tracks the changes that are made to the data. As a result, the calling method is relieved of that particular chore.

C.   **Incorrect:** Like the individual parameters, an XML document can easily be used to move data back and forth between the caller and the callee. But also like individual parameters, there is no automatic persistence of values, so the caller needs to keep track of what changed.

D.   **Incorrect:** The basic problem is the same as with answer C. The fact that the XML document is in a SOAP format does not make it any easier to track the changes to the parameter values.

Chapter 9: Case Scenario Answers

Case Scenario 1: Evaluating a Component

1.   Because more than 1,000,000 leads could be in a request, each of which could require two separate network requests, performance is a big factor for the simple reason that if each validation takes a second, it will take more than 10 days to process all of the leads. Ideally, any purchased component will take advantage of techniques such as caching to reduce the overhead of validation. But if not, then building the component allows the development team to customize the processing to minimize the overhead for the validation process.

2.   The second important criterion will be ease of customization. Things like customizations related to improving and monitoring performance will be quite important to the component. Support for this level of customization should contribute high marks to the component's purchasability. If none of the candidates support performance tuning to this level, that will lean much more heavily to a home-grown solution.

Case Scenario 2: Evaluating Data Abstraction

1.   Given the restrictions on the client, one of the design goals should be to take as much of the "heavy lifting" of the application away from the client as possible. In other words, if a process can be taken from the client and performed on the server, it should be. In the realm of data access, this means that stored procedures are more likely to be the data access approach of choice than dynamic SQL is. If the only type of statement being executed is a simple SQL statement, this choice is not obvious. But stored procedures can provide an opportunity to implement some business logic on the server, accomplishing the goal of removing functionality from the client.

2.   Assuming that the default choice is the stored procedure approach, then the use of dynamic SQL is most likely to be limited to where the need for truly dynamic SQL is required. There are some instances in which the criteria or the fields to be returned might vary based on the demands of the application. Although stored procedures can be created so that the stored procedures contain a (potentially) large number of *if* statements, that type of structure can become cumbersome to maintain. The linear logic required to dynamically build the SQL statements is much more suited to the traditional .NET languages.

Chapter 10: Lesson Review Answers

Lesson 1

1. **Correct Answers: C and D**

    A. **Incorrect:** Since the Web service is being called asynchronously, there is no way that success can be determined synchronously.

    B. **Incorrect:** The reason this option is incorrect is a little challenging to understand. The asynchronous success outcome assumes that there is a delay in determining the outcome but that the outcome is available before processing continues.

    C. **Correct:** Sending a batch update to a Web service is an excellent example of an optimistic success outcome scenario.

    D. **Correct:** Calling the Web service can easily result in a failure due to network problems, server problems, or data problems. Each of these falls into the abject failure category.

2. **Correct Answer: D**

    A. **Incorrect:** There really is no information to be gathered about the call that is exceptionally useful in a log. The exception itself will contain the reason that the call failed. The only exception might be if the Web service was hosted by a third party and your company had a service level agreement requiring a certain percentage of uptime.

    B. **Incorrect:** There are no details about the call itself that can be determined by looking at the code.

    C. **Incorrect:** Making a Web service call does not involve using resources that require clean-up prior to garbage collection.

    D. **Correct:** The fact that there are three possible endpoints mean that calls to the second and third are possible if the first one fails. Catching the *WebException* gives the caller the opportunity to validate successfully against the other Web services.

3. **Correct Answer: C**

    A. **Incorrect:** Although this technique might work, it is ugly for a number of reasons. The code would need to be embedded in each method, which clutters the procedure. It becomes easier for some developer to forget to add the code to the method. And if the mechanism ever needs to be modified, the number of required changes would be prohibitive.

    B. **Incorrect:** The Windows Forms mechanism that is started with the *Application.Run* statement actually has its own unhandled exception handling mechanism. So even though *Application.Run* is wrapped with the *Try-Catch* code, the *Application* object will handle the unhandled exception by displaying a message box.

C.   **Correct:** As mentioned in answer B, the *Application* object has its own unhandled exception handler. The only way to be notified when an unhandled exception occurs (and to suppress the default message box) is to create an event handler for the *ThreadException* event.

D.   **Incorrect:** Even though it might seem like using the *UnhandledException* event is acceptable, the same problem as described in the rationale for answer B still applies. An exception that is raised on the user interface thread for the Windows Forms application is handled by the default handler, which displays the message box. As a result, the *UnhandledException* event is never raised.

Lesson 2

1.   **Correct Answers: A and C**

A.   **Correct:** The fact that the application is distributed over a wide area increases the interest in operations when exceptions happen. Although it's possible to be notified of exceptions without using a framework, the ability to deploy updates to the configuration file from a central location would greatly increase the benefits of a framework.

B.   **Incorrect:** Handling exceptions using a framework on a single user application, especially one this small, is probably overkill. Not that it can't be done, but only that the effort involved isn't likely to be worth the potential gain.

C.   **Correct:** In this instance the framework is useful because it allows changes to be made to the configuration on the fly. For a service that is intended to keep running (as most Windows services do), this can be quite a benefit.

D.   **Incorrect:** A console application that performs a single task is unlikely to need an exception handling framework.

2.   **Correct Answer: D**

A.   **Incorrect:** Although a custom handler can be developed to provide the required functionality, it is not the simplest way to address the problem.

B.   **Incorrect:** The logging handler takes the information associated with the exception and puts it into a logging data store. This doesn't change the message that's included in the exception.

C.   **Incorrect:** Although using a replace handler will remove the sensitive information from the exception, the original exception will disappear, along with any useful information that it might contain.

D.   **Correct:** The wrapping handler creates a new exception, complete with a new *Message* property value. This eliminates the sensitive information from the display. And the original exception is placed into the *InnerException* property, so it's available if needed.

3. **Correct Answers: C and D**

    A. **Incorrect:** Although a custom handler can be developed to provide the required functionality, it is not the simplest way to address the problem.

    B. **Incorrect:** The logging handler takes the information associated with the exception and puts it into a logging data store. This doesn't change the message that is included in the exception.

    C. **Correct:** The replace handler converts one type of exception into an exception of a different type. Because it does so, the exception that is not currently being handled can be changed into one that is handled.

    D. **Correct:** Because the wrapping handler creates a new exception, it too can be used to convert the currently unhandled exception into one that will be recoverable.

Chapter 10: Case Scenario Answers

Case Scenario 1: Appropriate Exception Handling

1. The pattern shown in the question is not a good one. The exception is not being caught for any of the four valid reasons for catching exceptions. It appears that the developer thought that putting the name of the method in the *Message* property was an important detail to add. Unfortunately, that isn't adding any information because the method is already in the *StackTrace*.

    What's worse, the pattern hides the exception that was generated. Every exception, regardless of the cause, gets converted to an *ApplicationException* exception. So if the disk is full or there was a problem with security, it still looks like an application exception. This makes it difficult for any callers in the stack to determine what action should be taken.

2. For the pattern shown, the better way to go would be to not catch any exceptions. None of the four reasons for catching an exception apply here, so the *Try-Catch* block should be removed. Any caller who wants to catch and handle an exception is free to do so. Once the *Try-Catch* is removed, make sure that the unit tests are rerun to ensure that the change has not affected functionality.

Case Scenario 2: Appropriate Exception Handling—The Sequel

1. The pattern shown in the question is almost the exact duplicate of the one shown in Case Scenario 1, "Appropriate Exception Handling." The only difference is that the Exception Handling Application Block is being used. The use of the application block is not an alternative to good exception handling practices. This is one of the dangers of a framework. Using one is not the same as handling exceptions properly.

Chapter 11: Lesson Review Answers

Lesson 1

1. **Correct Answer: B**

    A. **Incorrect:** The application settings should not be used for updatable information. Also, the settings would then be shared across all of the users.

    B. **Correct:** This is the directory in which the user preference configuration information is stored.

    C. **Incorrect:** application.config is used when the application is a COM+ application, which this is not.

    D. **Incorrect:** Having everyone use the same config file will not save the last four files for the current user, not to mention the potential for problems when two applications update simultaneously.

2. **Correct Answer: B**

    A. **Incorrect:** The application settings should not be used for updatable information.

    B. **Correct:** This is the directory in which the user preference configuration information is stored.

    C. **Incorrect:** application.config is used when the application is a COM+ application, which this is not.

    D. **Incorrect:** Having everyone use the same config file will not save the last four files for the current user.

3. **Correct Answer: A**

    A. **Correct:** This is the only one of the choices that would provide working functionality.

    B. **Incorrect:** The user.config file is used for user-scoped settings. And the directory specified is incorrect.

    C. **Incorrect:** application.config is used when the application is a COM+ application, which this is not.

    D. **Incorrect:** Click-once functionality does not, by default, allow access to network resources.

Lesson 2

1. **Correct Answer: C**

    A. **Incorrect:** The use of a physical file would require that the client machine be turned on in order to update the version information.

B. **Incorrect:** The use of isolated storage would require that the client machine be turned on in order to update the version information.

C. **Correct:** Storing the version in a database provides a central location for the information that can be modified by the administrator as long as the database is running.

D. **Incorrect:** The use of the registry would require that the client machine be turned on in order to update the version information.

2. **Correct Answers: A and B**

A. **Correct:** The DataSet could certainly be stored in the physical file. Whether it should be is going to depend on the size of the DataSet and any concerns that might be raised about the possibility of a user modifying the cached values.

B. **Correct:** This is the most likely place to store the DataSet. Although a user could still modify it, it would take a much higher level of sophistication to be able to file and modify the saved result.

C. **Incorrect:** Because the application must be able to run outside the corporate network, being able to access the database is unlikely for all of the required situations.

D. **Incorrect:** Saving a serialized version of a DataSet object to store in the registry, although feasible, is not recommended. And there is a limit of approximately 2048 bytes on the size of a value in the registry and a limit of 64 KB as the total size of all values for a key.

3. **Correct Answer: B**

A. **Incorrect:** In many Smart Client environments, the application doesn't have access to write to the local file system. As a result, attempting to update the application's settings won't be successful.

B. **Correct:** The use of isolated storage provides the capabilities (both reading and writing) for storing the configuration information associated with Smart Client applications.

C. **Incorrect:** Because the application is expected to be used (at least some of the time) in a disconnected mode, storing the configuration information in a network database is not going to provide access often enough.

D. **Incorrect:** As with the local file system, Smart Client applications don't (by default) have access to update the registry.

Lesson 3

1. **Correct Answer: C**

A. **Incorrect:** Converting data, especially nonstring values, to strings is not a fast process.

B. **Incorrect:** Same as A, but the fact that you need to parse the XML document upon retrieval makes it even slower.

    C. **Correct:** Storing configuration information in a binary format is the fastest way to store and retrieve data.

    D. **Incorrect:** To MIME-encode the data is not an effective use of processing cycles because the data is again converted to and from strings.

2. **Correct Answer: C**

    A. **Incorrect:** The string format works right up to the point where a nonintrinsic data type is used. Since the class contains such a property, the string format is not appropriate.

    B. **Incorrect:** The XML serialization process will operate only on the readable and writable properties. So the read-only property would be ignored in this format.

    C. **Correct:** The binary format serializes the exact binary content of the object, including both read-only properties and nonintrinsic data types.

    D. **Incorrect:** No MIME-encoded provider is included with the .NET Framework.

3. **Correct Answers: A and B**

    A. **Correct:** The conversion of the object to a string format supports all of the requirements, especially the one that allows users to edit the value of the object while it is in its persisted state.

    B. **Correct:** An XML format also provides a viable solution, for the same reasons the string format does.

    C. **Incorrect:** The binary format does not allow users to edit the information while it is in the persisted format.

    D. **Incorrect:** There is no provider for a MIME-encoded format in the .NET Framework.

Chapter 11: Case Scenario Answers

Case Scenario 1: Sharing Configuration Information

1. The correct answer to this question is to use a custom configuration provider. Specifically, a provider should be created to retrieve information from the MySQL database and present it to the .NET applications as the configuration data. Although it's true that there is no MySQL data provider available out of the box, a number of third-party alternatives can be used instead.

    The reason for taking this approach has to do with ensuring that the configuration information can't get out of sync. The typical approaches to solving this type of problem include creating a common front end for configuration and using a trigger to cause updates to be automatically serialized.

The problem with using a front-end application is that it needs to be used. Although it's quite possible to create an application that would keep both sides in sync, there is no guarantee that the application will be used any time the configuration data is updated. As with pretty much any database, there are direct methods (such as executing SQL statements) that could update the configuration information without using the front end.

Which brings up the second possibility—the use of a trigger to keep the configuration data synchronized. Again, this is certainly a possibility, although it requires that the changes always be made on the MySQL side. There is no way to raise a trigger on the saving of a standard .NET config file. But the assumption is that the person writing the trigger knows where all of the configuration files that need to be updated are kept. And if (make that when) a new application is created, the trigger will have to be updated with that information as well. In other words, this solution is a fragile one that will work for a while but that has the possibility of being useless as time goes on and knowledgeable people move on to other positions.

Of course, there is the requirement for some additional configuration information, specifically the connection details for the MySQL database. But in the overall scheme of things, that is not overly challenging and can easily be placed into the standard application configuration file.

Which brings us back to the proposed solution. The main benefit is that there need be no remembering for it to work. To be completely open, what has to be "remembered" is that a custom provider is required to be used. But once it is, an object can easily be created from the configuration information. And if configuration information is modified, even if the structure of the data store is changed, the configuration option can easily adjust.

2. The biggest risk to the proposed solution is that the .NET applications now depend on the presence of the MySQL database in order to function. Precisely how good or bad this is depends on the specifics of the infrastructure, but even in the best-case scenario it is now necessary to have access to the database in order to launch the application. Even when you tell users about this requirement, it will still come as a shock the first time the database is unavailable and they can't launch the application.

The easiest way to mitigate this problem is to design a caching mechanism into the configuration provider. Perhaps as the configuration information is retrieved from MySQL, it can immediately be persisted into the .NET configuration file. In that manner, if the MySQL database is unavailable, the most recent values can be used instead.

Note that the feasibility of this mitigation depends in large part on the criticality of the configuration information. If the configuration data doesn't change regularly, "caching" it in app.config is a viable solution. Also, if missing any changes temporarily is not a significant problem, the caching might be possible. But as either of these variables moves toward a higher level of criticality, the less likely it is that a caching solution will be feasible.

Case Scenario 2: Securing Configuration Information

1. When it comes to providing isolation of configuration information, the isolated storage data store is the obvious choice. The information is placed into a storage location that is different for each individual. And, through the use of Windows roaming profiles, the isolated storage can follow the user as the user moves from workstation to workstation.

   Some of the other choices are certainly an option, however. A flat file could be used, as long as the storage location for the file is a shared drive that is accessible from every workstation. In order to ensure that unauthorized access is impossible, each user should have a different directory and the directory should be secured. Also, from a management perspective, the ability to access each of the user's configuration files could be a benefit if the application needs to be updated.

   A database is also an option for this type of configuration storage. As with both isolated storage and the flat file, the centralized nature lends itself to using the application on different machines. There is a little bit of a challenge with respect to keeping each user's data separate. The user ID must be included in the key to the database record in order to keep the data segregated from other users.

2. When it comes to encrypting the configuration information, there are two main choices. If a configuration file is structured in the same manner as the typical app.config (that is, like an XML document), then the aspnet_regiis command can be used to encrypt those sections that need to be secured. If, on the other hand, a database is used, then the data needs to be passed through an encryption and decryption process. One option to encrypt and decrypt the data stream is with a custom provider combined with the *CryptoStream* class.

Chapter 12: Lesson Review Answers

Lesson 1

1. **Correct Answer: A**
   A. **Correct:** This approach creates a separate unit testing project for each project in your application. This way, developers can run each test project individually.
   B. **Incorrect:** The .NET unit testing framework requires that you define a test project to house your unit tests. The framework would not run these tests.
   C. **Incorrect:** This approach is similar to B. The .NET unit testing framework requires that you define a test project to house your unit tests. The framework would not run these tests.
   D. **Incorrect:** If you create a single unit testing project for your application, you will be able to easily run all your tests as a group. However, it does not provide any isolation among the developer team.

2. **Correct Answers: C and D**

    A. **Incorrect:** Unit tests do not work well for testing the execution of the user interface. You will have to do manual testing or use a third-party tool for testing your Windows user interface.

    B. **Incorrect:** Unit tests test units of functionality in your code. An integration test should look at larger sections of code as they relate to working with other bits of code.

    C. **Correct:** Unit tests are very useful to developers trying to get up to speed on unfamiliar code. The unit tests serve as code-based documentation on exactly how the code should both work and fail.

    D. **Correct:** The existence of unit tests allows you to make changes to your code with confidence. You can execute the unit test as a smoke test prior to checking in changes to a build.

3. **Correct Answers: A and C**

    A. **Correct:** Unit tests are primarily used to test middle-tier objects.

    B. **Incorrect:** Unit tests do not test the viability of the user interface or its usability.

    C. **Correct:** Unit tests are great at testing code libraries. This includes libraries that access data.

    D. **Incorrect:** Unit tests are used to test application code. They are not used for testing things like SQL and database table structures or relationships.

4. **Correct Answer: B**

    A. **Incorrect:** A large number of passing tests is only one indication of quality. You must also ensure that those tests are covering the vast majority of the code in the application. For example, tests that all pass but cover only 10 percent of the code do not provide an accurate picture of quality.

    B. **Correct:** You want to set a metric for code coverage (typically 70 percent or better). If the test cases for the given build meet or exceed this value, you can pass the build on to the test team.

    C. **Incorrect:** This is an important statistic. A lot of new code late in a development cycle, for instance, can trigger an alarm. However, this is not an indication of the quality or coverage of your unit tests.

    D. **Incorrect:** This too is an important measure. You want to know how much code has changed from one build to the next. However, this does not indicate whether your unit tests have covered that code.

5. **Correct Answers: A, B, and C**

    A. **Correct:** These values represent the upper and lower bounds of the data type. The values are acceptable by your interface. Therefore, a good bounds check will determine how your application behaves at these bounds.

    B. **Correct:** You will want to check a numeric data type that is used in a calculation for how it behaves at zero (0) and negative one (−1). These values often have unforeseen consequences to calculations.

    C. **Correct:** Your bounds check should verify what happens in your method when you exceed its boundaries. These values exceed the boundaries by one.

    D. **Incorrect:** This is not an example of a boundary check. You may use similar values for your standard unit test, but they do not signify boundary checking.

Lesson 2

1. **Correct Answer: B**

    A. **Incorrect:** Bounds testing refers to verifying that a method still behaves as expected at, near, or beyond the bounds of its parameter's data types.

    B. **Correct:** Load testing is used to confirm that the application behaves as expected, given the target load.

    C. **Incorrect:** Performance testing helps you find performance issues with your code. It also verifies that the application performs to the required metrics. It is not meant to stress your application to a breaking point.

    D. **Incorrect:** Stress testing is the process of applying more and more concurrent users to the site until it no longer performs to expected metrics.

2. **Correct Answers: B and D**

    A. **Incorrect:** Integration testing should be done by testers after the code has been unit tested. Integration tests should also be a black box test.

    B. **Correct:** Integration testing is black box testing. As such, it should define a series of inputs and expected outputs for each test case.

    C. **Incorrect:** Testers should practice continuous integration testing. This reduces risk and cost for the application. After the application is complete, the integration tests should be run through again as a form of system testing.

    D. **Correct:** Integration tests help to test the reliability of your application. You can do this by repeatedly executing these tests.

3. **Correct Answers: B and C**

    A. **Incorrect:** A load test should test for expected, concurrent load. A stress test can be used to test for potential peaks or spikes in load. It is a good idea to use a stress test to make sure your application can withstand up to 1.5 times normal load.

    B. **Correct:** You need to set your user access distribution to match the actual, anticipated network access.

    C. **Correct:** You want to define a test distribution that mimics user interaction with your application.

D. **Incorrect:** There is no distribution defined by a single test. You should define two tests to mimic the way users work with your system.

4. **Correct Answer: D**

   A. **Incorrect:** You do not want your processors to be overtaxed. However, this metric should be monitored during stress testing and not during performance testing.

   B. **Incorrect:** The memory utilization metric is another stress indicator. It does not provide details on transaction performance.

   C. **Incorrect:** The requests per second indicate how many requests are coming into the server, not how pages are performing.

   D. **Correct:** The response time represents the average response time for requests. You can drill into this data to determine actual page response times.

5. **Correct Answers: A and C**

   A. **Correct:** Agents execute your tests. Controllers manage the agents.

   B. **Incorrect:** The test controller (and not the agent) tells the agents what tests to run, what data to use for those tests, and when to start and stop the tests.

   C. **Correct:** Agents send their test data back to the controller. The controller is used to review the aggregated agent results.

   D. **Incorrect:** Testers use clients to author and edit tests.

Chapter 12: Case Scenario Answers

Case Scenario: Evaluating a Testing Strategy

1. First, the developers will be working independently. Therefore, you should suggest creating a number of separate projects for storing unit tests. In addition, each developer is not concerned about any other developer's code; this is the responsibility of integration testing. Second, you should define a real metric for unit testing inside the test plan. It was suggested in the interviews that at least 75 percent code coverage be enforced. Finally, you should indicate that all unit test code coverage for a build be published to a central server for reporting. The project manager should not rely on word of mouth for this information. If you can't publish this data to a server, you need visual verification.

2. Your load test should be created to support at least 10 concurrent users during peak load. You arrive at that figure by adding the number of sales reps (5) to the total reviewers (5). This is your peak load. It is likely that your actual load will never approach this peak. To arrive at this figure, every user of the system would have to be working in the system at once.

   You should not define a hard target for stress testing. Rather, you should step the user load in perhaps 10 percent increments until you find a breaking point. You should also confirm that this breaking point exceeds 1.5 times the peak load. This will ensure that the application has some room to scale if new demands are placed on it.

3. The transactional unit tests verify the user business functions. From this perspective, you might prefer to create a single test and add to it and modify it as needed. This gives you one test to verify that the entire set of business transactions work or don't work.

   However, these tests will most likely also be used for defining the load, stress, and performance tests. For these tests it is important to simulate actual user load based on actual user behavior. In the case scenario the sales reps and reviewers work at different levels. You should therefore create separate transactional unit tests per test case or user activity. This will allow you to distribute these tests across the simulated user load.

4. First, you should suggest that the load test include network distribution as defined by the application support team (90 percent LAN, 10 percent VPN). Next, you ensure that the test team documents an actual user load pattern for the load tests. They need to segment the tests based on how users work. Last, it is important to define the number of concurrent users (see question 2) and what is meant by concurrent users. For the load tests concurrent users should be defined as the number of users working with the application. These users are working; they are not all executing simultaneous transactions. Therefore, you should use standard (or real) think times between transactions.

5. The testers need to set performance thresholds that should not be exceeded in order to verify that the load tests succeeded. Some simple thresholds include no rejected transactions (timeouts) and no errors. You should also define thresholds for processor and memory usage. For example, you might indicate that the load test should be considered as failed if the processor spikes above 80 percent for longer than 10 seconds. You would define a similar statement relative to memory usage.

6. First, the integration testing does not identify how the integration will be tested at the database level. There needs to be tests that confirm that data extracted from multiple systems gets into the database and is aggregated correctly. Second, the integration tests should define (or point to) actual test inputs and expected outputs. You should consider the tests to have been passed only after the results have been compared. Finally, the plan calls for building integration tests from use cases. This is okay, although more work needs to be done to identify communication issues and to determine what happens when things fail.

7. First, you should suggest that the test team also flood this quiet network with traffic patterns that exist in the real network. This is the only way you can determine how the application will behave on the production network. Second, the database requires more test data. You need to generate data that approximates the database as it will be in production. You should also suggest creating an automated means of initializing the data and cleaning it up before tests are run.

Chapter 13: Lesson Review Answers

Lesson 1

1. **Correct Answer: B**

    A. **Incorrect:** The *TestCleanup* attribute indicates a method should be run after each test is executed.

    B. **Correct:** The *TestInitialize* attribute indicates that the decorated method should be run before each unit test is run.

    C. **Incorrect:** The *ClassCleanup* attribute indicates a method should be run once after all tests are executed.

    D. **Incorrect:** The *ClassInitialize* attribute indicates a method should be run once before all tests are executed.

2. **Correct Answer: D**

    A. **Incorrect:** The *AreEqual* method is used to determine if two values are equal (not two objects).

    B. **Incorrect:** The *IsTrue* method checks a Boolean value (not an object). The second parameter is used for writing a message to the test results upon failure.

    C. **Incorrect:** The *IsInstanceOfType* method checks to see if an object is of a certain type.

    D. **Correct:** The *AreSame* method checks to verify that two objects are identical.

3. **Correct Answers: B and D**

    A. **Incorrect:** This method simply returns data from the database. Standard unit tests should cover this method.

    B. **Correct:** This method represents a key transaction in the system. It should therefore warrant additional testing.

    C. **Incorrect:** It should be sufficient to test these properties with standard unit tests.

    D. **Correct:** This method has a lot of business logic. In addition, several applications will share it. Therefore, you should consider writing additional unit tests for this method.

4. **Correct Answers: B and D**

    A. **Incorrect:** Use cases are meant to flush out requirements. Test cases are typically derived from use cases.

    B. **Correct:** Testers write test cases from use cases.

    C. **Incorrect:** Test cases are written for testers to verify that the system meets the requirements. However, developers can leverage test cases to help them write better unit tests.

    D. **Correct:** Test cases are made up of the steps a tester should take, the data the tester should enter, and the results the tester should expect.

5. **Correct Answers: C and D**

    A. **Incorrect:** Test case execution and full integration testing is the responsibility of the test team.

    B. **Incorrect:** Developers need only make sure that their calls to external libraries did not break the interface. They should not spend time verifying that the calls actually did what was intended. This is the responsibility of the tester and the author of the external library.

    C. **Correct:** Developers should verify that their code works not just on their machines but also in a simulated version of the test/production environment.

    D. **Correct:** Developers need to identify their dependencies. This includes looking at third-party libraries that they might be using and verifying these libraries against the configuration management plan.

Lesson 2

A. **Correct Answers: A and C**

    A. **Correct:** A code review helps you track code to standards.

    B. **Incorrect:** Code reviews do not have an effect on test cases.

    C. **Correct:** A code review is not a test; however, it often finds unforeseen consequences in code that would show themselves as bugs.

    D. **Incorrect:** Code reviews do not, by definition, concern themselves with requirements. They are meant to be technical.

B. **Correct Answers: A and C**

    A. **Correct:** A coding standard defines how developers should structure their code and handle errors.

    B. **Incorrect:** This is an example of an architecture standard.

    C. **Correct:** This represents a coding standard or rule.

    D. **Incorrect:** This is a naming (not coding) standard.

C. **Correct Answer: B**

    A. **Incorrect:** There is no such operation. You can call Extract Interface to define an interface from an existing class.

    B. **Correct:** You call Encapsulate Field to create a property from a field variable.

    C. **Incorrect:** There is no such operation. You can call Promote Local to Parameter to move a local variable to a method parameter.

    D. **Incorrect:** There is no such operation. You can call Extract Interface to define an interface from an existing class.

D. **Correct Answers: C and D**

A. **Incorrect:** The Code Analysis tool analyzes static code only.

B. **Incorrect:** You can configure the set of rules you wish to enforce with the Code Analysis tool.

C. **Correct:** When you select Run Code Analysis from Visual Studio, the issues are shown as warnings.

D. **Correct:** When an issue is shown in the Error List, you can right-click the issue and choose Show Error Help to view a possible resolution for the item.

Lesson 3

1. **Correct Answer: C**

A. **Incorrect:** This change can either be deferred or made. There should be no reason to escalate such a small item to the project stakeholders. In addition, if marketing is part of the decision, you should lean toward accepting this request.

B. **Incorrect:** This is a bug. It needs to be fixed without question. It is preventing testers from completing their test case.

C. **Correct:** This was a major miss by the team. However, a change this big, this late in the project, will require a decision from the project stakeholders.

D. **Incorrect:** This is a bug with a simple fix. It should be accommodated.

2. **Correct Answers: A, B, C, and D**

A. **Correct:** You should verify that both environments have the same versions of the deployed code.

B. **Correct:** You should verify the operating system, its configuration, and the .NET Framework setup.

C. **Correct:** Security is often the cause of code not working in a different environment.

D. **Correct:** You should check that the data being tested against is the same in both environments.

3. **Correct Answers: B and C**

A. **Incorrect:** You should not create an entire branch just for your fix. Instead, your fix should be released as part of the next, planned build.

B. **Correct:** You should update the deployment plan and release notes to indicate that the bug was fixed and in the new build. This will help testers to know what to expect. It will also help the build team get the right code on the test server.

C. **Correct:** You need to mark the bug as fixed in the bug tracking software. You might also decide to associate your change set with the work item in Team Systems.

D. **Incorrect:** There is no need to clutter the code comments with release and bug information.

Chapter 13: Case Scenario Answers

Case Scenario 1: Defining Unit Tests from a Test Case

1. You should consider creating a ClassInitialize or TestInitialize method to reset the database to the test data prior to running your unit tests.

   The connectivity to the reservation system and the location mapping service represents an integration test. You need to simply verify that you successfully call these interfaces.

2. You should consider creating a ScheduleMeeting test case that mimics the entire event registration process from a user's perspective. This will allow you to test the entire process without the user interface. It would call the same methods as each step in the wizard, in the same order. This will allow you to create a unit test that helps with integration testing and verification of the UI.

3. You should consider binding your unit test to the test data. This includes the expected results. This will allow you to make certain assertions based on the context of each row in the test data.

4. The alternate test case involves verifying how your code works when the third-party system raises an exception, is not available, or can't process the booking. This is integration testing. However, if you wrote the code to call those methods, you are on the hook for making sure they work in all scenarios. You should therefore create unit tests for these conditions.

Case Scenario 2: Performing a Code Review

1. You should start by defining development standards. You can't measure code without a target; developers can't be held to an undefined standard. You should get the team together and start defining what is acceptable. You should also create an architectural standard on how you implement database code, objects, services, user elements, and so on.

2. This should not be peer-to-peer. The developers are too inexperienced for this to work. Instead, the technical lead or senior developer (you) should handle the code reviews to get started.

3. The code reviews will immediately help by mentoring developers in terms of best practices. In addition, a second set of eyes will help find gaps in quality. Finally, code reviews create a no-place-to-hide environment. Code reviews will help identify developers who need additional training.

4. You should create a formal code review process. This will help the company keep a close eye on the quality of the code. It will also foster a knowledge base of known issues. Developers can use this repository as a learning tool. Management can use it to certify that the code is being written to standards.

Chapter 14: Lesson Review Answers

Lesson 1

1. **Correct Answer: B**

    A. **Incorrect:** Although a file copy would move the assembly containing the serviced component to the target system, Administrator rights are required to create the COM+ application in which the serviced component will be installed.

    B. **Correct:** The installer package can be configured to run the regsvcs utility at installation time, which will install the COM+ application and serviced component. Then the application no longer needs to be executed as an Administrator.

    C. **Incorrect:** Click Once deployment doesn't allow for configuration on the target system to be modified. This includes the registration of serviced components.

    D. **Incorrect:** Smart Client is just another name for the Click Once deployment technique.

2. **Correct Answer: A**

    A. **Correct:** The *WebBrowser* control has a specific dependency on a file (shdocvw.dll) that Visual Studio doesn't automatically detect. As a result, it is not included in the installation package unless it is added manually. Given the exception that occurred, this is the most likely scenario.

    B. **Incorrect:** Although missing registry entries are possible, it's unlikely that the absence of an entry would cause a *FileNotFoundException* to be raised.

    C. **Incorrect:** There is no requirement that an executable be signed (although it's considered a good practice to do so). And in no situation would having an unsigned executable cause a *FileNotFoundException* to be thrown.

    D. **Incorrect:** An incorrect version of a dependent assembly (assuming that the main executable has been signed) will not result in a *FileLoadException* being thrown.

3. **Correct Answer: B**

    A. **Incorrect:** Active Directory requires an MSI file to be created in order to be deployable using Group Policy. So even if you might be able to deploy an application using XCOPY, this style of deployment can't be used in the given scenario.

    B. **Correct:** The Windows installer package is generated as an MSI file, which is exactly what Active Directory needs to deploy the application using Group Policy.

    C. **Incorrect:** Click Once deployment is used to deploy an application by placing the executable on a Web server. As such, it is not appropriate for use with Group Policy.

    D. **Incorrect:** Smart Client is just another name for the Click Once deployment technique.

Lesson 2

1. **Correct Answer: B**

    A. **Incorrect:** The robustness requirement for an application affects its deployment. For example, an application that has been designed to be scalable might need to have the same component functionality deployed to more than one machine. Any deployment plan needs to take this replication into consideration.

    B. **Correct:** How the connection to a data source is determined doesn't affect the deployment. This is a class-level implementation detail that doesn't have any impact on deployment beyond ensuring that the correct configuration information is provided.

    C. **Incorrect:** The use of a service-based approach to design has a significant impact on deployment. The use of services implies that more than one machine could be involved, which means that two deployments should be created, one for the client and one for the server. This is true even if they will ultimately be placed on a single system, the reason being that it's better to identify the server and client components while the project is still fresh in everyone's mind.

    D. **Incorrect:** The integration of the new application with existing corporate artifacts affects the deployment in that consideration needs to be given to the communication channels and locations of the application components. The integration process might force the deployment of technologies that might not otherwise be required, for example.

2. **Correct Answer: B**

    A. **Incorrect:** The Application Connection Designer focuses on identifying the connections that exist between the components within an application.

    B. **Correct:** The Deployment Designer is used to map the systems for a particular application onto the current system infrastructure model. The result is a model of how the systems are to be deployed into the current environment.

    C. **Incorrect:** The Logical Datacenter Designer describes the systems that exist in the current environment. Although the information in this design is used to validate the deployment, it is not a model of the deployment.

    D. **Incorrect:** The System Designer is used to create the elements of deployment for one or more applications. The systems that are created can then be used in the Deployment Designer to actually model the deployment. However, on its own, the system design does not model a specific deployment.

3. **Correct Answer: A**

    A. **Correct:** The Application Connection Designer is used to create a model of the data connections that exist between the components in an application. Specifically, any flow of information between the components will be captured as part of this model.

   B. **Incorrect:** The Deployment Designer is used to map the systems for a particular application onto the current system infrastructure model.

   C. **Incorrect:** The Logical Datacenter Designer describes the systems that exist in the current environment. This information is used in the final deployment design and to validate that the current infrastructure supports the connection requirement of the deployed system.

   D. **Incorrect:** The System Designer is used to create the elements of deployment for one or more applications. Each system is actually a unit of deployment.

Chapter 14: Case Scenario Answers

Case Scenario 1: Choosing the Deployment Method

   1. There are really two parts to the user portion of the application. And it makes sense to have two separate installations due to some conflicting requirements. The COM+ portion of the application should be installed using a Windows Installer package. This allows the COM+ application to be properly registered (assuming that it's run using Administrator privileges). Also, the fact that it makes a permanent change to the user's machine means that the installer needs to run.

   The user interface portion of the application, on the other hand, should be deployed using a Click Once technology. This allows for the ongoing updating of the application by simply moving new assemblies to a central location. Also, there is no indication that any change to the user's machine is required over and above the COM+ component that has already been dealt with.

   2. The installation of the SQL Server database would best be accomplished through scripting. A script that creates the database and all of the contained objects should be created (or generated). That script can then be executed against the SQL Server system using osql.exe or through the SQL Server Management Studio.

Case Scenario 2: Choosing the Deployment Method

   1. The starting point for modeling the component deployment process is to create a logical datacenter design. This contains the servers and communication channels that exist within the infrastructure. Next, the components that make up the application are modeled using the Application Connection Designer. Once these elements have been completed, it becomes possible to create systems (using the System Designer) and map those systems onto the infrastructure model to ensure that the infrastructure can meet the application's functional and communication requirements.

2. The type of verification that should be performed depends on the specific requirements of the application. There is, however, an underlying theme among all of the verification steps—that being to determine if the installation was complete and if the components are operating as expected. In addition, the continued monitoring of the application's components can be implemented using some of the techniques that are used to verify the application. This can be useful in creating a proactive operational environment in which problems are detected prior (if possible) to their affecting the user's experience.

Chapter 15: Lesson Review Answers

Lesson 1

1. **Correct Answer: C**
   A. **Incorrect:** Although the graph view on Performance Monitor displays the most recent two minutes (or so) of values, it's not useful for post collection analysis unless someone is constantly watching the graph.
   B. **Incorrect:** Performance alerts are point-in-time warnings issued when a set of defined thresholds has been crossed. Although it could be used to alert operations that something important has happened, it is not useful when collecting data for evaluation.
   C. **Correct:** The log view is the best choice here because the information that is required for analysis is placed into a file in a format that can easily be used to identify the cause for the performance issue at some later time.
   D. **Incorrect:** The report view displays only the current value for a set of counters. This is not useful for analysis after the fact.

2. **Correct Answers: A and D**
   A. **Correct:** With every thrown exception, effort is expended collecting the information necessary to populate the appropriate exception object. As a result, too many exceptions will slow down the perceived response time of an application without affecting the other more obvious signs of performance (that is, CPU and memory).
   B. **Incorrect:** Object allocation is a very fast process and strings don't even need to go outside of the memory already allocated to the running process. As a result, although allocating strings does impair performance, it is rarely significant enough to notice in the absence of other, more serious, issues.
   C. **Incorrect:** The allocation of large objects does take longer (and requires more memory) than the allocation of smaller objects. However, given that memory issues don't appear to be playing a role in the problem, it's unlikely that this is the root cause of the degraded performance.

D. **Correct:** A possible reason for poor performance without memory or CPU problems is locking. A locked process doesn't use any CPU time and there is no gain in memory. Yet because it's waiting, the user will perceive slow response time.

Lesson 2

1. **Correct Answer: B**

    A. **Incorrect:** The purpose of an application flow-logic diagram is almost completely to document the dependencies between components.

    B. **Correct:** The component is a unit of deployment. It's quite possible for a component to contain multiple classes.

    C. **Incorrect:** In the diagram only the exposed interface is included. It should not be possible to access a component through anything but an interface.

    D. **Incorrect:** A circular reference occurs when Class A is dependent on Class B and Class B is dependent on Class A. Because the relationship is unidirectional, it is not possible to have a circular relationship.

2. **Correct Answers: A and B**

    A. **Correct:** With a complexity of 15, it is still relatively safe to make changes to the application without worrying significantly about side-effect bugs.

    B. **Correct:** Increasing the number of components has the effect of adding to the number of nodes, which would lower the value of the complexity.

    C. **Incorrect:** Decreasing the number of components by combining existing components actually raises the complexity.

    D. **Incorrect:** A complexity value of 15 is below the threshold of being very difficult to safely change.

3. **Correct Answer: A**

    A. **Correct:** Classes are explicitly not part of the application flow-logic diagram.

    B. **Incorrect:** The component is one of the basic elements of the application flow-logic diagram.

    C. **Incorrect:** The application flow-logic diagram is intended to model the dependencies that exist between components. As such, they are included in the diagram.

    D. **Incorrect:** The interface represents the methods through which the components in the application flow-logic diagram are related.

Chapter 15: Case Scenario Answers

Case Scenario 1: Tuning an Application

1. Given that the problem appears to be more prevalent when larger files are processed, it's more likely that the issue is related to memory. The contents of the file or the results of the processing are, perhaps, being loaded into memory before they're sent to the database. The way to validate this hypothesis is to use Task Manager to view the CPU and memory usage of the application while it is processing a large file. The same information is available through the Performance Monitor, with the % Processor Time and Working Set counters.

2. If memory is the source of the problem, the Private Bytes, Allocated Bytes/sec, and Large Object Heap size counters might provide some insight into the details. Also, monitoring the Gen 0, Gen 1, and Gen 2 heap sizes might reveal whether the problem is caused by poorly designed object lifetimes.

3. If the CPU is the source of the problem, then the Processor Queue Length or Context Switches/sec counters might provide some insight into the source.

Case Scenario 2: Diagramming an Application

1. The diagram should contain all the components in the application, along with the relationships among them in terms of the dependencies based on the exposed set of interfaces.

2. The application flow-logic diagram is not intended to model the class hierarchy. For this reason, the hierarchy should not be in the produced diagram.

3. Data access components (as well as user interface components) should not be included in the diagram. Their functionality is typically not complicated enough to measurably add to the complexity of the application. To put it another way, the data access component is responsible for retrieving data (whether it be through stored procedures or dynamic SQL) and updating data (using the same two techniques). The logic is generally quite simple and is unlikely to increase the difficulties in modifying or maintaining the application, which is ultimately what complexity is attempting to quantify.

Chapter 16: Lesson Review Answers

Lesson 1

1. **Correct Answers: B and C**

    A. **Incorrect:** The source of the audio track has no bearing on how the audio file can be downloaded. It does have an impact on the quality that *can* be stored, but not directly on the format that is most appropriate.

    B. **Correct:** The compression level of the audio track has a direct correlation to the size of the file. And delivering large files from a remote Web site can be challenging, depending on the bandwidth that is available. As a result, attempts should be made to ensure that the quality is appropriate for the client machines.

    C. **Correct:** The available bandwidth will affect the selected format because an attempt to minimize the size of the content is appropriate. As a result, the format should be compressed as much as is reasonable for the target system.

    D. **Incorrect:** Like the source of the sound, the sampling rate affects the quality of the sound that *can* be delivered. But it doesn't have an impact on the format that should be selected to actually deliver the content.

2. **Correct Answer: B**

    A. **Incorrect:** The multimedia content is stored on a central server and will therefore need to be distributed across the network in order to be played on the client computers. This process has the potential to cause a significant drain on the network capacity. The network engineers at the company where the software will be installed will definitely be interested in the requirements of your application.

    B. **Correct:** The licensing of the content isn't a concern for the people who deploy the software. Yes, they need to be aware of the DRM issues, but the retrieval of the licensing takes place at run time. When it comes to the installation process, the licensing is not an issue.

    C. **Incorrect:** The codecs that are required on the client computers should definitely be part of the installation instructions. After all, they are part of the set of software that needs to be installed before the application will function correctly.

    D. **Incorrect:** Because the application is playing video from a remote machine, the availability of that server is needed. The Quality of Service requirement is the latency that can be tolerated before the application appears to break. This is information that should be provided as part of the installation document for the application.

Lesson 2

1. **Correct Answer: A**

    A. **Correct:** The .NET Framework doesn't provide any support for playing video.

    B. **Incorrect:** The *DirectShow* class exposes a number of methods that can be used to start, pause, and stop video.

    C. **Incorrect:** The Media Control Interface exposes a method that accepts a command. The command can be used to play a particular file, either video or audio.

    D. **Incorrect:** No managed code classes support the playing of video.

2. **Correct Answer: D**

    A. **Incorrect:** The *PlaySound* function is used to play WAV files. As such, it can't be used to play MP3-formatted files.

    B. **Incorrect:** Like the *PlaySound* Win32 function, the *SoundPlayer* class supports only WAV files. In fact, if you dig under the cover of the *SoundPlayer* class, you will eventually get to a call to the *PlaySound* function to actually make the sound audible.

    C. **Incorrect:** The *SystemSound* class is used to play the sources associated with specific Windows events. It can't be used to play an arbitrary MP3-formatted file.

    D. **Correct:** By using the Windows Media Player SDK, you can play any audio format that Windows Media Player supports. This includes the MP3-formatted file described in the question.

3. **Correct Answer: C**

    A. **Incorrect:** The *AutoShow* property on the *IVideoWindow* is used to indicate whether the video is automatically rendered when the data stream arrives. It has nothing to do with blocking the user interface thread.

    B. **Incorrect:** The *RenderFile* method prepares the video stream to be rendered. It does not cause the content to be played.

    C. **Correct:** The *Run* method starts to render the content in the data stream. Once the stream has started, control returns to the calling program, leaving the content playing until a *Pause* or a *Stop* method is called.

    D. **Incorrect:** The *WaitForCompletion* method causes the current application to stop until the data stream has finished rendering. In other words, the thread is blocked until the content is finished, in direct contradiction to the requirements outlined in the question.

Chapter 16: Case Scenario Answer

Case Scenario: Delivering Multimedia Content

1. The limited bandwidth means that a compressed format for the audio stream would be a benefit. This eliminates WAV as a possible format only because the normal mode for WAV is not compressed. As to whether you want to use MP3 or WMA as the format, it really depends on the licensing issues, if there are any. The WMA format can be more easily integrated into the Windows Media Rights Manager if the generation and validation of licenses is required. As for the deployment requirements, since MP3 or WMA will be used, the run-time libraries for the Windows Media Player SDK need to be installed along with the application.

2. The specific codec you choose should be based on compression and cost considerations. Regardless of the selected format, the deployment requirement is the same. The *Direct-Show* class is deployed with the DirectX installation, so part of setting up the application will involve ensuring that this is done.

Index

System Requirements

We recommend that you use a computer that is not your primary workstation to do the lab exercises in this book because you will make changes to the operating system and application configuration.

Hardware Requirements

The following hardware is required to complete the lab exercises:

- Computer with a 600-MHz or faster processor (1 GHz recommended)
- 192 MB of RAM or more (512 MB recommended)
- 2 GB of available hard disk space
- DVD-ROM drive
- 1,024 x 768 or higher resolution display with 256 colors
- Keyboard and Microsoft mouse or compatible pointing device

Software Requirements

The following software is required to complete the practice exercises:

- One of the following operating systems:
    - Microsoft Windows 2000 with Service Pack 4
    - Windows XP with Service Pack 2
    - Windows XP Professional, x64 Editions (WOW)
    - Windows Server 2003 with Service Pack 1
    - Windows Server 2003, x64 Editions (WOW)
    - Windows Server 2003 R2
    - Windows Server 2003 R2, x64 Editions (WOW)
    - Windows Vista
- Visual Studio 2005 (A 90-day evaluation edition of Visual Studio 2005 Professional Edition is included on DVD with this book.)

IMPORTANT Evaluation edition is not the full retail product

The 90-day evaluation edition of Microsoft Visual Studio 2005 Professional Edition provided with this training kit is not the full retail product and is provided only for the purposes of training and evaluation. Microsoft and Microsoft Technical Support do not support this evaluation edition.

Information about any issues relating to the use of this evaluation edition with this training kit is posted to the Support section of the Microsoft Press Web site (www.microsoft.com/learning /support/books/). For information about ordering the full version of any Microsoft software, please call Microsoft Sales at (800) 426-9400 or visit www.microsoft.com.

IMPORTANT Visual Studio Team Suite

To complete the lab exercises for Chapter 13, Lesson 1, you will need to have Microsoft Visual Studio 2005 Team Edition for Software Developers installed on your computer. This is available as part of Visual Studio 2005 Team Suite. You can download a free 180-day trial version of Visual Studio 2005 Team Suite from http://www.microsoft.com/downloads/details.aspx?FamilyId=5677DDC4-5035-401F-95C3-CC6F46F6D8F7&displaylang=en. You will need to uninstall Visual Studio 2005 Professional to install Visual Studio Team Suite on the same computer.

To complete the lab exercises for Chapter 13, Lesson 1, you will need:

- 256 MB of RAM or more
- 3.3 GB available disk space to download Visual Studio Team Suite
- 2 GB available disk space to install Visual Studio Team Suite
- One of the following operating systems:
  - ❑ Microsoft Windows 2000 with Service Pack 4
  - ❑ Windows XP with Service Pack 2
  - ❑ Windows Server 2003 with Service Pack 1
    - ● Microsoft Windows 2000 with Service Pack 4
    - ● Windows XP with Service Pack 2
    - ● Windows Server 2003 with Service Pack 1
    - ● Windows Vista

Additional Resources for C# Developers

Published and Forthcoming Titles from Microsoft Press

Microsoft® Visual C#® 2005 Express Edition: Build a Program Now!
Patrice Pelland ● ISBN 0-7356-2229-9

In this lively, eye-opening, and hands-on book, all you need is a computer and the desire to learn how to program with Visual C# 2005 Express Edition. Featuring a full working edition of the software, this fun and highly visual guide walks you through a complete programming project—a desktop weather-reporting application—from start to finish. You'll get an unintimidating introduction to the Microsoft Visual Studio® development environment and learn how to put the lightweight, easy-to-use tools in Visual C# Express to work right away—creating, compiling, testing, and delivering your first, ready-to-use program. You'll get expert tips, coaching, and visual examples at each step of the way, along with pointers to additional learning resources.

Microsoft Visual C# 2005 *Step by Step*
John Sharp ● ISBN 0-7356-2129-2

Visual C#, a feature of Visual Studio 2005, is a modern programming language designed to deliver a productive environment for creating business frameworks and reusable object-oriented components. Now you can teach yourself essential techniques with Visual C#—and start building components and Microsoft Windows®–based applications—one step at a time. With *Step by Step*, you work at your own pace through hands-on, learn-by-doing exercises. Whether you're a beginning programmer or new to this particular language, you'll learn how, when, and why to use specific features of Visual C# 2005. Each chapter puts you to work, building your knowledge of core capabilities and guiding you as you create your first C#-based applications for Windows, data management, and the Web.

Programming Microsoft Visual C# 2005 Framework Reference
Francesco Balena ● ISBN 0-7356-2182-9

Complementing *Programming Microsoft Visual C# 2005 Core Reference*, this book covers a wide range of additional topics and information critical to Visual C# developers, including Windows Forms, working with Microsoft ADO.NET 2.0 and Microsoft ASP.NET 2.0, Web services, security, remoting, and much more. Packed with sample code and real-world examples, this book will help developers move from understanding to mastery.

Programming Microsoft Visual C# 2005 *Core Reference*
Donis Marshall ● ISBN 0-7356-2181-0

Get the in-depth reference and pragmatic, real-world insights you need to exploit the enhanced language features and core capabilities in Visual C# 2005. Programming expert Donis Marshall deftly builds your proficiency with classes, structs, and other fundamentals, and advances your expertise with more advanced topics such as debugging, threading, and memory management. Combining incisive reference with hands-on coding examples and best practices, this *Core Reference* focuses on mastering the C# skills you need to build innovative solutions for smart clients and the Web.

CLR via C#, Second Edition
Jeffrey Richter ● ISBN 0-7356-2163-2

In this new edition of Jeffrey Richter's popular book, you get focused, pragmatic guidance on how to exploit the common language runtime (CLR) functionality in Microsoft .NET Framework 2.0 for applications of all types—from Web Forms, Windows Forms, and Web services to solutions for Microsoft SQL Server™, Microsoft code names "Avalon" and "Indigo," consoles, Microsoft Windows NT® Service, and more. Targeted to advanced developers and software designers, this book takes you under the covers of .NET for an in-depth understanding of its structure, functions, and operational components, demonstrating the most practical ways to apply this knowledge to your own development efforts. You'll master fundamental design tenets for .NET and get hands-on insights for creating high-performance applications more easily and efficiently. The book features extensive code examples in Visual C# 2005.

Programming Microsoft Windows Forms
Charles Petzold ● ISBN 0-7356-2153-5

CLR via C++
Jeffrey Richter with Stanley B. Lippman
ISBN 0-7356-2248-5

Programming Microsoft Web Forms
Douglas J. Reilly ● ISBN 0-7356-2179-9

Debugging, Tuning, and Testing Microsoft .NET 2.0 Applications
John Robbins ● ISBN 0-7356-2202-7

For more information about Microsoft Press® books and other learning products,
visit: **www.microsoft.com/books** *and* **www.microsoft.com/learning**

Additional Resources for Visual Basic Developers

Published and Forthcoming Titles from Microsoft Press

Microsoft® Visual Basic® 2005 Express Edition: Build a Program Now!
Patrice Pelland • ISBN 0-7356-2213-2

Featuring a full working edition of the software, this fun and highly visual guide walks you through a complete programming project—a desktop weather-reporting application—from start to finish. You'll get an introduction to the Microsoft Visual Studio® development environment and learn how to put the lightweight, easy-to-use tools in Visual Basic Express to work right away—creating, compiling, testing, and delivering your first ready-to-use program. You'll get expert tips, coaching, and visual examples each step of the way, along with pointers to additional learning resources.

Microsoft Visual Basic 2005 *Step by Step*
Michael Halvorson • ISBN 0-7356-2131-4

With enhancements across its visual designers, code editor, language, and debugger that help accelerate the development and deployment of robust, elegant applications across the Web, a business group, or an enterprise, Visual Basic 2005 focuses on enabling developers to rapidly build applications. Now you can teach yourself the essentials of working with Visual Studio 2005 and the new features of the Visual Basic language—one step at a time. Each chapter puts you to work, showing you how, when, and why to use specific features of Visual Basic and guiding as you create actual components and working applications for Microsoft Windows®. You'll also explore data management and Web-based development topics.

Programming Microsoft Visual Basic 2005 *Core Reference*
Francesco Balena • ISBN 0-7356-2183-7

Get the expert insights, indispensable reference, and practical instruction needed to exploit the core language features and capabilities in Visual Basic 2005. Well-known Visual Basic programming author Francesco Balena expertly guides you through the fundamentals, including modules, keywords, and inheritance, and builds your mastery of more advanced topics such as delegates, assemblies, and My Namespace. Combining in-depth reference with extensive, hands-on code examples and best-practices advice, this *Core Reference* delivers the key resources that you need to develop professional-level programming skills for smart clients and the Web.

Programming Microsoft Visual Basic 2005 Framework Reference
Francesco Balena • ISBN 0-7356-2175-6

Complementing *Programming Microsoft Visual Basic 2005 Core Reference*, this book covers a wide range of additional topics and information critical to Visual Basic developers, including Windows Forms, working with Microsoft ADO.NET 2.0 and ASP.NET 2.0, Web services, security, remoting, and much more. Packed with sample code and real-world examples, this book will help developers move from understanding to mastery.

Programming Microsoft Windows Forms
Charles Petzold • ISBN 0-7356-2153-5

Programming Microsoft Web Forms
Douglas J. Reilly • ISBN 0-7356-2179-9

Debugging, Tuning, and Testing Microsoft .NET 2.0 Applications
John Robbins • ISBN 0-7356-2202-7

Microsoft ASP.NET 2.0 *Step by Step*
George Shepherd • ISBN 0-7356-2201-9

Microsoft ADO.NET 2.0 *Step by Step*
Rebecca Riordan • ISBN 0-7356-2164-0

Programming Microsoft ASP.NET 2.0 *Core Reference*
Dino Esposito • ISBN 0-7356-2176-4

For more information about Microsoft Press® books and other learning products, visit: **www.microsoft.com/books** *and* **www.microsoft.com/learning**

What do you think of this book?

We want to hear from you!

Do you have a few minutes to participate in a brief online survey?

Microsoft is interested in hearing your feedback so we can continually improve our books and learning resources for you.

To participate in our survey, please visit:

www.microsoft.com/learning/booksurvey/

...and enter this book's ISBN-10 number (appears above barcode on back cover*). As a thank-you to survey participants in the United States and Canada, each month we'll randomly select five respondents to win one of five $100 gift certificates from a leading online merchant. At the conclusion of the survey, you can enter the drawing by providing your e-mail address, which will be used for prize notification only.

Thanks in advance for your input. Your opinion counts!

* Where to find the ISBN-10 on back cover

Example only. Each book has unique ISBN.